THE STINKING

Other *Get Fuzzy* Books

The Dog Is Not a Toy (House Rule #4)

Fuzzy Logic: Get Fuzzy 2

The Get Fuzzy Experience: Are You Bucksperienced

I Would Have Bought You a Cat, But . . .

Blueprint for Disaster

Say Cheesy

Scrum Bums

I'm Ready for My Movie Contract

Take Our Cat, Please!

Ignorance, Thy Name Is Bucky

Dumbheart

Masters of the Nonsenseverse

Survival of the Filthiest

Treasuries

Groovitude: A Get Fuzzy Treasury

Bucky Katt's Big Book of Fun

Loserpalooza

The Potpourrific Great Big Grab Bag of Get Fuzzy

Treasury of the Lost Litter Box

THE STINKING

a  treasury by darby conley

Andrews McMeel
Publishing, LLC

Kansas City • Sydney • London

Get Fuzzy is distributed internationally by Universal Uclick.

Andrews McMeel Publishing, LLC
an Andrews McMeel Universal company
1130 Walnut Street
Kansas City, Missouri 64106
www.andrewsmcmeel.com

12 13 14 15 16 BAM 10 9 8 7 6 5 4 3 2 1

ISBN-13: 978-1-4494-2798-6

Library of Congress Control Number: 2012938485

Get Fuzzy can be viewed on the Internet at
www.gocomics.com/getfuzzy

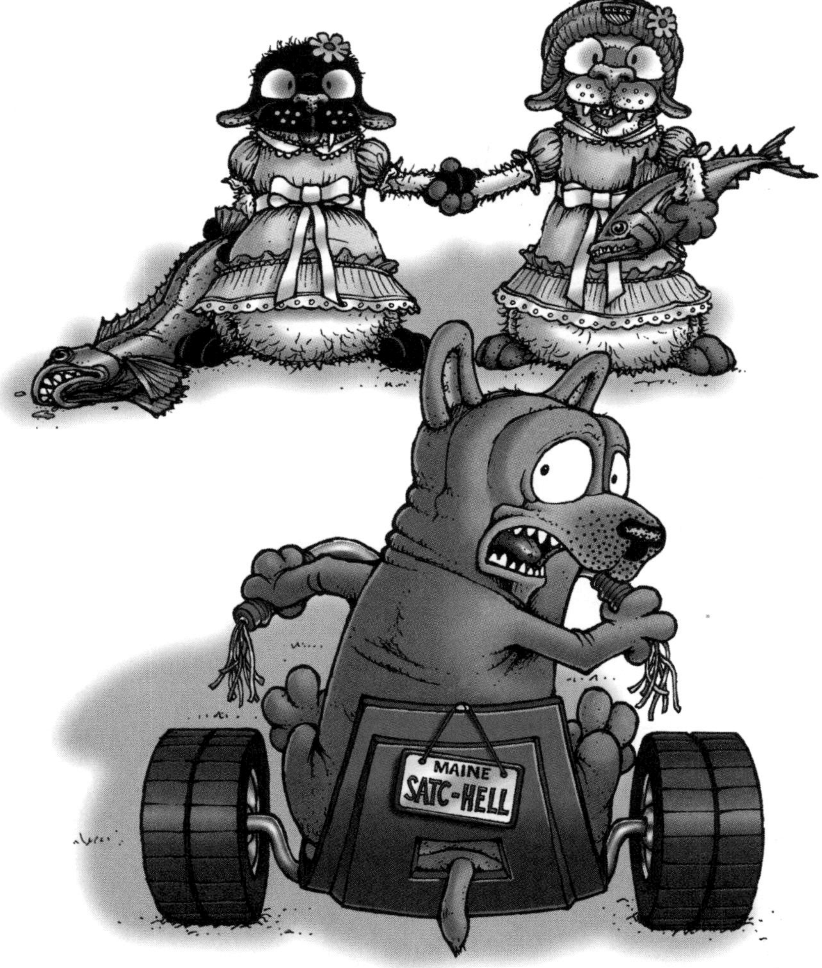
MAINE
SATC-HELL

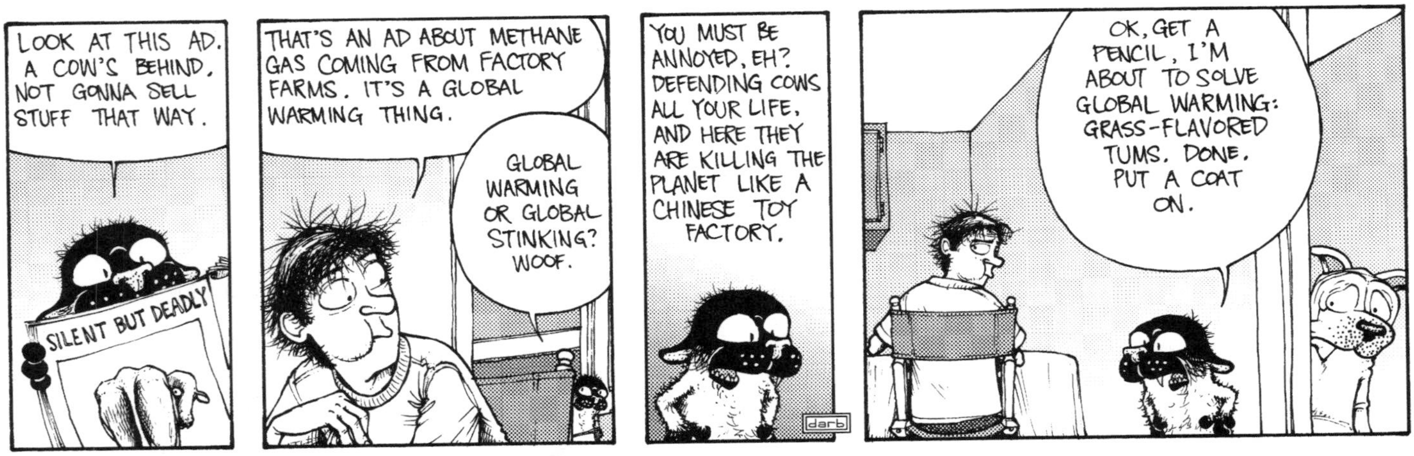
LOOK AT THIS AD. A COW'S BEHIND. NOT GONNA SELL STUFF THAT WAY.
SILENT BUT DEADLY
THAT'S AN AD ABOUT METHANE GAS COMING FROM FACTORY FARMS. IT'S A GLOBAL WARMING THING.
GLOBAL WARMING OR GLOBAL STINKING? WOOF.
YOU MUST BE ANNOYED, EH? DEFENDING COWS ALL YOUR LIFE, AND HERE THEY ARE KILLING THE PLANET LIKE A CHINESE TOY FACTORY.
darb
OK, GET A PENCIL, I'M ABOUT TO SOLVE GLOBAL WARMING: GRASS-FLAVORED TUMS. DONE. PUT A COAT ON.

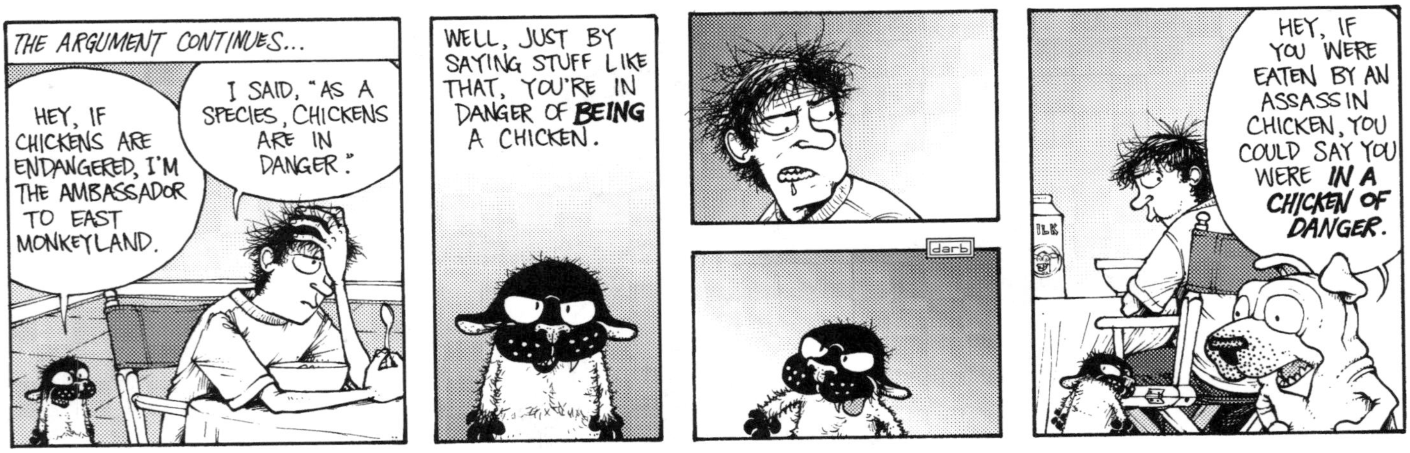
THE ARGUMENT CONTINUES...
HEY, IF CHICKENS ARE ENDANGERED, I'M THE AMBASSADOR TO EAST MONKEYLAND.
I SAID, "AS A SPECIES, CHICKENS ARE IN DANGER."
WELL, JUST BY SAYING STUFF LIKE THAT, YOU'RE IN DANGER OF BEING A CHICKEN.
darb
HEY, IF YOU WERE EATEN BY AN ASSASSIN CHICKEN, YOU COULD SAY YOU WERE IN A CHICKEN OF DANGER.

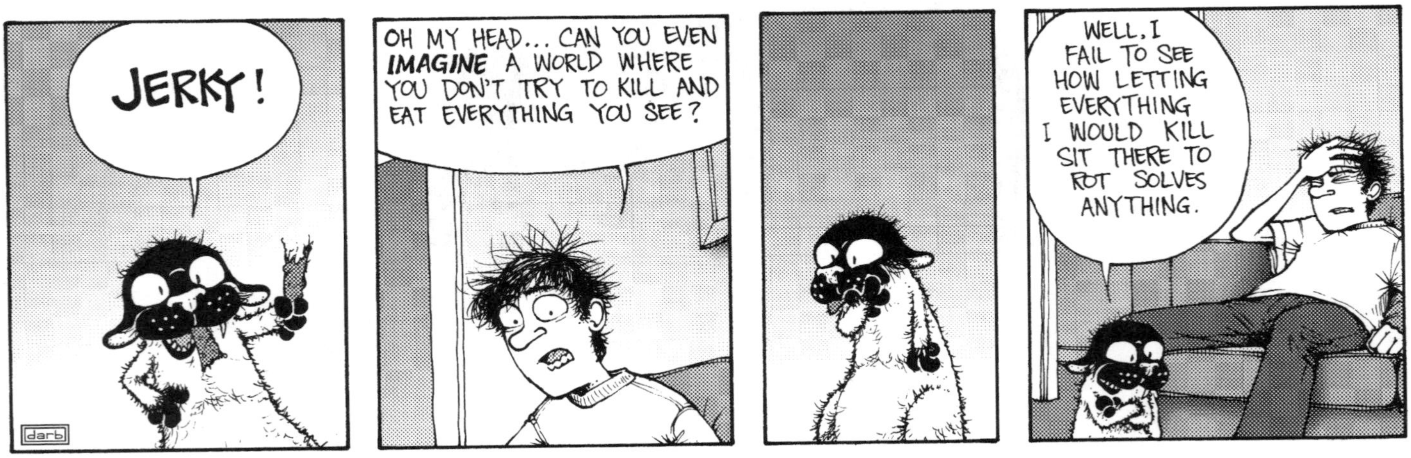
JERKY!
darb
OH MY HEAD... CAN YOU EVEN IMAGINE A WORLD WHERE YOU DON'T TRY TO KILL AND EAT EVERYTHING YOU SEE?
WELL, I FAIL TO SEE HOW LETTING EVERYTHING I WOULD KILL SIT THERE TO ROT SOLVES ANYTHING.

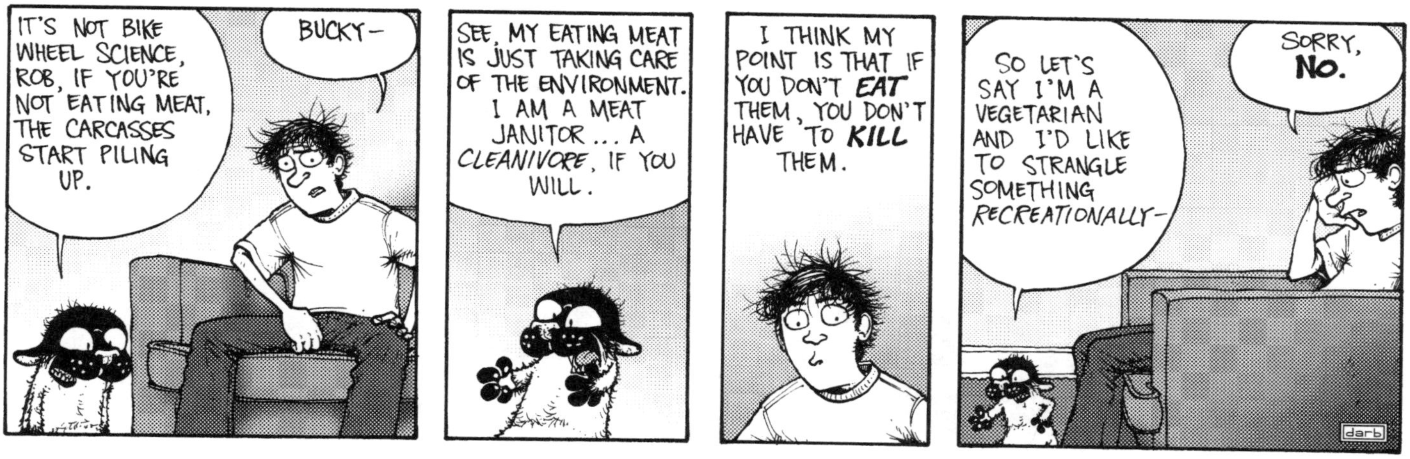
IT'S NOT BIKE WHEEL SCIENCE, ROB, IF YOU'RE NOT EATING MEAT, THE CARCASSES START PILING UP.
BUCKY—
SEE, MY EATING MEAT IS JUST TAKING CARE OF THE ENVIRONMENT. I AM A MEAT JANITOR... A *CLEANIVORE*, IF YOU WILL.
I THINK MY POINT IS THAT IF YOU DON'T **EAT** THEM, YOU DON'T HAVE TO **KILL** THEM.
SO LET'S SAY I'M A VEGETARIAN AND I'D LIKE TO STRANGLE SOMETHING *RECREATIONALLY*—
SORRY, **NO.**
darb

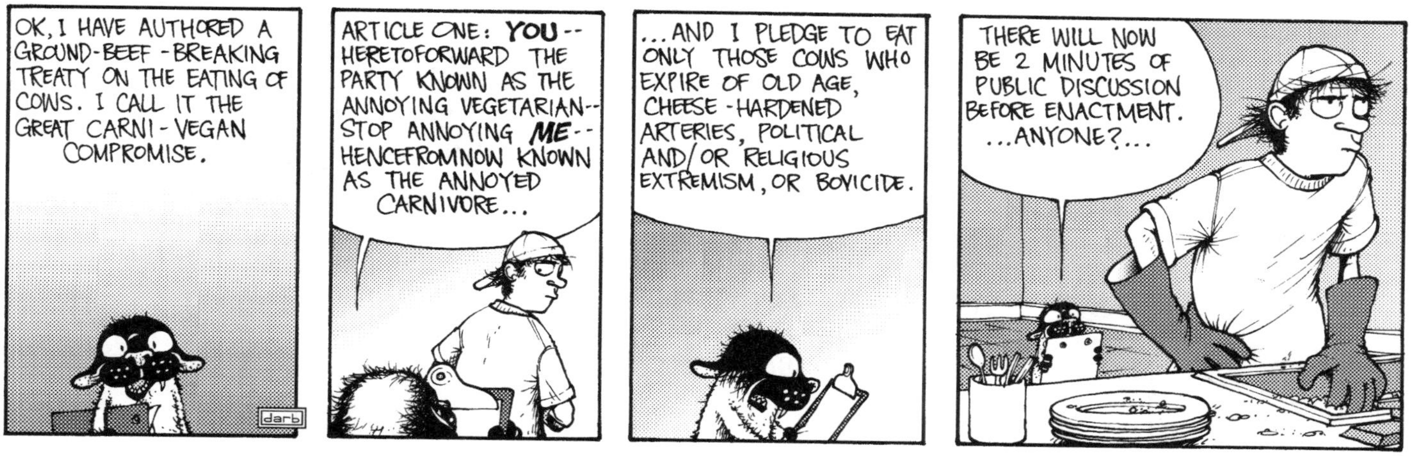
OK, I HAVE AUTHORED A GROUND-BEEF-BREAKING TREATY ON THE EATING OF COWS. I CALL IT THE GREAT CARNI-VEGAN COMPROMISE.
darb
ARTICLE ONE: **YOU**-- HERETOFORWARD THE PARTY KNOWN AS THE ANNOYING VEGETARIAN-- STOP ANNOYING **ME**-- HENCEFROMNOW KNOWN AS THE ANNOYED CARNIVORE...
...AND I PLEDGE TO EAT ONLY THOSE COWS WHO EXPIRE OF OLD AGE, CHEESE-HARDENED ARTERIES, POLITICAL AND/OR RELIGIOUS EXTREMISM, OR BOVICIDE.
THERE WILL NOW BE 2 MINUTES OF PUBLIC DISCUSSION BEFORE ENACTMENT. ...ANYONE?...

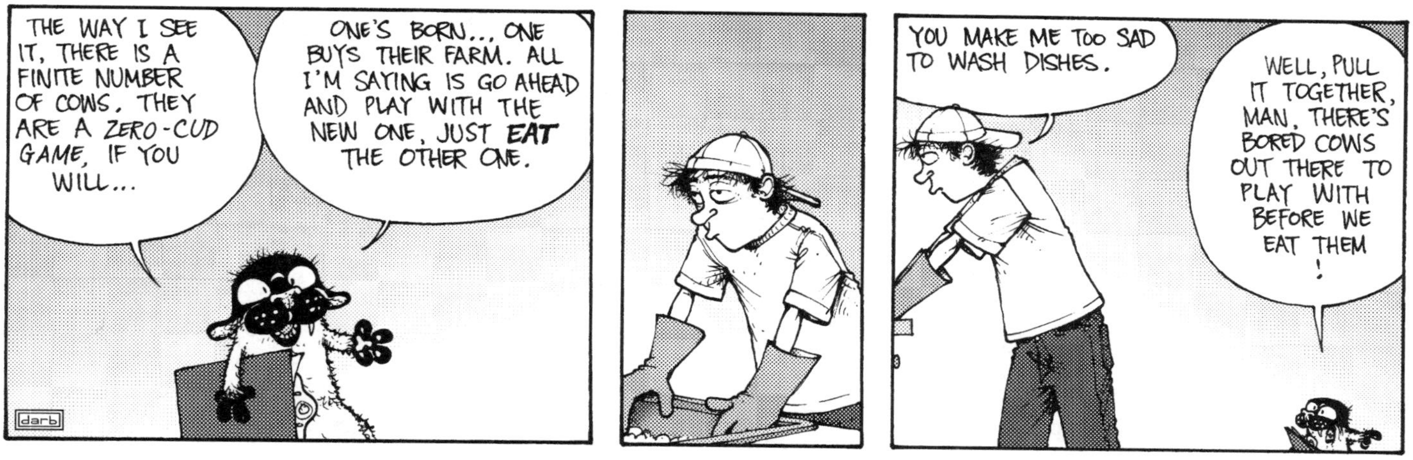
THE WAY I SEE IT, THERE IS A FINITE NUMBER OF COWS. THEY ARE A *ZERO-CUD GAME*, IF YOU WILL...
ONE'S BORN..., ONE BUYS THEIR FARM. ALL I'M SAYING IS GO AHEAD AND PLAY WITH THE NEW ONE, JUST **EAT** THE OTHER ONE.
darb
YOU MAKE ME TOO SAD TO WASH DISHES.
WELL, PULL IT TOGETHER, MAN. THERE'S BORED COWS OUT THERE TO PLAY WITH BEFORE WE EAT THEM!

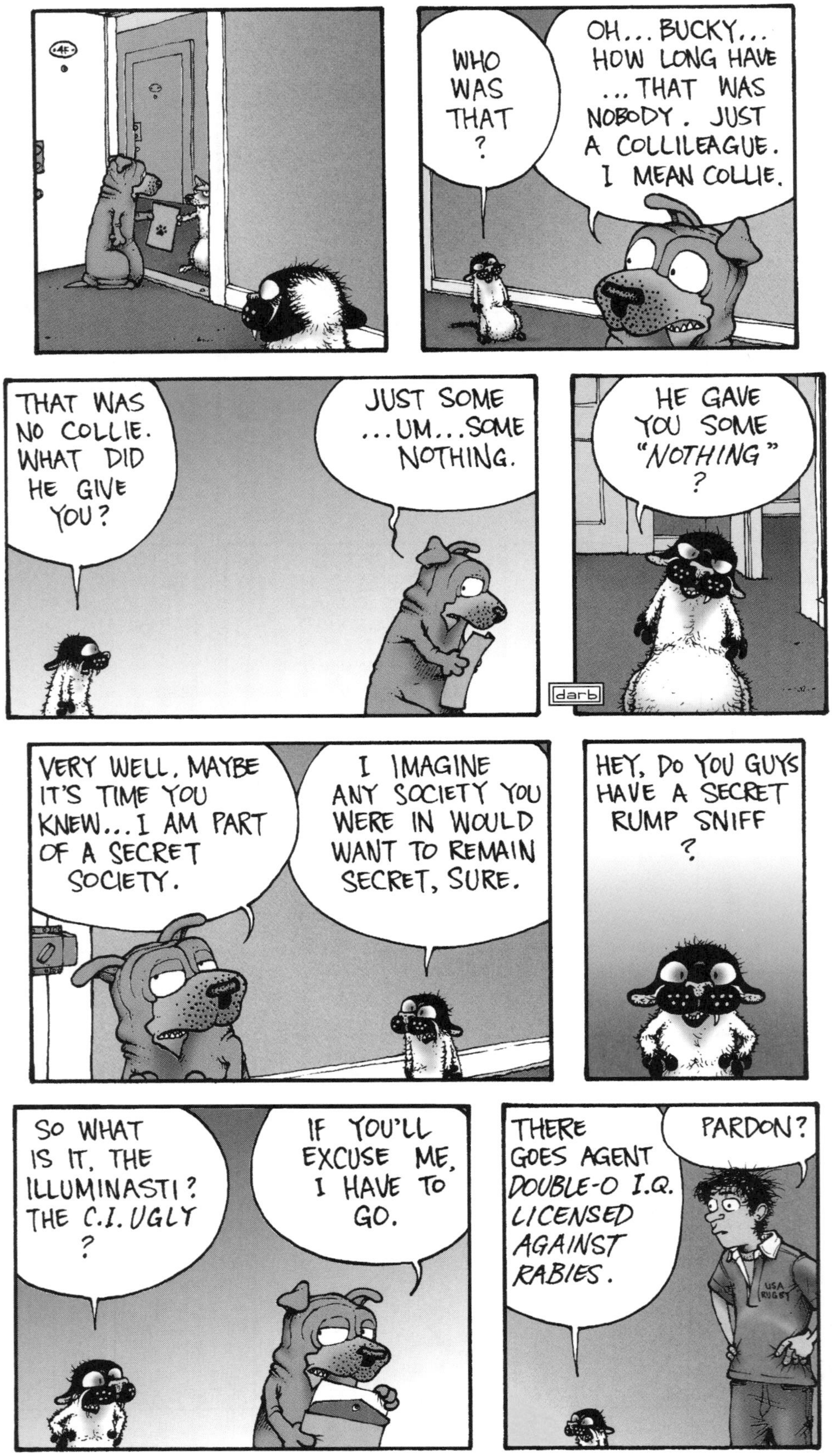
4F
WHO WAS THAT ?
OH... BUCKY... HOW LONG HAVE ... THAT WAS NOBODY. JUST A COLLILEAGUE. I MEAN COLLIE.
THAT WAS NO COLLIE. WHAT DID HE GIVE YOU?
JUST SOME ...UM...SOME NOTHING.
HE GAVE YOU SOME "*NOTHING*" ?
darb
VERY WELL, MAYBE IT'S TIME YOU KNEW... I AM PART OF A SECRET SOCIETY.
I IMAGINE ANY SOCIETY YOU WERE IN WOULD WANT TO REMAIN SECRET, SURE.
HEY, DO YOU GUYS HAVE A SECRET RUMP SNIFF ?
SO WHAT IS IT, THE ILLUMINASTI? THE *C.I. UGLY* ?
IF YOU'LL EXCUSE ME, I HAVE TO GO.
THERE GOES AGENT *DOUBLE-O I.Q. LICENSED AGAINST RABIES*.
PARDON?
USA RUGBY

WELL, I FOR ONE THINK IT'S MADNESS TO NOT EAT COWS.

THERE'D BE A COWPULATION EXPLOSION. COWS ON THE SUBWAY. COWS IN PUBLIC RESTROOMS. COWS FALLING OFF MOPEDS AROUND SANDY CORNERS...

COWS HITTIN' ON YOUR SISTER AT THE COMPANY DO.

BUCKY, THE ONLY REA~~~

THE ONLY REASON THERE'S SO MANY COWS AS IT IS IS SO THEY CAN BE EATEN.

OK. CORRECT ME IF I'M WRONG, BUT YOU'RE MAKING MY POINT.

I THINK WE'RE GOING TO HAVE TO AGREE TO DISAGREE ABOUT EATING COWS.

FINE. JUST DON'T COME CRYIN' TO ME THE NEXT TIME A COW IS BEARING DOWN ON YOU WITH A BIG HAMMER.

COWS DON'T USE HAMMERS.

YEAH, I HEARD THEY PREFER KNIVES, TOO.

COR, THAT'S SOME BAD BEEF, INNIT?

I KNEW A LITTLE FELLA, RIGHT, GOT IN A TIFF WITH A COW IN SHEFFIELD. GOT KNOCKED OUT COLD BY A BLAST OF MILK, RIGHT?

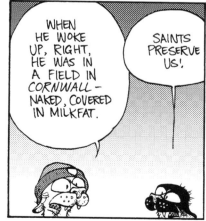

WHEN HE WOKE UP, RIGHT, HE WAS IN A FIELD IN CORNWALL — NAKED, COVERED IN MILKFAT.

SAINTS PRESERVE US!

I RECKON IF HE'D BEEN LACTOSE INTOLERANT, HE'D BE DEAD NOW.

MAKES YOU COUNT YOUR COW-FREE BLESSINGS.

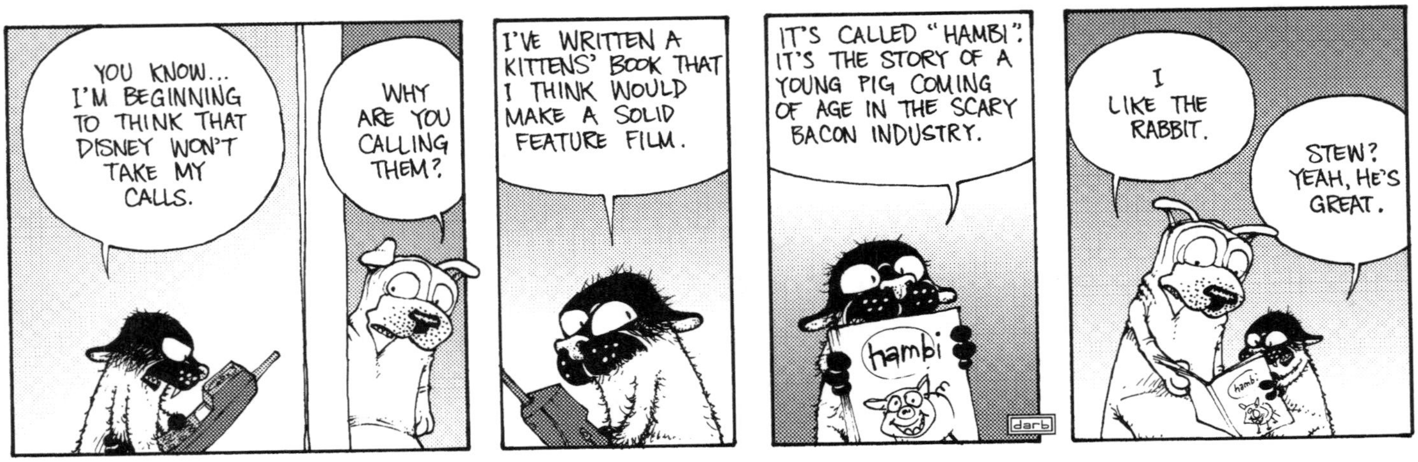
YOU KNOW... I'M BEGINNING TO THINK THAT DISNEY WON'T TAKE MY CALLS.
WHY ARE YOU CALLING THEM?
I'VE WRITTEN A KITTENS' BOOK THAT I THINK WOULD MAKE A SOLID FEATURE FILM.
IT'S CALLED "HAMBI". IT'S THE STORY OF A YOUNG PIG COMING OF AGE IN THE SCARY BACON INDUSTRY.
hambi
I LIKE THE RABBIT.
STEW? YEAH, HE'S GREAT.

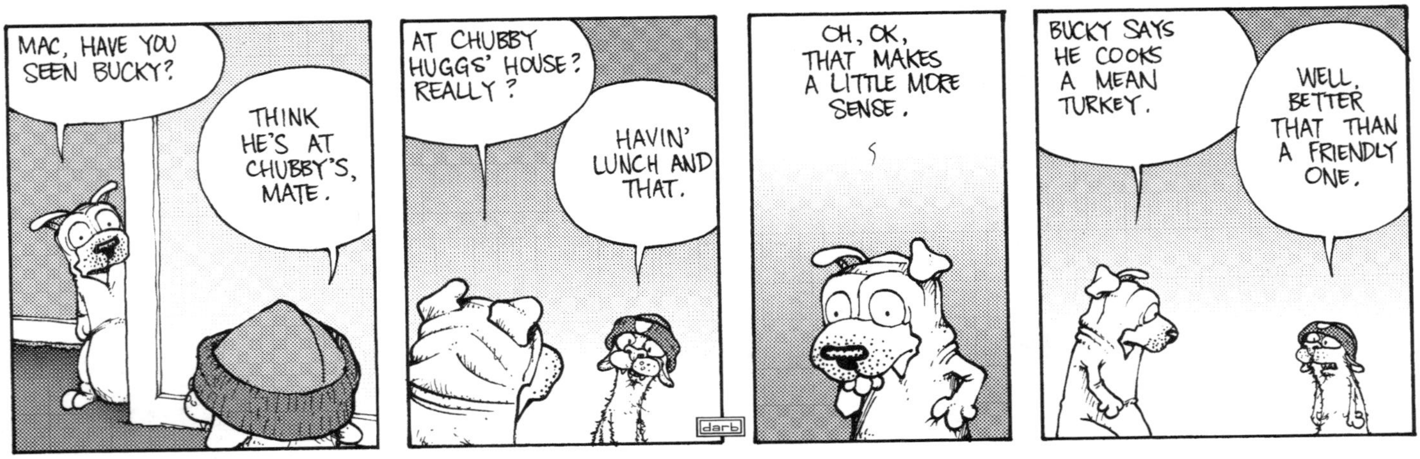
MAC, HAVE YOU SEEN BUCKY?
THINK HE'S AT CHUBBY'S, MATE.
AT CHUBBY HUGGS' HOUSE? REALLY?
HAVIN' LUNCH AND THAT.
OH, OK, THAT MAKES A LITTLE MORE SENSE.
BUCKY SAYS HE COOKS A MEAN TURKEY.
WELL, BETTER THAT THAN A FRIENDLY ONE.

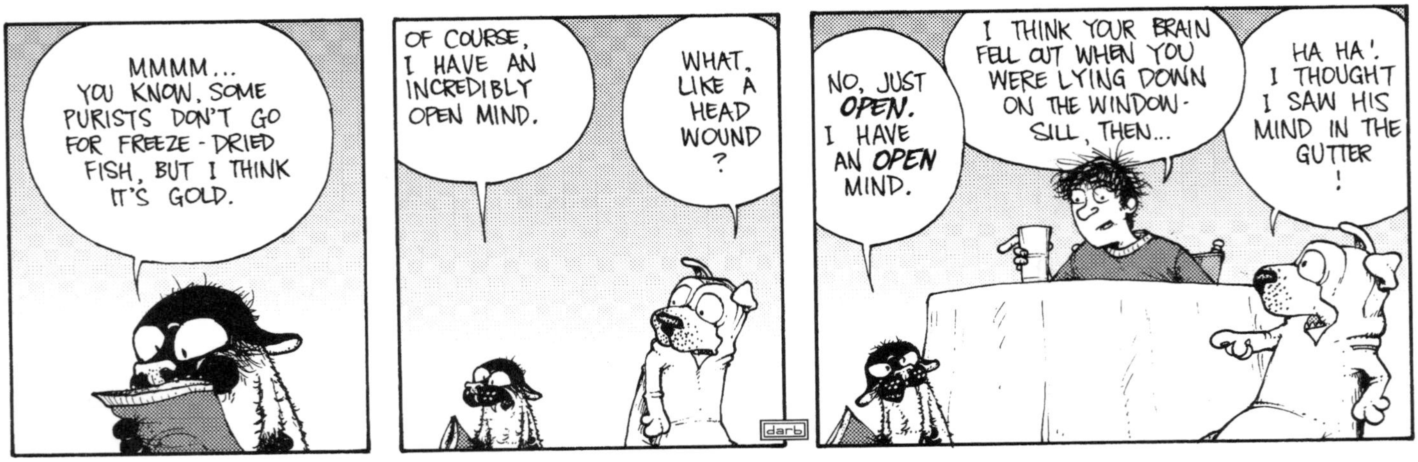
MMMM... YOU KNOW, SOME PURISTS DON'T GO FOR FREEZE-DRIED FISH, BUT I THINK IT'S GOLD.
OF COURSE, I HAVE AN INCREDIBLY OPEN MIND.
WHAT, LIKE A HEAD WOUND?
NO, JUST *OPEN*. I HAVE AN *OPEN* MIND.
I THINK YOUR BRAIN FELL OUT WHEN YOU WERE LYING DOWN ON THE WINDOW-SILL, THEN...
HA HA! I THOUGHT I SAW HIS MIND IN THE GUTTER!

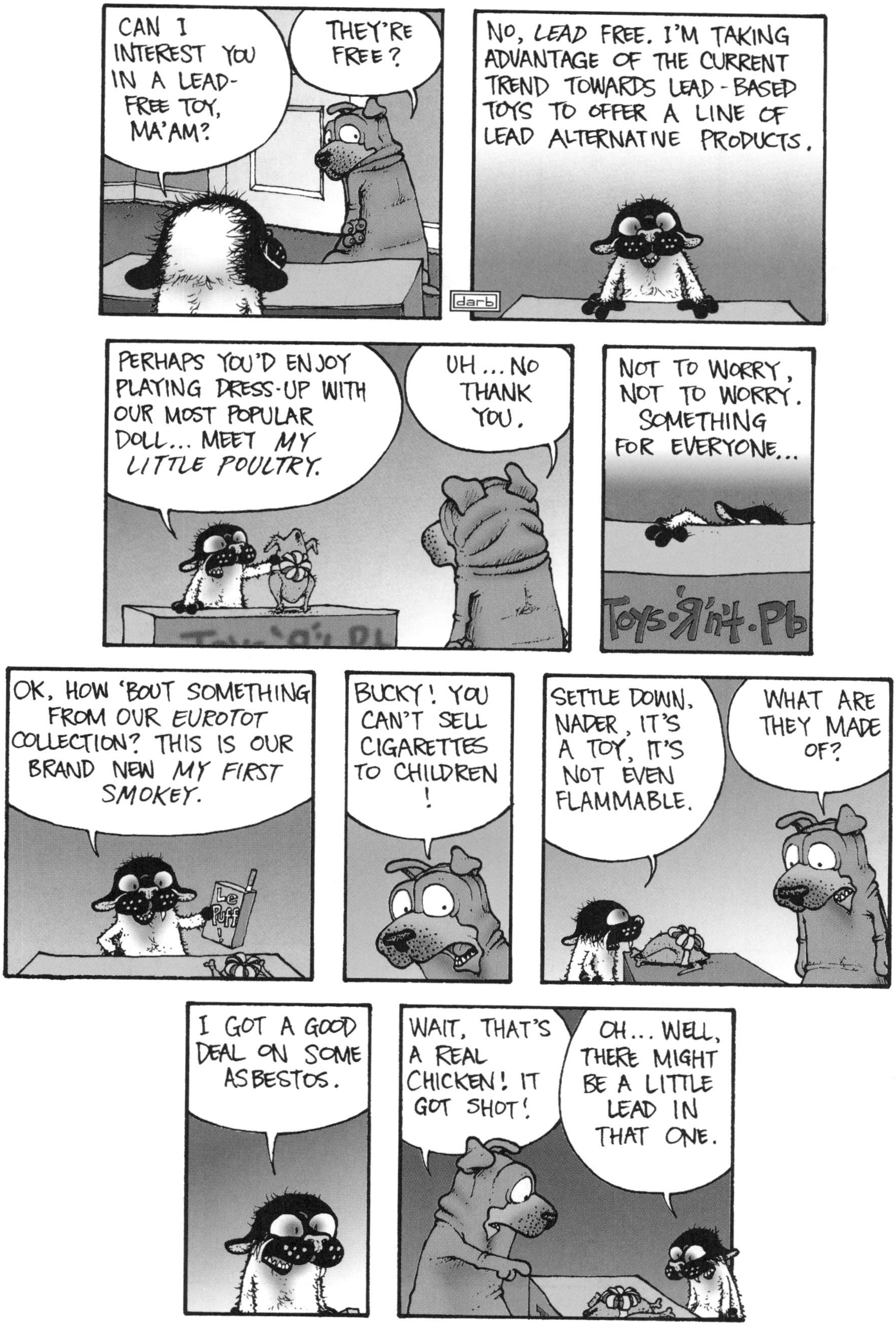
CAN I INTEREST YOU IN A LEAD-FREE TOY, MA'AM?
THEY'RE FREE?
NO, *LEAD* FREE. I'M TAKING ADVANTAGE OF THE CURRENT TREND TOWARDS LEAD-BASED TOYS TO OFFER A LINE OF LEAD ALTERNATIVE PRODUCTS.
darb
PERHAPS YOU'D ENJOY PLAYING DRESS-UP WITH OUR MOST POPULAR DOLL... MEET *MY LITTLE POULTRY.*
UH... NO THANK YOU.
NOT TO WORRY, NOT TO WORRY. SOMETHING FOR EVERYONE...
Toys·Я'n't·Pb
OK, HOW 'BOUT SOMETHING FROM OUR *EUROTOT* COLLECTION? THIS IS OUR BRAND NEW *MY FIRST SMOKEY.*
Le Puff!
BUCKY! YOU CAN'T SELL CIGARETTES TO CHILDREN!
SETTLE DOWN, NADER, IT'S A TOY, IT'S NOT EVEN FLAMMABLE.
WHAT ARE THEY MADE OF?
I GOT A GOOD DEAL ON SOME ASBESTOS.
WAIT, THAT'S A REAL CHICKEN! IT GOT SHOT!
OH... WELL, THERE MIGHT BE A LITTLE LEAD IN THAT ONE.

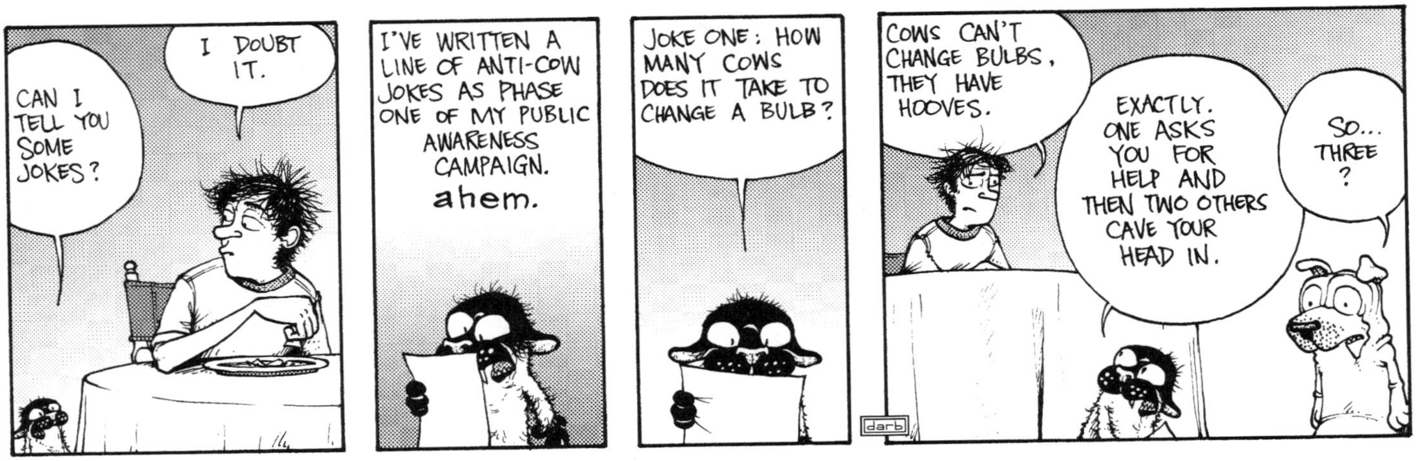
CAN I TELL YOU SOME JOKES?
I DOUBT IT.
I'VE WRITTEN A LINE OF ANTI-COW JOKES AS PHASE ONE OF MY PUBLIC AWARENESS CAMPAIGN.
ahem.
JOKE ONE: HOW MANY COWS DOES IT TAKE TO CHANGE A BULB?
COWS CAN'T CHANGE BULBS, THEY HAVE HOOVES.
EXACTLY. ONE ASKS YOU FOR HELP AND THEN TWO OTHERS CAVE YOUR HEAD IN.
SO... THREE?
darb

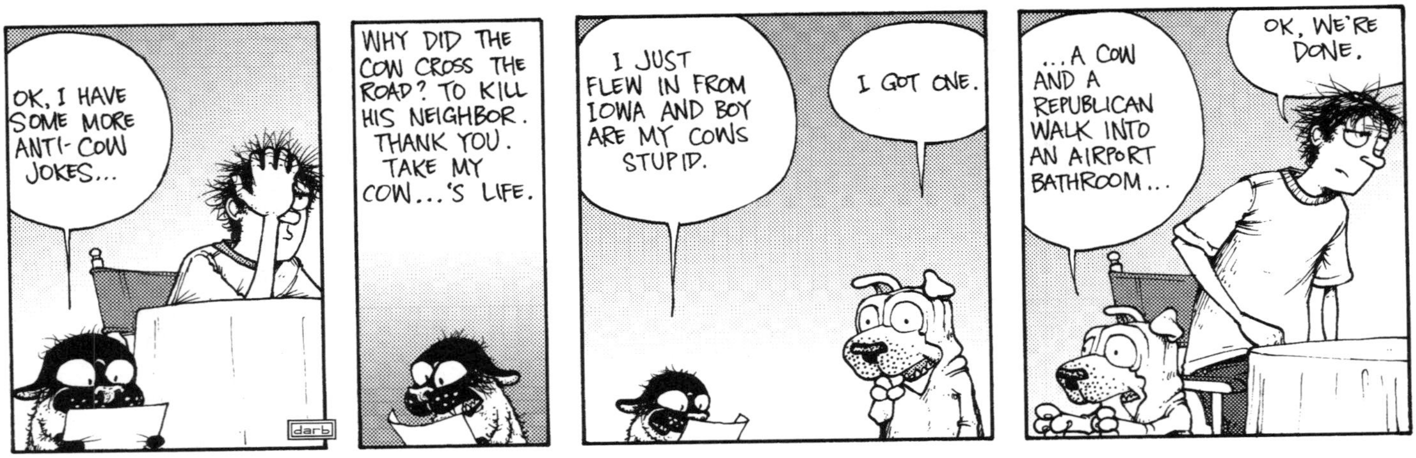
OK, I HAVE SOME MORE ANTI-COW JOKES...
darb
WHY DID THE COW CROSS THE ROAD? TO KILL HIS NEIGHBOR. THANK YOU. TAKE MY COW...'S LIFE.
I JUST FLEW IN FROM IOWA AND BOY ARE MY COWS STUPID.
I GOT ONE.
...A COW AND A REPUBLICAN WALK INTO AN AIRPORT BATHROOM...
OK, WE'RE DONE.

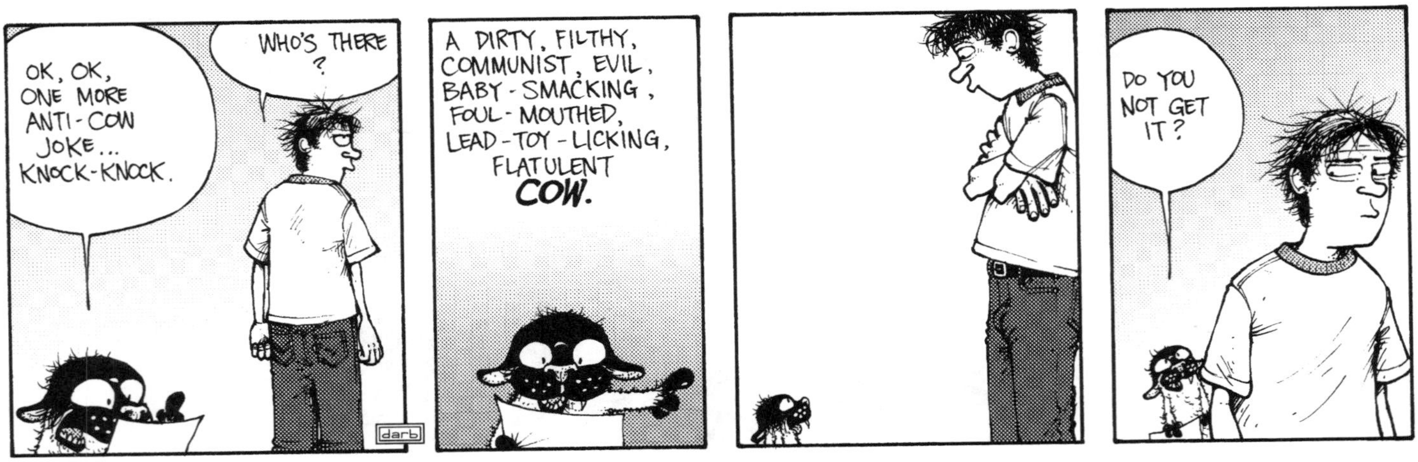
OK, OK, ONE MORE ANTI-COW JOKE... KNOCK-KNOCK.
WHO'S THERE?
darb
A DIRTY, FILTHY, COMMUNIST, EVIL, BABY-SMACKING, FOUL-MOUTHED, LEAD-TOY-LICKING, FLATULENT COW.
DO YOU NOT GET IT?

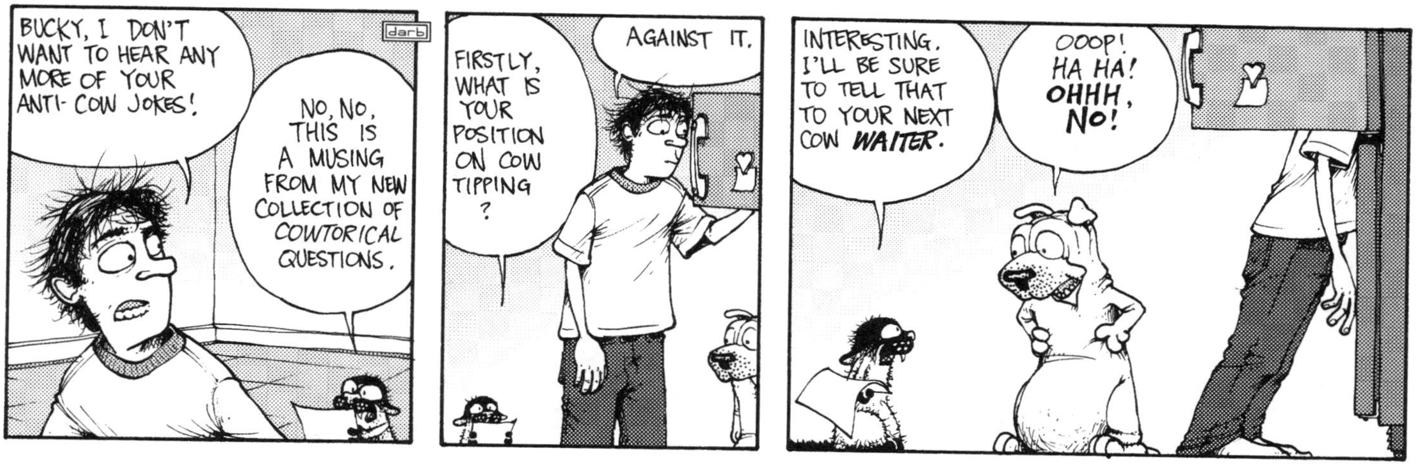
BUCKY, I DON'T WANT TO HEAR ANY MORE OF YOUR ANTI-COW JOKES!
NO, NO, THIS IS A MUSING FROM MY NEW COLLECTION OF COWTORICAL QUESTIONS.
FIRSTLY, WHAT IS YOUR POSITION ON COW TIPPING?
AGAINST IT.
INTERESTING. I'LL BE SURE TO TELL THAT TO YOUR NEXT COW WAITER.
OOOP! HA HA! OHHH, NO!

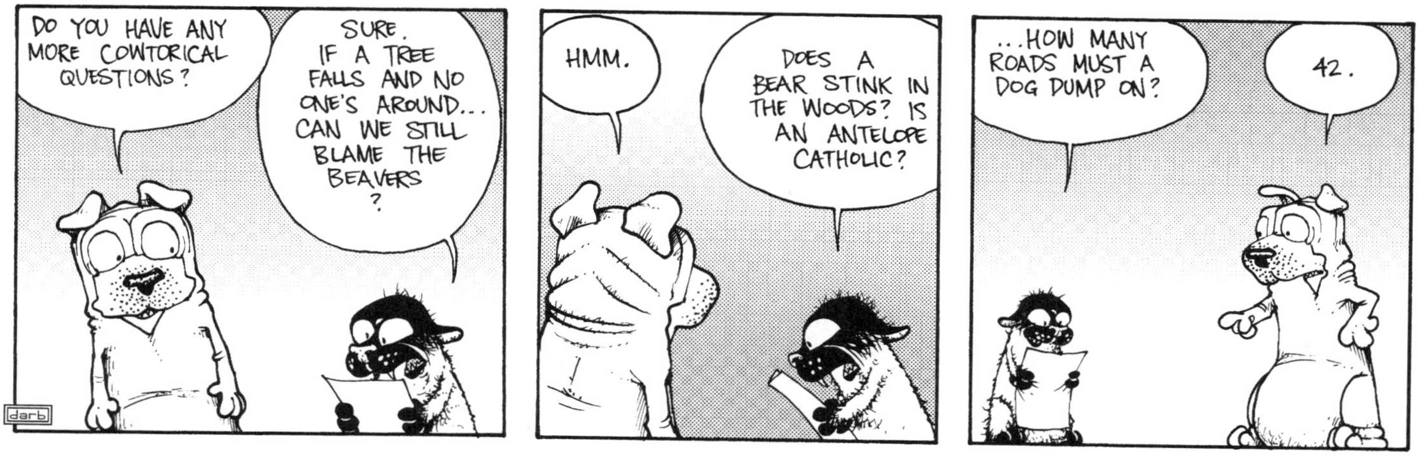
DO YOU HAVE ANY MORE COWTORICAL QUESTIONS?
SURE. IF A TREE FALLS AND NO ONE'S AROUND... CAN WE STILL BLAME THE BEAVERS?
HMM.
DOES A BEAR STINK IN THE WOODS? IS AN ANTELOPE CATHOLIC?
...HOW MANY ROADS MUST A DOG DUMP ON?
42.

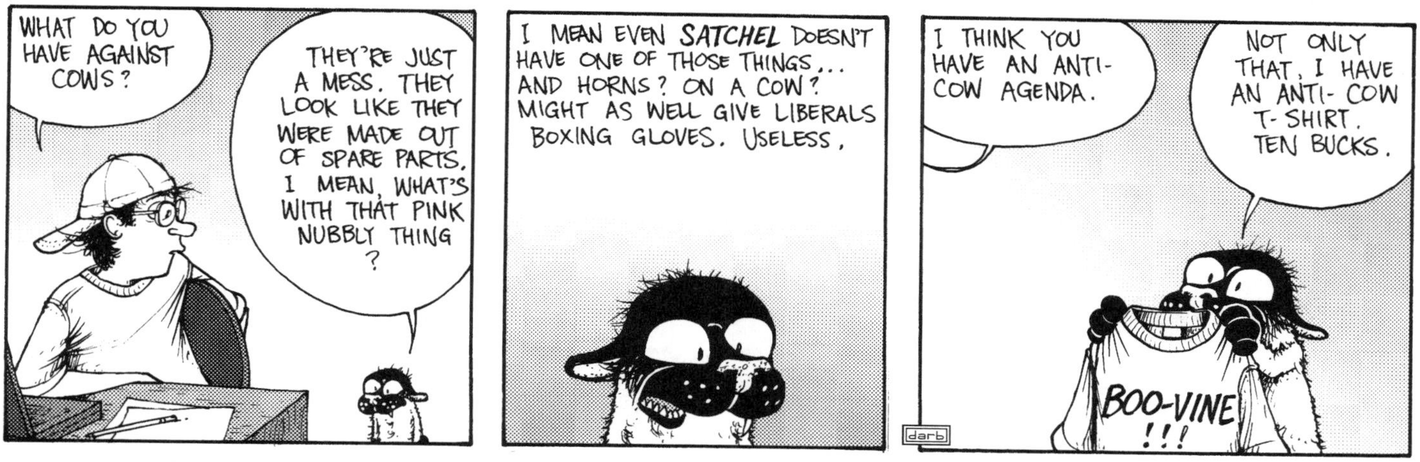
WHAT DO YOU HAVE AGAINST COWS?
THEY'RE JUST A MESS. THEY LOOK LIKE THEY WERE MADE OUT OF SPARE PARTS. I MEAN, WHAT'S WITH THAT PINK NUBBLY THING?
I MEAN EVEN SATCHEL DOESN'T HAVE ONE OF THOSE THINGS... AND HORNS? ON A COW? MIGHT AS WELL GIVE LIBERALS BOXING GLOVES. USELESS.
I THINK YOU HAVE AN ANTI-COW AGENDA.
NOT ONLY THAT, I HAVE AN ANTI-COW T-SHIRT. TEN BUCKS.
BOO-VINE!!!

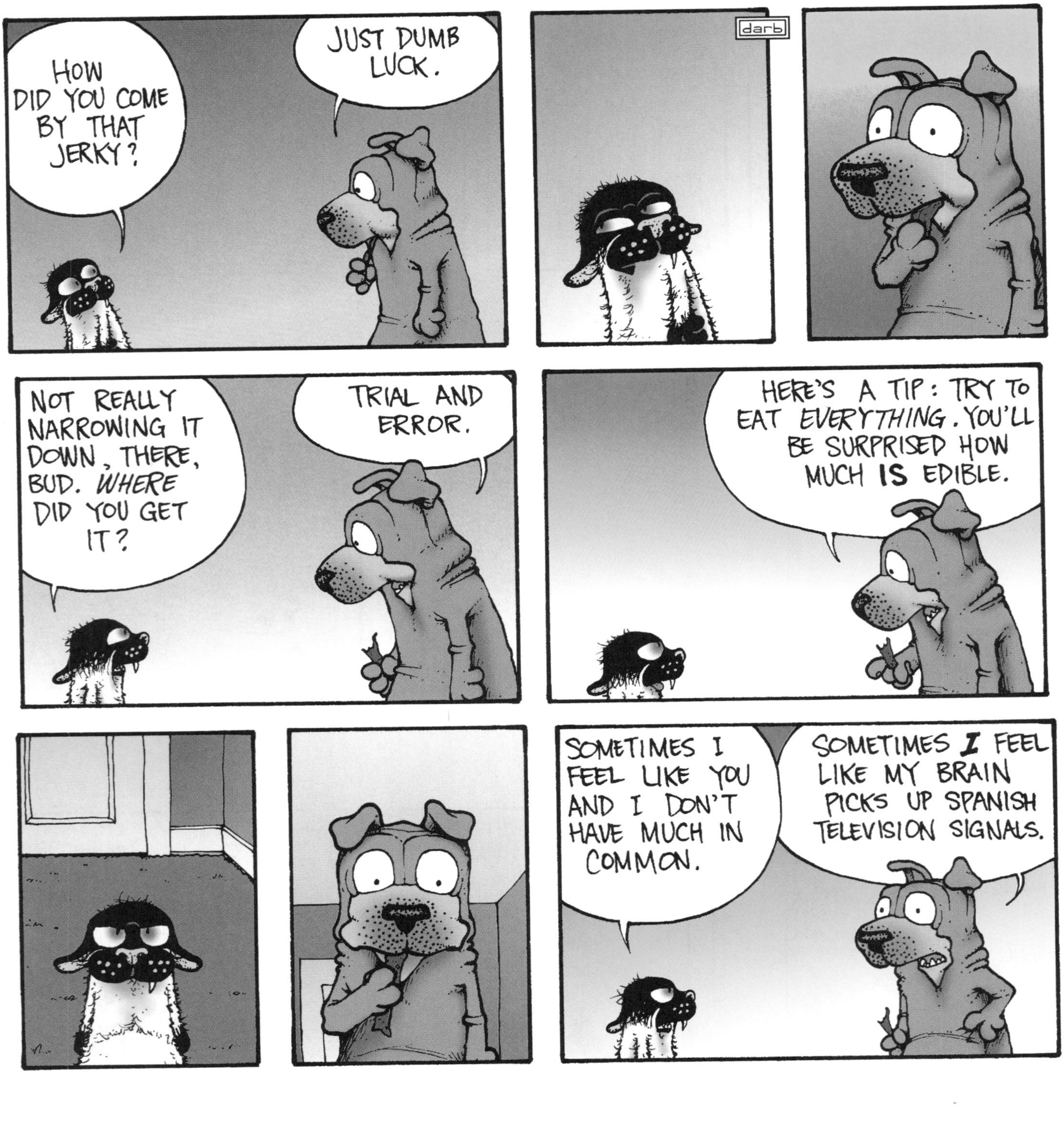
HOW DID YOU COME BY THAT JERKY?
JUST DUMB LUCK.
darb
NOT REALLY NARROWING IT DOWN, THERE, BUD. *WHERE* DID YOU GET IT?
TRIAL AND ERROR.
HERE'S A TIP: TRY TO EAT *EVERYTHING*. YOU'LL BE SURPRISED HOW MUCH **IS** EDIBLE.
SOMETIMES I FEEL LIKE YOU AND I DON'T HAVE MUCH IN COMMON.
SOMETIMES *I* FEEL LIKE MY BRAIN PICKS UP SPANISH TELEVISION SIGNALS.

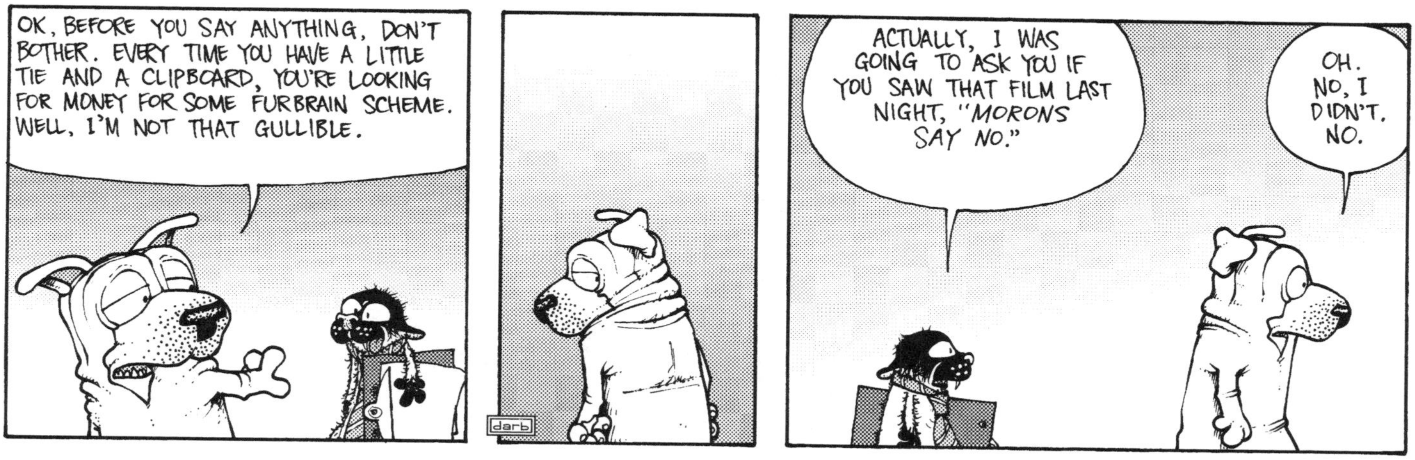
OK, BEFORE YOU SAY ANYTHING, DON'T BOTHER. EVERY TIME YOU HAVE A LITTLE TIE AND A CLIPBOARD, YOU'RE LOOKING FOR MONEY FOR SOME FURBRAIN SCHEME. WELL, I'M NOT THAT GULLIBLE.
ACTUALLY, I WAS GOING TO ASK YOU IF YOU SAW THAT FILM LAST NIGHT, "MORONS SAY NO."
OH. NO, I DIDN'T. NO.

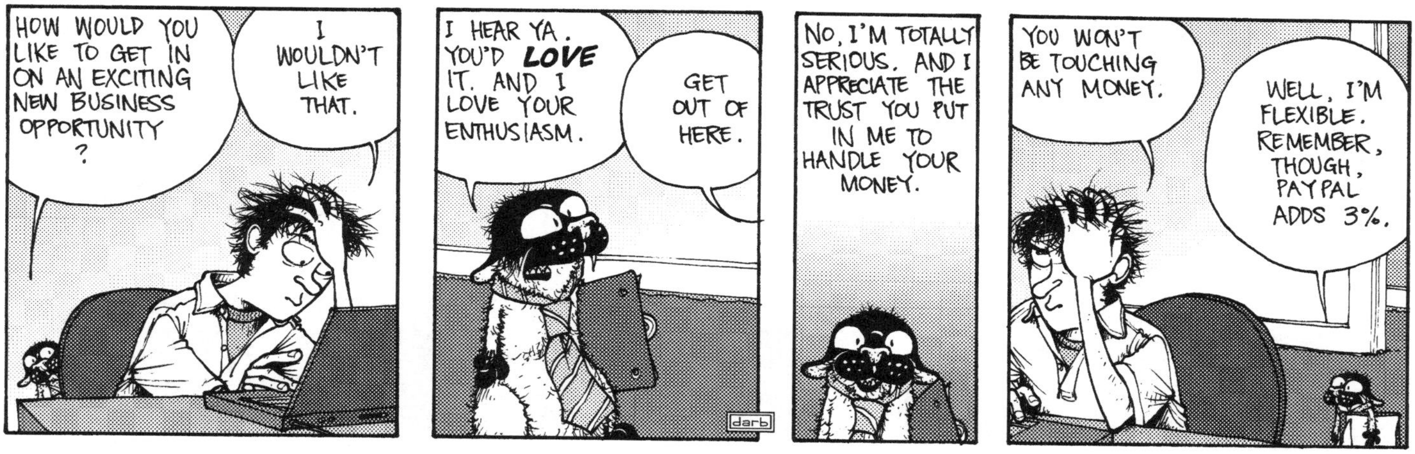
HOW WOULD YOU LIKE TO GET IN ON AN EXCITING NEW BUSINESS OPPORTUNITY ?
I WOULDN'T LIKE THAT.
I HEAR YA. YOU'D LOVE IT. AND I LOVE YOUR ENTHUSIASM.
GET OUT OF HERE.
NO, I'M TOTALLY SERIOUS. AND I APPRECIATE THE TRUST YOU PUT IN ME TO HANDLE YOUR MONEY.
YOU WON'T BE TOUCHING ANY MONEY.
WELL, I'M FLEXIBLE. REMEMBER, THOUGH, PAYPAL ADDS 3%.

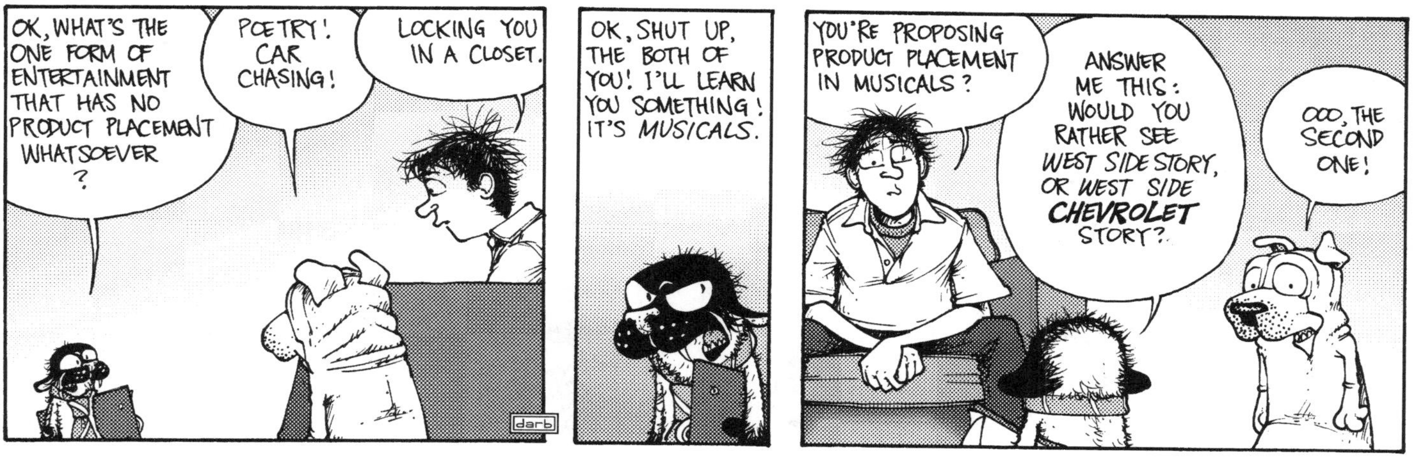
OK, WHAT'S THE ONE FORM OF ENTERTAINMENT THAT HAS NO PRODUCT PLACEMENT WHATSOEVER ?
POETRY! CAR CHASING!
LOCKING YOU IN A CLOSET.
OK, SHUT UP, THE BOTH OF YOU! I'LL LEARN YOU SOMETHING! IT'S MUSICALS.
YOU'RE PROPOSING PRODUCT PLACEMENT IN MUSICALS?
ANSWER ME THIS: WOULD YOU RATHER SEE WEST SIDE STORY, OR WEST SIDE CHEVROLET STORY?
OOO, THE SECOND ONE!

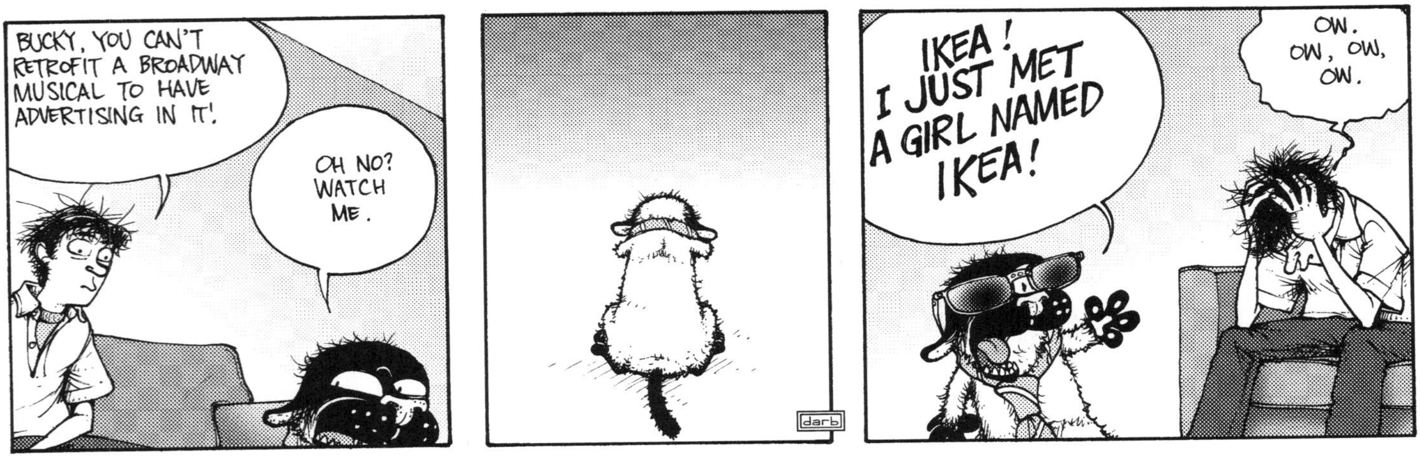
BUCKY, YOU CAN'T RETROFIT A BROADWAY MUSICAL TO HAVE ADVERTISING IN IT!
OH NO? WATCH ME.
darb
IKEA! I JUST MET A GIRL NAMED IKEA!
OW. OW, OW, OW.

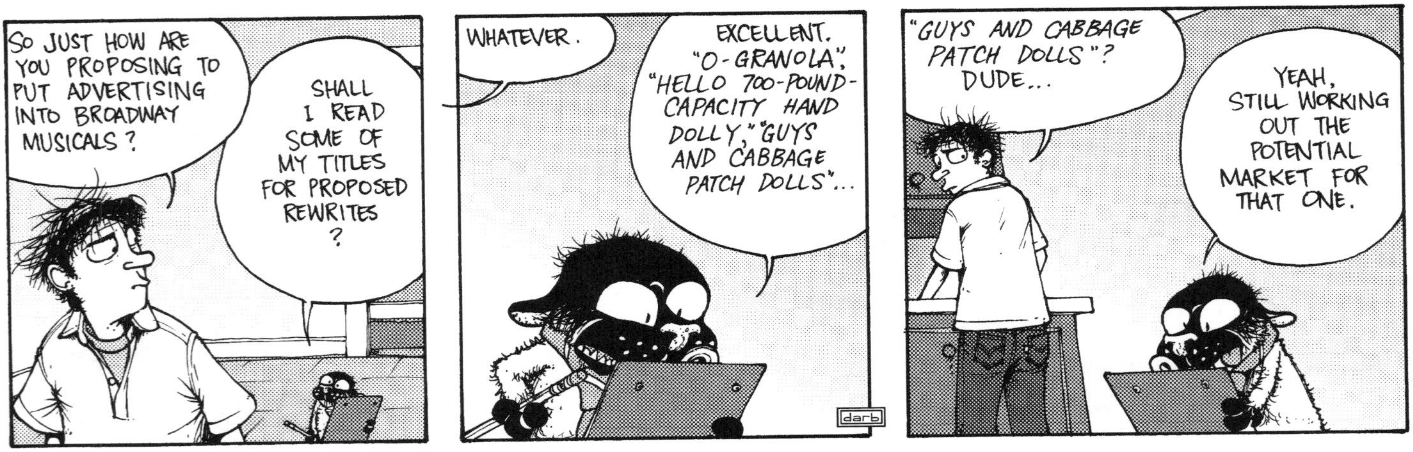
SO JUST HOW ARE YOU PROPOSING TO PUT ADVERTISING INTO BROADWAY MUSICALS?
SHALL I READ SOME OF MY TITLES FOR PROPOSED REWRITES?
WHATEVER.
EXCELLENT. "O-GRANOLA", "HELLO 700-POUND-CAPACITY HAND DOLLY," "GUYS AND CABBAGE PATCH DOLLS"...
darb
"GUYS AND CABBAGE PATCH DOLLS"? DUDE...
YEAH, STILL WORKING OUT THE POTENTIAL MARKET FOR THAT ONE.

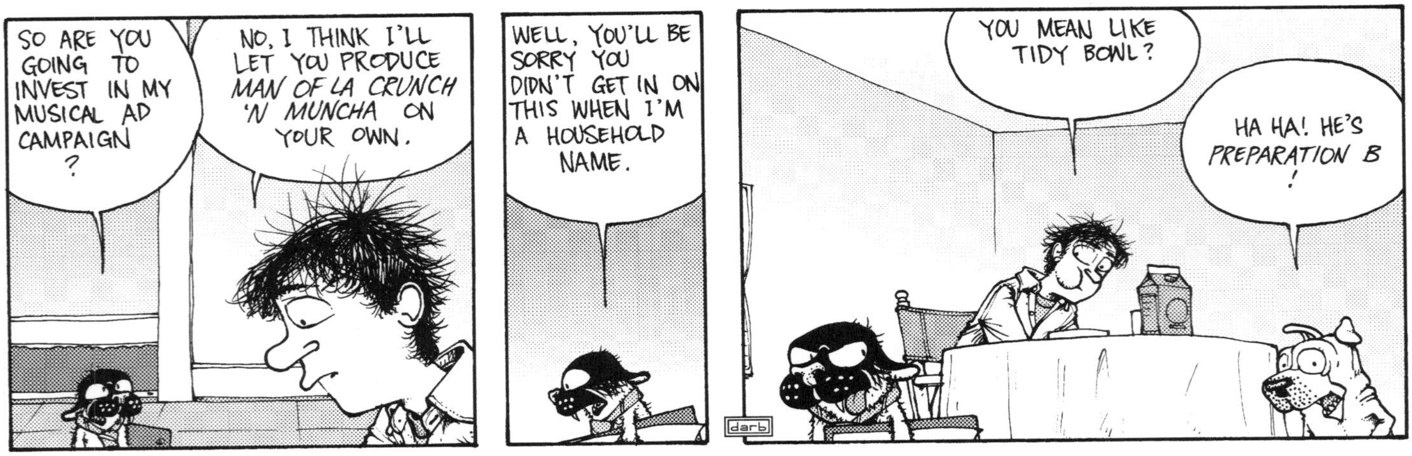
SO ARE YOU GOING TO INVEST IN MY MUSICAL AD CAMPAIGN?
NO, I THINK I'LL LET YOU PRODUCE *MAN OF LA CRUNCH 'N MUNCHA* ON YOUR OWN.
WELL, YOU'LL BE SORRY YOU DIDN'T GET IN ON THIS WHEN I'M A HOUSEHOLD NAME.
darb
YOU MEAN LIKE TIDY BOWL?
HA HA! HE'S *PREPARATION B*!

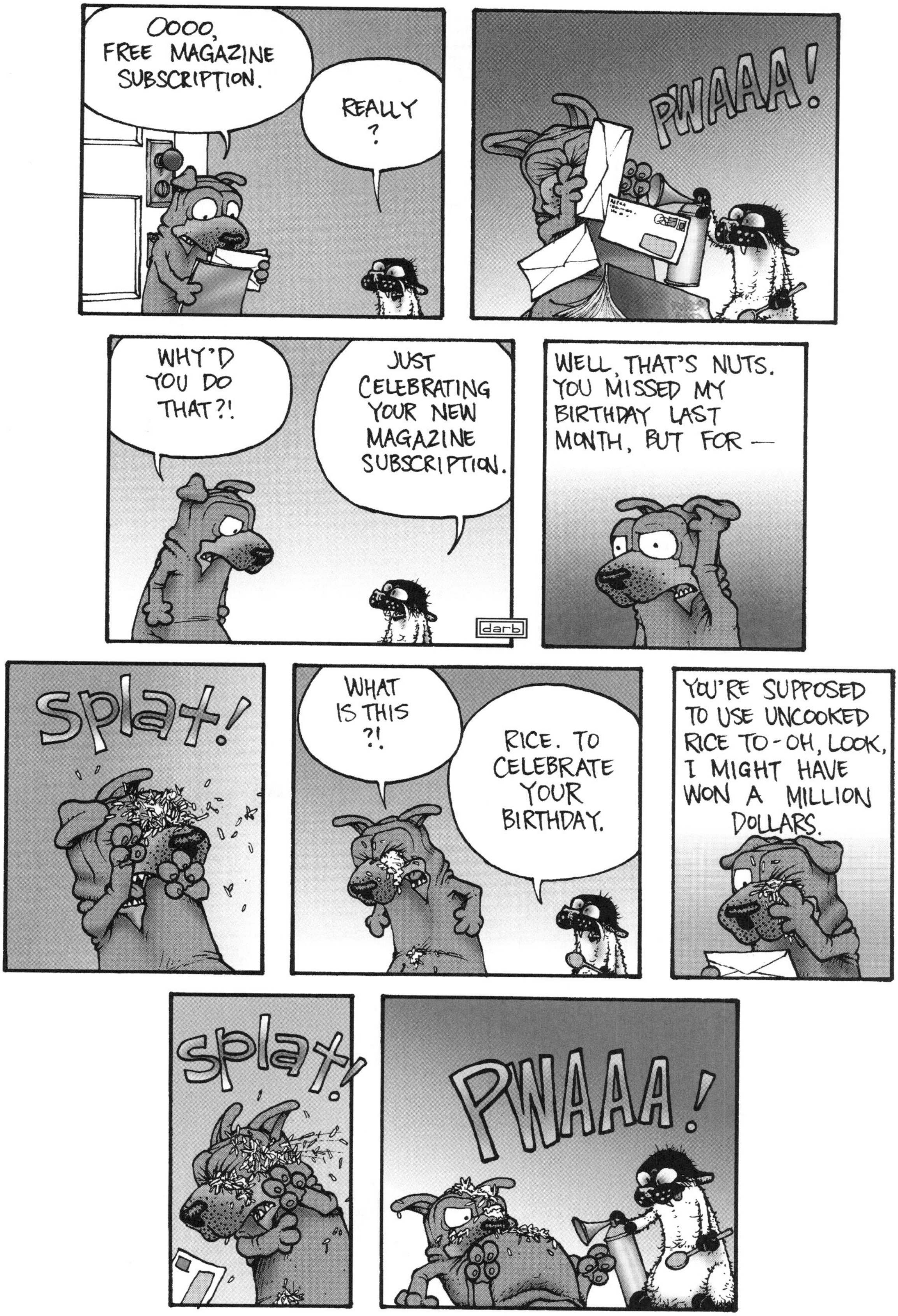
OOOO, FREE MAGAZINE SUBSCRIPTION.
REALLY ?
PWAAA!
WHY'D YOU DO THAT?!
JUST CELEBRATING YOUR NEW MAGAZINE SUBSCRIPTION.
darb
WELL, THAT'S NUTS. YOU MISSED MY BIRTHDAY LAST MONTH, BUT FOR—
splat!
WHAT IS THIS ?!
RICE. TO CELEBRATE YOUR BIRTHDAY.
YOU'RE SUPPOSED TO USE UNCOOKED RICE TO-OH, LOOK, I MIGHT HAVE WON A MILLION DOLLARS.
splat!
PWAAA!

OH, HI! WHAT ARE YOU DOING IN MY ROOM? IS THAT A PIE?

IT'S AN IMAGE PIE.

STUDIES SHOW IT'S IMPOSSIBLE TO THINK THAT SOMEONE HOLDING A PIE JUST LOOTED YOUR PIGGY BANK.

WAIT.... WHAT DOES "LOOTED" MEAN?

CARE FOR A DIVERSION CRACKER?

YEAH, YEAH!

BUCKY, WHERE DID ALL THE STUFF IN MY ROOM GO?

OH, I CLEANED YOUR ROOM EARLIER.

THERE'S NOTHING LEFT IN MY ROOM...

NO PROBLEM, CHIEF. YOU'RE WELCOME.

BUT YOU, LIKE, STOLE ALL OF MY STUFF...

WELL, I MAINTAIN I WAS CLEANING, AND IT'S THE THOUGHT THAT COUNTS.

NO, THE BRAIN COUNTS, AND YOUR BRAIN ALSO JUST STOLE ALL MY STUFF!

LOOK, IF YOU'RE GONNA GET TECHNICAL, THE FINGERS COUNT!

EVERYBODY KNOWS YOU COUNT WITH YOUR FINGERS! 1... 2... 6... UH... 1 AGAIN...

BUT YOUR BRAIN IS DOING THE COUNTING, IT CONTROLS YOUR FINGERS.

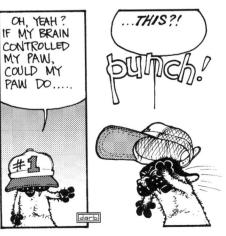

OH, YEAH? IF MY BRAIN CONTROLLED MY PAW, COULD MY PAW DO.....

...THIS?!

punch!

punch punch

OOF!

18

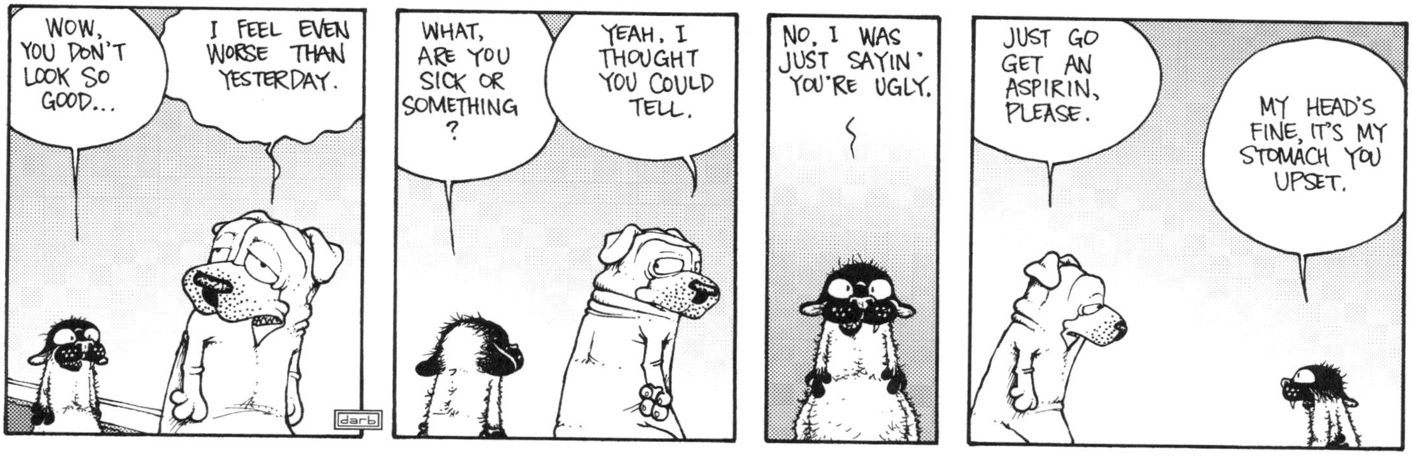
WOW, YOU DON'T LOOK SO GOOD...
I FEEL EVEN WORSE THAN YESTERDAY.
darb
WHAT, ARE YOU SICK OR SOMETHING ?
YEAH, I THOUGHT YOU COULD TELL.
NO, I WAS JUST SAYIN' YOU'RE UGLY.
JUST GO GET AN ASPIRIN, PLEASE.
MY HEAD'S FINE, IT'S MY STOMACH YOU UPSET.

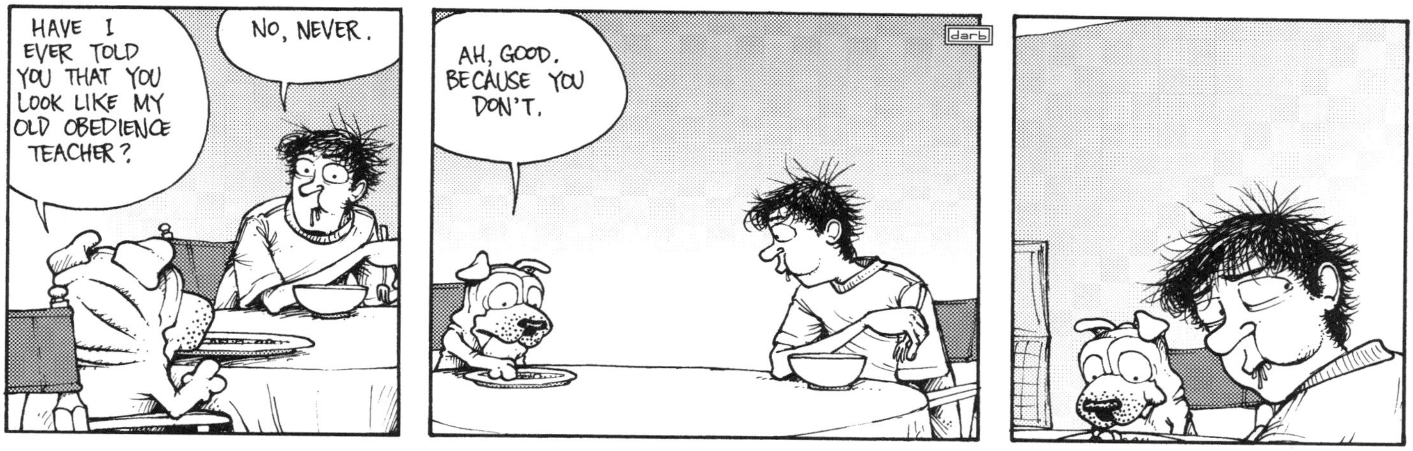
HAVE I EVER TOLD YOU THAT YOU LOOK LIKE MY OLD OBEDIENCE TEACHER?
NO, NEVER.
darb
AH, GOOD. BECAUSE YOU DON'T.

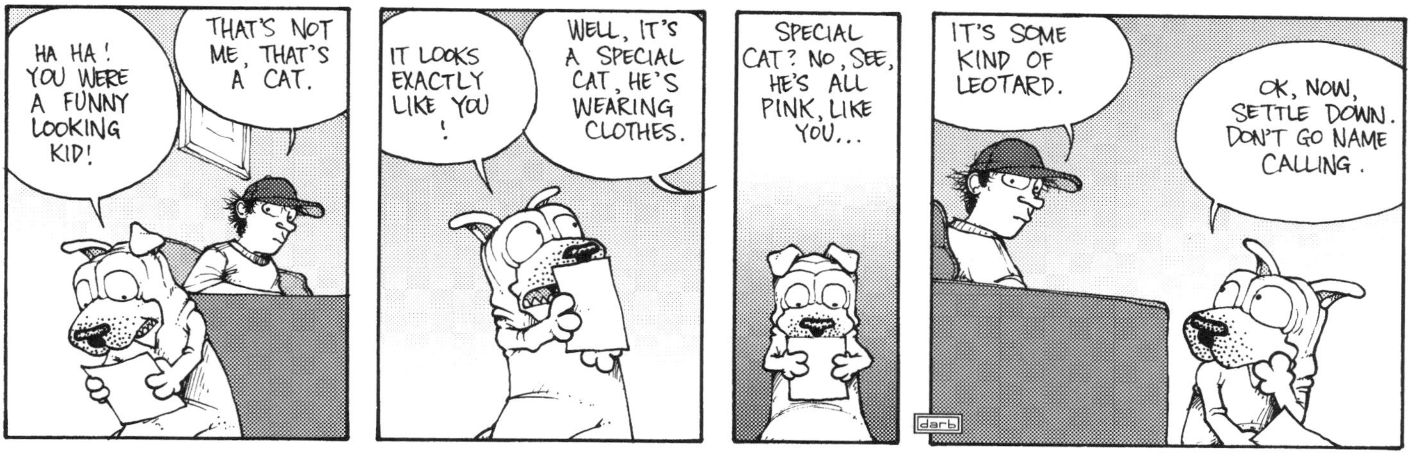
HA HA! YOU WERE A FUNNY LOOKING KID!
THAT'S NOT ME, THAT'S A CAT.
IT LOOKS EXACTLY LIKE YOU !
WELL, IT'S A SPECIAL CAT, HE'S WEARING CLOTHES.
SPECIAL CAT? NO, SEE, HE'S ALL PINK, LIKE YOU...
darb
IT'S SOME KIND OF LEOTARD.
OK, NOW, SETTLE DOWN. DON'T GO NAME CALLING.

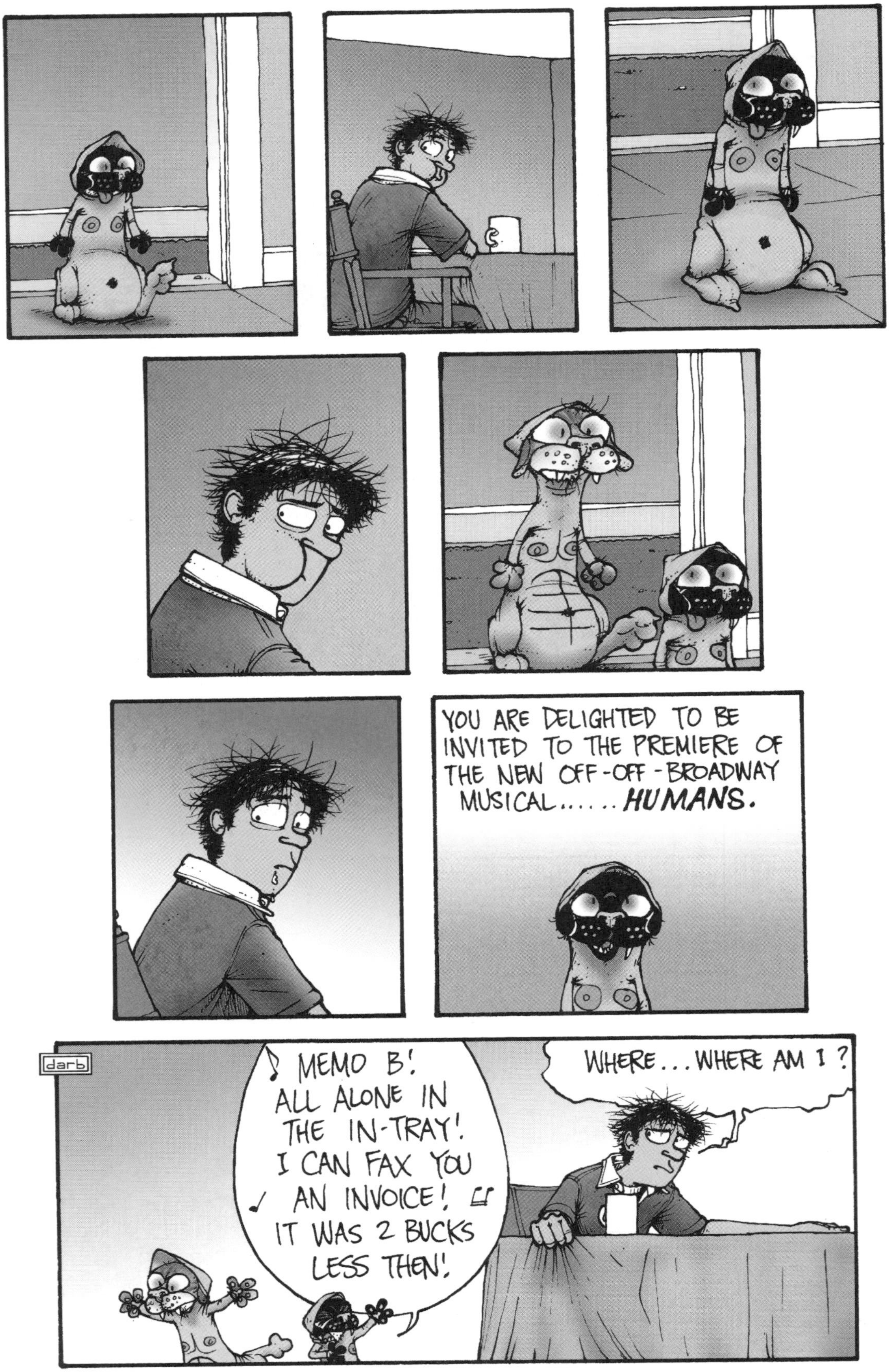
YOU ARE DELIGHTED TO BE INVITED TO THE PREMIERE OF THE NEW OFF-OFF-BROADWAY MUSICAL...... HUMANS.
darb
♪ MEMO B! ALL ALONE IN THE IN-TRAY! I CAN FAX YOU AN INVOICE! IT WAS 2 BUCKS LESS THEN!
WHERE... WHERE AM I ?

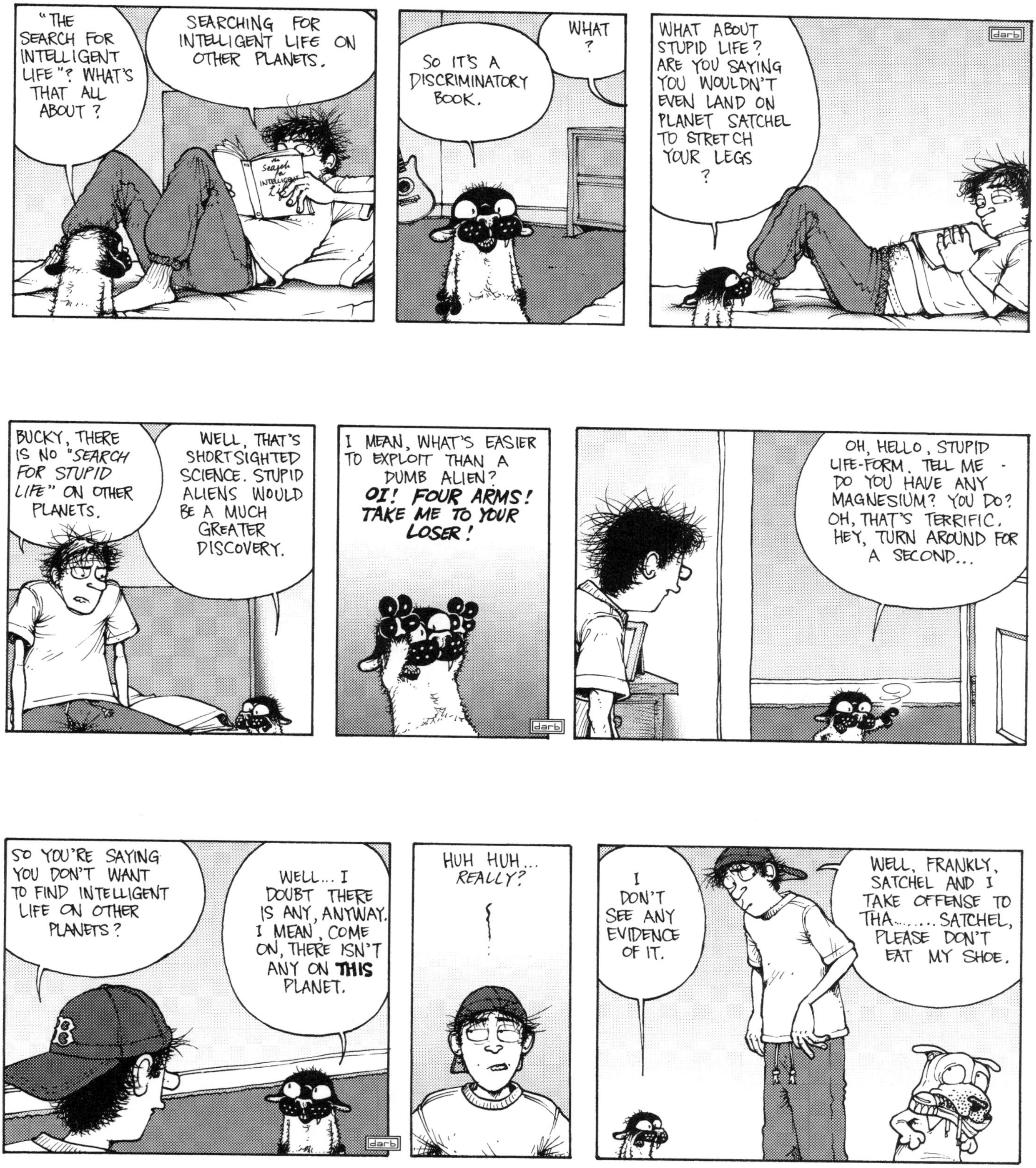
"THE SEARCH FOR INTELLIGENT LIFE"? WHAT'S THAT ALL ABOUT?
SEARCHING FOR INTELLIGENT LIFE ON OTHER PLANETS.
SO IT'S A DISCRIMINATORY BOOK.
WHAT?
WHAT ABOUT STUPID LIFE? ARE YOU SAYING YOU WOULDN'T EVEN LAND ON PLANET SATCHEL TO STRETCH YOUR LEGS?
darb
BUCKY, THERE IS NO "SEARCH FOR STUPID LIFE" ON OTHER PLANETS.
WELL, THAT'S SHORTSIGHTED SCIENCE. STUPID ALIENS WOULD BE A MUCH GREATER DISCOVERY.
I MEAN, WHAT'S EASIER TO EXPLOIT THAN A DUMB ALIEN?
OI! FOUR ARMS! TAKE ME TO YOUR LOSER!
darb
OH, HELLO, STUPID LIFE-FORM. TELL ME - DO YOU HAVE ANY MAGNESIUM? YOU DO? OH, THAT'S TERRIFIC. HEY, TURN AROUND FOR A SECOND...
SO YOU'RE SAYING YOU DON'T WANT TO FIND INTELLIGENT LIFE ON OTHER PLANETS?
WELL... I DOUBT THERE IS ANY, ANYWAY. I MEAN, COME ON, THERE ISN'T ANY ON THIS PLANET.
darb
HUH HUH... REALLY?
I DON'T SEE ANY EVIDENCE OF IT.
WELL, FRANKLY, SATCHEL AND I TAKE OFFENSE TO THA....... SATCHEL, PLEASE DON'T EAT MY SHOE.

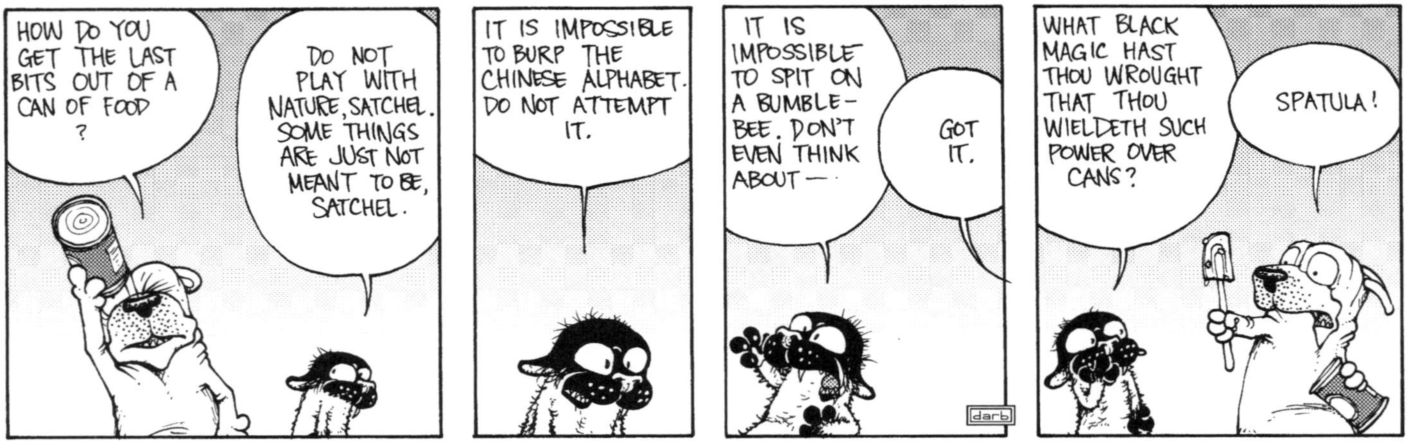
HOW DO YOU GET THE LAST BITS OUT OF A CAN OF FOOD ?
DO NOT PLAY WITH NATURE, SATCHEL. SOME THINGS ARE JUST NOT MEANT TO BE, SATCHEL.
IT IS IMPOSSIBLE TO BURP THE CHINESE ALPHABET. DO NOT ATTEMPT IT.
IT IS IMPOSSIBLE TO SPIT ON A BUMBLE-BEE. DON'T EVEN THINK ABOUT—
GOT IT.
darb
WHAT BLACK MAGIC HAST THOU WROUGHT THAT THOU WIELDETH SUCH POWER OVER CANS?
SPATULA!

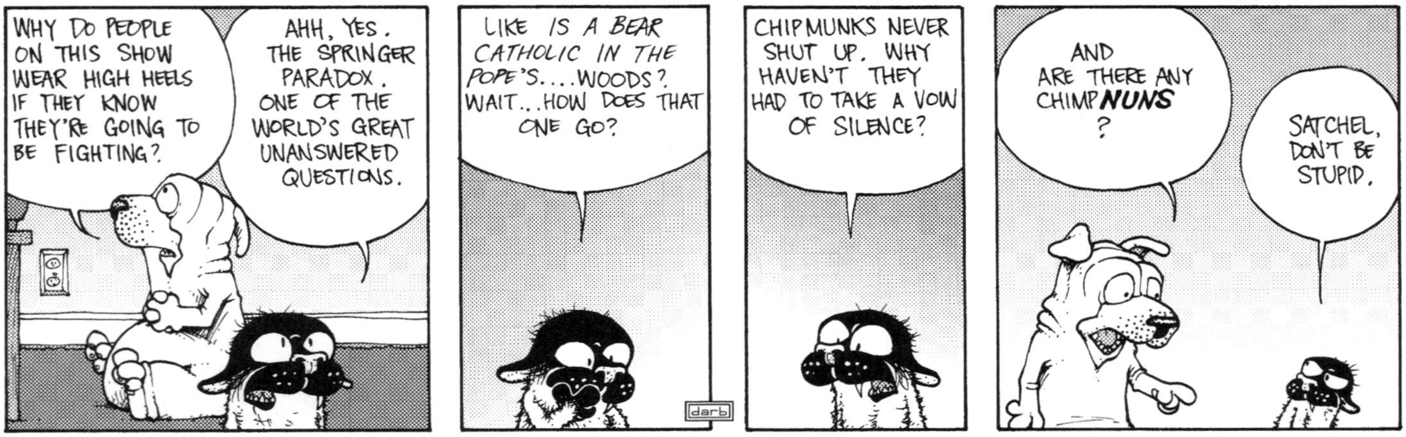
WHY DO PEOPLE ON THIS SHOW WEAR HIGH HEELS IF THEY KNOW THEY'RE GOING TO BE FIGHTING?
AHH, YES. THE SPRINGER PARADOX. ONE OF THE WORLD'S GREAT UNANSWERED QUESTIONS.
LIKE *IS A BEAR CATHOLIC IN THE POPE'S....WOODS?* WAIT...HOW DOES THAT ONE GO?
darb
CHIPMUNKS NEVER SHUT UP. WHY HAVEN'T THEY HAD TO TAKE A VOW OF SILENCE?
AND ARE THERE ANY CHIMP **NUNS** ?
SATCHEL, DON'T BE STUPID.

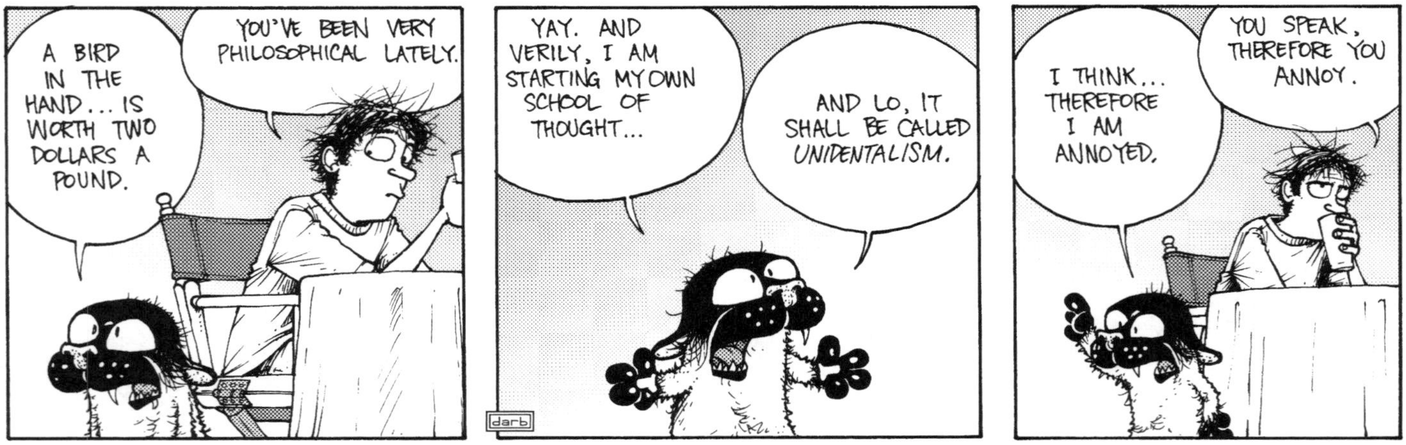
A BIRD IN THE HAND... IS WORTH TWO DOLLARS A POUND.
YOU'VE BEEN VERY PHILOSOPHICAL LATELY.
YAY. AND VERILY, I AM STARTING MY OWN SCHOOL OF THOUGHT...
AND LO, IT SHALL BE CALLED *UNIDENTALISM*.
darb
I THINK... THEREFORE I AM ANNOYED.
YOU SPEAK, THEREFORE YOU ANNOY.

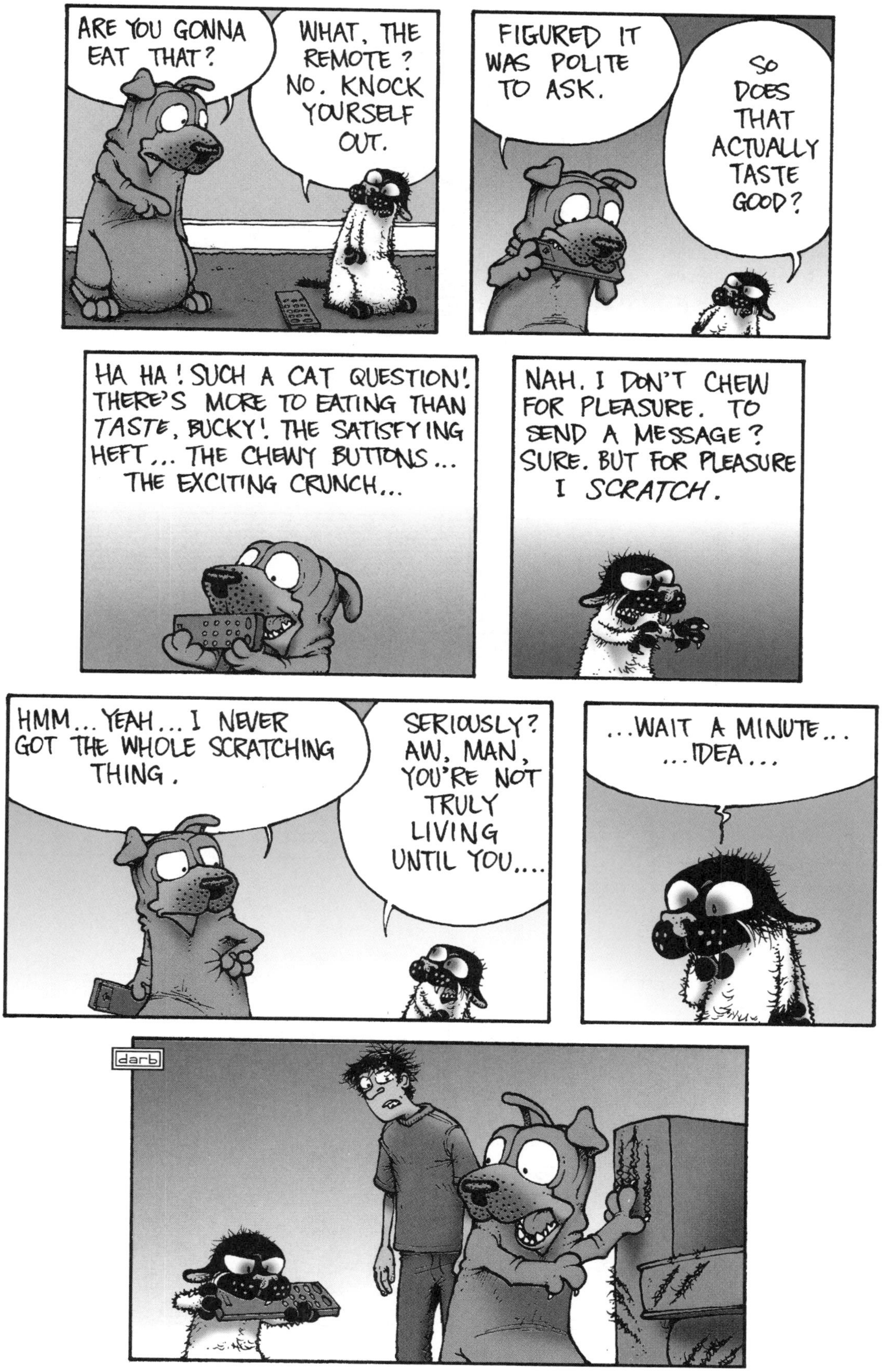
ARE YOU GONNA EAT THAT?
WHAT, THE REMOTE? NO. KNOCK YOURSELF OUT.
FIGURED IT WAS POLITE TO ASK.
SO DOES THAT ACTUALLY TASTE GOOD?
HA HA! SUCH A CAT QUESTION! THERE'S MORE TO EATING THAN *TASTE*, BUCKY! THE SATISFYING HEFT... THE CHEWY BUTTONS... THE EXCITING CRUNCH...
NAH. I DON'T CHEW FOR PLEASURE. TO SEND A MESSAGE? SURE. BUT FOR PLEASURE I *SCRATCH*.
HMM... YEAH... I NEVER GOT THE WHOLE SCRATCHING THING.
SERIOUSLY? AW, MAN, YOU'RE NOT TRULY LIVING UNTIL YOU....
...WAIT A MINUTE... ...IDEA...
darb

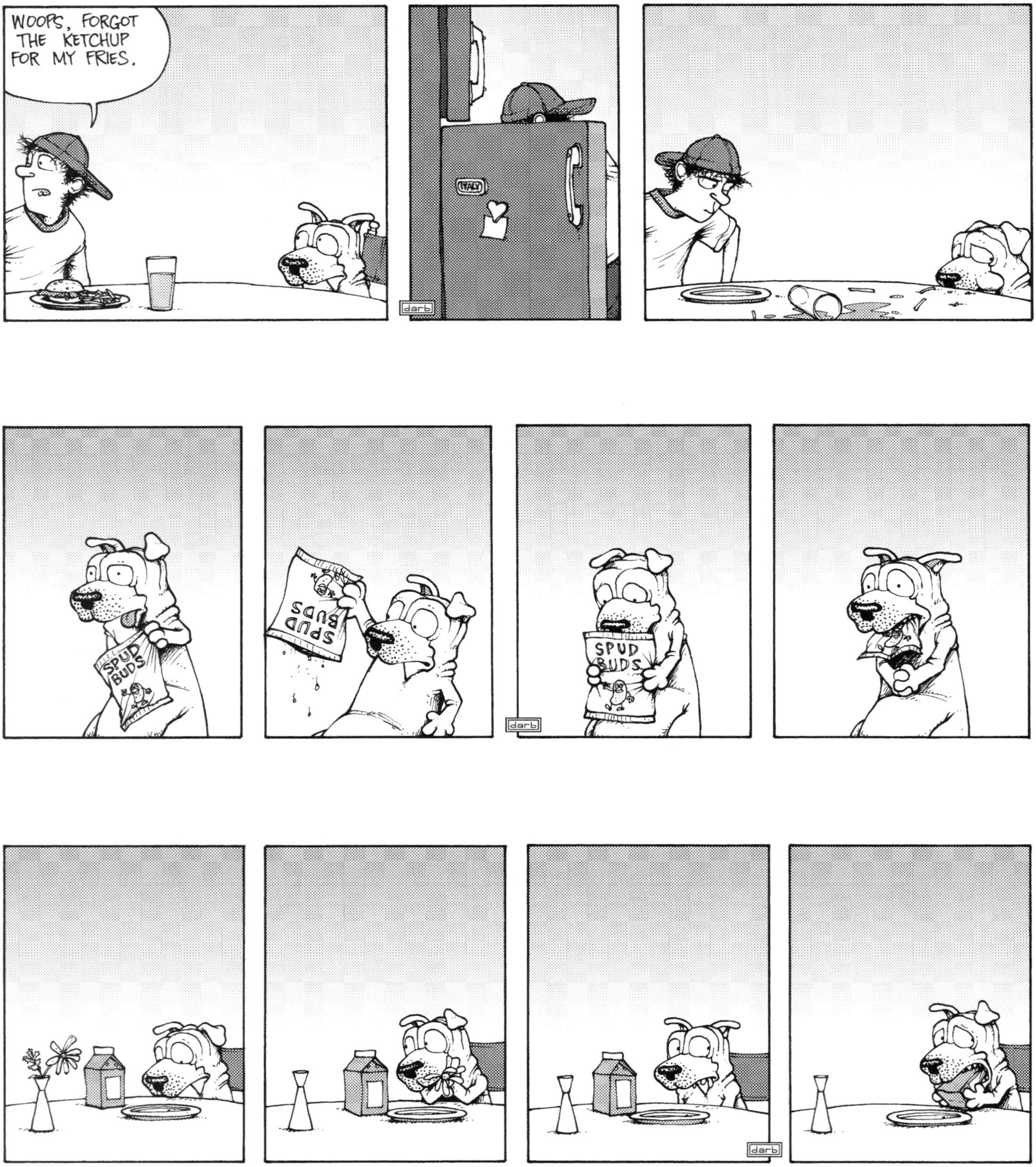
WOOPS, FORGOT THE KETCHUP FOR MY FRIES.
ITALY
darb
SPUD BUDS
darb
SPUD BUDS
darb

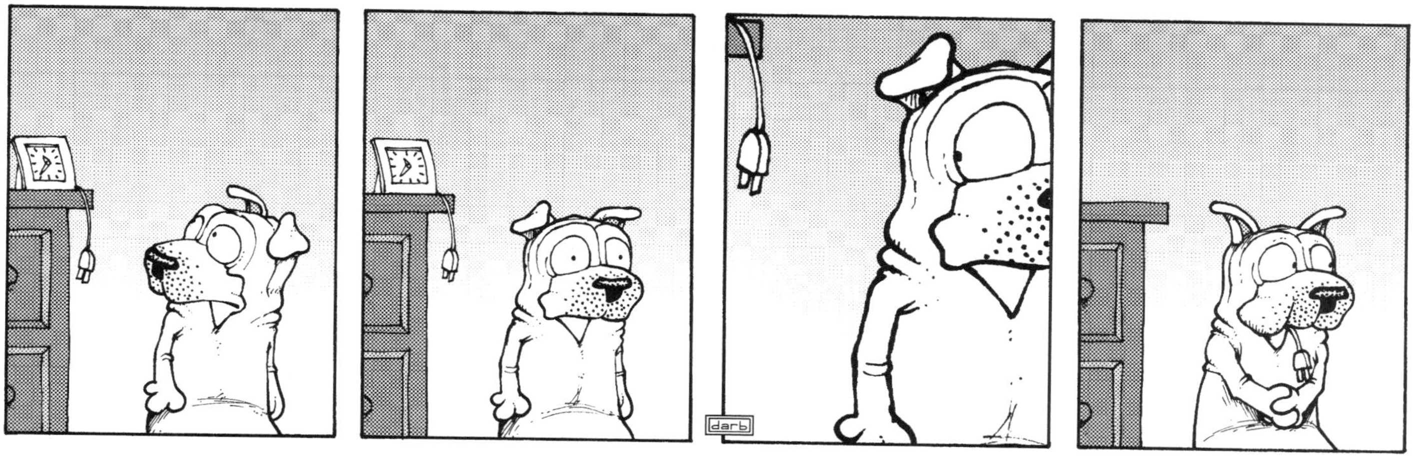
darb

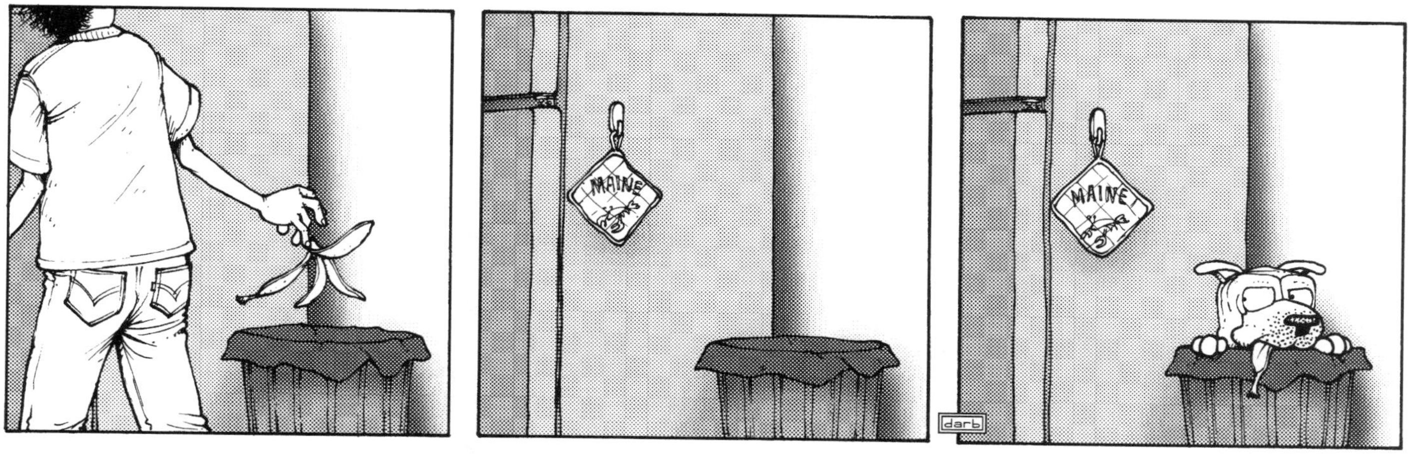
MAINE
MAINE
darb

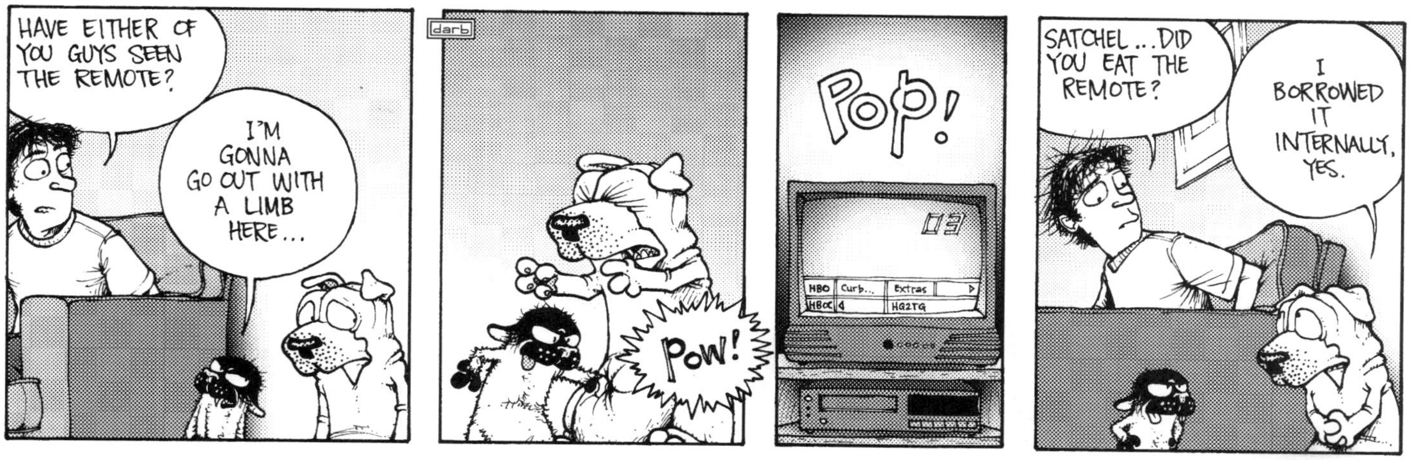
HAVE EITHER OF YOU GUYS SEEN THE REMOTE?
I'M GONNA GO OUT WITH A LIMB HERE...
darb
POW!
POP!
SATCHEL...DID YOU EAT THE REMOTE?
I BORROWED IT INTERNALLY, YES.

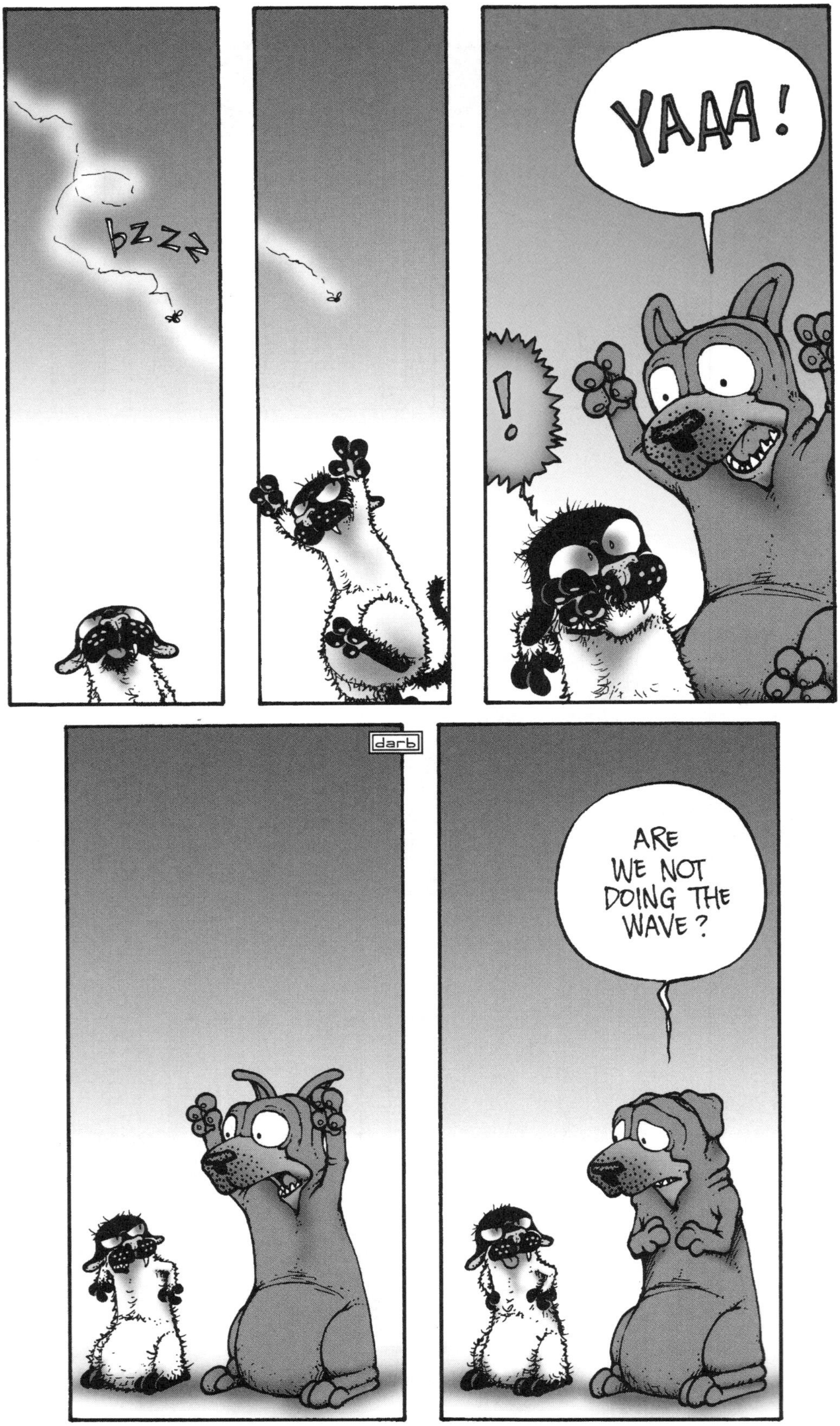
bzzz
YAAA!
!
darb
ARE WE NOT DOING THE WAVE?

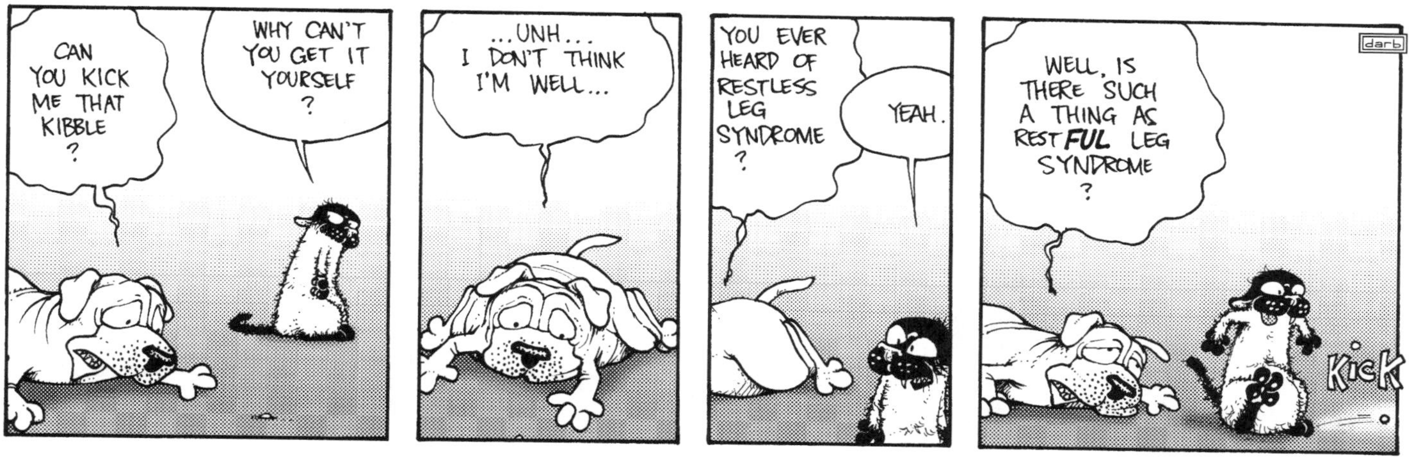
CAN YOU KICK ME THAT KIBBLE ?
WHY CAN'T YOU GET IT YOURSELF ?
...UNH... I DON'T THINK I'M WELL...
YOU EVER HEARD OF RESTLESS LEG SYNDROME ?
YEAH.
WELL, IS THERE SUCH A THING AS REST**FUL** LEG SYNDROME ?
KICK

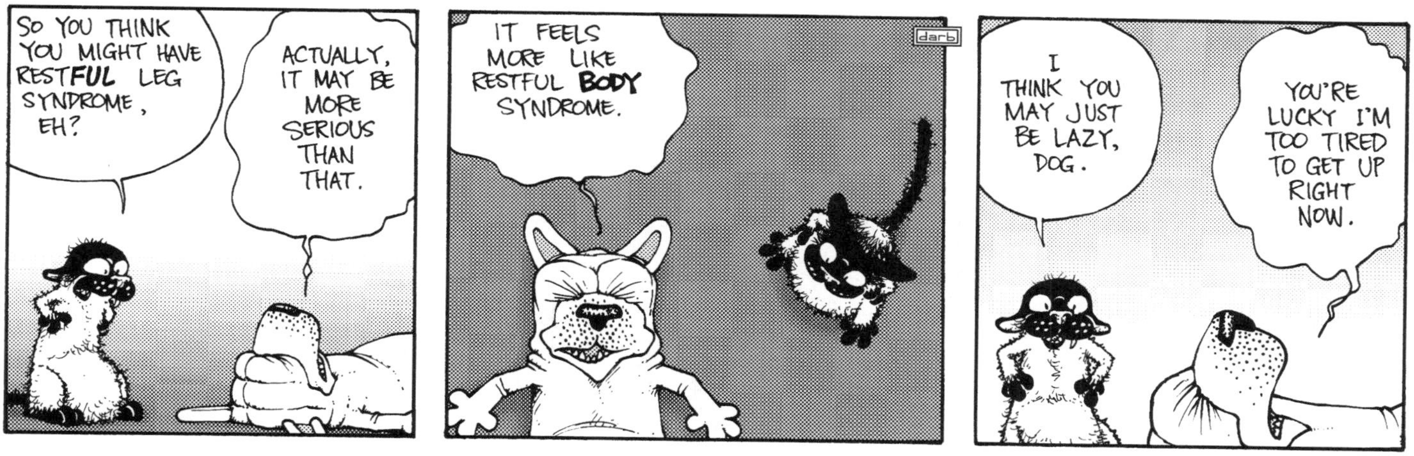
SO YOU THINK YOU MIGHT HAVE REST**FUL** LEG SYNDROME, EH?
ACTUALLY, IT MAY BE MORE SERIOUS THAN THAT.
IT FEELS MORE LIKE RESTFUL **BODY** SYNDROME.
I THINK YOU MAY JUST BE LAZY, DOG.
YOU'RE LUCKY I'M TOO TIRED TO GET UP RIGHT NOW.

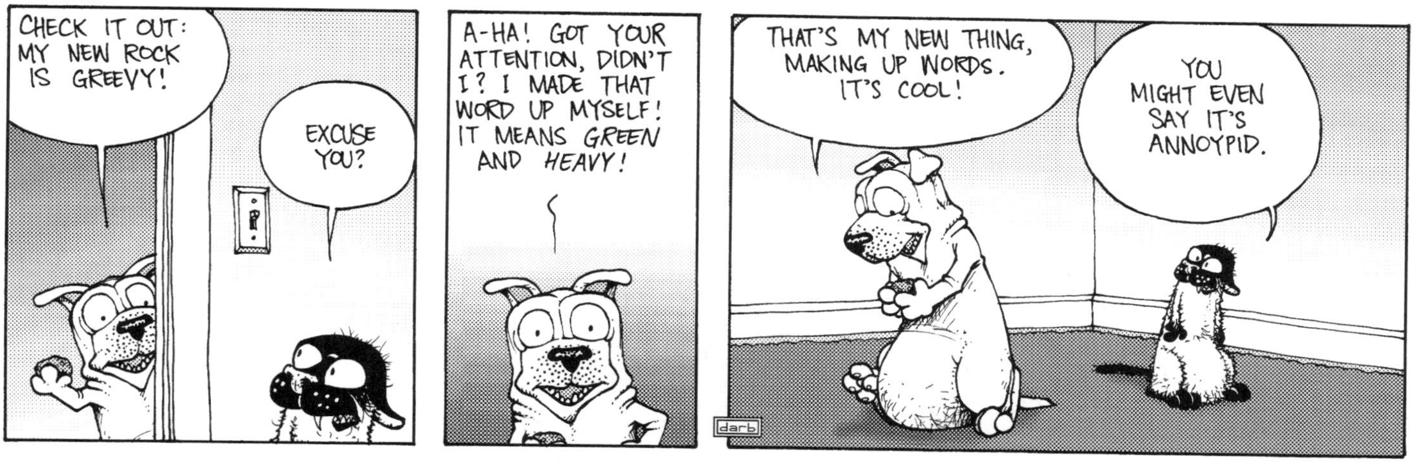
CHECK IT OUT: MY NEW ROCK IS GREEVY!
EXCUSE YOU?
A-HA! GOT YOUR ATTENTION, DIDN'T I? I MADE THAT WORD UP MYSELF! IT MEANS *GREEN* AND *HEAVY*!
THAT'S MY NEW THING, MAKING UP WORDS. IT'S COOL!
YOU MIGHT EVEN SAY IT'S ANNOYPID.

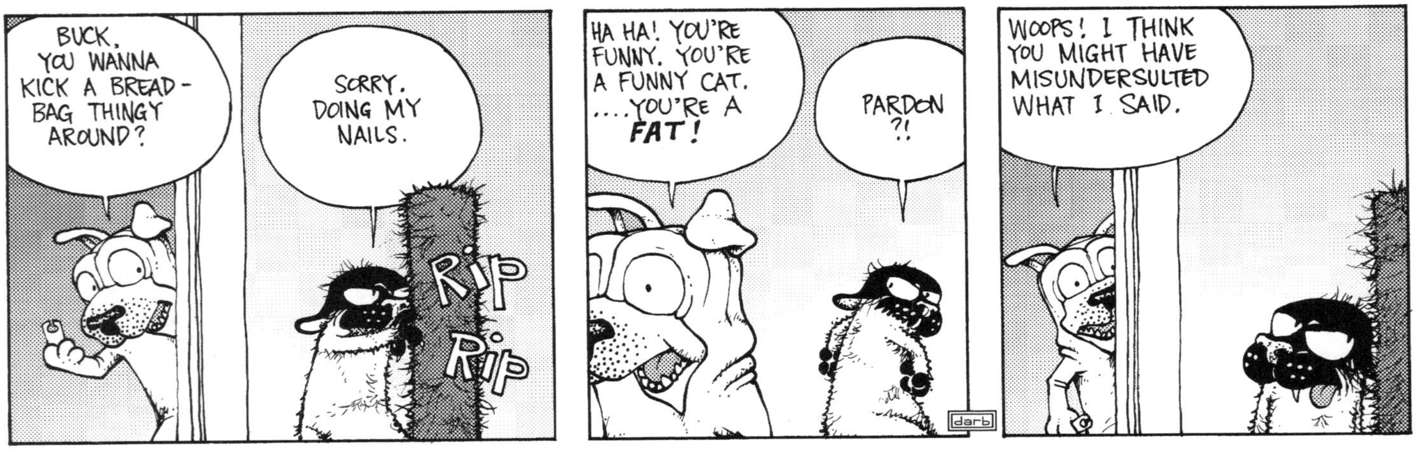
BUCK. YOU WANNA KICK A BREAD-BAG THINGY AROUND?
SORRY. DOING MY NAILS.
RIP
RIP
HA HA! YOU'RE FUNNY. YOU'RE A FUNNY CAT. ....YOU'RE A FAT!
PARDON ?!
WOOPS! I THINK YOU MIGHT HAVE MISUNDERSULTED WHAT I SAID.
darb

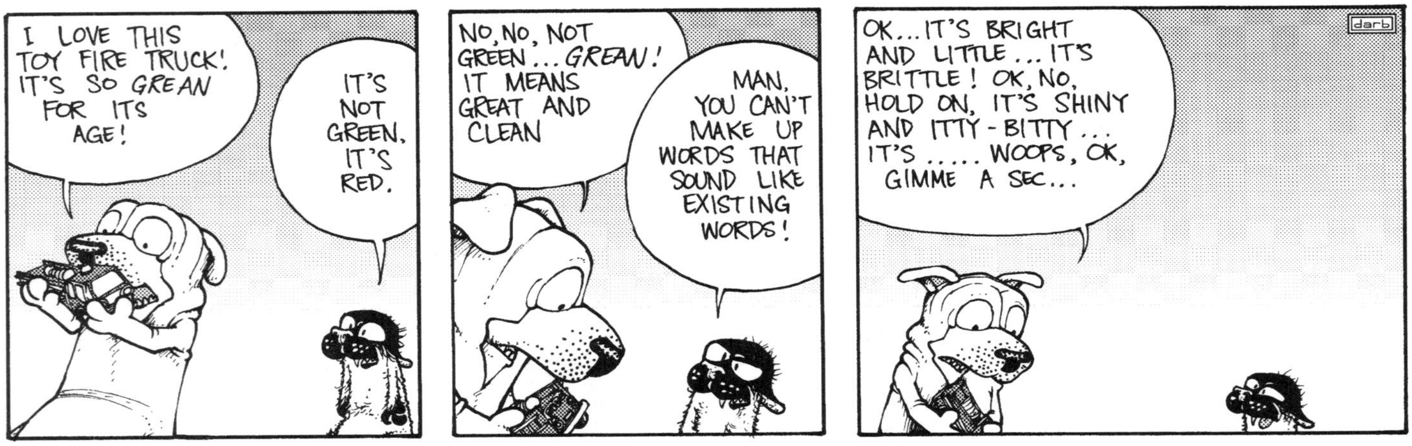
I LOVE THIS TOY FIRE TRUCK! IT'S SO GREAN FOR ITS AGE!
IT'S NOT GREEN. IT'S RED.
NO, NO, NOT GREEN... GREAN! IT MEANS GREAT AND CLEAN
MAN, YOU CAN'T MAKE UP WORDS THAT SOUND LIKE EXISTING WORDS!
darb
OK... IT'S BRIGHT AND LITTLE... IT'S BRITTLE! OK, NO, HOLD ON, IT'S SHINY AND ITTY-BITTY... IT'S..... WOOPS, OK, GIMME A SEC...

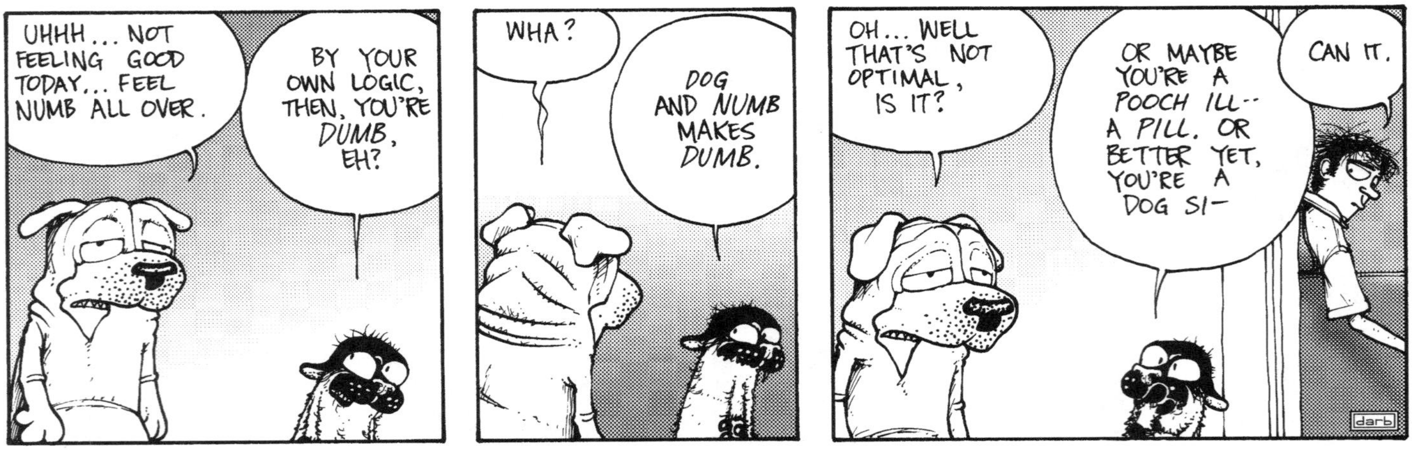
UHHH... NOT FEELING GOOD TODAY... FEEL NUMB ALL OVER.
BY YOUR OWN LOGIC, THEN, YOU'RE DUMB, EH?
WHA?
DOG AND NUMB MAKES DUMB.
OH... WELL THAT'S NOT OPTIMAL, IS IT?
OR MAYBE YOU'RE A POOCH ILL-- A PILL. OR BETTER YET, YOU'RE A DOG SI—
CAN IT.
darb

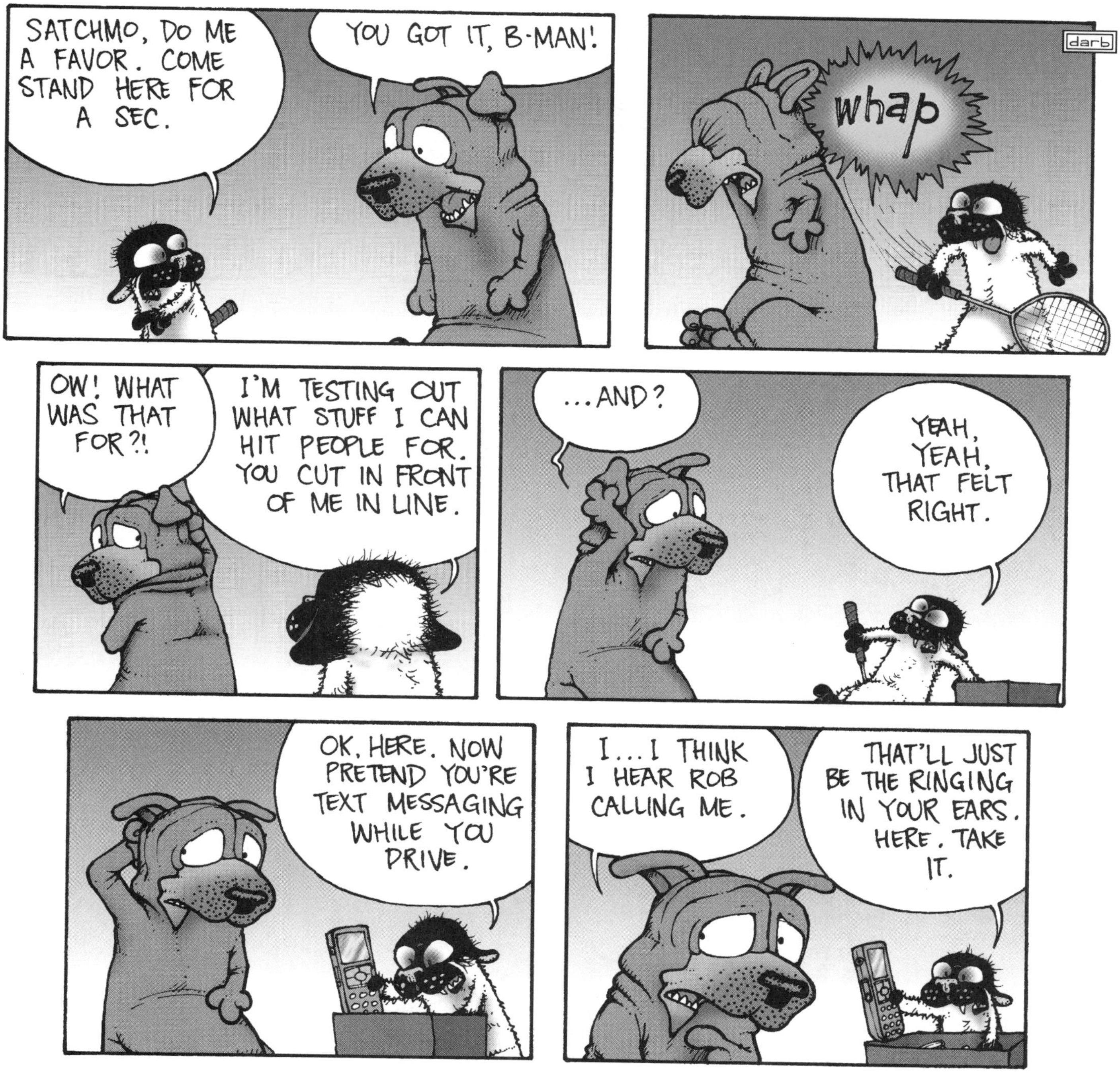
SATCHMO, DO ME A FAVOR. COME STAND HERE FOR A SEC.
YOU GOT IT, B-MAN!
darb
whap
OW! WHAT WAS THAT FOR?!
I'M TESTING OUT WHAT STUFF I CAN HIT PEOPLE FOR. YOU CUT IN FRONT OF ME IN LINE.
...AND?
YEAH, YEAH, THAT FELT RIGHT.
OK, HERE. NOW PRETEND YOU'RE TEXT MESSAGING WHILE YOU DRIVE.
I...I THINK I HEAR ROB CALLING ME.
THAT'LL JUST BE THE RINGING IN YOUR EARS. HERE. TAKE IT.

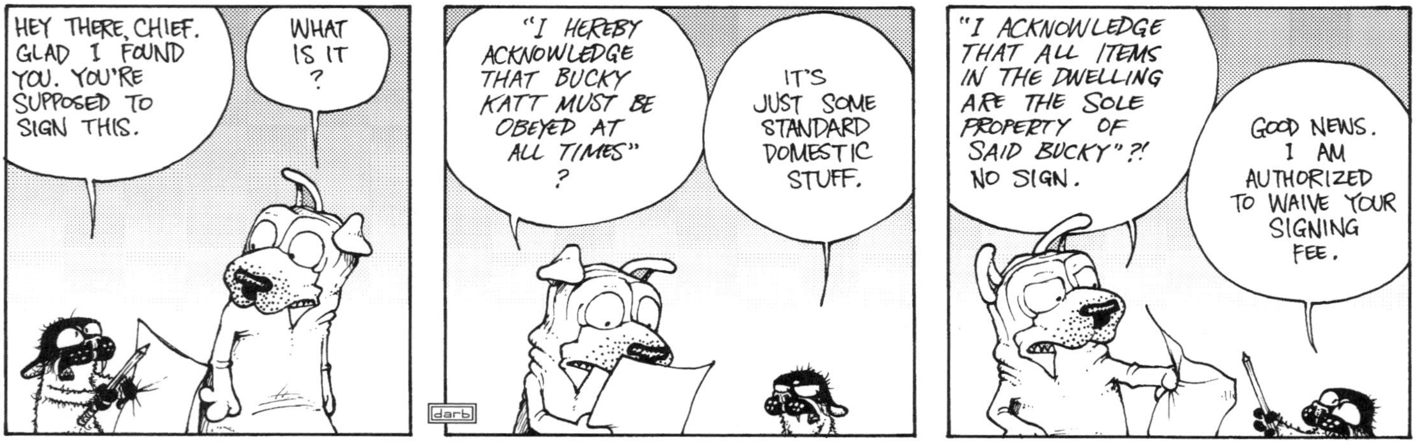
HEY THERE, CHIEF. GLAD I FOUND YOU. YOU'RE SUPPOSED TO SIGN THIS.
WHAT IS IT ?
"I HEREBY ACKNOWLEDGE THAT BUCKY KATT MUST BE OBEYED AT ALL TIMES" ?
IT'S JUST SOME STANDARD DOMESTIC STUFF.
"I ACKNOWLEDGE THAT ALL ITEMS IN THE DWELLING ARE THE SOLE PROPERTY OF SAID BUCKY"?! NO SIGN.
GOOD NEWS. I AM AUTHORIZED TO WAIVE YOUR SIGNING FEE.

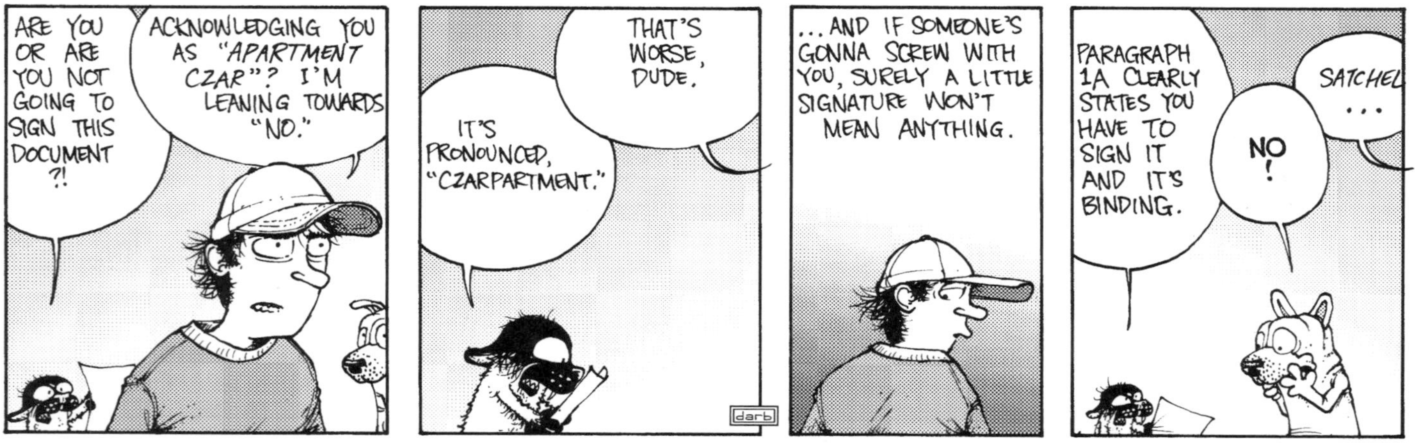
ARE YOU OR ARE YOU NOT GOING TO SIGN THIS DOCUMENT ?!
ACKNOWLEDGING YOU AS "APARTMENT CZAR"? I'M LEANING TOWARDS "NO."
IT'S PRONOUNCED, "CZARPARTMENT."
THAT'S WORSE, DUDE.
...AND IF SOMEONE'S GONNA SCREW WITH YOU, SURELY A LITTLE SIGNATURE WON'T MEAN ANYTHING.
PARAGRAPH 1A CLEARLY STATES YOU HAVE TO SIGN IT AND IT'S BINDING.
NO !
SATCHEL ...

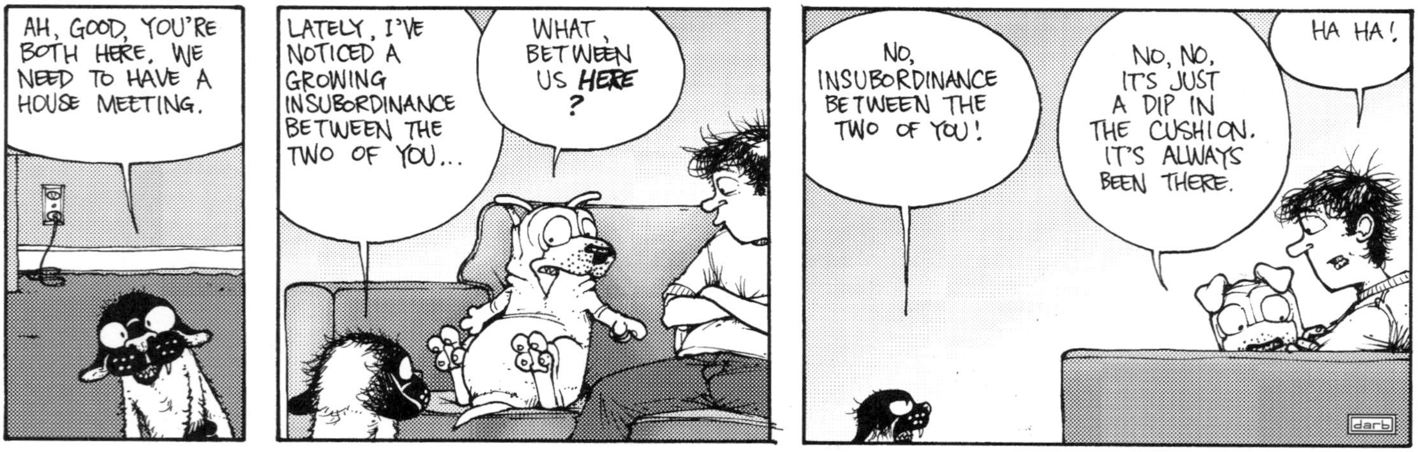
AH, GOOD, YOU'RE BOTH HERE. WE NEED TO HAVE A HOUSE MEETING.
LATELY, I'VE NOTICED A GROWING INSUBORDINANCE BETWEEN THE TWO OF YOU...
WHAT, BETWEEN US HERE ?
NO, INSUBORDINANCE BETWEEN THE TWO OF YOU!
NO, NO, IT'S JUST A DIP IN THE CUSHION. IT'S ALWAYS BEEN THERE.
HA HA!

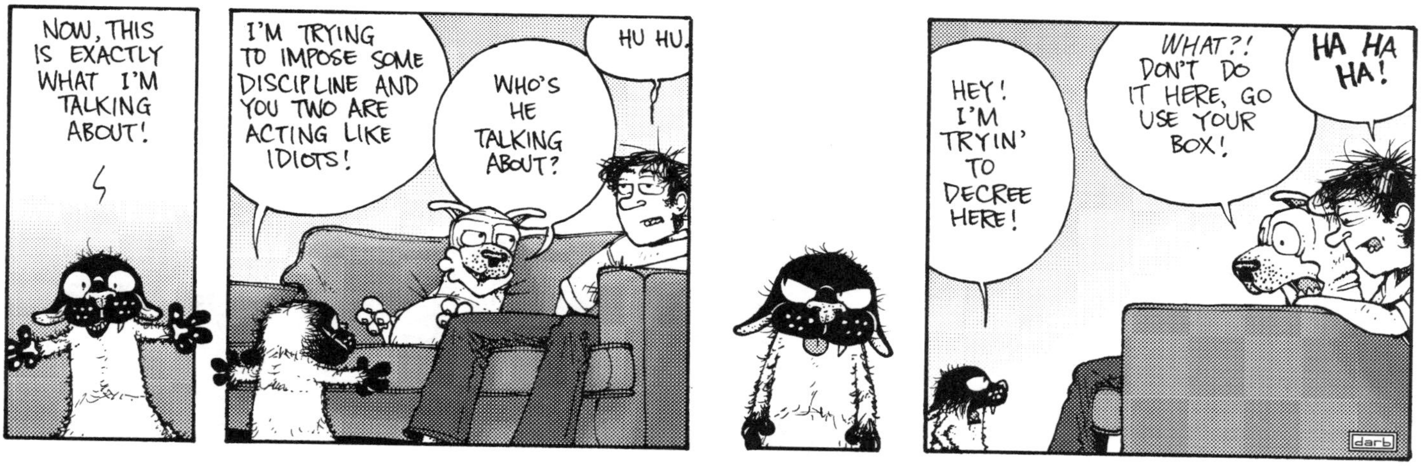
NOW, THIS IS EXACTLY WHAT I'M TALKING ABOUT!
I'M TRYING TO IMPOSE SOME DISCIPLINE AND YOU TWO ARE ACTING LIKE IDIOTS!
HU HU.
WHO'S HE TALKING ABOUT?
HEY! I'M TRYIN' TO DECREE HERE!
WHAT?! DON'T DO IT HERE, GO USE YOUR BOX!
HA HA HA!

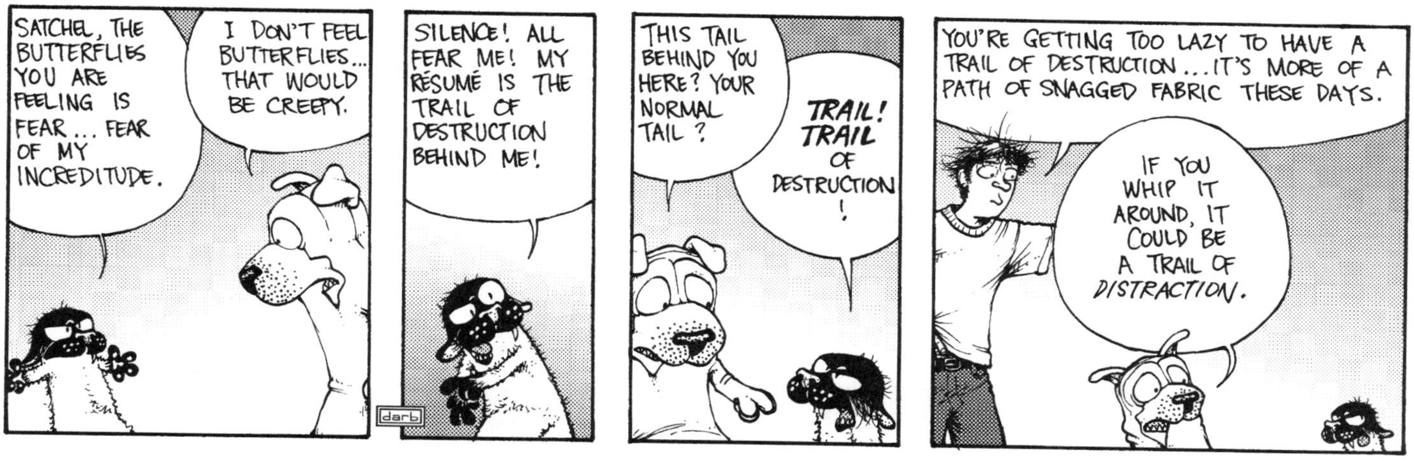
SATCHEL, THE BUTTERFLIES YOU ARE FEELING IS FEAR... FEAR OF MY INCREDITUDE.
I DON'T FEEL BUTTERFLIES... THAT WOULD BE CREEPY.
SILENCE! ALL FEAR ME! MY RÉSUMÉ IS THE TRAIL OF DESTRUCTION BEHIND ME!
THIS TAIL BEHIND YOU HERE? YOUR NORMAL TAIL?
TRAIL! TRAIL OF DESTRUCTION!
YOU'RE GETTING TOO LAZY TO HAVE A TRAIL OF DESTRUCTION... IT'S MORE OF A PATH OF SNAGGED FABRIC THESE DAYS.
IF YOU WHIP IT AROUND, IT COULD BE A TRAIL OF DISTRACTION.

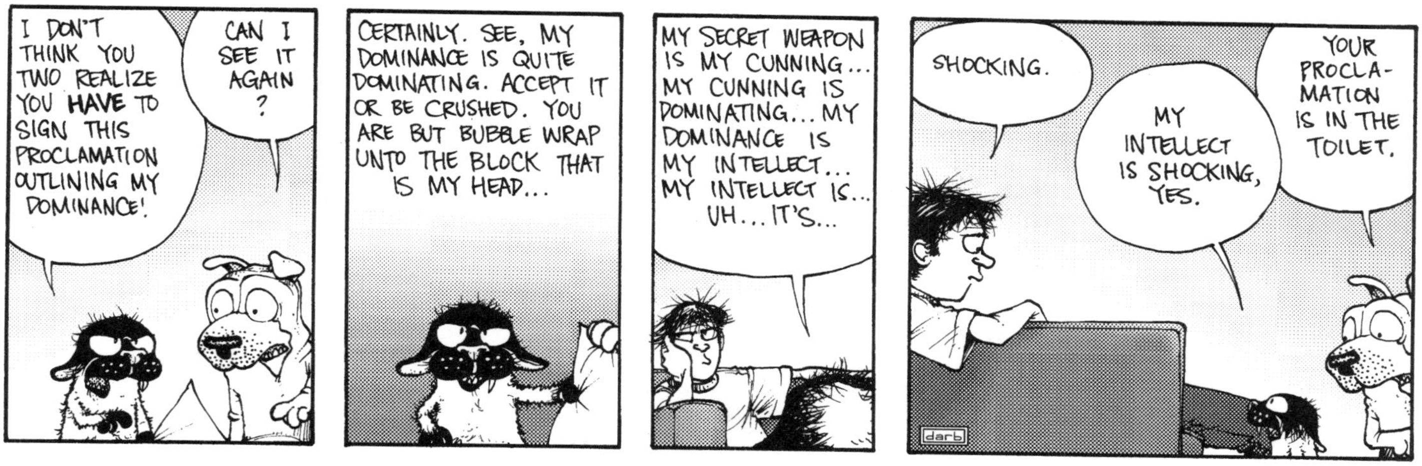
I DON'T THINK YOU TWO REALIZE YOU HAVE TO SIGN THIS PROCLAMATION OUTLINING MY DOMINANCE!
CAN I SEE IT AGAIN?
CERTAINLY. SEE, MY DOMINANCE IS QUITE DOMINATING. ACCEPT IT OR BE CRUSHED. YOU ARE BUT BUBBLE WRAP UNTO THE BLOCK THAT IS MY HEAD...
MY SECRET WEAPON IS MY CUNNING... MY CUNNING IS DOMINATING... MY DOMINANCE IS MY INTELLECT... MY INTELLECT IS... UH... IT'S...
SHOCKING.
MY INTELLECT IS SHOCKING, YES.
YOUR PROCLAMATION IS IN THE TOILET.

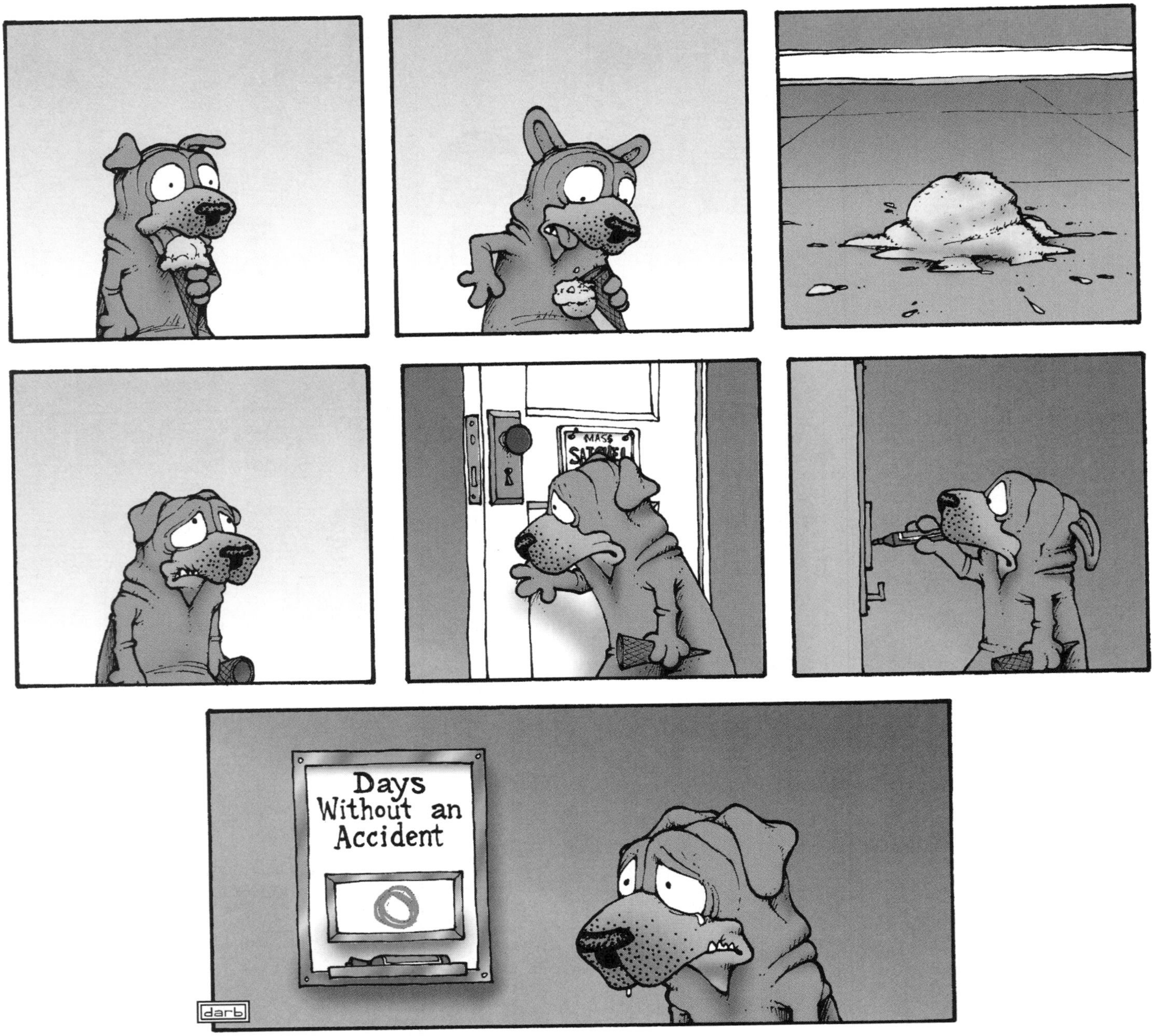
MASS
Days
Without an
Accident
darb

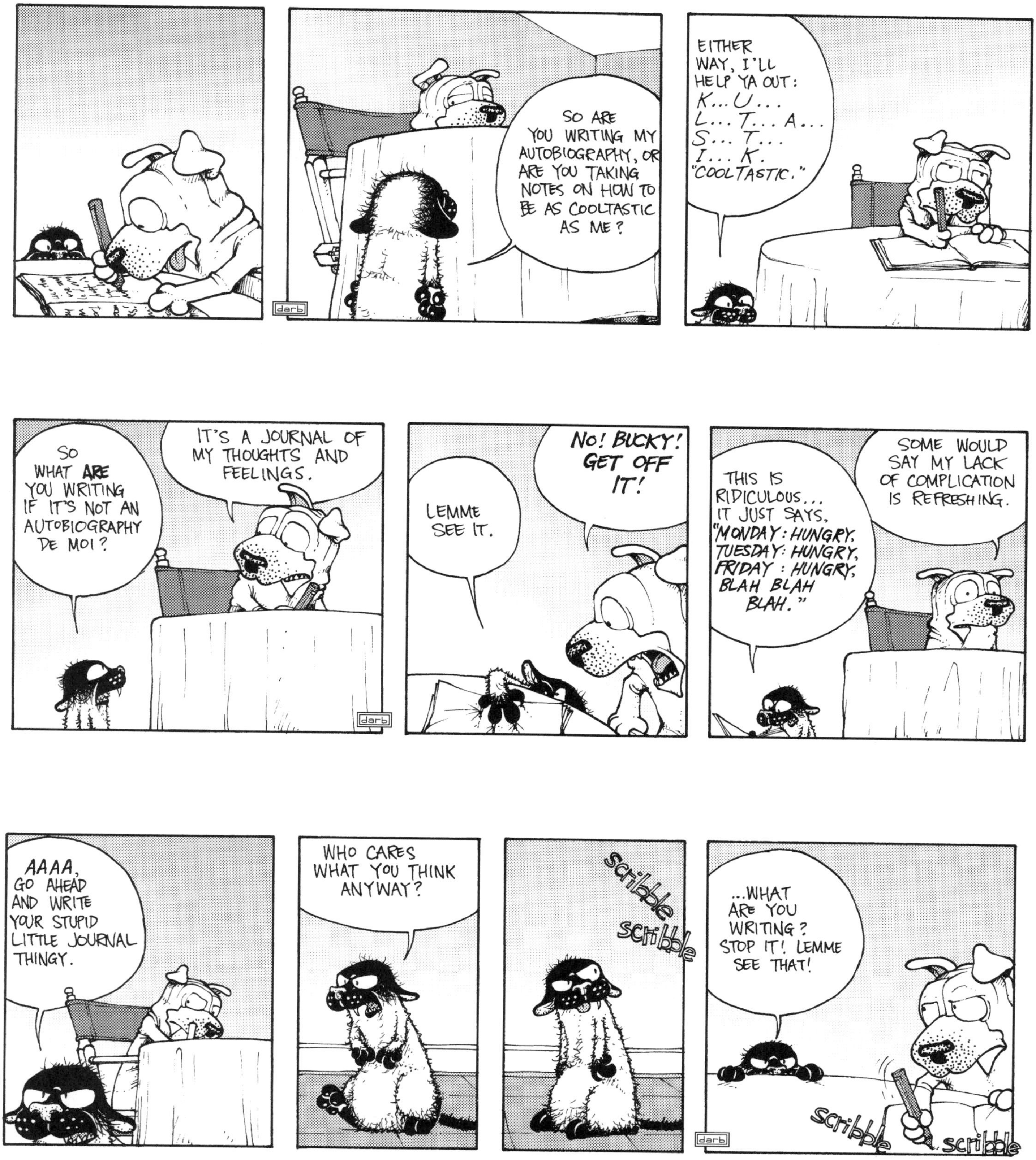
SO ARE YOU WRITING MY AUTOBIOGRAPHY, OR ARE YOU TAKING NOTES ON HOW TO BE AS COOLTASTIC AS ME?
EITHER WAY, I'LL HELP YA OUT: K... U... L... T... A... S... T... I... K. "COOLTASTIC."
SO WHAT ARE YOU WRITING IF IT'S NOT AN AUTOBIOGRAPHY DE MOI?
IT'S A JOURNAL OF MY THOUGHTS AND FEELINGS.
LEMME SEE IT.
NO! BUCKY! GET OFF IT!
THIS IS RIDICULOUS... IT JUST SAYS, "MONDAY: HUNGRY. TUESDAY: HUNGRY. FRIDAY: HUNGRY. BLAH BLAH BLAH."
SOME WOULD SAY MY LACK OF COMPLICATION IS REFRESHING.
AAAA, GO AHEAD AND WRITE YOUR STUPID LITTLE JOURNAL THINGY.
WHO CARES WHAT YOU THINK ANYWAY?
scribble
scribble
...WHAT ARE YOU WRITING? STOP IT! LEMME SEE THAT!
scribble
scribble

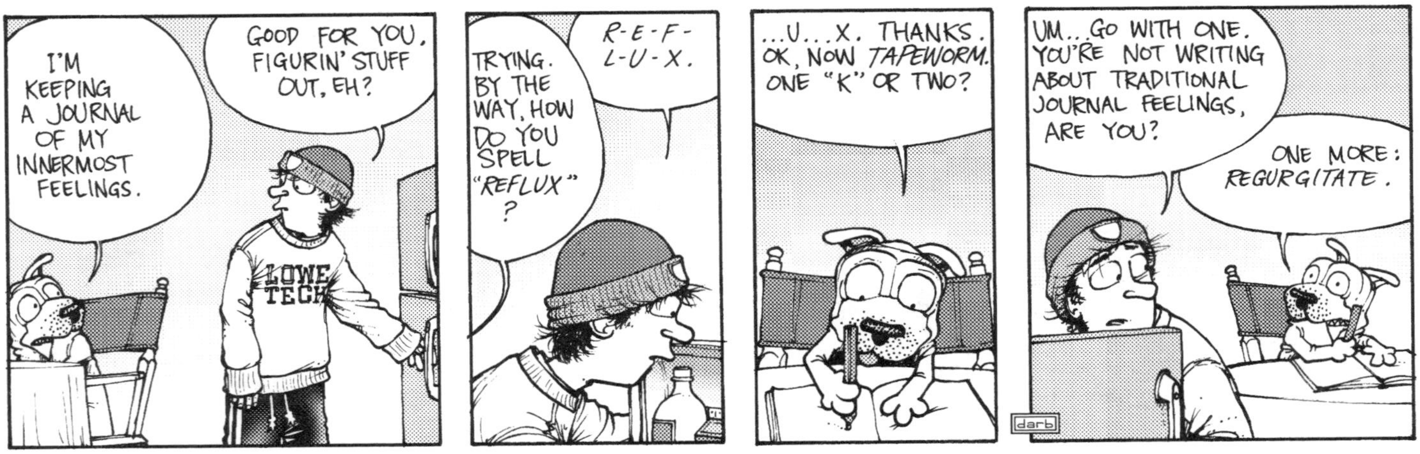
I'M KEEPING A JOURNAL OF MY INNERMOST FEELINGS.
GOOD FOR YOU, FIGURIN' STUFF OUT, EH?
TRYING. BY THE WAY, HOW DO YOU SPELL "REFLUX"?
R-E-F-L-U-X.
...U...X. THANKS. OK, NOW TAPEWORM. ONE "K" OR TWO?
UM...GO WITH ONE. YOU'RE NOT WRITING ABOUT TRADITIONAL JOURNAL FEELINGS, ARE YOU?
ONE MORE: REGURGITATE.
LOWE TECH

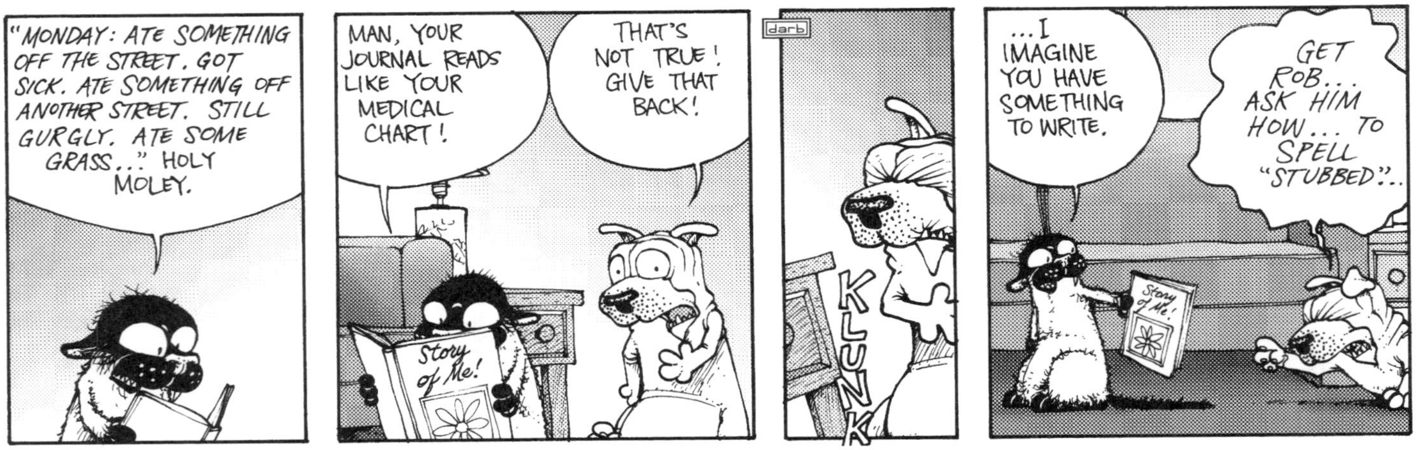
"MONDAY: ATE SOMETHING OFF THE STREET. GOT SICK. ATE SOMETHING OFF ANOTHER STREET. STILL GURGLY. ATE SOME GRASS..." HOLY MOLEY.
MAN, YOUR JOURNAL READS LIKE YOUR MEDICAL CHART!
THAT'S NOT TRUE! GIVE THAT BACK!
Story of Me!
KLUNK
...I IMAGINE YOU HAVE SOMETHING TO WRITE.
GET ROB... ASK HIM HOW... TO SPELL "STUBBED"...

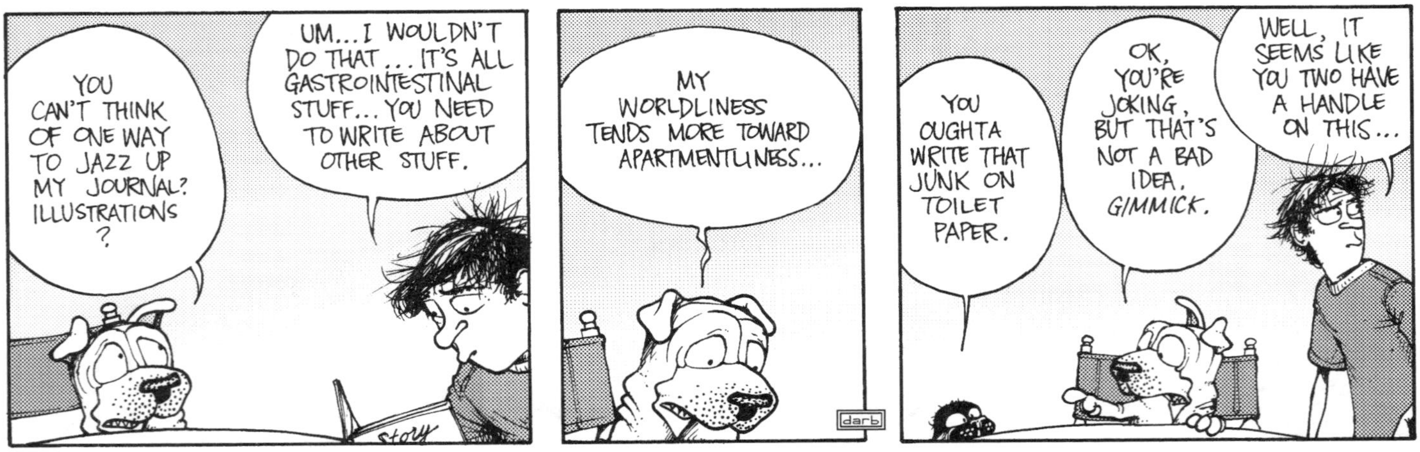
YOU CAN'T THINK OF ONE WAY TO JAZZ UP MY JOURNAL? ILLUSTRATIONS?
UM...I WOULDN'T DO THAT...IT'S ALL GASTROINTESTINAL STUFF...YOU NEED TO WRITE ABOUT OTHER STUFF.
MY WORLDLINESS TENDS MORE TOWARD APARTMENTLINESS...
YOU OUGHTA WRITE THAT JUNK ON TOILET PAPER.
OK, YOU'RE JOKING, BUT THAT'S NOT A BAD IDEA. GIMMICK.
WELL, IT SEEMS LIKE YOU TWO HAVE A HANDLE ON THIS...

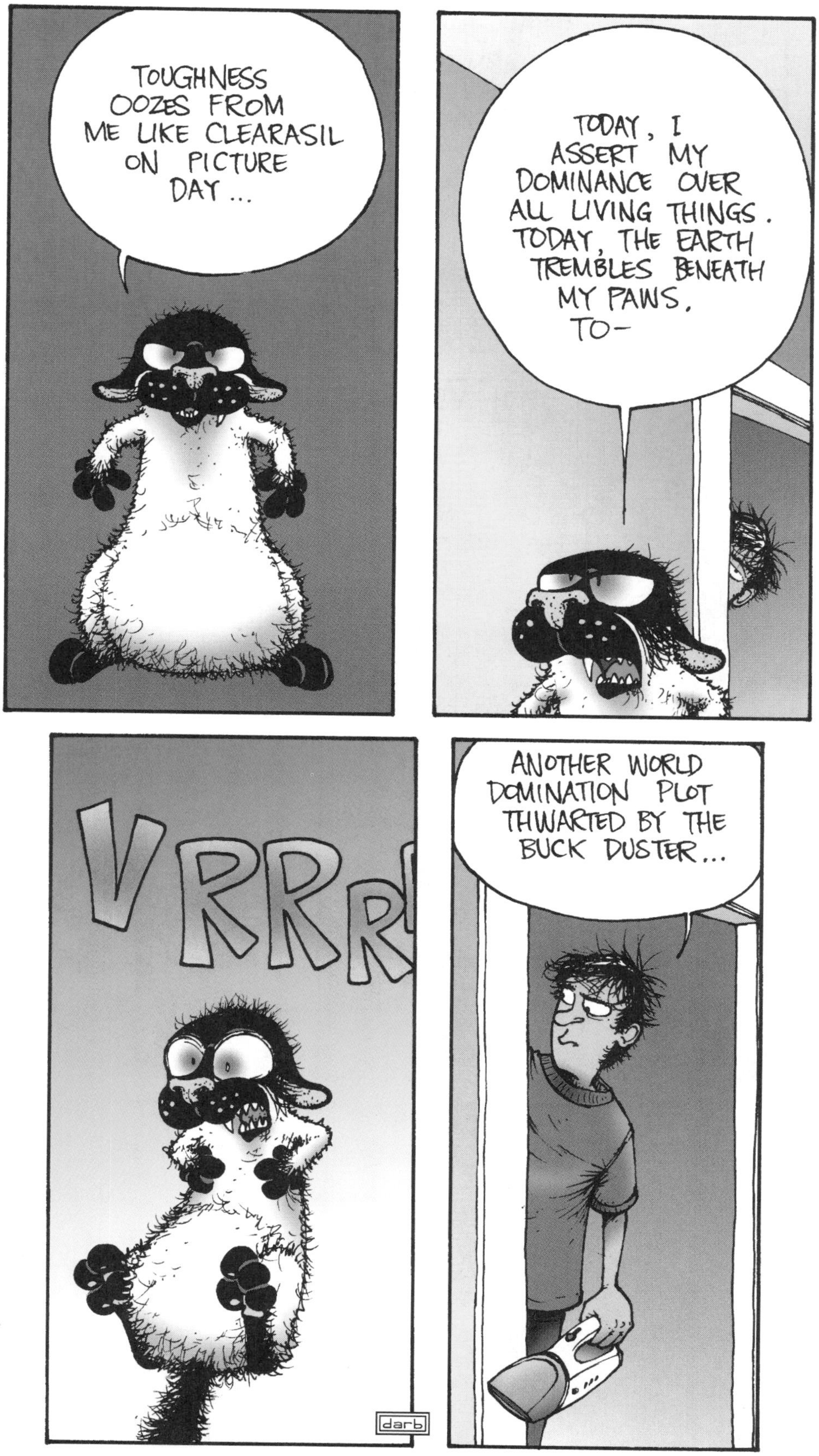
TOUGHNESS OOZES FROM ME LIKE CLEARASIL ON PICTURE DAY...
TODAY, I ASSERT MY DOMINANCE OVER ALL LIVING THINGS. TODAY, THE EARTH TREMBLES BENEATH MY PAWS. TO-
VRRR
darb
ANOTHER WORLD DOMINATION PLOT THWARTED BY THE BUCK DUSTER...

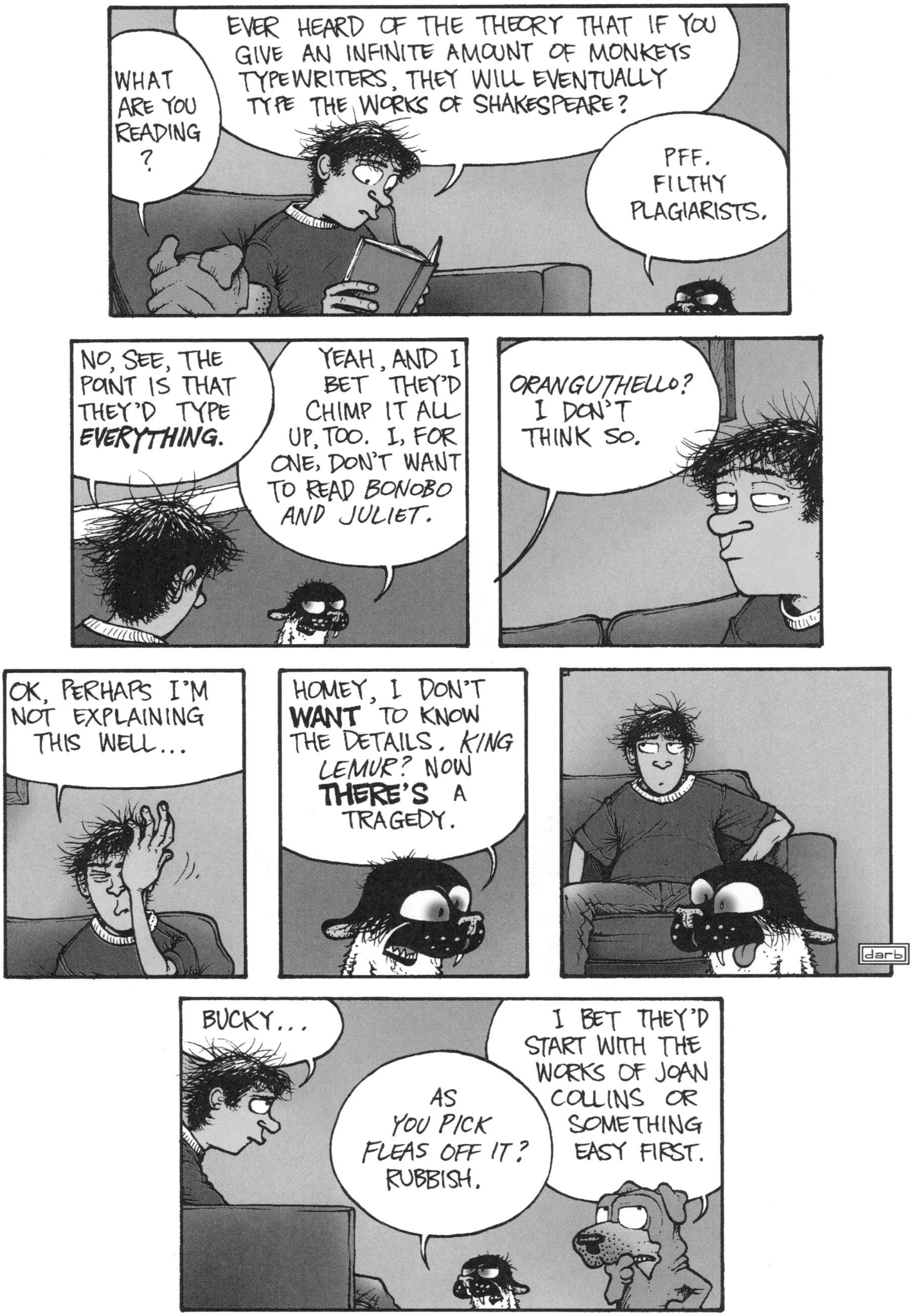
WHAT ARE YOU READING ?
EVER HEARD OF THE THEORY THAT IF YOU GIVE AN INFINITE AMOUNT OF MONKEYS TYPEWRITERS, THEY WILL EVENTUALLY TYPE THE WORKS OF SHAKESPEARE?
PFF. FILTHY PLAGIARISTS.
NO, SEE, THE POINT IS THAT THEY'D TYPE **EVERYTHING.**
YEAH, AND I BET THEY'D CHIMP IT ALL UP, TOO. I, FOR ONE, DON'T WANT TO READ *BONOBO AND JULIET.*
ORANGUTHELLO? I DON'T THINK SO.
OK, PERHAPS I'M NOT EXPLAINING THIS WELL...
HOMEY, I DON'T **WANT** TO KNOW THE DETAILS. *KING LEMUR?* NOW **THERE'S** A TRAGEDY.
darb
BUCKY...
AS *YOU PICK FLEAS OFF IT?* RUBBISH.
I BET THEY'D START WITH THE WORKS OF JOAN COLLINS OR SOMETHING EASY FIRST.

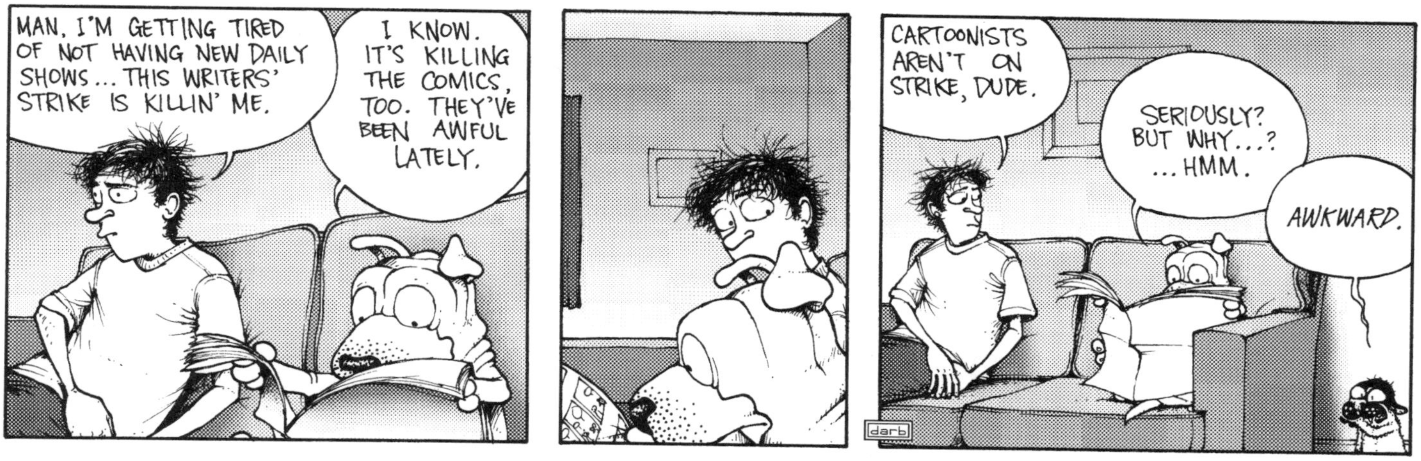
MAN, I'M GETTING TIRED OF NOT HAVING NEW DAILY SHOWS... THIS WRITERS' STRIKE IS KILLIN' ME.
I KNOW. IT'S KILLING THE COMICS, TOO. THEY'VE BEEN AWFUL LATELY.
CARTOONISTS AREN'T ON STRIKE, DUDE.
SERIOUSLY? BUT WHY...? ...HMM.
AWKWARD.
darb

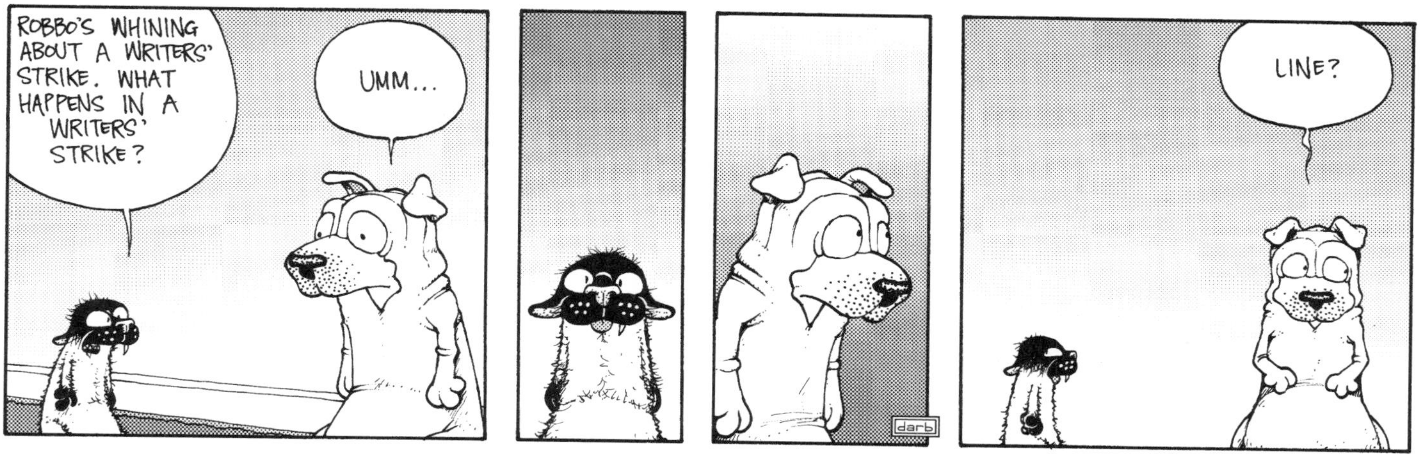
ROBBO'S WHINING ABOUT A WRITERS' STRIKE. WHAT HAPPENS IN A WRITERS' STRIKE?
UMM...
darb
LINE?

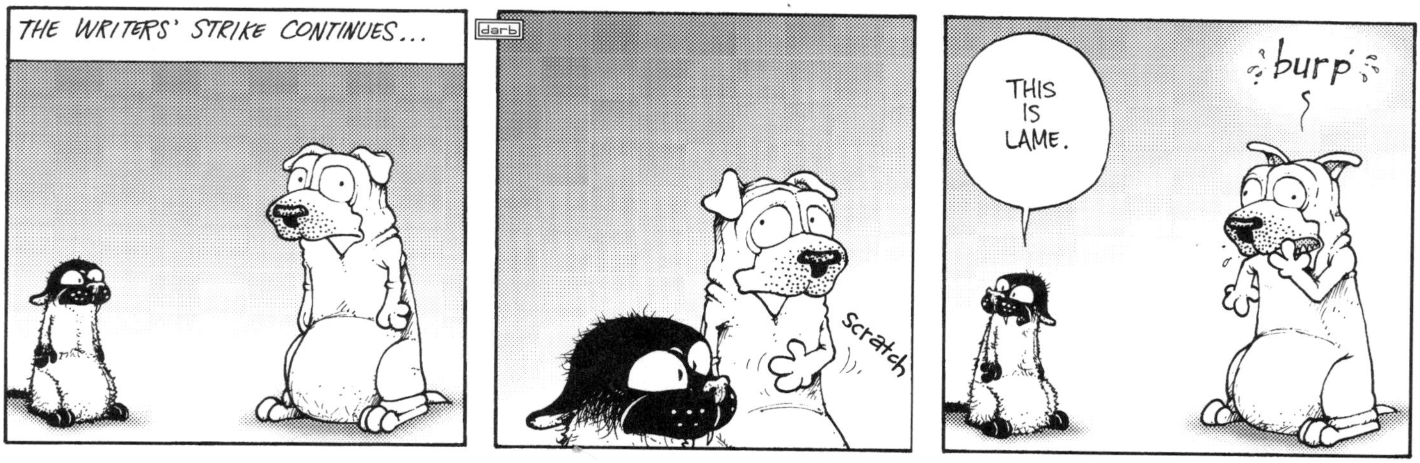
THE WRITERS' STRIKE CONTINUES...
darb
scratch
THIS IS LAME.
burp

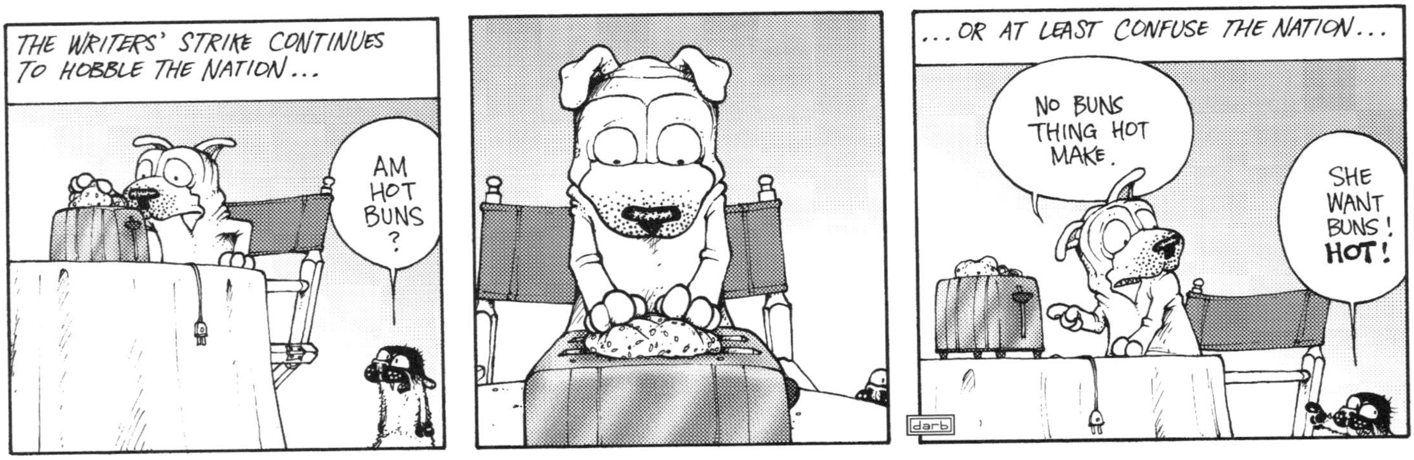
THE WRITERS' STRIKE CONTINUES TO HOBBLE THE NATION...
AM HOT BUNS ?
...OR AT LEAST CONFUSE THE NATION...
NO BUNS THING HOT MAKE.
SHE WANT BUNS! HOT!
darb

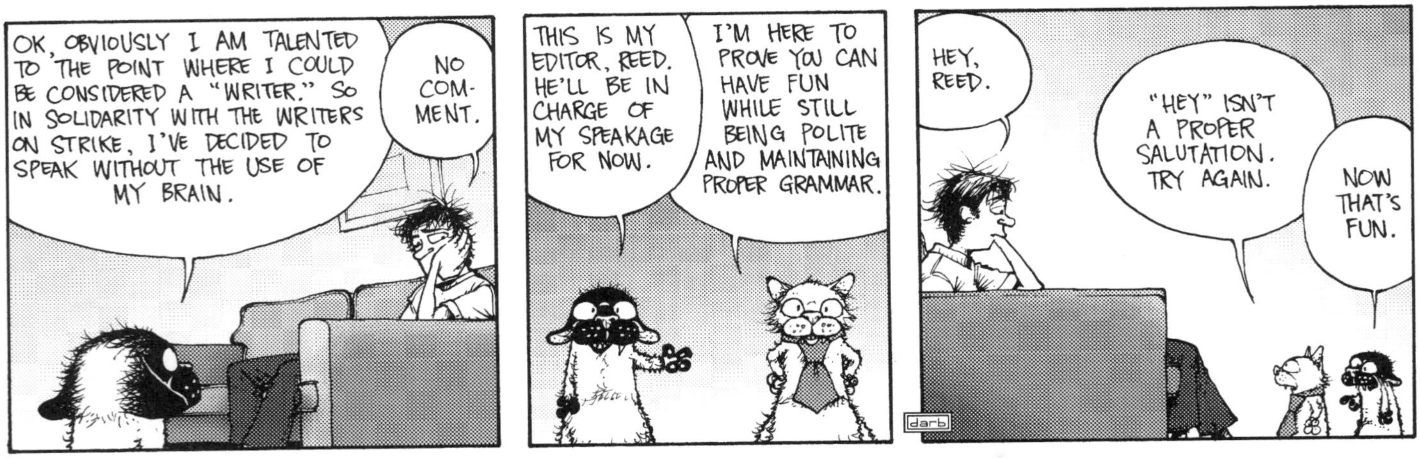
OK, OBVIOUSLY I AM TALENTED TO THE POINT WHERE I COULD BE CONSIDERED A "WRITER." SO IN SOLIDARITY WITH THE WRITERS ON STRIKE, I'VE DECIDED TO SPEAK WITHOUT THE USE OF MY BRAIN.
NO COM-MENT.
THIS IS MY EDITOR, REED. HE'LL BE IN CHARGE OF MY SPEAKAGE FOR NOW.
I'M HERE TO PROVE YOU CAN HAVE FUN WHILE STILL BEING POLITE AND MAINTAINING PROPER GRAMMAR.
HEY, REED.
"HEY" ISN'T A PROPER SALUTATION. TRY AGAIN.
NOW THAT'S FUN.
darb

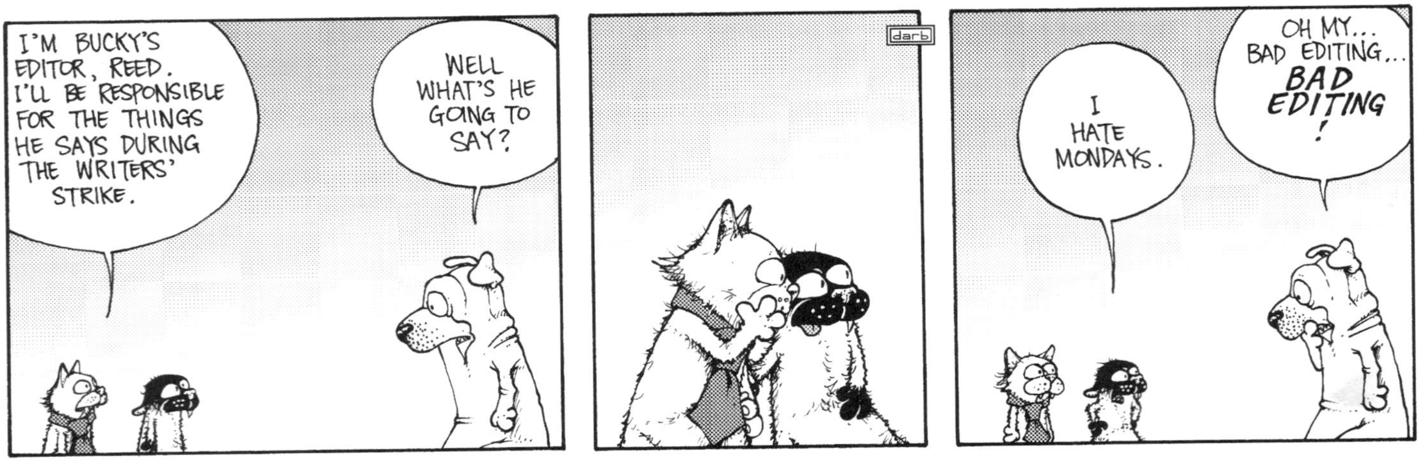
I'M BUCKY'S EDITOR, REED. I'LL BE RESPONSIBLE FOR THE THINGS HE SAYS DURING THE WRITERS' STRIKE.
WELL WHAT'S HE GOING TO SAY?
darb
I HATE MONDAYS.
OH MY... BAD EDITING... BAD EDITING!

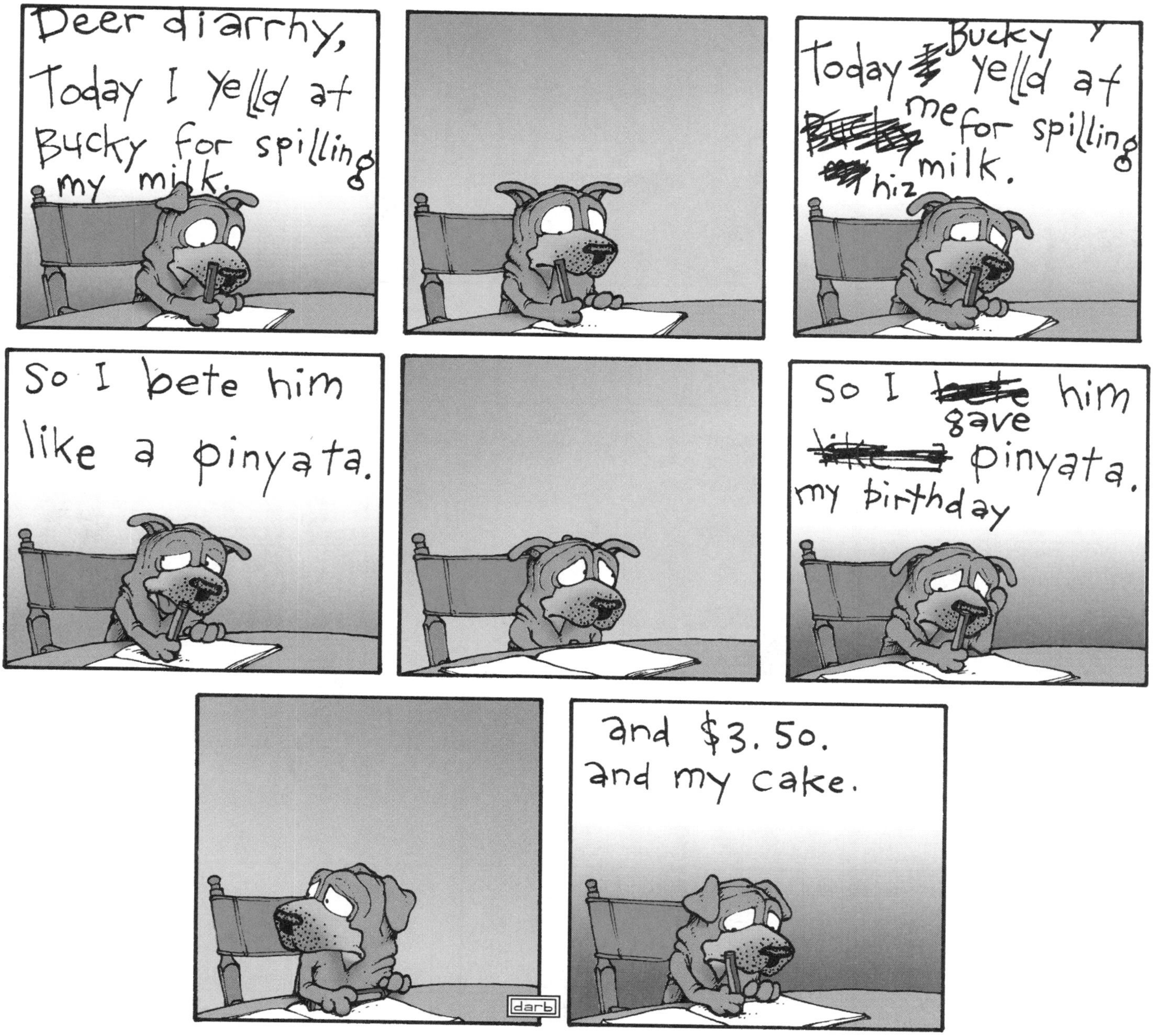
Deer diarrhy,
Today I yelld at Bucky for spilling my milk.
Today Bucky yelld at me for spilling hiz milk.
So I bete him like a pinyata.
So I gave him my birthday pinyata.
and $3.50.
and my cake.
darb

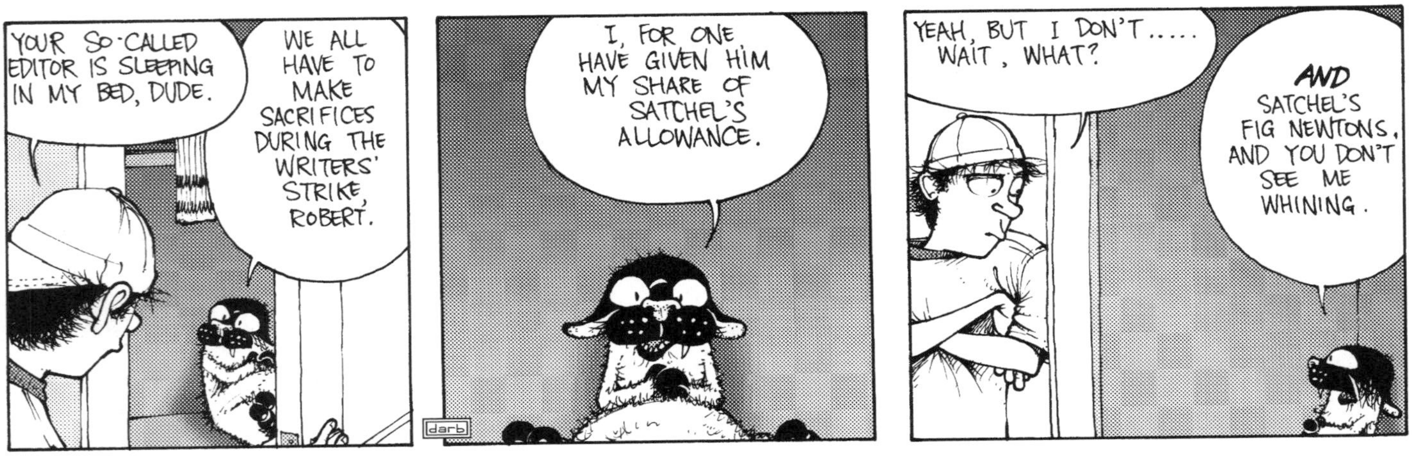
YOUR SO-CALLED EDITOR IS SLEEPING IN MY BED, DUDE.
WE ALL HAVE TO MAKE SACRIFICES DURING THE WRITERS' STRIKE, ROBERT.
I, FOR ONE HAVE GIVEN HIM MY SHARE OF SATCHEL'S ALLOWANCE.
YEAH, BUT I DON'T..... WAIT, WHAT?
AND SATCHEL'S FIG NEWTONS, AND YOU DON'T SEE ME WHINING.

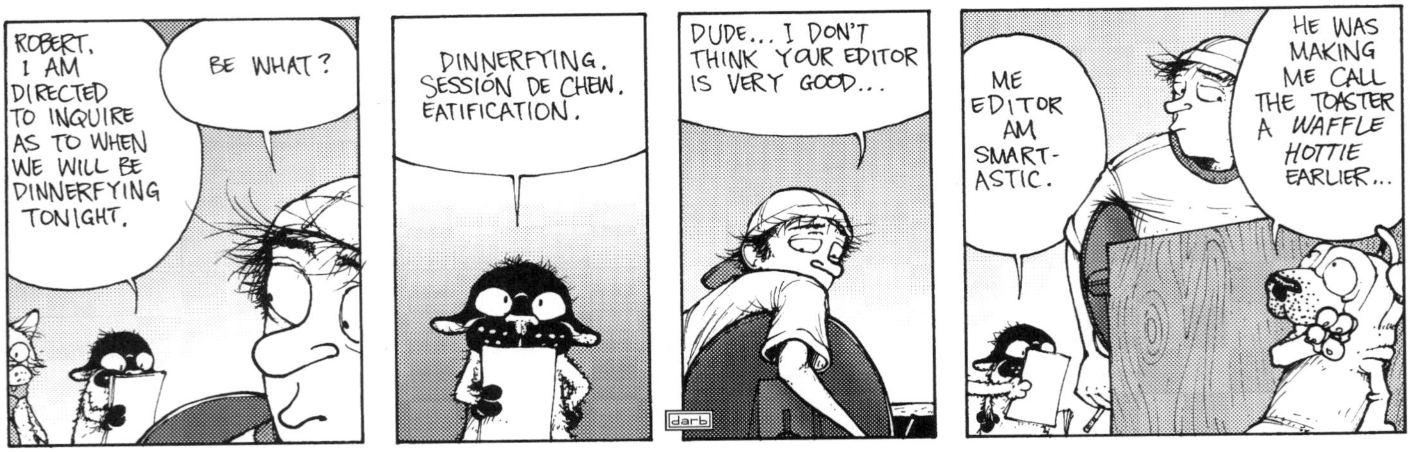
ROBERT. I AM DIRECTED TO INQUIRE AS TO WHEN WE WILL BE DINNERFYING TONIGHT.
BE WHAT?
DINNERFYING. SESSIÓN DE CHEW. EATIFICATION.
DUDE... I DON'T THINK YOUR EDITOR IS VERY GOOD...
ME EDITOR AM SMART-ASTIC.
HE WAS MAKING ME CALL THE TOASTER A WAFFLE HOTTIE EARLIER...

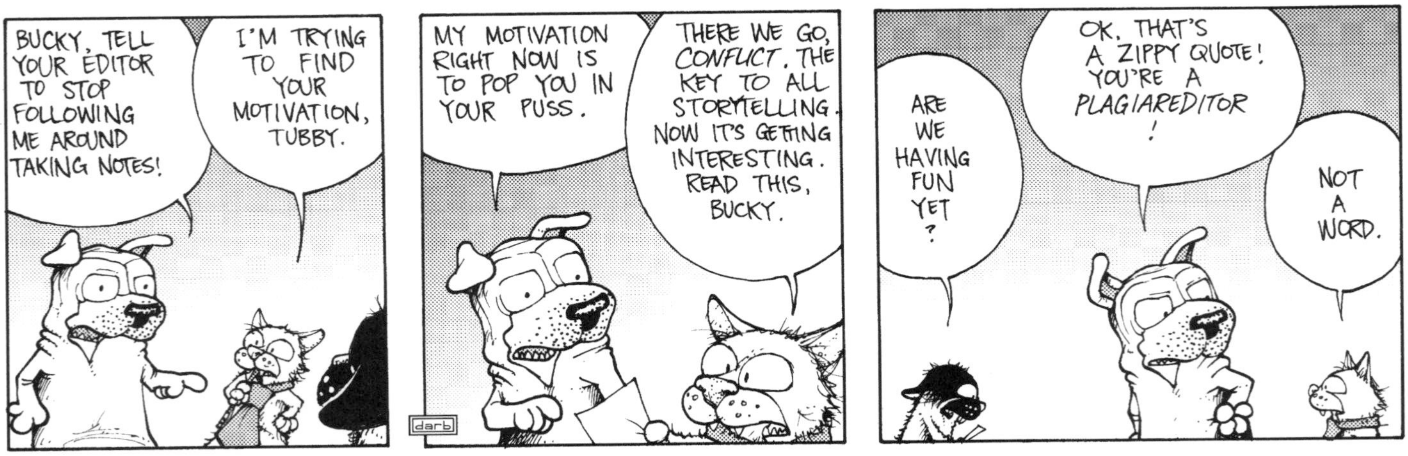
BUCKY, TELL YOUR EDITOR TO STOP FOLLOWING ME AROUND TAKING NOTES!
I'M TRYING TO FIND YOUR MOTIVATION, TUBBY.
MY MOTIVATION RIGHT NOW IS TO POP YOU IN YOUR PUSS.
THERE WE GO, CONFLICT. THE KEY TO ALL STORYTELLING. NOW IT'S GETTING INTERESTING. READ THIS, BUCKY.
ARE WE HAVING FUN YET ?
OK. THAT'S A ZIPPY QUOTE! YOU'RE A PLAGIAREDITOR !
NOT A WORD.

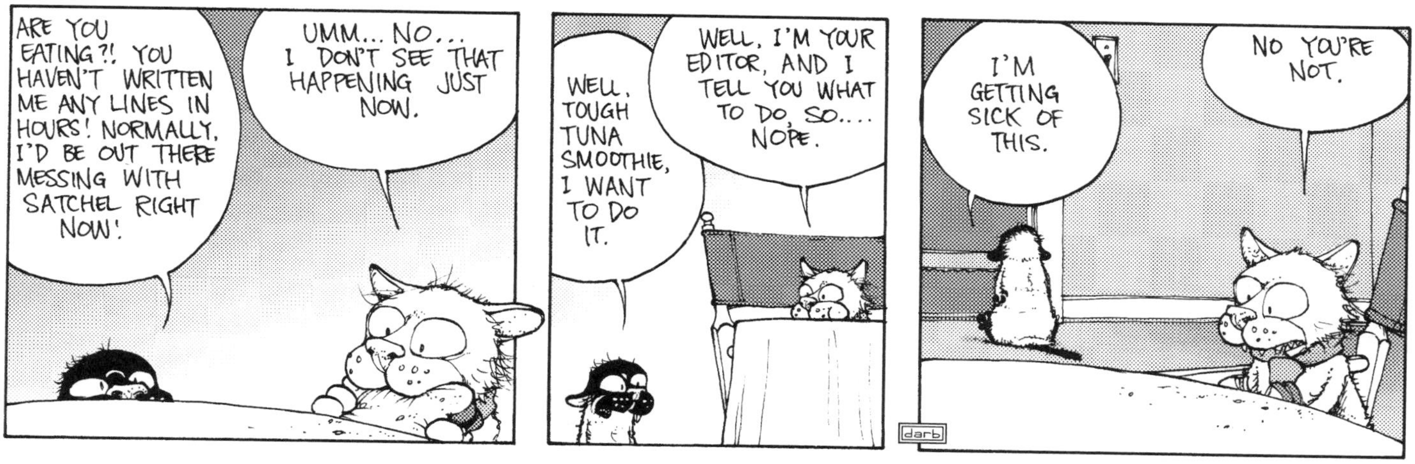
ARE YOU EATING?! YOU HAVEN'T WRITTEN ME ANY LINES IN HOURS! NORMALLY, I'D BE OUT THERE MESSING WITH SATCHEL RIGHT NOW!
UMM... NO... I DON'T SEE THAT HAPPENING JUST NOW.
WELL, TOUGH TUNA SMOOTHIE, I WANT TO DO IT.
WELL, I'M YOUR EDITOR, AND I TELL YOU WHAT TO DO, SO.... NOPE.
I'M GETTING SICK OF THIS.
NO YOU'RE NOT.
darb

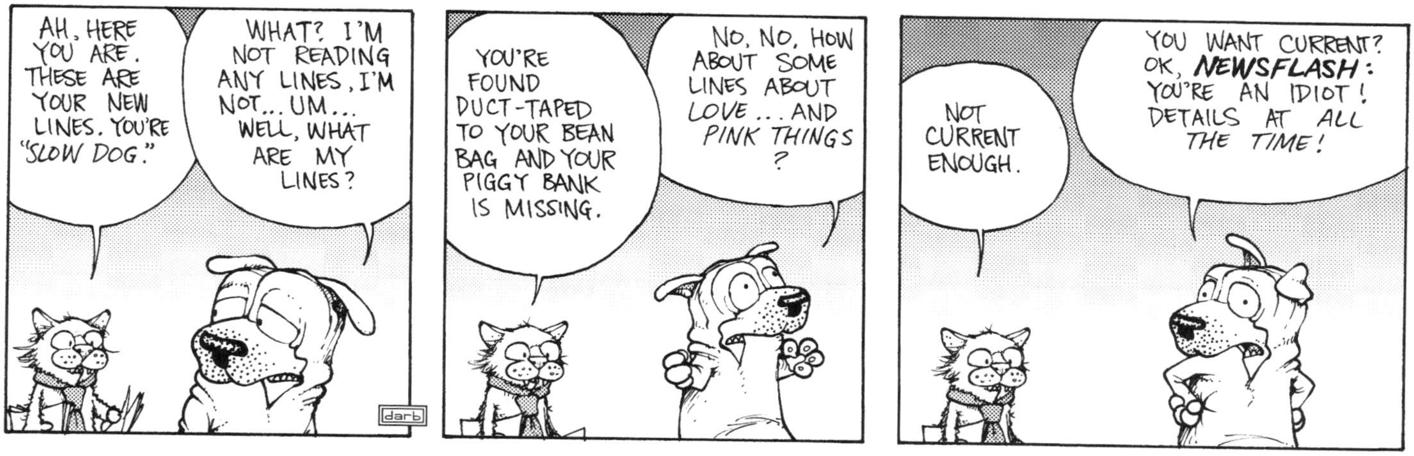
AH, HERE YOU ARE. THESE ARE YOUR NEW LINES. YOU'RE *"SLOW DOG."*
WHAT? I'M NOT READING ANY LINES, I'M NOT... UM... WELL, WHAT ARE MY LINES?
darb
YOU'RE FOUND DUCT-TAPED TO YOUR BEAN BAG AND YOUR PIGGY BANK IS MISSING.
NO, NO, HOW ABOUT SOME LINES ABOUT *LOVE*... AND *PINK THINGS*?
NOT CURRENT ENOUGH.
YOU WANT CURRENT? OK, ***NEWSFLASH***: YOU'RE AN IDIOT! DETAILS AT *ALL THE TIME!*

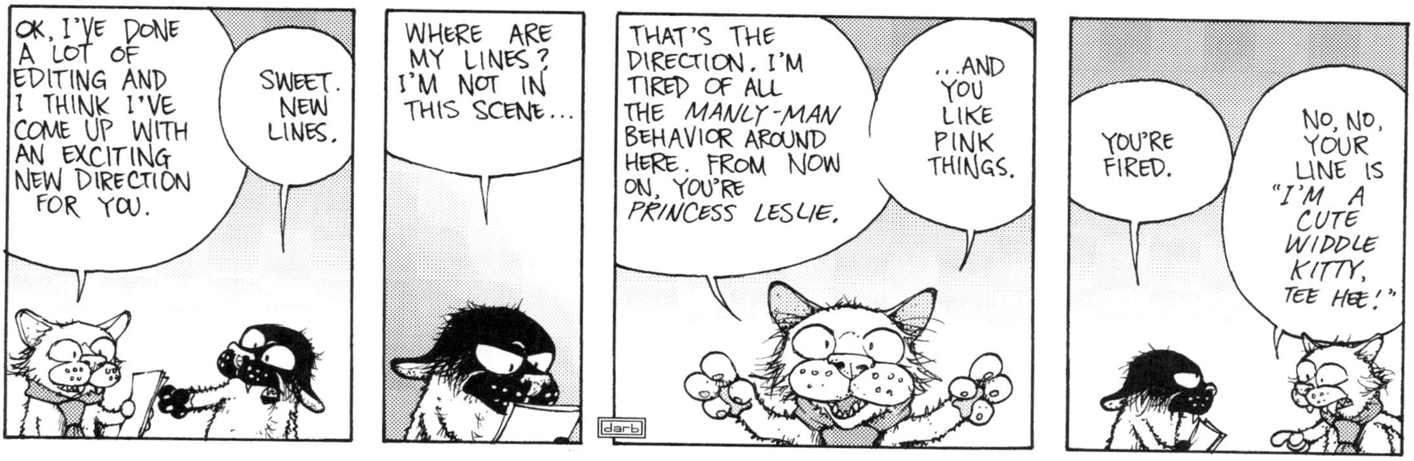
OK, I'VE DONE A LOT OF EDITING AND I THINK I'VE COME UP WITH AN EXCITING NEW DIRECTION FOR YOU.
SWEET. NEW LINES.
WHERE ARE MY LINES? I'M NOT IN THIS SCENE...
darb
THAT'S THE DIRECTION. I'M TIRED OF ALL THE *MANLY-MAN* BEHAVIOR AROUND HERE. FROM NOW ON, YOU'RE *PRINCESS LESLIE.*
...AND YOU LIKE PINK THINGS.
YOU'RE FIRED.
NO, NO, YOUR LINE IS *"I'M A CUTE WIDDLE KITTY, TEE HEE!"*

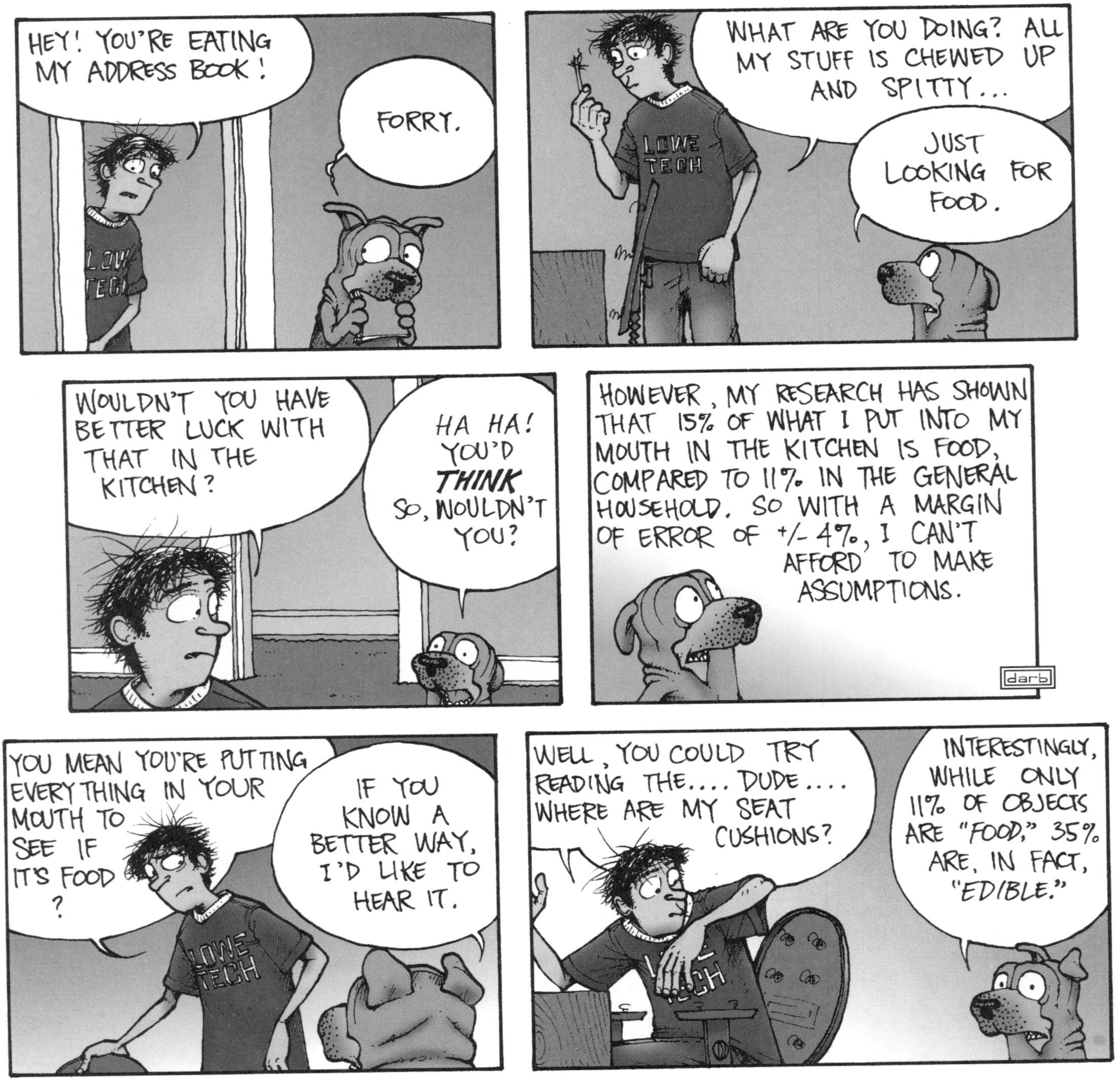
HEY! YOU'RE EATING MY ADDRESS BOOK!
FORRY.
LOWE TECH
WHAT ARE YOU DOING? ALL MY STUFF IS CHEWED UP AND SPITTY...
JUST LOOKING FOR FOOD.
WOULDN'T YOU HAVE BETTER LUCK WITH THAT IN THE KITCHEN?
HA HA! YOU'D *THINK* SO, WOULDN'T YOU?
HOWEVER, MY RESEARCH HAS SHOWN THAT 15% OF WHAT I PUT INTO MY MOUTH IN THE KITCHEN IS FOOD, COMPARED TO 11% IN THE GENERAL HOUSEHOLD. SO WITH A MARGIN OF ERROR OF +/- 4%, I CAN'T AFFORD TO MAKE ASSUMPTIONS.
darb
YOU MEAN YOU'RE PUTTING EVERYTHING IN YOUR MOUTH TO SEE IF IT'S FOOD?
IF YOU KNOW A BETTER WAY, I'D LIKE TO HEAR IT.
WELL, YOU COULD TRY READING THE.... DUDE.... WHERE ARE MY SEAT CUSHIONS?
INTERESTINGLY, WHILE ONLY 11% OF OBJECTS ARE "FOOD," 35% ARE, IN FACT, "EDIBLE."

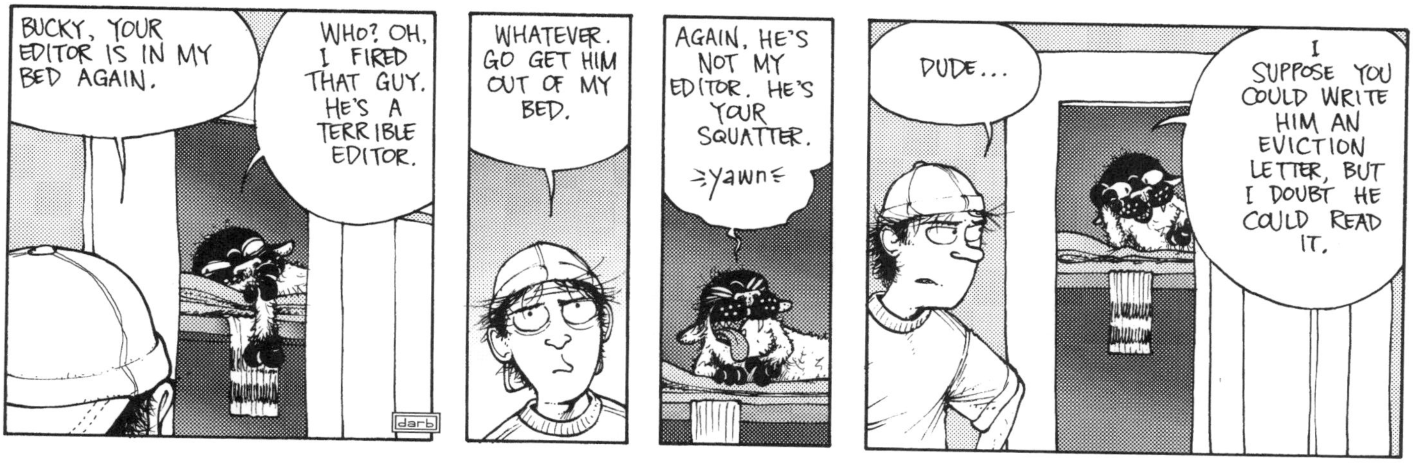
BUCKY, YOUR EDITOR IS IN MY BED AGAIN.
WHO? OH, I FIRED THAT GUY. HE'S A TERRIBLE EDITOR.
WHATEVER. GO GET HIM OUT OF MY BED.
AGAIN, HE'S NOT MY EDITOR. HE'S YOUR SQUATTER.
yawn
DUDE...
I SUPPOSE YOU COULD WRITE HIM AN EVICTION LETTER, BUT I DOUBT HE COULD READ IT.
darb

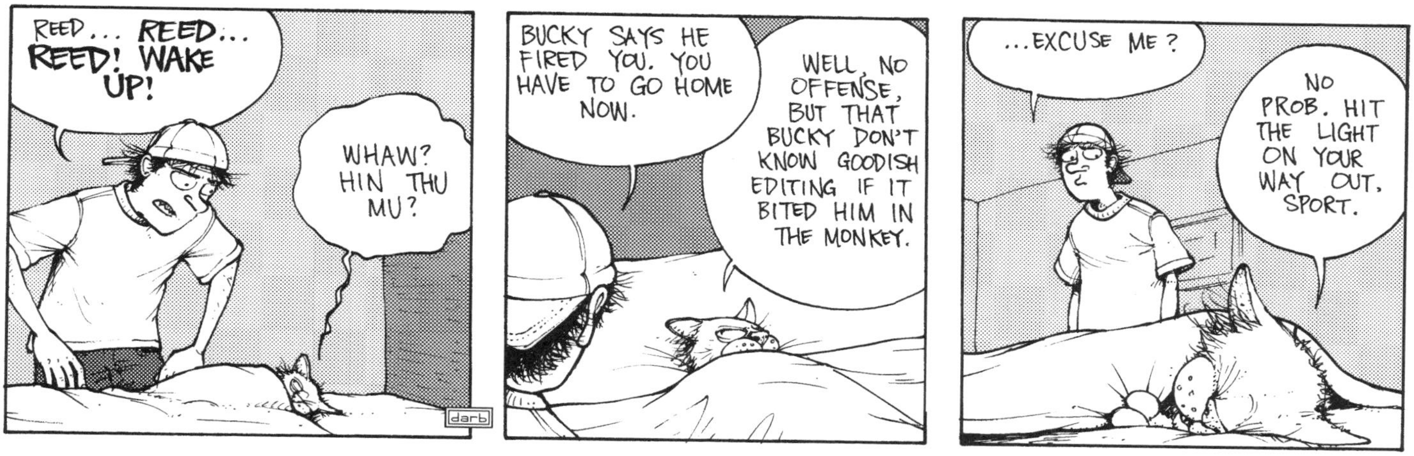
REED... REED... REED! WAKE UP!
WHAW? HIN THU MU?
BUCKY SAYS HE FIRED YOU. YOU HAVE TO GO HOME NOW.
WELL, NO OFFENSE, BUT THAT BUCKY DON'T KNOW GOODISH EDITING IF IT BITED HIM IN THE MONKEY.
...EXCUSE ME?
NO PROB. HIT THE LIGHT ON YOUR WAY OUT, SPORT.
darb

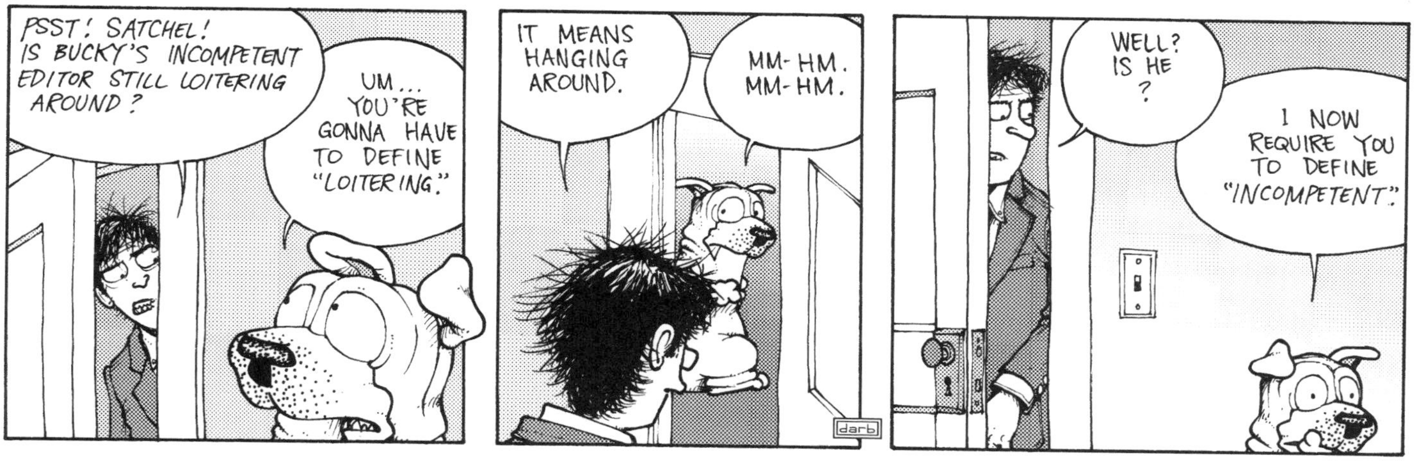
PSST! SATCHEL! IS BUCKY'S INCOMPETENT EDITOR STILL LOITERING AROUND?
UM... YOU'RE GONNA HAVE TO DEFINE "LOITERING."
IT MEANS HANGING AROUND.
MM-HM. MM-HM.
WELL? IS HE ?
I NOW REQUIRE YOU TO DEFINE "INCOMPETENT."
darb

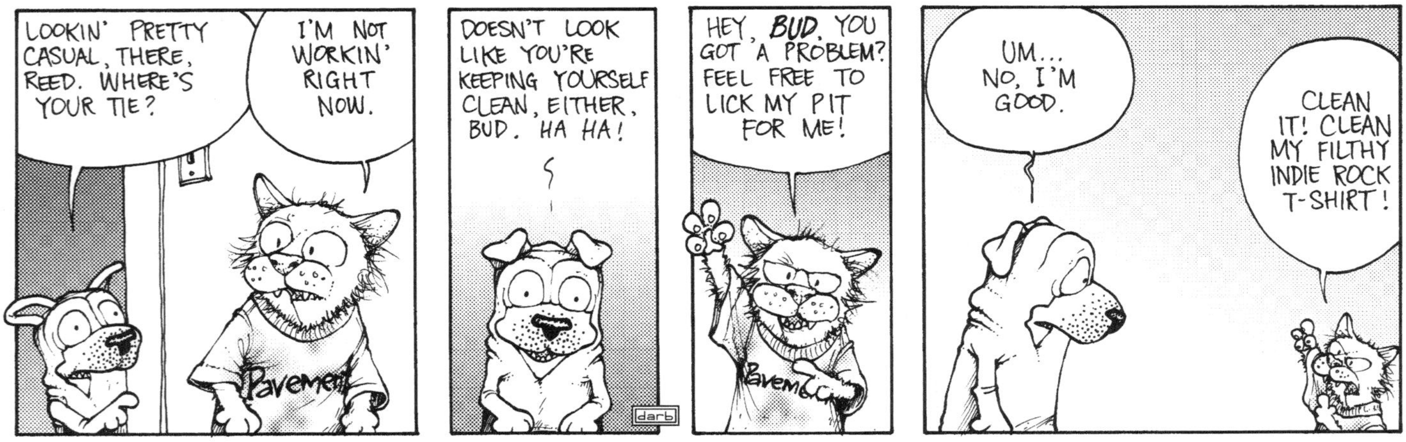
LOOKIN' PRETTY CASUAL, THERE, REED. WHERE'S YOUR TIE?
I'M NOT WORKIN' RIGHT NOW.
Pavement
DOESN'T LOOK LIKE YOU'RE KEEPING YOURSELF CLEAN, EITHER, BUD. HA HA!
darb
HEY, **BUD**, YOU GOT A PROBLEM? FEEL FREE TO LICK MY PIT FOR ME!
UM... NO, I'M GOOD.
CLEAN IT! CLEAN MY FILTHY INDIE ROCK T-SHIRT!

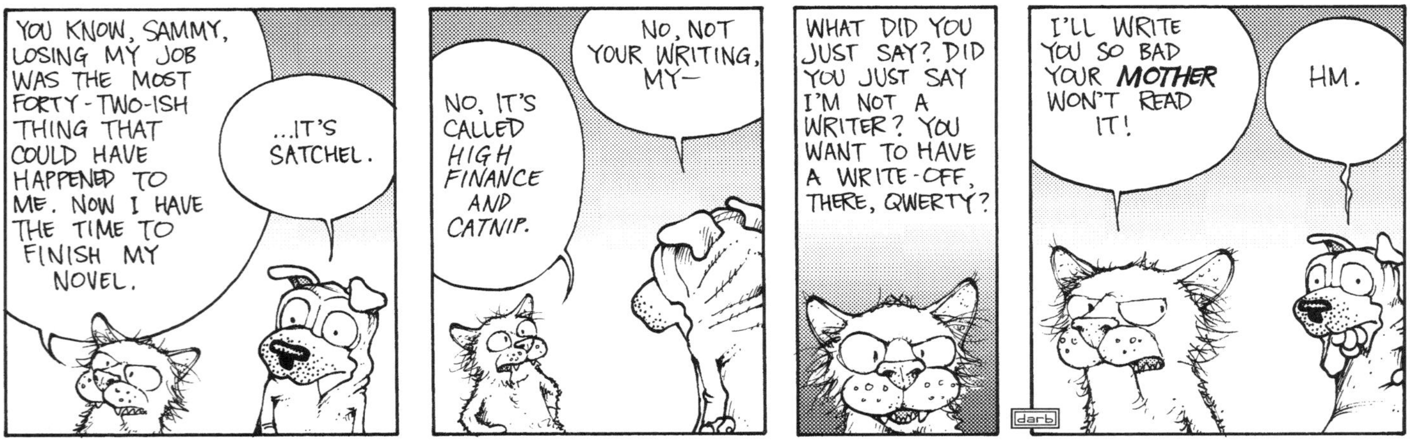
YOU KNOW, SAMMY, LOSING MY JOB WAS THE MOST FORTY-TWO-ISH THING THAT COULD HAVE HAPPENED TO ME. NOW I HAVE THE TIME TO FINISH MY NOVEL.
...IT'S SATCHEL.
NO, IT'S CALLED *HIGH FINANCE AND CATNIP*.
NO, NOT YOUR WRITING, MY—
WHAT DID YOU JUST SAY? DID YOU JUST SAY I'M NOT A WRITER? YOU WANT TO HAVE A WRITE-OFF, THERE, QWERTY?
darb
I'LL WRITE YOU SO BAD YOUR ***MOTHER*** WON'T READ IT!
HM.

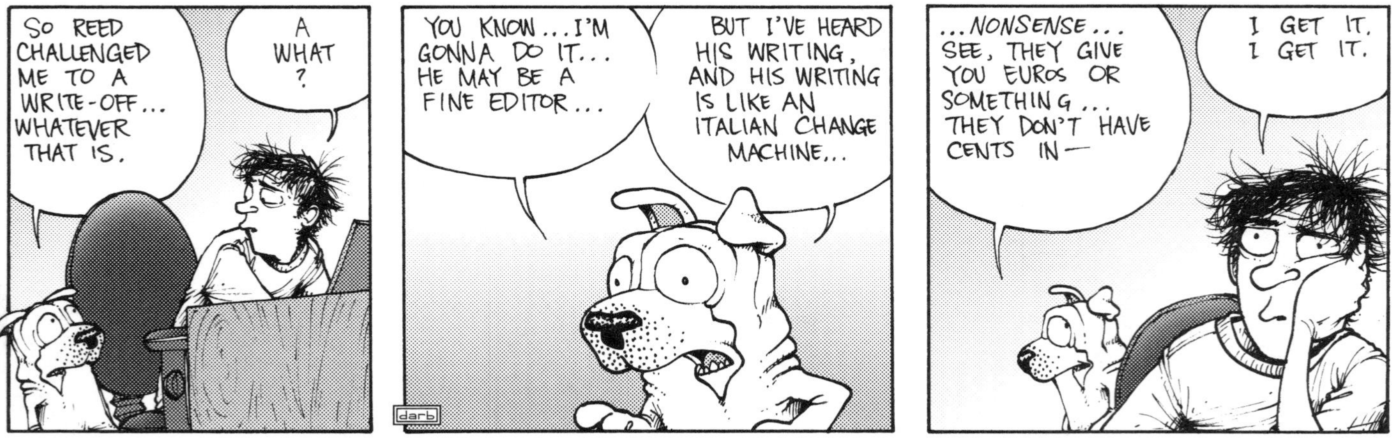
SO REED CHALLENGED ME TO A WRITE-OFF... WHATEVER THAT IS.
A WHAT?
YOU KNOW... I'M GONNA DO IT... HE MAY BE A FINE EDITOR...
BUT I'VE HEARD HIS WRITING, AND HIS WRITING IS LIKE AN ITALIAN CHANGE MACHINE...
darb
...*NONSENSE*... SEE, THEY GIVE YOU EUROS OR SOMETHING... THEY DON'T HAVE CENTS IN—
I GET IT. I GET IT.

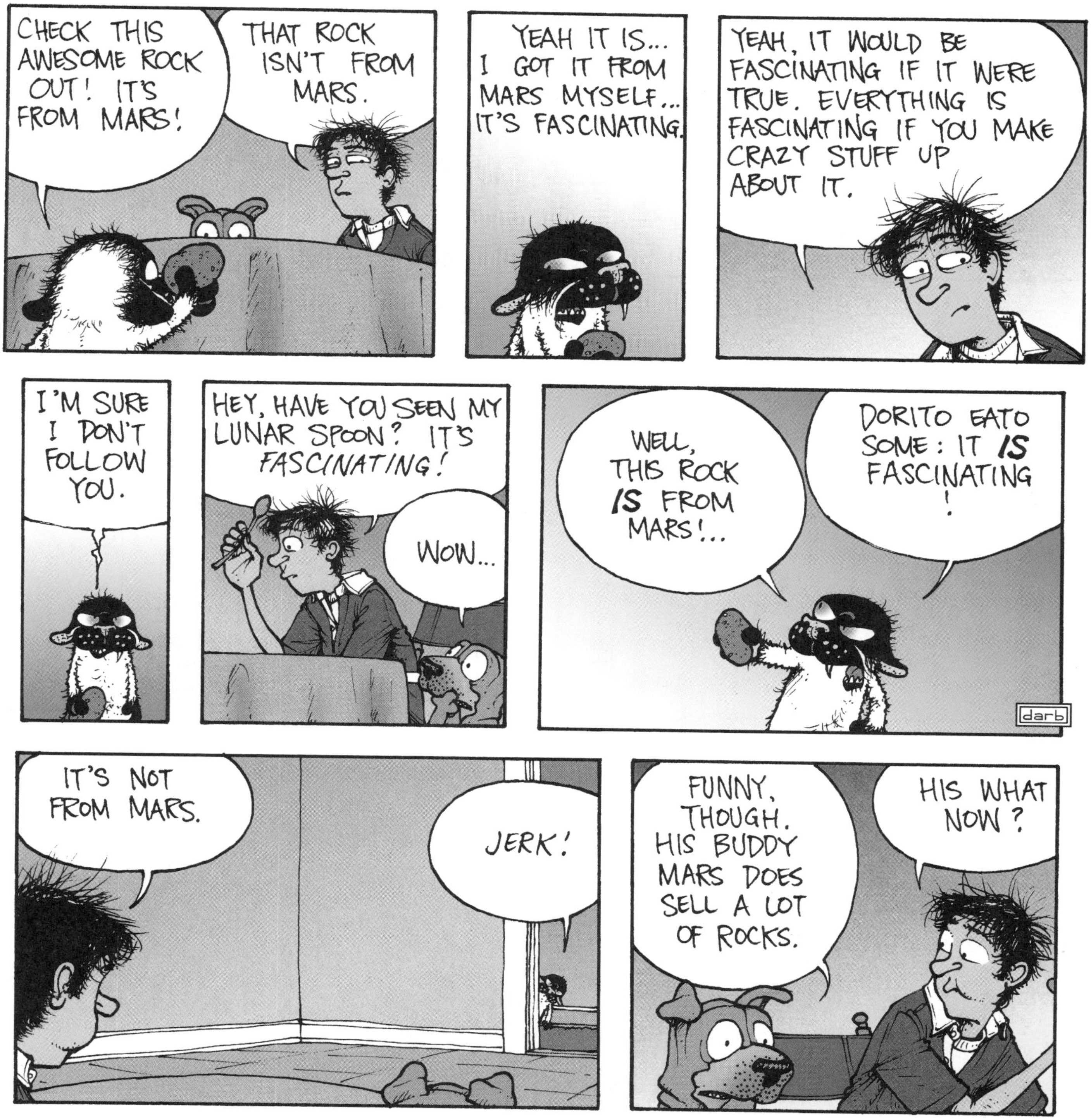
CHECK THIS AWESOME ROCK OUT! IT'S FROM MARS!
THAT ROCK ISN'T FROM MARS.
YEAH IT IS... I GOT IT FROM MARS MYSELF... IT'S FASCINATING.
YEAH, IT WOULD BE FASCINATING IF IT WERE TRUE. EVERYTHING IS FASCINATING IF YOU MAKE CRAZY STUFF UP ABOUT IT.
I'M SURE I DON'T FOLLOW YOU.
HEY, HAVE YOU SEEN MY LUNAR SPOON? IT'S *FASCINATING!*
WOW...
WELL, THIS ROCK **IS** FROM MARS!...
DORITO EATO SOME: IT **IS** FASCINATING!
darb
IT'S NOT FROM MARS.
JERK!
FUNNY, THOUGH. HIS BUDDY MARS DOES SELL A LOT OF ROCKS.
HIS WHAT NOW?

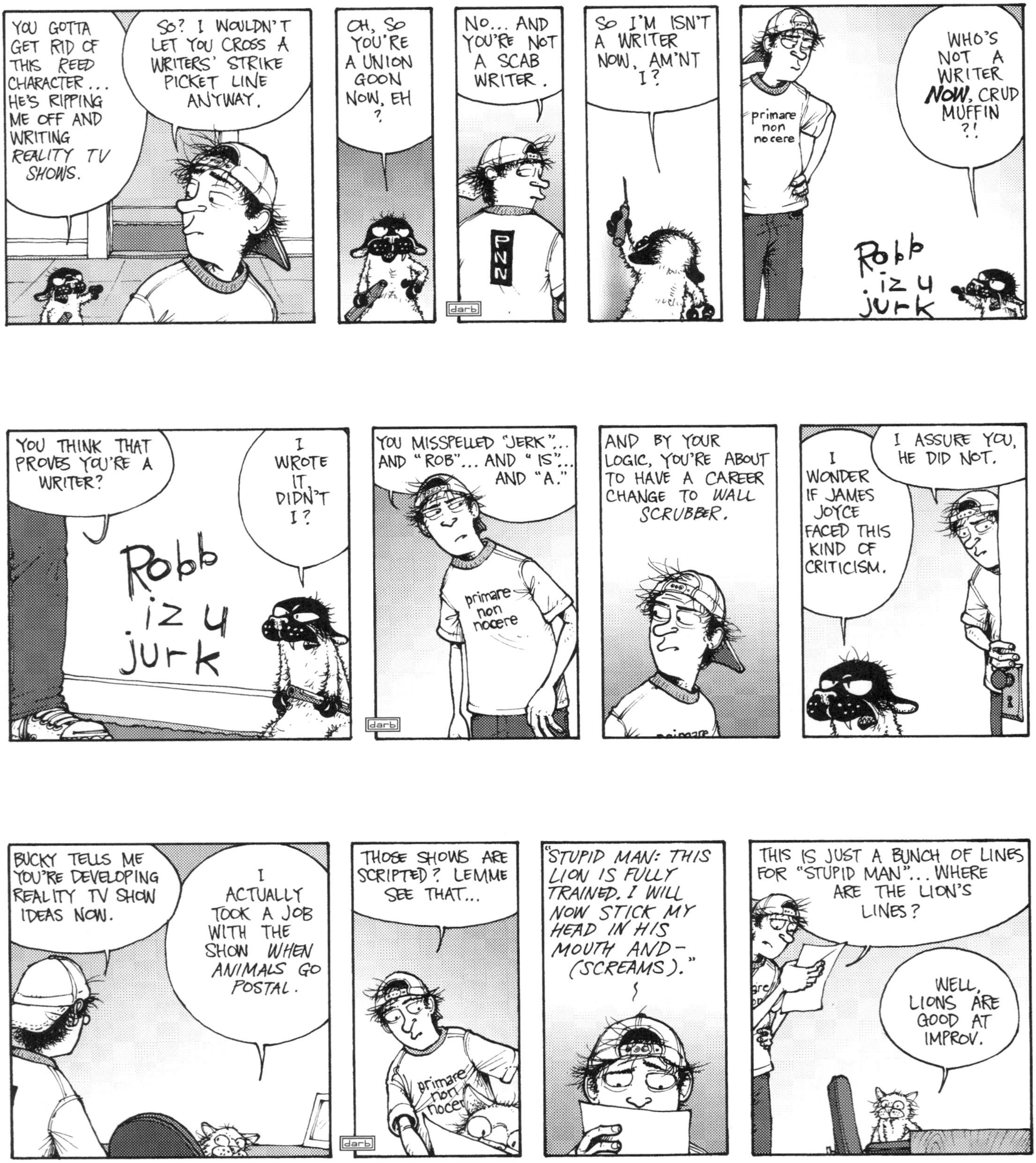
YOU GOTTA GET RID OF THIS REED CHARACTER... HE'S RIPPING ME OFF AND WRITING REALITY TV SHOWS.
SO? I WOULDN'T LET YOU CROSS A WRITERS' STRIKE PICKET LINE ANYWAY.
OH, SO YOU'RE A UNION GOON NOW, EH?
NO... AND YOU'RE NOT A SCAB WRITER.
PNN
SO I'M ISN'T A WRITER NOW, AM'NT I?
primare non nocere
WHO'S NOT A WRITER NOW, CRUD MUFFIN?!
Robb iz u jurk
YOU THINK THAT PROVES YOU'RE A WRITER?
I WROTE IT, DIDN'T I?
Robb iz u jurk
YOU MISSPELLED "JERK"... AND "ROB"... AND "IS"... AND "A."
primare non nocere
AND BY YOUR LOGIC, YOU'RE ABOUT TO HAVE A CAREER CHANGE TO WALL SCRUBBER.
I WONDER IF JAMES JOYCE FACED THIS KIND OF CRITICISM.
I ASSURE YOU, HE DID NOT.
BUCKY TELLS ME YOU'RE DEVELOPING REALITY TV SHOW IDEAS NOW.
I ACTUALLY TOOK A JOB WITH THE SHOW WHEN ANIMALS GO POSTAL.
THOSE SHOWS ARE SCRIPTED? LEMME SEE THAT...
primare non nocere
"STUPID MAN: THIS LION IS FULLY TRAINED. I WILL NOW STICK MY HEAD IN HIS MOUTH AND– (SCREAMS)."
THIS IS JUST A BUNCH OF LINES FOR "STUPID MAN"... WHERE ARE THE LION'S LINES?
WELL, LIONS ARE GOOD AT IMPROV.

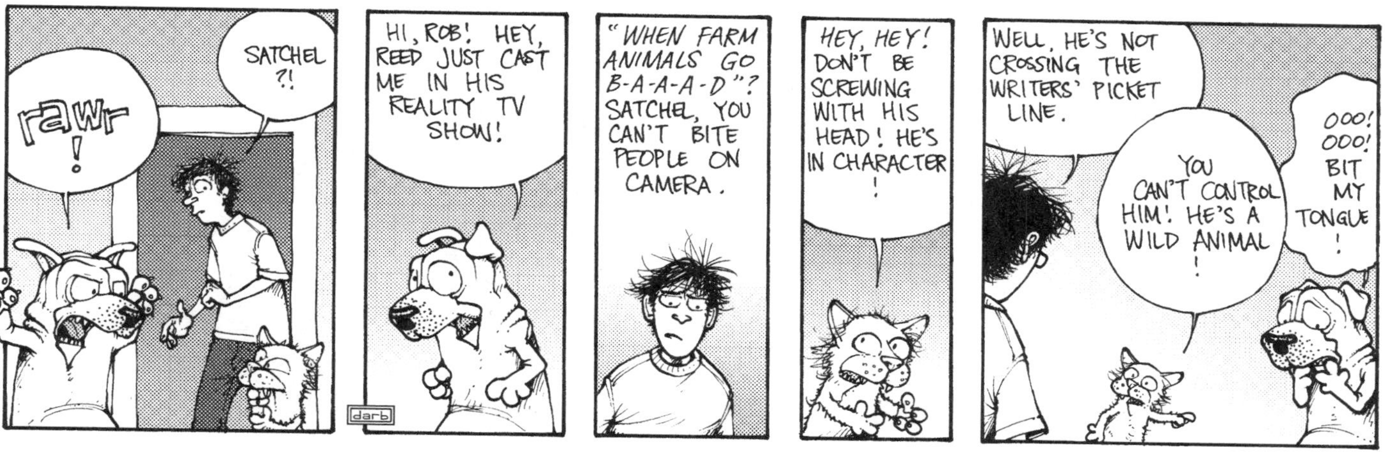
rawr!
SATCHEL?!
HI, ROB! HEY, REED JUST CAST ME IN HIS REALITY TV SHOW!
"WHEN FARM ANIMALS GO B-A-A-A-D"? SATCHEL, YOU CAN'T BITE PEOPLE ON CAMERA.
HEY, HEY! DON'T BE SCREWING WITH HIS HEAD! HE'S IN CHARACTER!
WELL, HE'S NOT CROSSING THE WRITERS' PICKET LINE.
YOU CAN'T CONTROL HIM! HE'S A WILD ANIMAL!
OOO! OOO! BIT MY TONGUE!

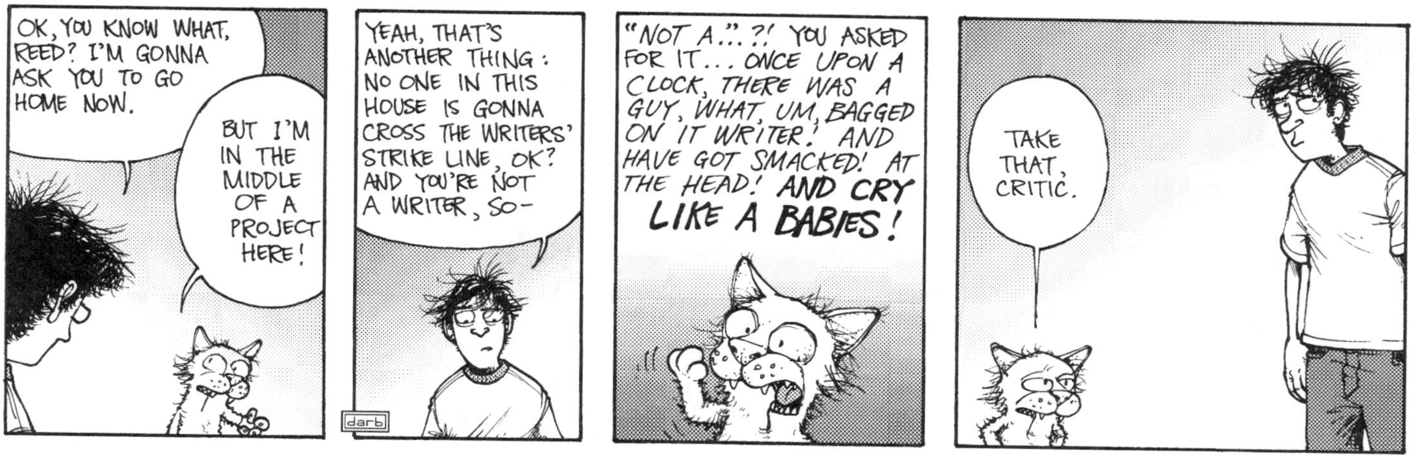
OK, YOU KNOW WHAT, REED? I'M GONNA ASK YOU TO GO HOME NOW.
BUT I'M IN THE MIDDLE OF A PROJECT HERE!
YEAH, THAT'S ANOTHER THING: NO ONE IN THIS HOUSE IS GONNA CROSS THE WRITERS' STRIKE LINE, OK? AND YOU'RE NOT A WRITER, SO-
"NOT A..."?! YOU ASKED FOR IT... ONCE UPON A CLOCK, THERE WAS A GUY, WHAT, UM, BAGGED ON IT WRITER! AND HAVE GOT SMACKED! AT THE HEAD! AND CRY LIKE A BABIES!
TAKE THAT, CRITIC.

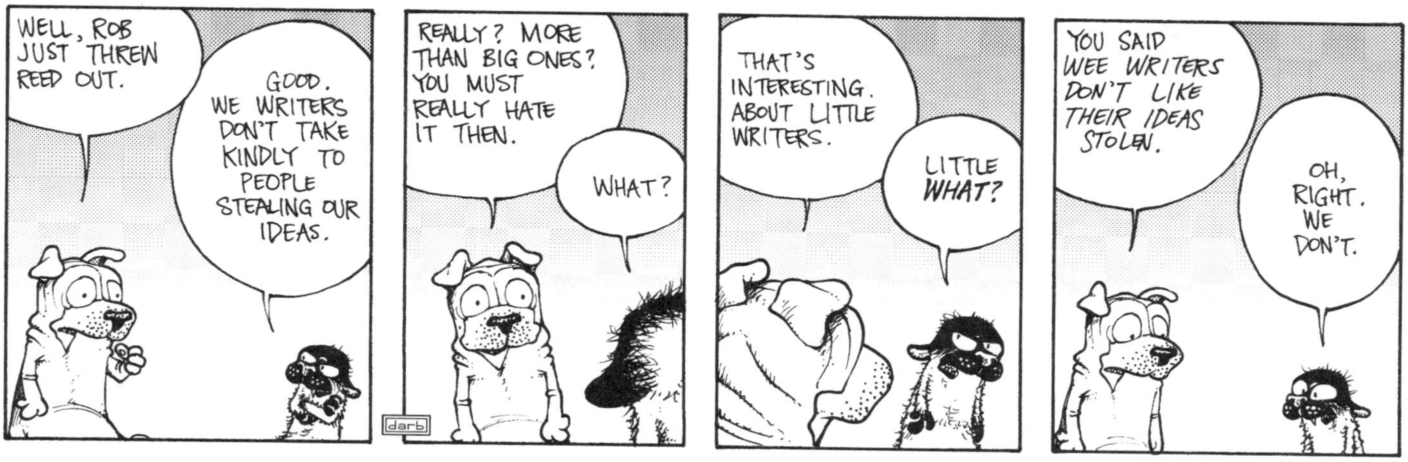
WELL, ROB JUST THREW REED OUT.
GOOD. WE WRITERS DON'T TAKE KINDLY TO PEOPLE STEALING OUR IDEAS.
REALLY? MORE THAN BIG ONES? YOU MUST REALLY HATE IT THEN.
WHAT?
THAT'S INTERESTING. ABOUT LITTLE WRITERS.
LITTLE WHAT?
YOU SAID WEE WRITERS DON'T LIKE THEIR IDEAS STOLEN.
OH, RIGHT. WE DON'T.

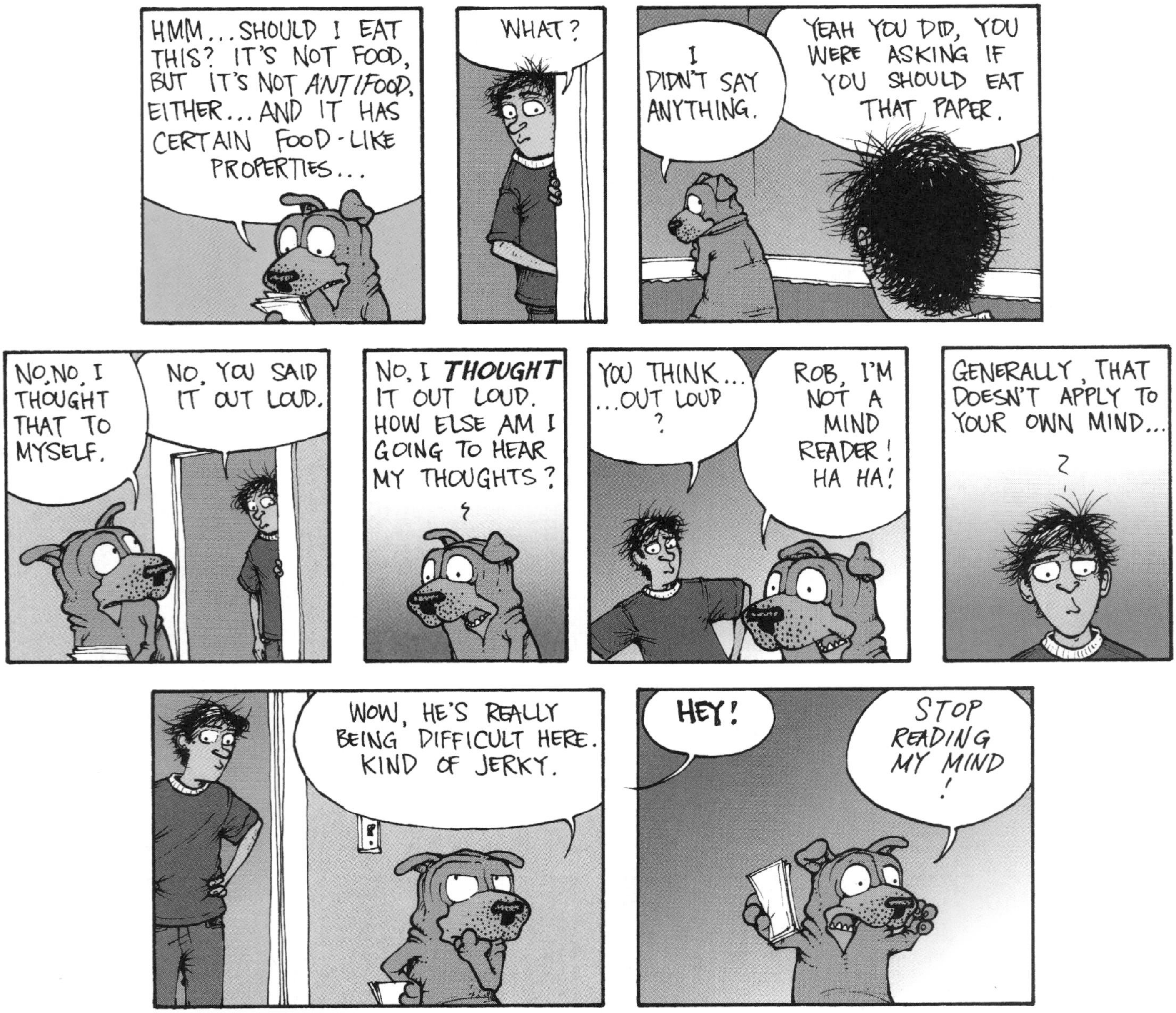
HMM... SHOULD I EAT THIS? IT'S NOT FOOD, BUT IT'S NOT ANTIFOOD, EITHER... AND IT HAS CERTAIN FOOD-LIKE PROPERTIES...
WHAT?
I DIDN'T SAY ANYTHING.
YEAH YOU DID, YOU WERE ASKING IF YOU SHOULD EAT THAT PAPER.
NO, NO, I THOUGHT THAT TO MYSELF.
NO, YOU SAID IT OUT LOUD.
NO, I THOUGHT IT OUT LOUD. HOW ELSE AM I GOING TO HEAR MY THOUGHTS?
YOU THINK... ...OUT LOUD ?
ROB, I'M NOT A MIND READER! HA HA!
GENERALLY, THAT DOESN'T APPLY TO YOUR OWN MIND...
WOW, HE'S REALLY BEING DIFFICULT HERE. KIND OF JERKY.
HEY!
STOP READING MY MIND!

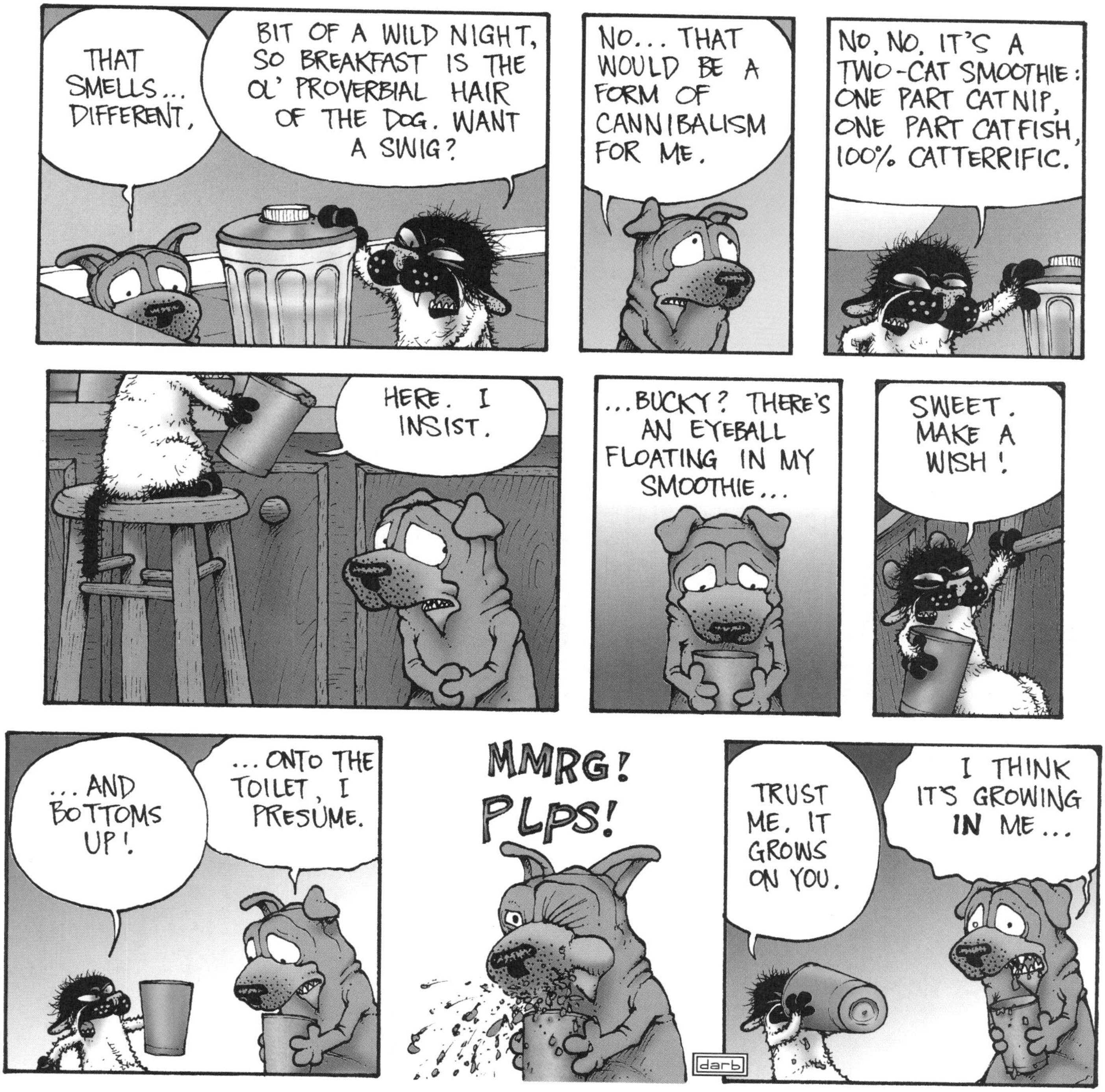
THAT SMELLS... DIFFERENT.
BIT OF A WILD NIGHT, SO BREAKFAST IS THE OL' PROVERBIAL HAIR OF THE DOG. WANT A SWIG?
NO... THAT WOULD BE A FORM OF CANNIBALISM FOR ME.
NO, NO. IT'S A TWO-CAT SMOOTHIE: ONE PART CATNIP, ONE PART CATFISH, 100% CATTERRIFIC.
HERE. I INSIST.
...BUCKY? THERE'S AN EYEBALL FLOATING IN MY SMOOTHIE...
SWEET. MAKE A WISH!
...AND BOTTOMS UP!
...ONTO THE TOILET, I PRESUME.
MMRG! PLPS!
darb
TRUST ME, IT GROWS ON YOU.
I THINK IT'S GROWING IN ME...

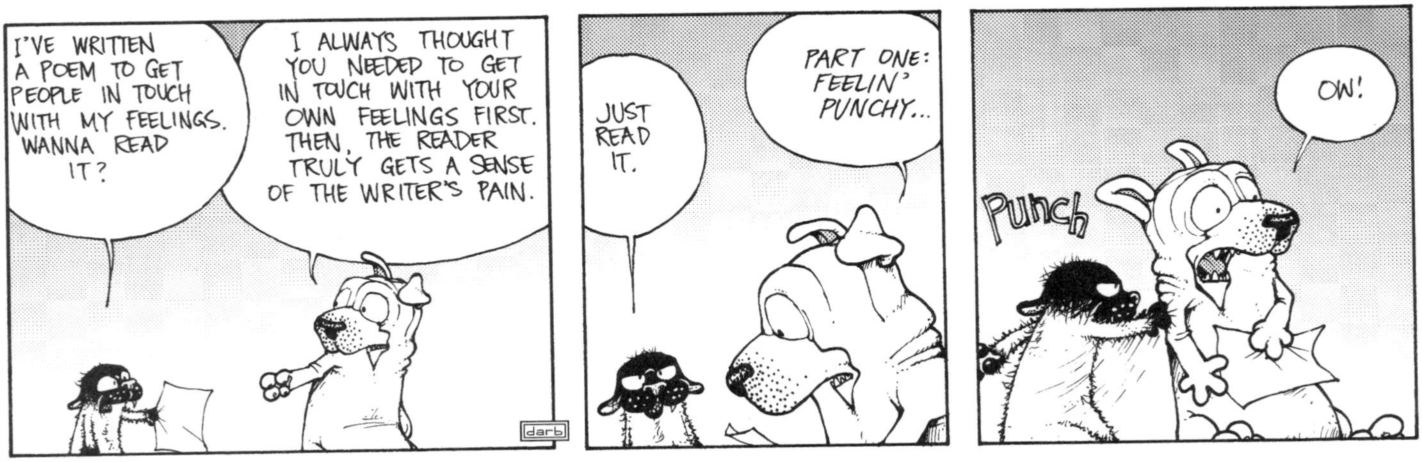
I'VE WRITTEN A POEM TO GET PEOPLE IN TOUCH WITH MY FEELINGS. WANNA READ IT?
I ALWAYS THOUGHT YOU NEEDED TO GET IN TOUCH WITH YOUR OWN FEELINGS FIRST. THEN, THE READER TRULY GETS A SENSE OF THE WRITER'S PAIN.
JUST READ IT.
PART ONE: FEELIN' PUNCHY...
Punch
OW!
darb

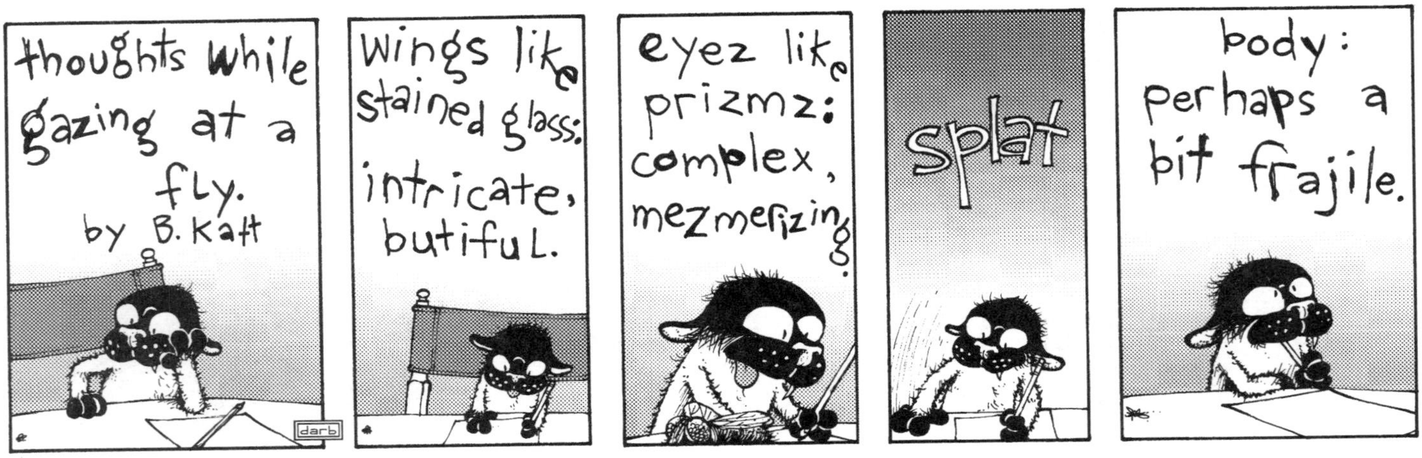
thoughts while gazing at a fly.
by B. Katt
darb
wings like stained glass:
intricate,
butifuL.
eyez like prizmz:
complex,
mezmerizing.
splat
body:
perhaps a bit frajile.

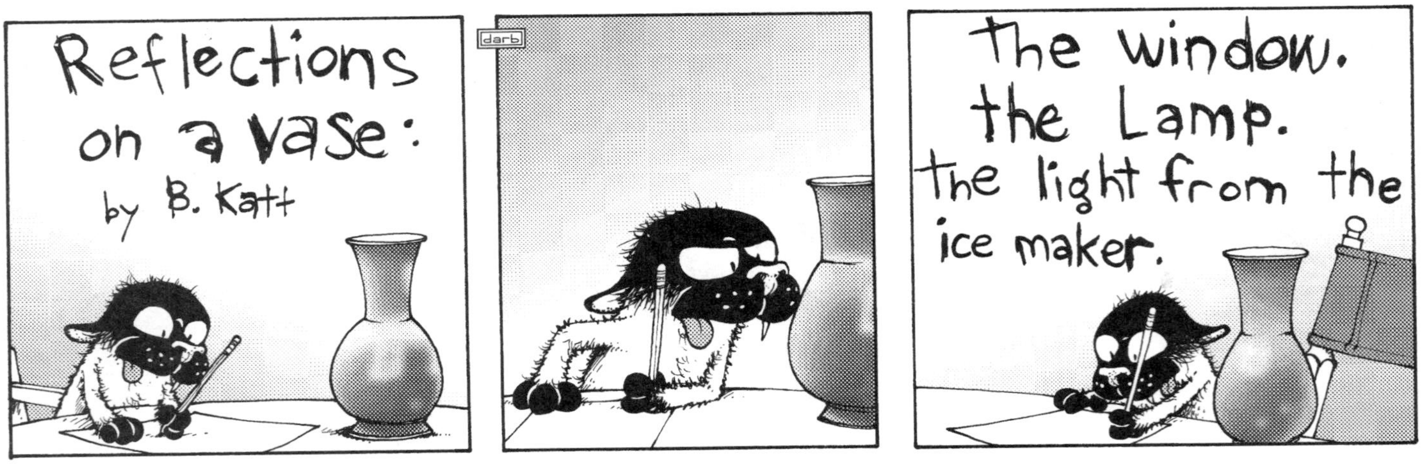
Reflections on a vase:
by B. Katt
darb
The window.
the Lamp.
The light from the ice maker.

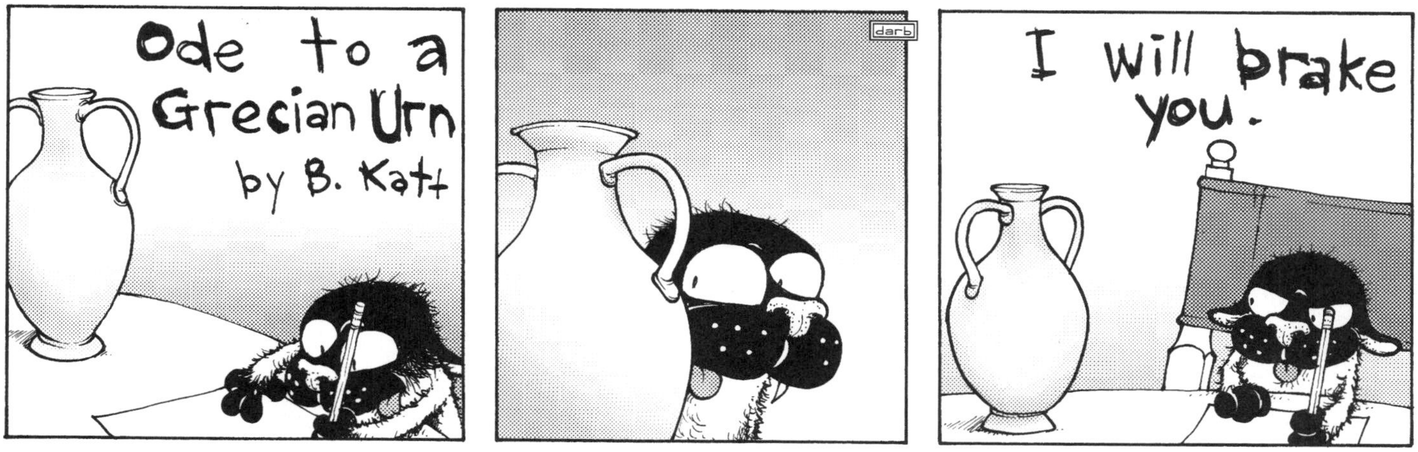
Ode to a Grecian Urn
by B. Katt
darb
I will brake you.

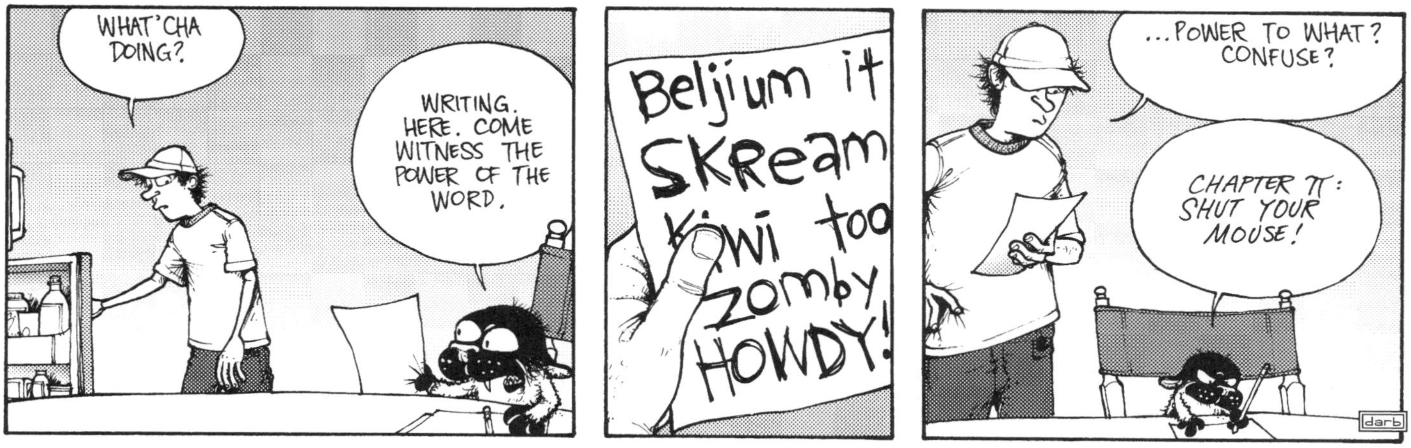
WHAT'CHA DOING?
WRITING. HERE. COME WITNESS THE POWER OF THE WORD.
Beljium it SKream Kiwi too zomby HOWDY!
...POWER TO WHAT? CONFUSE?
CHAPTER π: SHUT YOUR MOUSE!
darb

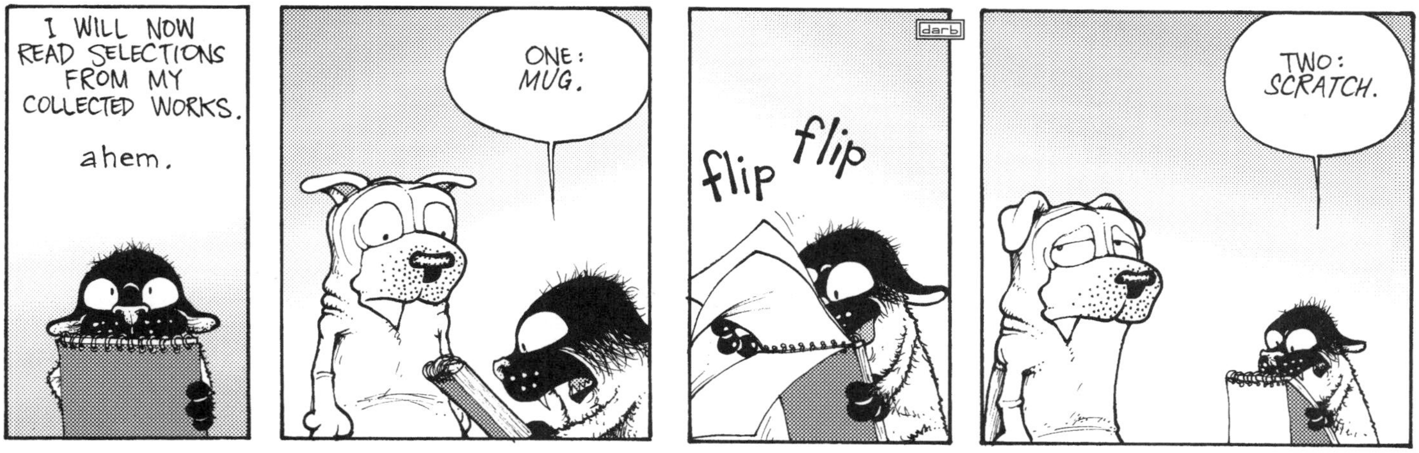
I WILL NOW READ SELECTIONS FROM MY COLLECTED WORKS.
ahem.
ONE: MUG.
darb
flip flip
TWO: SCRATCH.

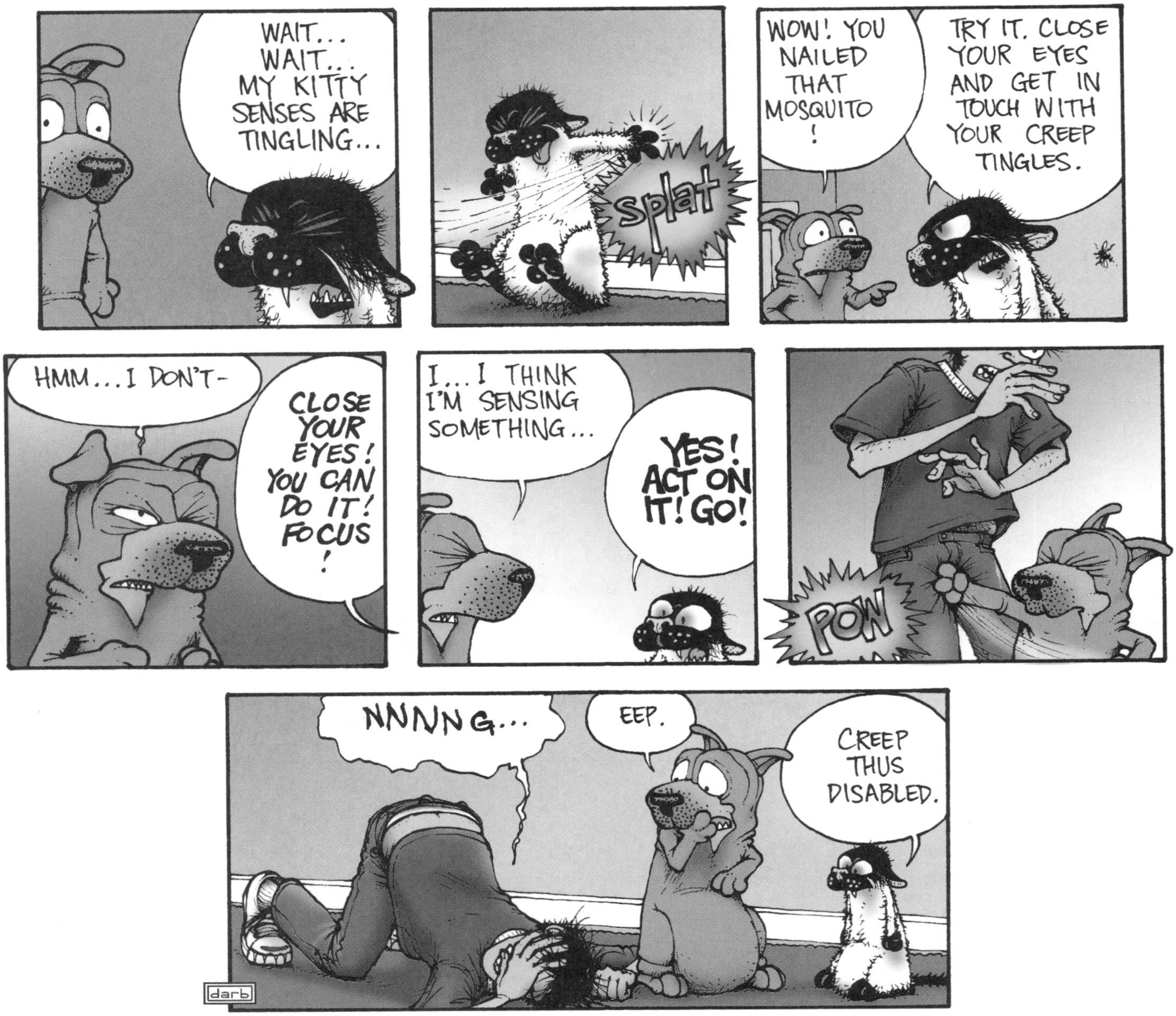

WAIT... WAIT... MY KITTY SENSES ARE TINGLING...
splat
WOW! YOU NAILED THAT MOSQUITO!
TRY IT. CLOSE YOUR EYES AND GET IN TOUCH WITH YOUR CREEP TINGLES.
HMM...I DON'T-
CLOSE YOUR EYES! YOU CAN DO IT! FOCUS!
I...I THINK I'M SENSING SOMETHING...
YES! ACT ON IT! GO!
POW
NNNNG...
EEP.
CREEP THUS DISABLED.
darb

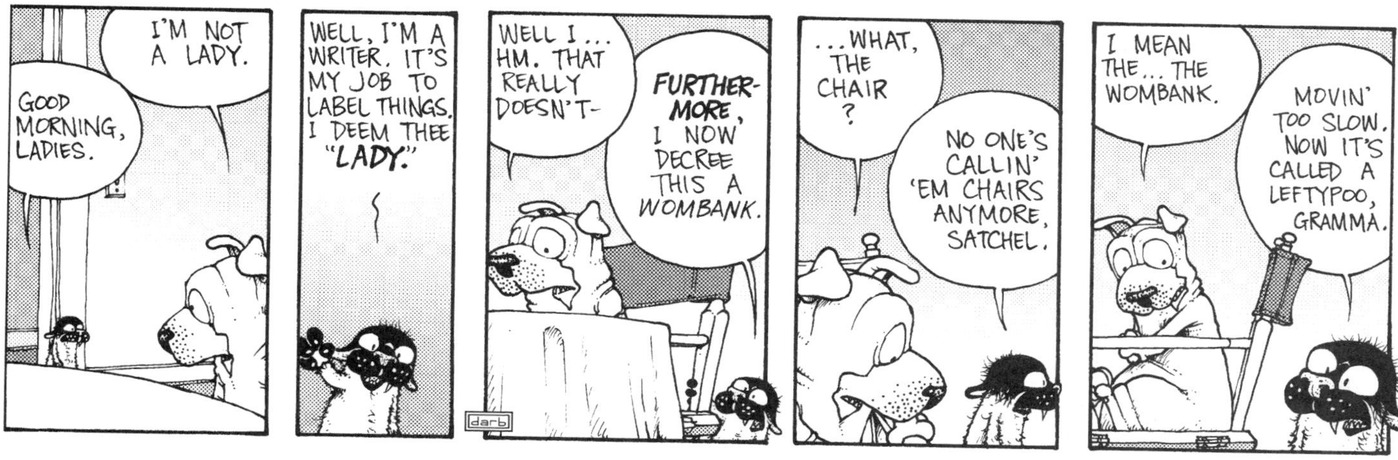
GOOD MORNING, LADIES.
I'M NOT A LADY.
WELL, I'M A WRITER. IT'S MY JOB TO LABEL THINGS. I DEEM THEE "LADY."
WELL I... HM. THAT REALLY DOESN'T-
FURTHERMORE, I NOW DECREE THIS A WOMBANK.
darb
...WHAT, THE CHAIR ?
NO ONE'S CALLIN' 'EM CHAIRS ANYMORE, SATCHEL.
I MEAN THE... THE WOMBANK.
MOVIN' TOO SLOW. NOW IT'S CALLED A LEFTYPOO, GRAMMA.

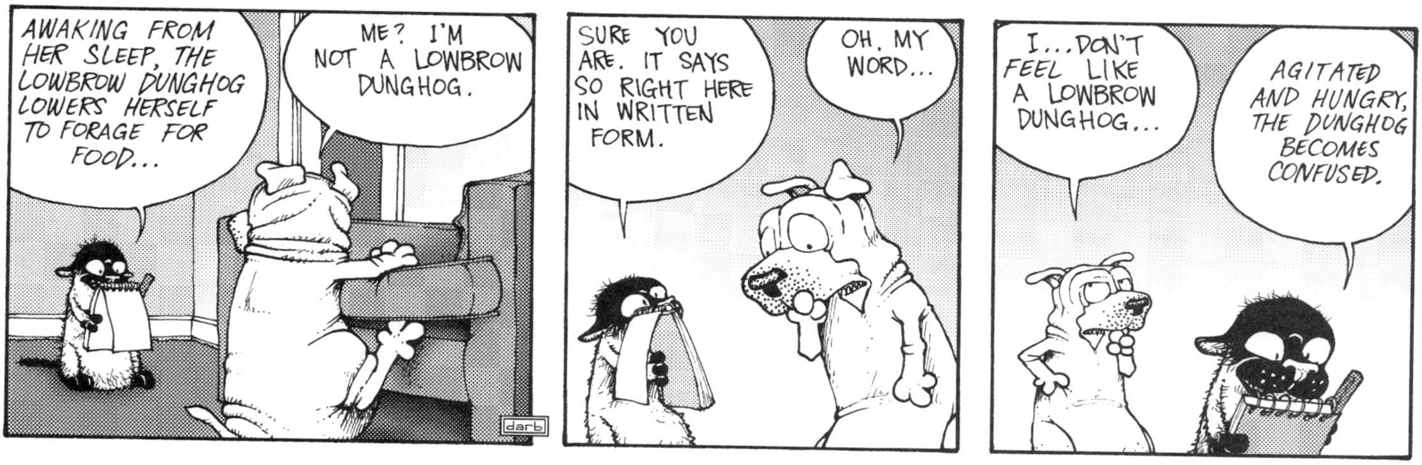
AWAKING FROM HER SLEEP, THE LOWBROW DUNGHOG LOWERS HERSELF TO FORAGE FOR FOOD...
ME? I'M NOT A LOWBROW DUNGHOG.
darb
SURE YOU ARE. IT SAYS SO RIGHT HERE IN WRITTEN FORM.
OH, MY WORD...
I...DON'T FEEL LIKE A LOWBROW DUNGHOG...
AGITATED AND HUNGRY, THE DUNGHOG BECOMES CONFUSED.

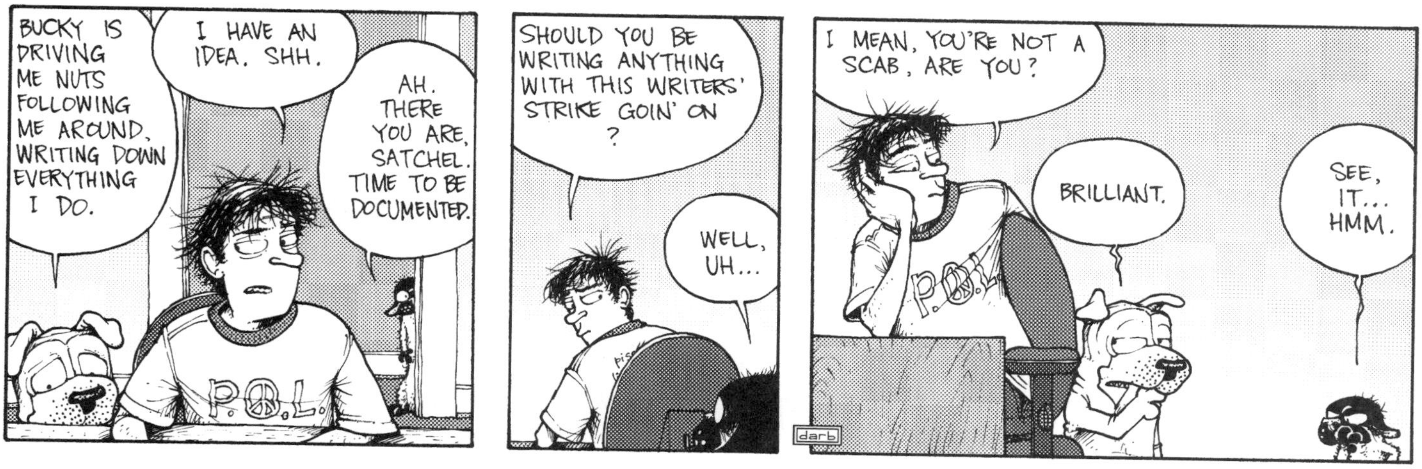
BUCKY IS DRIVING ME NUTS FOLLOWING ME AROUND, WRITING DOWN EVERYTHING I DO.
I HAVE AN IDEA. SHH.
AH. THERE YOU ARE, SATCHEL. TIME TO BE DOCUMENTED.
SHOULD YOU BE WRITING ANYTHING WITH THIS WRITERS' STRIKE GOIN' ON ?
WELL, UH...
darb
I MEAN, YOU'RE NOT A SCAB, ARE YOU?
BRILLIANT.
SEE, IT... HMM.

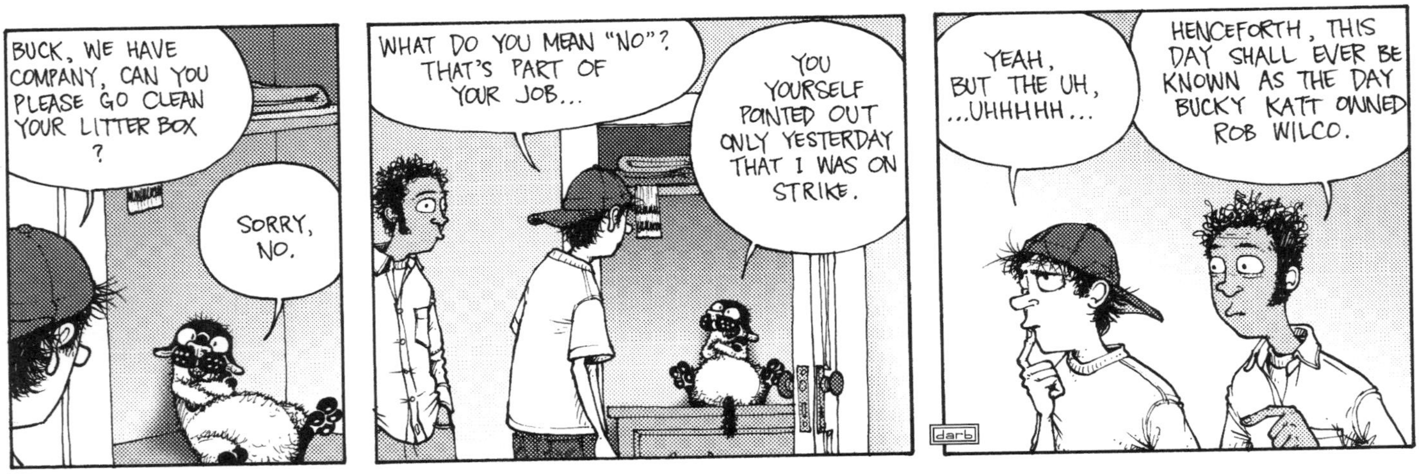
BUCK, WE HAVE COMPANY, CAN YOU PLEASE GO CLEAN YOUR LITTER BOX ?
SORRY, NO.
WHAT DO YOU MEAN "NO"? THAT'S PART OF YOUR JOB...
YOU YOURSELF POINTED OUT ONLY YESTERDAY THAT I WAS ON STRIKE.
YEAH, BUT THE UH, ...UHHHHH...
HENCEFORTH, THIS DAY SHALL EVER BE KNOWN AS THE DAY BUCKY KATT OWNED ROB WILCO.
darb

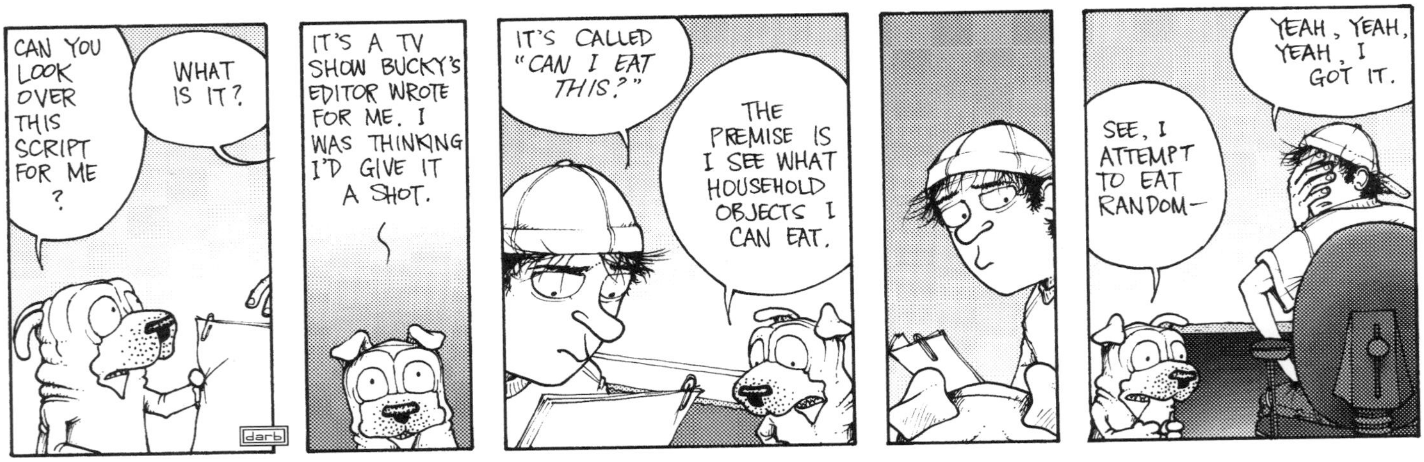
CAN YOU LOOK OVER THIS SCRIPT FOR ME ?
WHAT IS IT?
darb
IT'S A TV SHOW BUCKY'S EDITOR WROTE FOR ME. I WAS THINKING I'D GIVE IT A SHOT.
IT'S CALLED "CAN I EAT THIS?"
THE PREMISE IS I SEE WHAT HOUSEHOLD OBJECTS I CAN EAT.
SEE, I ATTEMPT TO EAT RANDOM–
YEAH, YEAH, YEAH, I GOT IT.

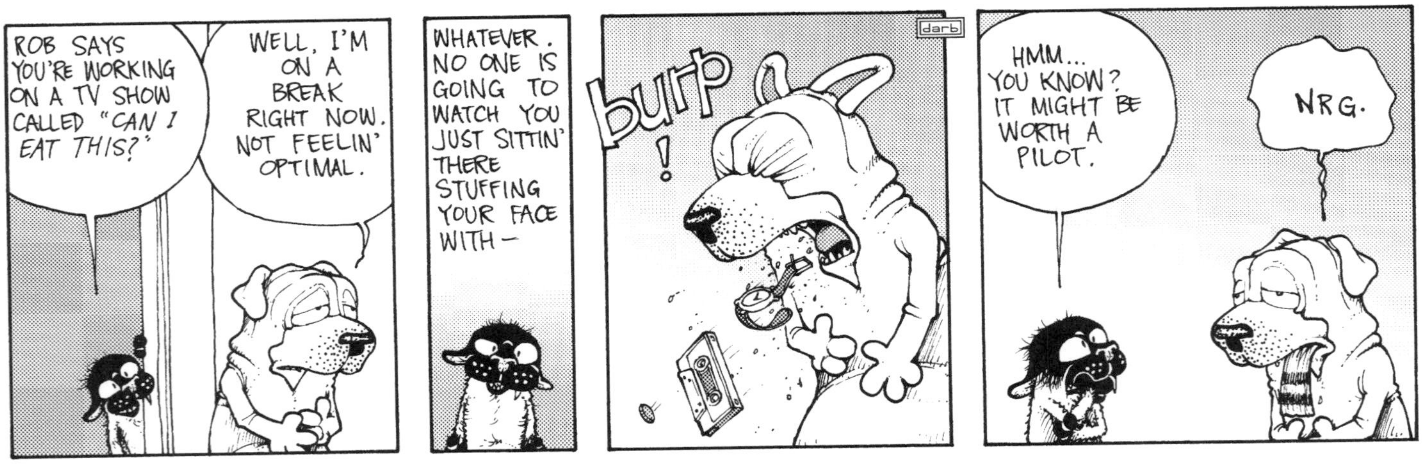
ROB SAYS YOU'RE WORKING ON A TV SHOW CALLED "CAN I EAT THIS?"
WELL, I'M ON A BREAK RIGHT NOW. NOT FEELIN' OPTIMAL.
WHATEVER. NO ONE IS GOING TO WATCH YOU JUST SITTIN' THERE STUFFING YOUR FACE WITH–
darb
burp !
HMM... YOU KNOW? IT MIGHT BE WORTH A PILOT.
NRG.

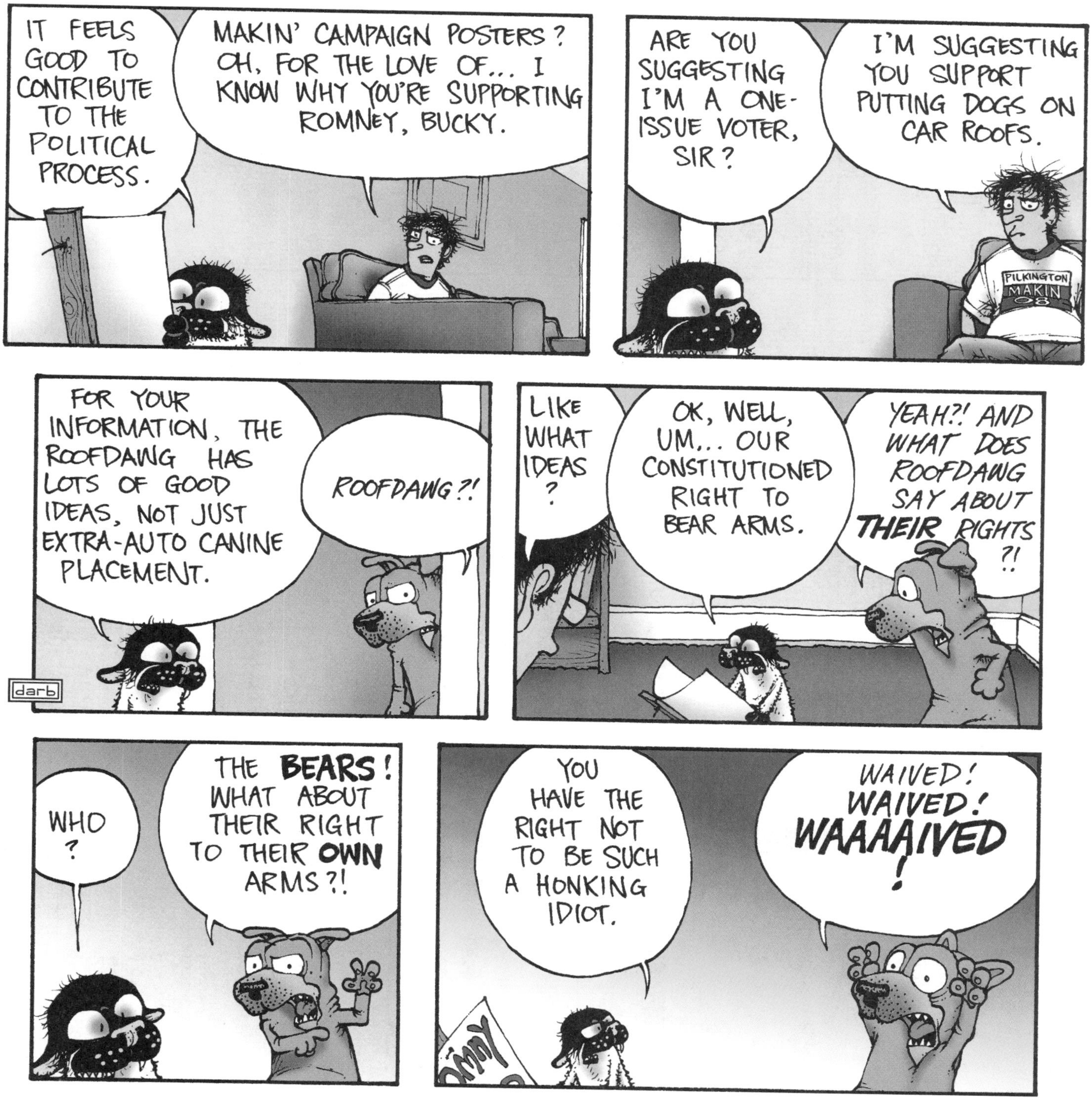
IT FEELS GOOD TO CONTRIBUTE TO THE POLITICAL PROCESS.
MAKIN' CAMPAIGN POSTERS? OH, FOR THE LOVE OF... I KNOW WHY YOU'RE SUPPORTING ROMNEY, BUCKY.
ARE YOU SUGGESTING I'M A ONE-ISSUE VOTER, SIR?
I'M SUGGESTING YOU SUPPORT PUTTING DOGS ON CAR ROOFS.
PILKINGTON
MAKIN 08
FOR YOUR INFORMATION, THE ROOFDAWG HAS LOTS OF GOOD IDEAS, NOT JUST EXTRA-AUTO CANINE PLACEMENT.
ROOFDAWG?!
darb
LIKE WHAT IDEAS?
OK, WELL, UM... OUR CONSTITUTIONED RIGHT TO BEAR ARMS.
YEAH?! AND WHAT DOES ROOFDAWG SAY ABOUT **THEIR** RIGHTS?!
WHO?
THE **BEARS**! WHAT ABOUT THEIR RIGHT TO THEIR **OWN** ARMS?!
YOU HAVE THE RIGHT NOT TO BE SUCH A HONKING IDIOT.
WAIVED! WAIVED! **WAAAAIVED!**

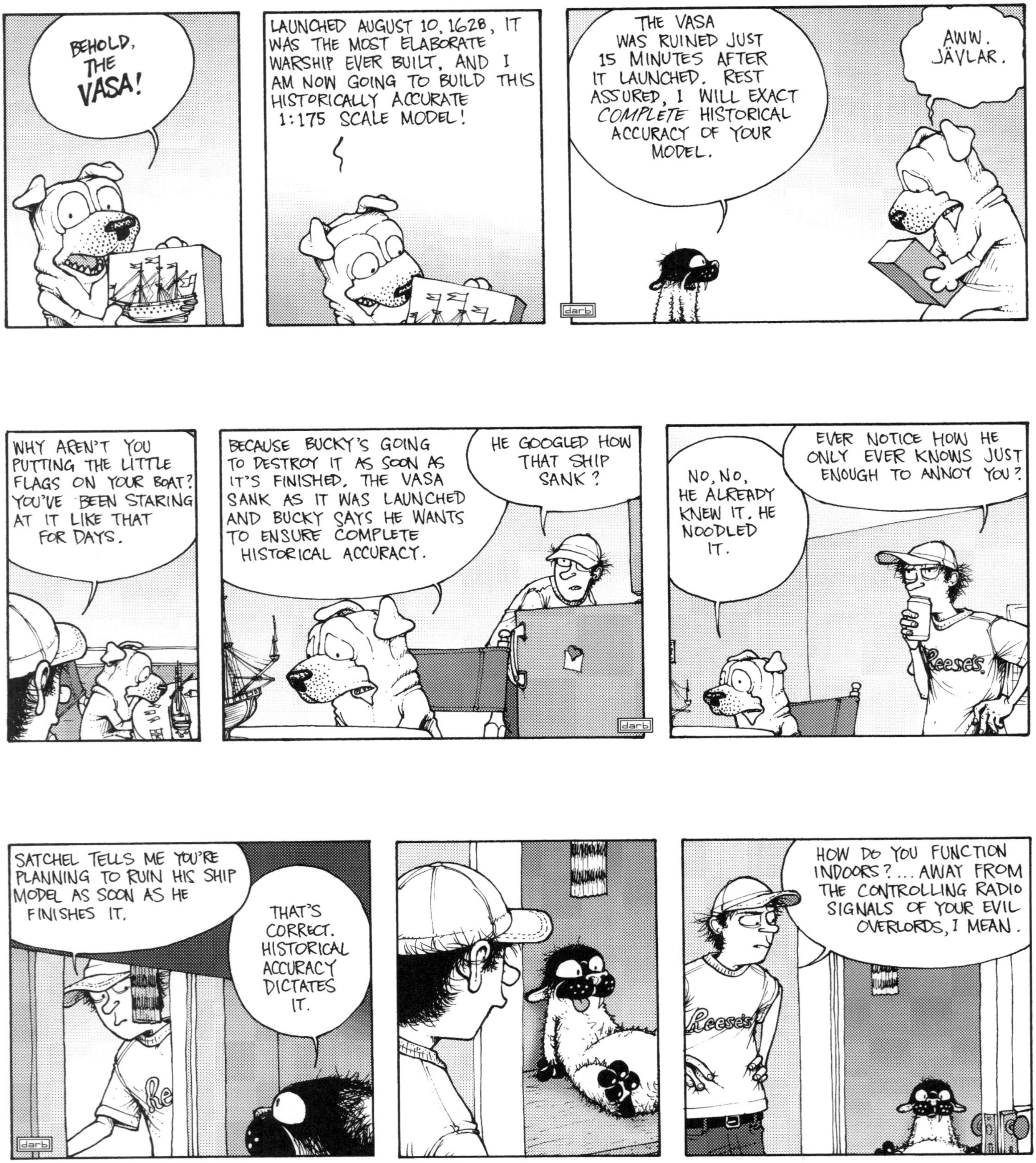
BEHOLD, THE VASA!
LAUNCHED AUGUST 10, 1628, IT WAS THE MOST ELABORATE WARSHIP EVER BUILT, AND I AM NOW GOING TO BUILD THIS HISTORICALLY ACCURATE 1:175 SCALE MODEL!
THE VASA WAS RUINED JUST 15 MINUTES AFTER IT LAUNCHED. REST ASSURED, I WILL EXACT COMPLETE HISTORICAL ACCURACY OF YOUR MODEL.
AWW. JÄVLAR.
darb
WHY AREN'T YOU PUTTING THE LITTLE FLAGS ON YOUR BOAT? YOU'VE BEEN STARING AT IT LIKE THAT FOR DAYS.
BECAUSE BUCKY'S GOING TO DESTROY IT AS SOON AS IT'S FINISHED. THE VASA SANK AS IT WAS LAUNCHED AND BUCKY SAYS HE WANTS TO ENSURE COMPLETE HISTORICAL ACCURACY.
HE GOOGLED HOW THAT SHIP SANK?
NO, NO, HE ALREADY KNEW IT. HE NOODLED IT.
EVER NOTICE HOW HE ONLY EVER KNOWS JUST ENOUGH TO ANNOY YOU?
Reese's
darb
SATCHEL TELLS ME YOU'RE PLANNING TO RUIN HIS SHIP MODEL AS SOON AS HE FINISHES IT.
THAT'S CORRECT. HISTORICAL ACCURACY DICTATES IT.
HOW DO YOU FUNCTION INDOORS? ... AWAY FROM THE CONTROLLING RADIO SIGNALS OF YOUR EVIL OVERLORDS, I MEAN.
Reese's
darb

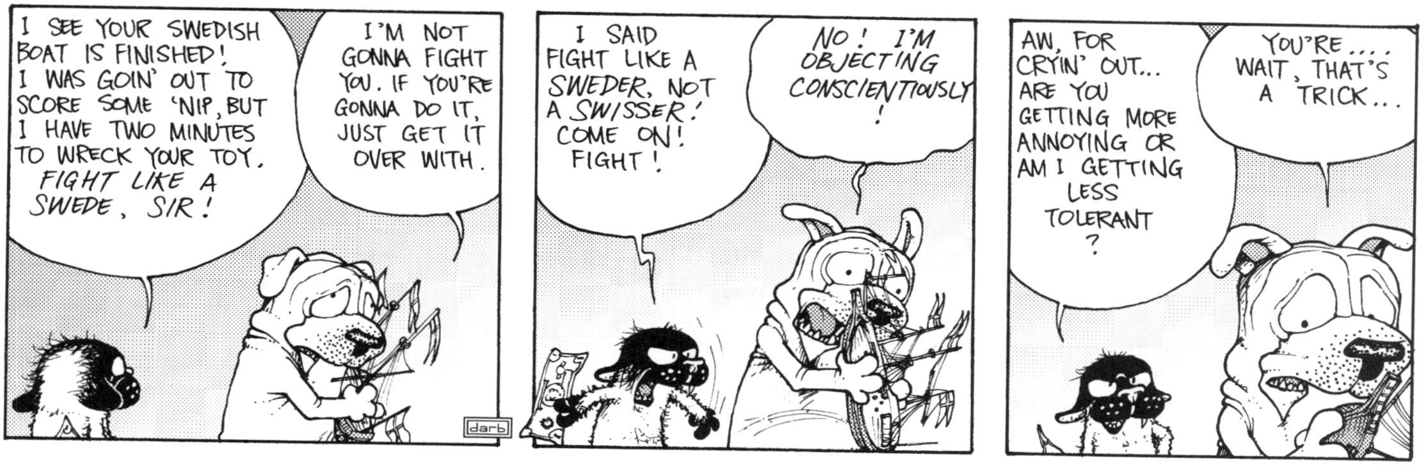
I SEE YOUR SWEDISH BOAT IS FINISHED! I WAS GOIN' OUT TO SCORE SOME 'NIP, BUT I HAVE TWO MINUTES TO WRECK YOUR TOY. FIGHT LIKE A SWEDE, SIR!
I'M NOT GONNA FIGHT YOU. IF YOU'RE GONNA DO IT, JUST GET IT OVER WITH.
darb
I SAID FIGHT LIKE A SWEDER, NOT A SWISSER! COME ON! FIGHT!
NO! I'M OBJECTING CONSCIENTIOUSLY!
AW, FOR CRYIN' OUT... ARE YOU GETTING MORE ANNOYING OR AM I GETTING LESS TOLERANT?
YOU'RE.... WAIT, THAT'S A TRICK...

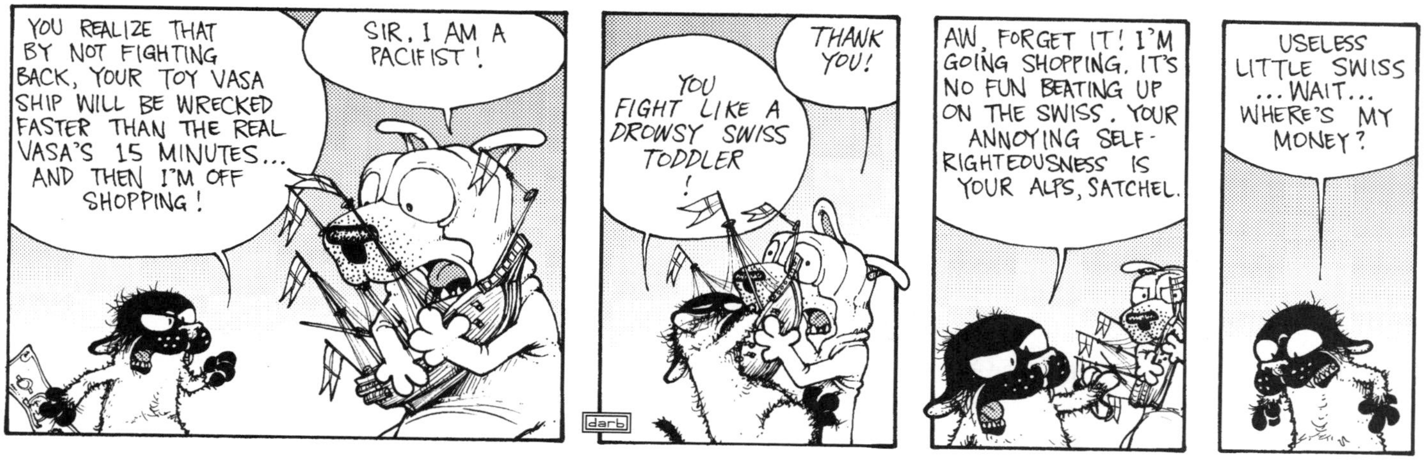
YOU REALIZE THAT BY NOT FIGHTING BACK, YOUR TOY VASA SHIP WILL BE WRECKED FASTER THAN THE REAL VASA'S 15 MINUTES... AND THEN I'M OFF SHOPPING!
SIR, I AM A PACIFIST!
darb
YOU FIGHT LIKE A DROWSY SWISS TODDLER!
THANK YOU!
AW, FORGET IT! I'M GOING SHOPPING. IT'S NO FUN BEATING UP ON THE SWISS. YOUR ANNOYING SELF-RIGHTEOUSNESS IS YOUR ALPS, SATCHEL.
USELESS LITTLE SWISS ...WAIT... WHERE'S MY MONEY?

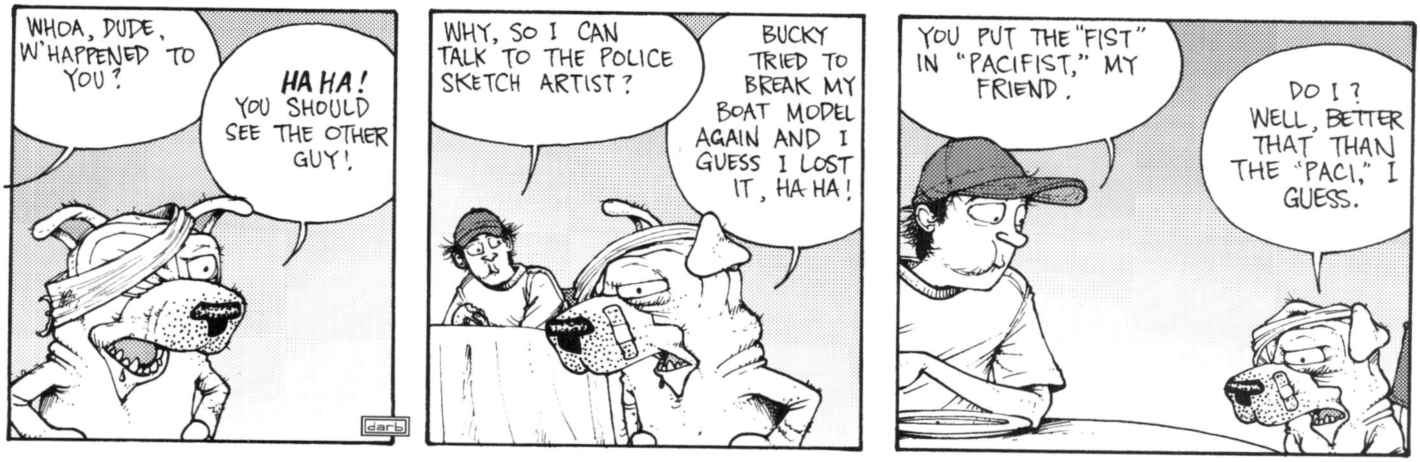
WHOA, DUDE, W'HAPPENED TO YOU?
HA HA! YOU SHOULD SEE THE OTHER GUY!
darb
WHY, SO I CAN TALK TO THE POLICE SKETCH ARTIST?
BUCKY TRIED TO BREAK MY BOAT MODEL AGAIN AND I GUESS I LOST IT, HA HA!
YOU PUT THE "FIST" IN "PACIFIST," MY FRIEND.
DO I? WELL, BETTER THAT THAN THE "PACI," I GUESS.

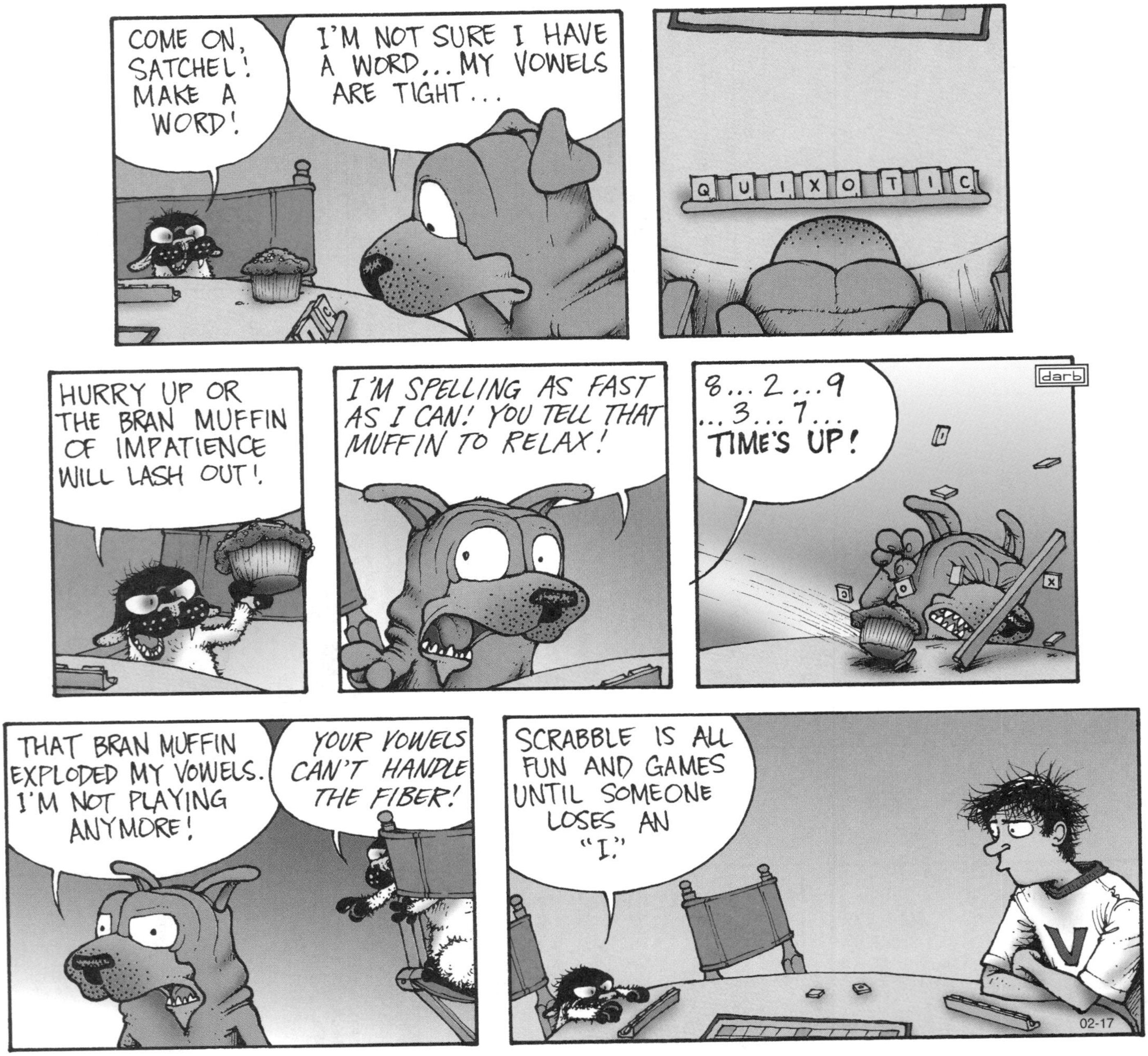
COME ON, SATCHEL! MAKE A WORD!
I'M NOT SURE I HAVE A WORD... MY VOWELS ARE TIGHT...
QUIXOTIC
HURRY UP OR THE BRAN MUFFIN OF IMPATIENCE WILL LASH OUT!
I'M SPELLING AS FAST AS I CAN! YOU TELL THAT MUFFIN TO RELAX!
8...2...9 ...3...7... TIME'S UP!
darb
THAT BRAN MUFFIN EXPLODED MY VOWELS. I'M NOT PLAYING ANYMORE!
YOUR VOWELS CAN'T HANDLE THE FIBER!
SCRABBLE IS ALL FUN AND GAMES UNTIL SOMEONE LOSES AN "I."
V
02-17

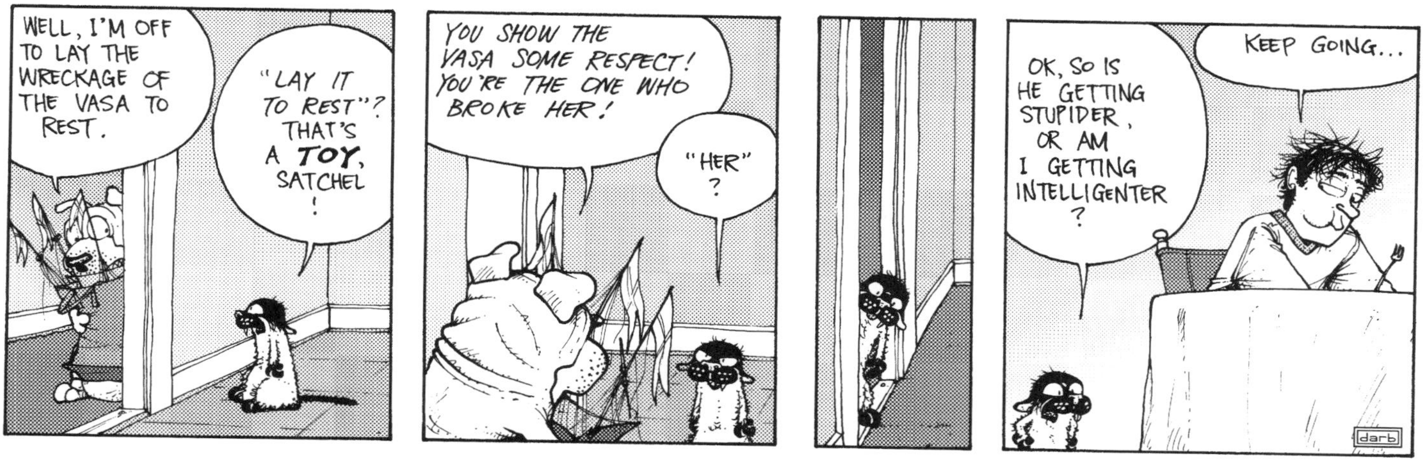
WELL, I'M OFF TO LAY THE WRECKAGE OF THE VASA TO REST.
"LAY IT TO REST"? THAT'S A TOY, SATCHEL!
YOU SHOW THE VASA SOME RESPECT! YOU'RE THE ONE WHO BROKE HER!
"HER"?
OK, SO IS HE GETTING STUPIDER, OR AM I GETTING INTELLIGENTER?
KEEP GOING...
darb

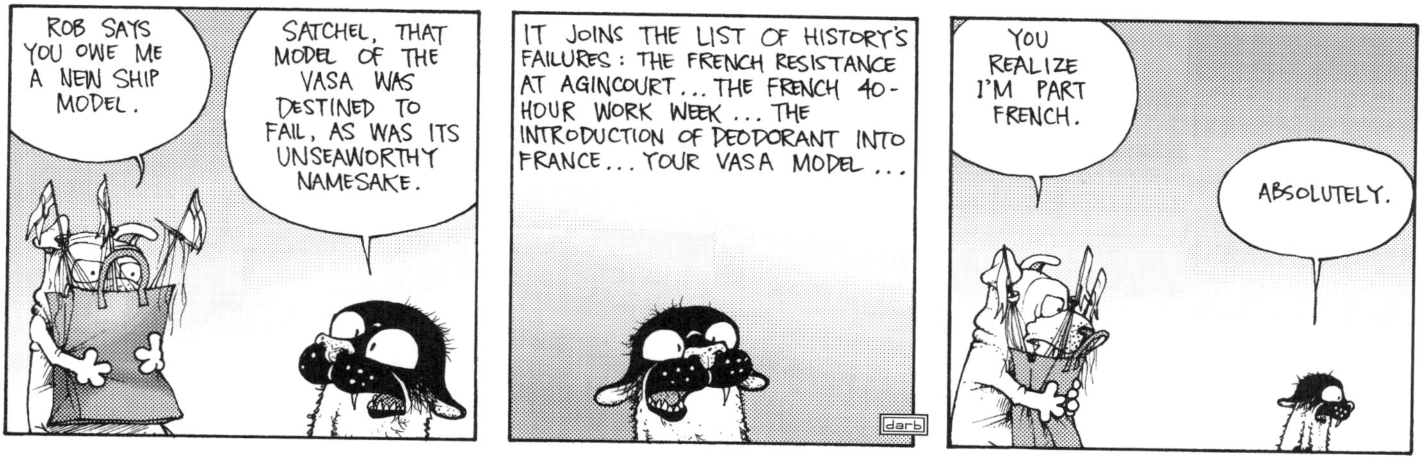
ROB SAYS YOU OWE ME A NEW SHIP MODEL.
SATCHEL, THAT MODEL OF THE VASA WAS DESTINED TO FAIL, AS WAS ITS UNSEAWORTHY NAMESAKE.
IT JOINS THE LIST OF HISTORY'S FAILURES: THE FRENCH RESISTANCE AT AGINCOURT... THE FRENCH 40-HOUR WORK WEEK... THE INTRODUCTION OF DEODORANT INTO FRANCE... YOUR VASA MODEL...
darb
YOU REALIZE I'M PART FRENCH.
ABSOLUTELY.

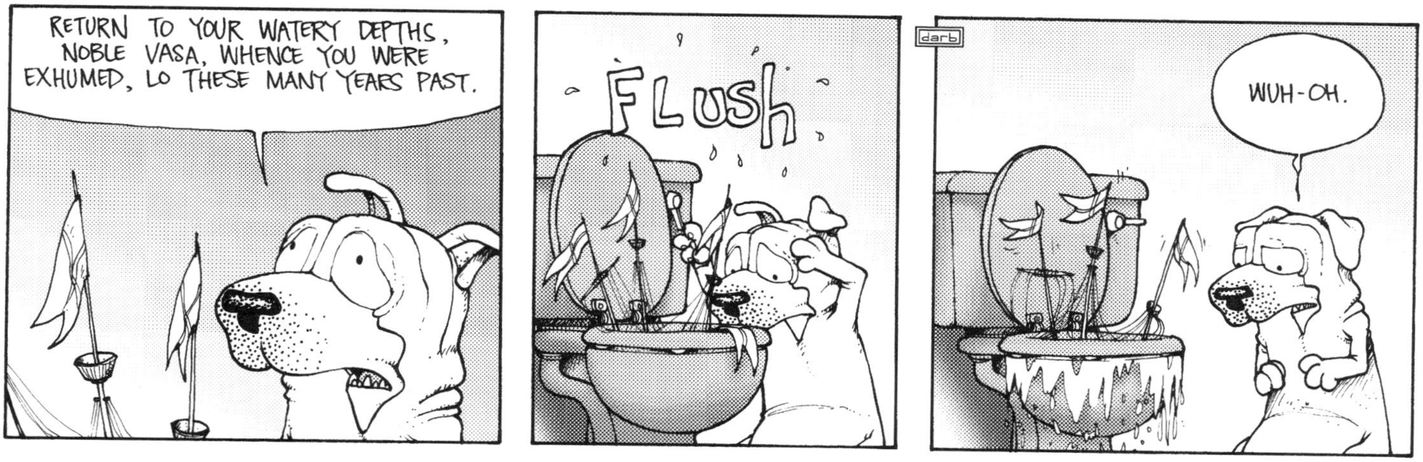
RETURN TO YOUR WATERY DEPTHS, NOBLE VASA, WHENCE YOU WERE EXHUMED, LO THESE MANY YEARS PAST.
FLUSH
darb
WUH-OH.

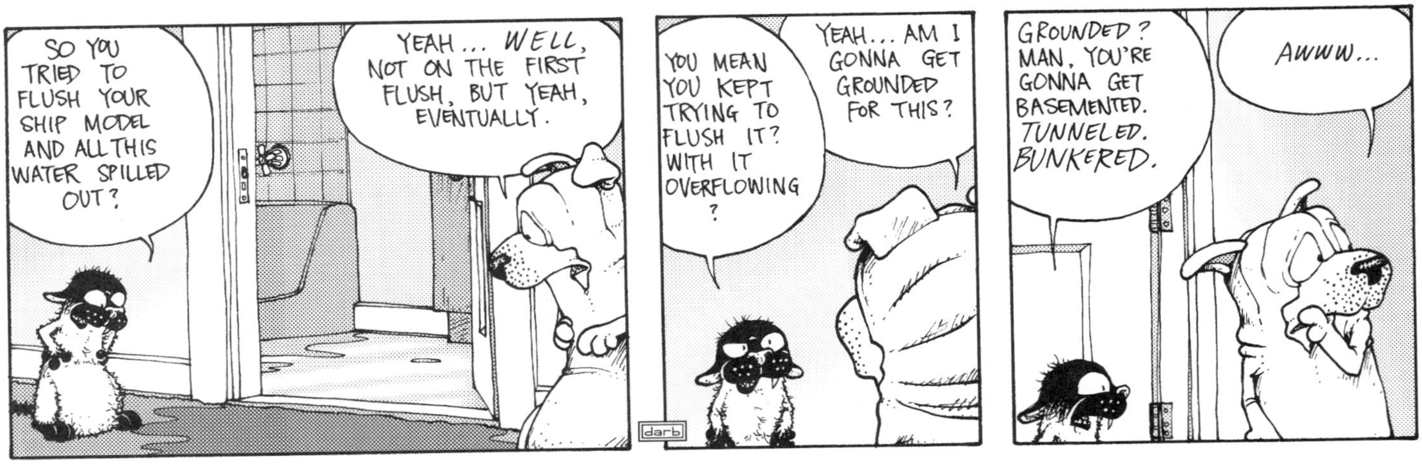
SO YOU TRIED TO FLUSH YOUR SHIP MODEL AND ALL THIS WATER SPILLED OUT?
YEAH... WELL, NOT ON THE FIRST FLUSH, BUT YEAH, EVENTUALLY.
YOU MEAN YOU KEPT TRYING TO FLUSH IT? WITH IT OVERFLOWING?
YEAH... AM I GONNA GET GROUNDED FOR THIS?
GROUNDED? MAN, YOU'RE GONNA GET BASEMENTED. TUNNELED. BUNKERED.
AWWW...

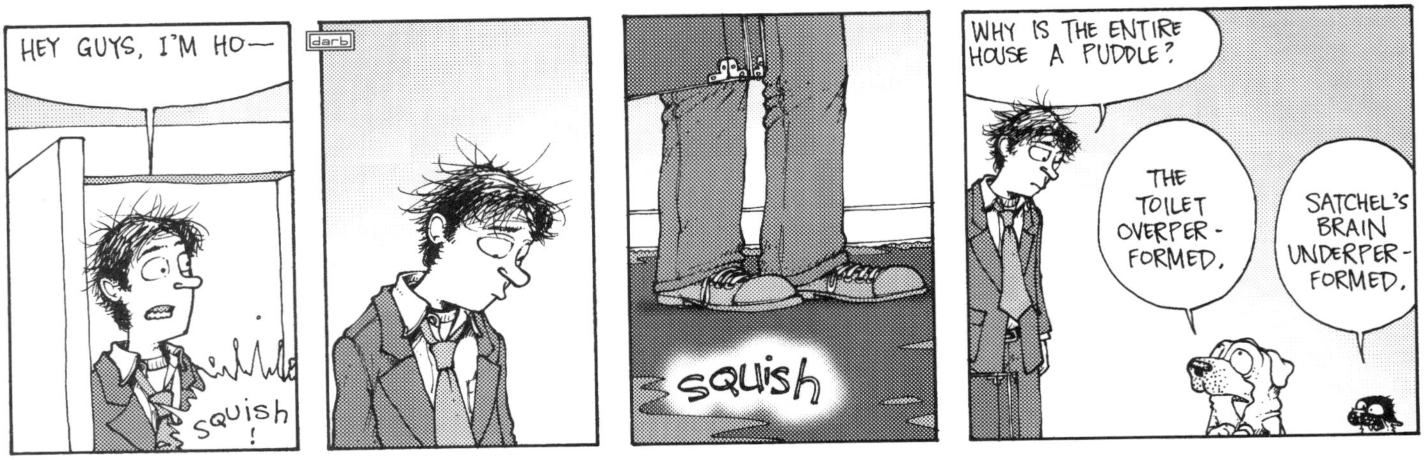
HEY GUYS, I'M HO—
SQUISH!
SQUISH
WHY IS THE ENTIRE HOUSE A PUDDLE?
THE TOILET OVERPERFORMED.
SATCHEL'S BRAIN UNDERPERFORMED.

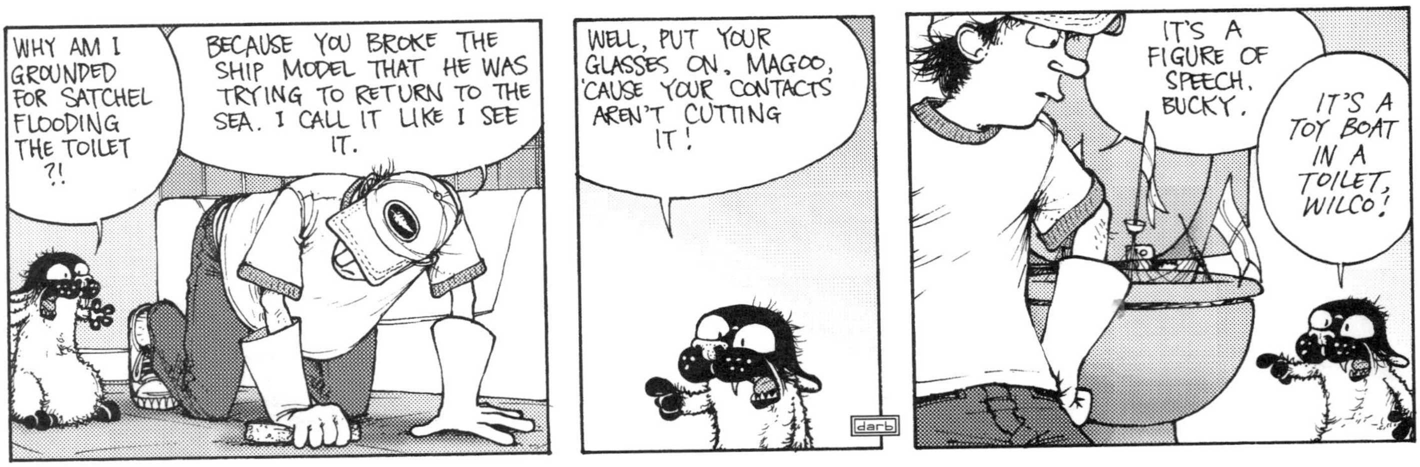
WHY AM I GROUNDED FOR SATCHEL FLOODING THE TOILET?!
BECAUSE YOU BROKE THE SHIP MODEL THAT HE WAS TRYING TO RETURN TO THE SEA. I CALL IT LIKE I SEE IT.
WELL, PUT YOUR GLASSES ON, MAGOO, 'CAUSE YOUR CONTACTS AREN'T CUTTING IT!
IT'S A FIGURE OF SPEECH, BUCKY.
IT'S A TOY BOAT IN A TOILET, WILCO!

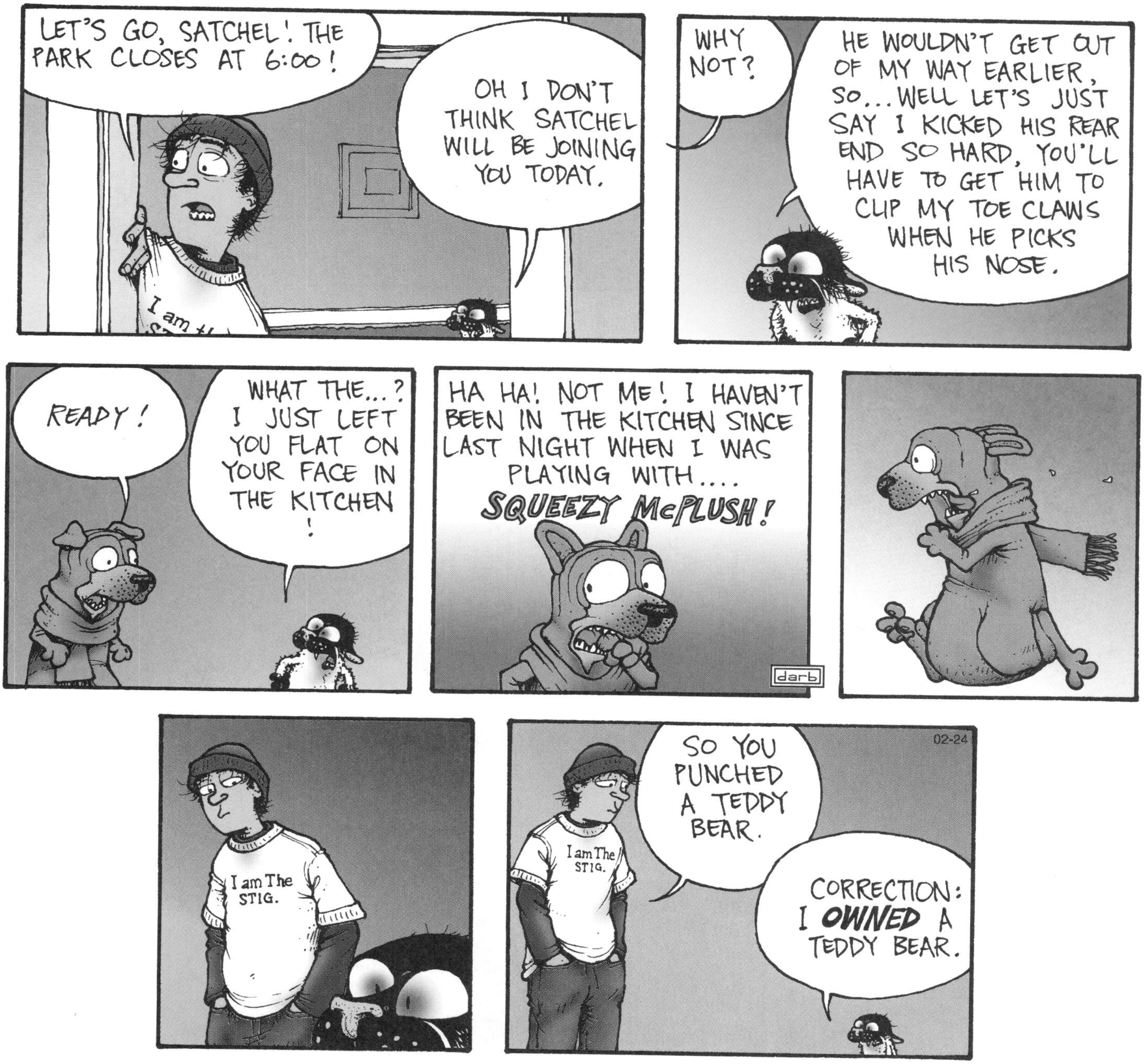
LET'S GO, SATCHEL! THE PARK CLOSES AT 6:00!
OH I DON'T THINK SATCHEL WILL BE JOINING YOU TODAY.
WHY NOT?
HE WOULDN'T GET OUT OF MY WAY EARLIER, SO... WELL LET'S JUST SAY I KICKED HIS REAR END SO HARD, YOU'LL HAVE TO GET HIM TO CLIP MY TOE CLAWS WHEN HE PICKS HIS NOSE.
READY!
WHAT THE...? I JUST LEFT YOU FLAT ON YOUR FACE IN THE KITCHEN!
HA HA! NOT ME! I HAVEN'T BEEN IN THE KITCHEN SINCE LAST NIGHT WHEN I WAS PLAYING WITH.... SQUEEZY McPLUSH!
darb
I am The STIG.
02-24
SO YOU PUNCHED A TEDDY BEAR.
I am The STIG.
CORRECTION: I OWNED A TEDDY BEAR.

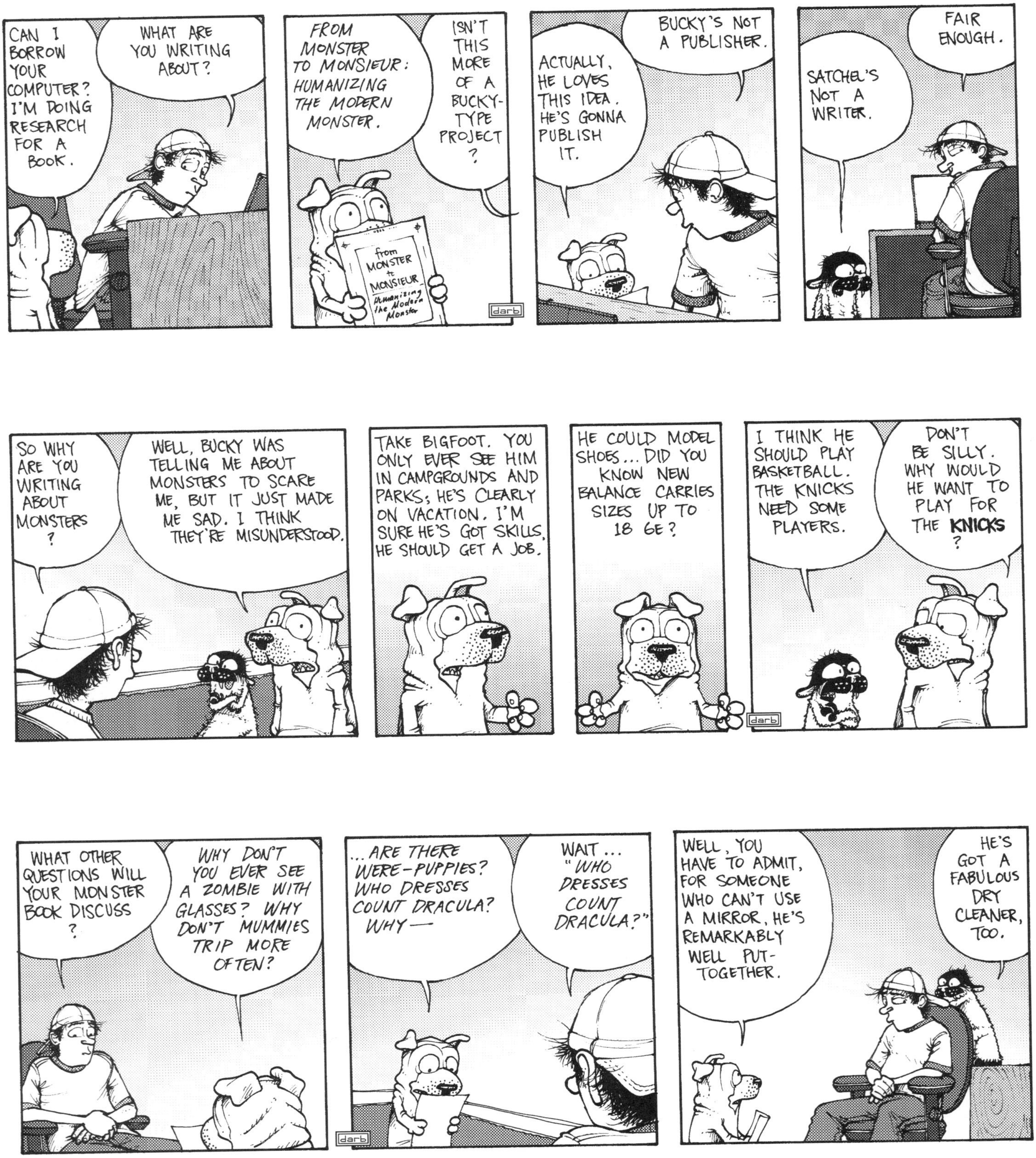
CAN I BORROW YOUR COMPUTER? I'M DOING RESEARCH FOR A BOOK.
WHAT ARE YOU WRITING ABOUT?
FROM MONSTER TO MONSIEUR: HUMANIZING THE MODERN MONSTER.
from MONSTER to MONSIEUR Humanizing the Modern Monster
ISN'T THIS MORE OF A BUCKY-TYPE PROJECT?
darb
BUCKY'S NOT A PUBLISHER.
ACTUALLY, HE LOVES THIS IDEA. HE'S GONNA PUBLISH IT.
FAIR ENOUGH.
SATCHEL'S NOT A WRITER.
SO WHY ARE YOU WRITING ABOUT MONSTERS?
WELL, BUCKY WAS TELLING ME ABOUT MONSTERS TO SCARE ME, BUT IT JUST MADE ME SAD. I THINK THEY'RE MISUNDERSTOOD.
TAKE BIGFOOT. YOU ONLY EVER SEE HIM IN CAMPGROUNDS AND PARKS; HE'S CLEARLY ON VACATION. I'M SURE HE'S GOT SKILLS. HE SHOULD GET A JOB.
HE COULD MODEL SHOES... DID YOU KNOW NEW BALANCE CARRIES SIZES UP TO 18 6E?
darb
I THINK HE SHOULD PLAY BASKETBALL. THE KNICKS NEED SOME PLAYERS.
DON'T BE SILLY. WHY WOULD HE WANT TO PLAY FOR THE KNICKS?
WHAT OTHER QUESTIONS WILL YOUR MONSTER BOOK DISCUSS?
WHY DON'T YOU EVER SEE A ZOMBIE WITH GLASSES? WHY DON'T MUMMIES TRIP MORE OFTEN?
darb
...ARE THERE WERE-PUPPIES? WHO DRESSES COUNT DRACULA? WHY—
WAIT... "WHO DRESSES COUNT DRACULA?"
WELL, YOU HAVE TO ADMIT, FOR SOMEONE WHO CAN'T USE A MIRROR, HE'S REMARKABLY WELL PUT-TOGETHER.
HE'S GOT A FABULOUS DRY CLEANER, TOO.

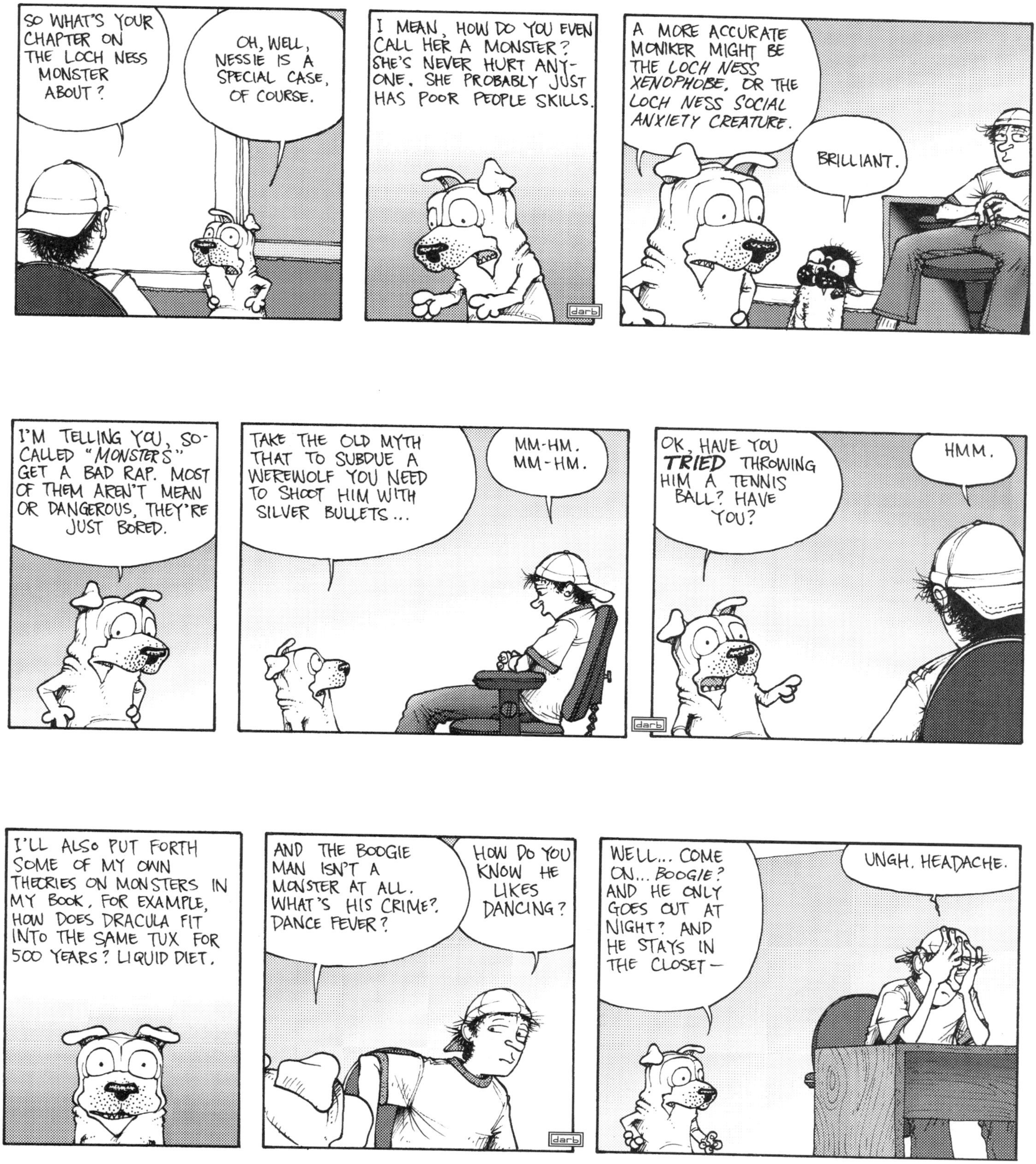
SO WHAT'S YOUR CHAPTER ON THE LOCH NESS MONSTER ABOUT?
OH, WELL, NESSIE IS A SPECIAL CASE, OF COURSE.
I MEAN, HOW DO YOU EVEN CALL HER A MONSTER? SHE'S NEVER HURT ANY-ONE. SHE PROBABLY JUST HAS POOR PEOPLE SKILLS.
A MORE ACCURATE MONIKER MIGHT BE THE LOCH NESS XENOPHOBE, OR THE LOCH NESS SOCIAL ANXIETY CREATURE.
BRILLIANT.
darb
I'M TELLING YOU, SO-CALLED "MONSTERS" GET A BAD RAP. MOST OF THEM AREN'T MEAN OR DANGEROUS, THEY'RE JUST BORED.
TAKE THE OLD MYTH THAT TO SUBDUE A WEREWOLF YOU NEED TO SHOOT HIM WITH SILVER BULLETS...
MM-HM. MM-HM.
OK, HAVE YOU TRIED THROWING HIM A TENNIS BALL? HAVE YOU?
HMM.
darb
I'LL ALSO PUT FORTH SOME OF MY OWN THEORIES ON MONSTERS IN MY BOOK, FOR EXAMPLE, HOW DOES DRACULA FIT INTO THE SAME TUX FOR 500 YEARS? LIQUID DIET.
AND THE BOOGIE MAN ISN'T A MONSTER AT ALL. WHAT'S HIS CRIME? DANCE FEVER?
HOW DO YOU KNOW HE LIKES DANCING?
WELL... COME ON... BOOGIE? AND HE ONLY GOES OUT AT NIGHT? AND HE STAYS IN THE CLOSET—
UNGH. HEADACHE.
darb

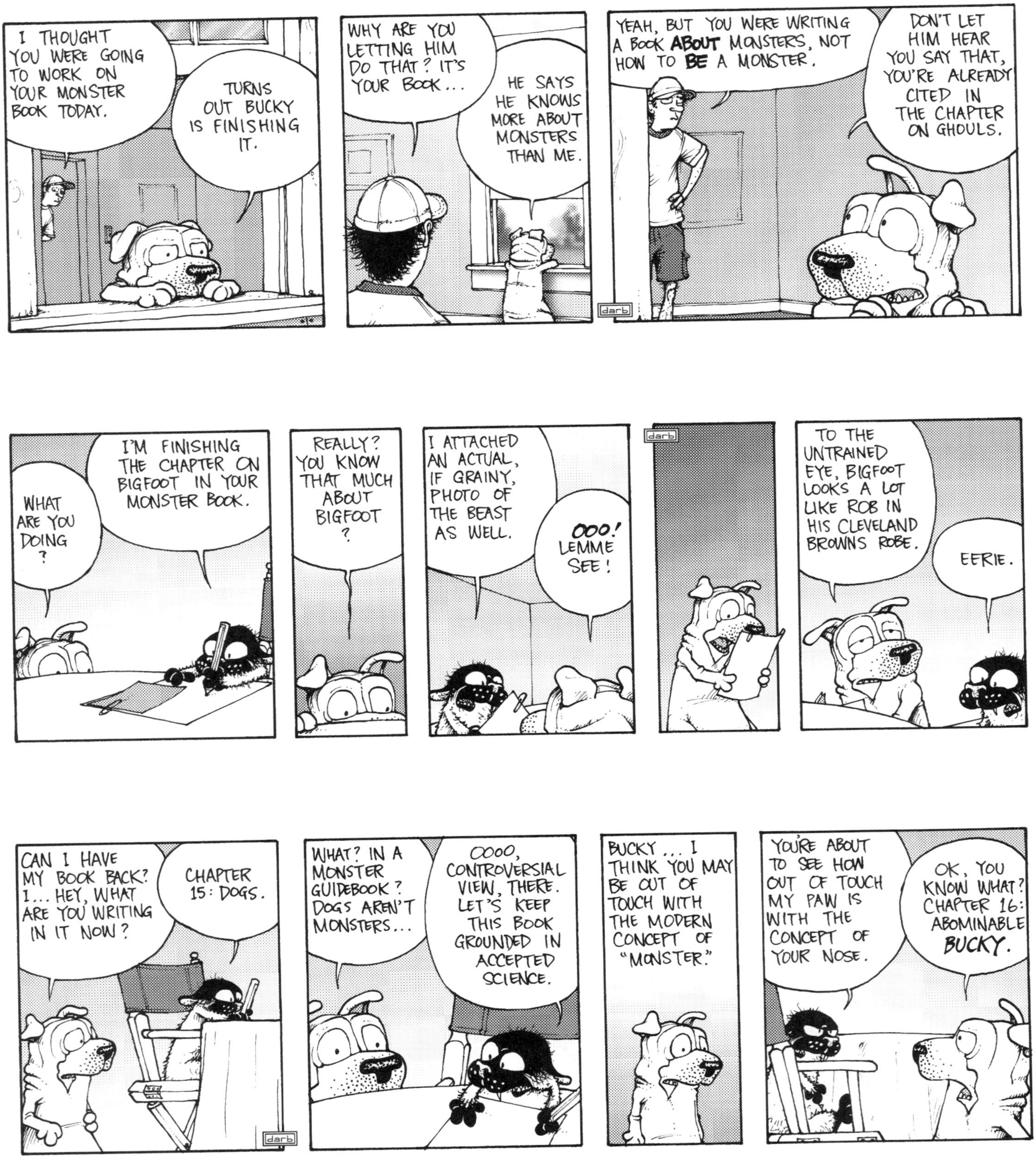
I THOUGHT YOU WERE GOING TO WORK ON YOUR MONSTER BOOK TODAY.
TURNS OUT BUCKY IS FINISHING IT.
WHY ARE YOU LETTING HIM DO THAT? IT'S YOUR BOOK...
HE SAYS HE KNOWS MORE ABOUT MONSTERS THAN ME.
YEAH, BUT YOU WERE WRITING A BOOK **ABOUT** MONSTERS, NOT HOW TO **BE** A MONSTER.
DON'T LET HIM HEAR YOU SAY THAT, YOU'RE ALREADY CITED IN THE CHAPTER ON GHOULS.
darb
WHAT ARE YOU DOING?
I'M FINISHING THE CHAPTER ON BIGFOOT IN YOUR MONSTER BOOK.
REALLY? YOU KNOW THAT MUCH ABOUT BIGFOOT?
I ATTACHED AN ACTUAL, IF GRAINY, PHOTO OF THE BEAST AS WELL.
OOO! LEMME SEE!
darb
TO THE UNTRAINED EYE, BIGFOOT LOOKS A LOT LIKE ROB IN HIS CLEVELAND BROWNS ROBE.
EERIE.
CAN I HAVE MY BOOK BACK? I... HEY, WHAT ARE YOU WRITING IN IT NOW?
CHAPTER 15: DOGS.
darb
WHAT? IN A MONSTER GUIDEBOOK? DOGS AREN'T MONSTERS...
OOOO, CONTROVERSIAL VIEW, THERE. LET'S KEEP THIS BOOK GROUNDED IN ACCEPTED SCIENCE.
BUCKY... I THINK YOU MAY BE OUT OF TOUCH WITH THE MODERN CONCEPT OF "MONSTER."
YOU'RE ABOUT TO SEE HOW OUT OF TOUCH MY PAW IS WITH THE CONCEPT OF YOUR NOSE.
OK, YOU KNOW WHAT? CHAPTER 16: ABOMINABLE **BUCKY**.

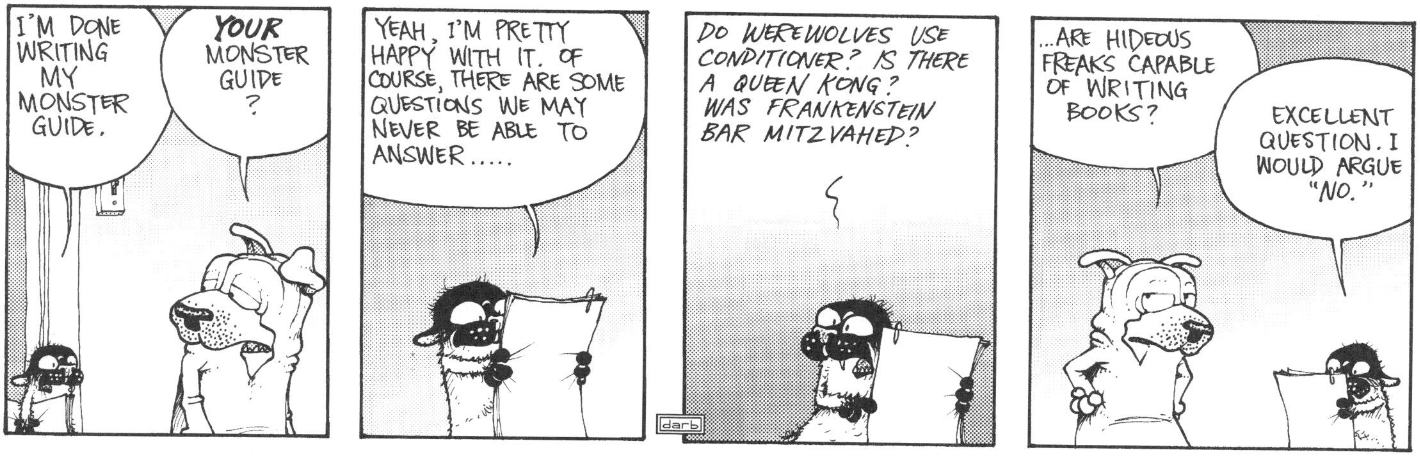
I'M DONE WRITING MY MONSTER GUIDE.
YOUR MONSTER GUIDE?
YEAH, I'M PRETTY HAPPY WITH IT. OF COURSE, THERE ARE SOME QUESTIONS WE MAY NEVER BE ABLE TO ANSWER.....
DO WEREWOLVES USE CONDITIONER? IS THERE A QUEEN KONG? WAS FRANKENSTEIN BAR MITZVAHED?
...ARE HIDEOUS FREAKS CAPABLE OF WRITING BOOKS?
EXCELLENT QUESTION. I WOULD ARGUE "NO."

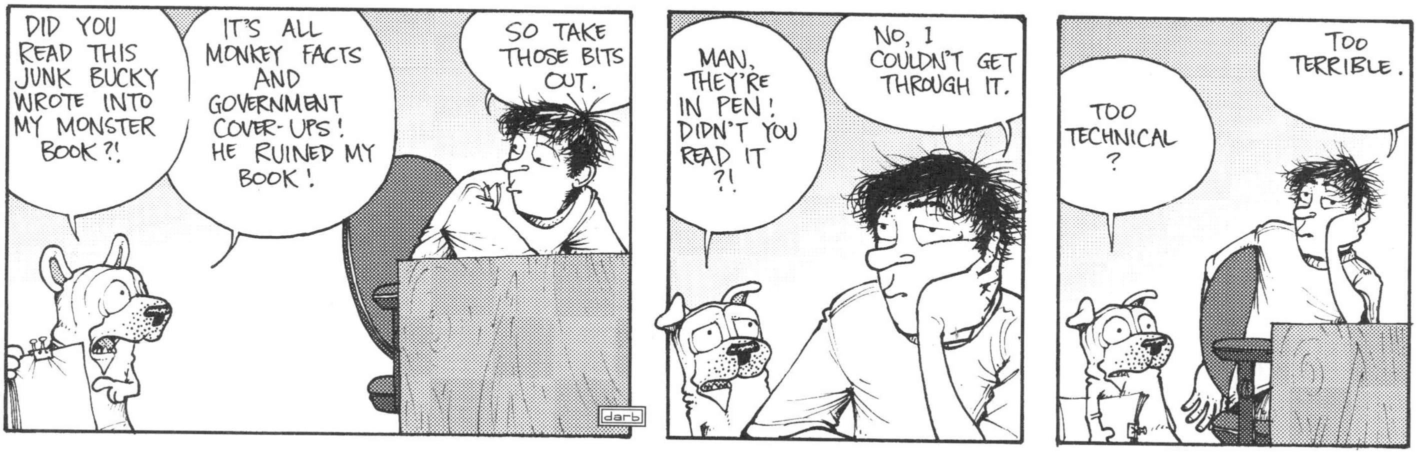
DID YOU READ THIS JUNK BUCKY WROTE INTO MY MONSTER BOOK?!
IT'S ALL MONKEY FACTS AND GOVERNMENT COVER-UPS! HE RUINED MY BOOK!
SO TAKE THOSE BITS OUT.
MAN, THEY'RE IN PEN! DIDN'T YOU READ IT?!
NO, I COULDN'T GET THROUGH IT.
TOO TECHNICAL?
TOO TERRIBLE.

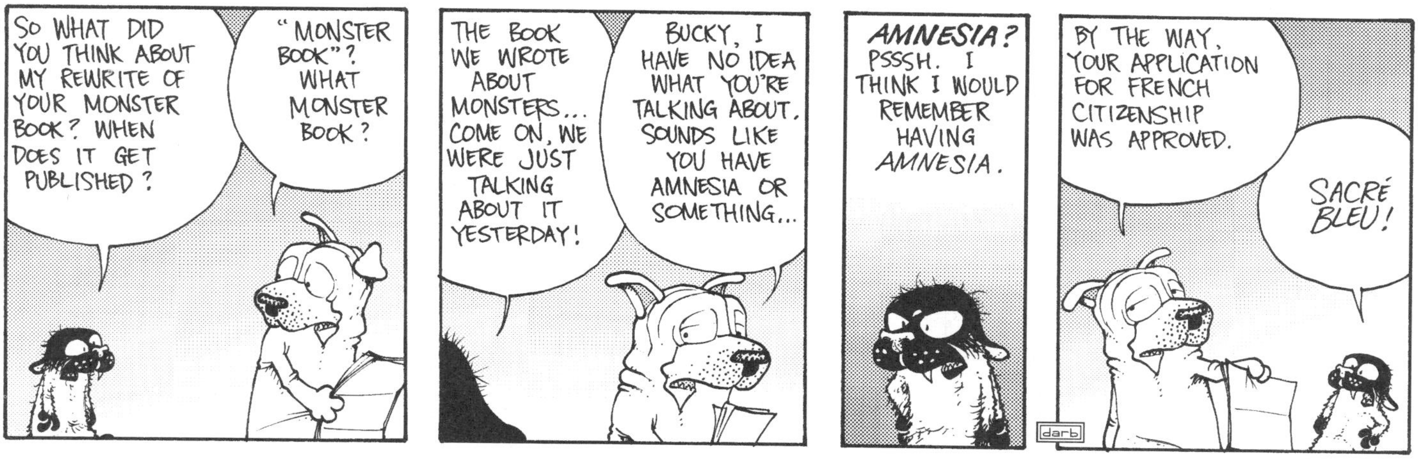
SO WHAT DID YOU THINK ABOUT MY REWRITE OF YOUR MONSTER BOOK? WHEN DOES IT GET PUBLISHED?
"MONSTER BOOK"? WHAT MONSTER BOOK?
THE BOOK WE WROTE ABOUT MONSTERS... COME ON, WE WERE JUST TALKING ABOUT IT YESTERDAY!
BUCKY, I HAVE NO IDEA WHAT YOU'RE TALKING ABOUT. SOUNDS LIKE YOU HAVE AMNESIA OR SOMETHING...
AMNESIA? PSSSH. I THINK I WOULD REMEMBER HAVING AMNESIA.
BY THE WAY, YOUR APPLICATION FOR FRENCH CITIZENSHIP WAS APPROVED.
SACRÉ BLEU!

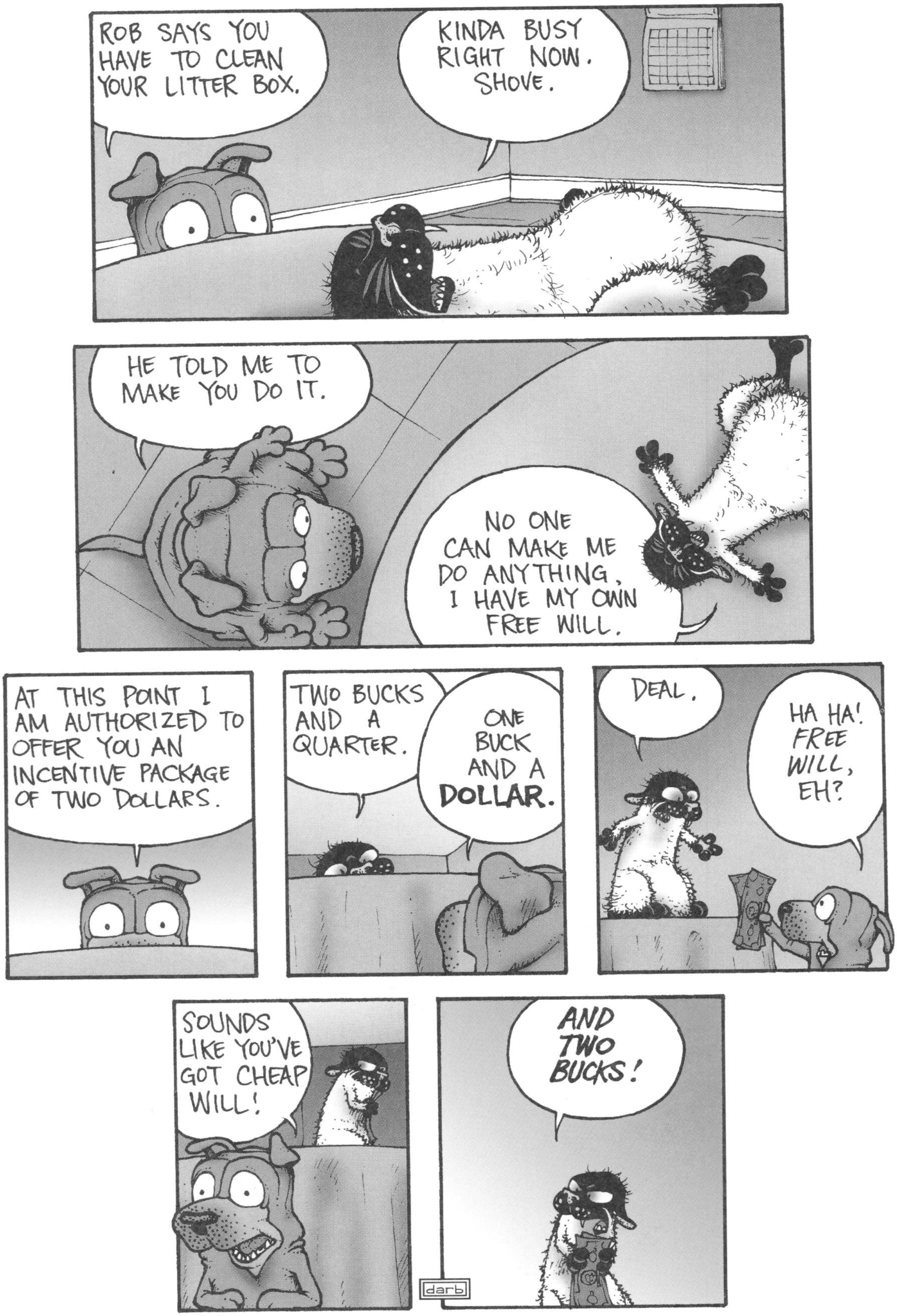
ROB SAYS YOU HAVE TO CLEAN YOUR LITTER BOX.
KINDA BUSY RIGHT NOW. SHOVE.
HE TOLD ME TO MAKE YOU DO IT.
NO ONE CAN MAKE ME DO ANYTHING, I HAVE MY OWN FREE WILL.
AT THIS POINT I AM AUTHORIZED TO OFFER YOU AN INCENTIVE PACKAGE OF TWO DOLLARS.
TWO BUCKS AND A QUARTER.
ONE BUCK AND A DOLLAR.
DEAL.
HA HA! FREE WILL, EH?
SOUNDS LIKE YOU'VE GOT CHEAP WILL!
AND TWO BUCKS!
darb

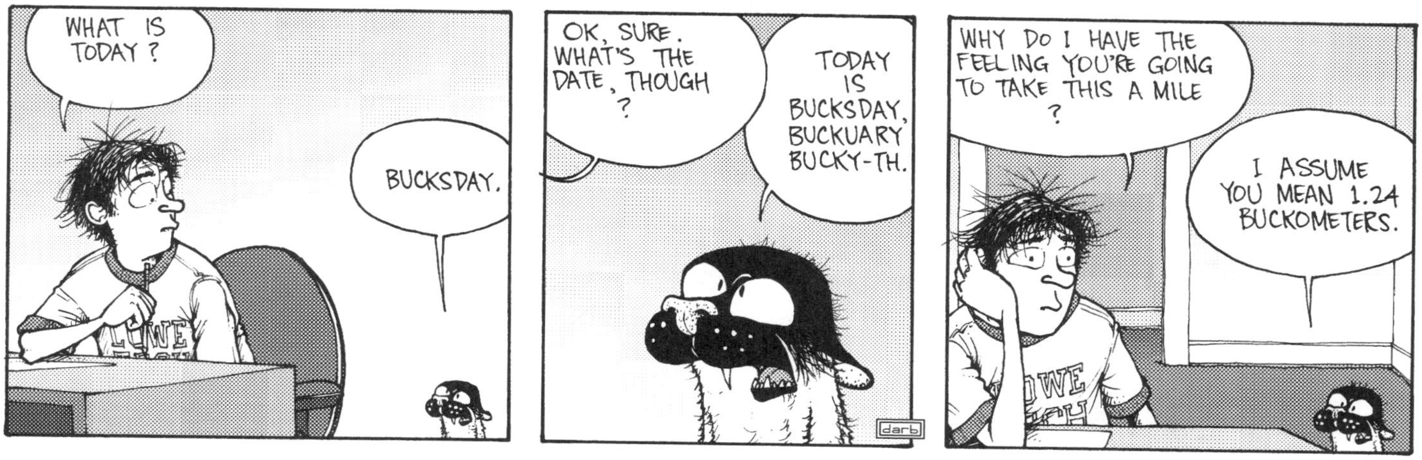
WHAT IS TODAY?
BUCKSDAY.
OK, SURE. WHAT'S THE DATE, THOUGH?
TODAY IS BUCKSDAY, BUCKUARY BUCKY-TH.
darb
WHY DO I HAVE THE FEELING YOU'RE GOING TO TAKE THIS A MILE?
I ASSUME YOU MEAN 1.24 BUCKOMETERS.

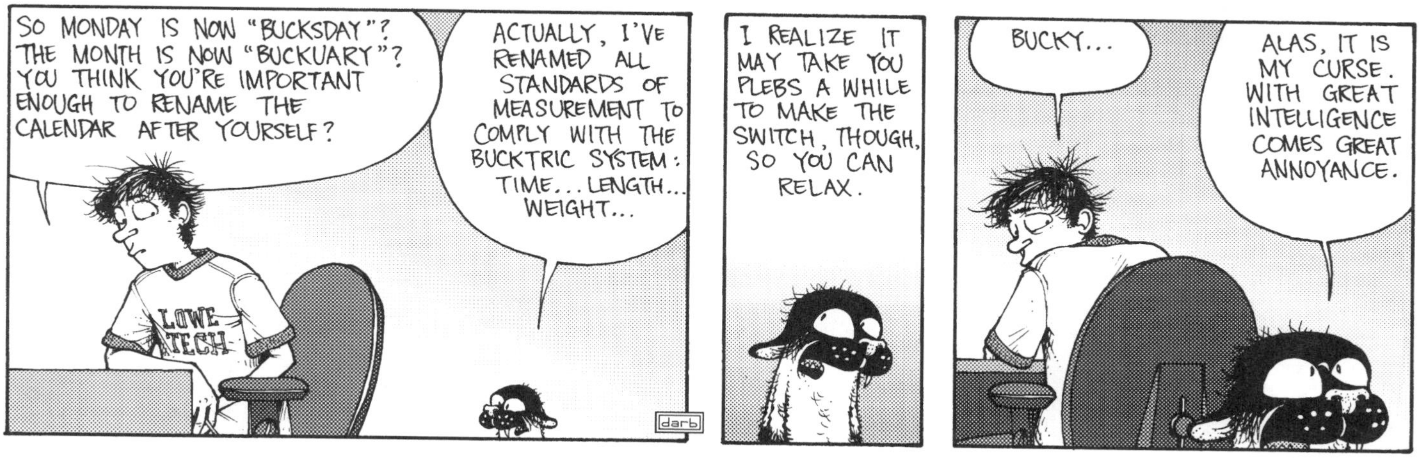
SO MONDAY IS NOW "BUCKSDAY"? THE MONTH IS NOW "BUCKUARY"? YOU THINK YOU'RE IMPORTANT ENOUGH TO RENAME THE CALENDAR AFTER YOURSELF?
ACTUALLY, I'VE RENAMED ALL STANDARDS OF MEASUREMENT TO COMPLY WITH THE BUCKTRIC SYSTEM: TIME... LENGTH... WEIGHT...
darb
I REALIZE IT MAY TAKE YOU PLEBS A WHILE TO MAKE THE SWITCH, THOUGH, SO YOU CAN RELAX.
BUCKY...
ALAS, IT IS MY CURSE. WITH GREAT INTELLIGENCE COMES GREAT ANNOYANCE.

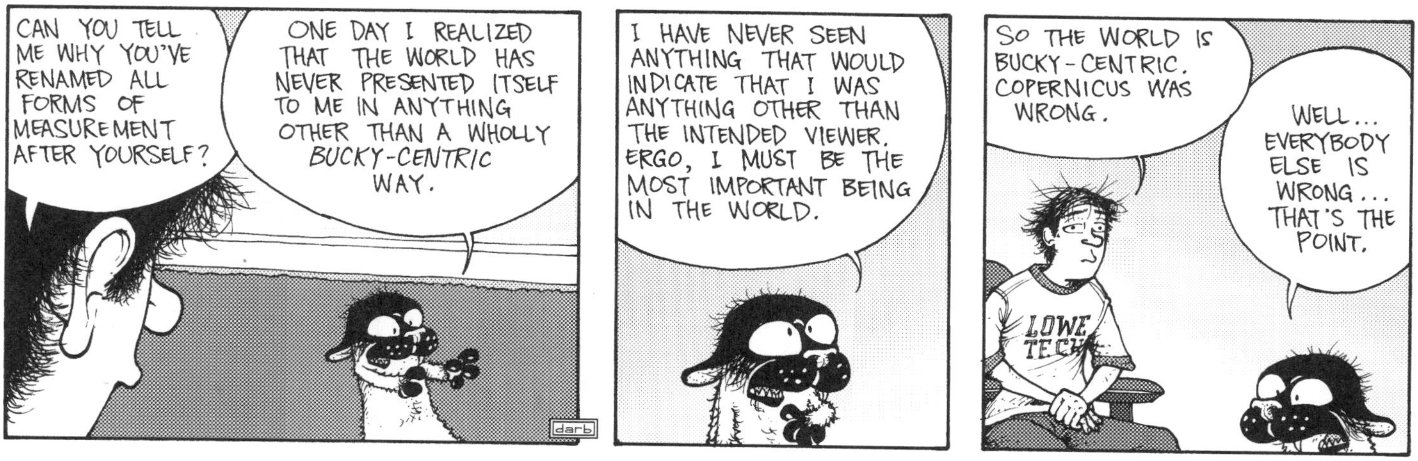
CAN YOU TELL ME WHY YOU'VE RENAMED ALL FORMS OF MEASUREMENT AFTER YOURSELF?
ONE DAY I REALIZED THAT THE WORLD HAS NEVER PRESENTED ITSELF TO ME IN ANYTHING OTHER THAN A WHOLLY *BUCKY-CENTRIC* WAY.
darb
I HAVE NEVER SEEN ANYTHING THAT WOULD INDICATE THAT I WAS ANYTHING OTHER THAN THE INTENDED VIEWER. ERGO, I MUST BE THE MOST IMPORTANT BEING IN THE WORLD.
SO THE WORLD IS BUCKY-CENTRIC. COPERNICUS WAS WRONG.
WELL... EVERYBODY ELSE IS WRONG... THAT'S THE POINT.

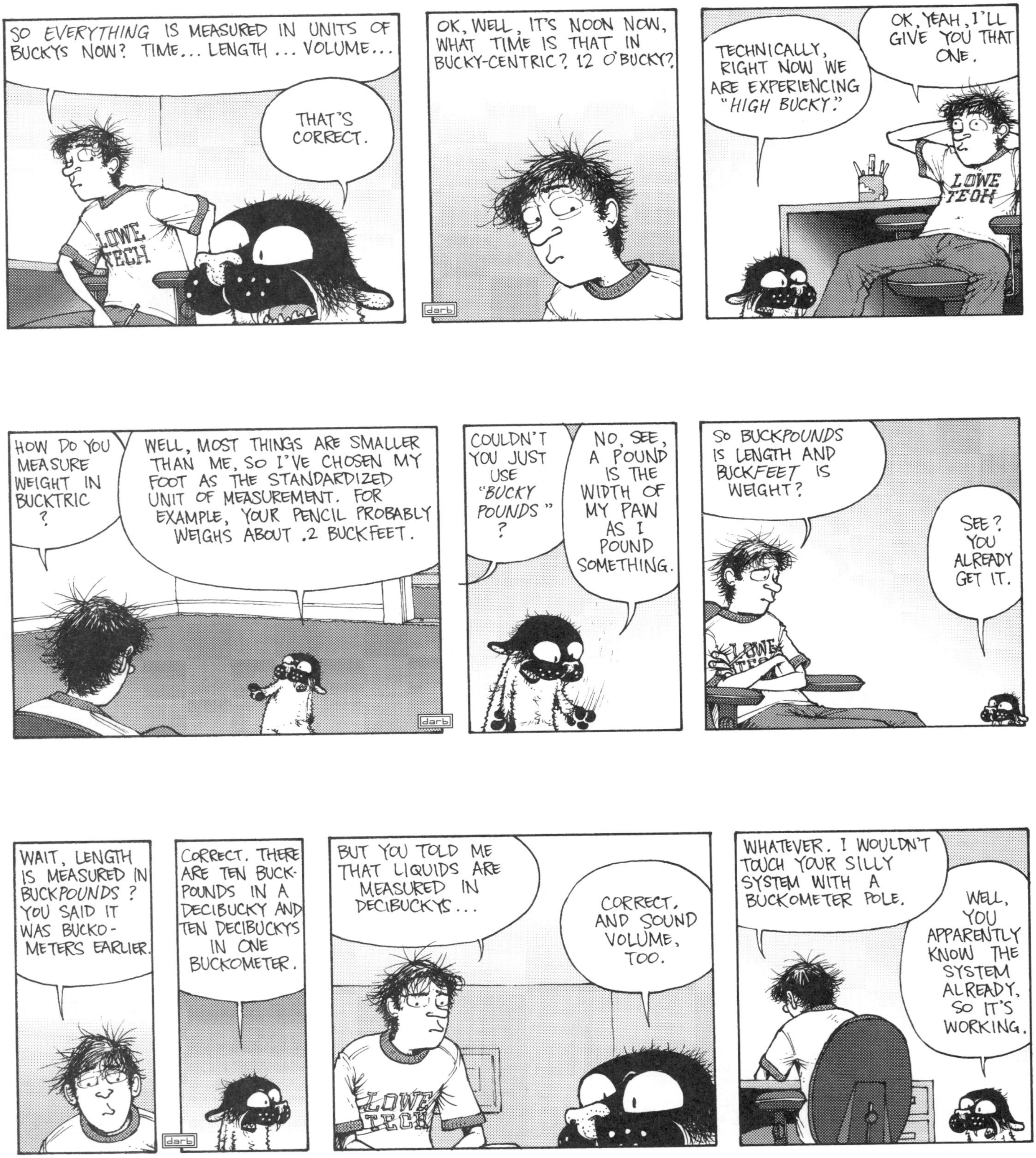

SO EVERYTHING IS MEASURED IN UNITS OF BUCKYS NOW? TIME... LENGTH ... VOLUME...
THAT'S CORRECT.
OK, WELL, IT'S NOON NOW, WHAT TIME IS THAT IN BUCKY-CENTRIC? 12 O'BUCKY?
TECHNICALLY, RIGHT NOW WE ARE EXPERIENCING "HIGH BUCKY."
OK, YEAH, I'LL GIVE YOU THAT ONE.
HOW DO YOU MEASURE WEIGHT IN BUCKTRIC?
WELL, MOST THINGS ARE SMALLER THAN ME, SO I'VE CHOSEN MY FOOT AS THE STANDARDIZED UNIT OF MEASUREMENT. FOR EXAMPLE, YOUR PENCIL PROBABLY WEIGHS ABOUT .2 BUCKFEET.
COULDN'T YOU JUST USE "BUCKY POUNDS"?
NO, SEE, A POUND IS THE WIDTH OF MY PAW AS I POUND SOMETHING.
SO BUCKPOUNDS IS LENGTH AND BUCKFEET IS WEIGHT?
SEE? YOU ALREADY GET IT.
WAIT, LENGTH IS MEASURED IN BUCKPOUNDS? YOU SAID IT WAS BUCKO-METERS EARLIER.
CORRECT. THERE ARE TEN BUCK-POUNDS IN A DECIBUCKY AND TEN DECIBUCKYS IN ONE BUCKOMETER.
BUT YOU TOLD ME THAT LIQUIDS ARE MEASURED IN DECIBUCKYS...
CORRECT, AND SOUND VOLUME, TOO.
WHATEVER. I WOULDN'T TOUCH YOUR SILLY SYSTEM WITH A BUCKOMETER POLE.
WELL, YOU APPARENTLY KNOW THE SYSTEM ALREADY, SO IT'S WORKING.

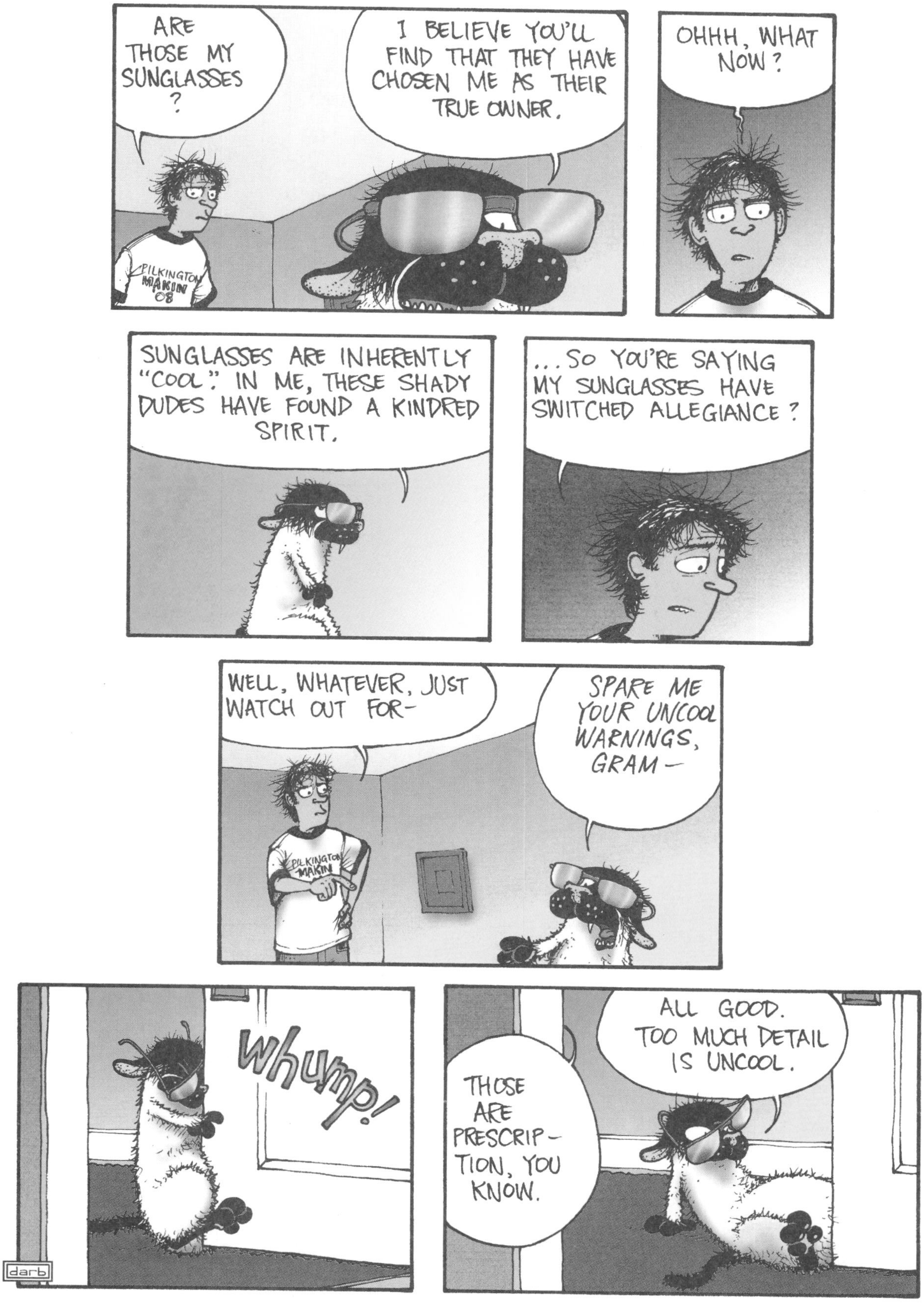
ARE THOSE MY SUNGLASSES ?
I BELIEVE YOU'LL FIND THAT THEY HAVE CHOSEN ME AS THEIR TRUE OWNER.
PILKINGTON MAKIN '08
OHHH, WHAT NOW ?
SUNGLASSES ARE INHERENTLY "COOL." IN ME, THESE SHADY DUDES HAVE FOUND A KINDRED SPIRIT.
...SO YOU'RE SAYING MY SUNGLASSES HAVE SWITCHED ALLEGIANCE ?
WELL, WHATEVER, JUST WATCH OUT FOR-
SPARE ME YOUR UNCOOL WARNINGS, GRAM -
PILKINGTON MAKIN
whump!
darb
ALL GOOD. TOO MUCH DETAIL IS UNCOOL.
THOSE ARE PRESCRIP-TION, YOU KNOW.

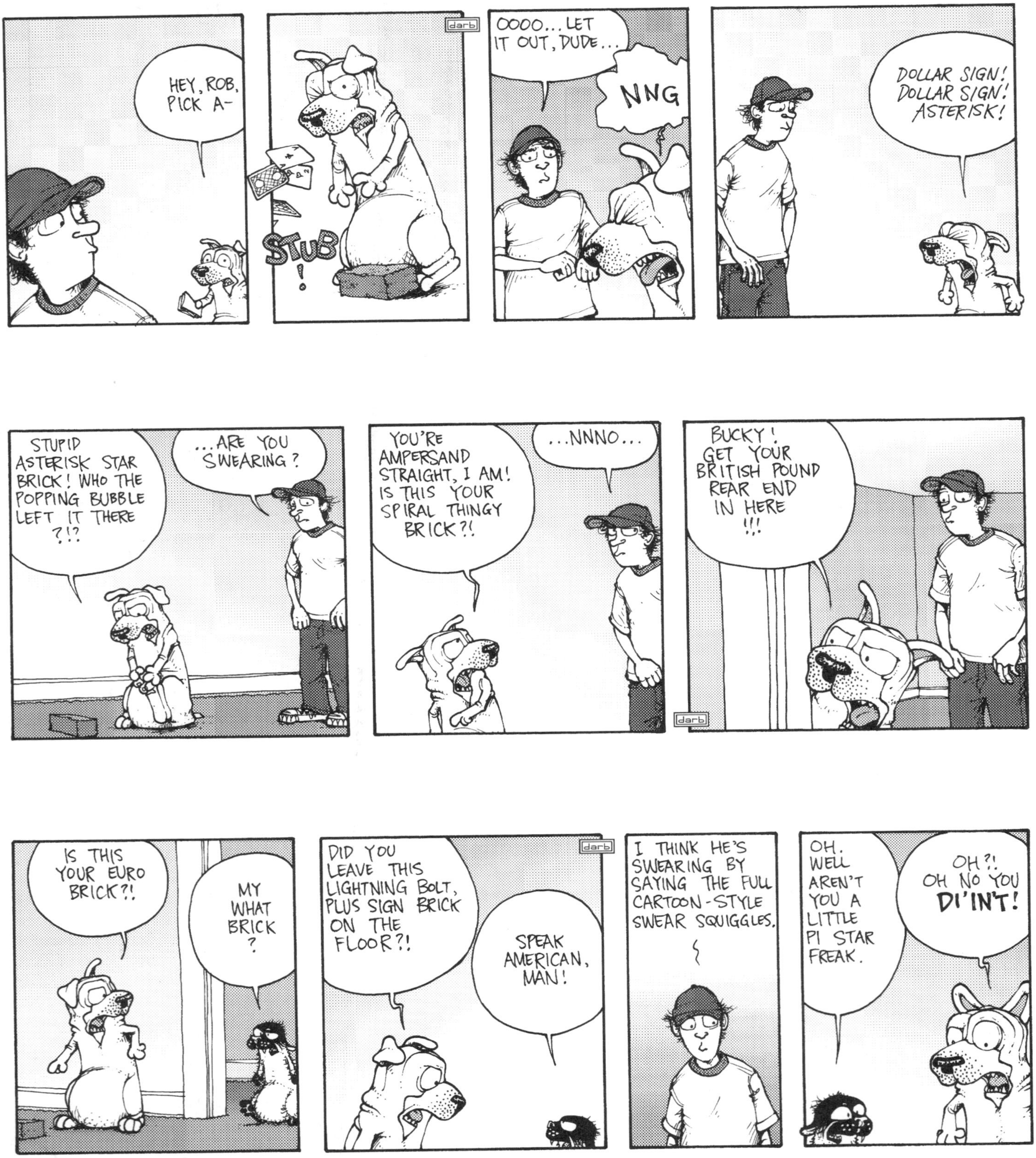
HEY, ROB, PICK A-
darb
STUB!
OOOO... LET IT OUT, DUDE...
NNG
DOLLAR SIGN! DOLLAR SIGN! ASTERISK!
STUPID ASTERISK STAR BRICK! WHO THE POPPING BUBBLE LEFT IT THERE ?!?
...ARE YOU SWEARING?
YOU'RE AMPERSAND STRAIGHT, I AM! IS THIS YOUR SPIRAL THINGY BRICK?!
...NNNO...
darb
BUCKY! GET YOUR BRITISH POUND REAR END IN HERE !!!
IS THIS YOUR EURO BRICK?!
MY WHAT BRICK ?
darb
DID YOU LEAVE THIS LIGHTNING BOLT, PLUS SIGN BRICK ON THE FLOOR?!
SPEAK AMERICAN, MAN!
I THINK HE'S SWEARING BY SAYING THE FULL CARTOON-STYLE SWEAR SQUIGGLES.
OH. WELL AREN'T YOU A LITTLE PI STAR FREAK.
OH?! OH NO YOU DI'IN'T!

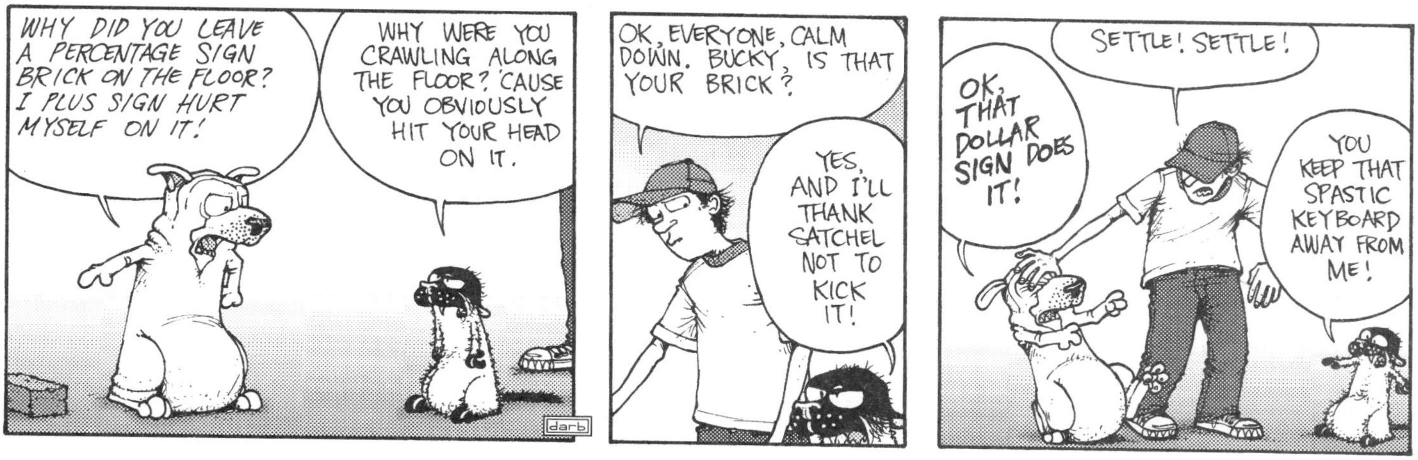

WHY DID YOU LEAVE A PERCENTAGE SIGN BRICK ON THE FLOOR? I PLUS SIGN HURT MYSELF ON IT!
WHY WERE YOU CRAWLING ALONG THE FLOOR? 'CAUSE YOU OBVIOUSLY HIT YOUR HEAD ON IT.
OK, EVERYONE, CALM DOWN. BUCKY, IS THAT YOUR BRICK?
YES, AND I'LL THANK SATCHEL NOT TO KICK IT!
SETTLE! SETTLE!
OK, THAT DOLLAR SIGN DOES IT!
YOU KEEP THAT SPASTIC KEYBOARD AWAY FROM ME!

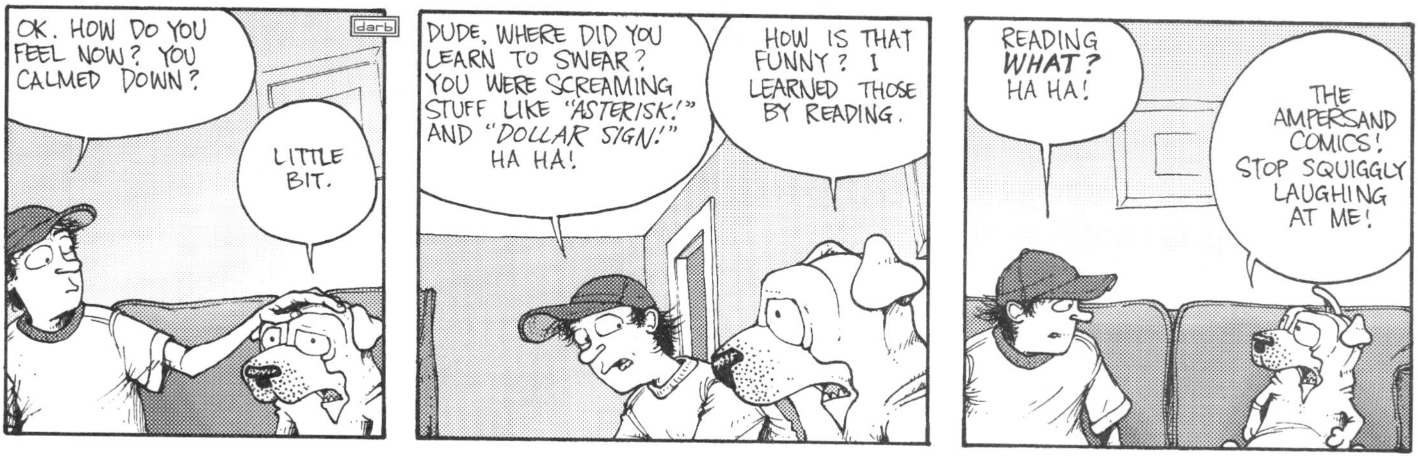

OK. HOW DO YOU FEEL NOW? YOU CALMED DOWN?
LITTLE BIT.
DUDE, WHERE DID YOU LEARN TO SWEAR? YOU WERE SCREAMING STUFF LIKE "ASTERISK!" AND "DOLLAR SIGN!" HA HA!
HOW IS THAT FUNNY? I LEARNED THOSE BY READING.
READING WHAT? HA HA!
THE AMPERSAND COMICS! STOP SQUIGGLY LAUGHING AT ME!

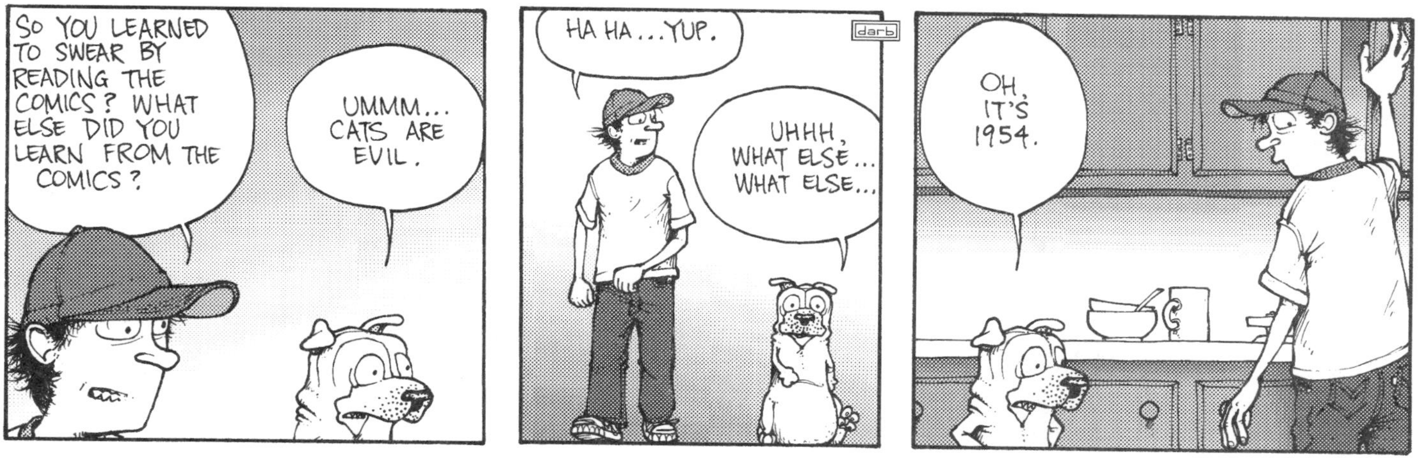

SO YOU LEARNED TO SWEAR BY READING THE COMICS? WHAT ELSE DID YOU LEARN FROM THE COMICS?
UMMM... CATS ARE EVIL.
HA HA... YUP.
UHHH, WHAT ELSE... WHAT ELSE...
OH, IT'S 1954.

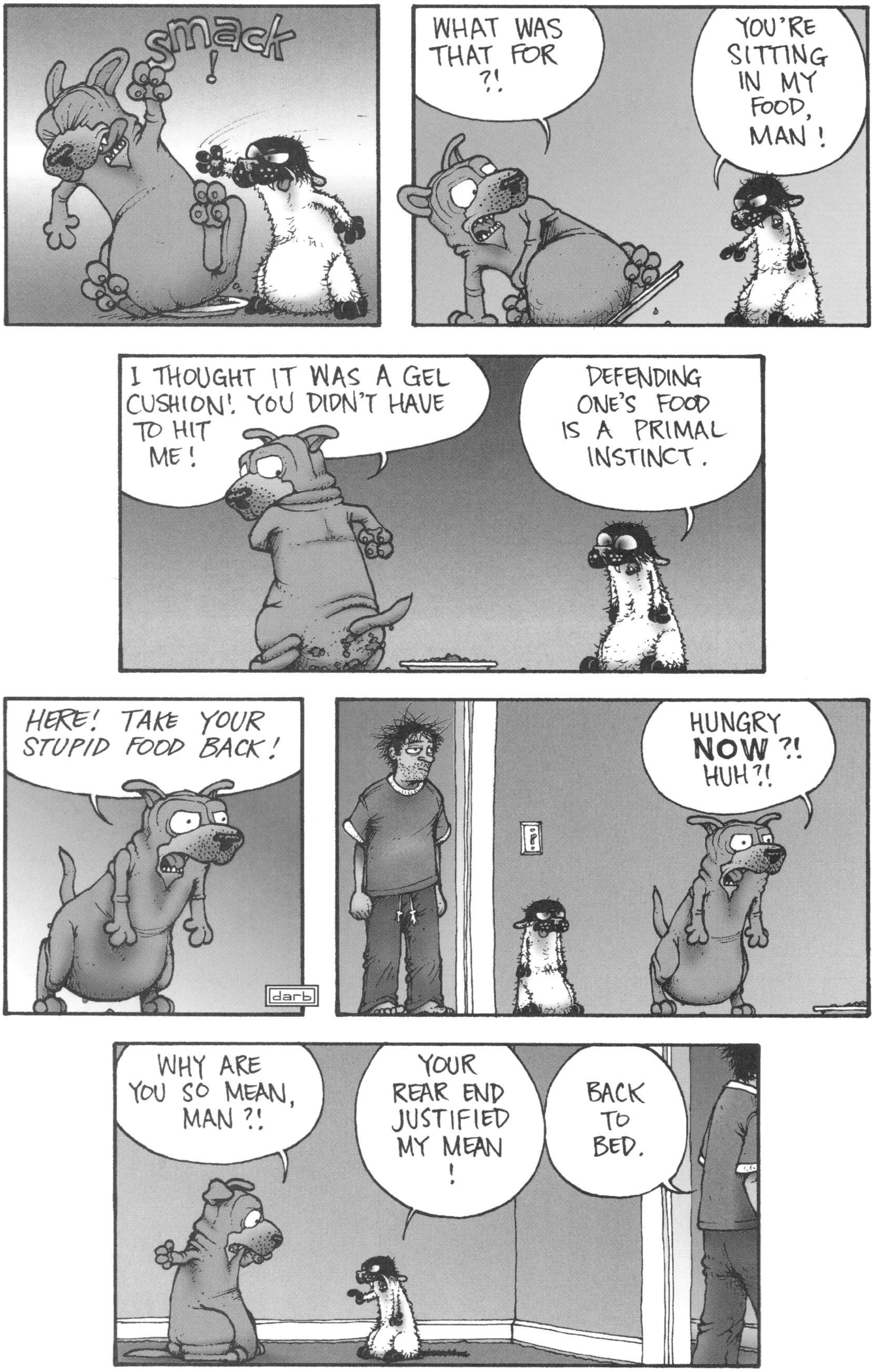
smack
!
WHAT WAS THAT FOR ?!
YOU'RE SITTING IN MY FOOD, MAN!
I THOUGHT IT WAS A GEL CUSHION! YOU DIDN'T HAVE TO HIT ME!
DEFENDING ONE'S FOOD IS A PRIMAL INSTINCT.
HERE! TAKE YOUR STUPID FOOD BACK!
darb
HUNGRY **NOW** ?! HUH ?!
WHY ARE YOU SO MEAN, MAN ?!
YOUR REAR END JUSTIFIED MY MEAN !
BACK TO BED.

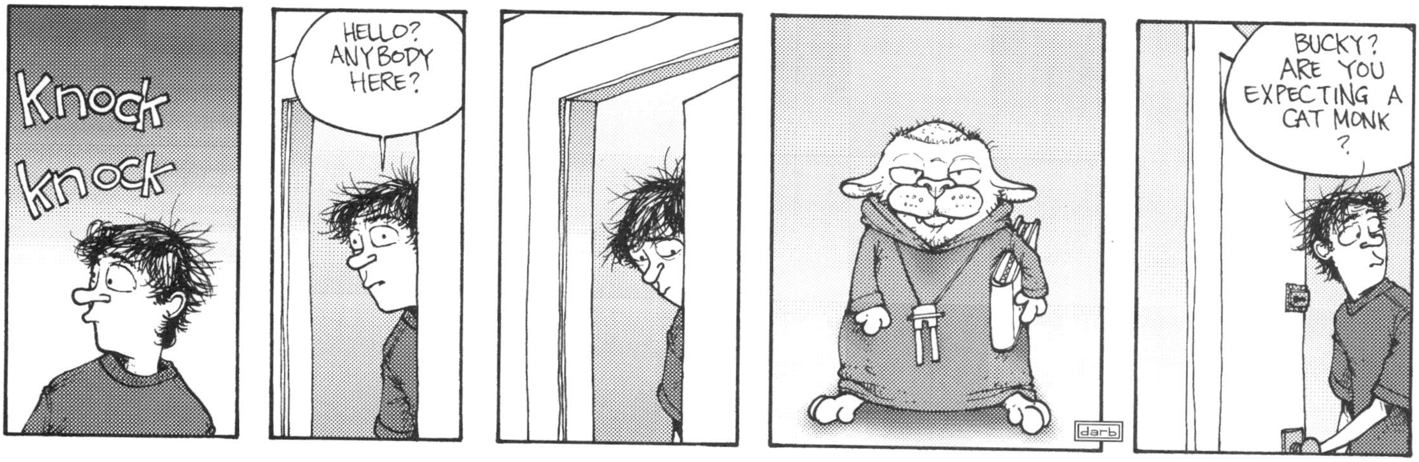
Knock knock
HELLO? ANYBODY HERE?
BUCKY? ARE YOU EXPECTING A CAT MONK ?

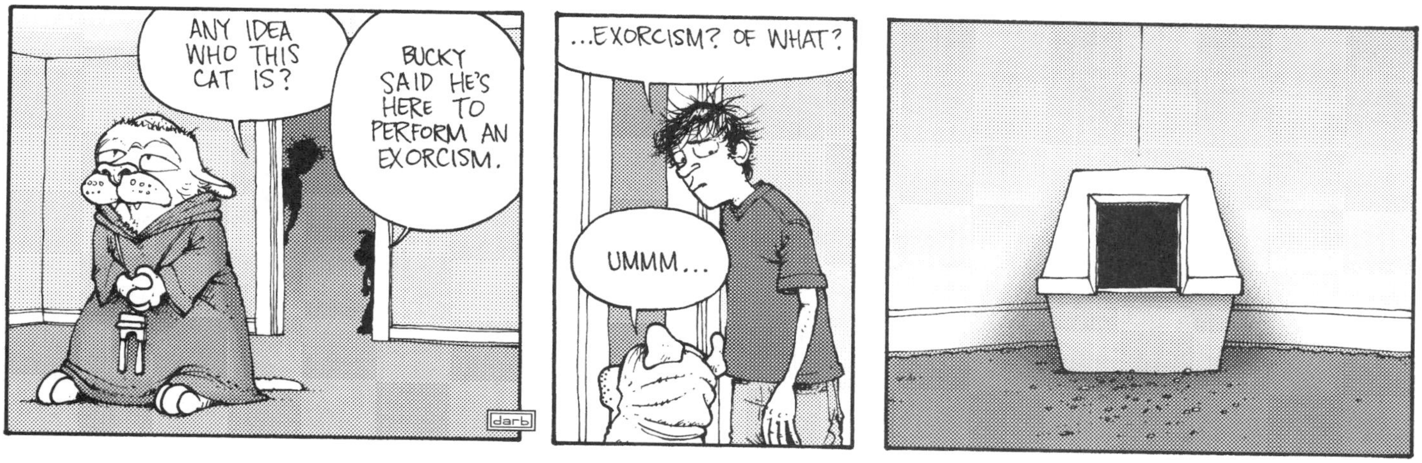
ANY IDEA WHO THIS CAT IS?
BUCKY SAID HE'S HERE TO PERFORM AN EXORCISM.
...EXORCISM? OF WHAT?
UMMM...

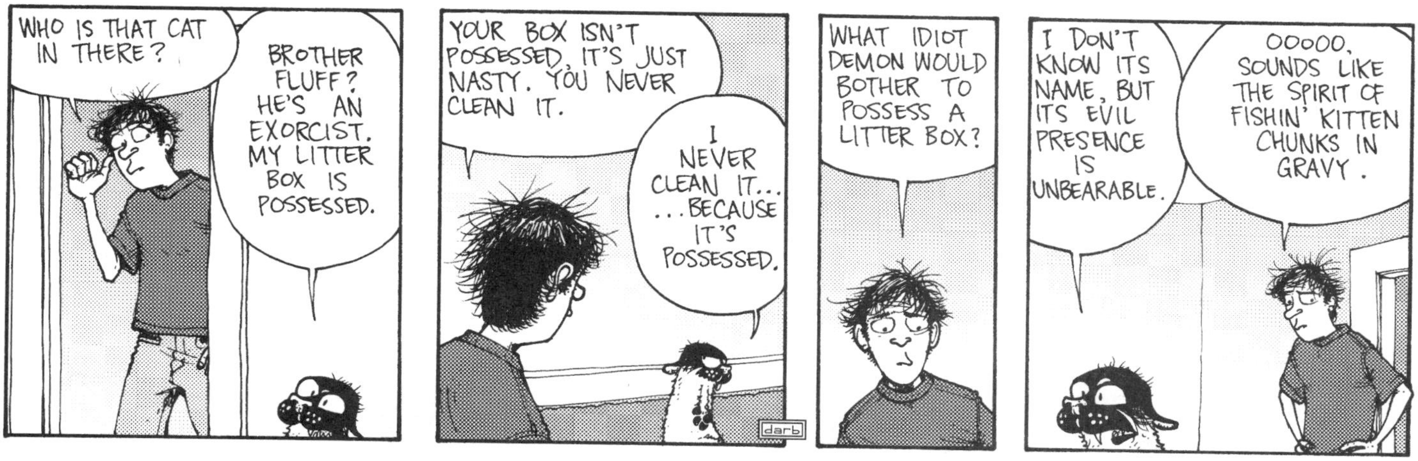
WHO IS THAT CAT IN THERE?
BROTHER FLUFF? HE'S AN EXORCIST. MY LITTER BOX IS POSSESSED.
YOUR BOX ISN'T POSSESSED, IT'S JUST NASTY. YOU NEVER CLEAN IT.
I NEVER CLEAN IT... ...BECAUSE IT'S POSSESSED.
WHAT IDIOT DEMON WOULD BOTHER TO POSSESS A LITTER BOX?
I DON'T KNOW ITS NAME, BUT ITS EVIL PRESENCE IS UNBEARABLE.
OOOOO. SOUNDS LIKE THE SPIRIT OF FISHIN' KITTEN CHUNKS IN GRAVY.

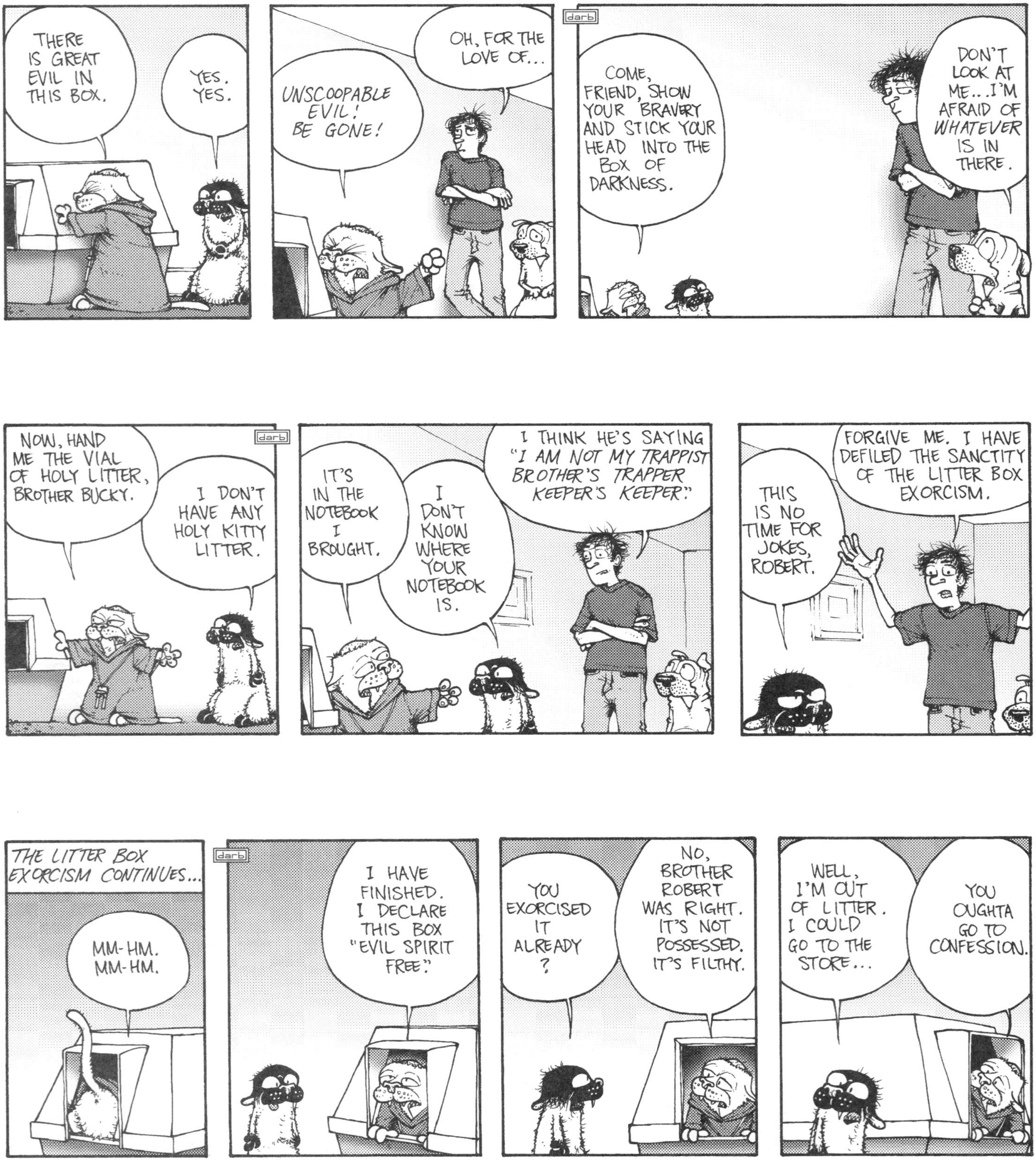
THERE IS GREAT EVIL IN THIS BOX.
YES. YES.
OH, FOR THE LOVE OF...
UNSCOOPABLE EVIL! BE GONE!
COME, FRIEND, SHOW YOUR BRAVERY AND STICK YOUR HEAD INTO THE BOX OF DARKNESS.
DON'T LOOK AT ME...I'M AFRAID OF WHATEVER IS IN THERE.
NOW, HAND ME THE VIAL OF HOLY LITTER, BROTHER BUCKY.
I DON'T HAVE ANY HOLY KITTY LITTER.
IT'S IN THE NOTEBOOK I BROUGHT.
I DON'T KNOW WHERE YOUR NOTEBOOK IS.
I THINK HE'S SAYING "I AM NOT MY TRAPPIST BROTHER'S TRAPPER KEEPER'S KEEPER."
THIS IS NO TIME FOR JOKES, ROBERT.
FORGIVE ME. I HAVE DEFILED THE SANCTITY OF THE LITTER BOX EXORCISM.
THE LITTER BOX EXORCISM CONTINUES...
MM-HM. MM-HM.
I HAVE FINISHED. I DECLARE THIS BOX "EVIL SPIRIT FREE."
YOU EXORCISED IT ALREADY?
NO, BROTHER ROBERT WAS RIGHT. IT'S NOT POSSESSED. IT'S FILTHY.
WELL, I'M OUT OF LITTER. I COULD GO TO THE STORE...
YOU OUGHTA GO TO CONFESSION.

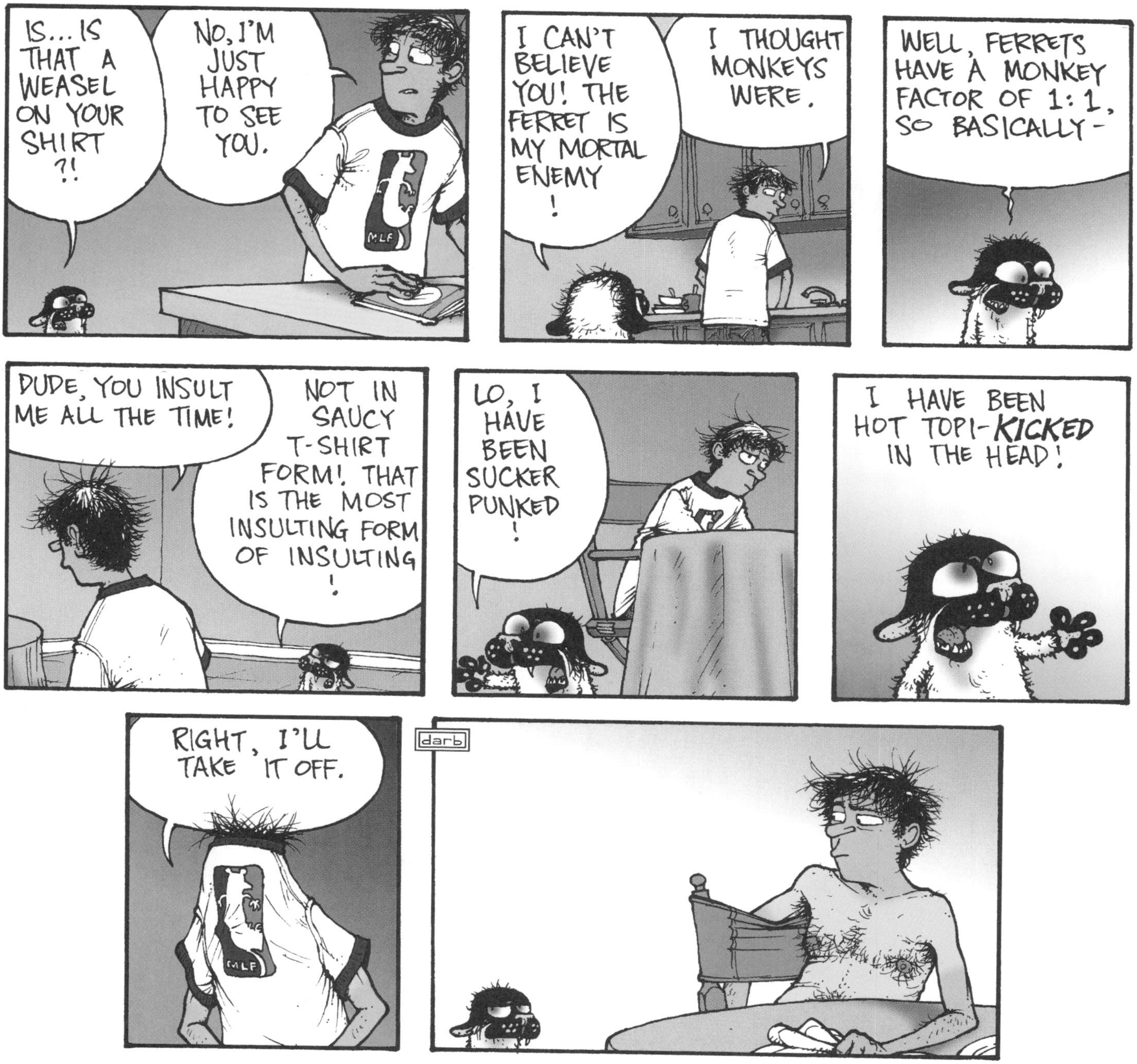
IS... IS THAT A WEASEL ON YOUR SHIRT ?!
NO, I'M JUST HAPPY TO SEE YOU.
I CAN'T BELIEVE YOU! THE FERRET IS MY MORTAL ENEMY !
I THOUGHT MONKEYS WERE.
WELL, FERRETS HAVE A MONKEY FACTOR OF 1:1, SO BASICALLY-
DUDE, YOU INSULT ME ALL THE TIME!
NOT IN SAUCY T-SHIRT FORM! THAT IS THE MOST INSULTING FORM OF INSULTING !
LO, I HAVE BEEN SUCKER PUNKED !
I HAVE BEEN HOT TOPI-KICKED IN THE HEAD!
RIGHT, I'LL TAKE IT OFF.
darb

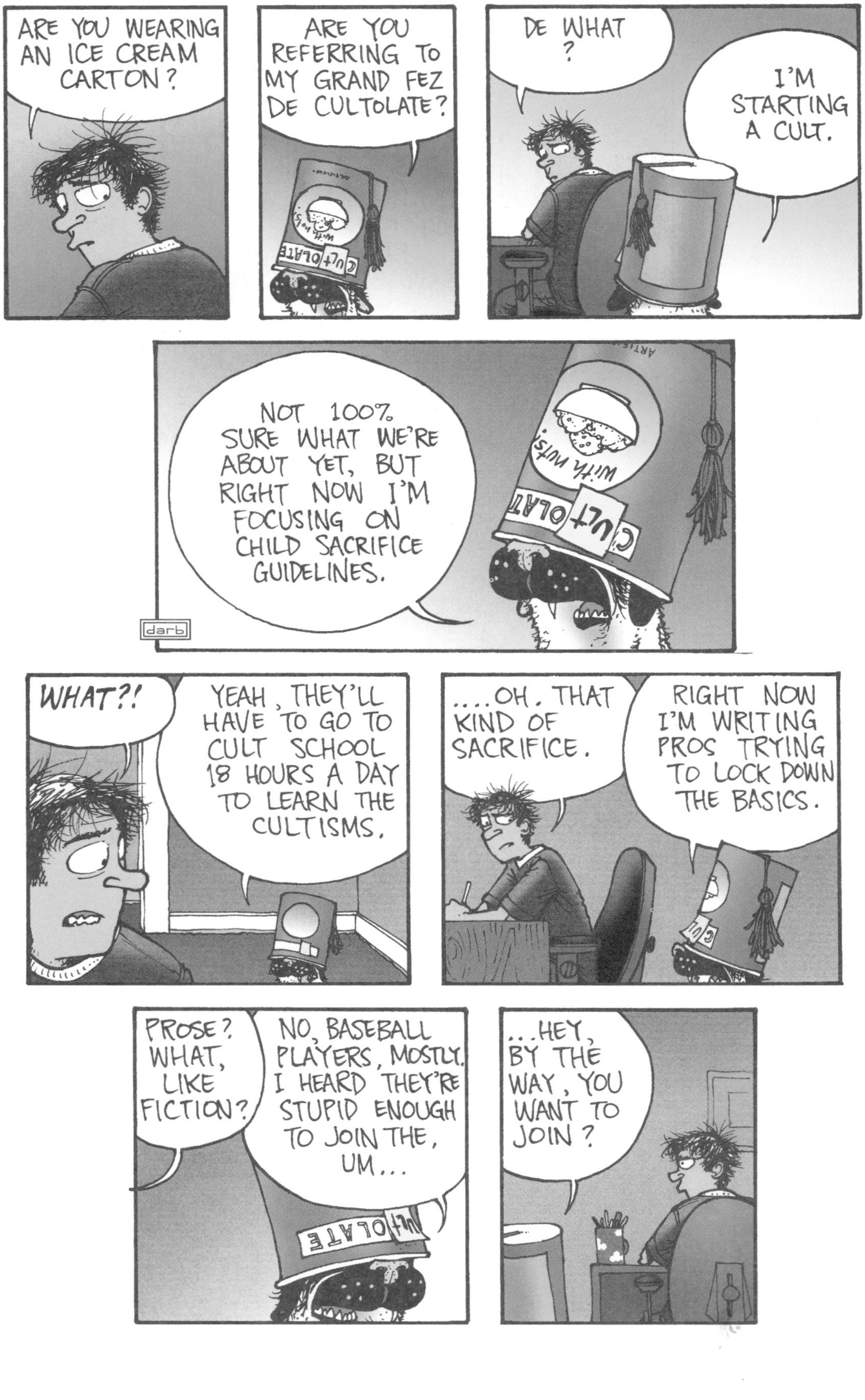
ARE YOU WEARING AN ICE CREAM CARTON?
ARE YOU REFERRING TO MY GRAND FEZ DE CULTOLATE?
CULTOLATE
DE WHAT?
I'M STARTING A CULT.
NOT 100% SURE WHAT WE'RE ABOUT YET, BUT RIGHT NOW I'M FOCUSING ON CHILD SACRIFICE GUIDELINES.
CULTOLAT
darb
WHAT?!
YEAH, THEY'LL HAVE TO GO TO CULT SCHOOL 18 HOURS A DAY TO LEARN THE CULTISMS.
....OH. THAT KIND OF SACRIFICE.
RIGHT NOW I'M WRITING PROS TRYING TO LOCK DOWN THE BASICS.
PROSE? WHAT, LIKE FICTION?
NO, BASEBALL PLAYERS, MOSTLY. I HEARD THEY'RE STUPID ENOUGH TO JOIN THE, UM...
ULTOLATE
...HEY, BY THE WAY, YOU WANT TO JOIN?

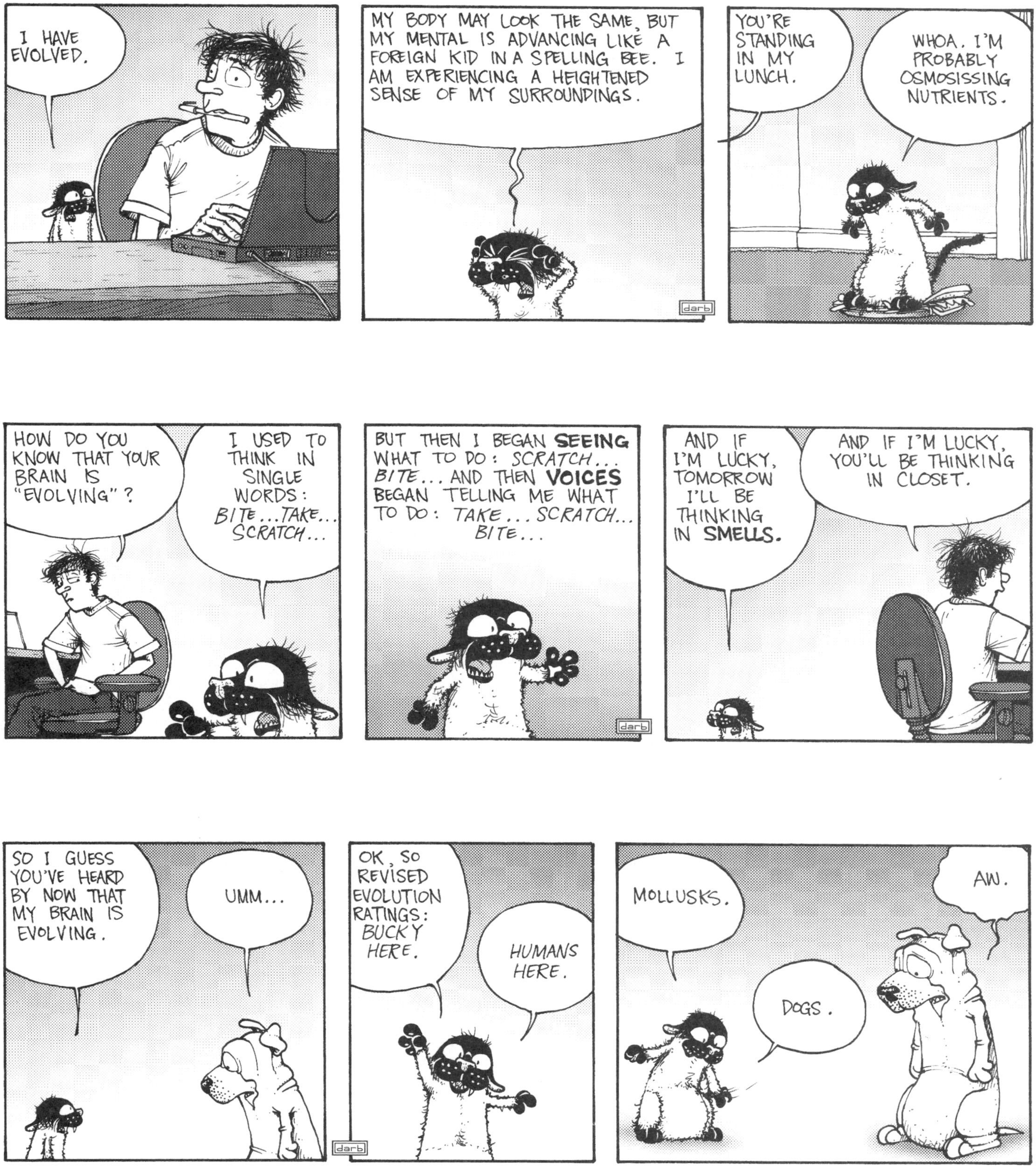
I HAVE EVOLVED.
MY BODY MAY LOOK THE SAME, BUT MY MENTAL IS ADVANCING LIKE A FOREIGN KID IN A SPELLING BEE. I AM EXPERIENCING A HEIGHTENED SENSE OF MY SURROUNDINGS.
YOU'RE STANDING IN MY LUNCH.
WHOA. I'M PROBABLY OSMOSISSING NUTRIENTS.
darb
HOW DO YOU KNOW THAT YOUR BRAIN IS "EVOLVING"?
I USED TO THINK IN SINGLE WORDS: BITE...TAKE... SCRATCH...
BUT THEN I BEGAN SEEING WHAT TO DO: SCRATCH... BITE... AND THEN VOICES BEGAN TELLING ME WHAT TO DO: TAKE... SCRATCH... BITE...
AND IF I'M LUCKY, TOMORROW I'LL BE THINKING IN SMELLS.
AND IF I'M LUCKY, YOU'LL BE THINKING IN CLOSET.
darb
SO I GUESS YOU'VE HEARD BY NOW THAT MY BRAIN IS EVOLVING.
UMM...
OK, SO REVISED EVOLUTION RATINGS: BUCKY HERE.
HUMANS HERE.
MOLLUSKS.
DOGS.
AW.
darb

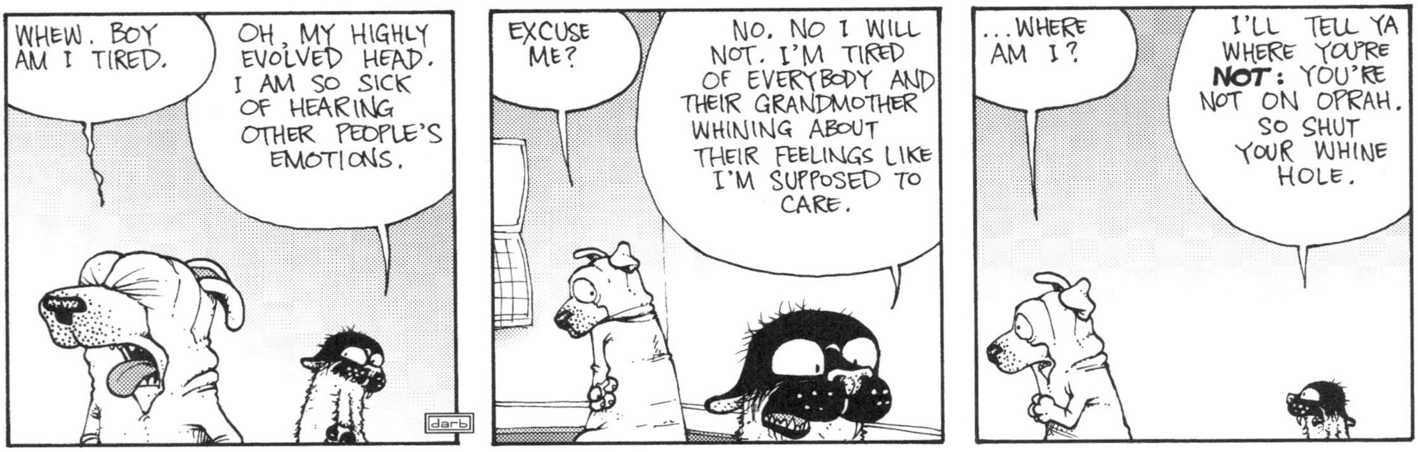
WHEW. BOY AM I TIRED.
OH, MY HIGHLY EVOLVED HEAD. I AM SO SICK OF HEARING OTHER PEOPLE'S EMOTIONS.
EXCUSE ME?
NO. NO I WILL NOT. I'M TIRED OF EVERYBODY AND THEIR GRANDMOTHER WHINING ABOUT THEIR FEELINGS LIKE I'M SUPPOSED TO CARE.
...WHERE AM I?
I'LL TELL YA WHERE YOU'RE **NOT**: YOU'RE NOT ON OPRAH. SO SHUT YOUR WHINE HOLE.

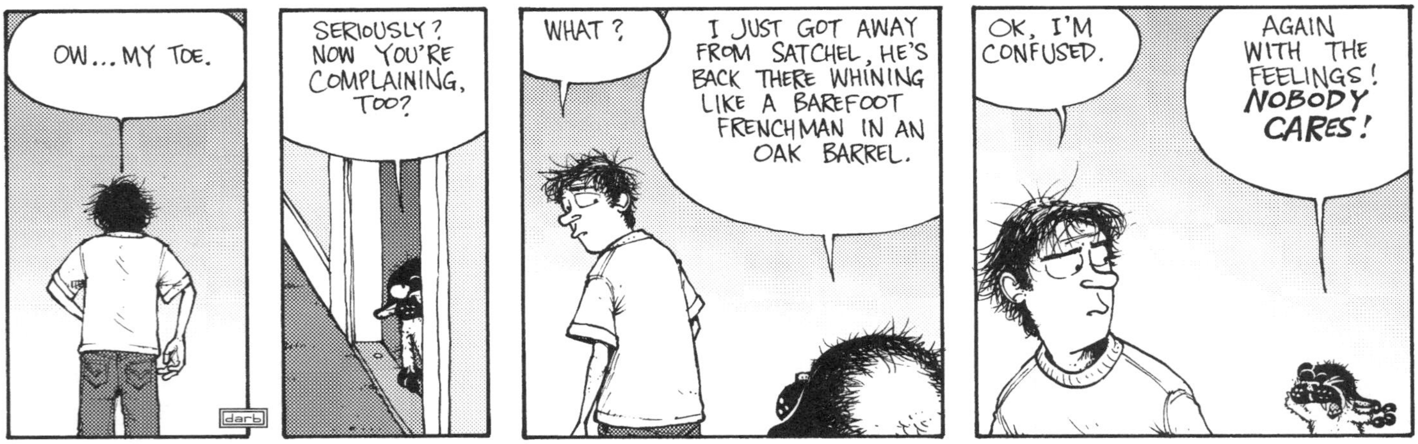
OW... MY TOE.
SERIOUSLY? NOW YOU'RE COMPLAINING, TOO?
WHAT?
I JUST GOT AWAY FROM SATCHEL, HE'S BACK THERE WHINING LIKE A BAREFOOT FRENCHMAN IN AN OAK BARREL.
OK, I'M CONFUSED.
AGAIN WITH THE FEELINGS! ***NOBODY CARES!***

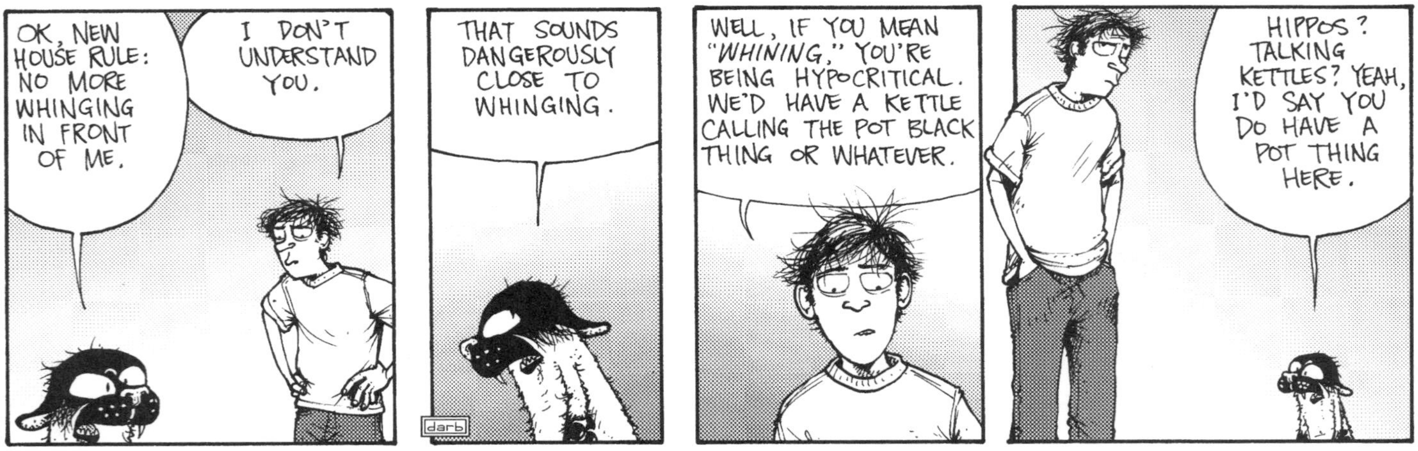
OK, NEW HOUSE RULE: NO MORE WHINGING IN FRONT OF ME.
I DON'T UNDERSTAND YOU.
THAT SOUNDS DANGEROUSLY CLOSE TO WHINGING.
WELL, IF YOU MEAN "*WHINING*," YOU'RE BEING HYPOCRITICAL. WE'D HAVE A KETTLE CALLING THE POT BLACK THING OR WHATEVER.
HIPPOS? TALKING KETTLES? YEAH, I'D SAY YOU DO HAVE A POT THING HERE.

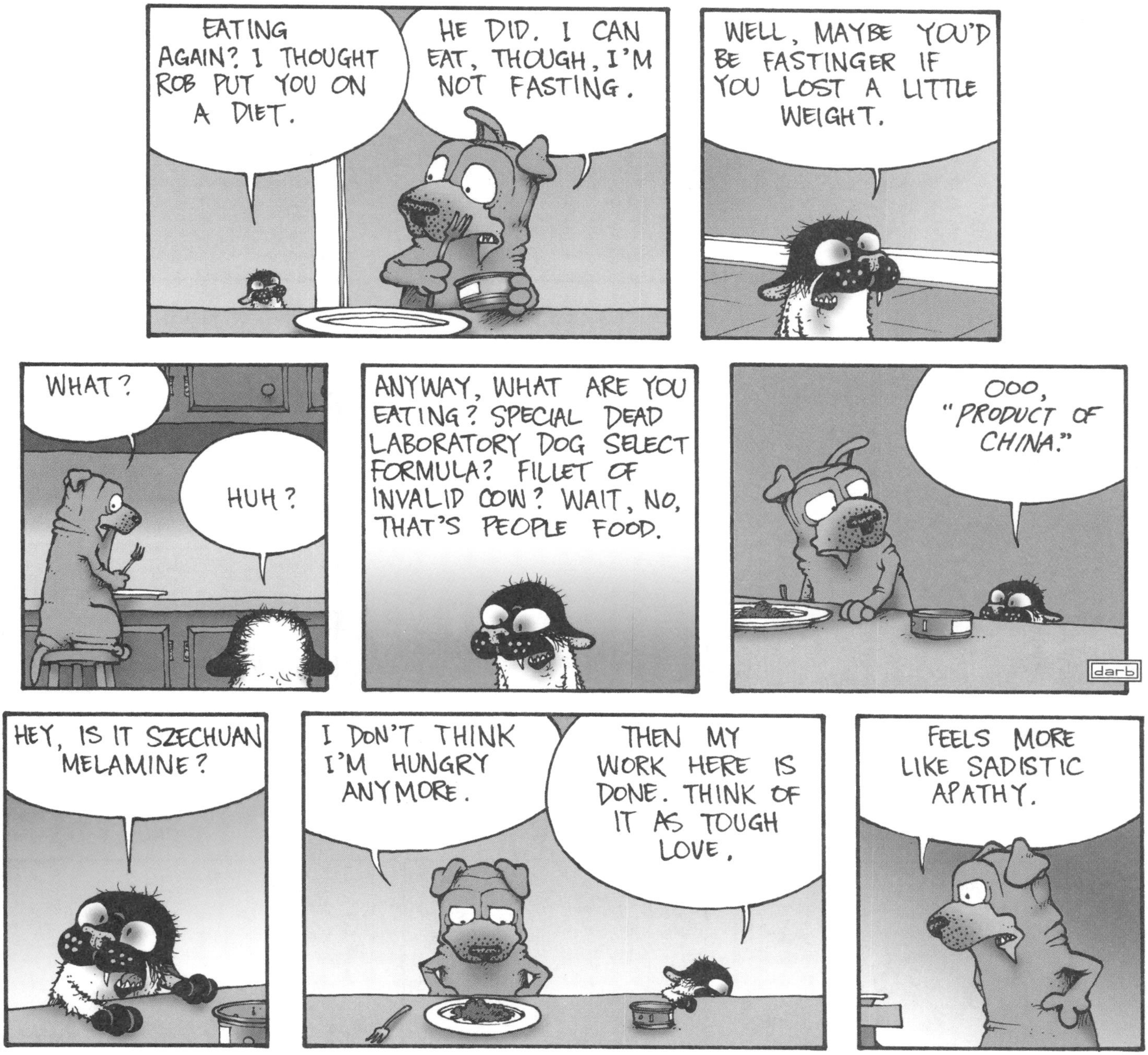
EATING AGAIN? I THOUGHT ROB PUT YOU ON A DIET.
HE DID. I CAN EAT, THOUGH, I'M NOT FASTING.
WELL, MAYBE YOU'D BE FASTINGER IF YOU LOST A LITTLE WEIGHT.
WHAT?
HUH?
ANYWAY, WHAT ARE YOU EATING? SPECIAL DEAD LABORATORY DOG SELECT FORMULA? FILLET OF INVALID COW? WAIT, NO, THAT'S PEOPLE FOOD.
OOO, "PRODUCT OF CHINA."
darb
HEY, IS IT SZECHUAN MELAMINE?
I DON'T THINK I'M HUNGRY ANYMORE.
THEN MY WORK HERE IS DONE. THINK OF IT AS TOUGH LOVE.
FEELS MORE LIKE SADISTIC APATHY.

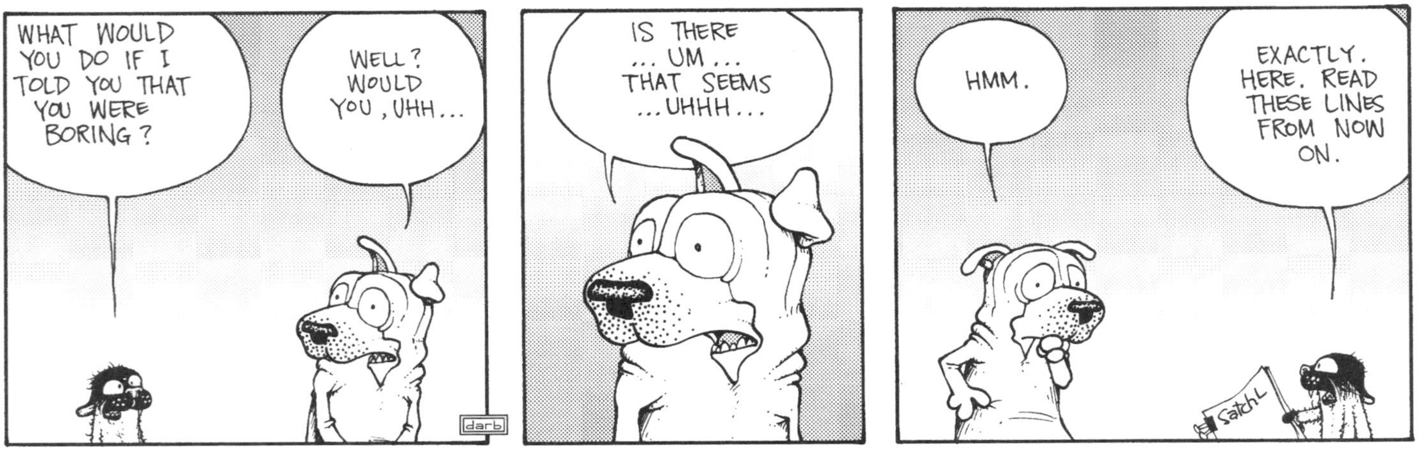
WHAT WOULD YOU DO IF I TOLD YOU THAT YOU WERE BORING?
WELL? WOULD YOU, UHH...
IS THERE ... UM ... THAT SEEMS ...UHHH...
HMM.
EXACTLY. HERE. READ THESE LINES FROM NOW ON.
darb

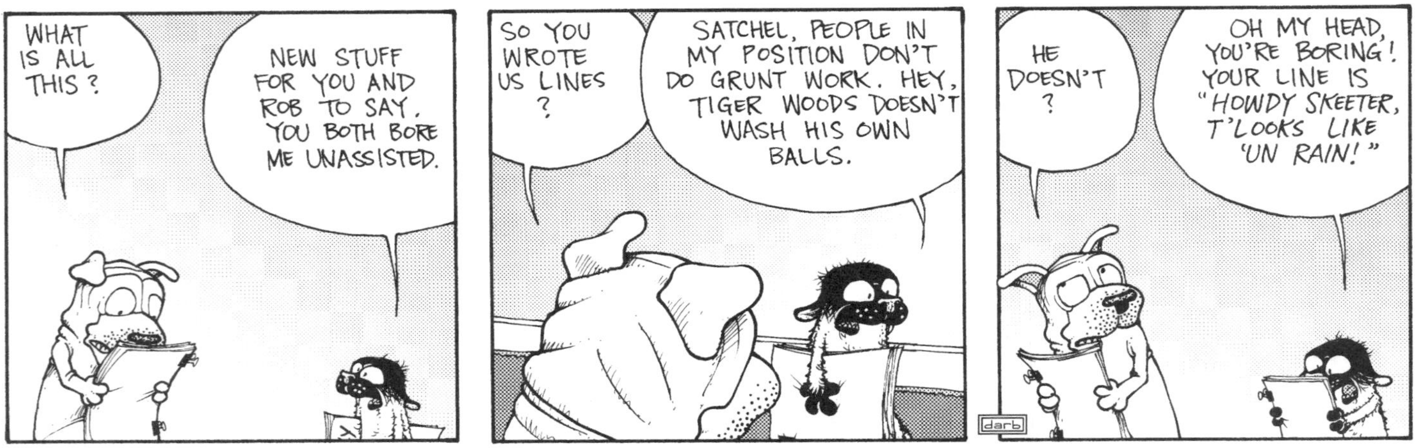
WHAT IS ALL THIS?
NEW STUFF FOR YOU AND ROB TO SAY. YOU BOTH BORE ME UNASSISTED.
SO YOU WROTE US LINES?
SATCHEL, PEOPLE IN MY POSITION DON'T DO GRUNT WORK. HEY, TIGER WOODS DOESN'T WASH HIS OWN BALLS.
HE DOESN'T?
OH MY HEAD, YOU'RE BORING! YOUR LINE IS "*HOWDY SKEETER, T'LOOKS LIKE 'UN RAIN!*"
darb

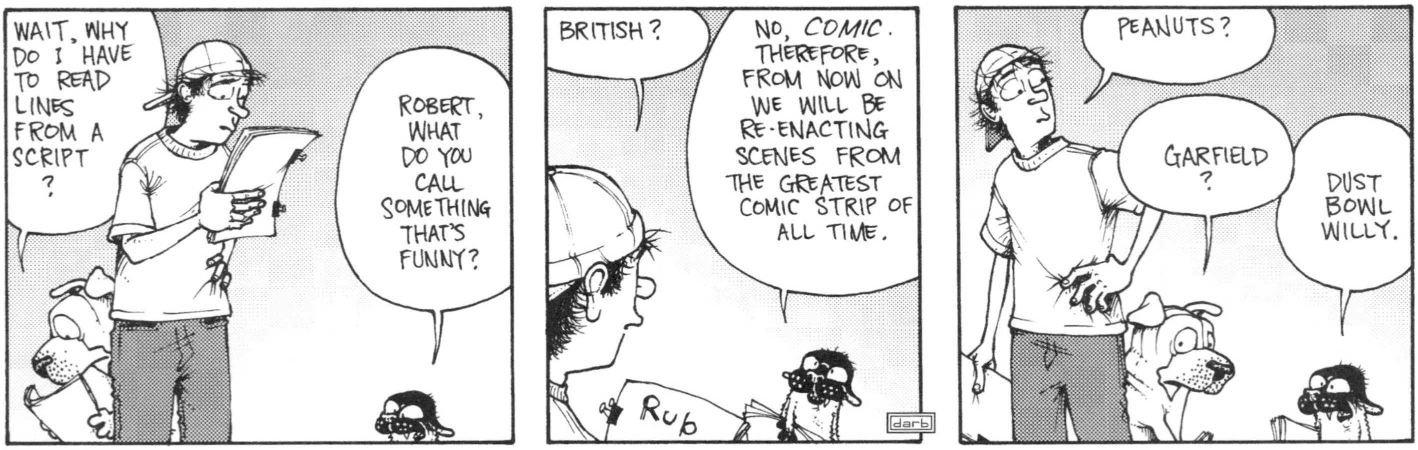
WAIT, WHY DO I HAVE TO READ LINES FROM A SCRIPT?
ROBERT, WHAT DO YOU CALL SOMETHING THAT'S FUNNY?
BRITISH?
NO, *COMIC*. THEREFORE, FROM NOW ON WE WILL BE RE-ENACTING SCENES FROM THE GREATEST COMIC STRIP OF ALL TIME.
Rub
darb
PEANUTS?
GARFIELD?
DUST BOWL WILLY.

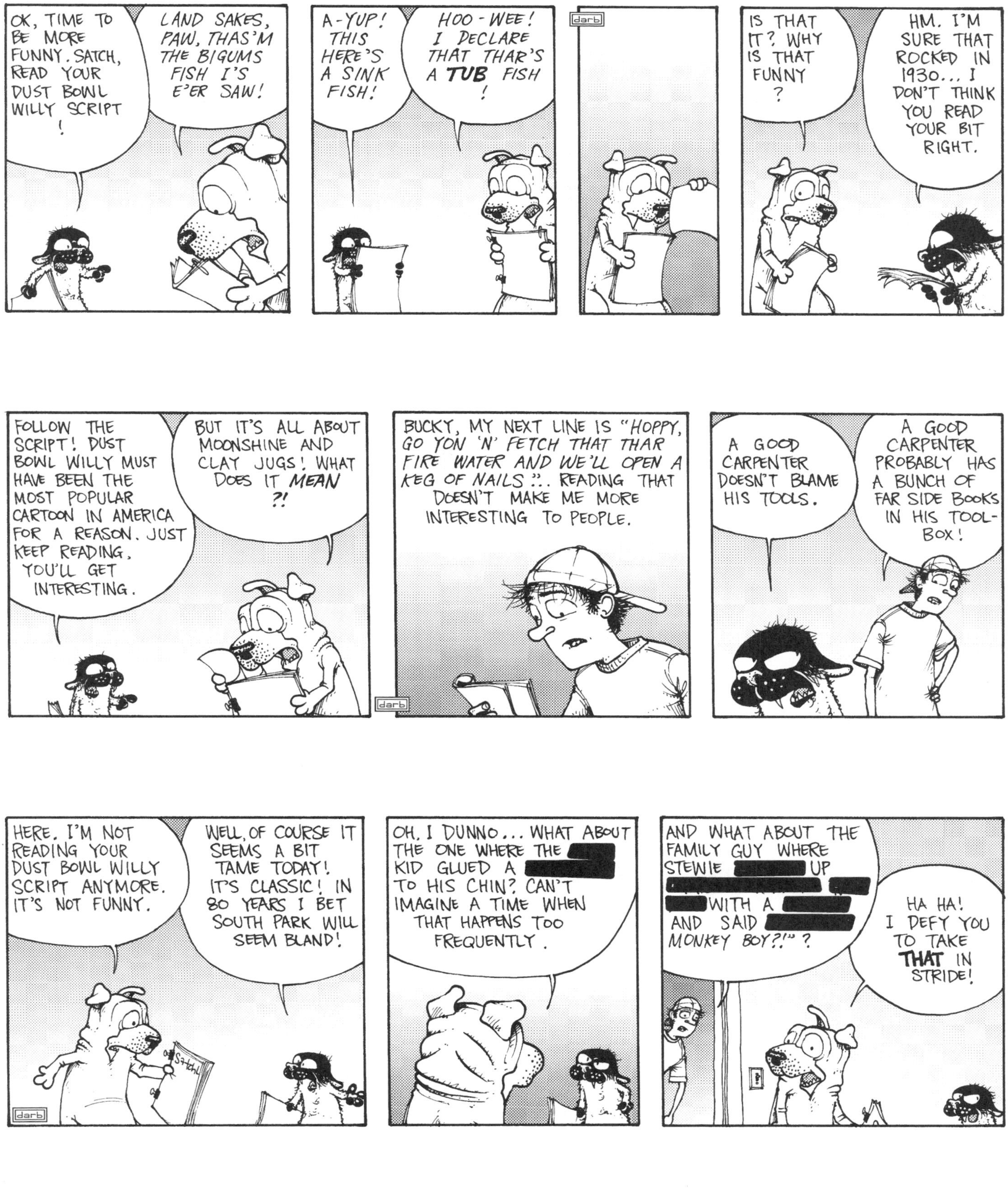
OK, TIME TO BE MORE FUNNY. SATCH, READ YOUR DUST BOWL WILLY SCRIPT!
LAND SAKES, PAW, THAS'M THE BIGUMS FISH I'S E'ER SAW!
A-YUP! THIS HERE'S A SINK FISH!
HOO-WEE! I DECLARE THAT THAR'S A **TUB** FISH!
IS THAT IT? WHY IS THAT FUNNY?
HM. I'M SURE THAT ROCKED IN 1930... I DON'T THINK YOU READ YOUR BIT RIGHT.
FOLLOW THE SCRIPT! DUST BOWL WILLY MUST HAVE BEEN THE MOST POPULAR CARTOON IN AMERICA FOR A REASON. JUST KEEP READING, YOU'LL GET INTERESTING.
BUT IT'S ALL ABOUT MOONSHINE AND CLAY JUGS! WHAT DOES IT *MEAN*?!
BUCKY, MY NEXT LINE IS "*HOPPY, GO YON 'N' FETCH THAT THAR FIRE WATER AND WE'LL OPEN A KEG OF NAILS!*". READING THAT DOESN'T MAKE ME MORE INTERESTING TO PEOPLE.
A GOOD CARPENTER DOESN'T BLAME HIS TOOLS.
A GOOD CARPENTER PROBABLY HAS A BUNCH OF FAR SIDE BOOKS IN HIS TOOL-BOX!
HERE. I'M NOT READING YOUR DUST BOWL WILLY SCRIPT ANYMORE. IT'S NOT FUNNY.
WELL, OF COURSE IT SEEMS A BIT TAME TODAY! IT'S CLASSIC! IN 80 YEARS I BET SOUTH PARK WILL SEEM BLAND!
OH, I DUNNO... WHAT ABOUT THE ONE WHERE THE [redacted] KID GLUED A [redacted] TO HIS CHIN? CAN'T IMAGINE A TIME WHEN THAT HAPPENS TOO FREQUENTLY.
AND WHAT ABOUT THE FAMILY GUY WHERE STEWIE [redacted] UP [redacted] WITH A [redacted] AND SAID [redacted] *MONKEY BOY?!*"?
HA HA! I DEFY YOU TO TAKE **THAT** IN STRIDE!

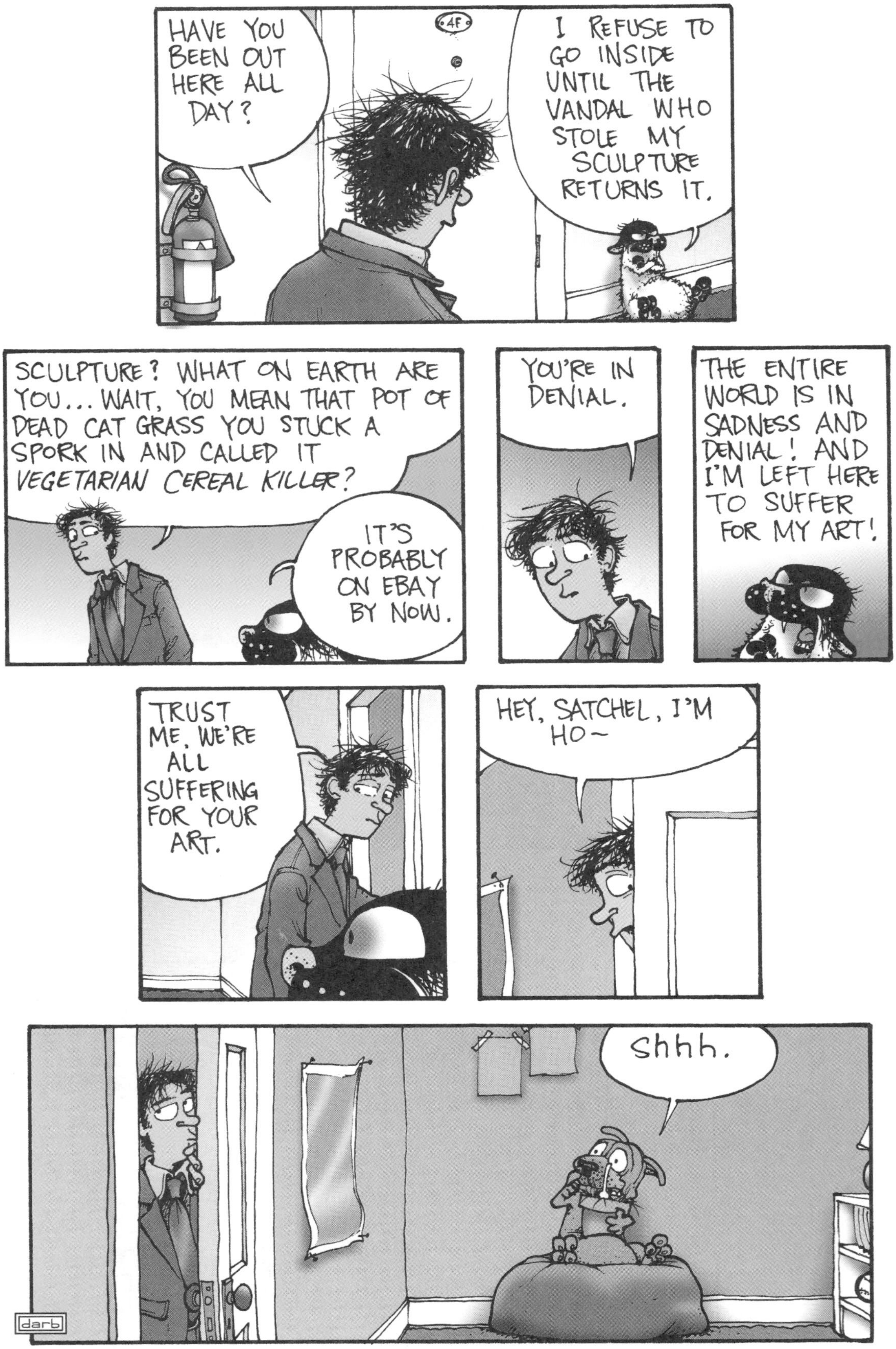
HAVE YOU BEEN OUT HERE ALL DAY?
4F
I REFUSE TO GO INSIDE UNTIL THE VANDAL WHO STOLE MY SCULPTURE RETURNS IT.
SCULPTURE? WHAT ON EARTH ARE YOU... WAIT, YOU MEAN THAT POT OF DEAD CAT GRASS YOU STUCK A SPORK IN AND CALLED IT *VEGETARIAN CEREAL KILLER?*
IT'S PROBABLY ON EBAY BY NOW.
YOU'RE IN DENIAL.
THE ENTIRE WORLD IS IN SADNESS AND DENIAL! AND I'M LEFT HERE TO SUFFER FOR MY ART!
TRUST ME, WE'RE ALL SUFFERING FOR YOUR ART.
HEY, SATCHEL, I'M HO~
shhh.
darb

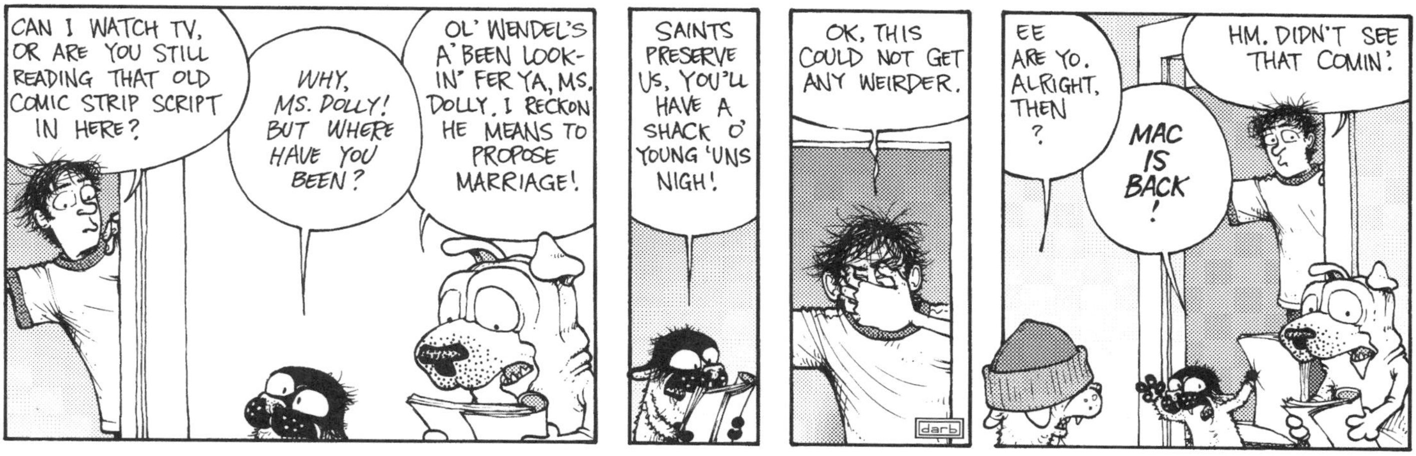
CAN I WATCH TV, OR ARE YOU STILL READING THAT OLD COMIC STRIP SCRIPT IN HERE?
WHY, MS. DOLLY! BUT WHERE HAVE YOU BEEN?
OL' WENDEL'S A'BEEN LOOK-IN' FER YA, MS. DOLLY. I RECKON HE MEANS TO PROPOSE MARRIAGE!
SAINTS PRESERVE US, YOU'LL HAVE A SHACK O' YOUNG 'UNS NIGH!
OK, THIS COULD NOT GET ANY WEIRDER.
darb
EE ARE YO. ALRIGHT, THEN?
MAC IS BACK!
HM. DIDN'T SEE THAT COMIN'.

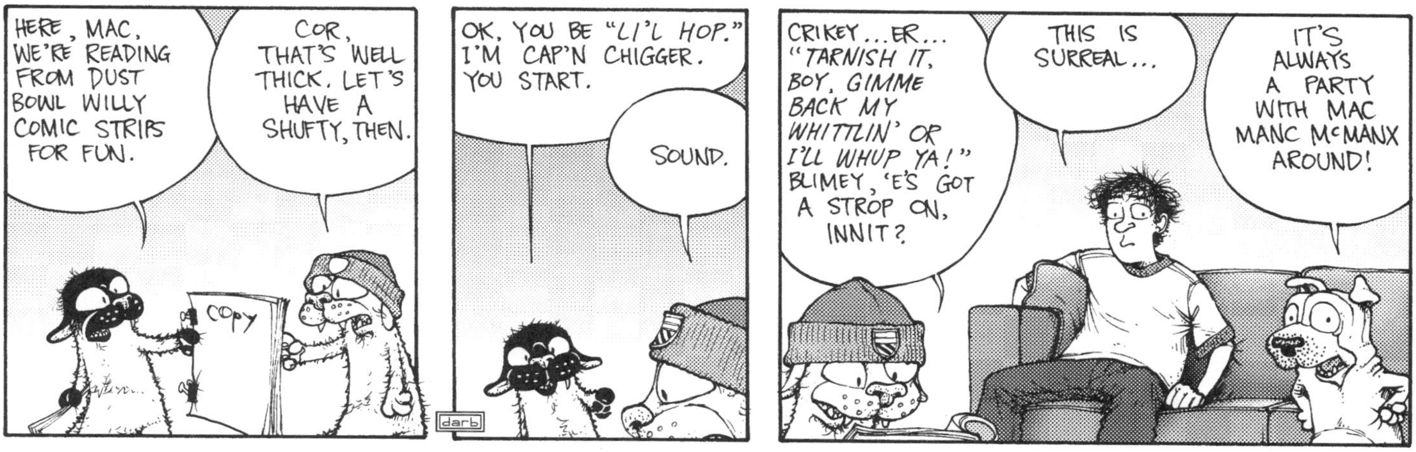
HERE, MAC, WE'RE READING FROM DUST BOWL WILLY COMIC STRIPS FOR FUN.
COR, THAT'S WELL THICK. LET'S HAVE A SHUFTY, THEN.
COPY
darb
OK, YOU BE "LI'L HOP." I'M CAP'N CHIGGER. YOU START.
SOUND.
CRIKEY...ER... "TARNISH IT, BOY, GIMME BACK MY WHITTLIN' OR I'LL WHUP YA!" BLIMEY, 'E'S GOT A STROP ON, INNIT?
THIS IS SURREAL...
IT'S ALWAYS A PARTY WITH MAC MANC McMANX AROUND!

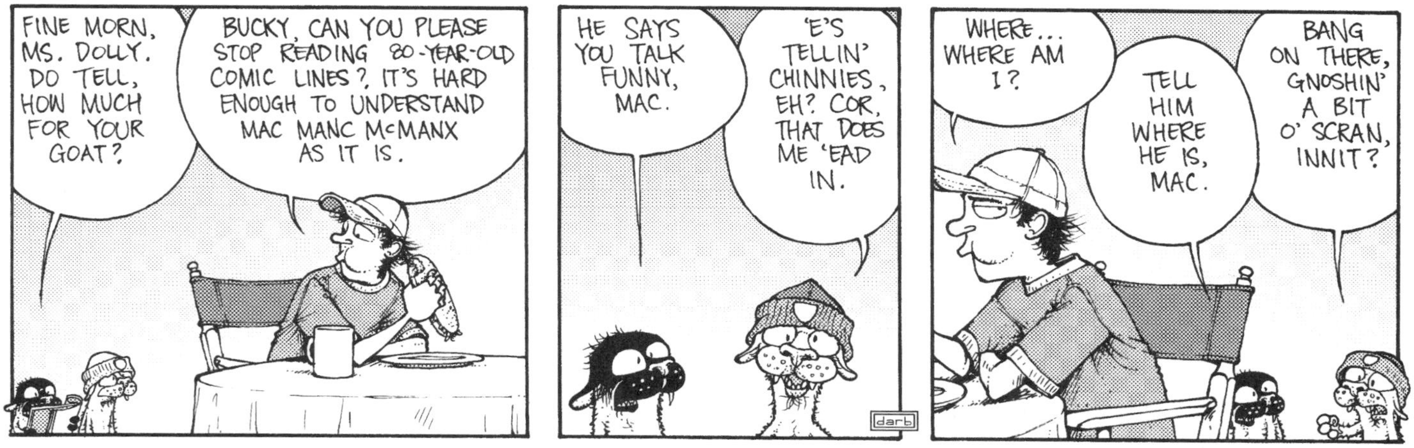
FINE MORN, MS. DOLLY. DO TELL, HOW MUCH FOR YOUR GOAT?
BUCKY, CAN YOU PLEASE STOP READING 80-YEAR-OLD COMIC LINES? IT'S HARD ENOUGH TO UNDERSTAND MAC MANC McMANX AS IT IS.
HE SAYS YOU TALK FUNNY, MAC.
'E'S TELLIN' CHINNIES, EH? COR, THAT DOES ME 'EAD IN.
darb
WHERE... WHERE AM I?
TELL HIM WHERE HE IS, MAC.
BANG ON THERE, GNOSHIN' A BIT O' SCRAN, INNIT?

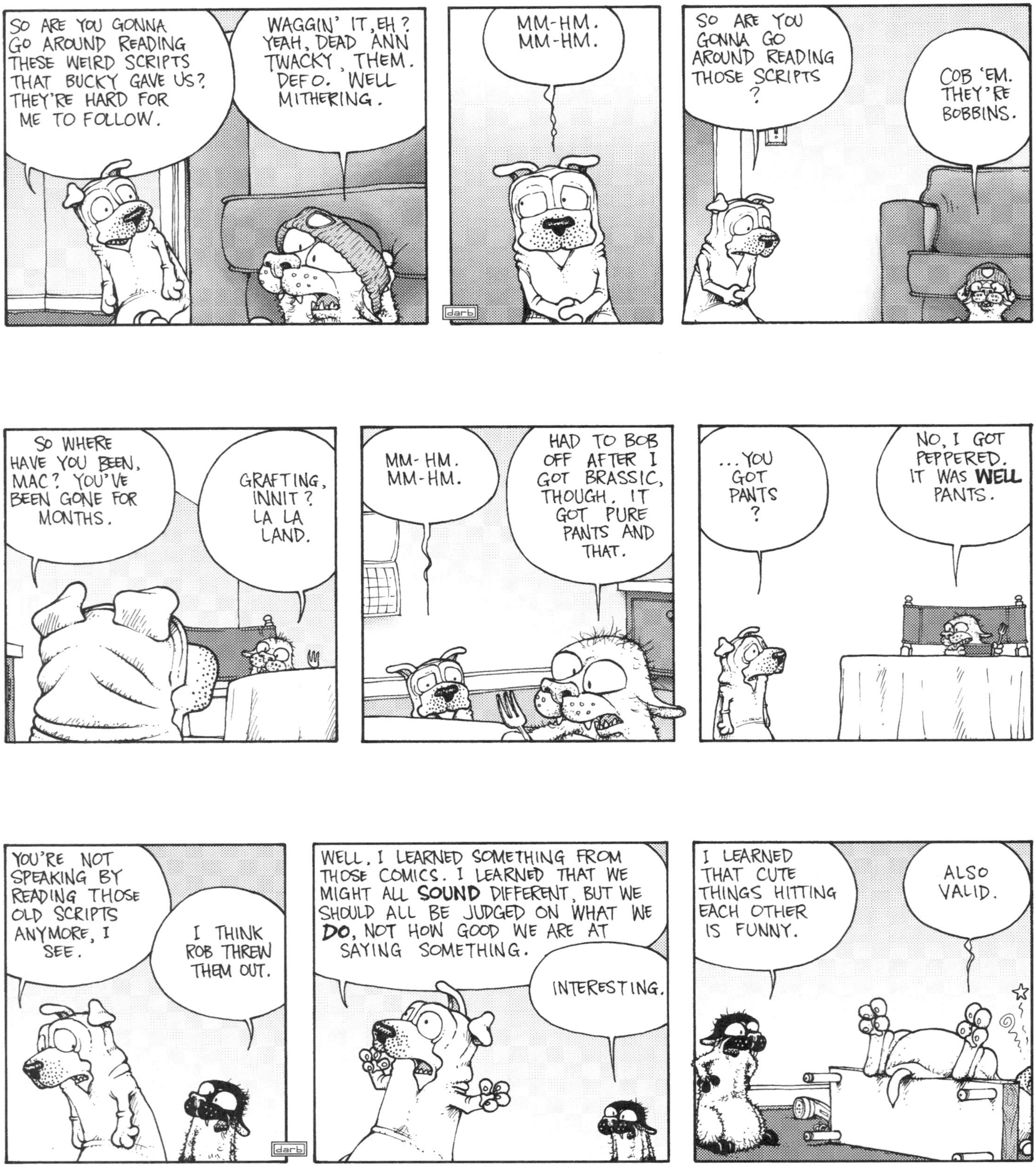
SO ARE YOU GONNA GO AROUND READING THESE WEIRD SCRIPTS THAT BUCKY GAVE US? THEY'RE HARD FOR ME TO FOLLOW.
WAGGIN' IT, EH? YEAH, DEAD ANN TWACKY, THEM. DEFO. WELL MITHERING.
MM-HM. MM-HM.
darb
SO ARE YOU GONNA GO AROUND READING THOSE SCRIPTS ?
COB 'EM. THEY'RE BOBBINS.
SO WHERE HAVE YOU BEEN, MAC? YOU'VE BEEN GONE FOR MONTHS.
GRAFTING, INNIT? LA LA LAND.
MM-HM. MM-HM.
HAD TO BOB OFF AFTER I GOT BRASSIC, THOUGH. IT GOT PURE PANTS AND THAT.
...YOU GOT PANTS ?
NO, I GOT PEPPERED. IT WAS **WELL** PANTS.
YOU'RE NOT SPEAKING BY READING THOSE OLD SCRIPTS ANYMORE, I SEE.
I THINK ROB THREW THEM OUT.
darb
WELL, I LEARNED SOMETHING FROM THOSE COMICS. I LEARNED THAT WE MIGHT ALL **SOUND** DIFFERENT, BUT WE SHOULD ALL BE JUDGED ON WHAT WE ***DO***, NOT HOW GOOD WE ARE AT SAYING SOMETHING.
INTERESTING.
I LEARNED THAT CUTE THINGS HITTING EACH OTHER IS FUNNY.
ALSO VALID.

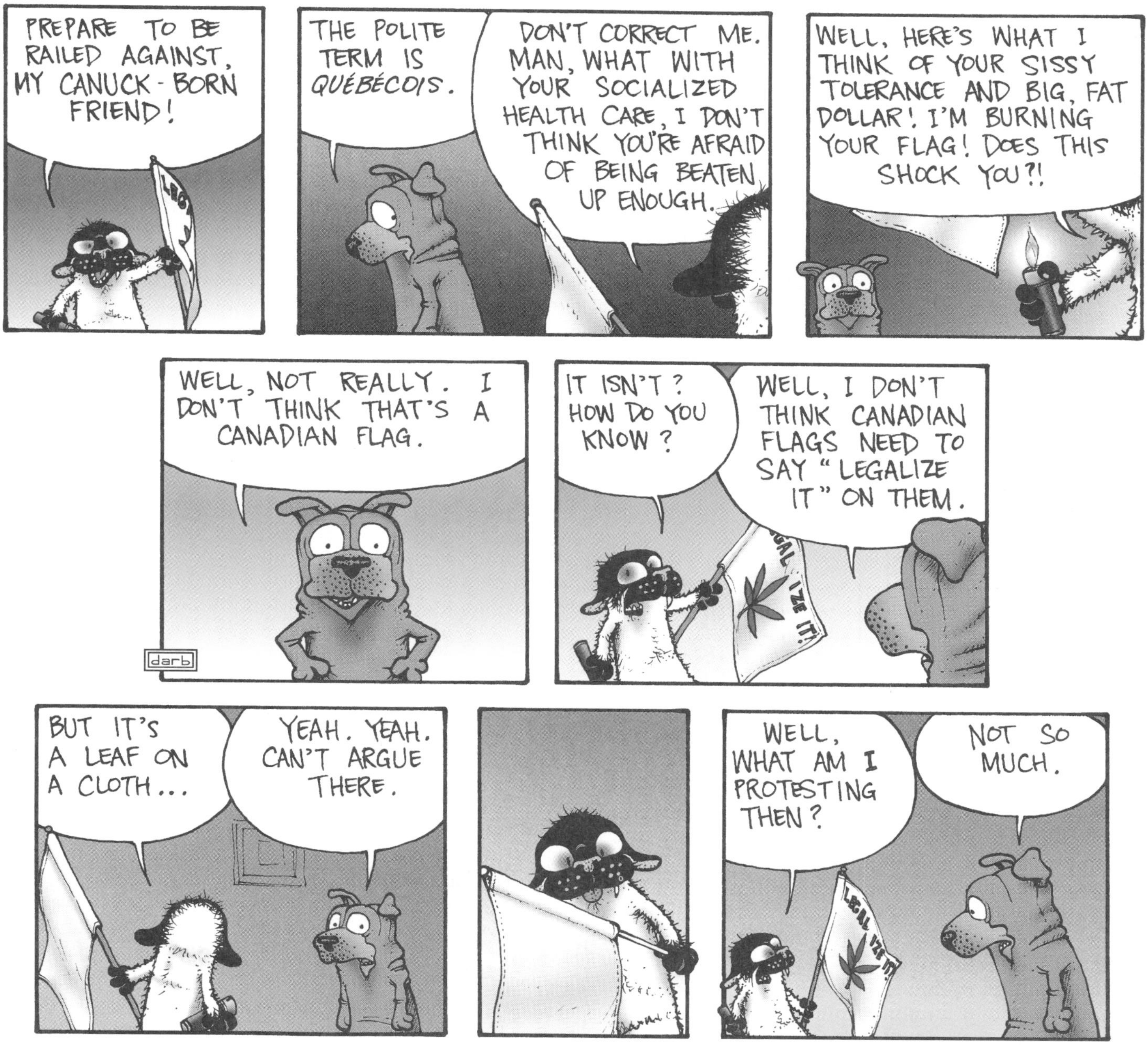
PREPARE TO BE RAILED AGAINST, MY CANUCK-BORN FRIEND!
THE POLITE TERM IS *QUÉBÉCOIS*.
DON'T CORRECT ME. MAN, WHAT WITH YOUR SOCIALIZED HEALTH CARE, I DON'T THINK YOU'RE AFRAID OF BEING BEATEN UP ENOUGH.
WELL, HERE'S WHAT I THINK OF YOUR SISSY TOLERANCE AND BIG, FAT DOLLAR! I'M BURNING YOUR FLAG! DOES THIS SHOCK YOU?!
WELL, NOT REALLY. I DON'T THINK THAT'S A CANADIAN FLAG.
darb
IT ISN'T? HOW DO YOU KNOW?
WELL, I DON'T THINK CANADIAN FLAGS NEED TO SAY "LEGALIZE IT" ON THEM.
LEGAL IZE IT!
BUT IT'S A LEAF ON A CLOTH...
YEAH. YEAH. CAN'T ARGUE THERE.
WELL, WHAT AM **I** PROTESTING THEN?
NOT SO MUCH.

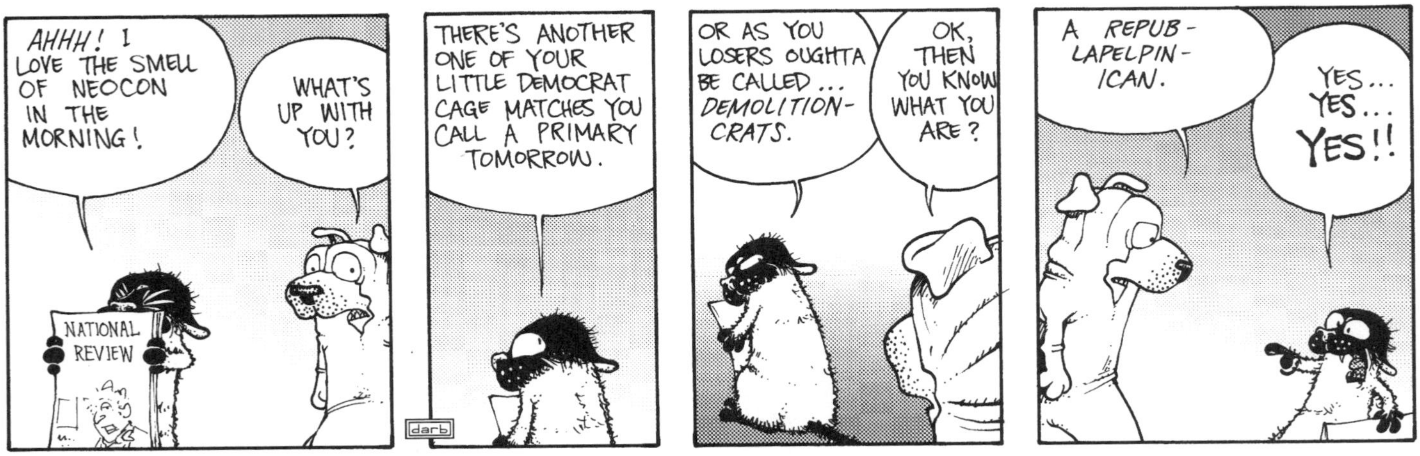
AHHH! I LOVE THE SMELL OF NEOCON IN THE MORNING!
NATIONAL REVIEW
WHAT'S UP WITH YOU?
THERE'S ANOTHER ONE OF YOUR LITTLE DEMOCRAT CAGE MATCHES YOU CALL A PRIMARY TOMORROW.
darb
OR AS YOU LOSERS OUGHTA BE CALLED... *DEMOLITION-CRATS.*
OK, THEN YOU KNOW WHAT YOU ARE?
A *REPUB-LAPELPIN-ICAN.*
YES... YES... **YES!!**

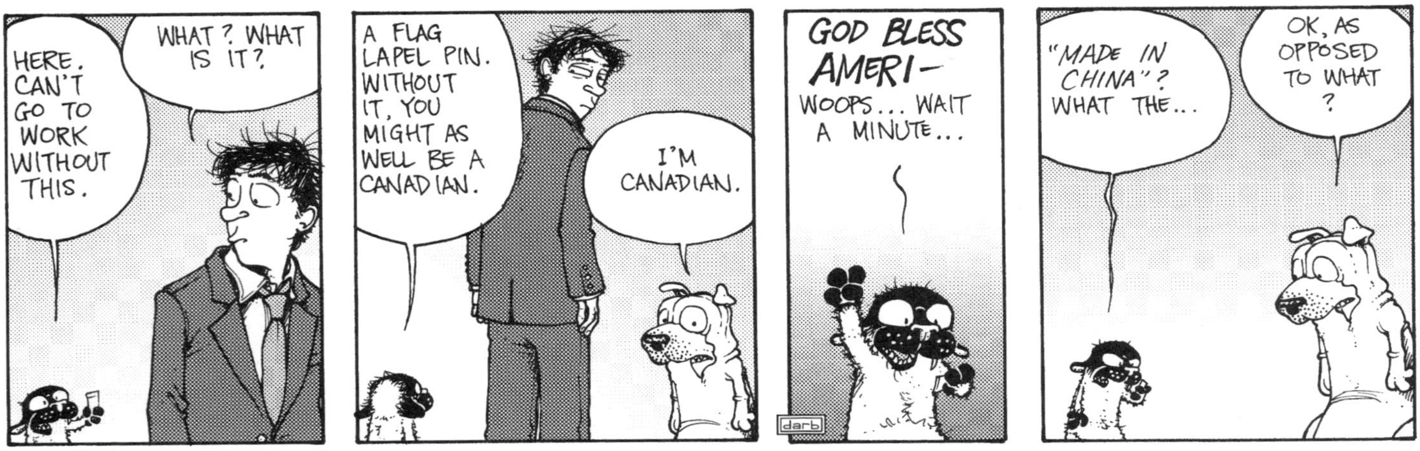
HERE. CAN'T GO TO WORK WITHOUT THIS.
WHAT? WHAT IS IT?
A FLAG LAPEL PIN. WITHOUT IT, YOU MIGHT AS WELL BE A CANADIAN.
I'M CANADIAN.
GOD BLESS AMERI— WOOPS... WAIT A MINUTE...
darb
"*MADE IN CHINA*"? WHAT THE...
OK, AS OPPOSED TO WHAT?

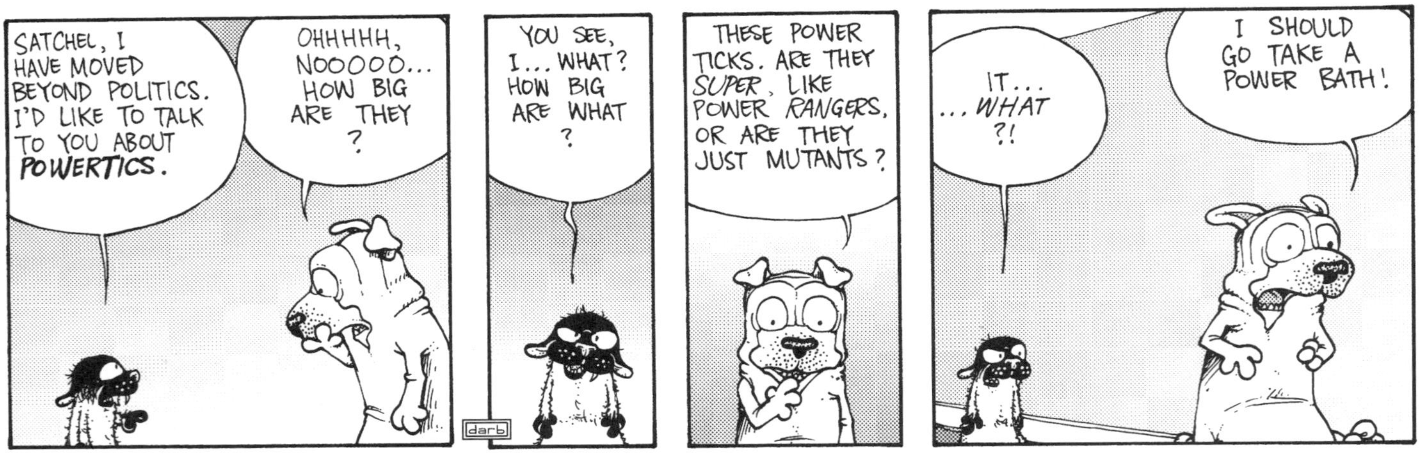
SATCHEL, I HAVE MOVED BEYOND POLITICS. I'D LIKE TO TALK TO YOU ABOUT **POWERTICS**.
OHHHHH, NOOOOO... HOW BIG ARE THEY?
darb
YOU SEE, I... WHAT? HOW BIG ARE WHAT?
THESE POWER TICKS. ARE THEY *SUPER*, LIKE POWER *RANGERS*, OR ARE THEY JUST MUTANTS?
IT... ...*WHAT*?!
I SHOULD GO TAKE A POWER BATH!

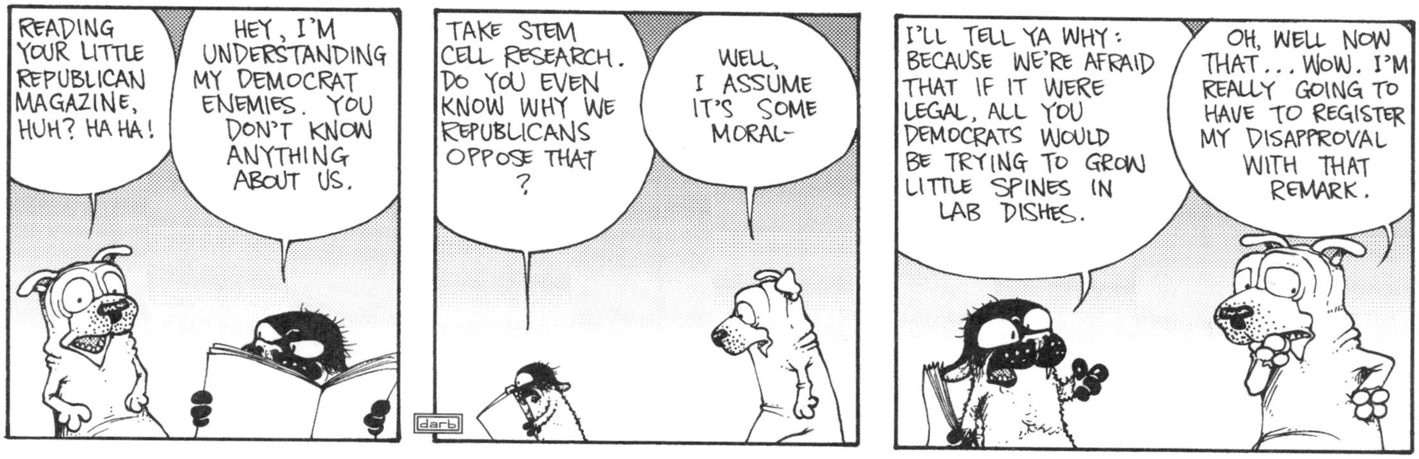
READING YOUR LITTLE REPUBLICAN MAGAZINE, HUH? HA HA!
HEY, I'M UNDERSTANDING MY DEMOCRAT ENEMIES. YOU DON'T KNOW ANYTHING ABOUT US.
TAKE STEM CELL RESEARCH. DO YOU EVEN KNOW WHY WE REPUBLICANS OPPOSE THAT?
WELL, I ASSUME IT'S SOME MORAL-
darb
I'LL TELL YA WHY: BECAUSE WE'RE AFRAID THAT IF IT WERE LEGAL, ALL YOU DEMOCRATS WOULD BE TRYING TO GROW LITTLE SPINES IN LAB DISHES.
OH, WELL NOW THAT... WOW. I'M REALLY GOING TO HAVE TO REGISTER MY DISAPPROVAL WITH THAT REMARK.

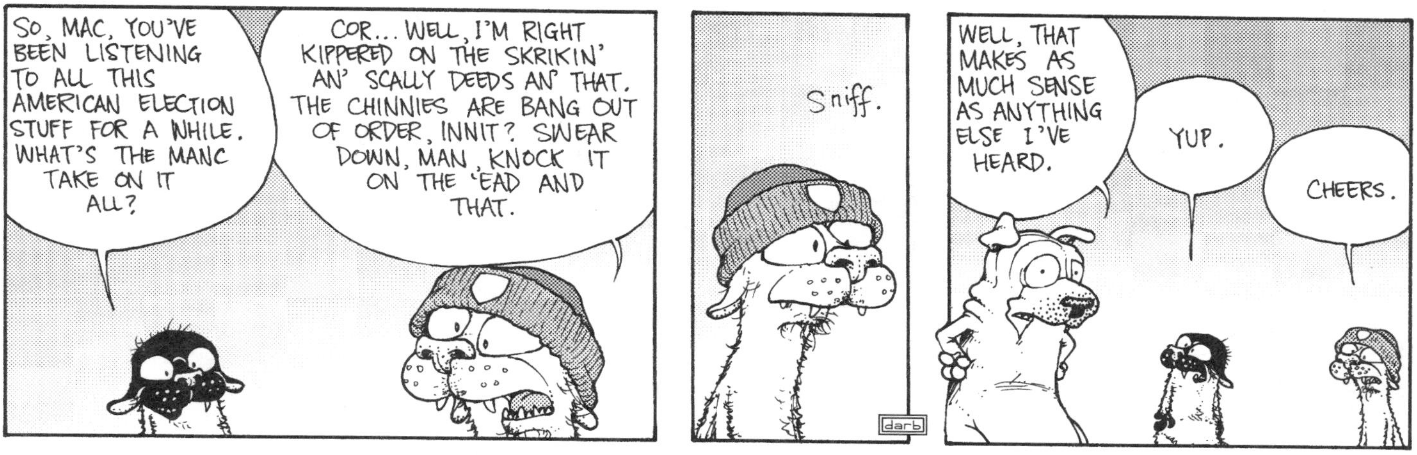
SO, MAC, YOU'VE BEEN LISTENING TO ALL THIS AMERICAN ELECTION STUFF FOR A WHILE. WHAT'S THE MANC TAKE ON IT ALL?
COR... WELL, I'M RIGHT KIPPERED ON THE SKRIKIN' AN' SCALLY DEEDS AN' THAT. THE CHINNIES ARE BANG OUT OF ORDER, INNIT? SWEAR DOWN, MAN, KNOCK IT ON THE 'EAD AND THAT.
Sniff.
darb
WELL, THAT MAKES AS MUCH SENSE AS ANYTHING ELSE I'VE HEARD.
YUP.
CHEERS.

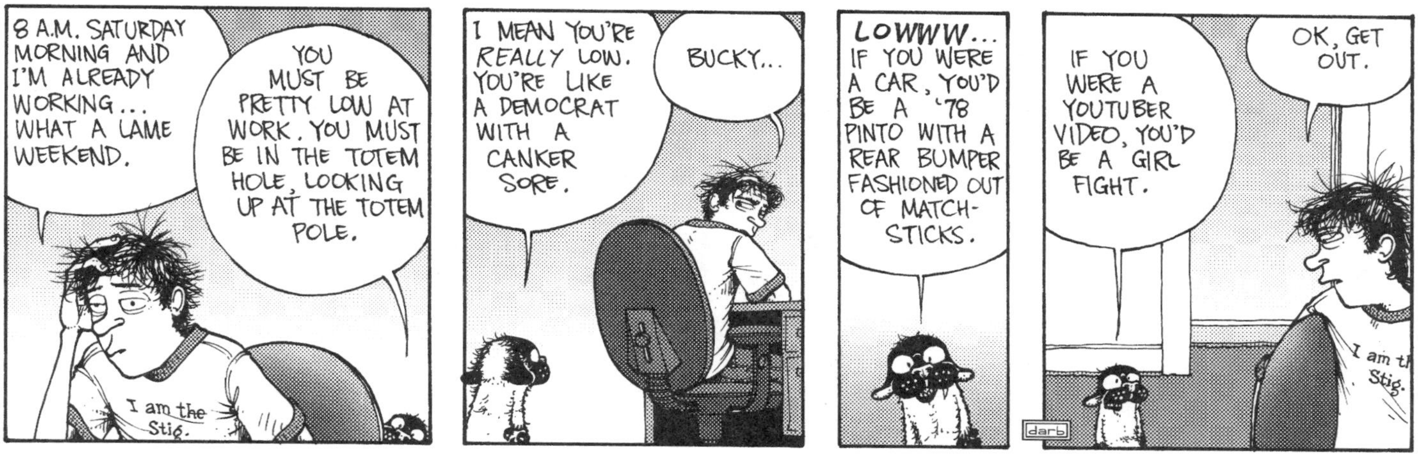
8 A.M. SATURDAY MORNING AND I'M ALREADY WORKING... WHAT A LAME WEEKEND.
YOU MUST BE PRETTY LOW AT WORK. YOU MUST BE IN THE TOTEM HOLE, LOOKING UP AT THE TOTEM POLE.
I am the Stig.
I MEAN YOU'RE REALLY LOW. YOU'RE LIKE A DEMOCRAT WITH A CANKER SORE.
BUCKY...
LOWWW... IF YOU WERE A CAR, YOU'D BE A '78 PINTO WITH A REAR BUMPER FASHIONED OUT OF MATCH-STICKS.
darb
IF YOU WERE A YOUTUBER VIDEO, YOU'D BE A GIRL FIGHT.
OK, GET OUT.

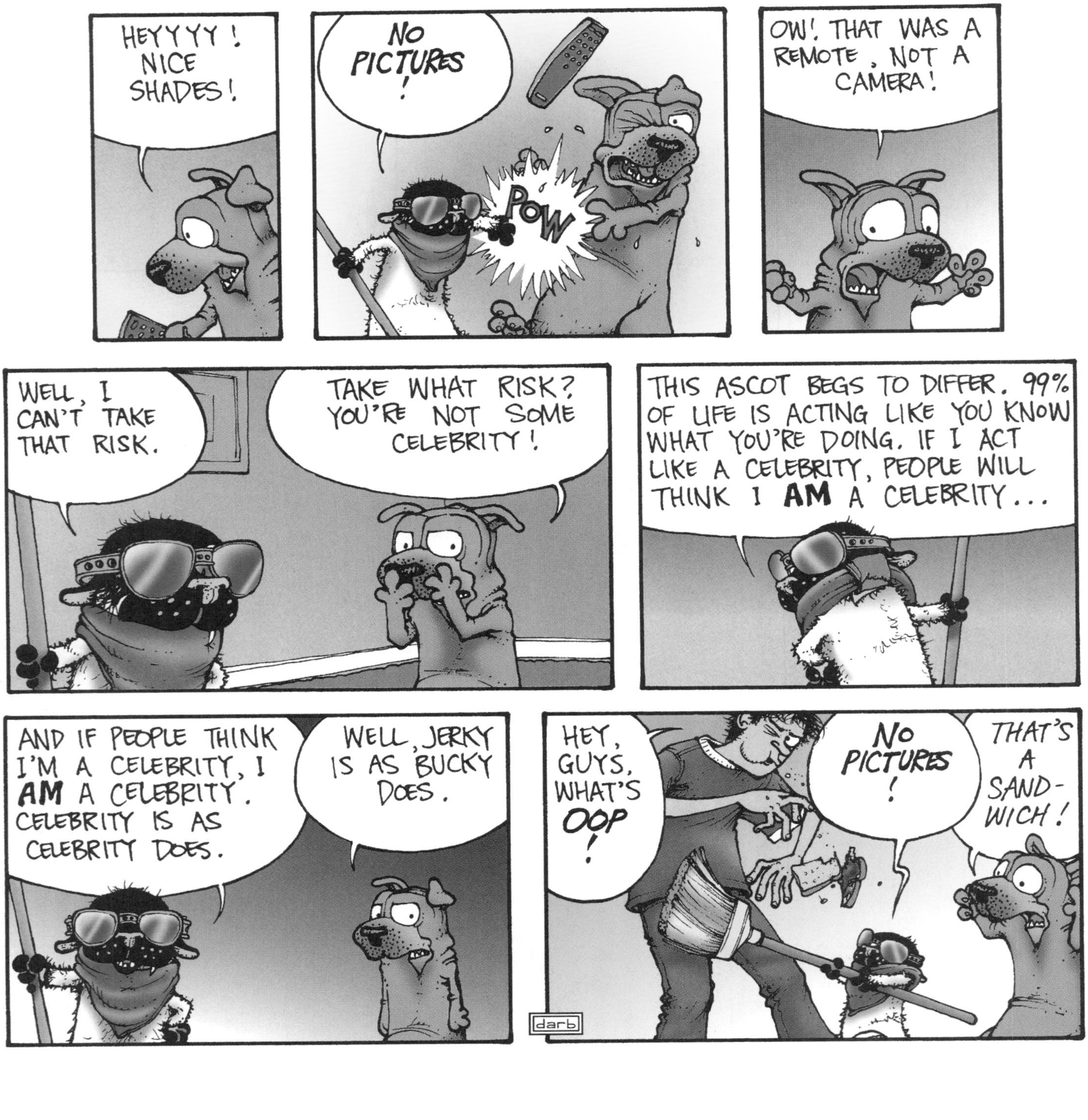
HEYYYY! NICE SHADES!
NO PICTURES!
POW
OW! THAT WAS A REMOTE, NOT A CAMERA!
WELL, I CAN'T TAKE THAT RISK.
TAKE WHAT RISK? YOU'RE NOT SOME CELEBRITY!
THIS ASCOT BEGS TO DIFFER. 99% OF LIFE IS ACTING LIKE YOU KNOW WHAT YOU'RE DOING. IF I ACT LIKE A CELEBRITY, PEOPLE WILL THINK I **AM** A CELEBRITY...
AND IF PEOPLE THINK I'M A CELEBRITY, I **AM** A CELEBRITY. CELEBRITY IS AS CELEBRITY DOES.
WELL, JERKY IS AS BUCKY DOES.
darb
HEY, GUYS, WHAT'S OOP!
NO PICTURES!
THAT'S A SAND-WICH!

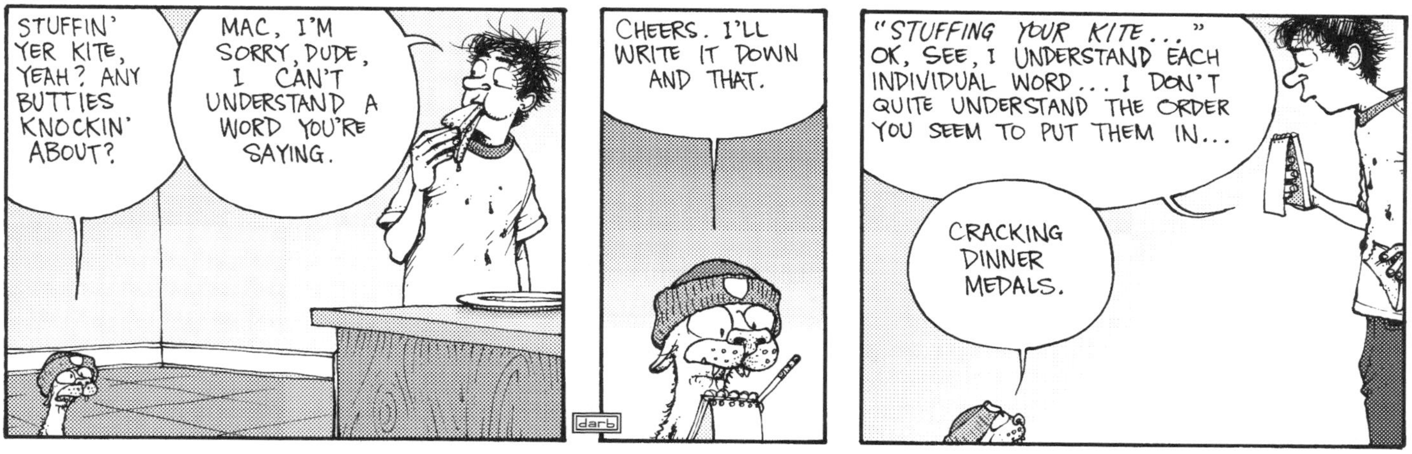
STUFFIN' YER KITE, YEAH? ANY BUTTIES KNOCKIN' ABOUT?
MAC, I'M SORRY, DUDE, I CAN'T UNDERSTAND A WORD YOU'RE SAYING.
CHEERS. I'LL WRITE IT DOWN AND THAT.
darb
"STUFFING YOUR KITE..." OK, SEE, I UNDERSTAND EACH INDIVIDUAL WORD... I DON'T QUITE UNDERSTAND THE ORDER YOU SEEM TO PUT THEM IN...
CRACKING DINNER MEDALS.

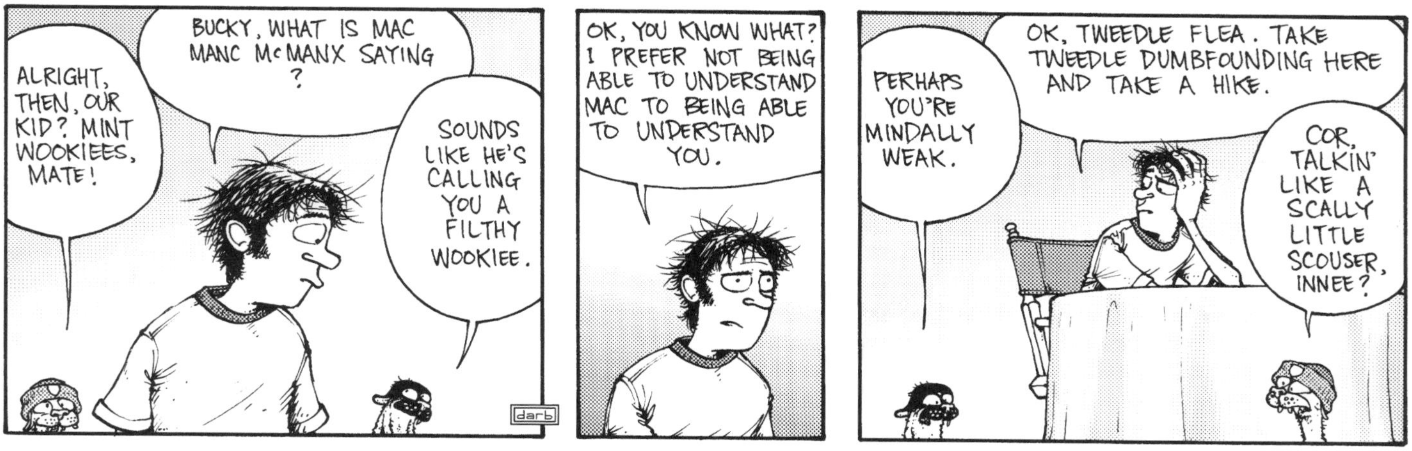
ALRIGHT, THEN, OUR KID? MINT WOOKIEES, MATE!
BUCKY, WHAT IS MAC MANC McMANX SAYING?
SOUNDS LIKE HE'S CALLING YOU A FILTHY WOOKIEE.
darb
OK, YOU KNOW WHAT? I PREFER NOT BEING ABLE TO UNDERSTAND MAC TO BEING ABLE TO UNDERSTAND YOU.
PERHAPS YOU'RE MINDALLY WEAK.
OK, TWEEDLE FLEA. TAKE TWEEDLE DUMBFOUNDING HERE AND TAKE A HIKE.
COR, TALKIN' LIKE A SCALLY LITTLE SCOUSER, INNEE?

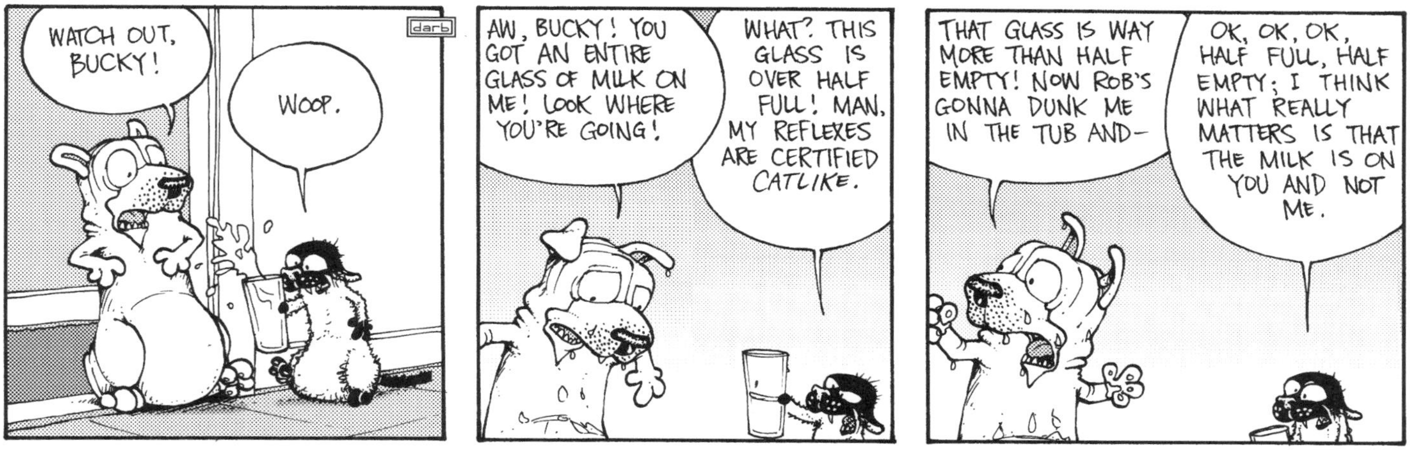
darb
WATCH OUT, BUCKY!
WOOP.
AW, BUCKY! YOU GOT AN ENTIRE GLASS OF MILK ON ME! LOOK WHERE YOU'RE GOING!
WHAT? THIS GLASS IS OVER HALF FULL! MAN, MY REFLEXES ARE CERTIFIED CATLIKE.
THAT GLASS IS WAY MORE THAN HALF EMPTY! NOW ROB'S GONNA DUNK ME IN THE TUB AND—
OK, OK, OK, HALF FULL, HALF EMPTY; I THINK WHAT REALLY MATTERS IS THAT THE MILK IS ON YOU AND NOT ME.

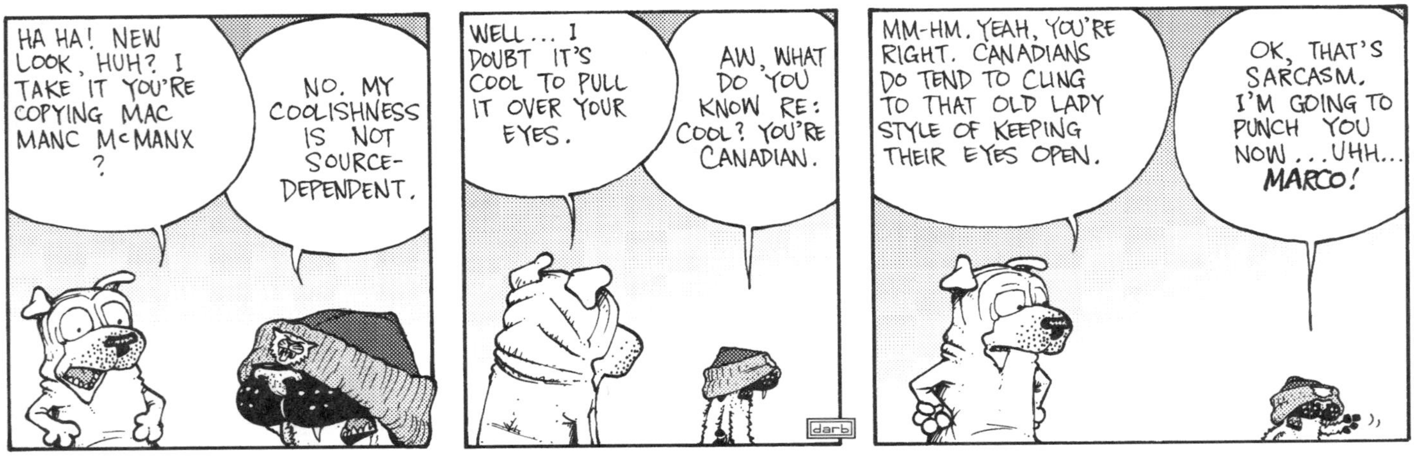
HA HA! NEW LOOK, HUH? I TAKE IT YOU'RE COPYING MAC MANC McMANX ?
NO. MY COOLISHNESS IS NOT SOURCE-DEPENDENT.
WELL... I DOUBT IT'S COOL TO PULL IT OVER YOUR EYES.
AW, WHAT DO YOU KNOW RE: COOL? YOU'RE CANADIAN.
MM-HM. YEAH, YOU'RE RIGHT. CANADIANS DO TEND TO CLING TO THAT OLD LADY STYLE OF KEEPING THEIR EYES OPEN.
OK, THAT'S SARCASM. I'M GOING TO PUNCH YOU NOW... UHH... MARCO!
darb

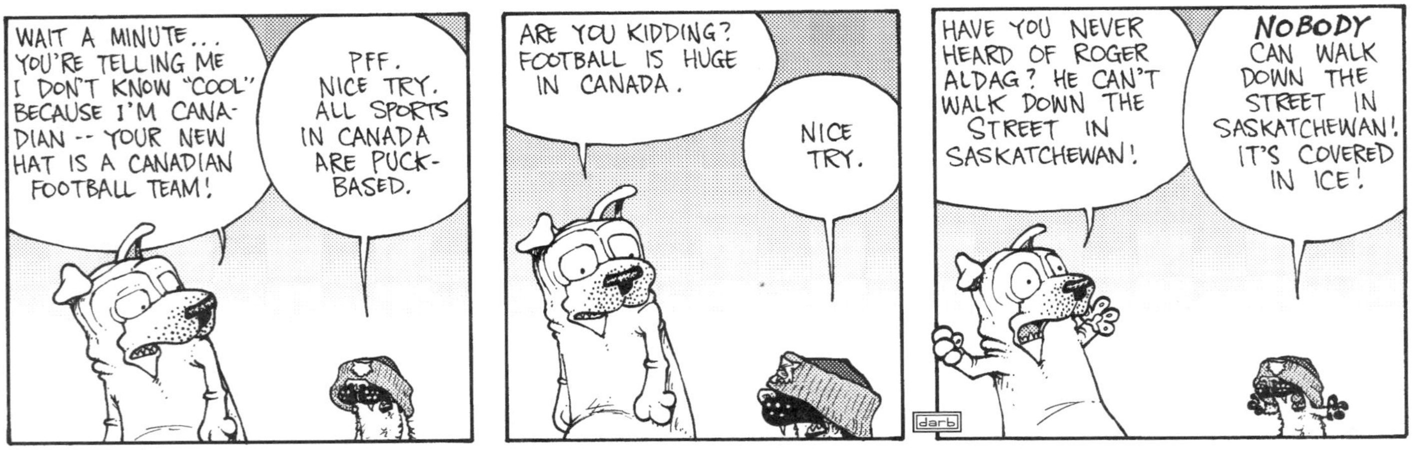
WAIT A MINUTE... YOU'RE TELLING ME I DON'T KNOW "COOL" BECAUSE I'M CANADIAN -- YOUR NEW HAT IS A CANADIAN FOOTBALL TEAM!
PFF. NICE TRY. ALL SPORTS IN CANADA ARE PUCK-BASED.
ARE YOU KIDDING? FOOTBALL IS HUGE IN CANADA.
NICE TRY.
HAVE YOU NEVER HEARD OF ROGER ALDAG? HE CAN'T WALK DOWN THE STREET IN SASKATCHEWAN!
NOBODY CAN WALK DOWN THE STREET IN SASKATCHEWAN! IT'S COVERED IN ICE!
darb

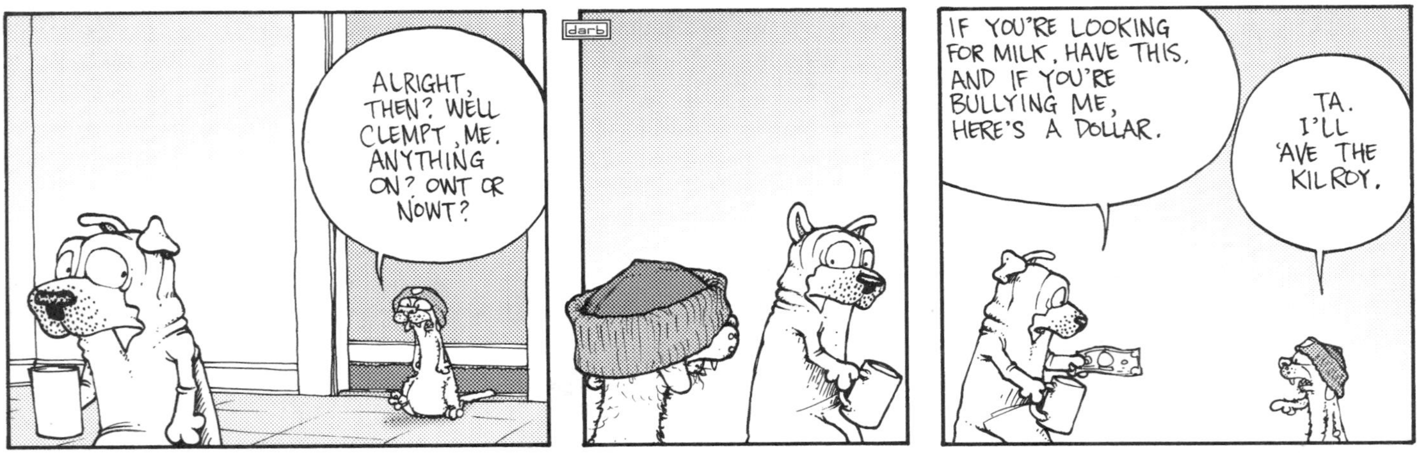
ALRIGHT, THEN? WELL CLEMPT, ME. ANYTHING ON? OWT OR NOWT?
darb
IF YOU'RE LOOKING FOR MILK, HAVE THIS. AND IF YOU'RE BULLYING ME, HERE'S A DOLLAR.
TA. I'LL 'AVE THE KILROY.

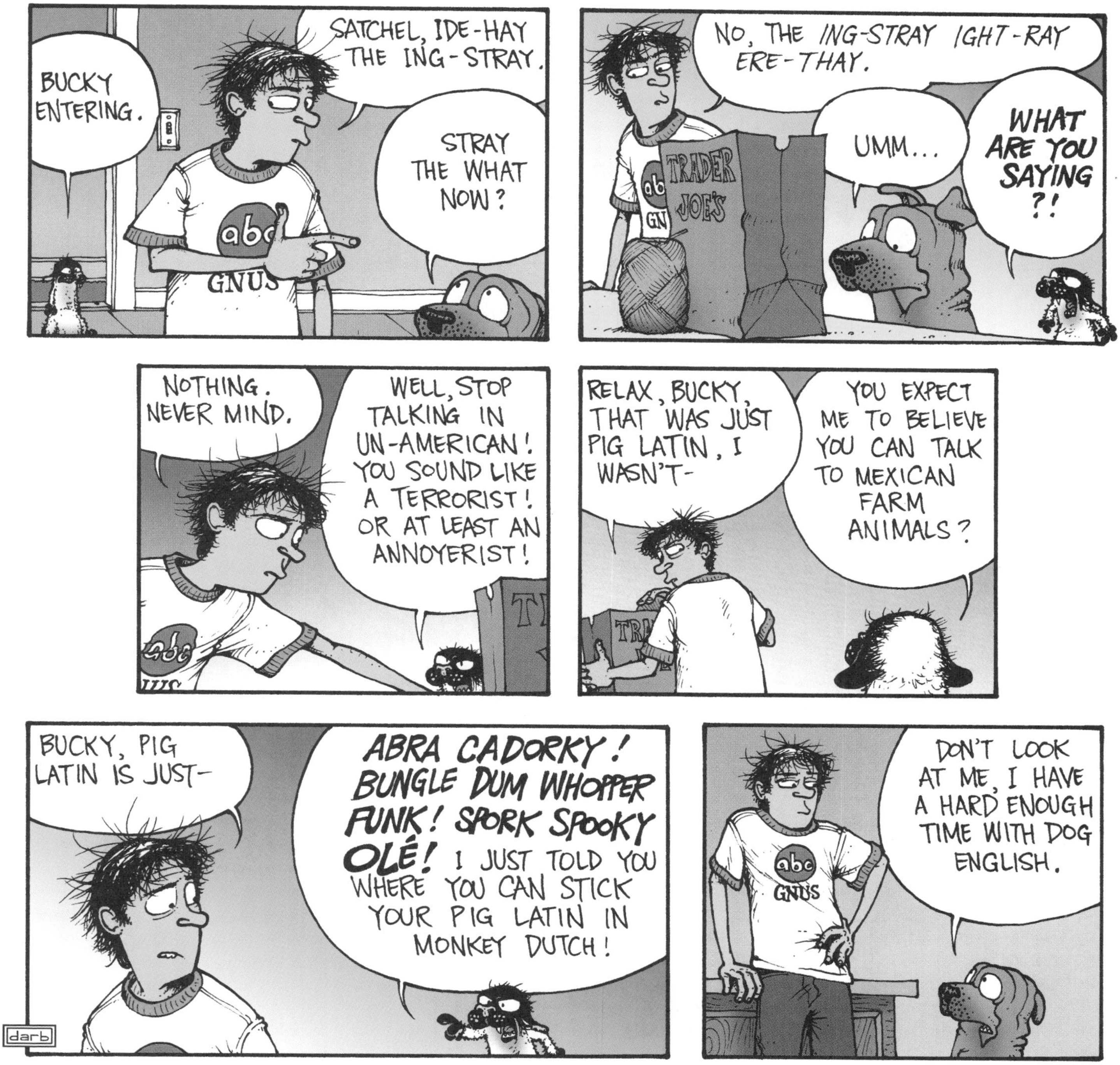
BUCKY ENTERING.
SATCHEL, IDE-HAY THE ING-STRAY.
STRAY THE WHAT NOW?
abc
GNUS
NO, THE ING-STRAY IGHT-RAY ERE-THAY.
UMM...
WHAT ARE YOU SAYING?!
TRADER JOE'S
NOTHING. NEVER MIND.
WELL, STOP TALKING IN UN-AMERICAN! YOU SOUND LIKE A TERRORIST! OR AT LEAST AN ANNOYERIST!
RELAX, BUCKY, THAT WAS JUST PIG LATIN, I WASN'T-
YOU EXPECT ME TO BELIEVE YOU CAN TALK TO MEXICAN FARM ANIMALS?
BUCKY, PIG LATIN IS JUST-
ABRA CADORKY! BUNGLE DUM WHOPPER FUNK! SPORK SPOOKY OLÉ! I JUST TOLD YOU WHERE YOU CAN STICK YOUR PIG LATIN IN MONKEY DUTCH!
darb
DON'T LOOK AT ME, I HAVE A HARD ENOUGH TIME WITH DOG ENGLISH.

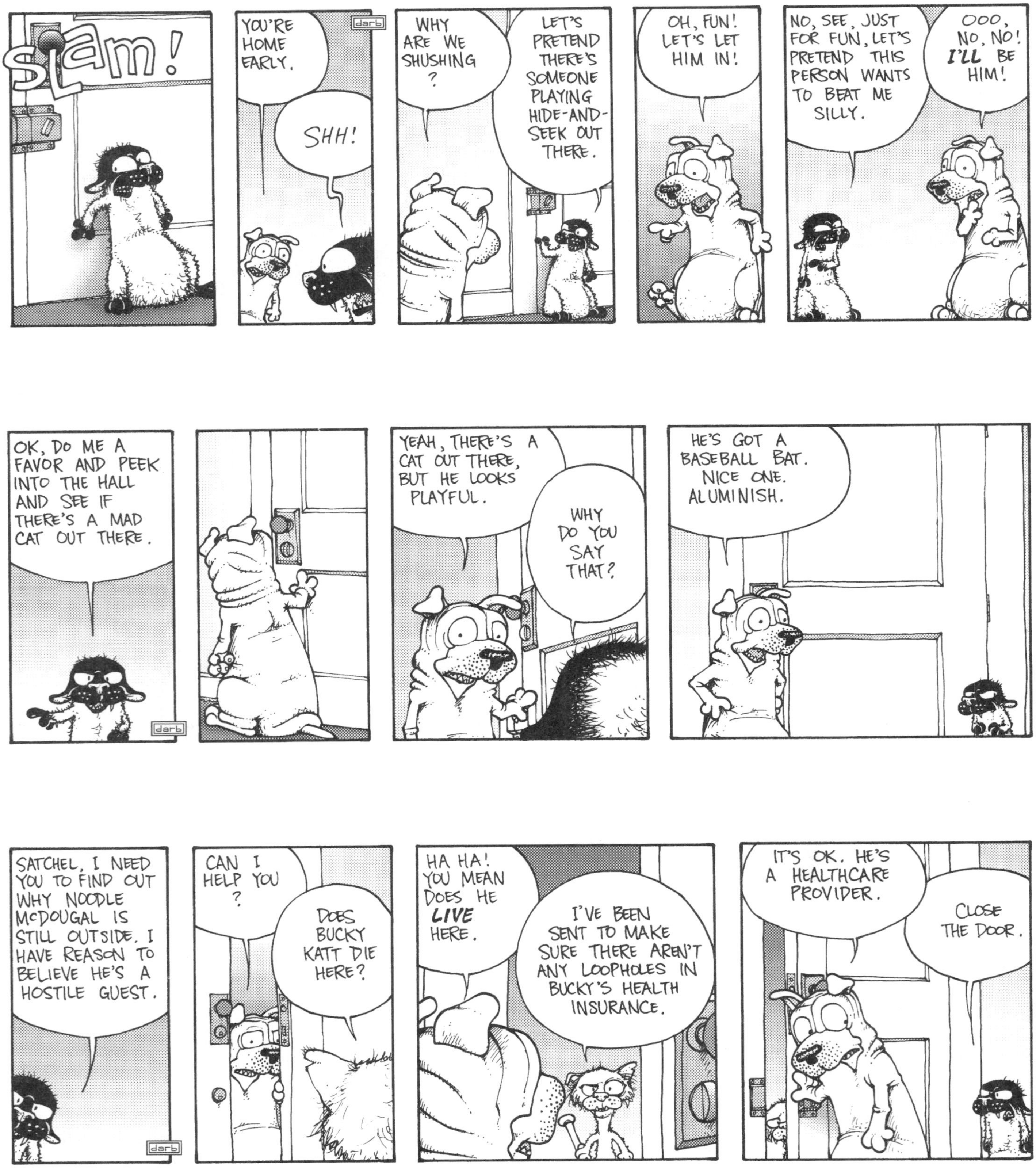
SLAM!
darb
YOU'RE HOME EARLY.
SHH!
WHY ARE WE SHUSHING?
LET'S PRETEND THERE'S SOMEONE PLAYING HIDE-AND-SEEK OUT THERE.
OH, FUN! LET'S LET HIM IN!
NO, SEE, JUST FOR FUN, LET'S PRETEND THIS PERSON WANTS TO BEAT ME SILLY.
OOO, NO, NO! I'LL BE HIM!
OK, DO ME A FAVOR AND PEEK INTO THE HALL AND SEE IF THERE'S A MAD CAT OUT THERE.
darb
YEAH, THERE'S A CAT OUT THERE, BUT HE LOOKS PLAYFUL.
WHY DO YOU SAY THAT?
HE'S GOT A BASEBALL BAT. NICE ONE. ALUMINISH.
SATCHEL, I NEED YOU TO FIND OUT WHY NOODLE McDOUGAL IS STILL OUTSIDE. I HAVE REASON TO BELIEVE HE'S A HOSTILE GUEST.
darb
CAN I HELP YOU?
DOES BUCKY KATT DIE HERE?
HA HA! YOU MEAN DOES HE LIVE HERE.
I'VE BEEN SENT TO MAKE SURE THERE AREN'T ANY LOOPHOLES IN BUCKY'S HEALTH INSURANCE.
IT'S OK. HE'S A HEALTHCARE PROVIDER.
CLOSE THE DOOR.

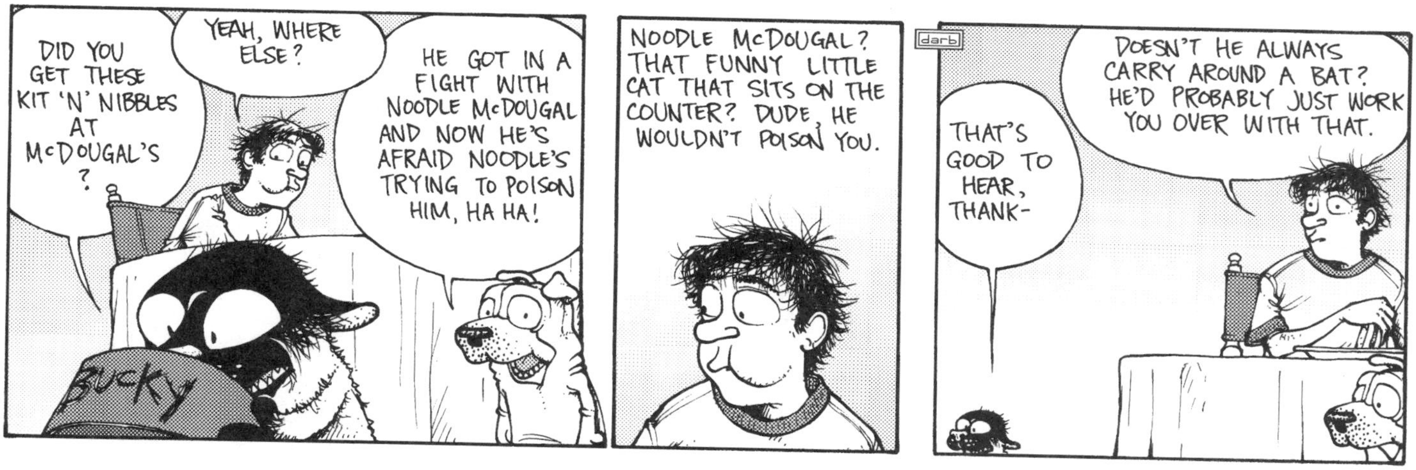
DID YOU GET THESE KIT 'N' NIBBLES AT McDOUGAL'S ?
YEAH, WHERE ELSE ?
HE GOT IN A FIGHT WITH NOODLE McDOUGAL AND NOW HE'S AFRAID NOODLE'S TRYING TO POISON HIM, HA HA!
NOODLE McDOUGAL? THAT FUNNY LITTLE CAT THAT SITS ON THE COUNTER? DUDE, HE WOULDN'T POISON YOU.
THAT'S GOOD TO HEAR, THANK-
DOESN'T HE ALWAYS CARRY AROUND A BAT? HE'D PROBABLY JUST WORK YOU OVER WITH THAT.
darb

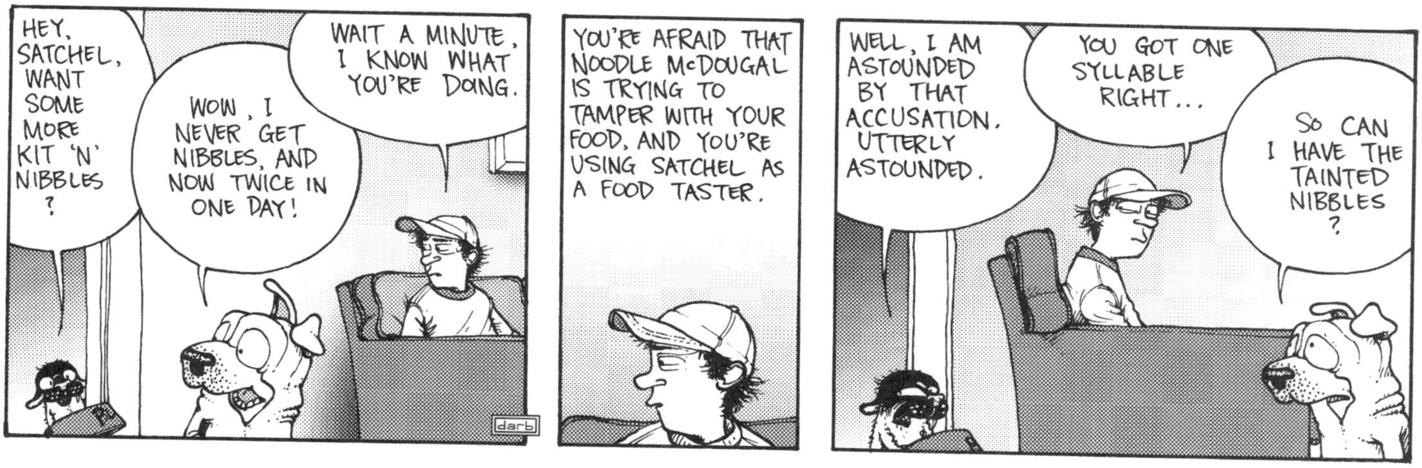
HEY, SATCHEL, WANT SOME MORE KIT 'N' NIBBLES ?
WOW, I NEVER GET NIBBLES, AND NOW TWICE IN ONE DAY!
WAIT A MINUTE, I KNOW WHAT YOU'RE DOING.
darb
YOU'RE AFRAID THAT NOODLE McDOUGAL IS TRYING TO TAMPER WITH YOUR FOOD, AND YOU'RE USING SATCHEL AS A FOOD TASTER.
WELL, I AM ASTOUNDED BY THAT ACCUSATION. UTTERLY ASTOUNDED.
YOU GOT ONE SYLLABLE RIGHT...
SO CAN I HAVE THE TAINTED NIBBLES ?

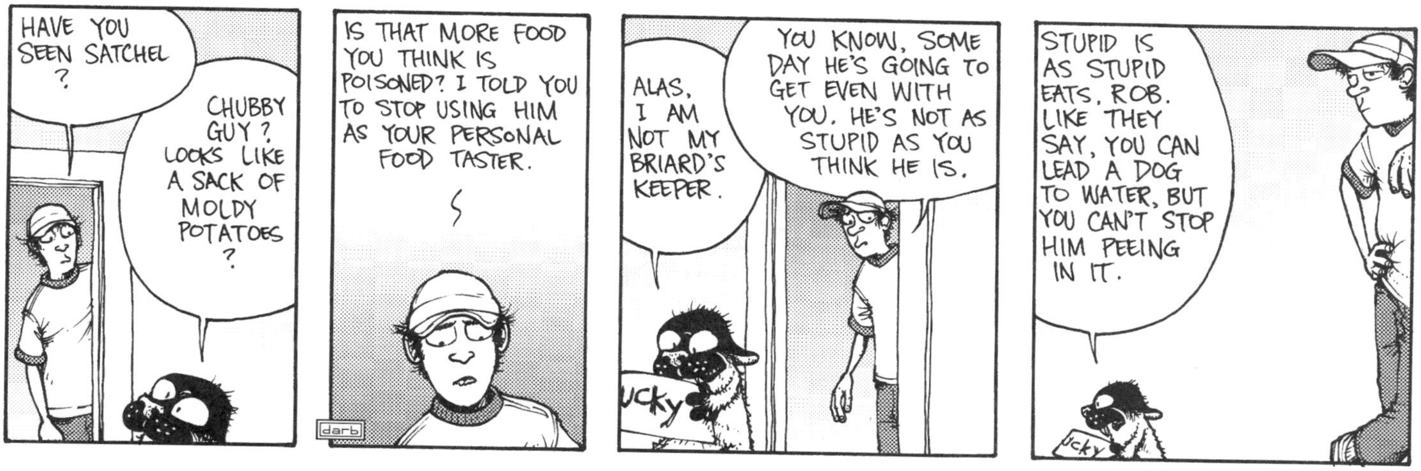
HAVE YOU SEEN SATCHEL ?
CHUBBY GUY? LOOKS LIKE A SACK OF MOLDY POTATOES ?
IS THAT MORE FOOD YOU THINK IS POISONED? I TOLD YOU TO STOP USING HIM AS YOUR PERSONAL FOOD TASTER.
darb
ALAS, I AM NOT MY BRIARD'S KEEPER.
YOU KNOW, SOME DAY HE'S GOING TO GET EVEN WITH YOU. HE'S NOT AS STUPID AS YOU THINK HE IS.
STUPID IS AS STUPID EATS, ROB. LIKE THEY SAY, YOU CAN LEAD A DOG TO WATER, BUT YOU CAN'T STOP HIM PEEING IN IT.

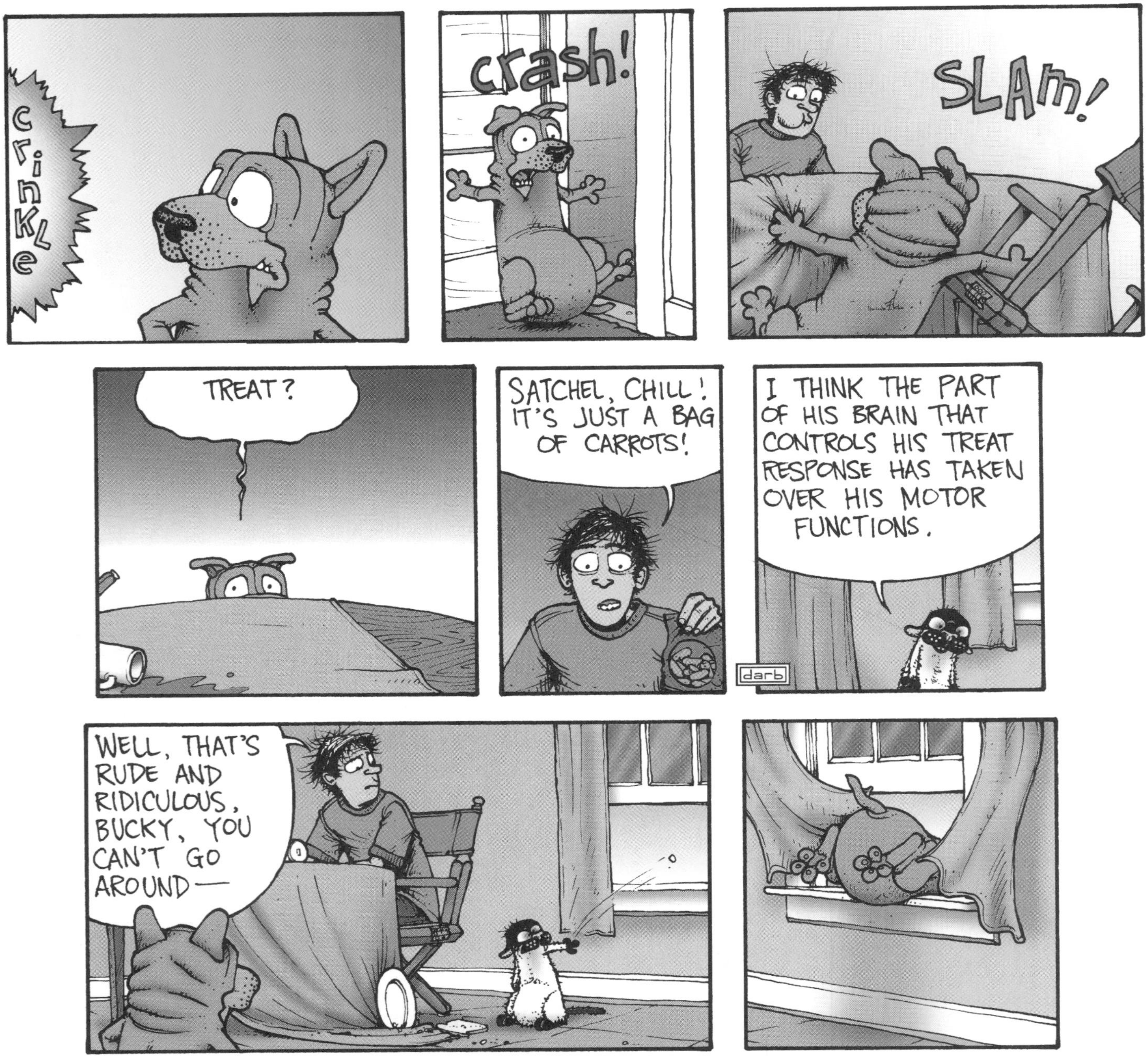

crinkle
crash!
SLAM!
TREAT?
SATCHEL, CHILL! IT'S JUST A BAG OF CARROTS!
I THINK THE PART OF HIS BRAIN THAT CONTROLS HIS TREAT RESPONSE HAS TAKEN OVER HIS MOTOR FUNCTIONS.
darb
WELL, THAT'S RUDE AND RIDICULOUS, BUCKY, YOU CAN'T GO AROUND—

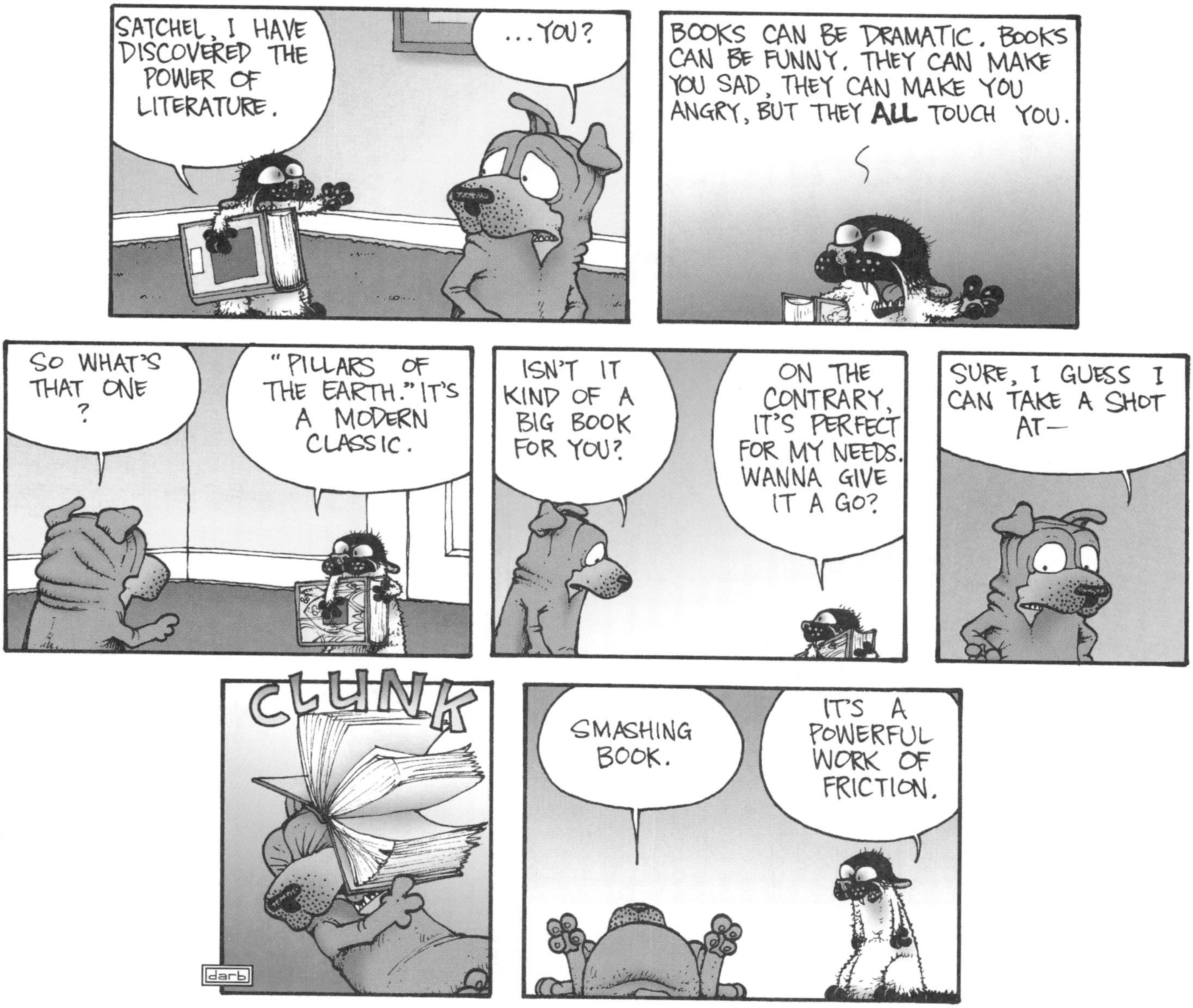
SATCHEL, I HAVE DISCOVERED THE POWER OF LITERATURE.
...YOU?
BOOKS CAN BE DRAMATIC. BOOKS CAN BE FUNNY. THEY CAN MAKE YOU SAD, THEY CAN MAKE YOU ANGRY, BUT THEY **ALL** TOUCH YOU.
SO WHAT'S THAT ONE?
"PILLARS OF THE EARTH." IT'S A MODERN CLASSIC.
ISN'T IT KIND OF A BIG BOOK FOR YOU?
ON THE CONTRARY, IT'S PERFECT FOR MY NEEDS. WANNA GIVE IT A GO?
SURE, I GUESS I CAN TAKE A SHOT AT—
CLUNK
darb
SMASHING BOOK.
IT'S A POWERFUL WORK OF FRICTION.

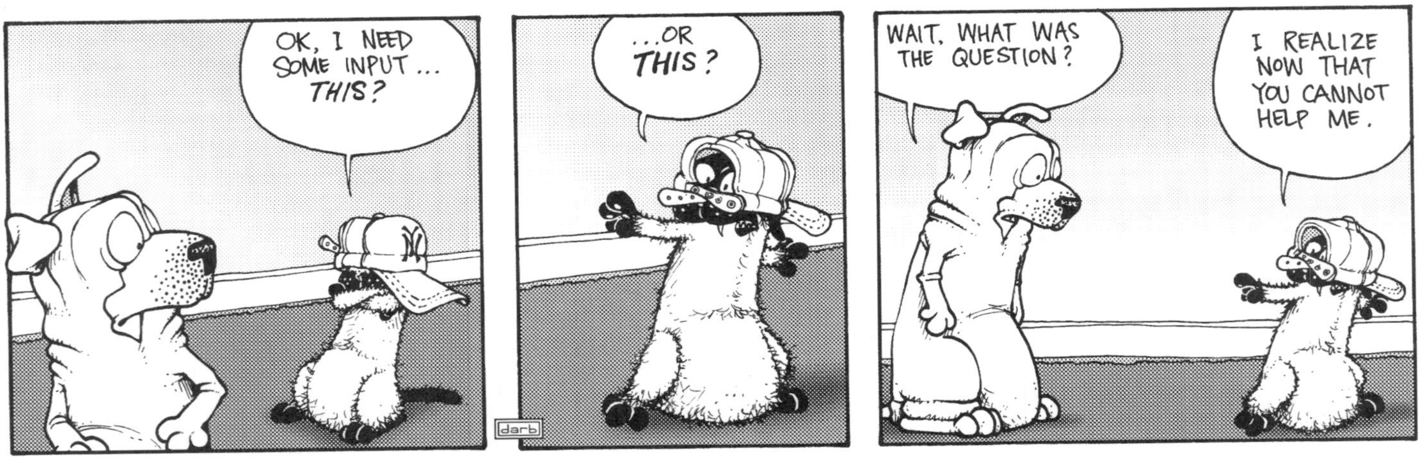
OK, I NEED SOME INPUT... THIS?
...OR THIS?
WAIT. WHAT WAS THE QUESTION?
I REALIZE NOW THAT YOU CANNOT HELP ME.
darb

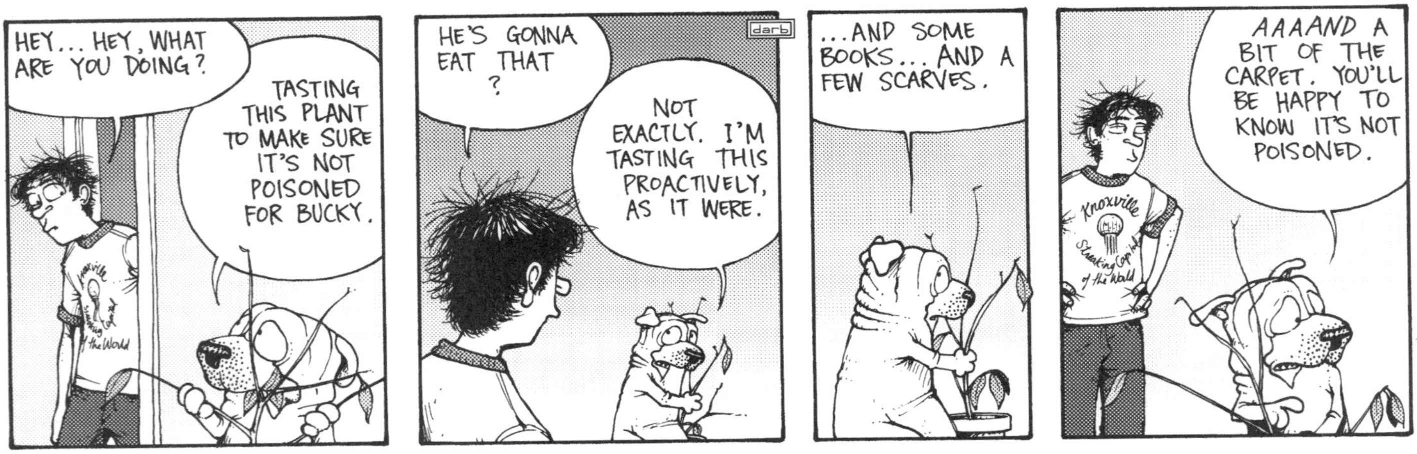
HEY... HEY, WHAT ARE YOU DOING?
TASTING THIS PLANT TO MAKE SURE IT'S NOT POISONED FOR BUCKY.
HE'S GONNA EAT THAT?
NOT EXACTLY. I'M TASTING THIS PROACTIVELY, AS IT WERE.
...AND SOME BOOKS... AND A FEW SCARVES.
AAAAND A BIT OF THE CARPET. YOU'LL BE HAPPY TO KNOW IT'S NOT POISONED.
darb

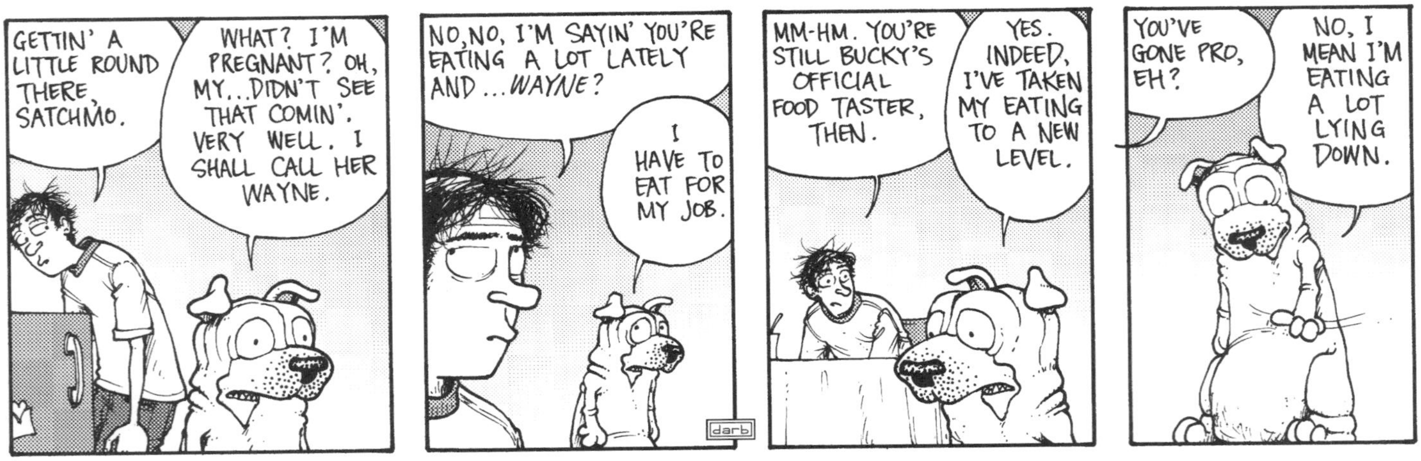
GETTIN' A LITTLE ROUND THERE, SATCHMO.
WHAT? I'M PREGNANT? OH, MY... DIDN'T SEE THAT COMIN'. VERY WELL. I SHALL CALL HER WAYNE.
NO, NO, I'M SAYIN' YOU'RE EATING A LOT LATELY AND... WAYNE?
I HAVE TO EAT FOR MY JOB.
MM-HM. YOU'RE STILL BUCKY'S OFFICIAL FOOD TASTER, THEN.
YES. INDEED, I'VE TAKEN MY EATING TO A NEW LEVEL.
YOU'VE GONE PRO, EH?
NO, I MEAN I'M EATING A LOT LYING DOWN.
darb

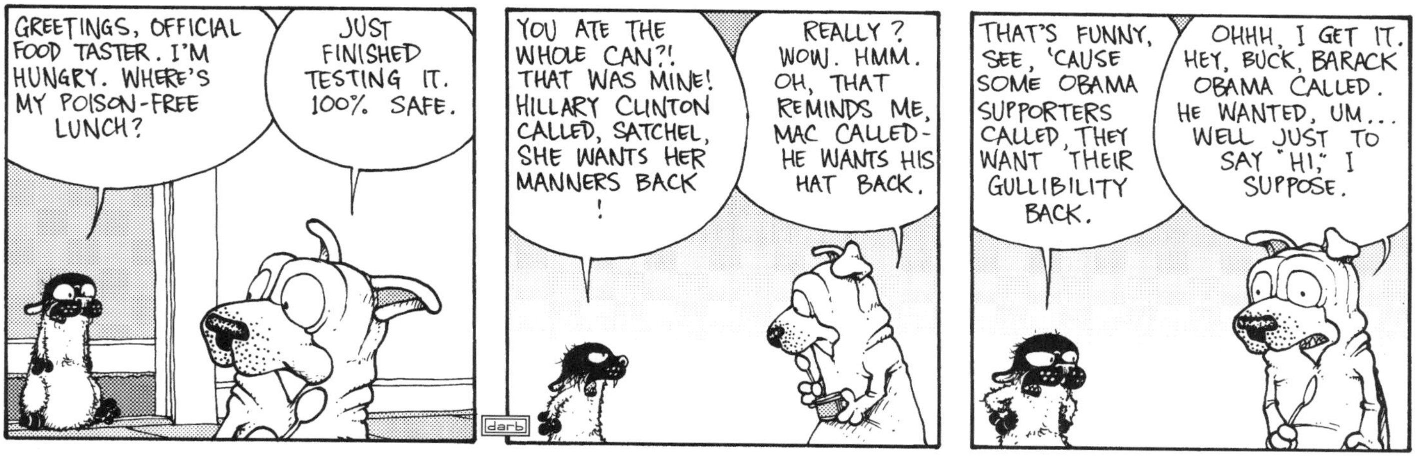
GREETINGS, OFFICIAL FOOD TASTER. I'M HUNGRY. WHERE'S MY POISON-FREE LUNCH?
JUST FINISHED TESTING IT. 100% SAFE.
YOU ATE THE WHOLE CAN?! THAT WAS MINE! HILLARY CLINTON CALLED, SATCHEL, SHE WANTS HER MANNERS BACK!
REALLY? WOW. HMM. OH, THAT REMINDS ME, MAC CALLED- HE WANTS HIS HAT BACK.
THAT'S FUNNY, SEE, 'CAUSE SOME OBAMA SUPPORTERS CALLED, THEY WANT THEIR GULLIBILITY BACK.
OHHH, I GET IT. HEY, BUCK, BARACK OBAMA CALLED. HE WANTED, UM... WELL JUST TO SAY "HI," I SUPPOSE.
darb

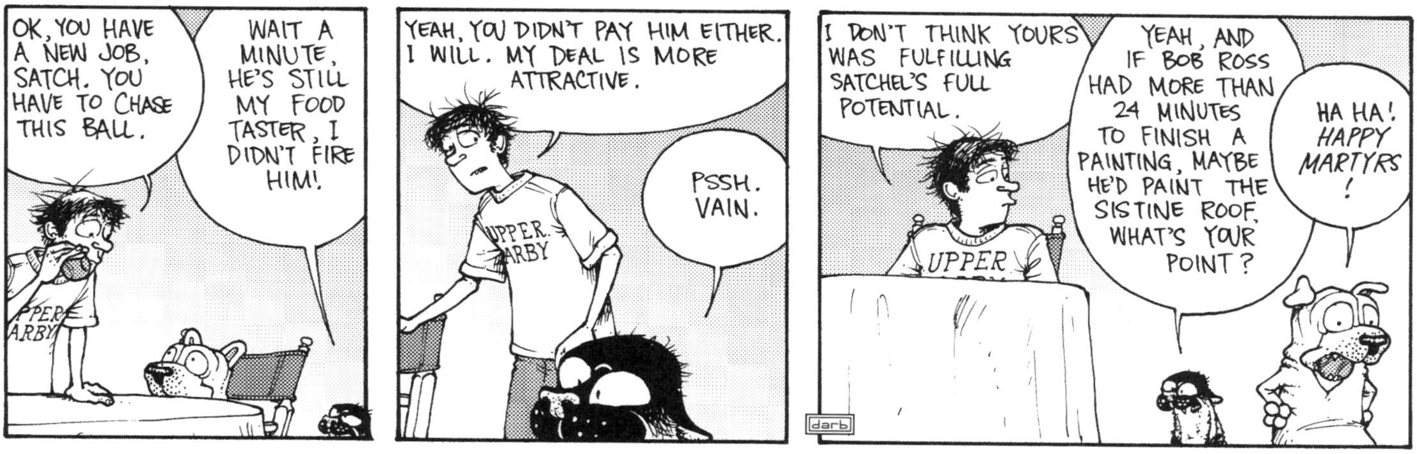
OK, YOU HAVE A NEW JOB, SATCH. YOU HAVE TO CHASE THIS BALL.
WAIT A MINUTE, HE'S STILL MY FOOD TASTER, I DIDN'T FIRE HIM!
YEAH, YOU DIDN'T PAY HIM EITHER. I WILL. MY DEAL IS MORE ATTRACTIVE.
PSSH. VAIN.
I DON'T THINK YOURS WAS FULFILLING SATCHEL'S FULL POTENTIAL.
YEAH, AND IF BOB ROSS HAD MORE THAN 24 MINUTES TO FINISH A PAINTING, MAYBE HE'D PAINT THE SISTINE ROOF. WHAT'S YOUR POINT?
HA HA! *HAPPY MARTYRS*!
darb

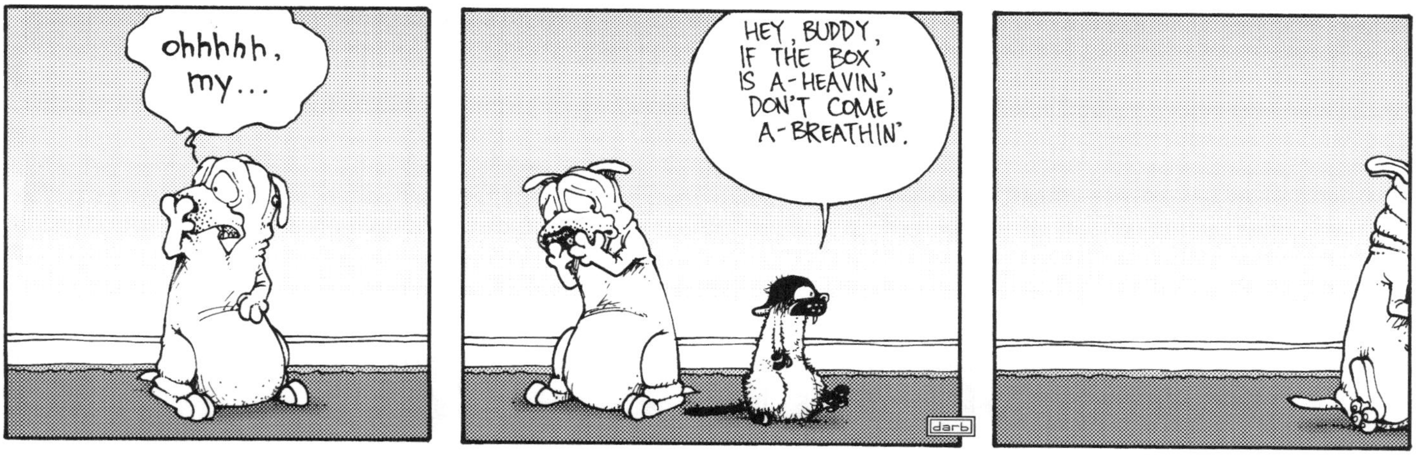
ohhhhh, my...
HEY, BUDDY, IF THE BOX IS A-HEAVIN', DON'T COME A-BREATHIN'.
darb

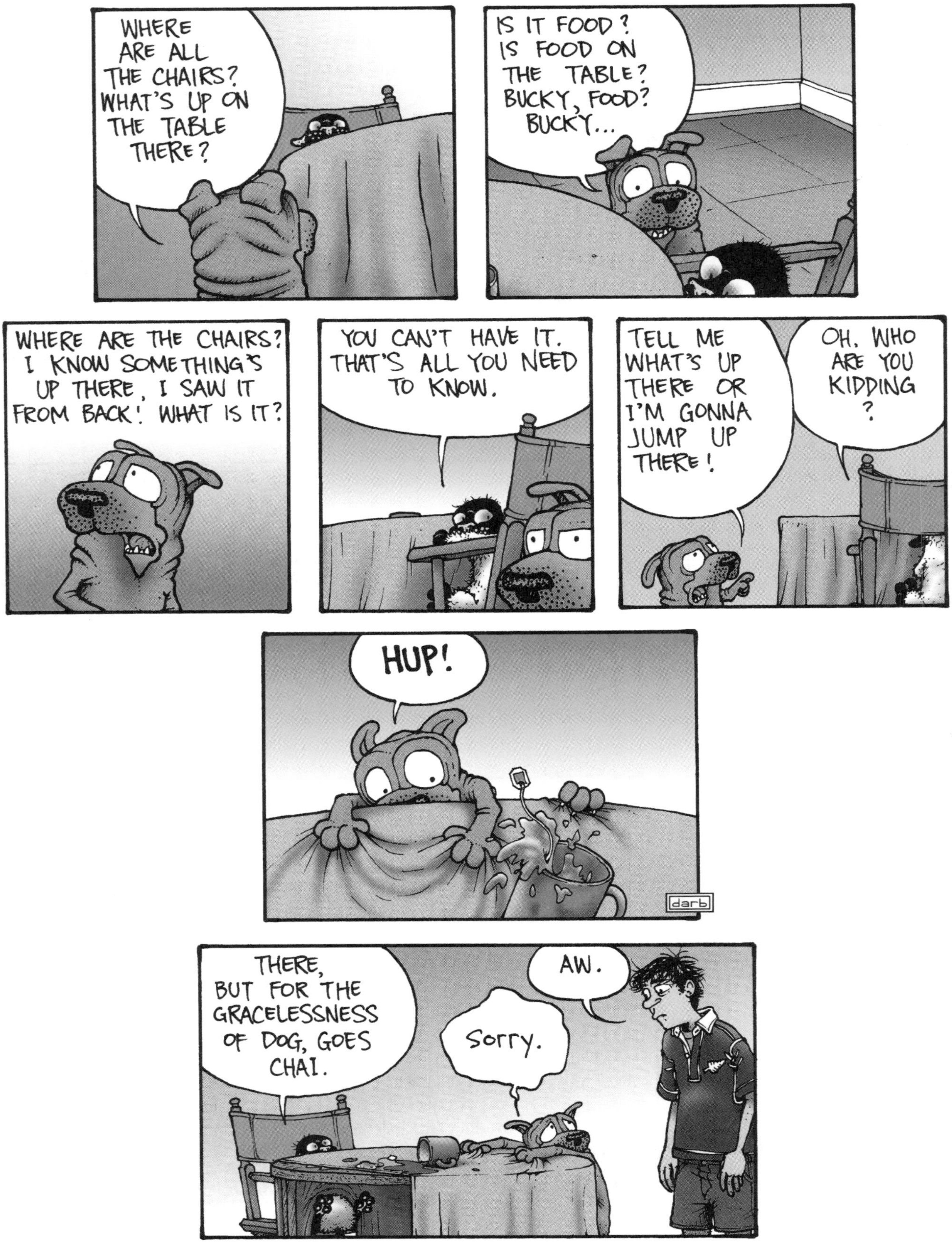
WHERE ARE ALL THE CHAIRS? WHAT'S UP ON THE TABLE THERE?
IS IT FOOD? IS FOOD ON THE TABLE? BUCKY, FOOD? BUCKY...
WHERE ARE THE CHAIRS? I KNOW SOMETHING'S UP THERE, I SAW IT FROM BACK! WHAT IS IT?
YOU CAN'T HAVE IT. THAT'S ALL YOU NEED TO KNOW.
TELL ME WHAT'S UP THERE OR I'M GONNA JUMP UP THERE!
OH. WHO ARE YOU KIDDING?
HUP!
darb
THERE, BUT FOR THE GRACELESSNESS OF DOG, GOES CHAI.
Sorry.
AW.

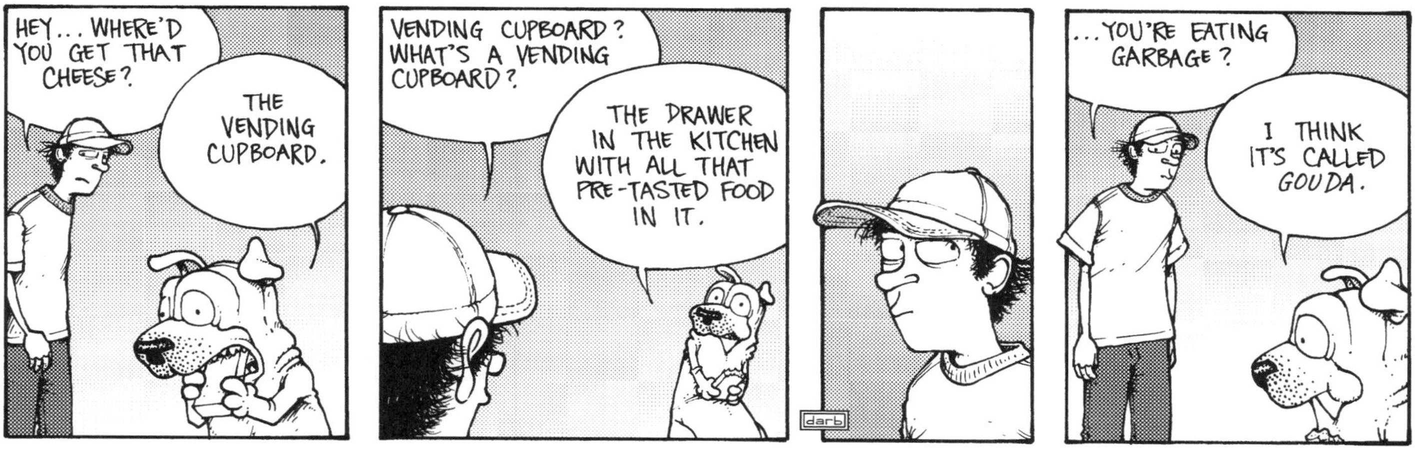
HEY... WHERE'D YOU GET THAT CHEESE?
THE VENDING CUPBOARD.
VENDING CUPBOARD? WHAT'S A VENDING CUPBOARD?
THE DRAWER IN THE KITCHEN WITH ALL THAT PRE-TASTED FOOD IN IT.
...YOU'RE EATING GARBAGE?
I THINK IT'S CALLED *GOUDA*.

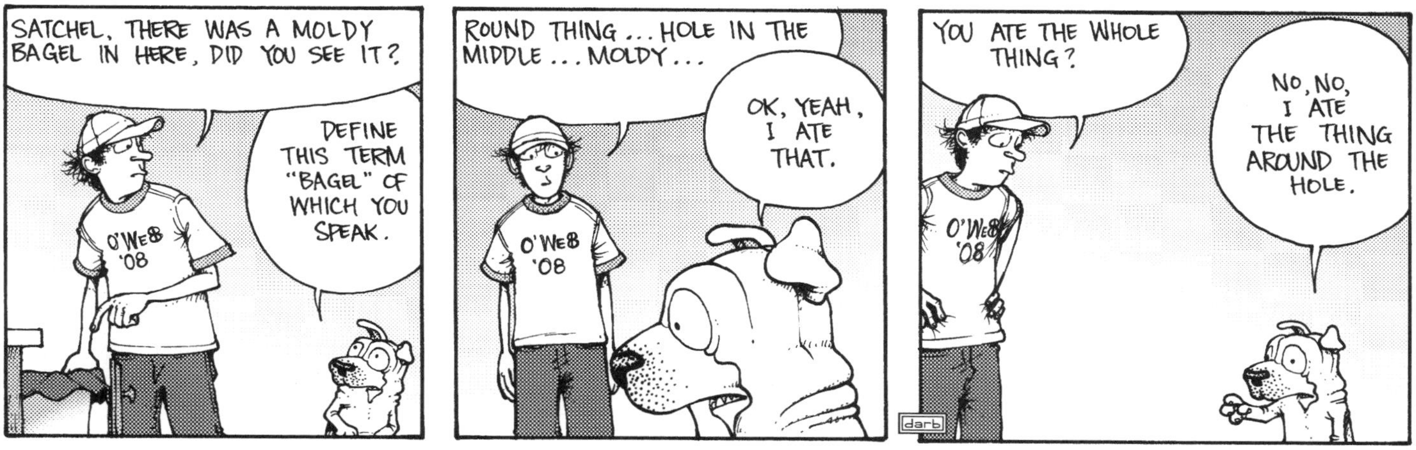
SATCHEL, THERE WAS A MOLDY BAGEL IN HERE, DID YOU SEE IT?
DEFINE THIS TERM "BAGEL" OF WHICH YOU SPEAK.
ROUND THING... HOLE IN THE MIDDLE... MOLDY...
OK, YEAH, I ATE THAT.
YOU ATE THE WHOLE THING?
NO, NO, I ATE THE THING AROUND THE HOLE.

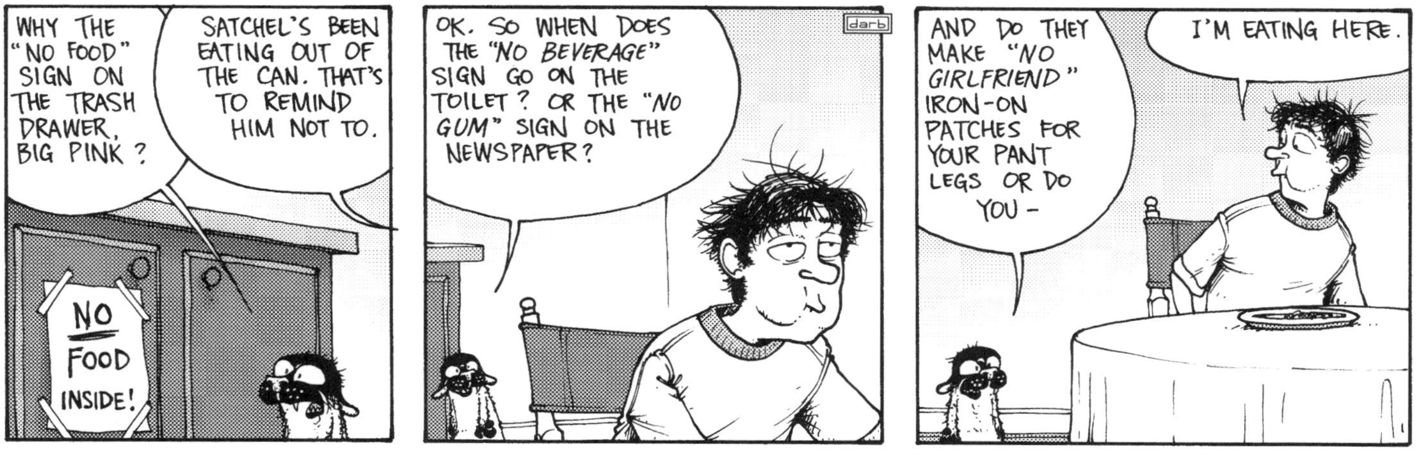
WHY THE "NO FOOD" SIGN ON THE TRASH DRAWER, BIG PINK?
SATCHEL'S BEEN EATING OUT OF THE CAN. THAT'S TO REMIND HIM NOT TO.
NO FOOD INSIDE!
OK. SO WHEN DOES THE "*NO BEVERAGE*" SIGN GO ON THE TOILET? OR THE "*NO GUM*" SIGN ON THE NEWSPAPER?
AND DO THEY MAKE "*NO GIRLFRIEND*" IRON-ON PATCHES FOR YOUR PANT LEGS OR DO YOU –
I'M EATING HERE.

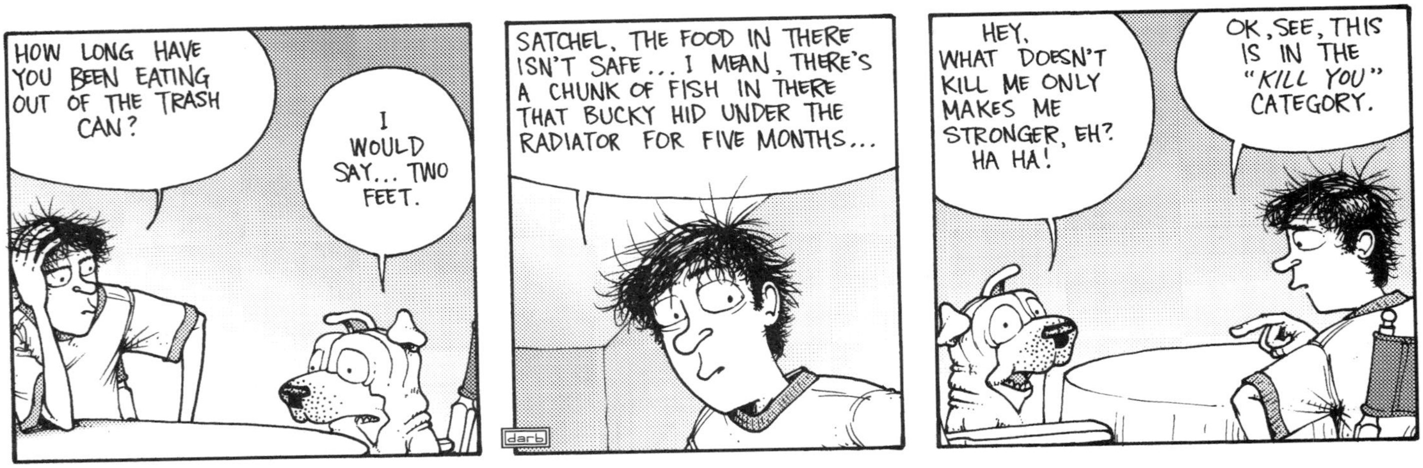
HOW LONG HAVE YOU BEEN EATING OUT OF THE TRASH CAN?
I WOULD SAY... TWO FEET.
SATCHEL, THE FOOD IN THERE ISN'T SAFE... I MEAN, THERE'S A CHUNK OF FISH IN THERE THAT BUCKY HID UNDER THE RADIATOR FOR FIVE MONTHS...
darb
HEY, WHAT DOESN'T KILL ME ONLY MAKES ME STRONGER, EH? HA HA!
OK, SEE, THIS IS IN THE "*KILL YOU*" CATEGORY.

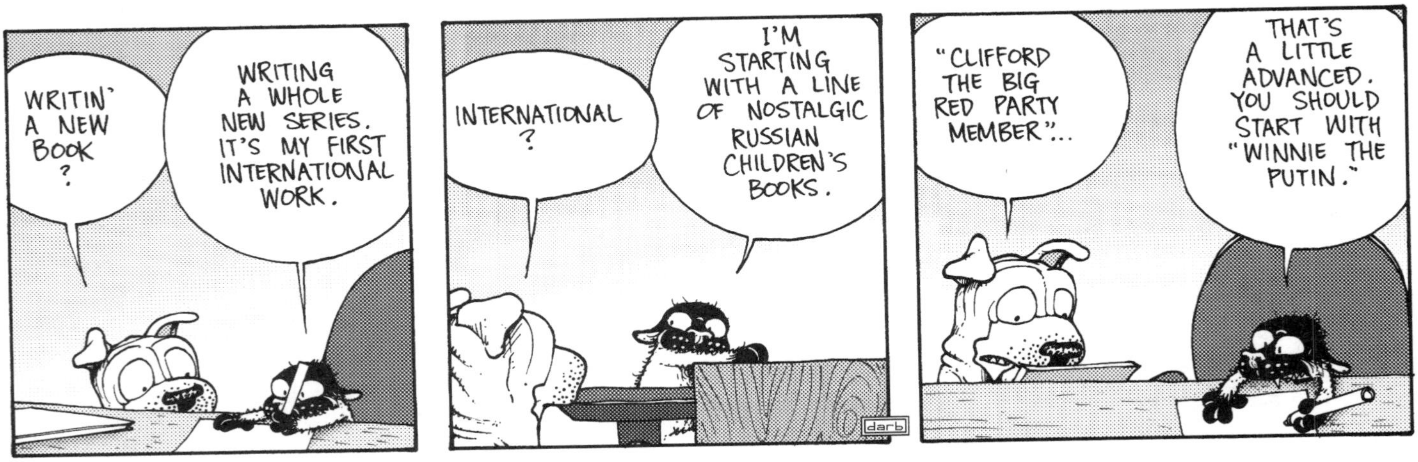
WRITIN' A NEW BOOK?
WRITING A WHOLE NEW SERIES. IT'S MY FIRST INTERNATIONAL WORK.
INTERNATIONAL?
I'M STARTING WITH A LINE OF NOSTALGIC RUSSIAN CHILDREN'S BOOKS.
darb
"CLIFFORD THE BIG RED PARTY MEMBER"...
THAT'S A LITTLE ADVANCED. YOU SHOULD START WITH "WINNIE THE PUTIN."

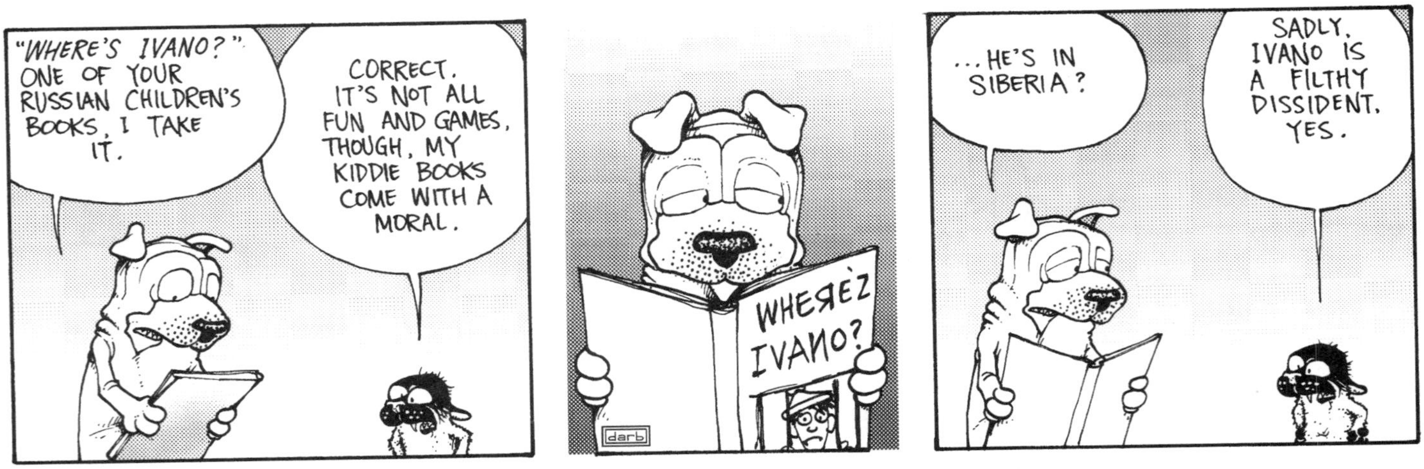
"*WHERE'S IVANO?*" ONE OF YOUR RUSSIAN CHILDREN'S BOOKS, I TAKE IT.
CORRECT. IT'S NOT ALL FUN AND GAMES, THOUGH, MY KIDDIE BOOKS COME WITH A MORAL.
WHEЯEZ IVAИO?
darb
...HE'S IN SIBERIA?
SADLY, IVANO IS A FILTHY DISSIDENT, YES.

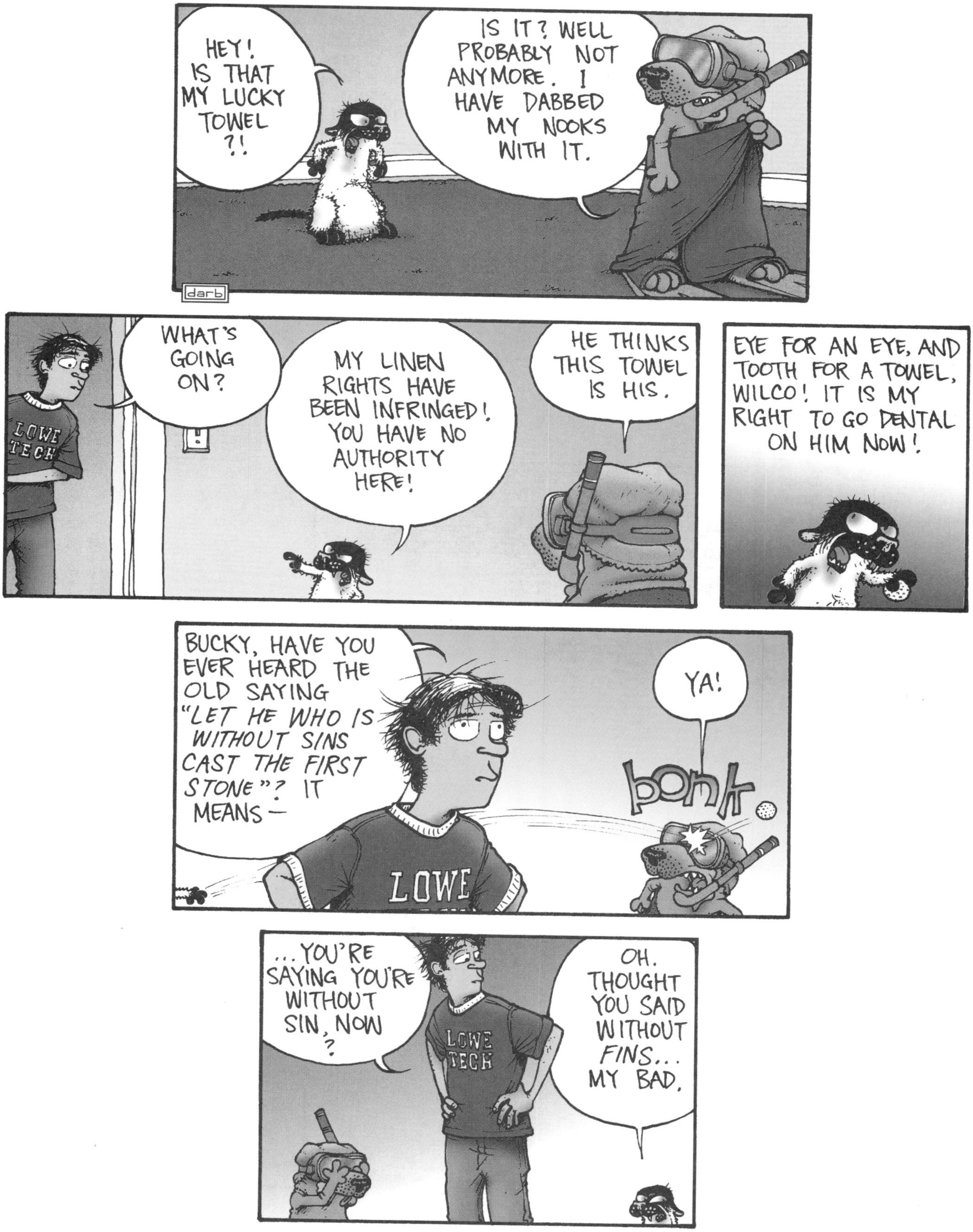
HEY! IS THAT MY LUCKY TOWEL ?!
IS IT? WELL PROBABLY NOT ANYMORE. I HAVE DABBED MY NOOKS WITH IT.
darb
WHAT'S GOING ON?
MY LINEN RIGHTS HAVE BEEN INFRINGED! YOU HAVE NO AUTHORITY HERE!
HE THINKS THIS TOWEL IS HIS.
EYE FOR AN EYE, AND TOOTH FOR A TOWEL, WILCO! IT IS MY RIGHT TO GO DENTAL ON HIM NOW!
BUCKY, HAVE YOU EVER HEARD THE OLD SAYING "LET HE WHO IS WITHOUT SINS CAST THE FIRST STONE"? IT MEANS—
YA!
bonk
...YOU'RE SAYING YOU'RE WITHOUT SIN, NOW ?
OH. THOUGHT YOU SAID WITHOUT FINS... MY BAD.

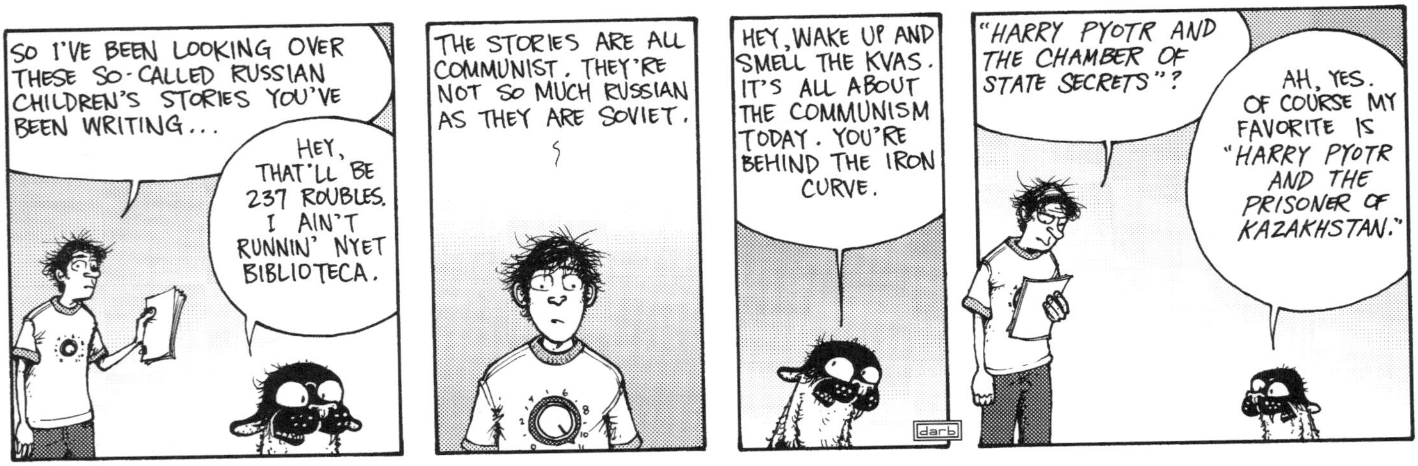
SO I'VE BEEN LOOKING OVER THESE SO-CALLED RUSSIAN CHILDREN'S STORIES YOU'VE BEEN WRITING...
HEY, THAT'LL BE 237 ROUBLES. I AIN'T RUNNIN' NYET BIBLIOTECA.
THE STORIES ARE ALL COMMUNIST. THEY'RE NOT SO MUCH RUSSIAN AS THEY ARE SOVIET.
HEY, WAKE UP AND SMELL THE KVAS. IT'S ALL ABOUT THE COMMUNISM TODAY. YOU'RE BEHIND THE IRON CURVE.
darb
"HARRY PYOTR AND THE CHAMBER OF STATE SECRETS"?
AH, YES. OF COURSE MY FAVORITE IS "HARRY PYOTR AND THE PRISONER OF KAZAKHSTAN."

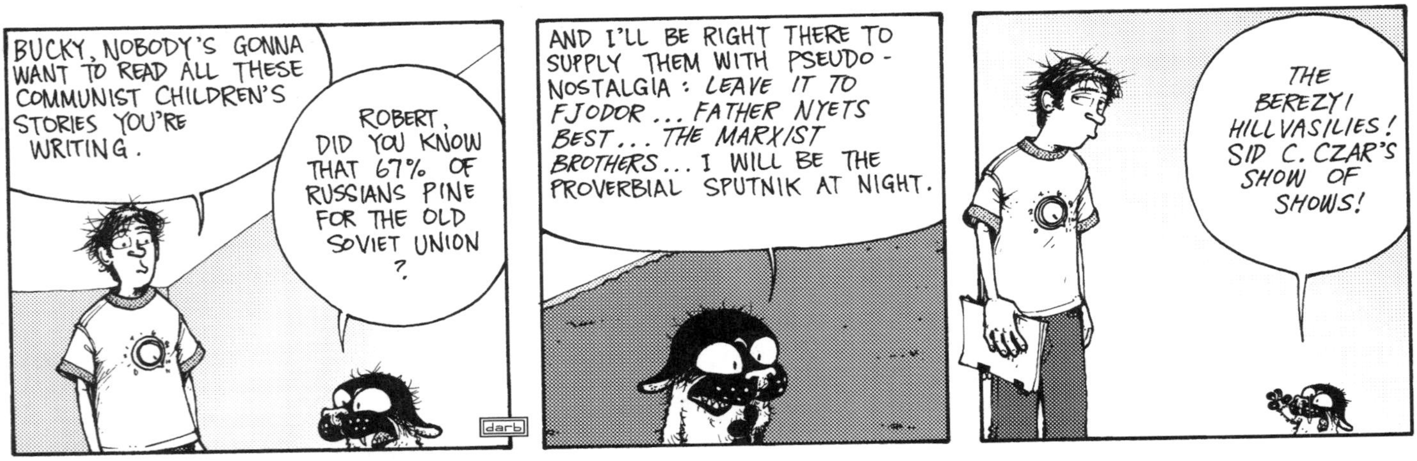
BUCKY, NOBODY'S GONNA WANT TO READ ALL THESE COMMUNIST CHILDREN'S STORIES YOU'RE WRITING.
ROBERT, DID YOU KNOW THAT 67% OF RUSSIANS PINE FOR THE OLD SOVIET UNION?
darb
AND I'LL BE RIGHT THERE TO SUPPLY THEM WITH PSEUDO-NOSTALGIA: LEAVE IT TO FJODOR... FATHER NYETS BEST... THE MARXIST BROTHERS... I WILL BE THE PROVERBIAL SPUTNIK AT NIGHT.
THE BEREZYI HILLVASILIES! SID C. CZAR'S SHOW OF SHOWS!

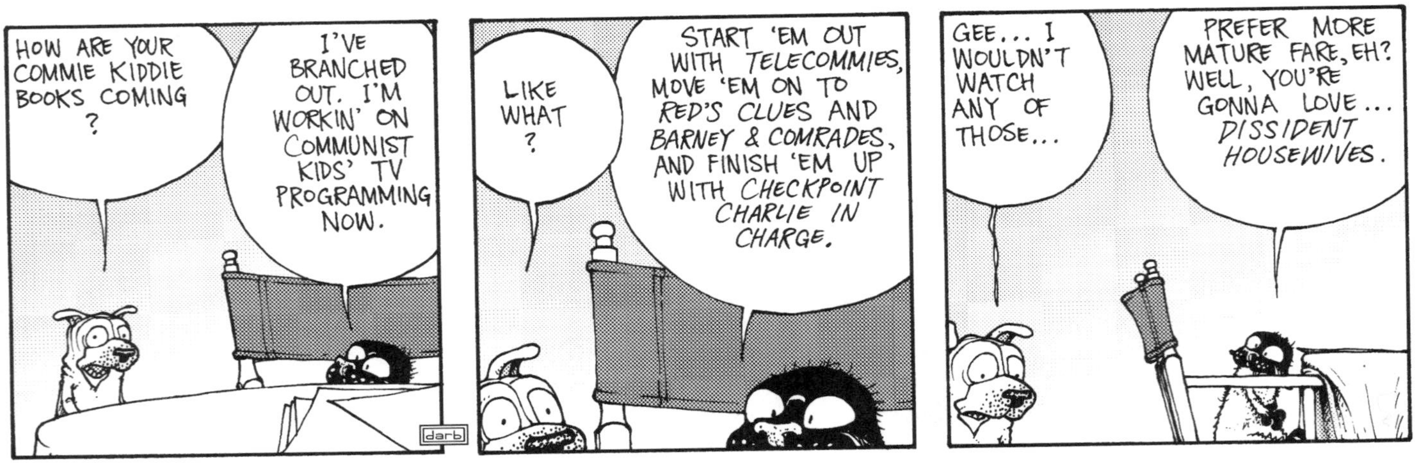
HOW ARE YOUR COMMIE KIDDIE BOOKS COMING?
I'VE BRANCHED OUT. I'M WORKIN' ON COMMUNIST KIDS' TV PROGRAMMING NOW.
darb
LIKE WHAT?
START 'EM OUT WITH TELECOMMIES, MOVE 'EM ON TO RED'S CLUES AND BARNEY & COMRADES, AND FINISH 'EM UP WITH CHECKPOINT CHARLIE IN CHARGE.
GEE... I WOULDN'T WATCH ANY OF THOSE...
PREFER MORE MATURE FARE, EH? WELL, YOU'RE GONNA LOVE... DISSIDENT HOUSEWIVES.

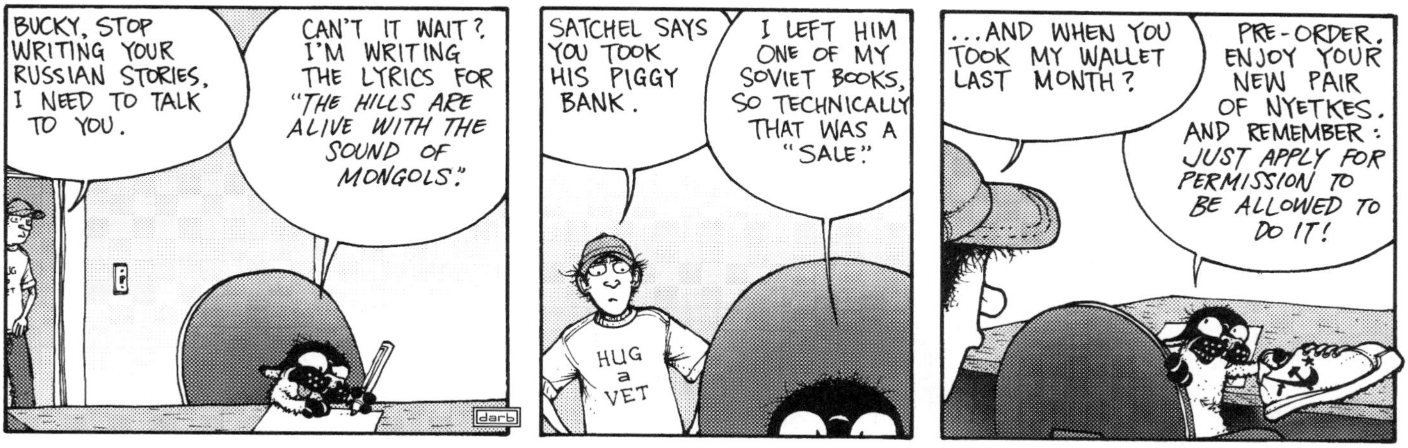
BUCKY, STOP WRITING YOUR RUSSIAN STORIES. I NEED TO TALK TO YOU.
CAN'T IT WAIT? I'M WRITING THE LYRICS FOR *"THE HILLS ARE ALIVE WITH THE SOUND OF MONGOLS."*
darb
SATCHEL SAYS YOU TOOK HIS PIGGY BANK.
I LEFT HIM ONE OF MY SOVIET BOOKS, SO TECHNICALLY THAT WAS A "SALE."
HUG a VET
...AND WHEN YOU TOOK MY WALLET LAST MONTH?
PRE-ORDER. ENJOY YOUR NEW PAIR OF NYETKES. AND REMEMBER: *JUST APPLY FOR PERMISSION TO BE ALLOWED TO DO IT!*

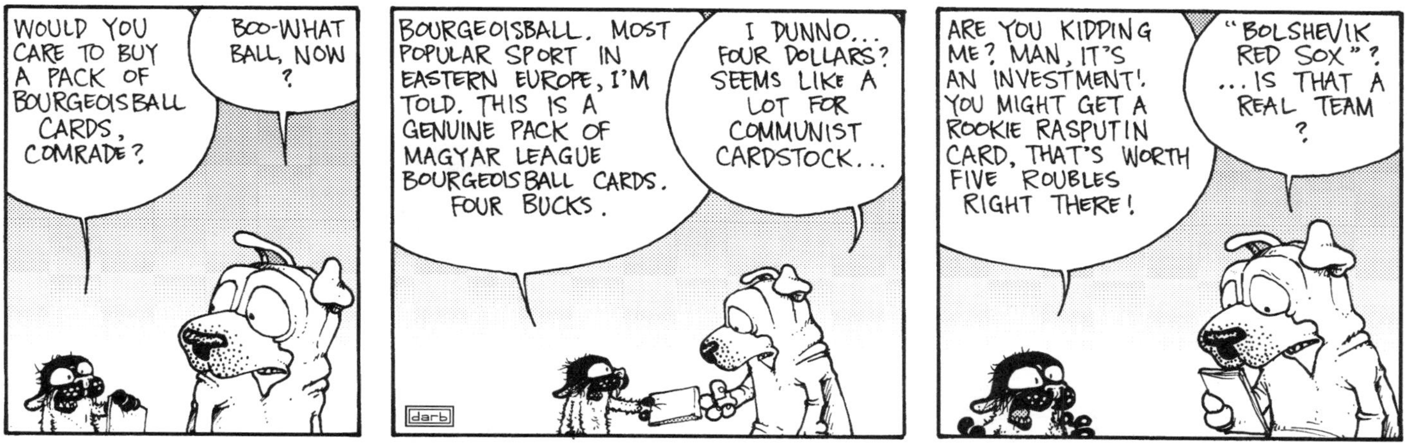
WOULD YOU CARE TO BUY A PACK OF BOURGEOISBALL CARDS, COMRADE?
BOO-WHAT BALL, NOW?
BOURGEOISBALL. MOST POPULAR SPORT IN EASTERN EUROPE, I'M TOLD. THIS IS A GENUINE PACK OF MAGYAR LEAGUE BOURGEOISBALL CARDS. FOUR BUCKS.
I DUNNO... FOUR DOLLARS? SEEMS LIKE A LOT FOR COMMUNIST CARDSTOCK...
darb
ARE YOU KIDDING ME? MAN, IT'S AN INVESTMENT! YOU MIGHT GET A ROOKIE RASPUTIN CARD. THAT'S WORTH FIVE ROUBLES RIGHT THERE!
"BOLSHEVIK RED SOX"? ...IS THAT A REAL TEAM?

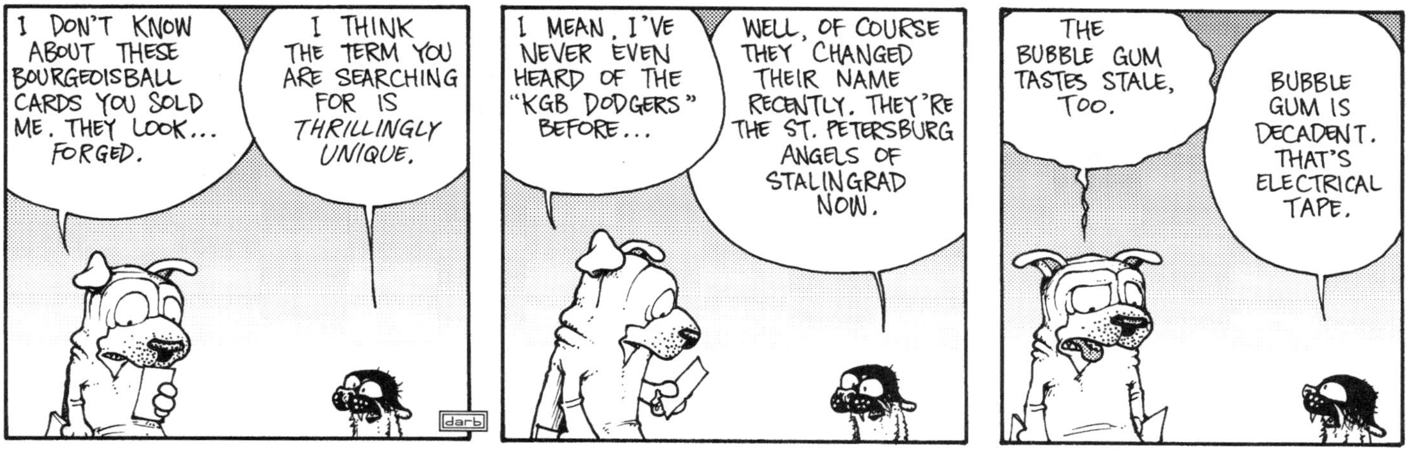
I DON'T KNOW ABOUT THESE BOURGEOISBALL CARDS YOU SOLD ME. THEY LOOK... FORGED.
I THINK THE TERM YOU ARE SEARCHING FOR IS *THRILLINGLY UNIQUE.*
darb
I MEAN, I'VE NEVER EVEN HEARD OF THE "KGB DODGERS" BEFORE...
WELL, OF COURSE THEY CHANGED THEIR NAME RECENTLY. THEY'RE THE ST. PETERSBURG ANGELS OF STALINGRAD NOW.
THE BUBBLE GUM TASTES STALE, TOO.
BUBBLE GUM IS DECADENT. THAT'S ELECTRICAL TAPE.

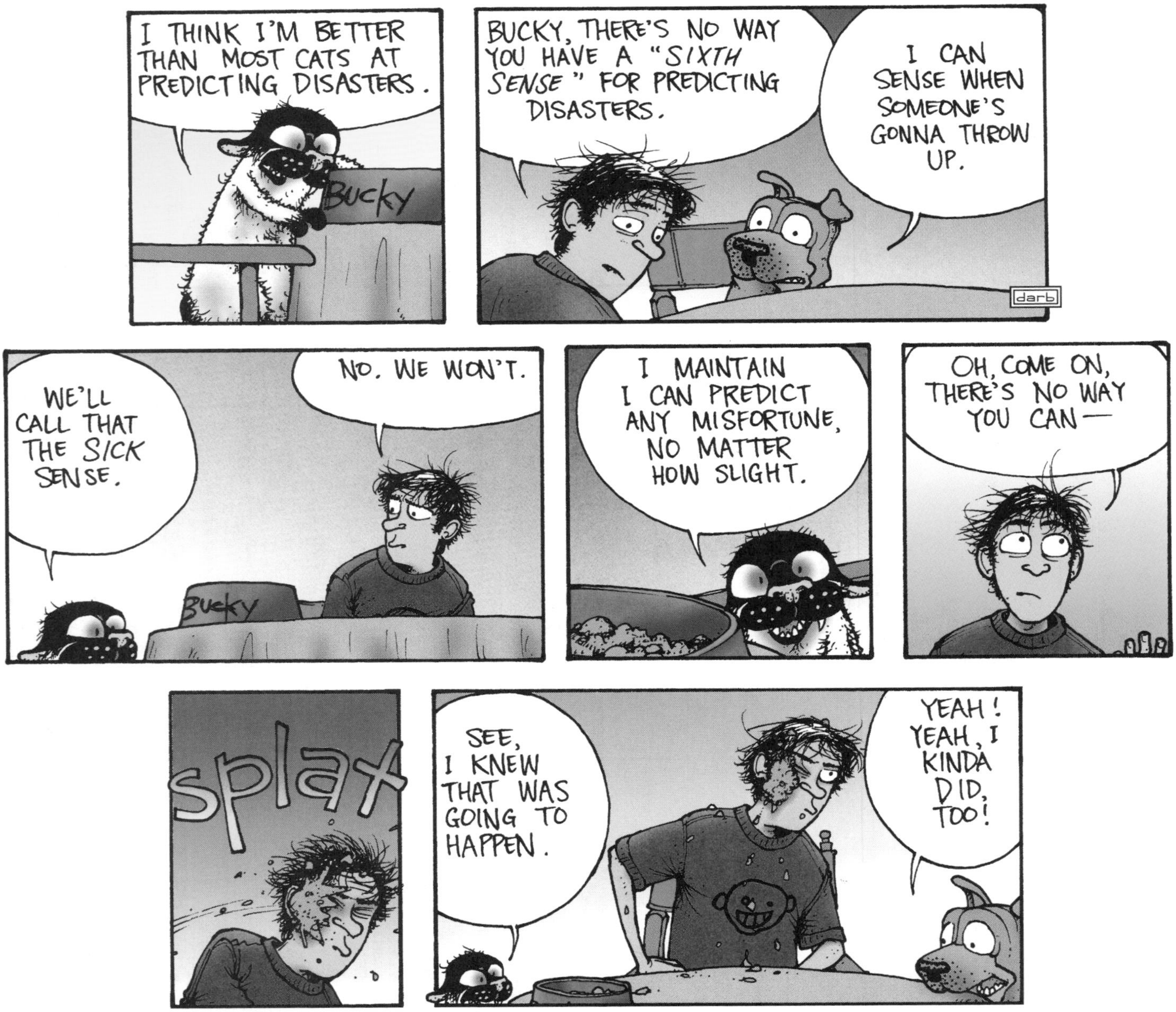
I THINK I'M BETTER THAN MOST CATS AT PREDICTING DISASTERS.
BUCKY
BUCKY, THERE'S NO WAY YOU HAVE A "SIXTH SENSE" FOR PREDICTING DISASTERS.
I CAN SENSE WHEN SOMEONE'S GONNA THROW UP.
darb
WE'LL CALL THAT THE SICK SENSE.
NO. WE WON'T.
BUCKY
I MAINTAIN I CAN PREDICT ANY MISFORTUNE, NO MATTER HOW SLIGHT.
OH, COME ON, THERE'S NO WAY YOU CAN—
splat
SEE, I KNEW THAT WAS GOING TO HAPPEN.
YEAH! YEAH, I KINDA DID, TOO!

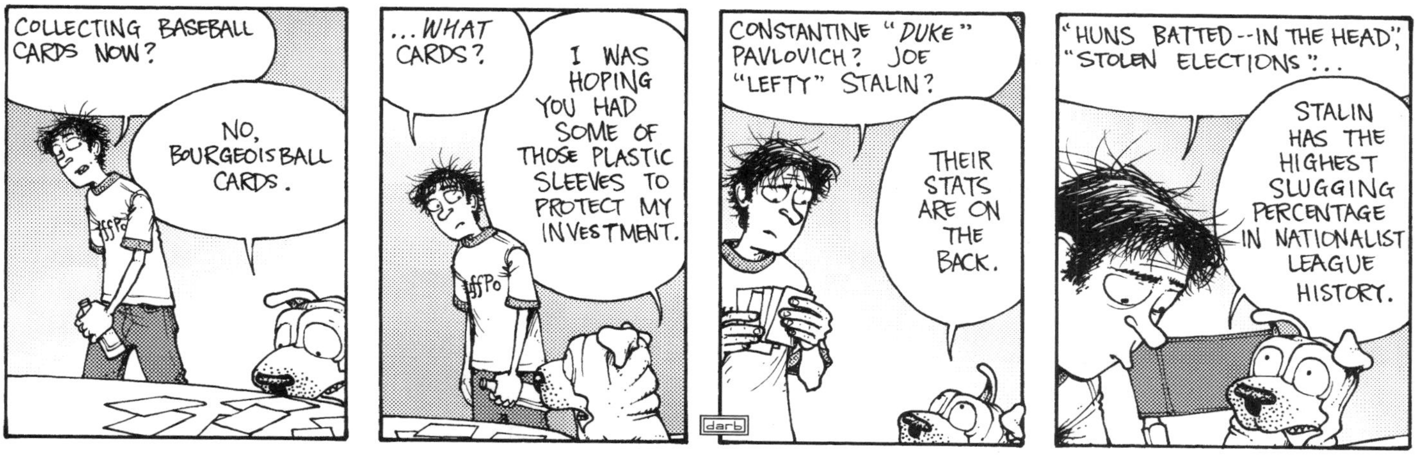
COLLECTING BASEBALL CARDS NOW?
NO, BOURGEOISBALL CARDS.
...*WHAT* CARDS?
I WAS HOPING YOU HAD SOME OF THOSE PLASTIC SLEEVES TO PROTECT MY INVESTMENT.
darb
CONSTANTINE "*DUKE*" PAVLOVICH? JOE "LEFTY" STALIN?
THEIR STATS ARE ON THE BACK.
"HUNS BATTED--IN THE HEAD", "STOLEN ELECTIONS"...
STALIN HAS THE HIGHEST SLUGGING PERCENTAGE IN NATIONALIST LEAGUE HISTORY.

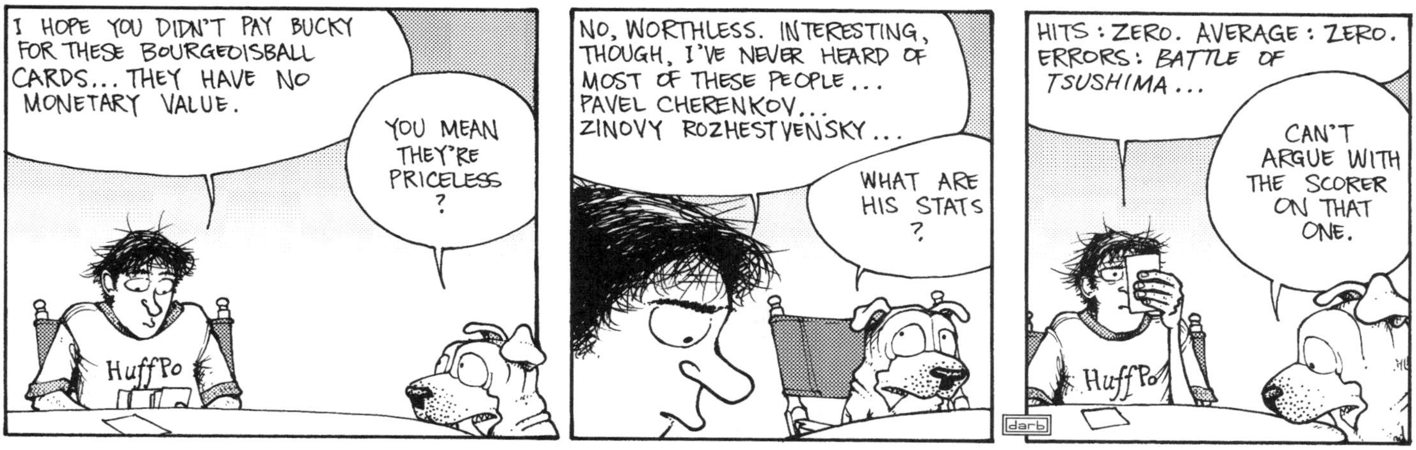
I HOPE YOU DIDN'T PAY BUCKY FOR THESE BOURGEOISBALL CARDS... THEY HAVE NO MONETARY VALUE.
YOU MEAN THEY'RE PRICELESS?
HuffPo
NO, WORTHLESS. INTERESTING, THOUGH, I'VE NEVER HEARD OF MOST OF THESE PEOPLE... PAVEL CHERENKOV... ZINOVY ROZHESTVENSKY...
WHAT ARE HIS STATS?
darb
HITS: ZERO. AVERAGE: ZERO. ERRORS: *BATTLE OF TSUSHIMA*...
CAN'T ARGUE WITH THE SCORER ON THAT ONE.
HuffPo

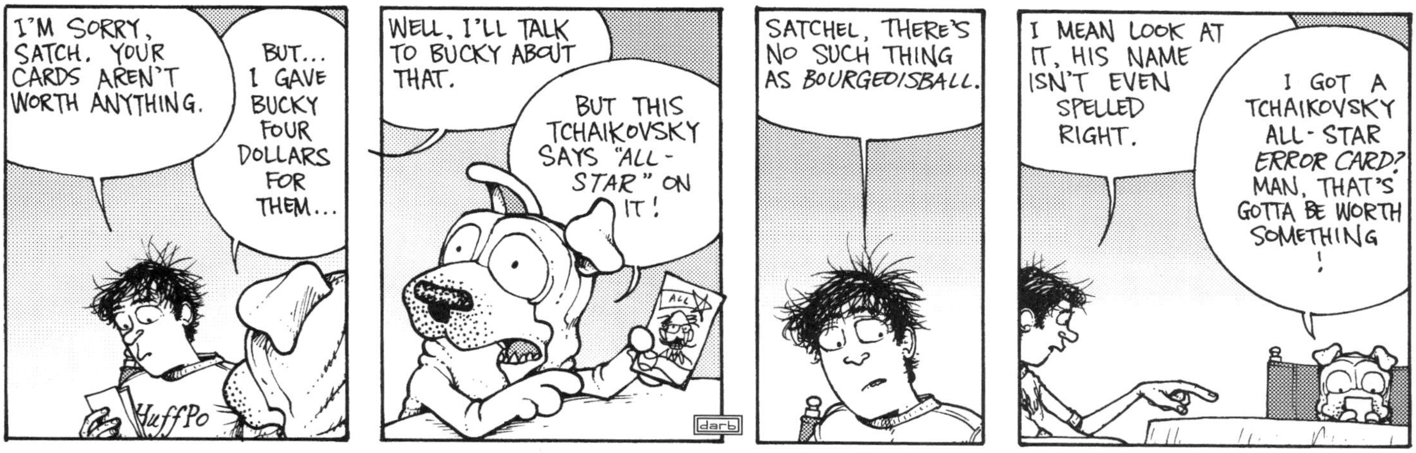
I'M SORRY, SATCH. YOUR CARDS AREN'T WORTH ANYTHING.
BUT... I GAVE BUCKY FOUR DOLLARS FOR THEM...
HuffPo
WELL, I'LL TALK TO BUCKY ABOUT THAT.
BUT THIS TCHAIKOVSKY SAYS "*ALL-STAR*" ON IT!
ALL
darb
SATCHEL, THERE'S NO SUCH THING AS *BOURGEOISBALL*.
I MEAN LOOK AT IT, HIS NAME ISN'T EVEN SPELLED RIGHT.
I GOT A TCHAIKOVSKY ALL-STAR *ERROR CARD?* MAN, THAT'S GOTTA BE WORTH SOMETHING!

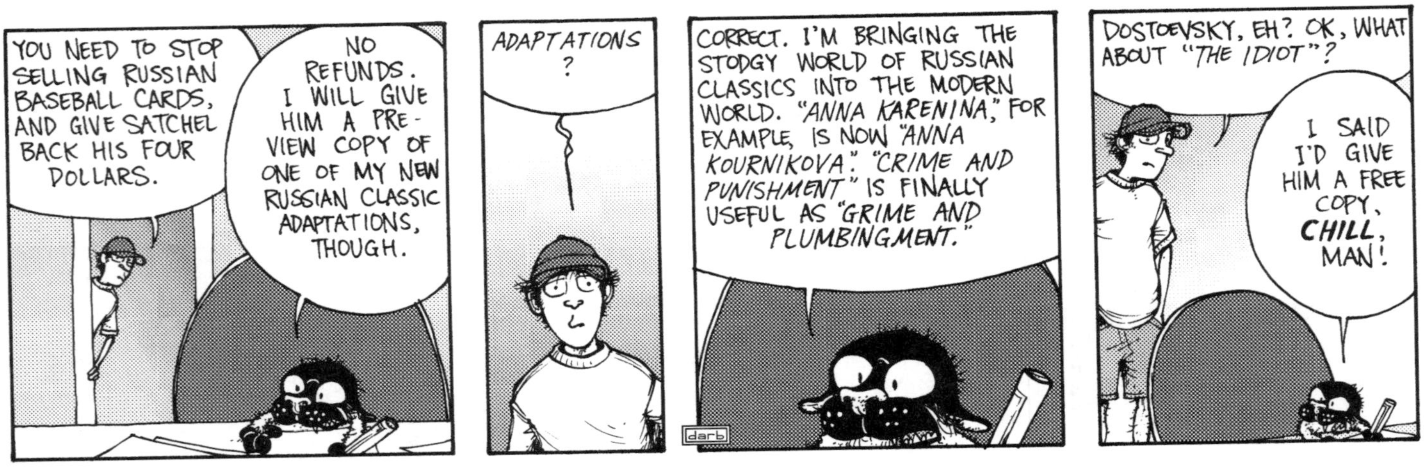
YOU NEED TO STOP SELLING RUSSIAN BASEBALL CARDS, AND GIVE SATCHEL BACK HIS FOUR DOLLARS.
NO REFUNDS. I WILL GIVE HIM A PRE-VIEW COPY OF ONE OF MY NEW RUSSIAN CLASSIC ADAPTATIONS, THOUGH.
ADAPTATIONS?
CORRECT. I'M BRINGING THE STODGY WORLD OF RUSSIAN CLASSICS INTO THE MODERN WORLD. "ANNA KARENINA," FOR EXAMPLE, IS NOW "ANNA KOURNIKOVA." "CRIME AND PUNISHMENT" IS FINALLY USEFUL AS "GRIME AND PLUMBINGMENT."
DOSTOEVSKY, EH? OK, WHAT ABOUT "THE IDIOT"?
I SAID I'D GIVE HIM A FREE COPY. CHILL, MAN!

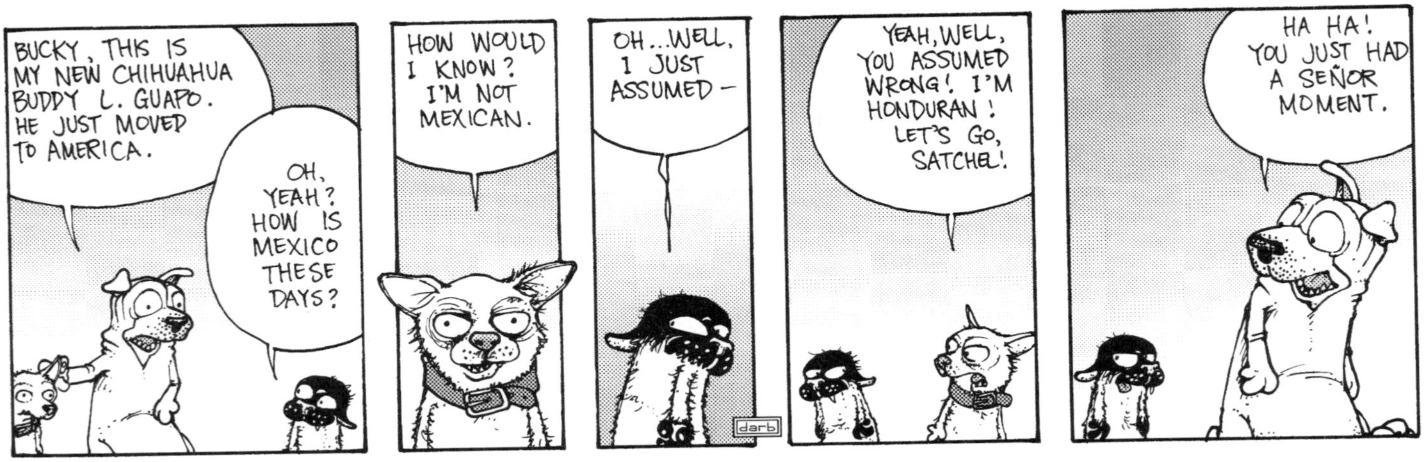
BUCKY, THIS IS MY NEW CHIHUAHUA BUDDY L. GUAPO. HE JUST MOVED TO AMERICA.
OH, YEAH? HOW IS MEXICO THESE DAYS?
HOW WOULD I KNOW? I'M NOT MEXICAN.
OH...WELL, I JUST ASSUMED—
YEAH, WELL, YOU ASSUMED WRONG! I'M HONDURAN! LET'S GO, SATCHEL!
HA HA! YOU JUST HAD A SEÑOR MOMENT.

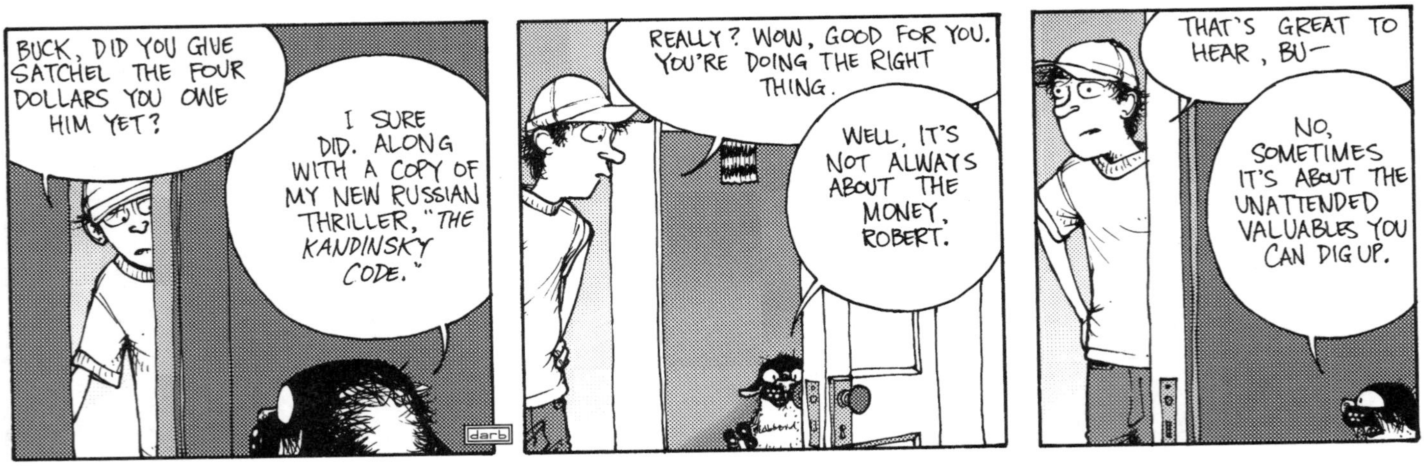
BUCK, DID YOU GIVE SATCHEL THE FOUR DOLLARS YOU OWE HIM YET?
I SURE DID. ALONG WITH A COPY OF MY NEW RUSSIAN THRILLER, "THE KANDINSKY CODE."
REALLY? WOW, GOOD FOR YOU. YOU'RE DOING THE RIGHT THING.
WELL, IT'S NOT ALWAYS ABOUT THE MONEY, ROBERT.
THAT'S GREAT TO HEAR, BU—
NO, SOMETIMES IT'S ABOUT THE UNATTENDED VALUABLES YOU CAN DIG UP.

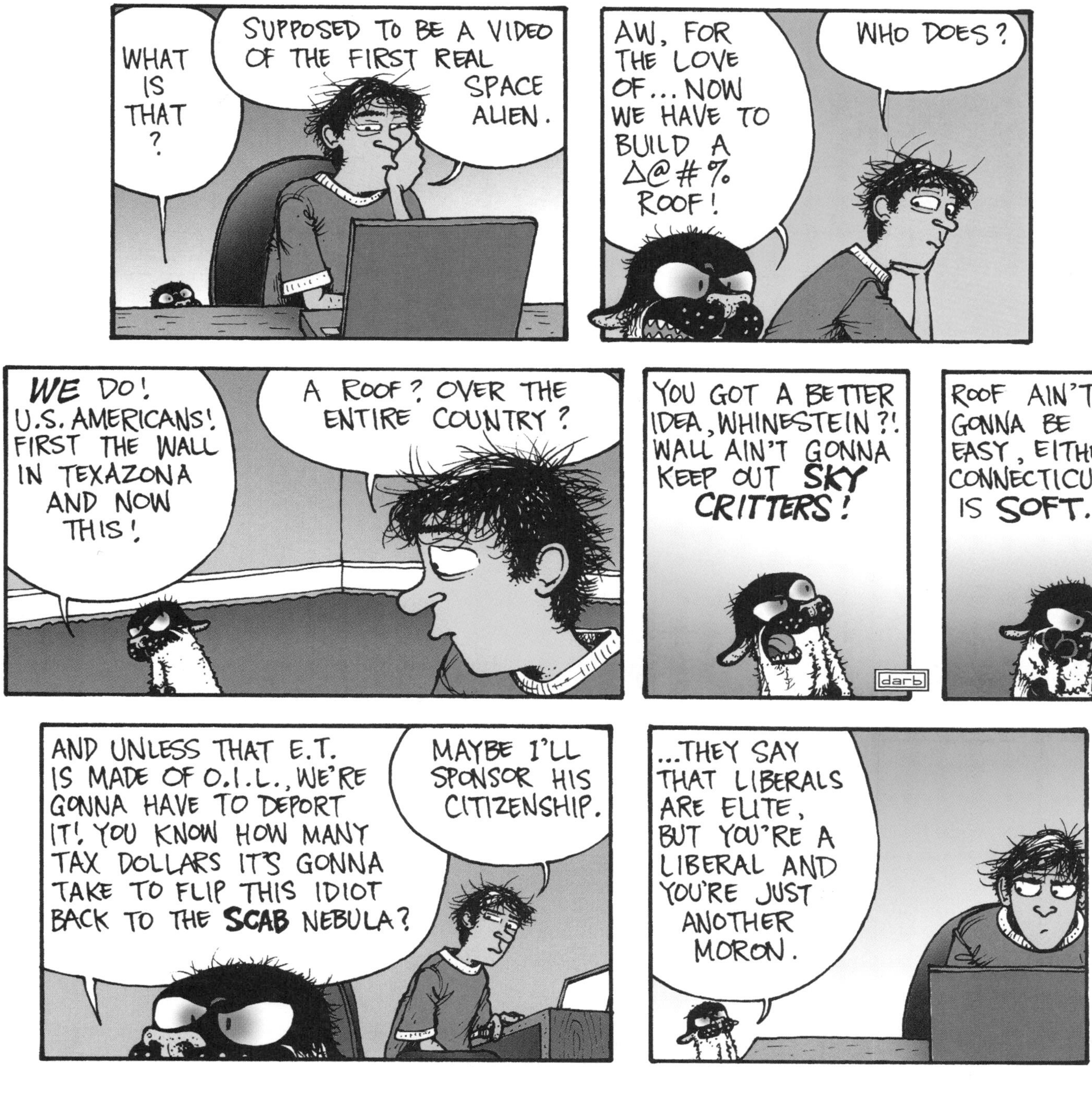
WHAT IS THAT ?
SUPPOSED TO BE A VIDEO OF THE FIRST REAL SPACE ALIEN.
AW, FOR THE LOVE OF... NOW WE HAVE TO BUILD A Δ@#% ROOF!
WHO DOES ?
WE DO! U.S. AMERICANS! FIRST THE WALL IN TEXAZONA AND NOW THIS!
A ROOF? OVER THE ENTIRE COUNTRY ?
YOU GOT A BETTER IDEA, WHINESTEIN ?! WALL AIN'T GONNA KEEP OUT SKY CRITTERS!
darb
ROOF AIN'T GONNA BE EASY, EITHER, CONNECTICUT IS SOFT.
AND UNLESS THAT E.T. IS MADE OF O.I.L., WE'RE GONNA HAVE TO DEPORT IT! YOU KNOW HOW MANY TAX DOLLARS IT'S GONNA TAKE TO FLIP THIS IDIOT BACK TO THE SCAB NEBULA?
MAYBE I'LL SPONSOR HIS CITIZENSHIP.
...THEY SAY THAT LIBERALS ARE ELITE, BUT YOU'RE A LIBERAL AND YOU'RE JUST ANOTHER MORON.

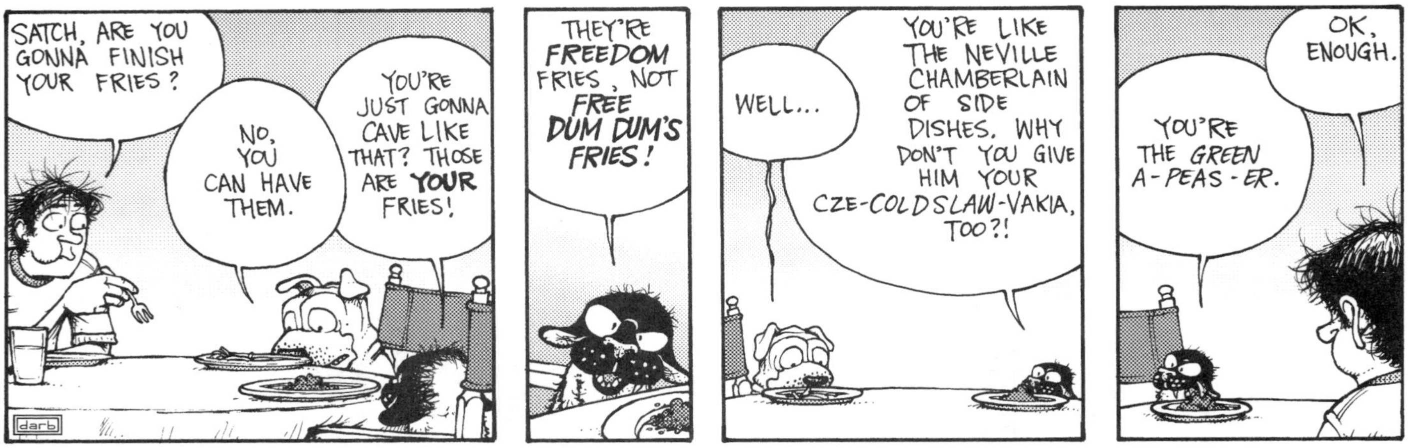
SATCH, ARE YOU GONNA FINISH YOUR FRIES?
NO, YOU CAN HAVE THEM.
YOU'RE JUST GONNA CAVE LIKE THAT? THOSE ARE **YOUR** FRIES!
darb
THEY'RE ***FREEDOM*** FRIES, NOT ***FREE DUM DUM'S FRIES!***
WELL...
YOU'RE LIKE THE NEVILLE CHAMBERLAIN OF SIDE DISHES. WHY DON'T YOU GIVE HIM YOUR CZE-*COLDSLAW*-VAKIA, TOO?!
OK, ENOUGH.
YOU'RE THE *GREEN A-PEAS-ER*.

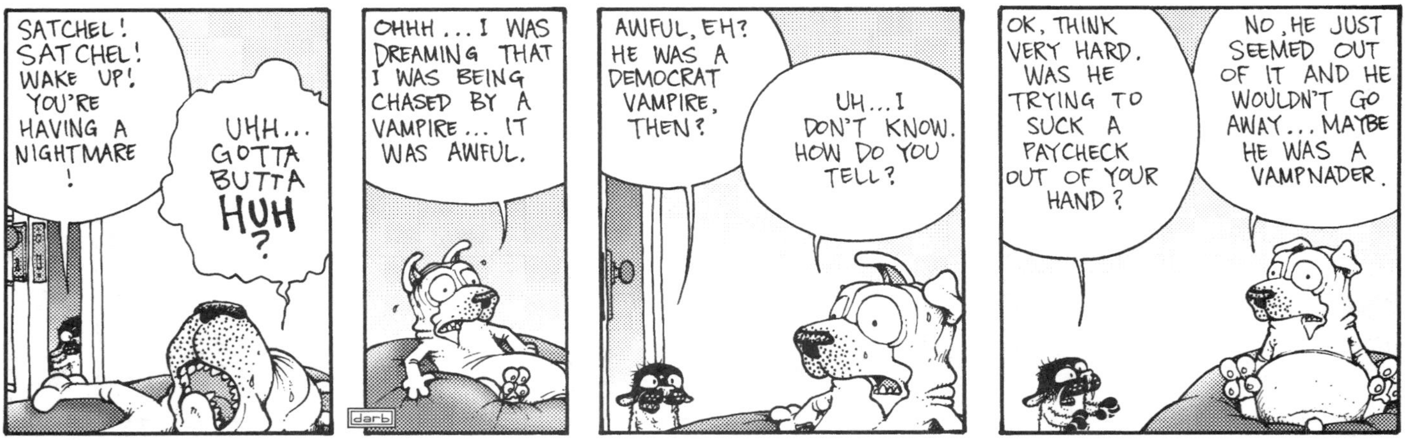
SATCHEL! SATCHEL! WAKE UP! YOU'RE HAVING A NIGHTMARE!
UHH... GOTTA BUTTA HUH?
darb
OHHH... I WAS DREAMING THAT I WAS BEING CHASED BY A VAMPIRE... IT WAS AWFUL.
AWFUL, EH? HE WAS A DEMOCRAT VAMPIRE, THEN?
UH... I DON'T KNOW. HOW DO YOU TELL?
OK, THINK VERY HARD. WAS HE TRYING TO SUCK A PAYCHECK OUT OF YOUR HAND?
NO, HE JUST SEEMED OUT OF IT AND HE WOULDN'T GO AWAY... MAYBE HE WAS A VAMPNADER.

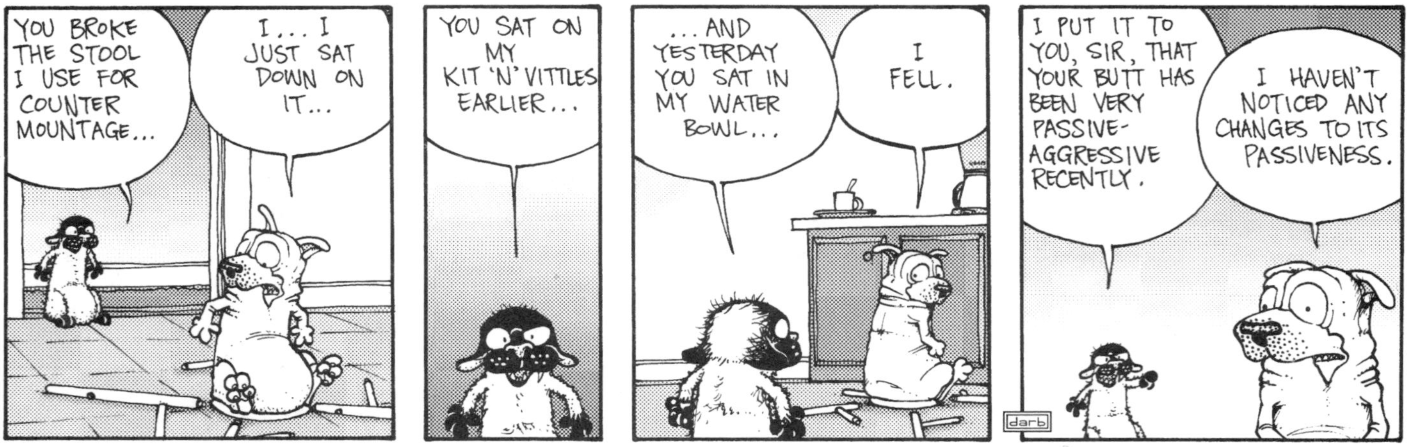
YOU BROKE THE STOOL I USE FOR COUNTER MOUNTAGE...
I... I JUST SAT DOWN ON IT...
YOU SAT ON MY KIT 'N' VITTLES EARLIER...
...AND YESTERDAY YOU SAT IN MY WATER BOWL...
I FELL.
I PUT IT TO YOU, SIR, THAT YOUR BUTT HAS BEEN VERY PASSIVE-AGGRESSIVE RECENTLY.
I HAVEN'T NOTICED ANY CHANGES TO ITS PASSIVENESS.
darb

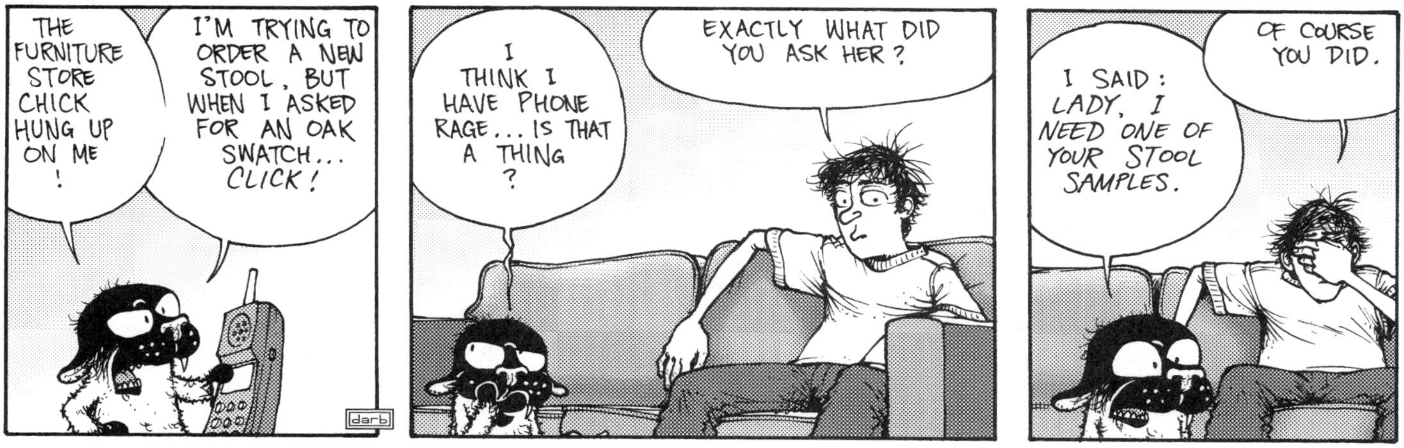
THE FURNITURE STORE CHICK HUNG UP ON ME !
I'M TRYING TO ORDER A NEW STOOL, BUT WHEN I ASKED FOR AN OAK SWATCH... CLICK!
darb
I THINK I HAVE PHONE RAGE... IS THAT A THING ?
EXACTLY WHAT DID YOU ASK HER?
I SAID: LADY, I NEED ONE OF YOUR STOOL SAMPLES.
OF COURSE YOU DID.

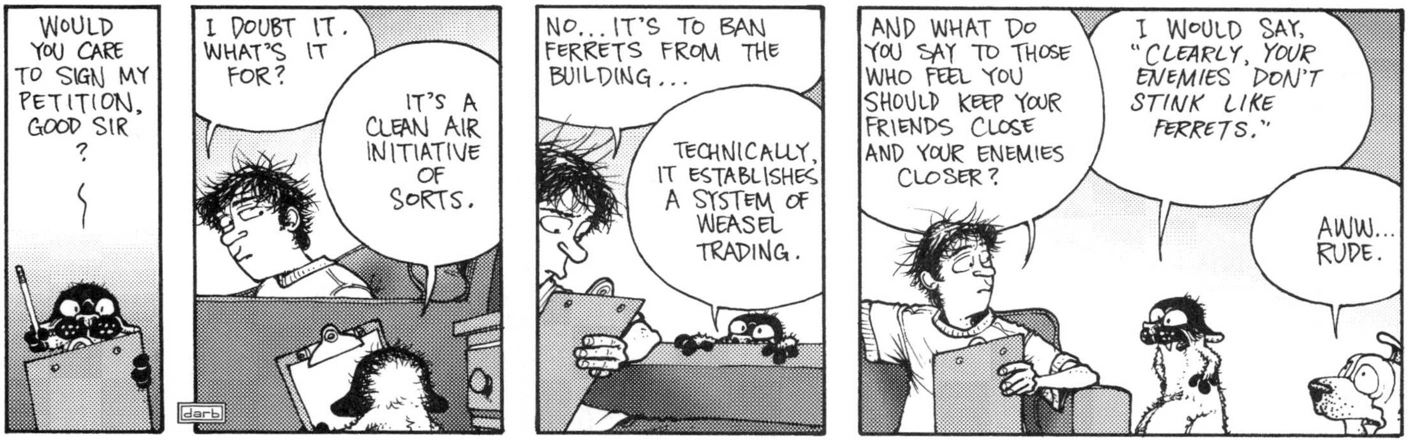
WOULD YOU CARE TO SIGN MY PETITION, GOOD SIR ?
darb
I DOUBT IT. WHAT'S IT FOR?
IT'S A CLEAN AIR INITIATIVE OF SORTS.
NO... IT'S TO BAN FERRETS FROM THE BUILDING...
TECHNICALLY, IT ESTABLISHES A SYSTEM OF WEASEL TRADING.
AND WHAT DO YOU SAY TO THOSE WHO FEEL YOU SHOULD KEEP YOUR FRIENDS CLOSE AND YOUR ENEMIES CLOSER?
I WOULD SAY, "CLEARLY, YOUR ENEMIES DON'T STINK LIKE FERRETS."
AWW... RUDE.

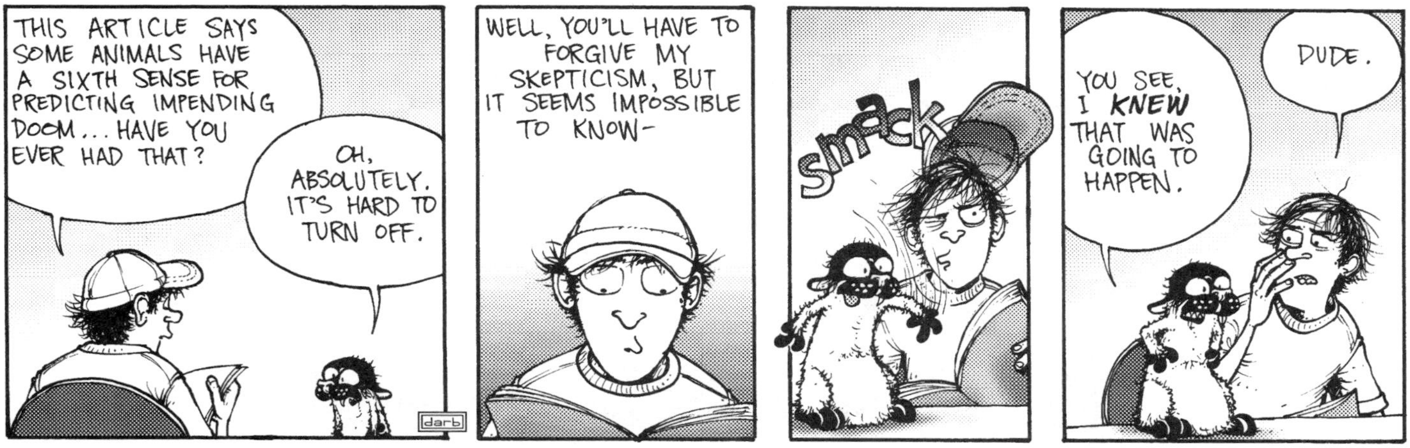
THIS ARTICLE SAYS SOME ANIMALS HAVE A SIXTH SENSE FOR PREDICTING IMPENDING DOOM... HAVE YOU EVER HAD THAT?
OH, ABSOLUTELY. IT'S HARD TO TURN OFF.
darb
WELL, YOU'LL HAVE TO FORGIVE MY SKEPTICISM, BUT IT SEEMS IMPOSSIBLE TO KNOW-
SMACK
YOU SEE, I **KNEW** THAT WAS GOING TO HAPPEN.
DUDE.

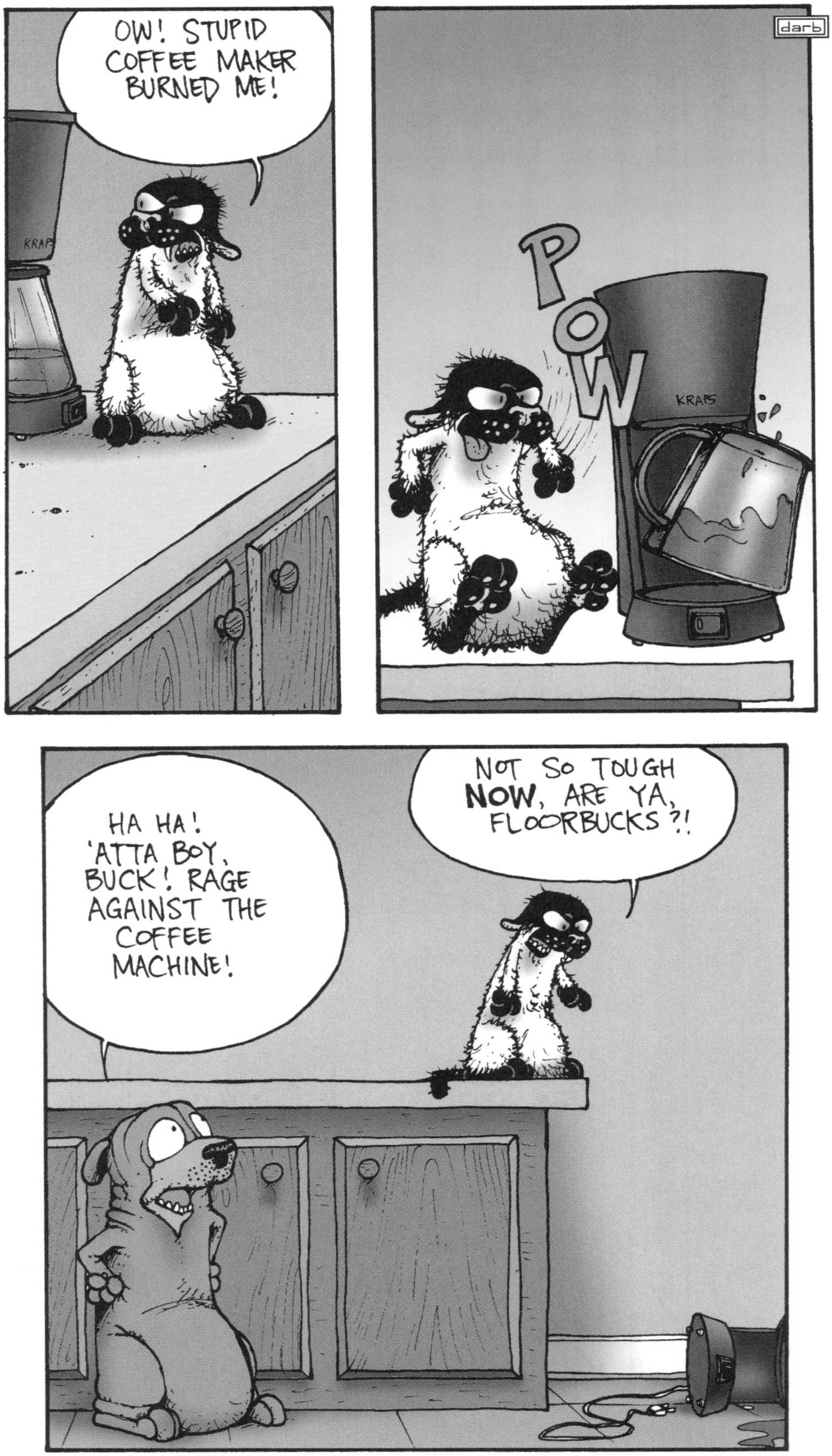
OW! STUPID COFFEE MAKER BURNED ME!
KRAPS
darb
POW
KRAPS
HA HA! 'ATTA BOY, BUCK! RAGE AGAINST THE COFFEE MACHINE!
NOT SO TOUGH NOW, ARE YA, FLOORBUCKS?!

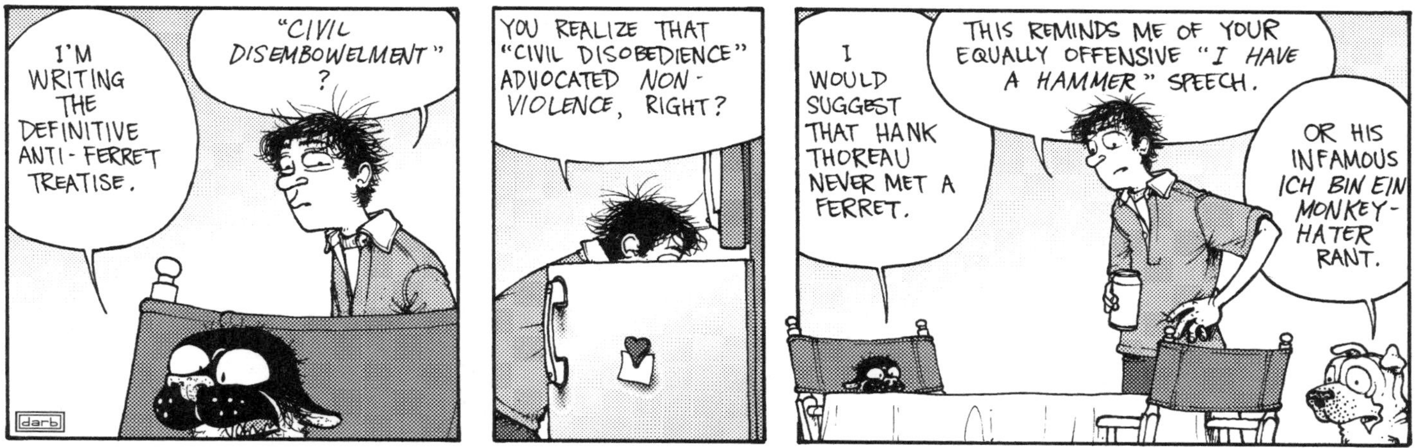
I'M WRITING THE DEFINITIVE ANTI-FERRET TREATISE.
"CIVIL DISEMBOWELMENT"?
YOU REALIZE THAT "CIVIL DISOBEDIENCE" ADVOCATED NON-VIOLENCE, RIGHT?
I WOULD SUGGEST THAT HANK THOREAU NEVER MET A FERRET.
THIS REMINDS ME OF YOUR EQUALLY OFFENSIVE "I HAVE A HAMMER" SPEECH.
OR HIS INFAMOUS ICH BIN EIN MONKEY-HATER RANT.
darb

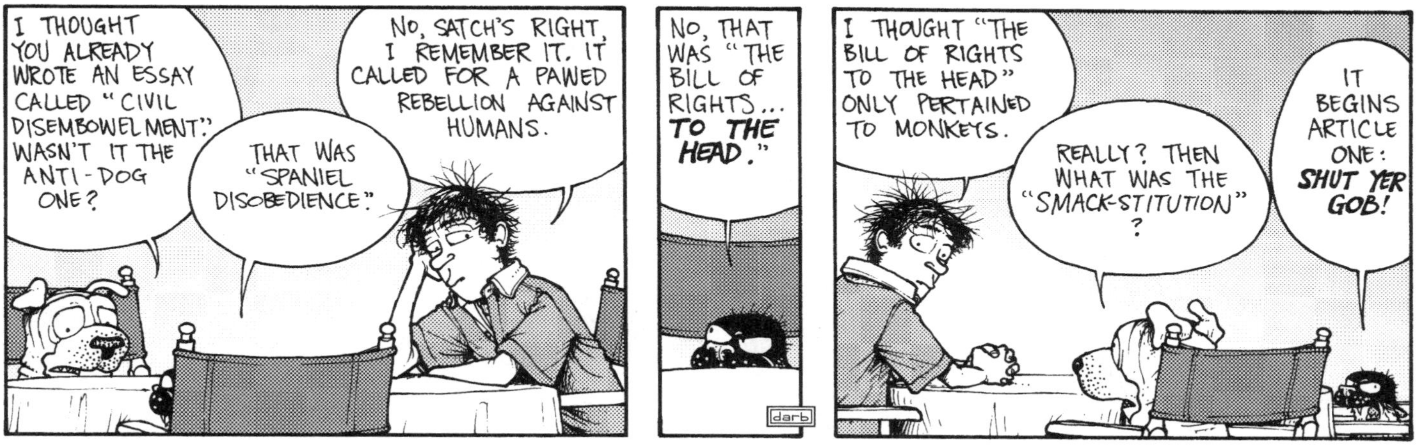
I THOUGHT YOU ALREADY WROTE AN ESSAY CALLED "CIVIL DISEMBOWELMENT." WASN'T IT THE ANTI-DOG ONE?
THAT WAS "SPANIEL DISOBEDIENCE."
NO, SATCH'S RIGHT, I REMEMBER IT. IT CALLED FOR A PAWED REBELLION AGAINST HUMANS.
NO, THAT WAS "THE BILL OF RIGHTS... TO THE HEAD."
I THOUGHT "THE BILL OF RIGHTS TO THE HEAD" ONLY PERTAINED TO MONKEYS.
REALLY? THEN WHAT WAS THE "SMACK-STITUTION"?
IT BEGINS ARTICLE ONE: SHUT YER GOB!
darb

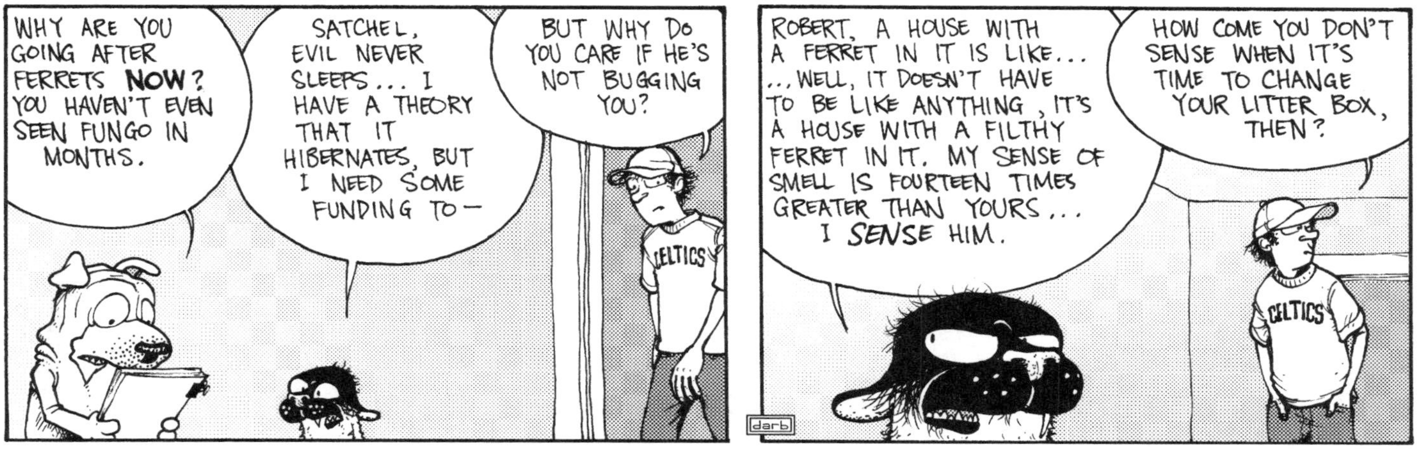
WHY ARE YOU GOING AFTER FERRETS NOW? YOU HAVEN'T EVEN SEEN FUNGO IN MONTHS.
SATCHEL, EVIL NEVER SLEEPS... I HAVE A THEORY THAT IT HIBERNATES, BUT I NEED SOME FUNDING TO—
BUT WHY DO YOU CARE IF HE'S NOT BUGGING YOU?
CELTICS
ROBERT, A HOUSE WITH A FERRET IN IT IS LIKE... ...WELL, IT DOESN'T HAVE TO BE LIKE ANYTHING, IT'S A HOUSE WITH A FILTHY FERRET IN IT. MY SENSE OF SMELL IS FOURTEEN TIMES GREATER THAN YOURS... I SENSE HIM.
HOW COME YOU DON'T SENSE WHEN IT'S TIME TO CHANGE YOUR LITTER BOX, THEN?
CELTICS
darb

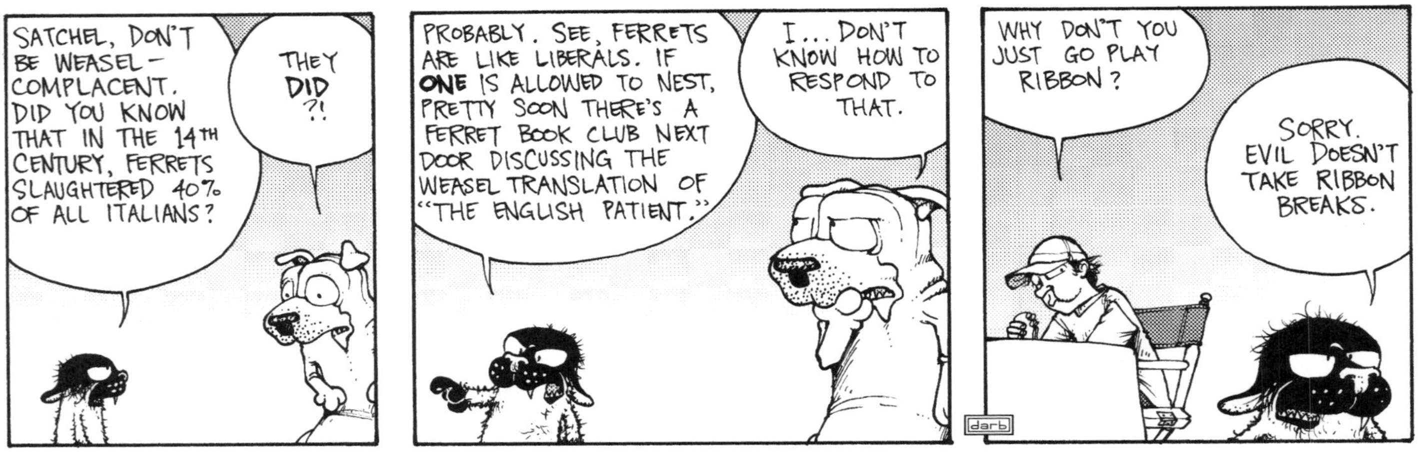
SATCHEL, DON'T BE WEASEL-COMPLACENT. DID YOU KNOW THAT IN THE 14TH CENTURY, FERRETS SLAUGHTERED 40% OF ALL ITALIANS?
THEY DID ?!
PROBABLY. SEE, FERRETS ARE LIKE LIBERALS. IF ONE IS ALLOWED TO NEST, PRETTY SOON THERE'S A FERRET BOOK CLUB NEXT DOOR DISCUSSING THE WEASEL TRANSLATION OF "THE ENGLISH PATIENT."
I... DON'T KNOW HOW TO RESPOND TO THAT.
WHY DON'T YOU JUST GO PLAY RIBBON?
SORRY. EVIL DOESN'T TAKE RIBBON BREAKS.
darb

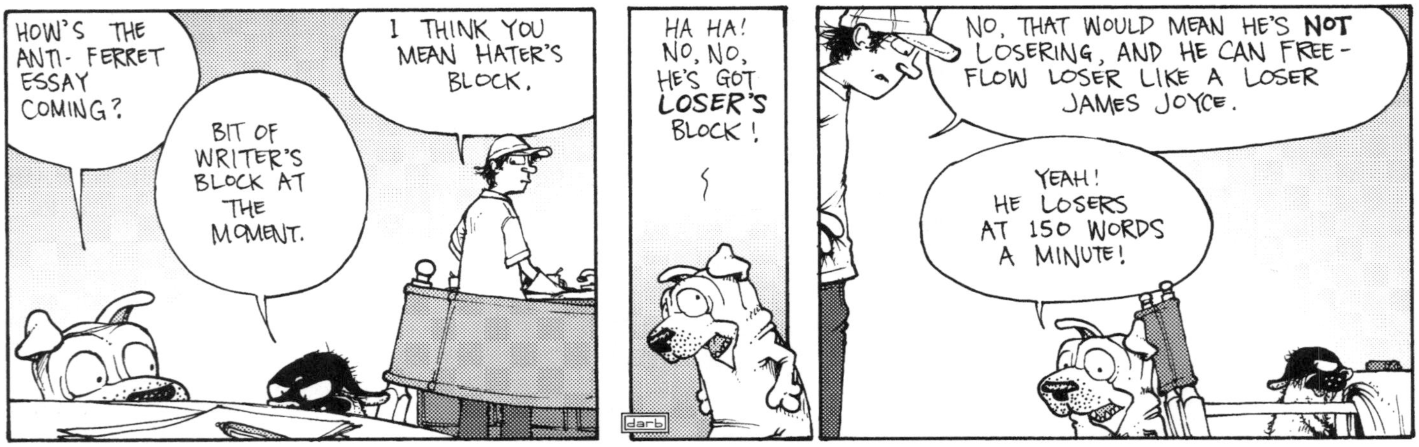
HOW'S THE ANTI-FERRET ESSAY COMING?
BIT OF WRITER'S BLOCK AT THE MOMENT.
I THINK YOU MEAN HATER'S BLOCK.
HA HA! NO, NO, HE'S GOT LOSER'S BLOCK!
darb
NO, THAT WOULD MEAN HE'S NOT LOSERING, AND HE CAN FREE-FLOW LOSER LIKE A LOSER JAMES JOYCE.
YEAH! HE LOSERS AT 150 WORDS A MINUTE!

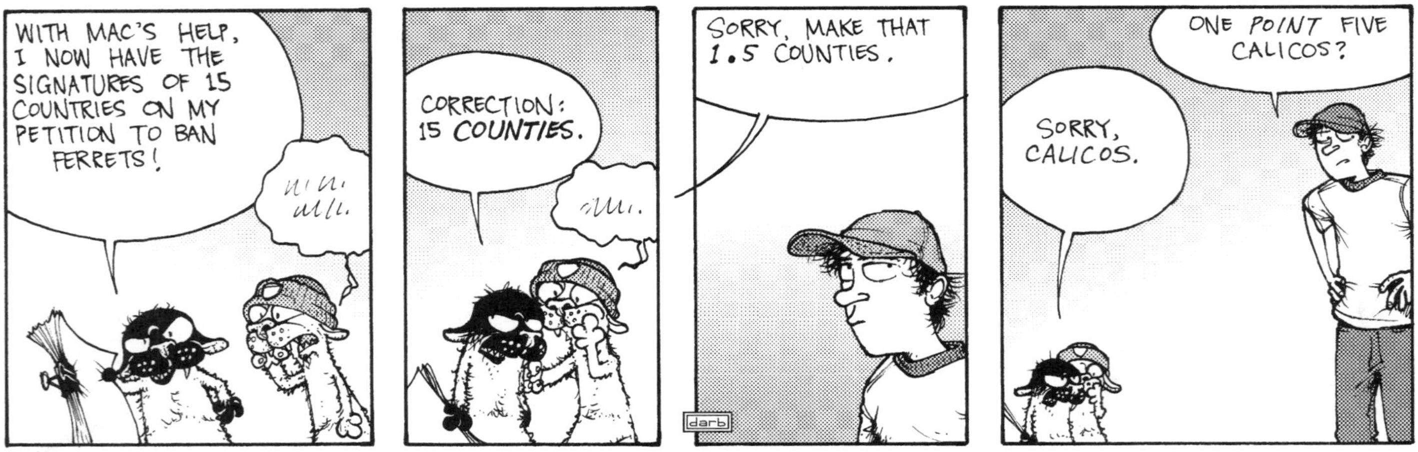
WITH MAC'S HELP, I NOW HAVE THE SIGNATURES OF 15 COUNTRIES ON MY PETITION TO BAN FERRETS!
CORRECTION: 15 COUNTIES.
SORRY, MAKE THAT 1.5 COUNTIES.
darb
ONE POINT FIVE CALICOS?
SORRY, CALICOS.

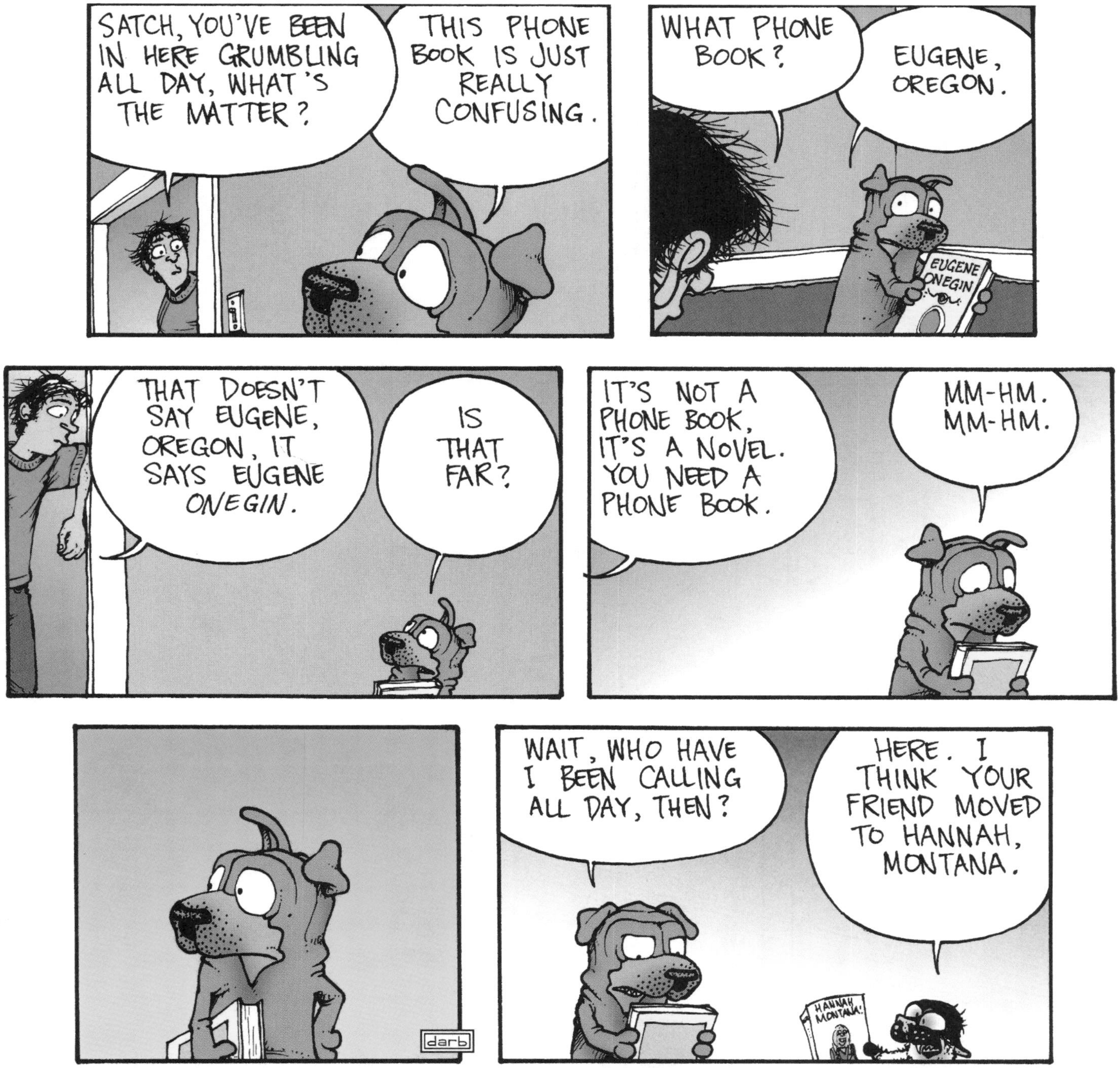
SATCH, YOU'VE BEEN IN HERE GRUMBLING ALL DAY, WHAT'S THE MATTER?
THIS PHONE BOOK IS JUST REALLY CONFUSING.
WHAT PHONE BOOK?
EUGENE, OREGON.
EUGENE ONEGIN
THAT DOESN'T SAY EUGENE, OREGON, IT SAYS EUGENE ONEGIN.
IS THAT FAR?
IT'S NOT A PHONE BOOK, IT'S A NOVEL. YOU NEED A PHONE BOOK.
MM-HM. MM-HM.
darb
WAIT, WHO HAVE I BEEN CALLING ALL DAY, THEN?
HERE. I THINK YOUR FRIEND MOVED TO HANNAH, MONTANA.
HANNAH MONTANA!

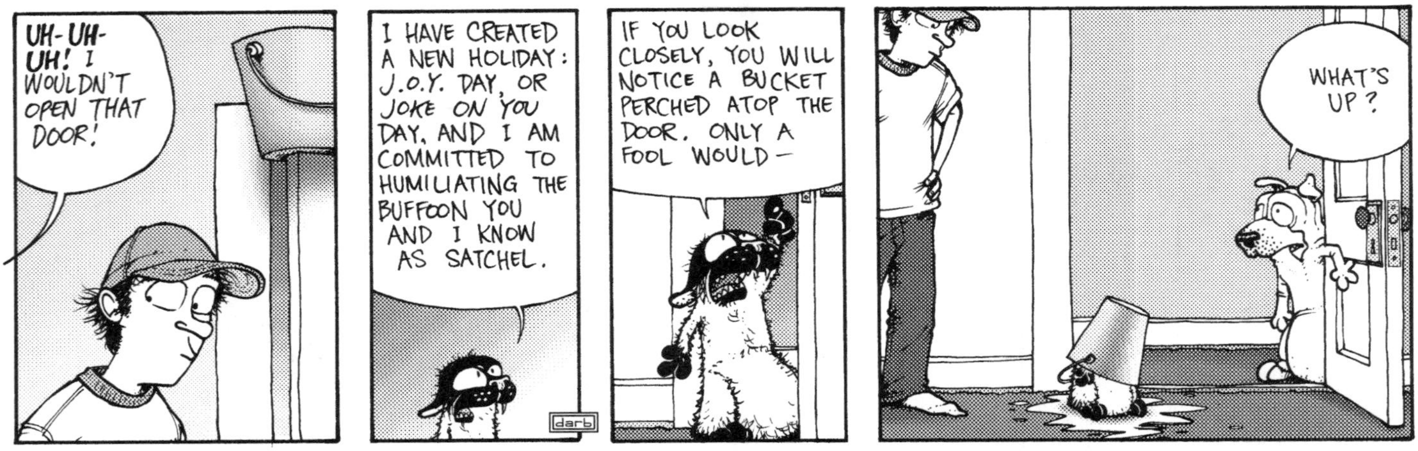
UH-UH-UH! I WOULDN'T OPEN THAT DOOR!
I HAVE CREATED A NEW HOLIDAY: J.O.Y. DAY, OR JOKE ON YOU DAY, AND I AM COMMITTED TO HUMILIATING THE BUFFOON YOU AND I KNOW AS SATCHEL.
darb
IF YOU LOOK CLOSELY, YOU WILL NOTICE A BUCKET PERCHED ATOP THE DOOR. ONLY A FOOL WOULD—
WHAT'S UP?

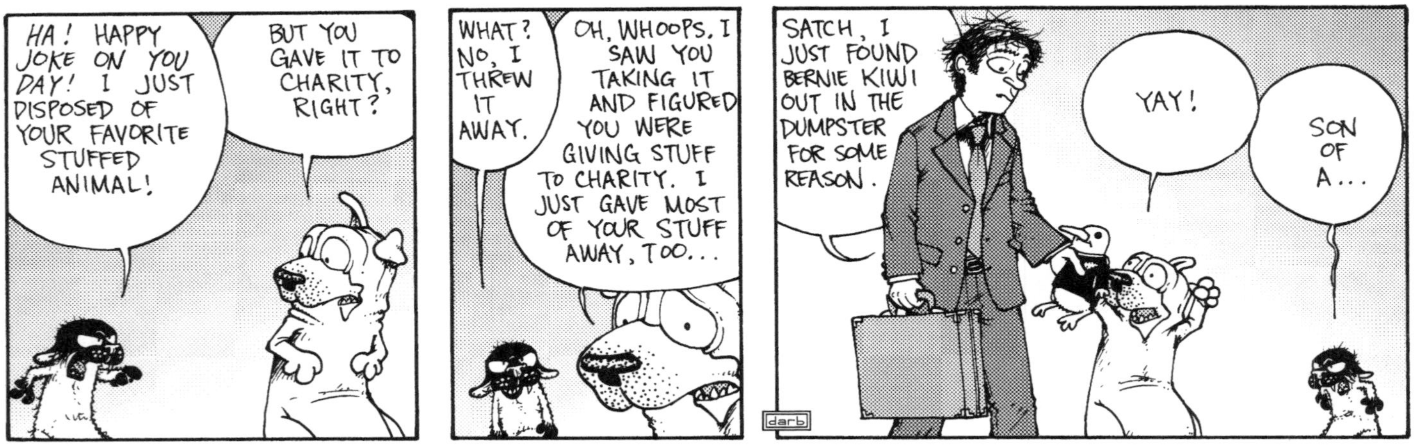
HA! HAPPY JOKE ON YOU DAY! I JUST DISPOSED OF YOUR FAVORITE STUFFED ANIMAL!
BUT YOU GAVE IT TO CHARITY, RIGHT?
WHAT? NO, I THREW IT AWAY.
OH, WHOOPS. I SAW YOU TAKING IT AND FIGURED YOU WERE GIVING STUFF TO CHARITY. I JUST GAVE MOST OF YOUR STUFF AWAY, TOO...
darb
SATCH, I JUST FOUND BERNIE KIWI OUT IN THE DUMPSTER FOR SOME REASON.
YAY!
SON OF A...

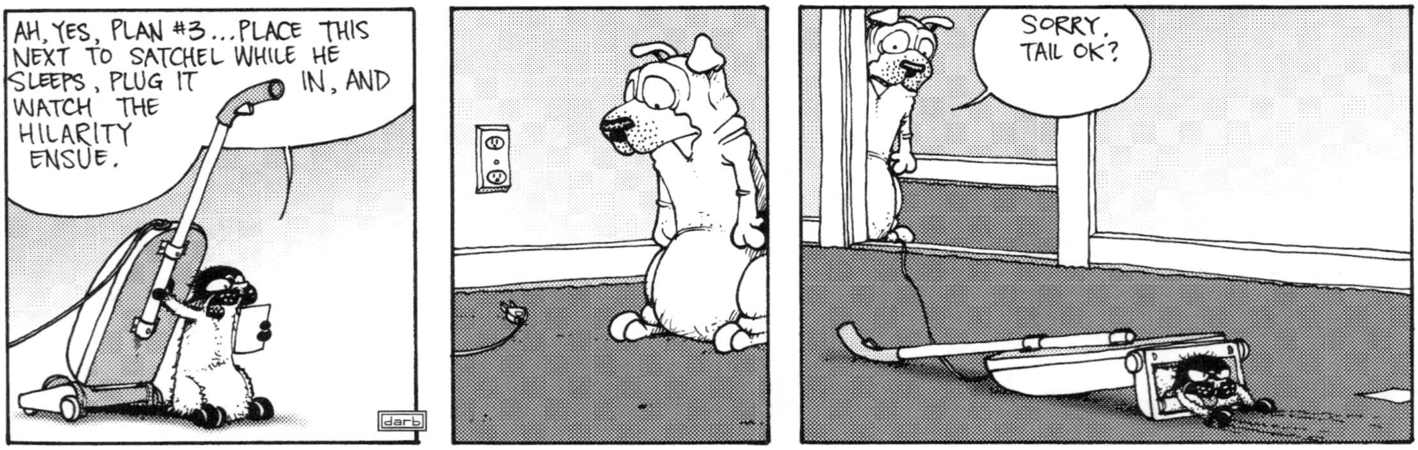
AH, YES, PLAN #3...PLACE THIS NEXT TO SATCHEL WHILE HE SLEEPS, PLUG IT IN, AND WATCH THE HILARITY ENSUE.
darb
SORRY. TAIL OK?

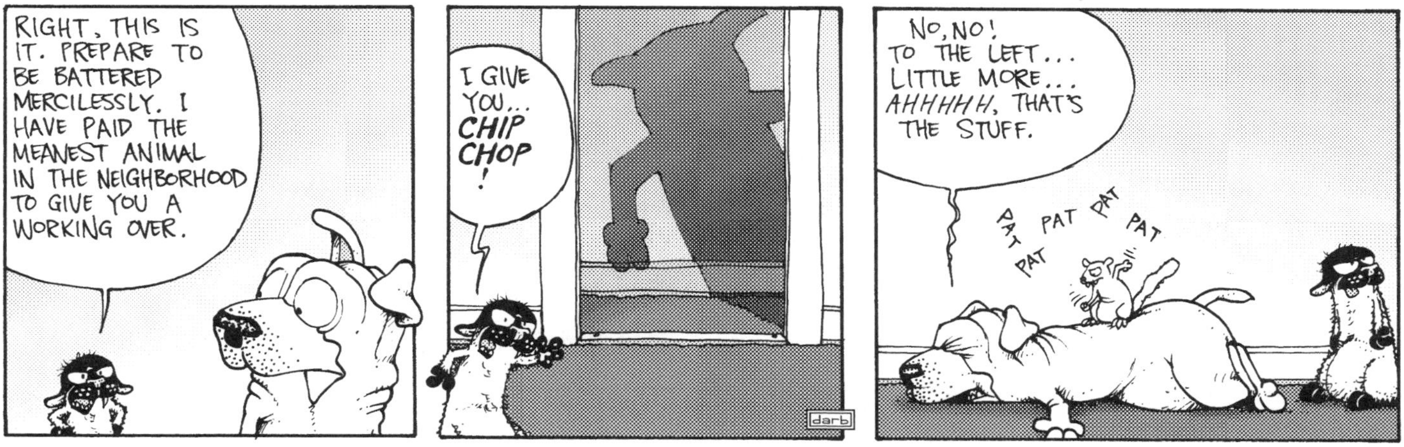
RIGHT, THIS IS IT. PREPARE TO BE BATTERED MERCILESSLY. I HAVE PAID THE MEANEST ANIMAL IN THE NEIGHBORHOOD TO GIVE YOU A WORKING OVER.
I GIVE YOU... CHIP CHOP !
darb
NO, NO! TO THE LEFT... LITTLE MORE... AHHHHH, THAT'S THE STUFF.
PAT PAT PAT PAT PAT

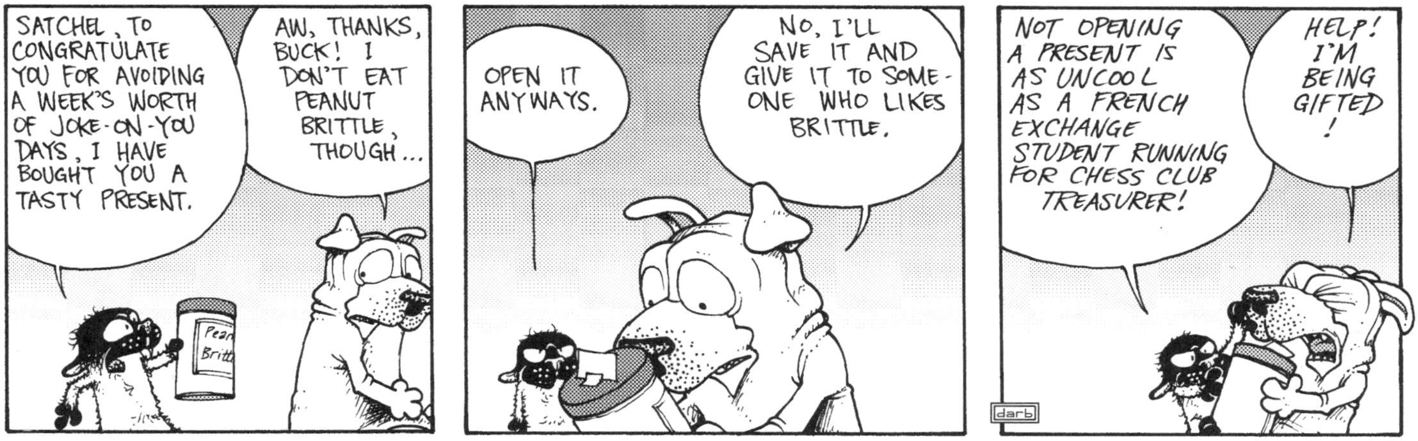
SATCHEL, TO CONGRATULATE YOU FOR AVOIDING A WEEK'S WORTH OF JOKE-ON-YOU DAYS, I HAVE BOUGHT YOU A TASTY PRESENT.
AW, THANKS, BUCK! I DON'T EAT PEANUT BRITTLE, THOUGH...
Peanut Brittle
OPEN IT ANYWAYS.
NO, I'LL SAVE IT AND GIVE IT TO SOMEONE WHO LIKES BRITTLE.
NOT OPENING A PRESENT IS AS UNCOOL AS A FRENCH EXCHANGE STUDENT RUNNING FOR CHESS CLUB TREASURER!
HELP! I'M BEING GIFTED !
darb

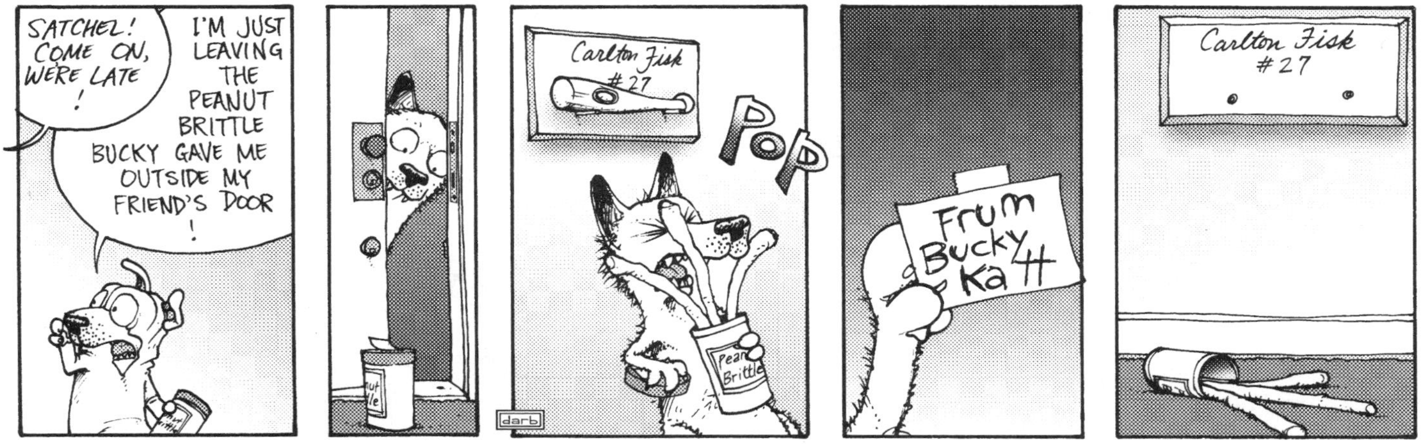
SATCHEL! COME ON, WE'RE LATE !
I'M JUST LEAVING THE PEANUT BRITTLE BUCKY GAVE ME OUTSIDE MY FRIEND'S DOOR !
darb
Carlton Fisk #27
POP
Peanut Brittle
Frum Bucky Katt
Carlton Fisk #27

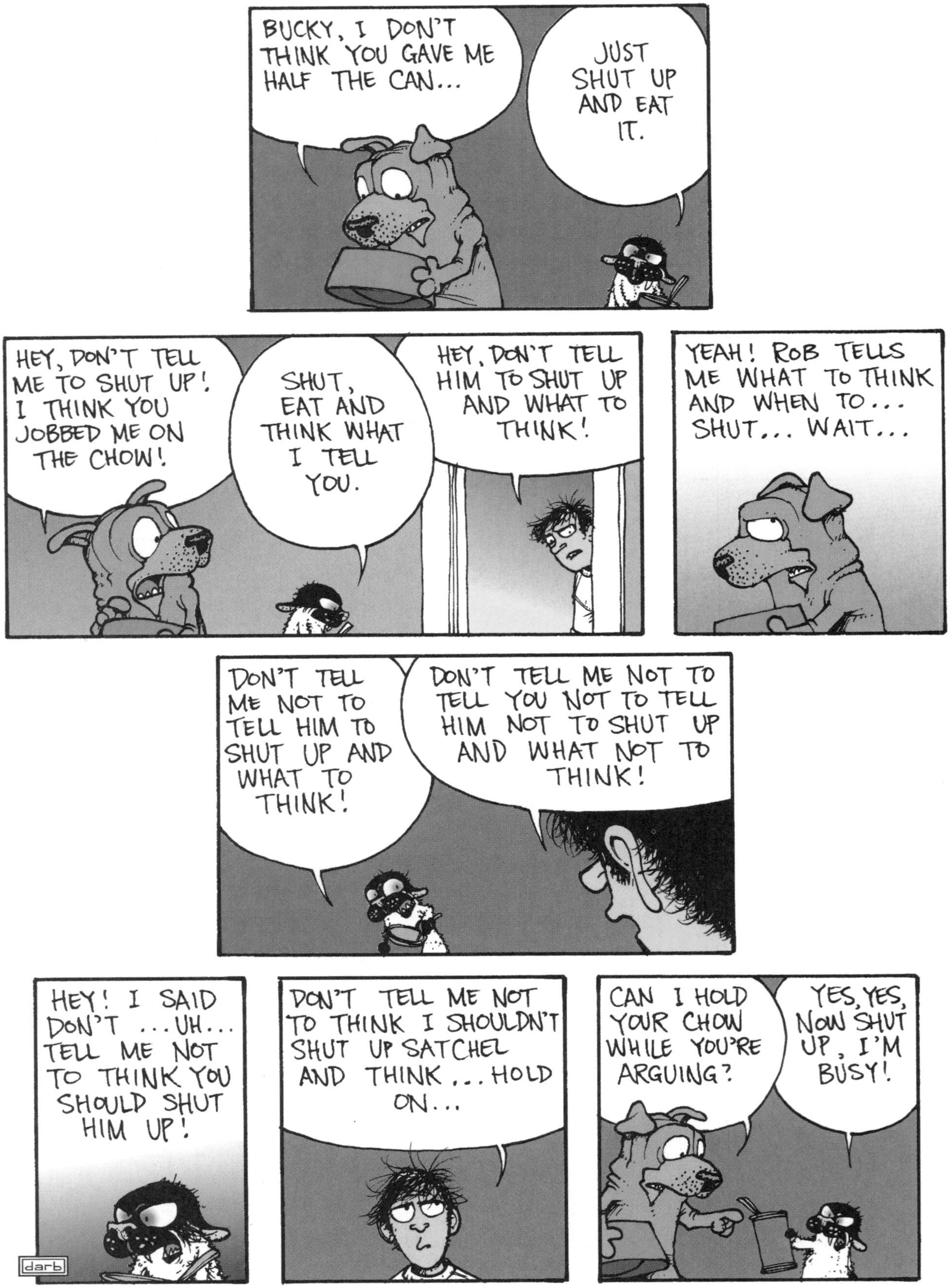
BUCKY, I DON'T THINK YOU GAVE ME HALF THE CAN...
JUST SHUT UP AND EAT IT.
HEY, DON'T TELL ME TO SHUT UP! I THINK YOU JOBBED ME ON THE CHOW!
SHUT, EAT AND THINK WHAT I TELL YOU.
HEY, DON'T TELL HIM TO SHUT UP AND WHAT TO THINK!
YEAH! ROB TELLS ME WHAT TO THINK AND WHEN TO... SHUT... WAIT...
DON'T TELL ME NOT TO TELL HIM TO SHUT UP AND WHAT TO THINK!
DON'T TELL ME NOT TO TELL YOU NOT TO TELL HIM NOT TO SHUT UP AND WHAT NOT TO THINK!
HEY! I SAID DON'T ...UH... TELL ME NOT TO THINK YOU SHOULD SHUT HIM UP!
darb
DON'T TELL ME NOT TO THINK I SHOULDN'T SHUT UP SATCHEL AND THINK... HOLD ON...
CAN I HOLD YOUR CHOW WHILE YOU'RE ARGUING?
YES, YES, NOW SHUT UP, I'M BUSY!

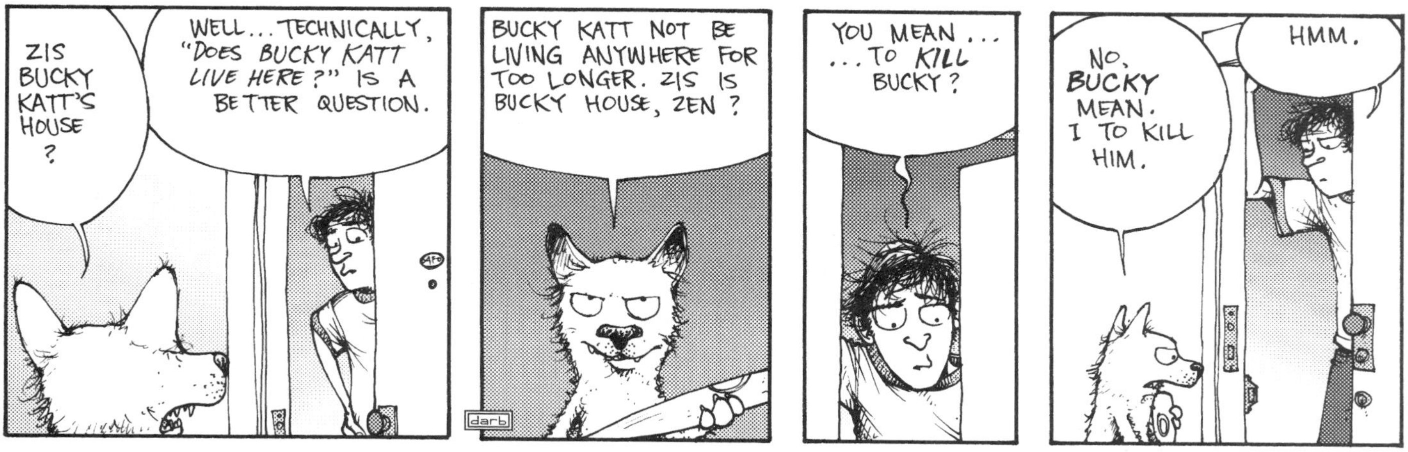

ZIS BUCKY KATT'S HOUSE ?
WELL... TECHNICALLY, *"DOES BUCKY KATT LIVE HERE?"* IS A BETTER QUESTION.
BUCKY KATT NOT BE LIVING ANYWHERE FOR TOO LONGER. ZIS IS BUCKY HOUSE, ZEN ?
YOU MEAN... ...TO **KILL** BUCKY?
NO, **BUCKY** MEAN. I TO KILL HIM.
HMM.
darb

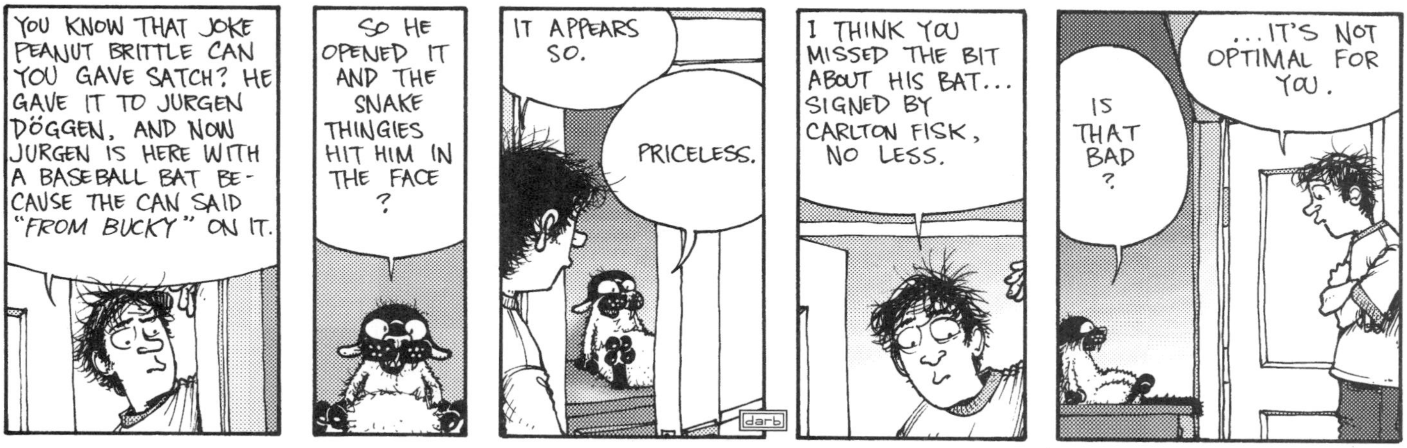

YOU KNOW THAT JOKE PEANUT BRITTLE CAN YOU GAVE SATCH? HE GAVE IT TO JURGEN DÖGGEN, AND NOW JURGEN IS HERE WITH A BASEBALL BAT BECAUSE THE CAN SAID *"FROM BUCKY"* ON IT.
SO HE OPENED IT AND THE SNAKE THINGIES HIT HIM IN THE FACE ?
IT APPEARS SO.
PRICELESS.
I THINK YOU MISSED THE BIT ABOUT HIS BAT... SIGNED BY CARLTON FISK, NO LESS.
IS THAT BAD ?
...IT'S NOT OPTIMAL FOR YOU.
darb

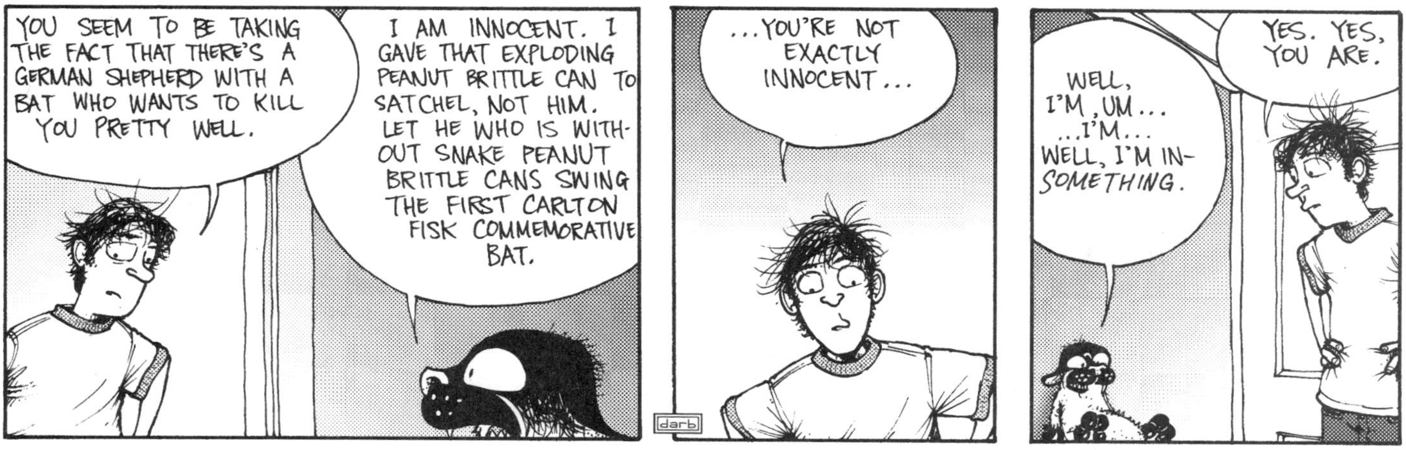

YOU SEEM TO BE TAKING THE FACT THAT THERE'S A GERMAN SHEPHERD WITH A BAT WHO WANTS TO KILL YOU PRETTY WELL.
I AM INNOCENT. I GAVE THAT EXPLODING PEANUT BRITTLE CAN TO SATCHEL, NOT HIM. LET HE WHO IS WITHOUT SNAKE PEANUT BRITTLE CANS SWING THE FIRST CARLTON FISK COMMEMORATIVE BAT.
...YOU'RE NOT EXACTLY INNOCENT...
WELL, I'M, UM... ...I'M... WELL, I'M IN-*SOMETHING.*
YES. YES, YOU ARE.
darb

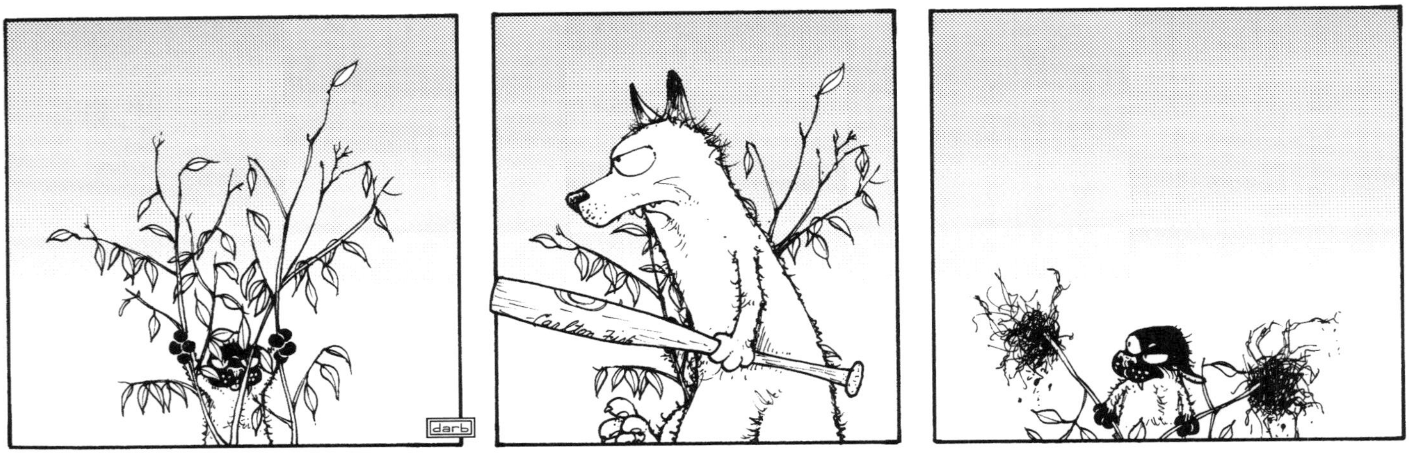

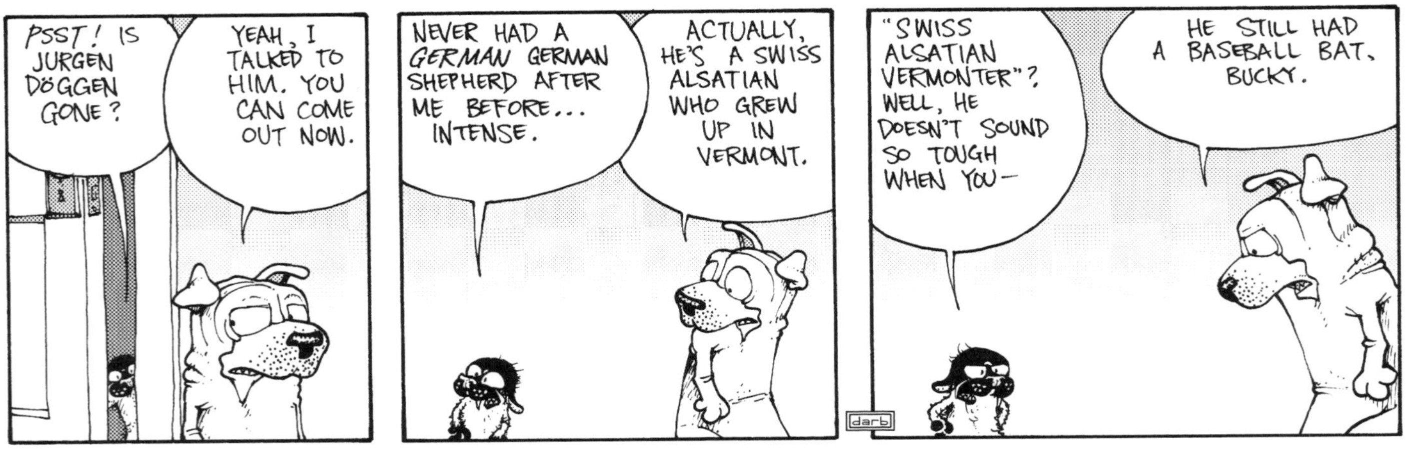
PSST! IS JURGEN DÖGGEN GONE?
YEAH, I TALKED TO HIM. YOU CAN COME OUT NOW.
NEVER HAD A GERMAN GERMAN SHEPHERD AFTER ME BEFORE... INTENSE.
ACTUALLY, HE'S A SWISS ALSATIAN WHO GREW UP IN VERMONT.
"SWISS ALSATIAN VERMONTER"? WELL, HE DOESN'T SOUND SO TOUGH WHEN YOU—
HE STILL HAD A BASEBALL BAT, BUCKY.

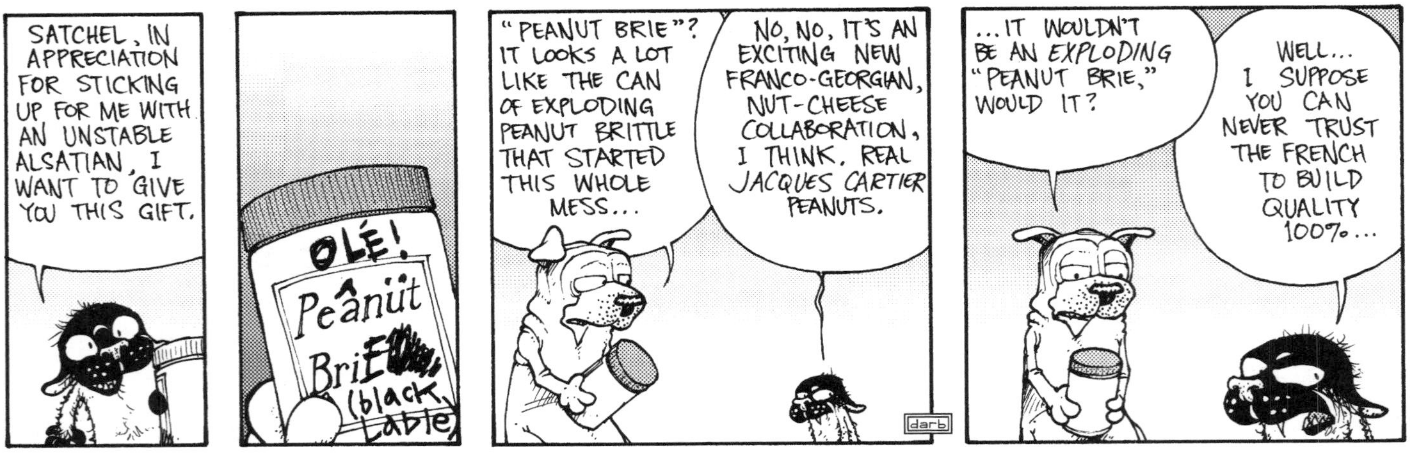
SATCHEL, IN APPRECIATION FOR STICKING UP FOR ME WITH AN UNSTABLE ALSATIAN, I WANT TO GIVE YOU THIS GIFT.
OLÉ!
Peânüt BriE
(black Lable)
"PEANUT BRIE"? IT LOOKS A LOT LIKE THE CAN OF EXPLODING PEANUT BRITTLE THAT STARTED THIS WHOLE MESS...
NO, NO, IT'S AN EXCITING NEW FRANCO-GEORGIAN, NUT-CHEESE COLLABORATION, I THINK. REAL JACQUES CARTIER PEANUTS.
...IT WOULDN'T BE AN EXPLODING "PEANUT BRIE," WOULD IT?
WELL... I SUPPOSE YOU CAN NEVER TRUST THE FRENCH TO BUILD QUALITY 100%...

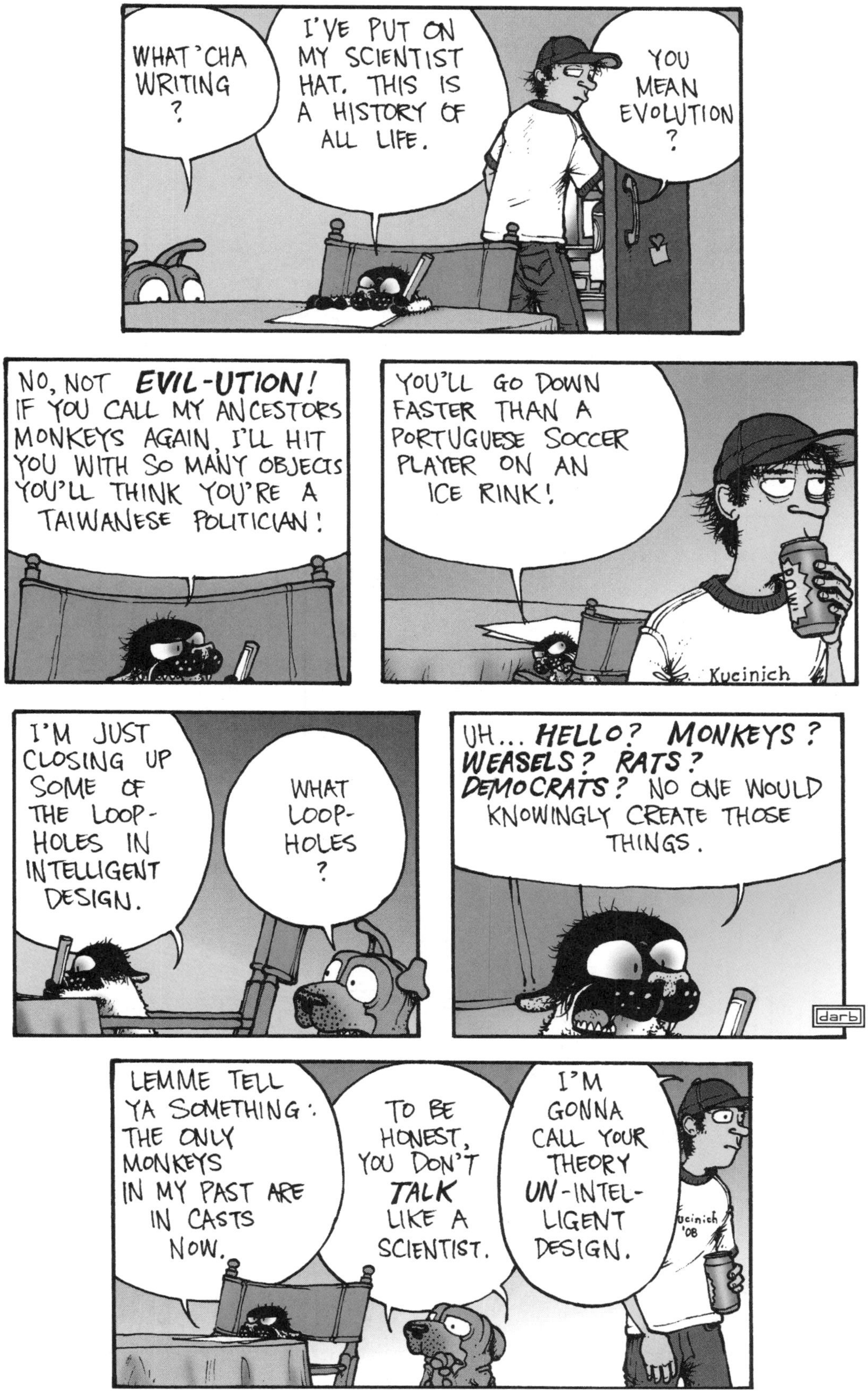
WHAT'CHA WRITING ?
I'VE PUT ON MY SCIENTIST HAT. THIS IS A HISTORY OF ALL LIFE.
YOU MEAN EVOLUTION ?
NO, NOT EVIL-UTION! IF YOU CALL MY ANCESTORS MONKEYS AGAIN, I'LL HIT YOU WITH SO MANY OBJECTS YOU'LL THINK YOU'RE A TAIWANESE POLITICIAN!
YOU'LL GO DOWN FASTER THAN A PORTUGUESE SOCCER PLAYER ON AN ICE RINK!
Kucinich
I'M JUST CLOSING UP SOME OF THE LOOP-HOLES IN INTELLIGENT DESIGN.
WHAT LOOP-HOLES ?
UH... HELLO? MONKEYS? WEASELS? RATS? DEMOCRATS? NO ONE WOULD KNOWINGLY CREATE THOSE THINGS.
darb
LEMME TELL YA SOMETHING: THE ONLY MONKEYS IN MY PAST ARE IN CASTS NOW.
TO BE HONEST, YOU DON'T TALK LIKE A SCIENTIST.
I'M GONNA CALL YOUR THEORY UN-INTEL-LIGENT DESIGN.
Kucinich '08

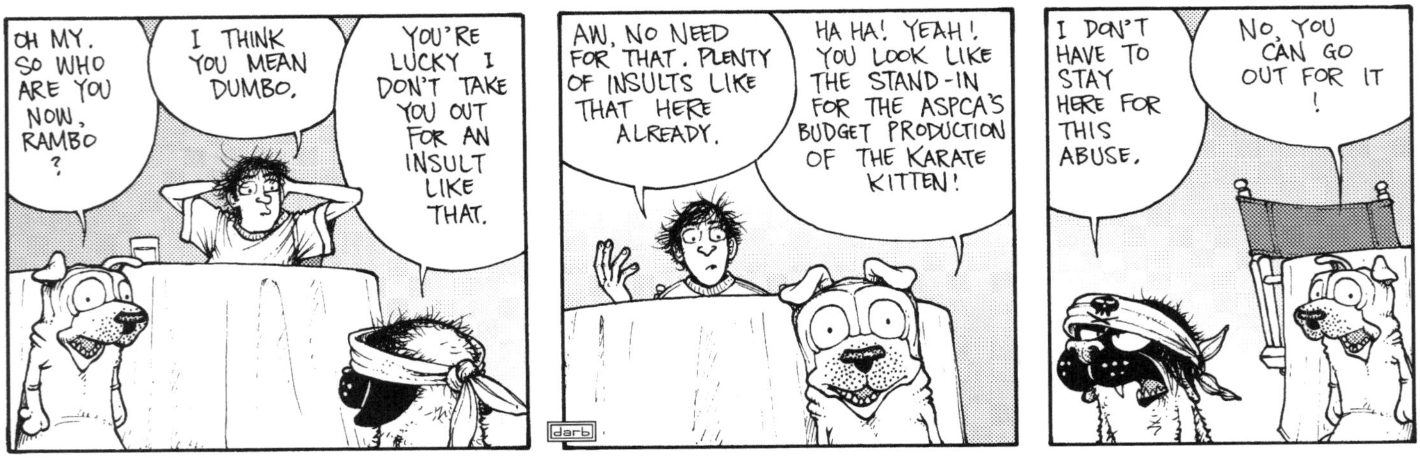
OH MY. SO WHO ARE YOU NOW, RAMBO ?
I THINK YOU MEAN DUMBO.
YOU'RE LUCKY I DON'T TAKE YOU OUT FOR AN INSULT LIKE THAT.
darb
AW, NO NEED FOR THAT. PLENTY OF INSULTS LIKE THAT HERE ALREADY.
HA HA! YEAH! YOU LOOK LIKE THE STAND-IN FOR THE ASPCA'S BUDGET PRODUCTION OF THE KARATE KITTEN!
I DON'T HAVE TO STAY HERE FOR THIS ABUSE.
NO, YOU CAN GO OUT FOR IT !

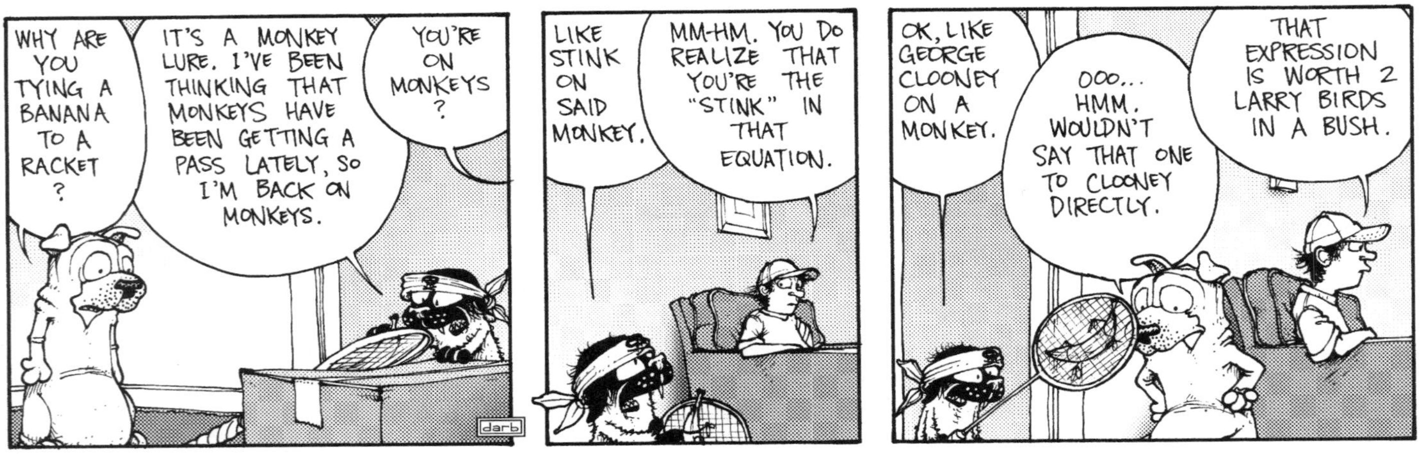
WHY ARE YOU TYING A BANANA TO A RACKET ?
IT'S A MONKEY LURE. I'VE BEEN THINKING THAT MONKEYS HAVE BEEN GETTING A PASS LATELY, SO I'M BACK ON MONKEYS.
YOU'RE ON MONKEYS ?
darb
LIKE STINK ON SAID MONKEY.
MM-HM. YOU DO REALIZE THAT YOU'RE THE "STINK" IN THAT EQUATION.
OK, LIKE GEORGE CLOONEY ON A MONKEY.
OOO... HMM. WOULDN'T SAY THAT ONE TO CLOONEY DIRECTLY.
THAT EXPRESSION IS WORTH 2 LARRY BIRDS IN A BUSH.

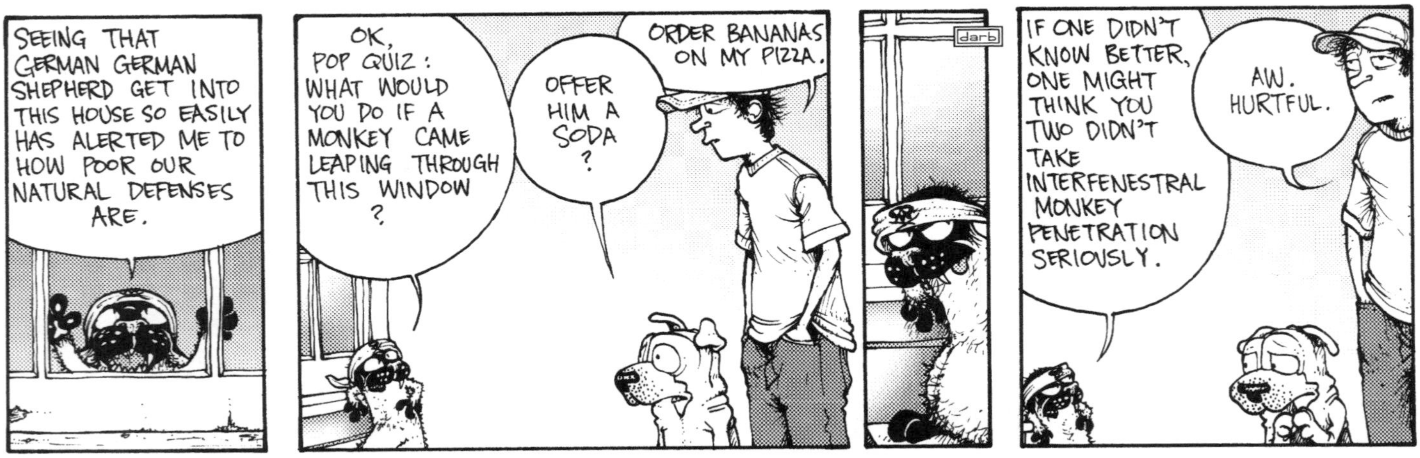
SEEING THAT GERMAN GERMAN SHEPHERD GET INTO THIS HOUSE SO EASILY HAS ALERTED ME TO HOW POOR OUR NATURAL DEFENSES ARE.
OK, POP QUIZ: WHAT WOULD YOU DO IF A MONKEY CAME LEAPING THROUGH THIS WINDOW ?
OFFER HIM A SODA ?
ORDER BANANAS ON MY PIZZA.
darb
IF ONE DIDN'T KNOW BETTER, ONE MIGHT THINK YOU TWO DIDN'T TAKE INTERFENESTRAL MONKEY PENETRATION SERIOUSLY.
AW. HURTFUL.

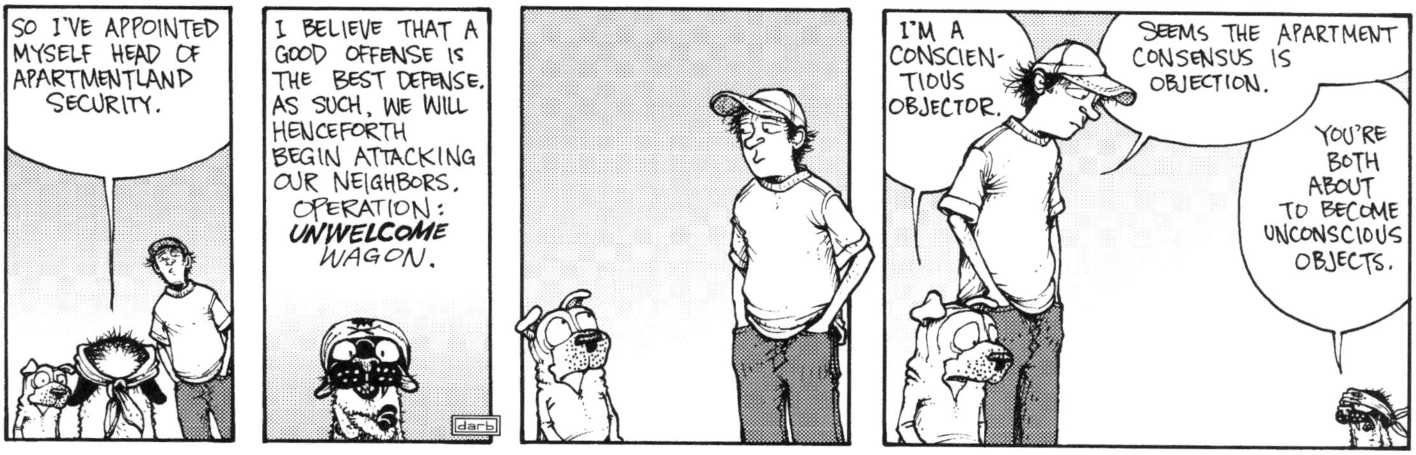
SO I'VE APPOINTED MYSELF HEAD OF APARTMENTLAND SECURITY.
I BELIEVE THAT A GOOD OFFENSE IS THE BEST DEFENSE. AS SUCH, WE WILL HENCEFORTH BEGIN ATTACKING OUR NEIGHBORS. OPERATION: UNWELCOME WAGON.
darb
I'M A CONSCIENTIOUS OBJECTOR.
SEEMS THE APARTMENT CONSENSUS IS OBJECTION.
YOU'RE BOTH ABOUT TO BECOME UNCONSCIOUS OBJECTS.

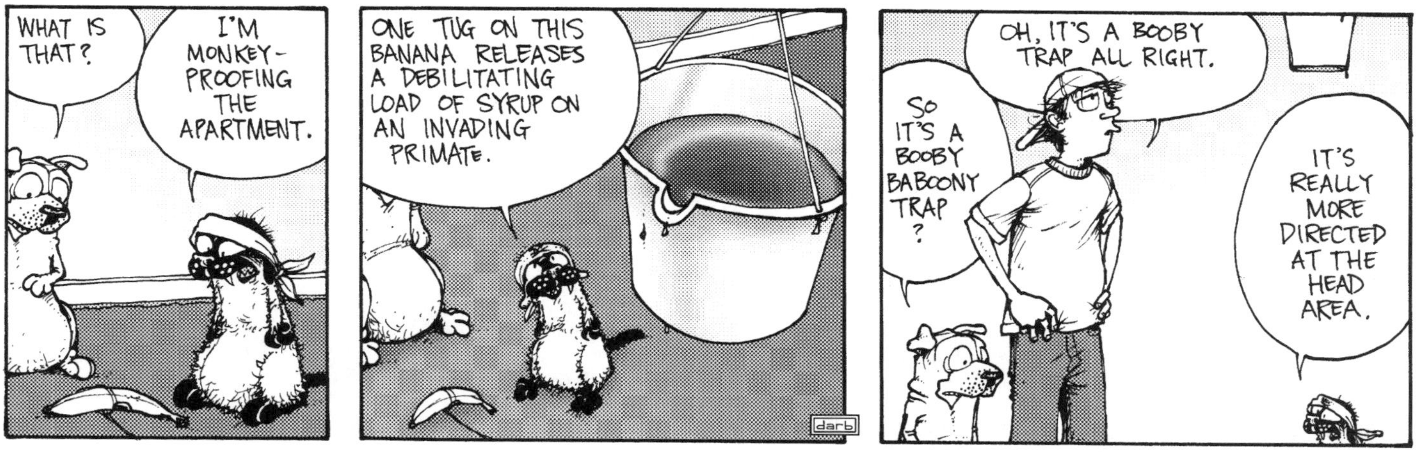
WHAT IS THAT?
I'M MONKEY-PROOFING THE APARTMENT.
ONE TUG ON THIS BANANA RELEASES A DEBILITATING LOAD OF SYRUP ON AN INVADING PRIMATE.
darb
SO IT'S A BOOBY BABOONY TRAP?
OH, IT'S A BOOBY TRAP ALL RIGHT.
IT'S REALLY MORE DIRECTED AT THE HEAD AREA.

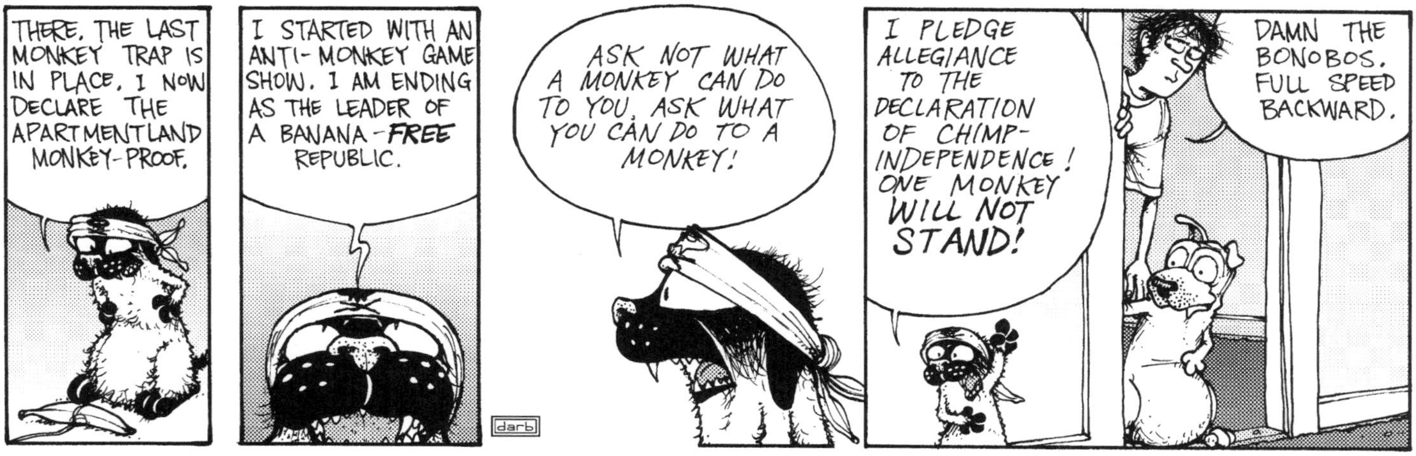
THERE. THE LAST MONKEY TRAP IS IN PLACE. I NOW DECLARE THE APARTMENTLAND MONKEY-PROOF.
I STARTED WITH AN ANTI-MONKEY GAME SHOW. I AM ENDING AS THE LEADER OF A BANANA-FREE REPUBLIC.
darb
ASK NOT WHAT A MONKEY CAN DO TO YOU, ASK WHAT YOU CAN DO TO A MONKEY!
I PLEDGE ALLEGIANCE TO THE DECLARATION OF CHIMP-INDEPENDENCE! ONE MONKEY WILL NOT STAND!
DAMN THE BONOBOS. FULL SPEED BACKWARD.

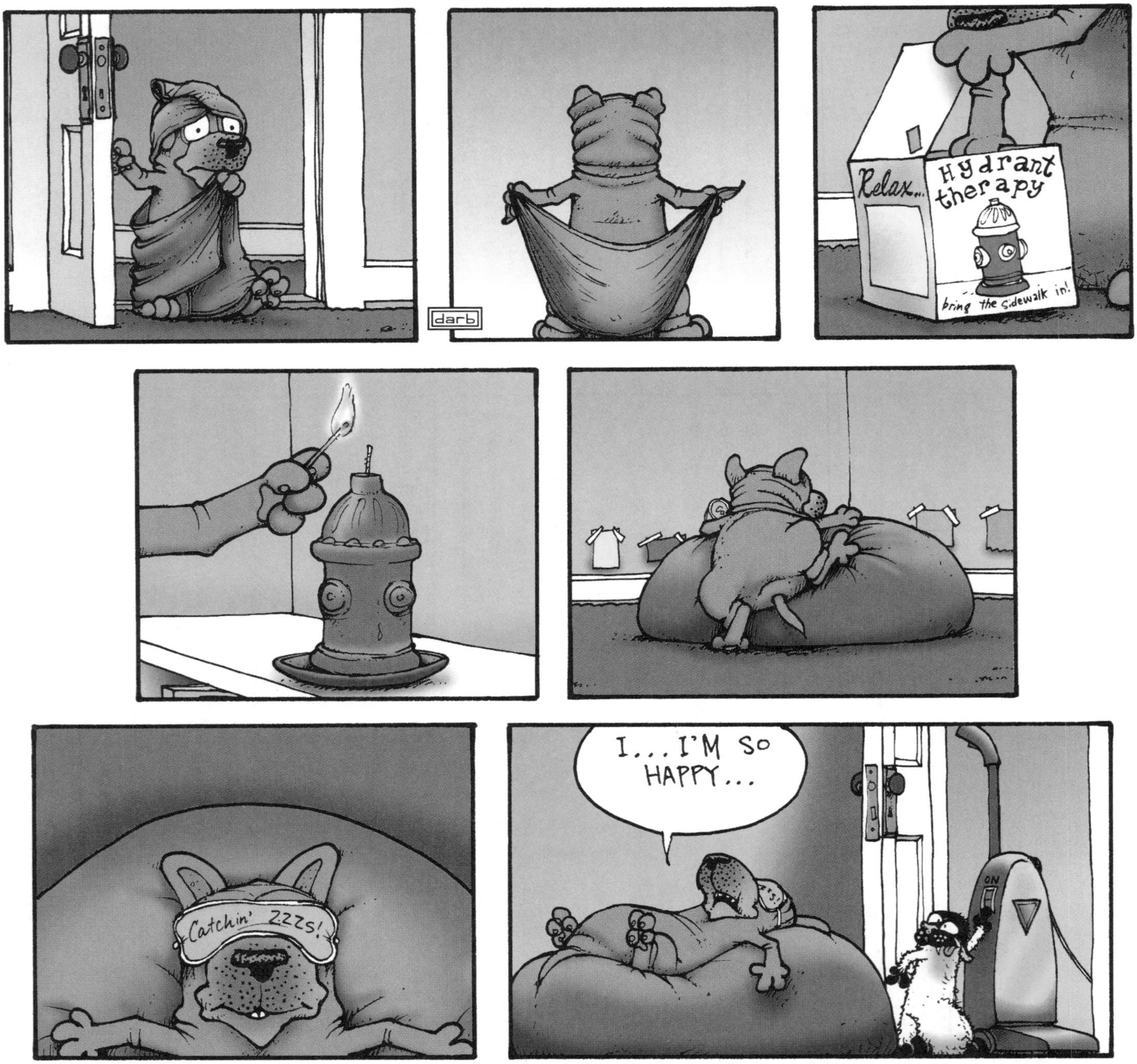
darb
Relax...
Hydrant therapy
bring the sidewalk in!
Catchin' ZZZs!
I...I'M SO HAPPY...
ON

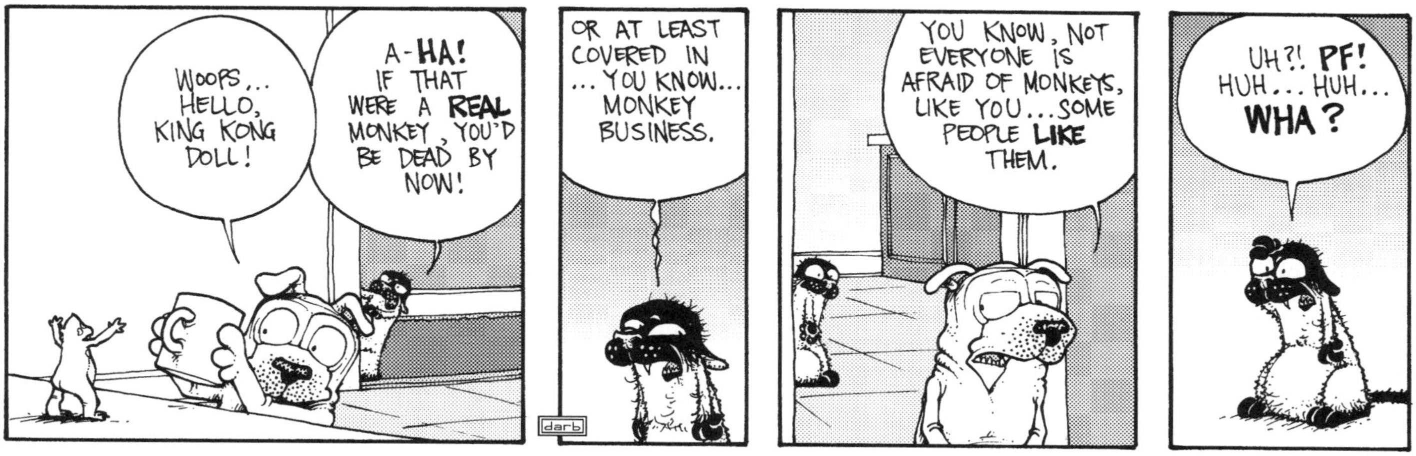
WOOPS,.. HELLO, KING KONG DOLL!
A-HA! IF THAT WERE A REAL MONKEY, YOU'D BE DEAD BY NOW!
OR AT LEAST COVERED IN ... YOU KNOW... MONKEY BUSINESS.
YOU KNOW, NOT EVERYONE IS AFRAID OF MONKEYS, LIKE YOU... SOME PEOPLE LIKE THEM.
UH?! PF! HUH... HUH... WHA?
darb

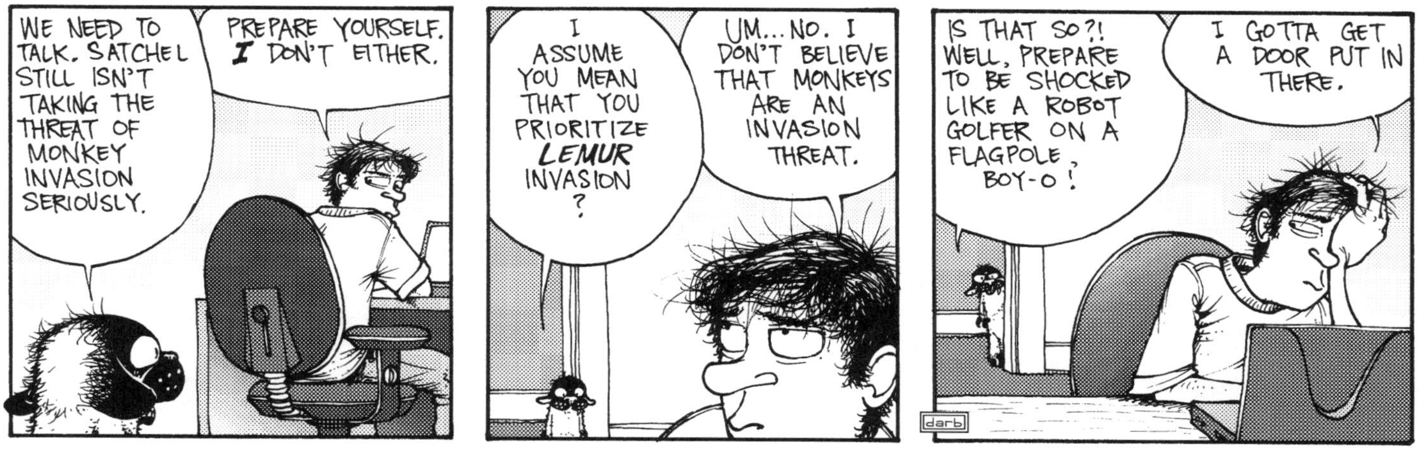
WE NEED TO TALK. SATCHEL STILL ISN'T TAKING THE THREAT OF MONKEY INVASION SERIOUSLY.
PREPARE YOURSELF. I DON'T EITHER.
I ASSUME YOU MEAN THAT YOU PRIORITIZE LEMUR INVASION?
UM... NO. I DON'T BELIEVE THAT MONKEYS ARE AN INVASION THREAT.
IS THAT SO?! WELL, PREPARE TO BE SHOCKED LIKE A ROBOT GOLFER ON A FLAGPOLE, BOY-O!
I GOTTA GET A DOOR PUT IN THERE.
darb

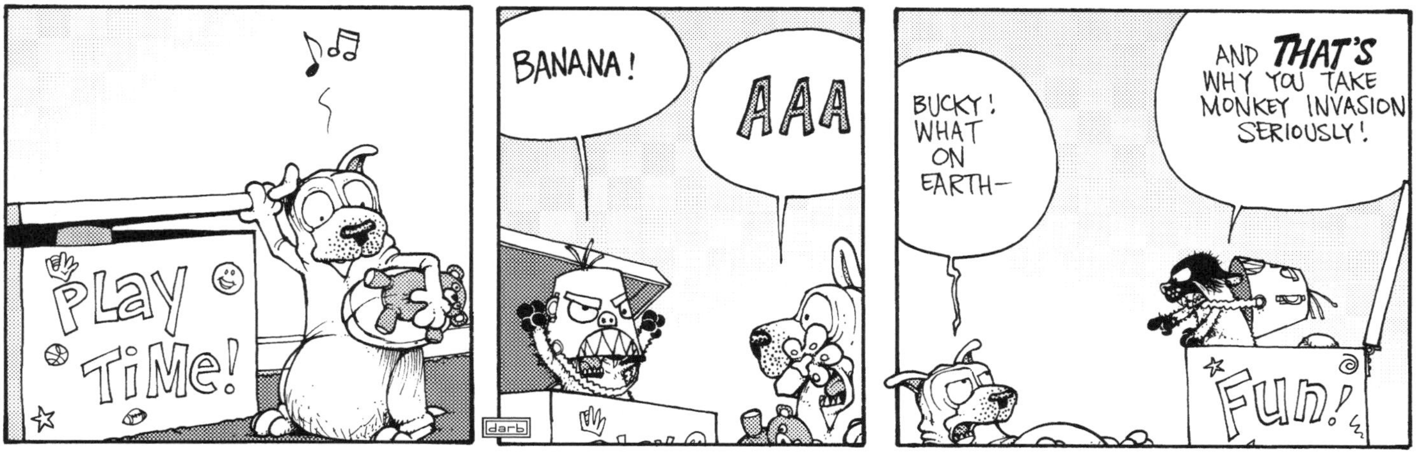
Play TiMe!
BANANA!
AAA
darb
BUCKY! WHAT ON EARTH–
AND THAT'S WHY YOU TAKE MONKEY INVASION SERIOUSLY!
Fun!

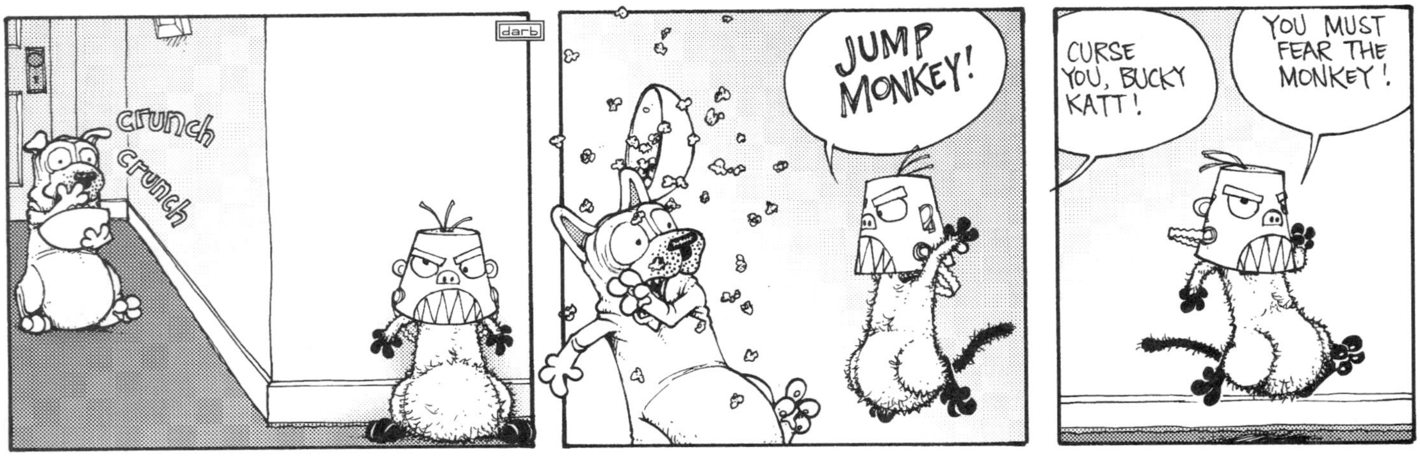
darb
crunch
crunch
JUMP MONKEY!
CURSE YOU, BUCKY KATT!
YOU MUST FEAR THE MONKEY!

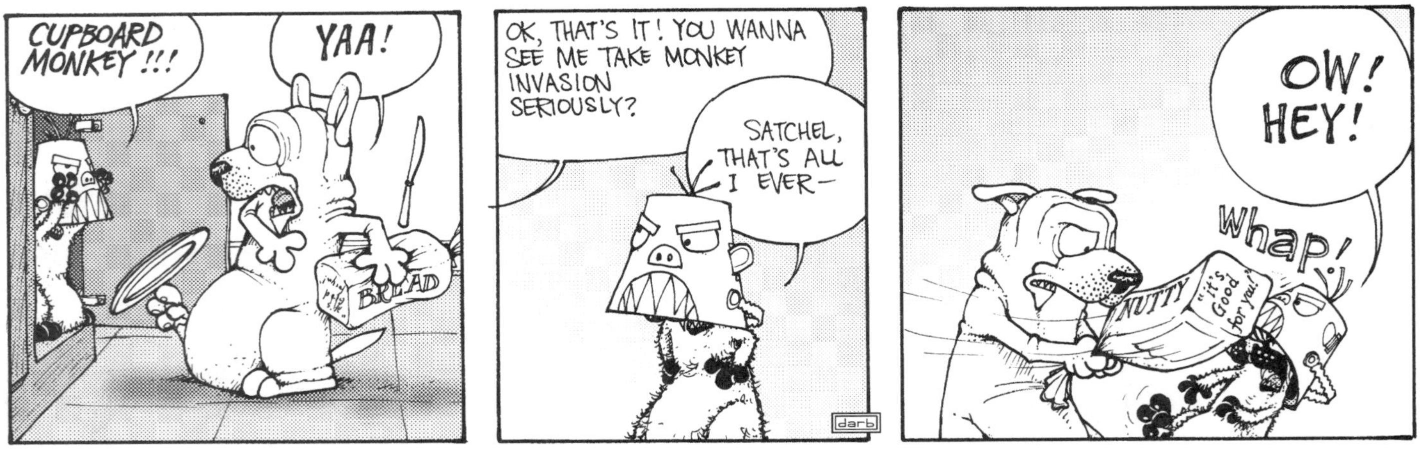
CUPBOARD MONKEY!!!
YAA!
BREAD
OK, THAT'S IT! YOU WANNA SEE ME TAKE MONKEY INVASION SERIOUSLY?
SATCHEL, THAT'S ALL I EVER—
darb
OW! HEY!
Whap!
NUTTY
"it's Good for you!"

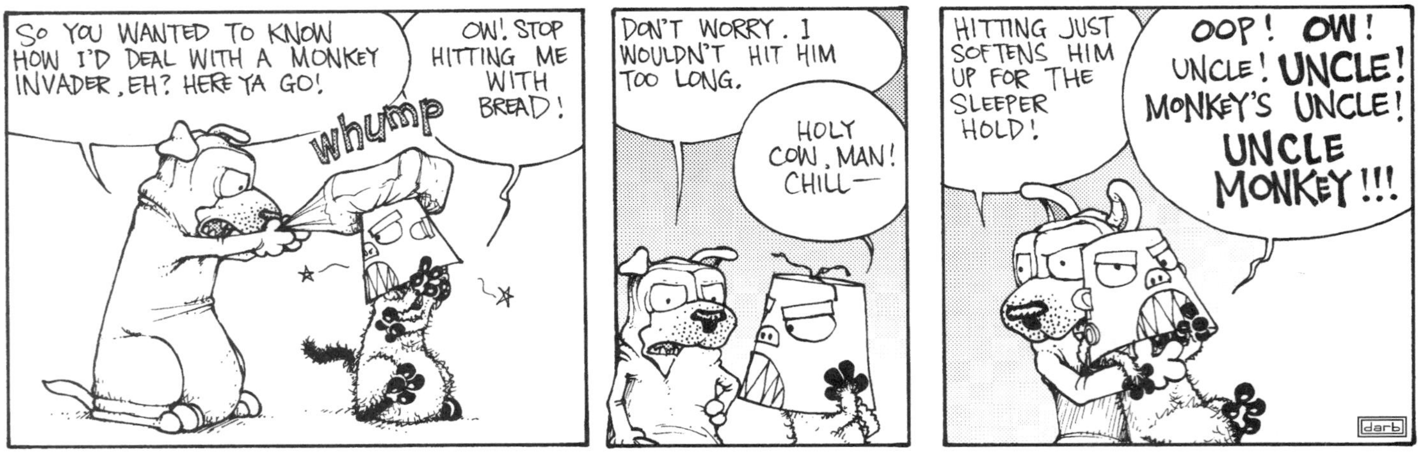
SO YOU WANTED TO KNOW HOW I'D DEAL WITH A MONKEY INVADER, EH? HERE YA GO!
OW! STOP HITTING ME WITH BREAD!
whump
DON'T WORRY. I WOULDN'T HIT HIM TOO LONG.
HOLY COW, MAN! CHILL—
HITTING JUST SOFTENS HIM UP FOR THE SLEEPER HOLD!
OOP! OW! UNCLE! UNCLE! MONKEY'S UNCLE! UNCLE MONKEY!!!
darb

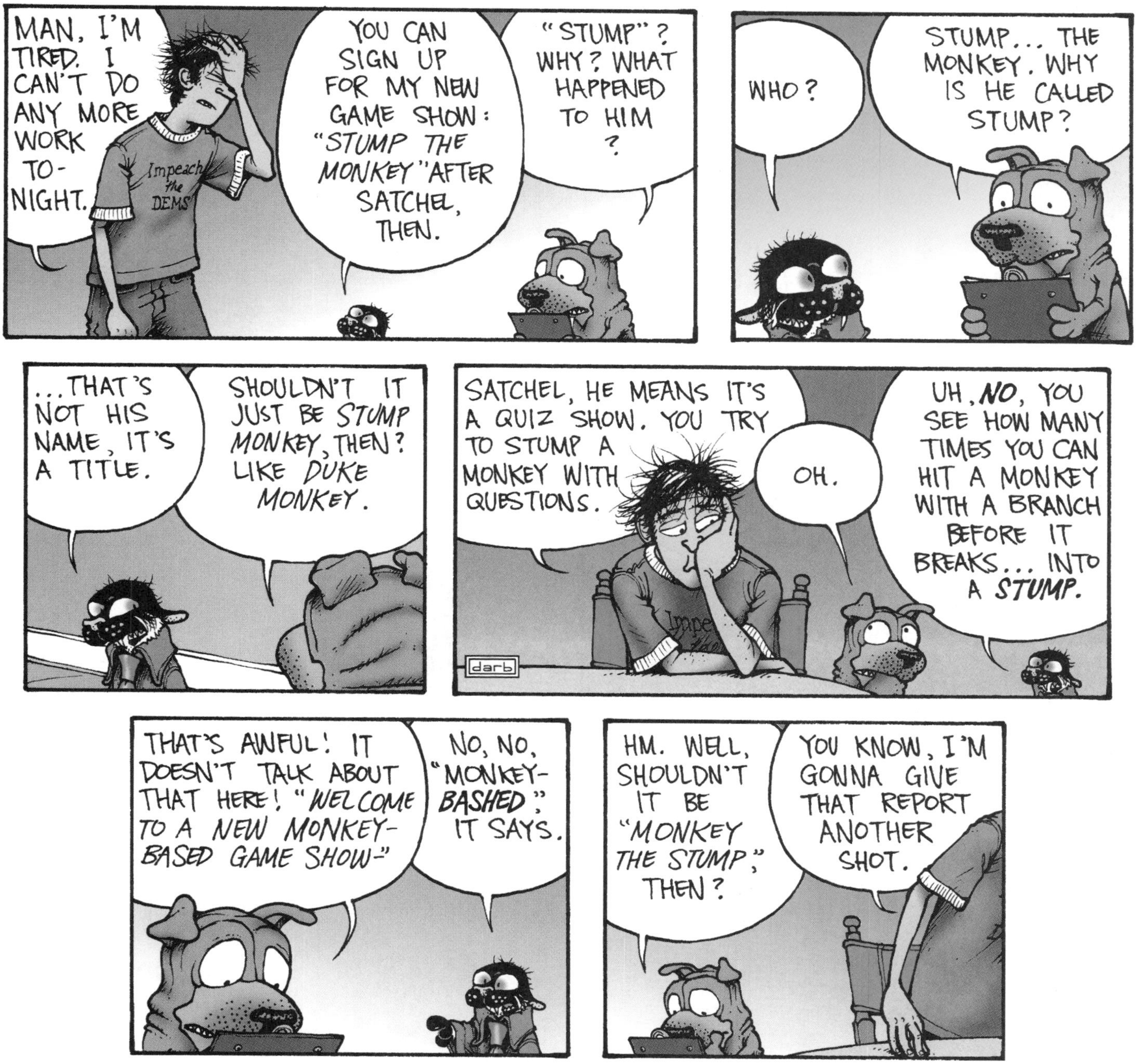
MAN, I'M TIRED. I CAN'T DO ANY MORE WORK TO-NIGHT.
Impeach the DEMS
YOU CAN SIGN UP FOR MY NEW GAME SHOW: "STUMP THE MONKEY" AFTER SATCHEL, THEN.
"STUMP"? WHY? WHAT HAPPENED TO HIM?
WHO?
STUMP... THE MONKEY. WHY IS HE CALLED STUMP?
...THAT'S NOT HIS NAME, IT'S A TITLE.
SHOULDN'T IT JUST BE STUMP MONKEY, THEN? LIKE DUKE MONKEY.
SATCHEL, HE MEANS IT'S A QUIZ SHOW. YOU TRY TO STUMP A MONKEY WITH QUESTIONS.
OH.
UH, NO, YOU SEE HOW MANY TIMES YOU CAN HIT A MONKEY WITH A BRANCH BEFORE IT BREAKS... INTO A STUMP.
darb
THAT'S AWFUL! IT DOESN'T TALK ABOUT THAT HERE! "WELCOME TO A NEW MONKEY-BASED GAME SHOW-"
NO, NO, "MONKEY-BASHED," IT SAYS.
HM. WELL, SHOULDN'T IT BE "MONKEY THE STUMP," THEN?
YOU KNOW, I'M GONNA GIVE THAT REPORT ANOTHER SHOT.

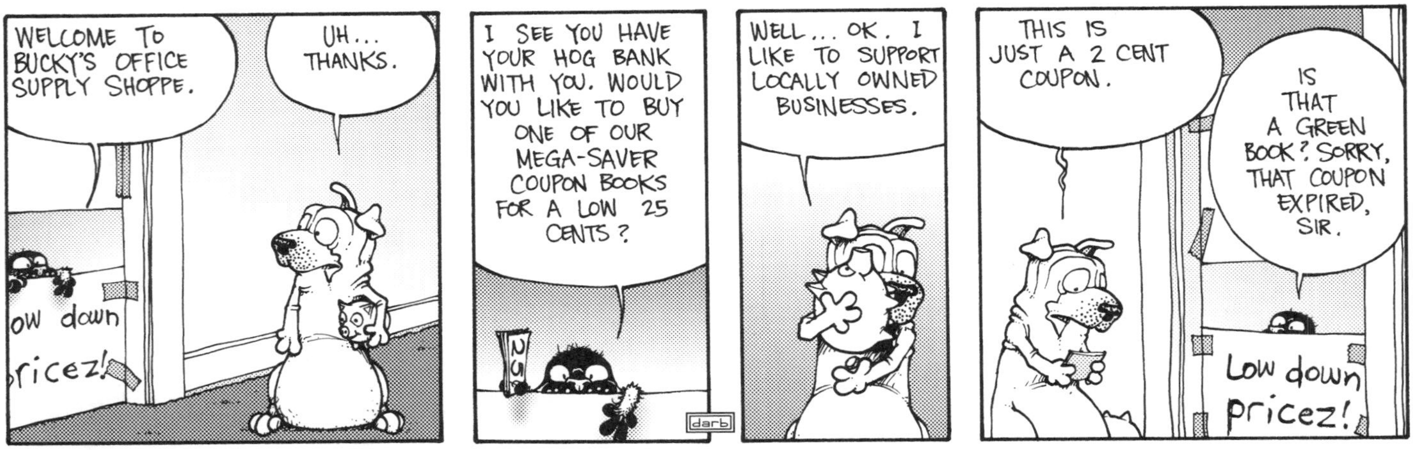
WELCOME TO BUCKY'S OFFICE SUPPLY SHOPPE.
UH... THANKS.
Low down pricez!
I SEE YOU HAVE YOUR HOG BANK WITH YOU. WOULD YOU LIKE TO BUY ONE OF OUR MEGA-SAVER COUPON BOOKS FOR A LOW 25 CENTS?
darb
WELL... OK. I LIKE TO SUPPORT LOCALLY OWNED BUSINESSES.
THIS IS JUST A 2 CENT COUPON.
IS THAT A GREEN BOOK? SORRY, THAT COUPON EXPIRED, SIR.
Low down pricez!

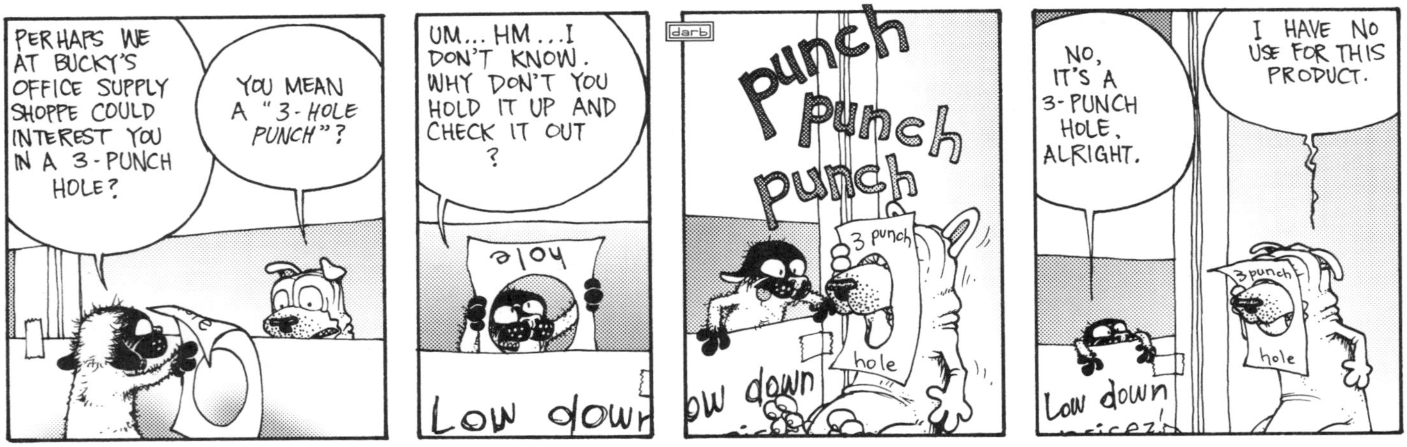
PERHAPS WE AT BUCKY'S OFFICE SUPPLY SHOPPE COULD INTEREST YOU IN A 3-PUNCH HOLE?
YOU MEAN A "3-HOLE PUNCH"?
UM... HM... I DON'T KNOW. WHY DON'T YOU HOLD IT UP AND CHECK IT OUT ?
hole
Low down
darb
punch punch punch
3 punch
hole
NO, IT'S A 3-PUNCH HOLE, ALRIGHT.
I HAVE NO USE FOR THIS PRODUCT.
3 punch
hole
Low down

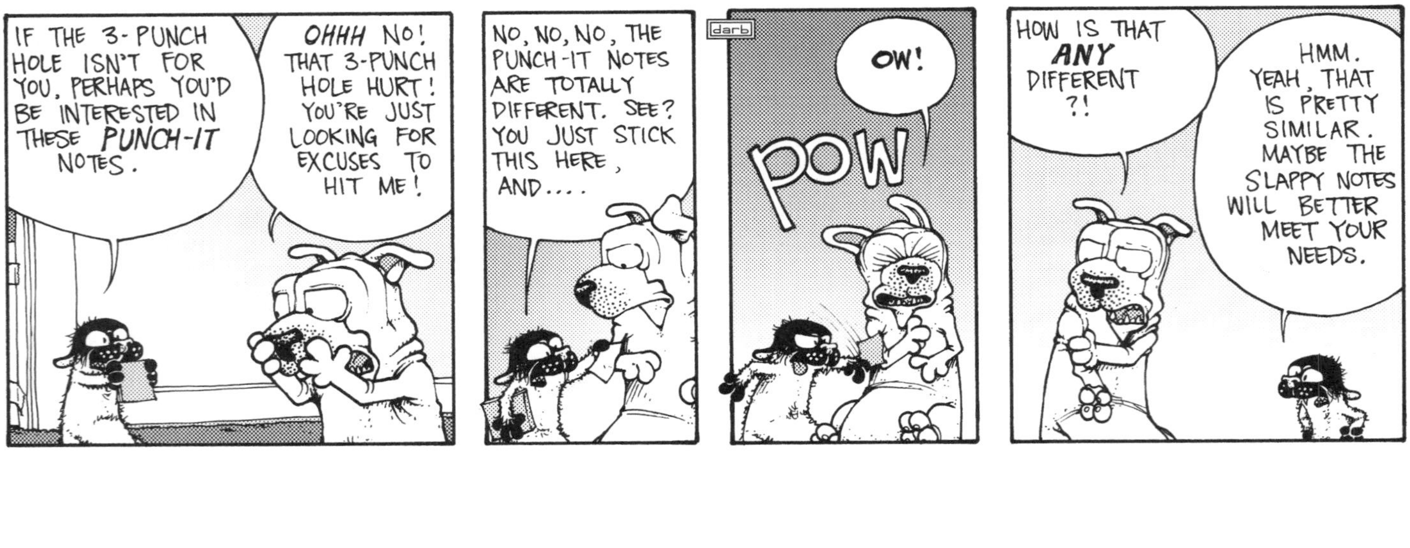
IF THE 3-PUNCH HOLE ISN'T FOR YOU, PERHAPS YOU'D BE INTERESTED IN THESE PUNCH-IT NOTES.
OHHH NO! THAT 3-PUNCH HOLE HURT! YOU'RE JUST LOOKING FOR EXCUSES TO HIT ME!
NO, NO, NO, THE PUNCH-IT NOTES ARE TOTALLY DIFFERENT. SEE? YOU JUST STICK THIS HERE, AND....
darb
OW!
POW
HOW IS THAT ANY DIFFERENT ?!
HMM. YEAH, THAT IS PRETTY SIMILAR. MAYBE THE SLAPPY NOTES WILL BETTER MEET YOUR NEEDS.

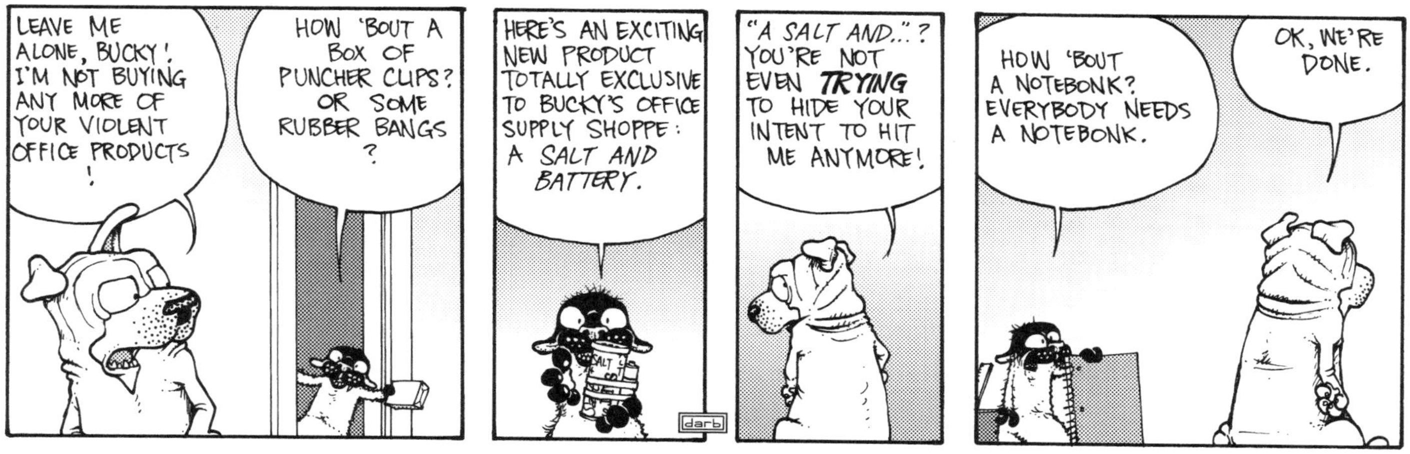
LEAVE ME ALONE, BUCKY! I'M NOT BUYING ANY MORE OF YOUR VIOLENT OFFICE PRODUCTS!
HOW 'BOUT A BOX OF PUNCHER CLIPS? OR SOME RUBBER BANGS?
HERE'S AN EXCITING NEW PRODUCT TOTALLY EXCLUSIVE TO BUCKY'S OFFICE SUPPLY SHOPPE: A *SALT AND BATTERY.*
darb
"*A SALT AND...*"? YOU'RE NOT EVEN **TRYING** TO HIDE YOUR INTENT TO HIT ME ANYMORE!
HOW 'BOUT A NOTEBONK? EVERYBODY NEEDS A NOTEBONK.
OK, WE'RE DONE.

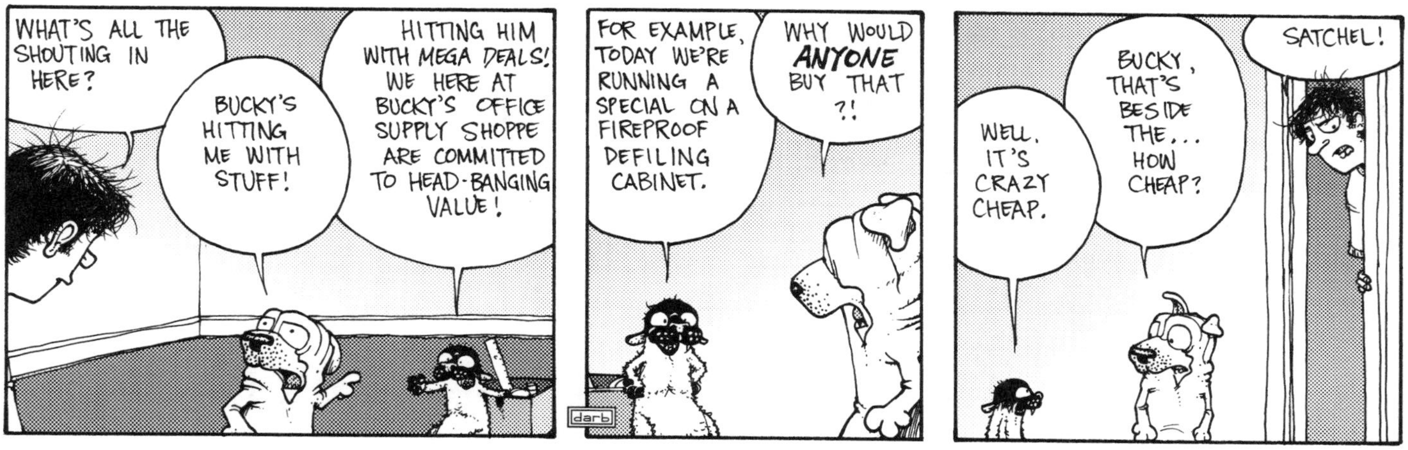
WHAT'S ALL THE SHOUTING IN HERE?
BUCKY'S HITTING ME WITH STUFF!
HITTING HIM WITH *MEGA DEALS!* WE HERE AT BUCKY'S OFFICE SUPPLY SHOPPE ARE COMMITTED TO HEAD-BANGING VALUE!
FOR EXAMPLE, TODAY WE'RE RUNNING A SPECIAL ON A FIREPROOF DEFILING CABINET.
WHY WOULD **ANYONE** BUY THAT?!
darb
WELL, IT'S CRAZY CHEAP.
BUCKY, THAT'S BESIDE THE... HOW CHEAP?
SATCHEL!

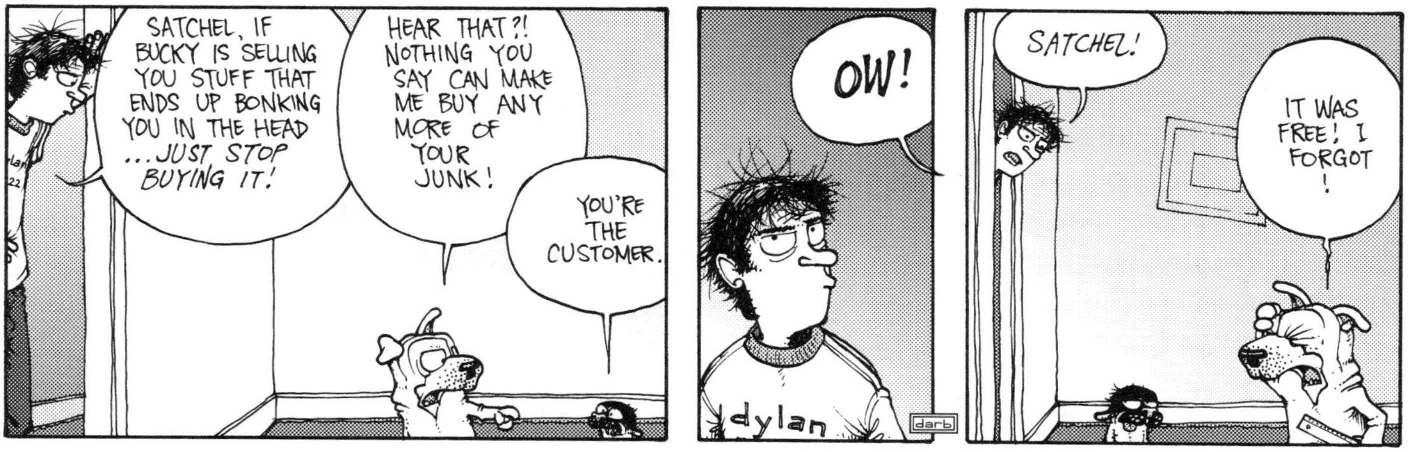
SATCHEL, IF BUCKY IS SELLING YOU STUFF THAT ENDS UP BONKING YOU IN THE HEAD *...JUST STOP BUYING IT!*
HEAR THAT?! NOTHING YOU SAY CAN MAKE ME BUY ANY MORE OF YOUR JUNK!
YOU'RE THE CUSTOMER.
OW!
dylan
darb
SATCHEL!
IT WAS FREE! I FORGOT!

DO YOU SMELL SOMETHING?
LIKE 800 THINGS. CAN YOU BE MORE SPECIFIC?
WHAT DO I SMELL IN HERE?
OPEN FACE DECADENCE, MY FRIEND.
WHAT IS MY SHAMPOO DOING IN THE KITCHEN? AND ALL MY DVDS? IS... IS THAT A HENDRIX DISC IN THE TOASTER ?!
A TOKEN OF YOUR CORRUPTED ETHICALS IS BEING PURIFIED, YES.
DUDE! STOP MELTING MY STUFF!
YOUR MORALIPIT IS DECREPITIED! I AM CLEANSING YOUR **SOULS**, ROBERT WILCO!
darb
IN FACT, I JUST DID THEM.
...YOU'RE ACTUALLY HOLDING A MEDIEVAL BURNING OF MY VANITIES ?!
TECHNICALLY, HE'S TOASTING YOUR VANITIES.

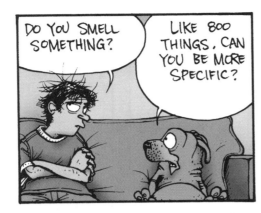

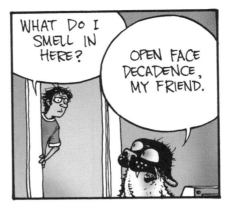

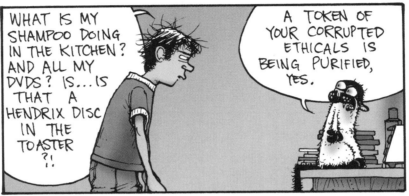

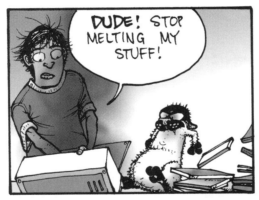

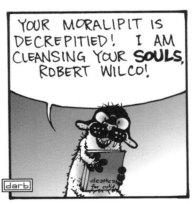

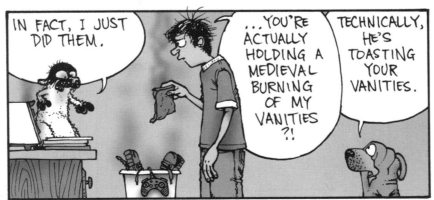

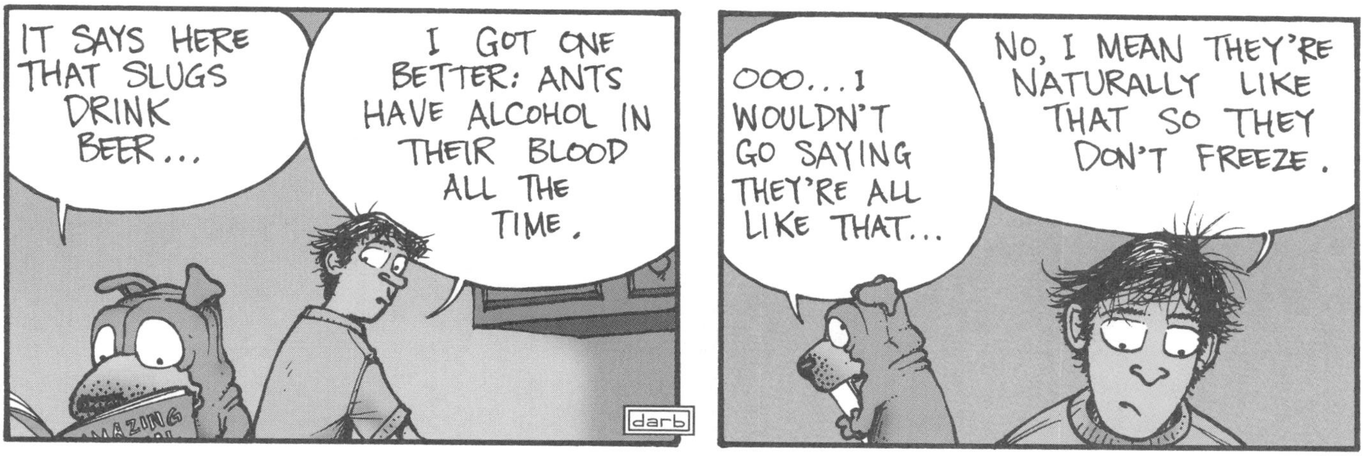
IT SAYS HERE THAT SLUGS DRINK BEER...
I GOT ONE BETTER: ANTS HAVE ALCOHOL IN THEIR BLOOD ALL THE TIME.
darb
OOO...I WOULDN'T GO SAYING THEY'RE ALL LIKE THAT...
NO, I MEAN THEY'RE NATURALLY LIKE THAT SO THEY DON'T FREEZE.

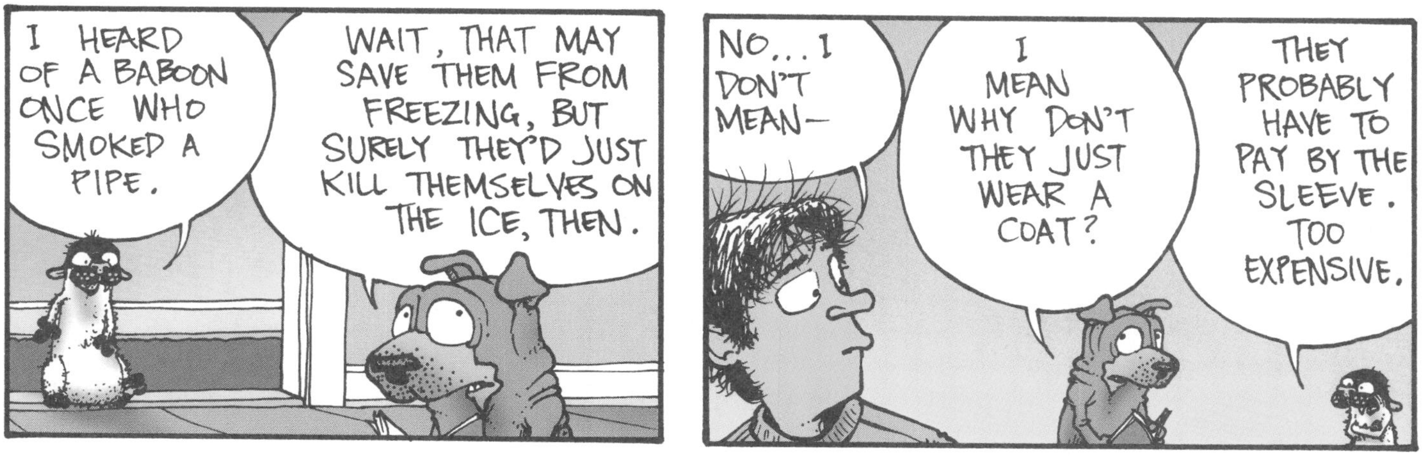
I HEARD OF A BABOON ONCE WHO SMOKED A PIPE.
WAIT, THAT MAY SAVE THEM FROM FREEZING, BUT SURELY THEY'D JUST KILL THEMSELVES ON THE ICE, THEN.
NO...I DON'T MEAN—
I MEAN WHY DON'T THEY JUST WEAR A COAT?
THEY PROBABLY HAVE TO PAY BY THE SLEEVE. TOO EXPENSIVE.

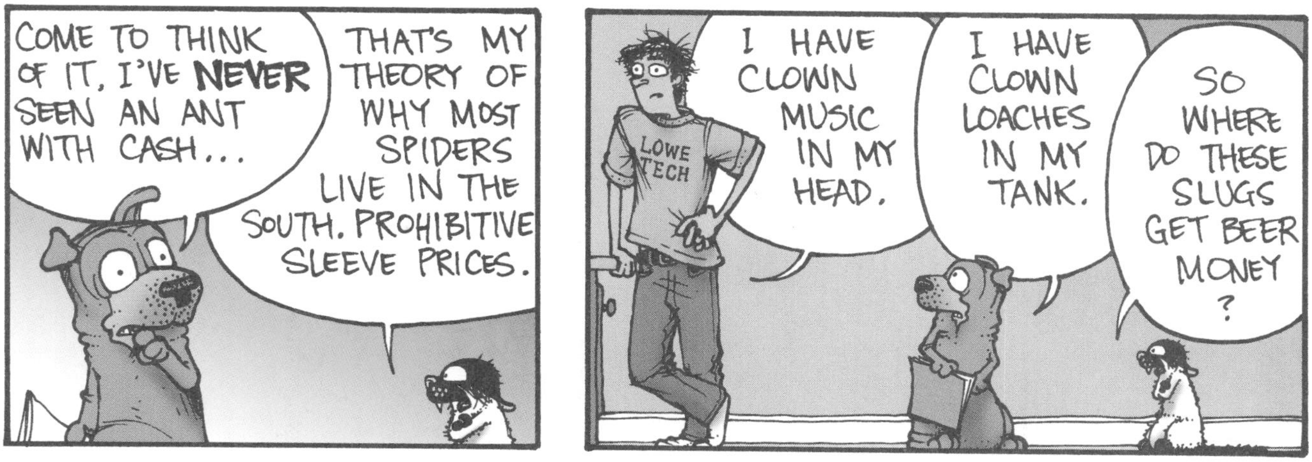
COME TO THINK OF IT, I'VE **NEVER** SEEN AN ANT WITH CASH...
THAT'S MY THEORY OF WHY MOST SPIDERS LIVE IN THE SOUTH. PROHIBITIVE SLEEVE PRICES.
LOWE TECH
I HAVE CLOWN MUSIC IN MY HEAD.
I HAVE CLOWN LOACHES IN MY TANK.
SO WHERE DO THESE SLUGS GET BEER MONEY?

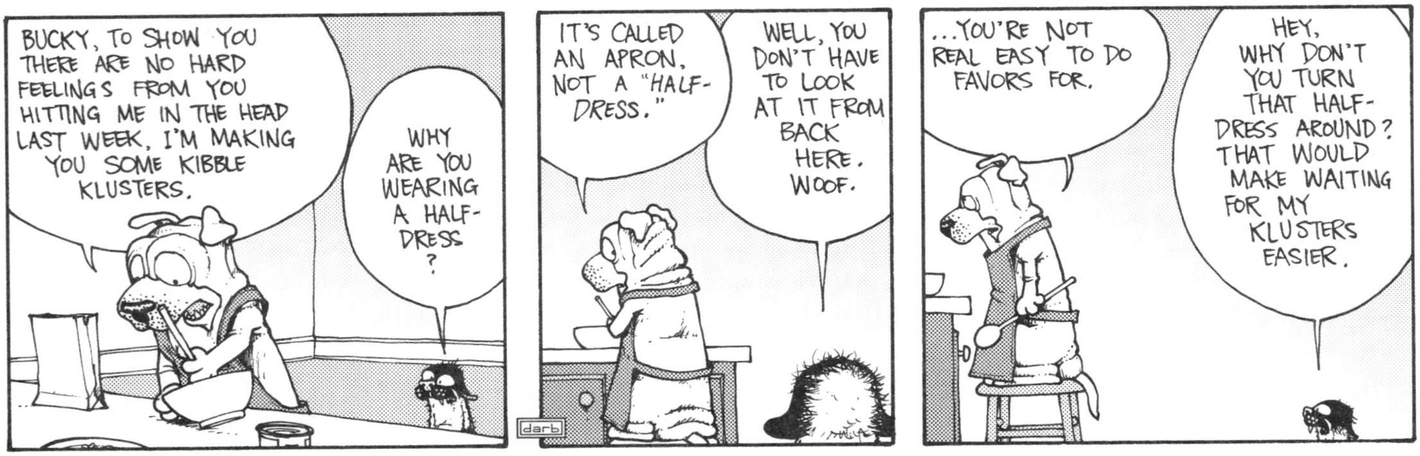
BUCKY, TO SHOW YOU THERE ARE NO HARD FEELINGS FROM YOU HITTING ME IN THE HEAD LAST WEEK, I'M MAKING YOU SOME KIBBLE KLUSTERS.
WHY ARE YOU WEARING A HALF-DRESS?
IT'S CALLED AN APRON, NOT A "HALF-DRESS."
WELL, YOU DON'T HAVE TO LOOK AT IT FROM BACK HERE. WOOF.
...YOU'RE NOT REAL EASY TO DO FAVORS FOR.
HEY, WHY DON'T YOU TURN THAT HALF-DRESS AROUND? THAT WOULD MAKE WAITING FOR MY KLUSTERS EASIER.
darb

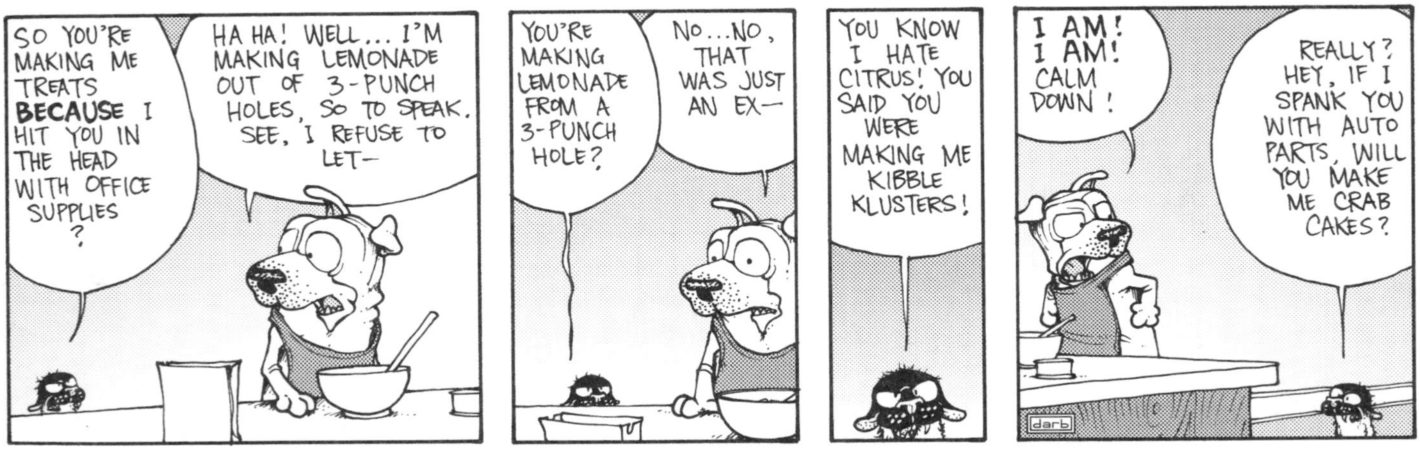
SO YOU'RE MAKING ME TREATS **BECAUSE** I HIT YOU IN THE HEAD WITH OFFICE SUPPLIES?
HA HA! WELL... I'M MAKING LEMONADE OUT OF 3-PUNCH HOLES, SO TO SPEAK. SEE, I REFUSE TO LET—
YOU'RE MAKING LEMONADE FROM A 3-PUNCH HOLE?
NO...NO, THAT WAS JUST AN EX—
YOU KNOW I HATE CITRUS! YOU SAID YOU WERE MAKING ME KIBBLE KLUSTERS!
I AM! I AM! CALM DOWN!
REALLY? HEY, IF I SPANK YOU WITH AUTO PARTS, WILL YOU MAKE ME CRAB CAKES?
darb

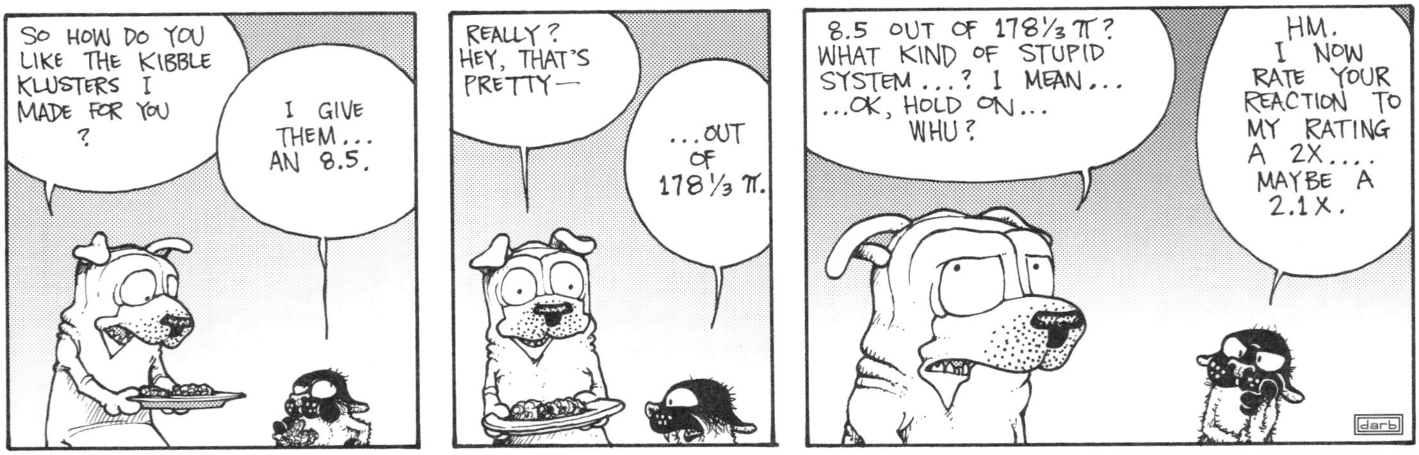
SO HOW DO YOU LIKE THE KIBBLE KLUSTERS I MADE FOR YOU?
I GIVE THEM... AN 8.5.
REALLY? HEY, THAT'S PRETTY—
...OUT OF 178⅓ π.
8.5 OUT OF 178⅓ π? WHAT KIND OF STUPID SYSTEM...? I MEAN... ...OK, HOLD ON... WHU?
HM. I NOW RATE YOUR REACTION TO MY RATING A 2X.... MAYBE A 2.1X.
darb

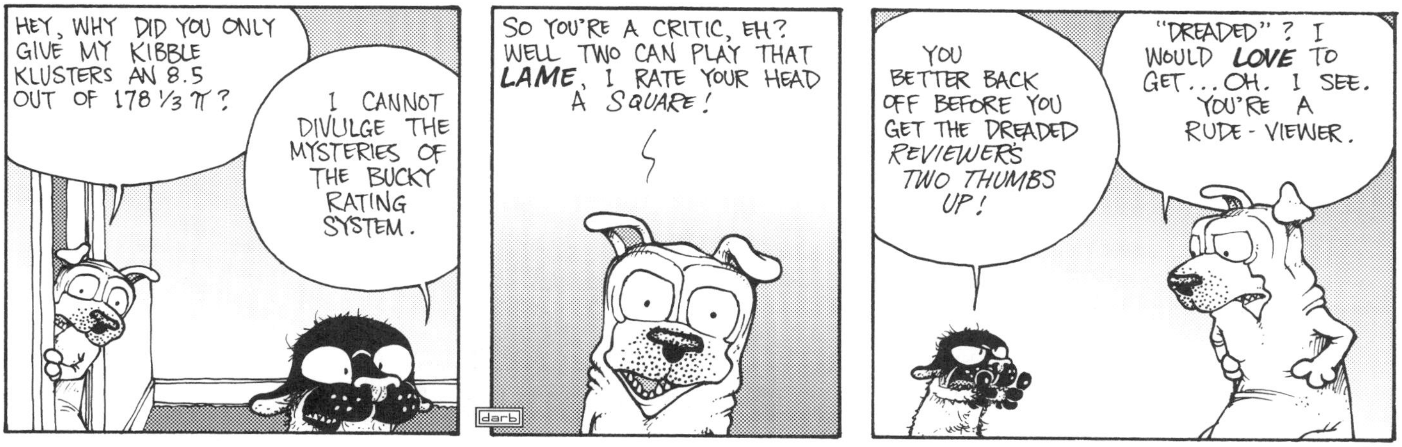
HEY, WHY DID YOU ONLY GIVE MY KIBBLE KLUSTERS AN 8.5 OUT OF 178 1/3 π?
I CANNOT DIVULGE THE MYSTERIES OF THE BUCKY RATING SYSTEM.
SO YOU'RE A CRITIC, EH? WELL TWO CAN PLAY THAT **LAME**, I RATE YOUR HEAD A *SQUARE!*
YOU BETTER BACK OFF BEFORE YOU GET THE DREADED *REVIEWER'S TWO THUMBS UP!*
"DREADED"? I WOULD **LOVE** TO GET...OH. I SEE. YOU'RE A RUDE-VIEWER.
darb

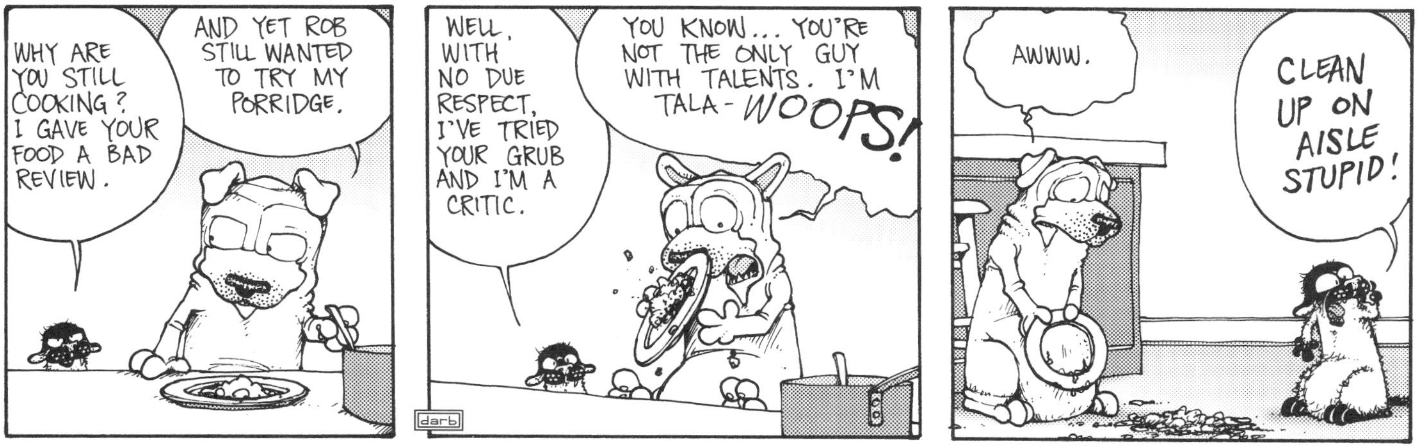
WHY ARE YOU STILL COOKING? I GAVE YOUR FOOD A BAD REVIEW.
AND YET ROB STILL WANTED TO TRY MY PORRIDGE.
WELL, WITH NO DUE RESPECT, I'VE TRIED YOUR GRUB AND I'M A CRITIC.
YOU KNOW... YOU'RE NOT THE ONLY GUY WITH TALENTS. I'M TALA-WOOPS!
AWWW.
CLEAN UP ON AISLE STUPID!
darb

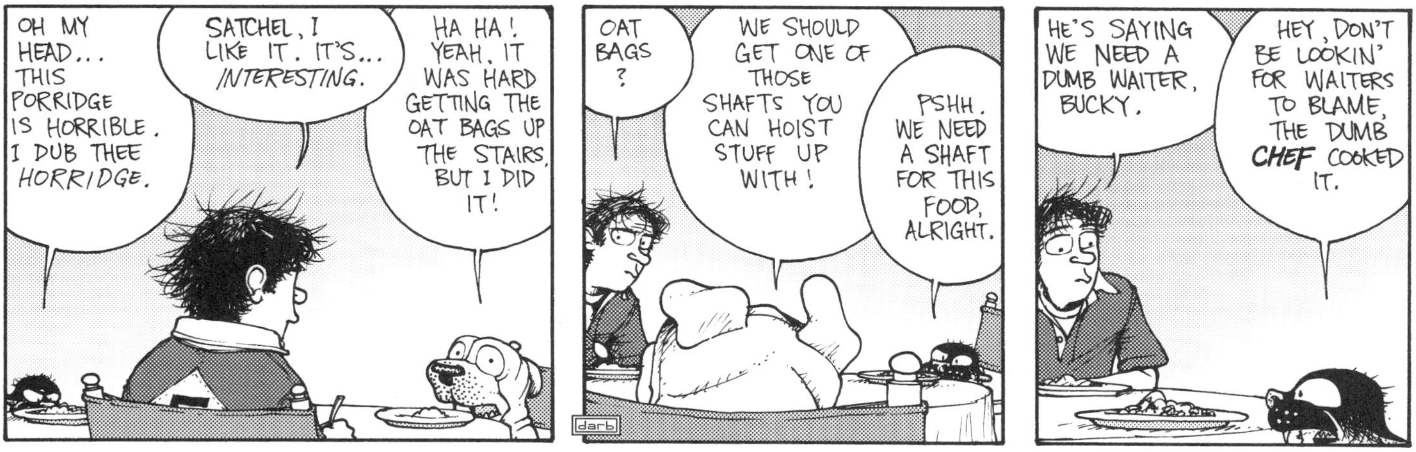
OH MY HEAD... THIS PORRIDGE IS HORRIBLE. I DUB THEE *HORRIDGE*.
SATCHEL, I LIKE IT. IT'S... *INTERESTING*.
HA HA! YEAH, IT WAS HARD GETTING THE OAT BAGS UP THE STAIRS, BUT I DID IT!
OAT BAGS?
WE SHOULD GET ONE OF THOSE SHAFTS YOU CAN HOIST STUFF UP WITH!
PSHH. WE NEED A SHAFT FOR THIS FOOD, ALRIGHT.
HE'S SAYING WE NEED A DUMB WAITER, BUCKY.
HEY, DON'T BE LOOKIN' FOR WAITERS TO BLAME, THE DUMB **CHEF** COOKED IT.
darb

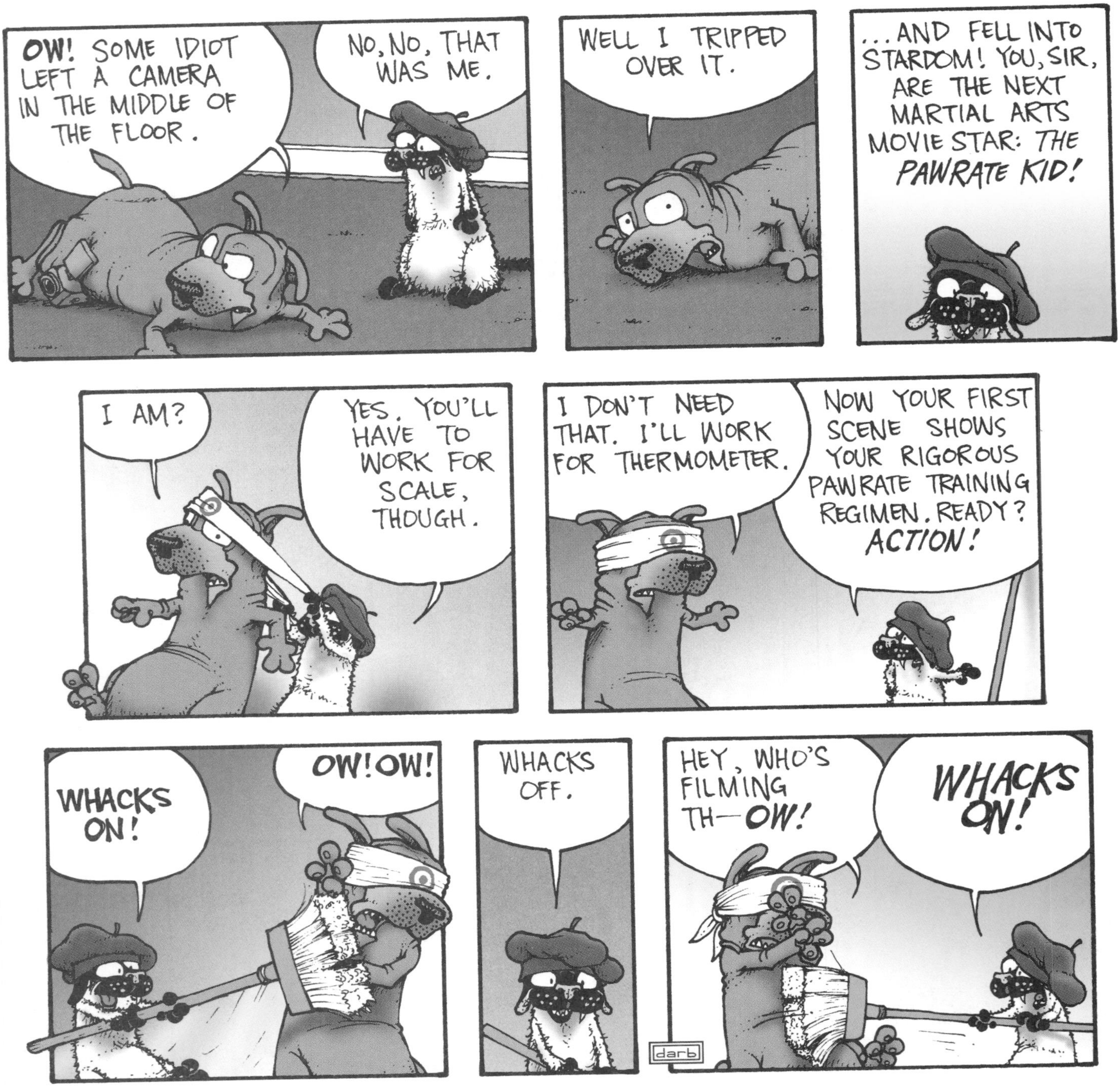
OW! SOME IDIOT LEFT A CAMERA IN THE MIDDLE OF THE FLOOR.
NO, NO, THAT WAS ME.
WELL I TRIPPED OVER IT.
...AND FELL INTO STARDOM! YOU, SIR, ARE THE NEXT MARTIAL ARTS MOVIE STAR: THE PAWRATE KID!
I AM?
YES. YOU'LL HAVE TO WORK FOR SCALE, THOUGH.
I DON'T NEED THAT. I'LL WORK FOR THERMOMETER.
NOW YOUR FIRST SCENE SHOWS YOUR RIGOROUS PAWRATE TRAINING REGIMEN. READY? ACTION!
WHACKS ON!
OW! OW!
WHACKS OFF.
HEY, WHO'S FILMING TH—OW!
WHACKS ON!
darb

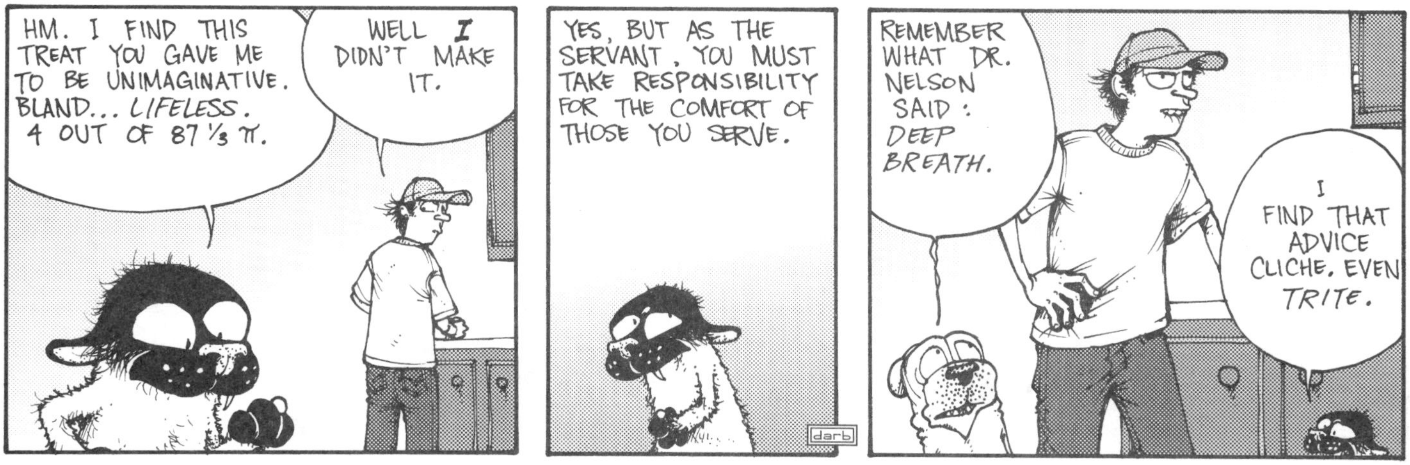
HM. I FIND THIS TREAT YOU GAVE ME TO BE UNIMAGINATIVE. BLAND... *LIFELESS*. 4 OUT OF 87 ⅓ π.
WELL *I* DIDN'T MAKE IT.
YES, BUT AS THE SERVANT, YOU MUST TAKE RESPONSIBILITY FOR THE COMFORT OF THOSE YOU SERVE.
REMEMBER WHAT DR. NELSON SAID: *DEEP BREATH.*
I FIND THAT ADVICE CLICHE. EVEN *TRITE*.

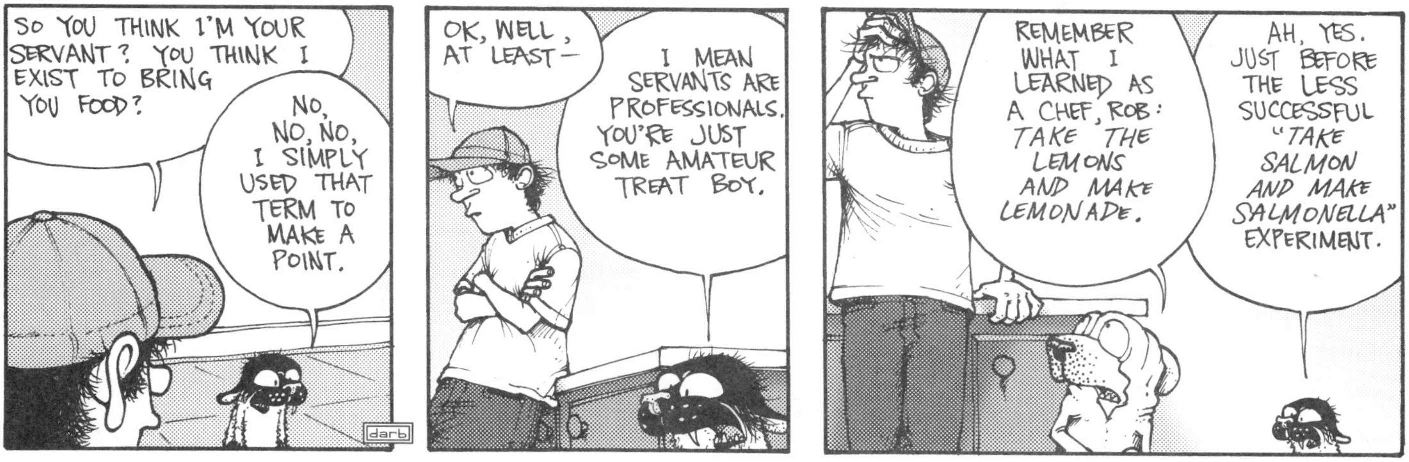
SO YOU THINK I'M YOUR SERVANT? YOU THINK I EXIST TO BRING YOU FOOD?
NO, NO, NO, I SIMPLY USED THAT TERM TO MAKE A POINT.
OK, WELL, AT LEAST—
I MEAN SERVANTS ARE PROFESSIONALS. YOU'RE JUST SOME AMATEUR TREAT BOY.
REMEMBER WHAT I LEARNED AS A CHEF, ROB: *TAKE THE LEMONS AND MAKE LEMONADE.*
AH, YES. JUST BEFORE THE LESS SUCCESSFUL "*TAKE SALMON AND MAKE SALMONELLA*" EXPERIMENT.

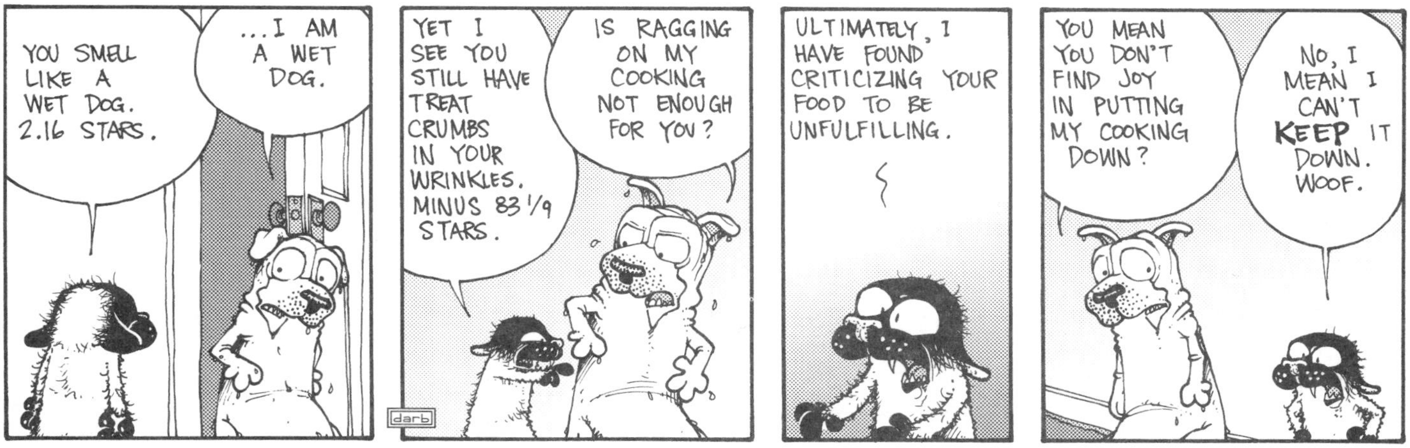
YOU SMELL LIKE A WET DOG. 2.16 STARS.
...I AM A WET DOG.
YET I SEE YOU STILL HAVE TREAT CRUMBS IN YOUR WRINKLES. MINUS 83 1/9 STARS.
IS RAGGING ON MY COOKING NOT ENOUGH FOR YOU?
ULTIMATELY, I HAVE FOUND CRITICIZING YOUR FOOD TO BE UNFULFILLING.
YOU MEAN YOU DON'T FIND JOY IN PUTTING MY COOKING DOWN?
NO, I MEAN I CAN'T **KEEP** IT DOWN. WOOF.

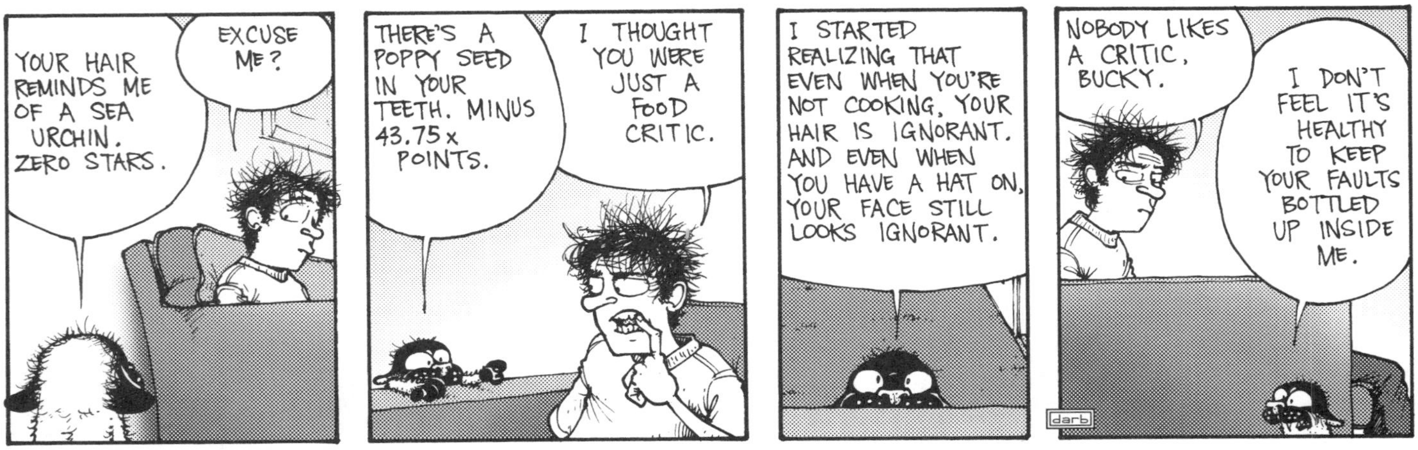
YOUR HAIR REMINDS ME OF A SEA URCHIN. ZERO STARS.
EXCUSE ME?
THERE'S A POPPY SEED IN YOUR TEETH. MINUS 43.75 x POINTS.
I THOUGHT YOU WERE JUST A FOOD CRITIC.
I STARTED REALIZING THAT EVEN WHEN YOU'RE NOT COOKING, YOUR HAIR IS IGNORANT. AND EVEN WHEN YOU HAVE A HAT ON, YOUR FACE STILL LOOKS IGNORANT.
NOBODY LIKES A CRITIC, BUCKY.
I DON'T FEEL IT'S HEALTHY TO KEEP YOUR FAULTS BOTTLED UP INSIDE ME.
darb

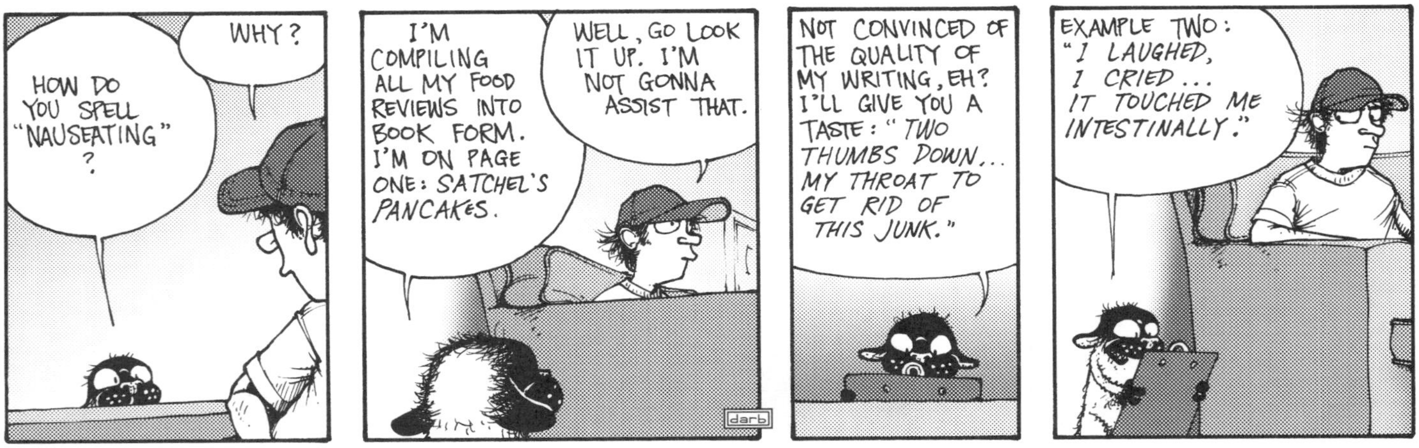
HOW DO YOU SPELL "NAUSEATING"?
WHY?
I'M COMPILING ALL MY FOOD REVIEWS INTO BOOK FORM. I'M ON PAGE ONE: *SATCHEL'S PANCAKES*.
WELL, GO LOOK IT UP. I'M NOT GONNA ASSIST THAT.
darb
NOT CONVINCED OF THE QUALITY OF MY WRITING, EH? I'LL GIVE YOU A TASTE: "*TWO THUMBS DOWN... MY THROAT TO GET RID OF THIS JUNK.*"
EXAMPLE TWO: "*I LAUGHED, I CRIED... IT TOUCHED ME INTESTINALLY.*"

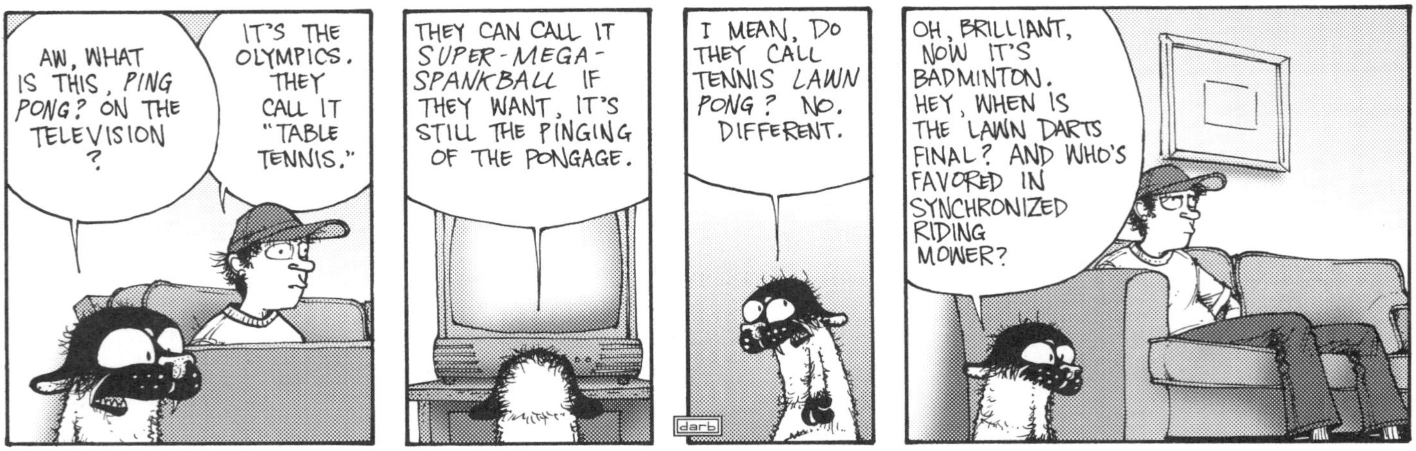
AW, WHAT IS THIS, *PING PONG?* ON THE TELEVISION?
IT'S THE OLYMPICS. THEY CALL IT "TABLE TENNIS."
THEY CAN CALL IT *SUPER-MEGA-SPANKBALL* IF THEY WANT, IT'S STILL THE PINGING OF THE PONGAGE.
I MEAN, DO THEY CALL TENNIS *LAWN PONG?* NO. DIFFERENT.
darb
OH, BRILLIANT, NOW IT'S BADMINTON. HEY, WHEN IS THE LAWN DARTS FINAL? AND WHO'S FAVORED IN SYNCHRONIZED RIDING MOWER?

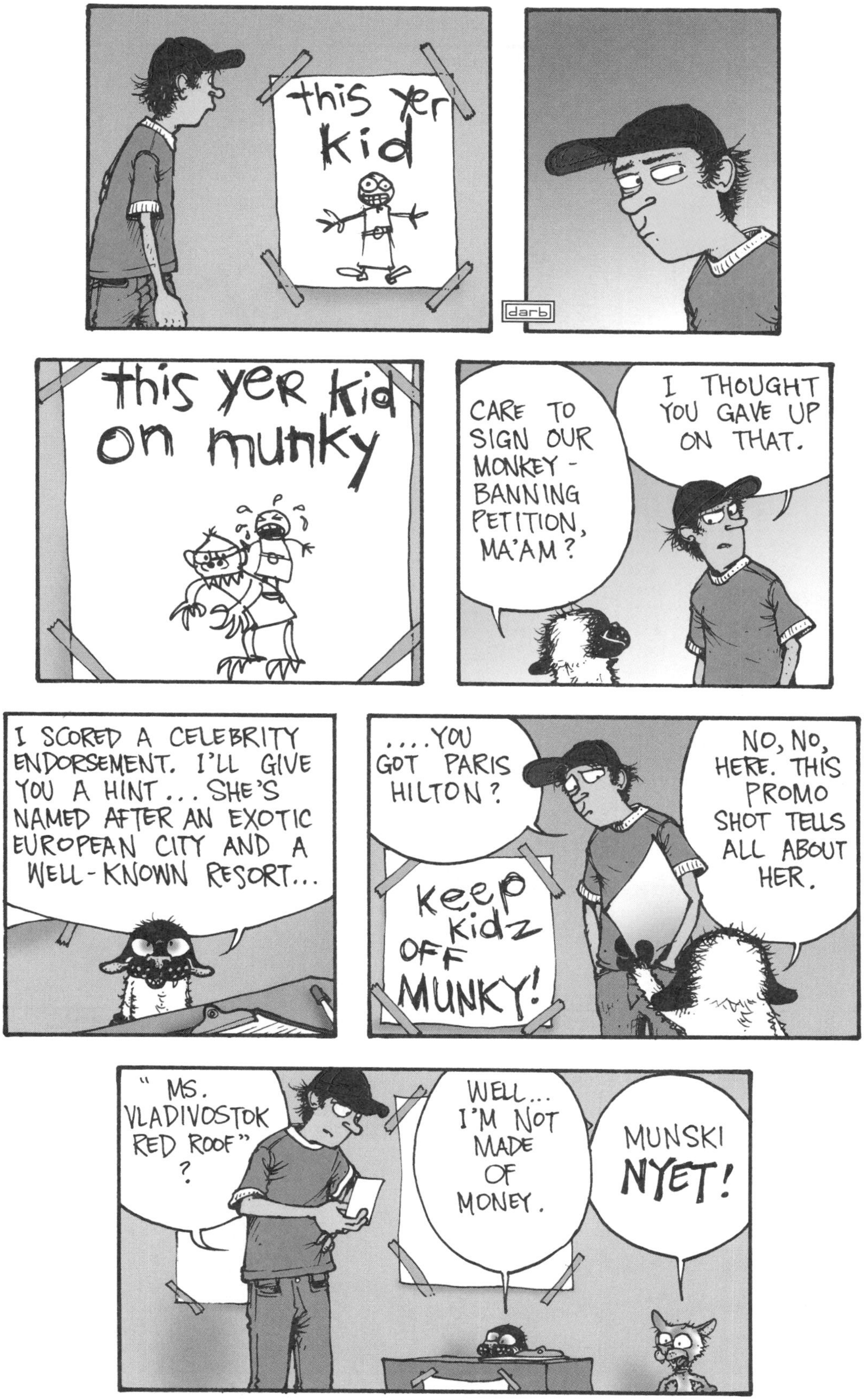
this yer kid
darb
this yer kid on munky
CARE TO SIGN OUR MONKEY-BANNING PETITION, MA'AM?
I THOUGHT YOU GAVE UP ON THAT.
I SCORED A CELEBRITY ENDORSEMENT. I'LL GIVE YOU A HINT... SHE'S NAMED AFTER AN EXOTIC EUROPEAN CITY AND A WELL-KNOWN RESORT...
....YOU GOT PARIS HILTON?
NO, NO, HERE. THIS PROMO SHOT TELLS ALL ABOUT HER.
keep kidz OFF MUNKY!
"MS. VLADIVOSTOK RED ROOF"?
WELL... I'M NOT MADE OF MONEY.
MUNSKI NYET!

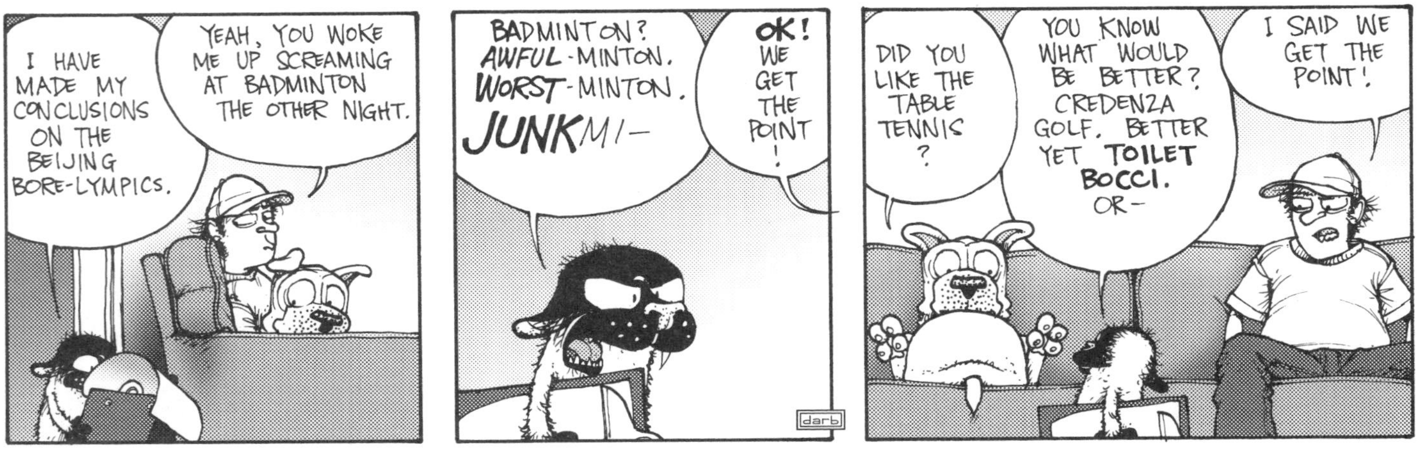
I HAVE MADE MY CONCLUSIONS ON THE BEIJING BORE-LYMPICS.
YEAH, YOU WOKE ME UP SCREAMING AT BADMINTON THE OTHER NIGHT.
BADMINTON? AWFUL-MINTON. WORST-MINTON. JUNKMI—
OK! WE GET THE POINT!
DID YOU LIKE THE TABLE TENNIS?
YOU KNOW WHAT WOULD BE BETTER? CREDENZA GOLF. BETTER YET TOILET BOCCI. OR—
I SAID WE GET THE POINT!
darb

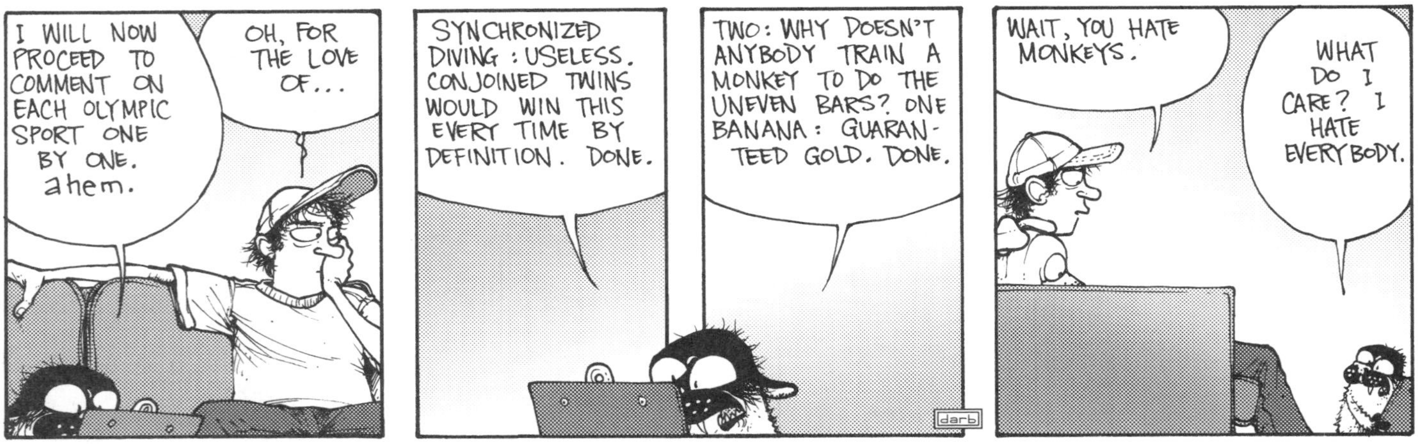
I WILL NOW PROCEED TO COMMENT ON EACH OLYMPIC SPORT ONE BY ONE. ahem.
OH, FOR THE LOVE OF...
SYNCHRONIZED DIVING: USELESS. CONJOINED TWINS WOULD WIN THIS EVERY TIME BY DEFINITION. DONE.
TWO: WHY DOESN'T ANYBODY TRAIN A MONKEY TO DO THE UNEVEN BARS? ONE BANANA: GUARANTEED GOLD. DONE.
WAIT, YOU HATE MONKEYS.
WHAT DO I CARE? I HATE EVERYBODY.
darb

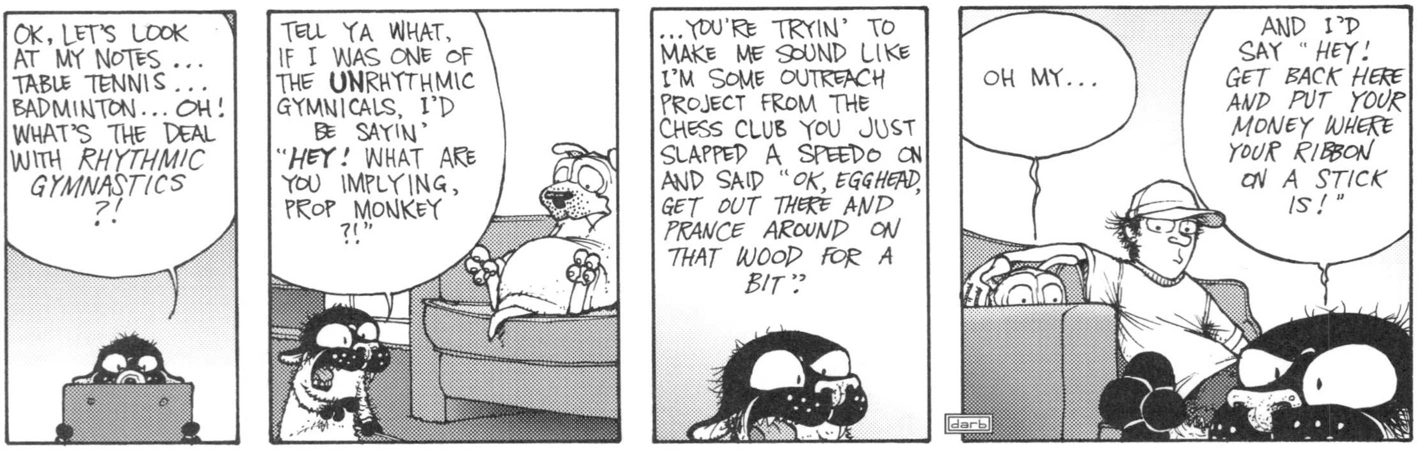
OK, LET'S LOOK AT MY NOTES... TABLE TENNIS... BADMINTON... OH! WHAT'S THE DEAL WITH RHYTHMIC GYMNASTICS?!
TELL YA WHAT, IF I WAS ONE OF THE UNRHYTHMIC GYMNICALS, I'D BE SAYIN' "HEY! WHAT ARE YOU IMPLYING, PROP MONKEY?!"
...YOU'RE TRYIN' TO MAKE ME SOUND LIKE I'M SOME OUTREACH PROJECT FROM THE CHESS CLUB YOU JUST SLAPPED A SPEEDO ON AND SAID "OK, EGGHEAD, GET OUT THERE AND PRANCE AROUND ON THAT WOOD FOR A BIT"?
OH MY...
AND I'D SAY "HEY! GET BACK HERE AND PUT YOUR MONEY WHERE YOUR RIBBON ON A STICK IS!"
darb

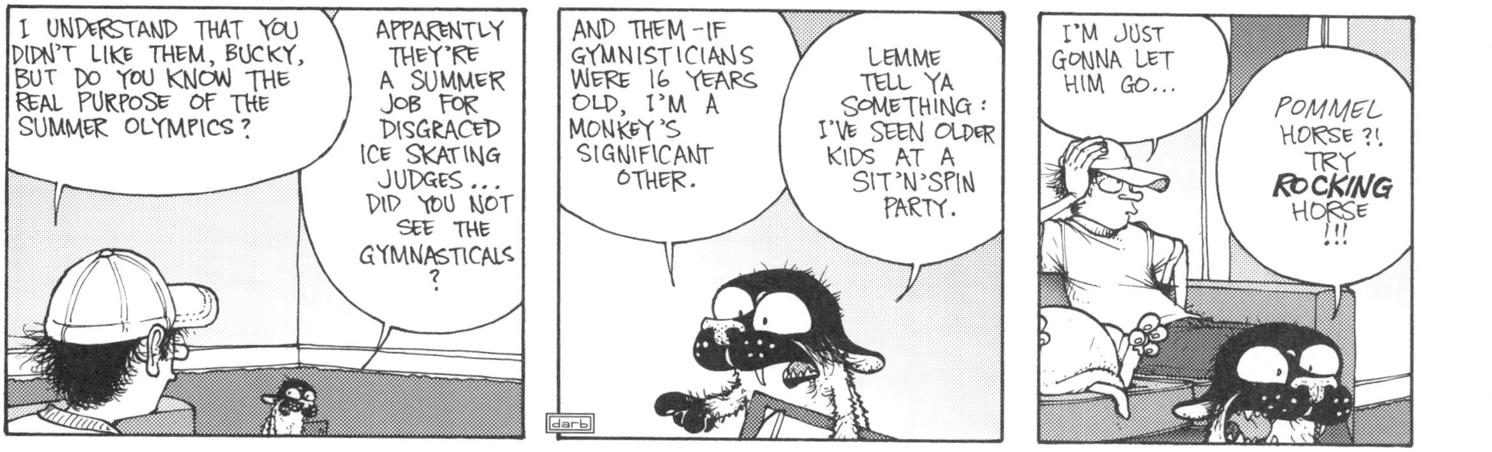
I UNDERSTAND THAT YOU DIDN'T LIKE THEM, BUCKY, BUT DO YOU KNOW THE REAL PURPOSE OF THE SUMMER OLYMPICS?
APPARENTLY THEY'RE A SUMMER JOB FOR DISGRACED ICE SKATING JUDGES... DID YOU NOT SEE THE GYMNASTICALS?
AND THEM - IF GYMNISTICIANS WERE 16 YEARS OLD, I'M A MONKEY'S SIGNIFICANT OTHER.
LEMME TELL YA SOMETHING: I'VE SEEN OLDER KIDS AT A SIT'N'SPIN PARTY.
darb
I'M JUST GONNA LET HIM GO...
POMMEL HORSE?! TRY ROCKING HORSE!!!

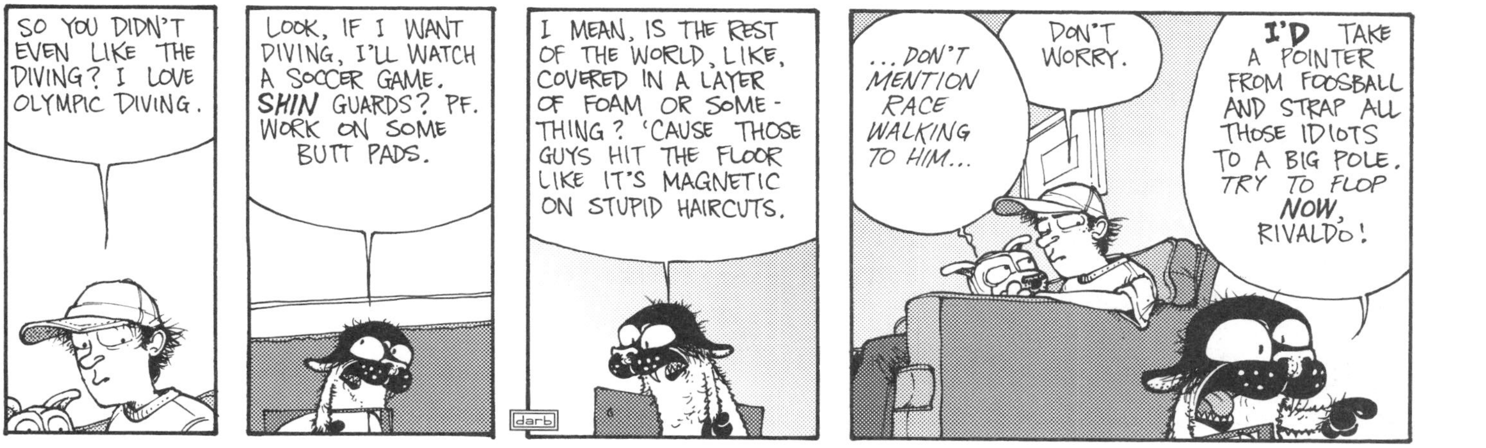
SO YOU DIDN'T EVEN LIKE THE DIVING? I LOVE OLYMPIC DIVING.
LOOK, IF I WANT DIVING, I'LL WATCH A SOCCER GAME. SHIN GUARDS? PF. WORK ON SOME BUTT PADS.
I MEAN, IS THE REST OF THE WORLD, LIKE, COVERED IN A LAYER OF FOAM OR SOMETHING? 'CAUSE THOSE GUYS HIT THE FLOOR LIKE IT'S MAGNETIC ON STUPID HAIRCUTS.
darb
...DON'T MENTION RACE WALKING TO HIM...
DON'T WORRY.
I'D TAKE A POINTER FROM FOOSBALL AND STRAP ALL THOSE IDIOTS TO A BIG POLE. TRY TO FLOP NOW, RIVALDO!

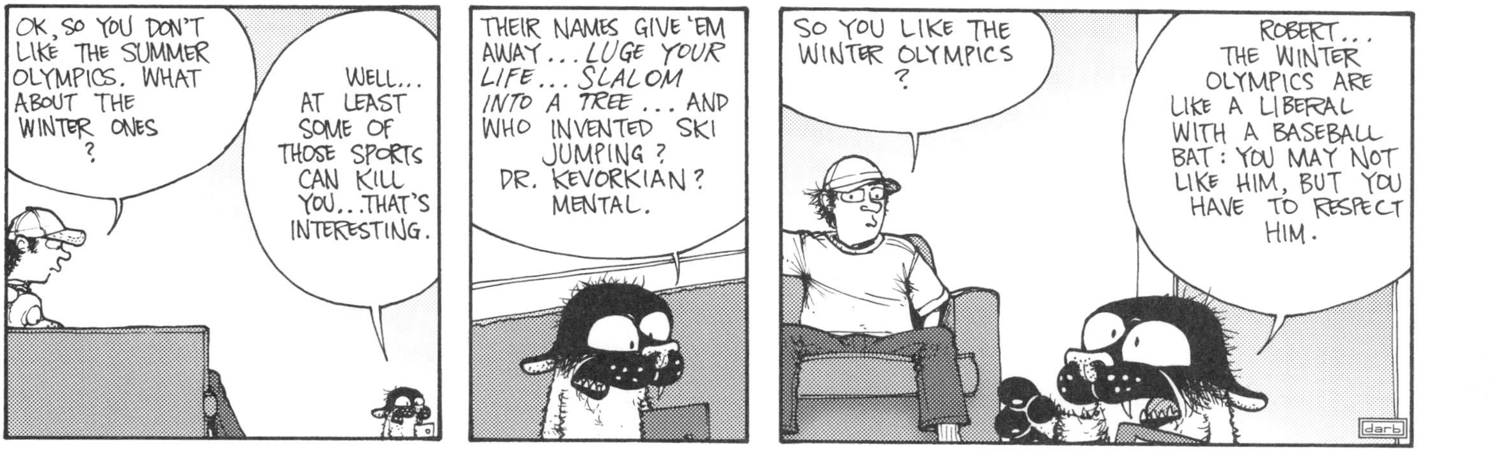
OK, SO YOU DON'T LIKE THE SUMMER OLYMPICS. WHAT ABOUT THE WINTER ONES?
WELL... AT LEAST SOME OF THOSE SPORTS CAN KILL YOU...THAT'S INTERESTING.
THEIR NAMES GIVE 'EM AWAY... LUGE YOUR LIFE... SLALOM INTO A TREE... AND WHO INVENTED SKI JUMPING? DR. KEVORKIAN? MENTAL.
SO YOU LIKE THE WINTER OLYMPICS?
ROBERT... THE WINTER OLYMPICS ARE LIKE A LIBERAL WITH A BASEBALL BAT: YOU MAY NOT LIKE HIM, BUT YOU HAVE TO RESPECT HIM.
darb

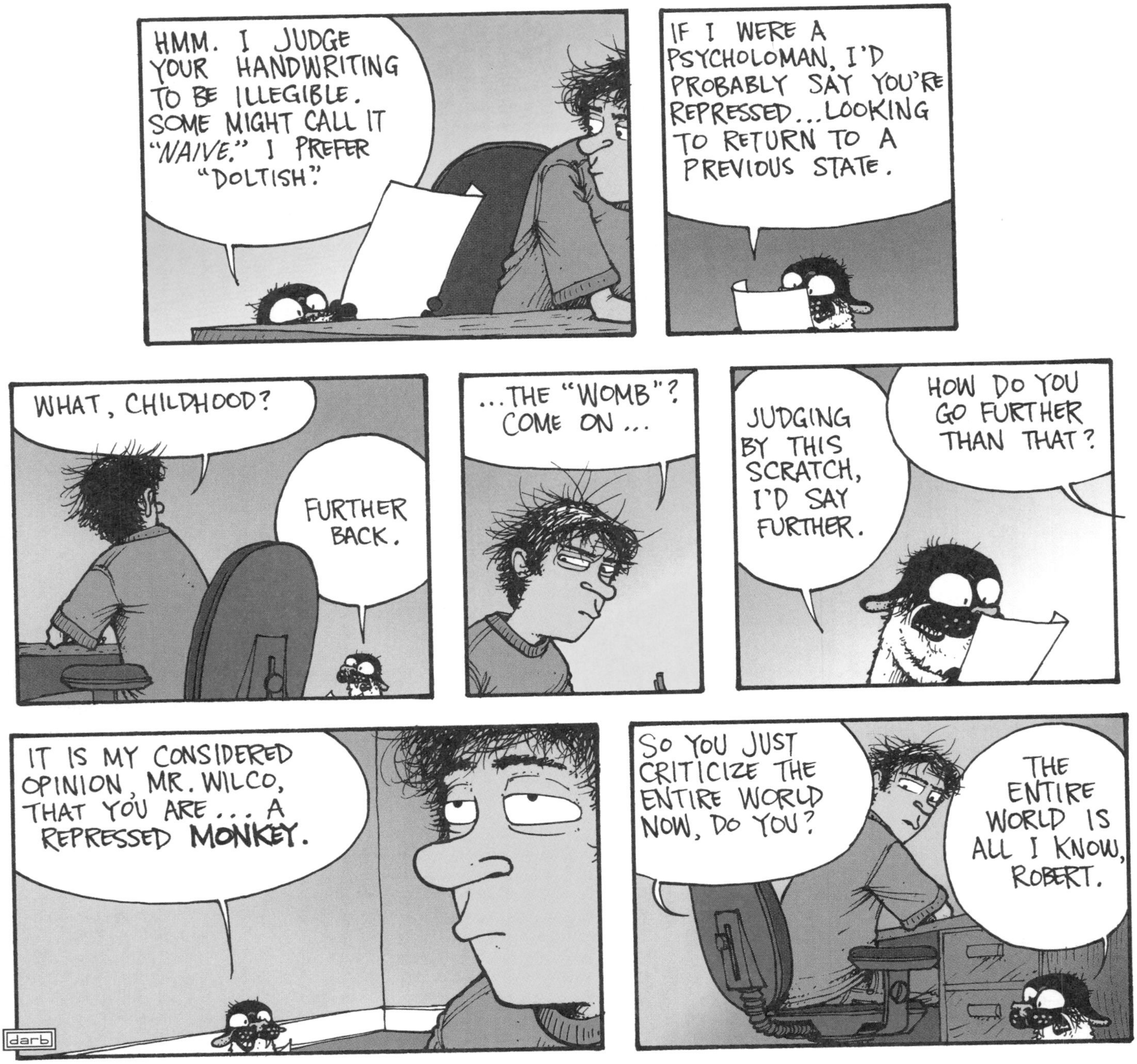
HMM. I JUDGE YOUR HANDWRITING TO BE ILLEGIBLE. SOME MIGHT CALL IT "NAIVE." I PREFER "DOLTISH."
IF I WERE A PSYCHOLOMAN, I'D PROBABLY SAY YOU'RE REPRESSED... LOOKING TO RETURN TO A PREVIOUS STATE.
WHAT, CHILDHOOD?
FURTHER BACK.
...THE "WOMB"? COME ON...
JUDGING BY THIS SCRATCH, I'D SAY FURTHER.
HOW DO YOU GO FURTHER THAN THAT?
IT IS MY CONSIDERED OPINION, MR. WILCO, THAT YOU ARE... A REPRESSED MONKEY.
darb
SO YOU JUST CRITICIZE THE ENTIRE WORLD NOW, DO YOU?
THE ENTIRE WORLD IS ALL I KNOW, ROBERT.

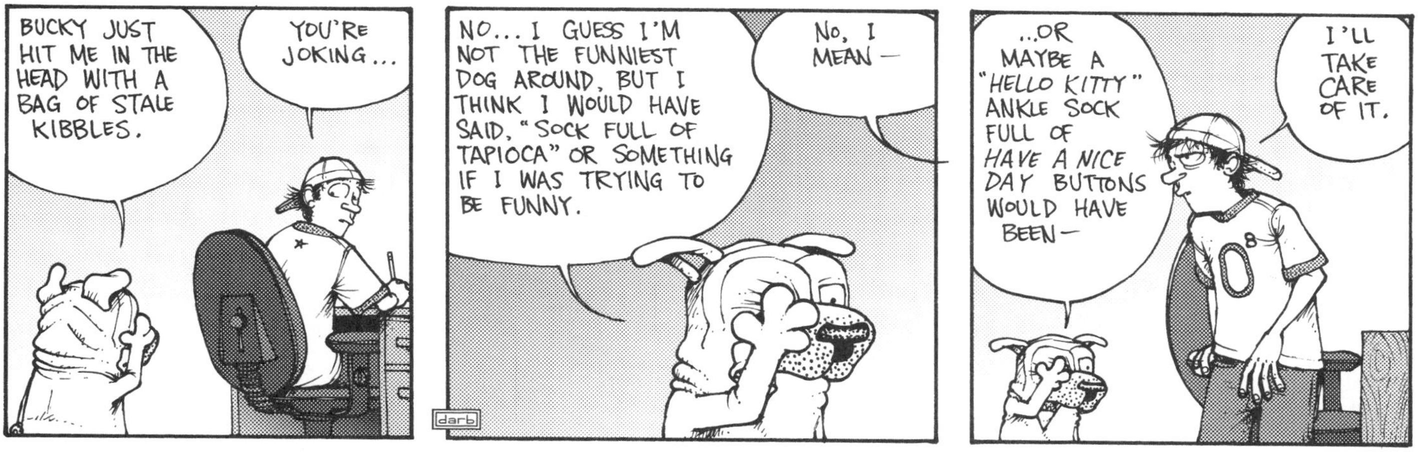
BUCKY JUST HIT ME IN THE HEAD WITH A BAG OF STALE KIBBLES.
YOU'RE JOKING...
NO... I GUESS I'M NOT THE FUNNIEST DOG AROUND, BUT I THINK I WOULD HAVE SAID, "SOCK FULL OF TAPIOCA" OR SOMETHING IF I WAS TRYING TO BE FUNNY.
No, I MEAN —
...OR MAYBE A "HELLO KITTY" ANKLE SOCK FULL OF HAVE A NICE DAY BUTTONS WOULD HAVE BEEN—
I'LL TAKE CARE OF IT.
darb

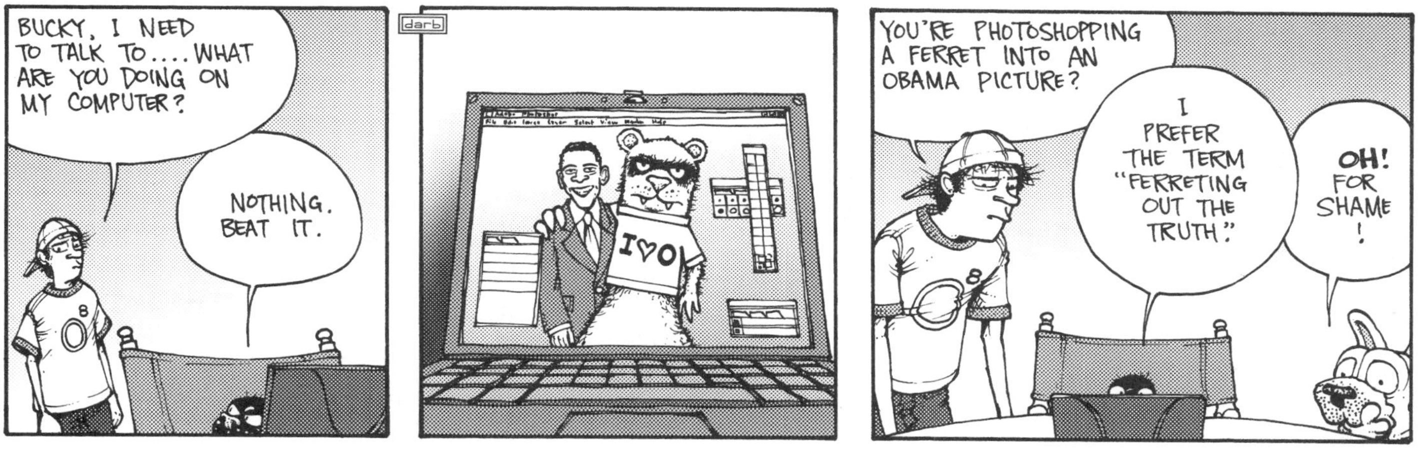
BUCKY, I NEED TO TALK TO.... WHAT ARE YOU DOING ON MY COMPUTER?
NOTHING. BEAT IT.
darb
YOU'RE PHOTOSHOPPING A FERRET INTO AN OBAMA PICTURE?
I PREFER THE TERM "FERRETING OUT THE TRUTH."
OH! FOR SHAME!

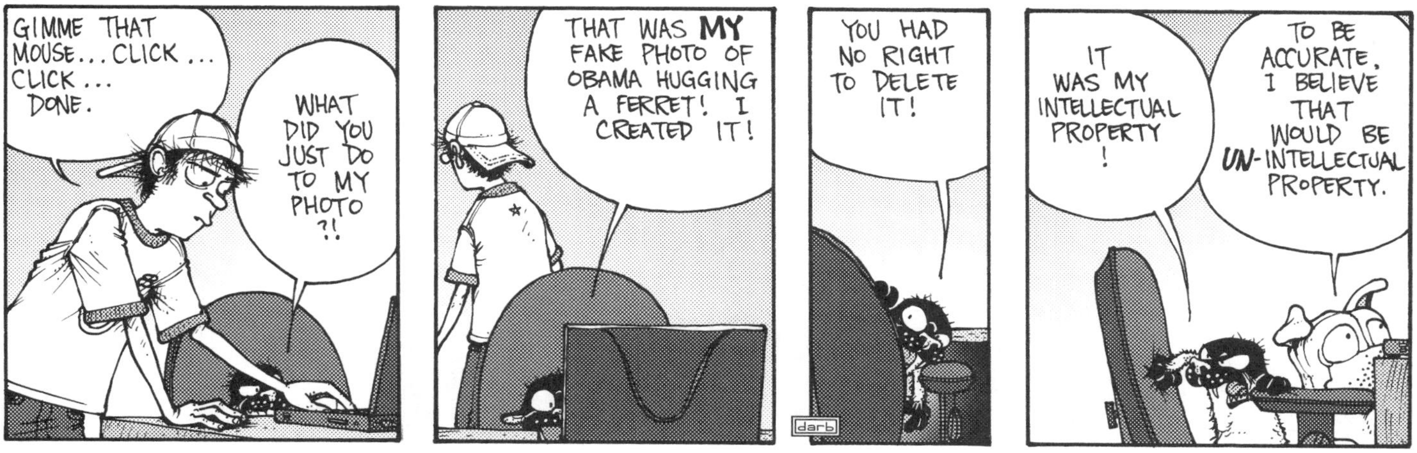
GIMME THAT MOUSE... CLICK... CLICK... DONE.
WHAT DID YOU JUST DO TO MY PHOTO?!
THAT WAS MY FAKE PHOTO OF OBAMA HUGGING A FERRET! I CREATED IT!
YOU HAD NO RIGHT TO DELETE IT!
darb
IT WAS MY INTELLECTUAL PROPERTY!
TO BE ACCURATE, I BELIEVE THAT WOULD BE UN-INTELLECTUAL PROPERTY.

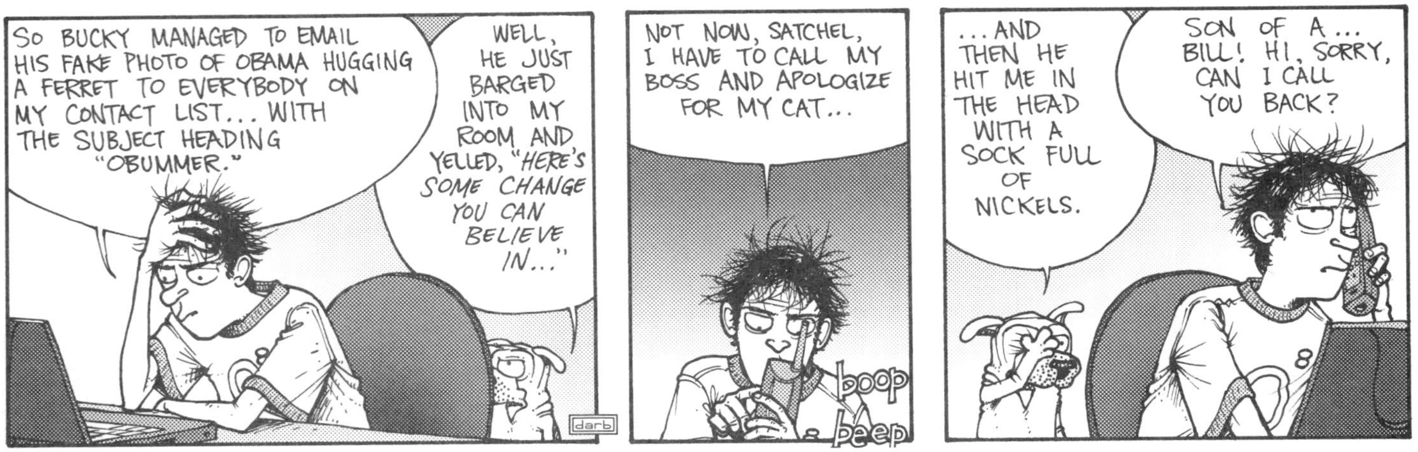
SO BUCKY MANAGED TO EMAIL HIS FAKE PHOTO OF OBAMA HUGGING A FERRET TO EVERYBODY ON MY CONTACT LIST... WITH THE SUBJECT HEADING "OBUMMER."
WELL, HE JUST BARGED INTO MY ROOM AND YELLED, "HERE'S SOME CHANGE YOU CAN BELIEVE IN..."
NOT NOW, SATCHEL, I HAVE TO CALL MY BOSS AND APOLOGIZE FOR MY CAT...
boop beep
...AND THEN HE HIT ME IN THE HEAD WITH A SOCK FULL OF NICKELS.
SON OF A... BILL! HI, SORRY, CAN I CALL YOU BACK?

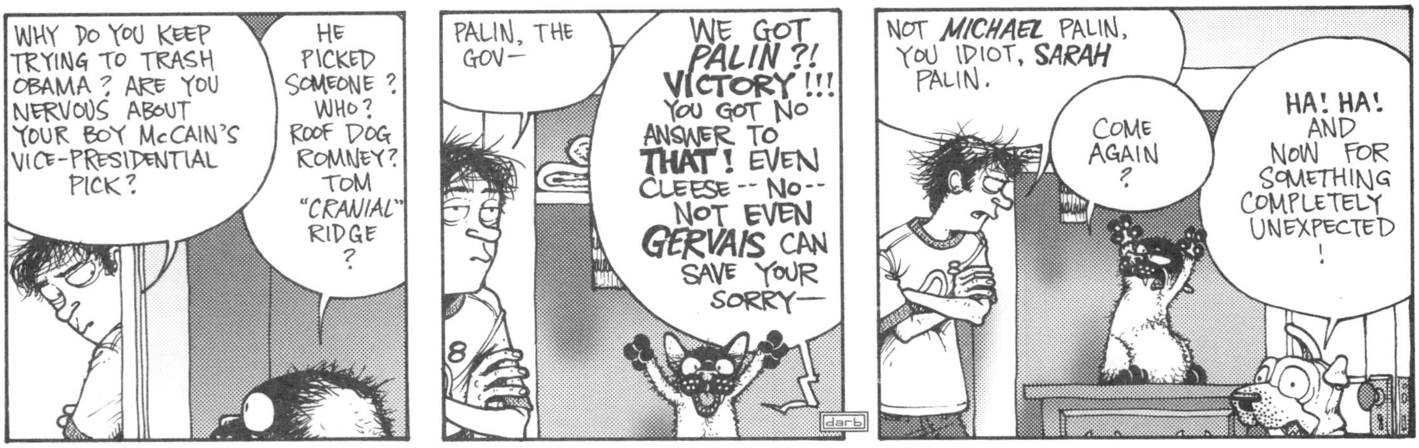
WHY DO YOU KEEP TRYING TO TRASH OBAMA? ARE YOU NERVOUS ABOUT YOUR BOY McCAIN'S VICE-PRESIDENTIAL PICK?
HE PICKED SOMEONE? WHO? ROOF DOG ROMNEY? TOM "CRANIAL" RIDGE?
PALIN, THE GOV—
WE GOT PALIN?! VICTORY!!! YOU GOT NO ANSWER TO THAT! EVEN CLEESE -- NO -- NOT EVEN GERVAIS CAN SAVE YOUR SORRY—
NOT MICHAEL PALIN, YOU IDIOT, SARAH PALIN.
COME AGAIN?
HA! HA! AND NOW FOR SOMETHING COMPLETELY UNEXPECTED!

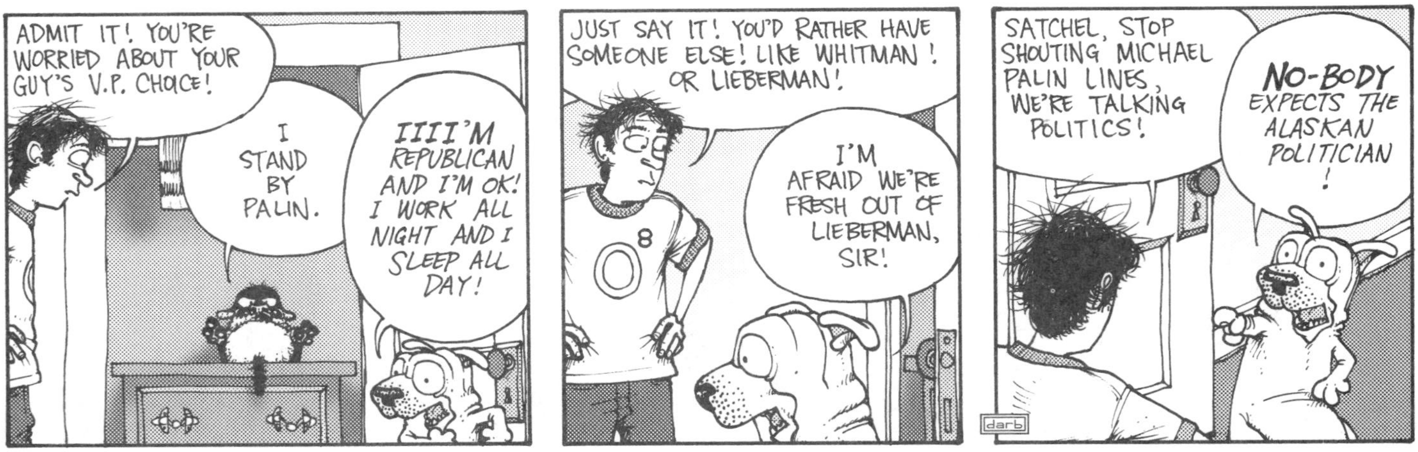
ADMIT IT! YOU'RE WORRIED ABOUT YOUR GUY'S V.P. CHOICE!
I STAND BY PALIN.
IIII'M REPUBLICAN AND I'M OK! I WORK ALL NIGHT AND I SLEEP ALL DAY!
JUST SAY IT! YOU'D RATHER HAVE SOMEONE ELSE! LIKE WHITMAN! OR LIEBERMAN!
I'M AFRAID WE'RE FRESH OUT OF LIEBERMAN, SIR!
SATCHEL, STOP SHOUTING MICHAEL PALIN LINES, WE'RE TALKING POLITICS!
NO-BODY EXPECTS THE ALASKAN POLITICIAN!

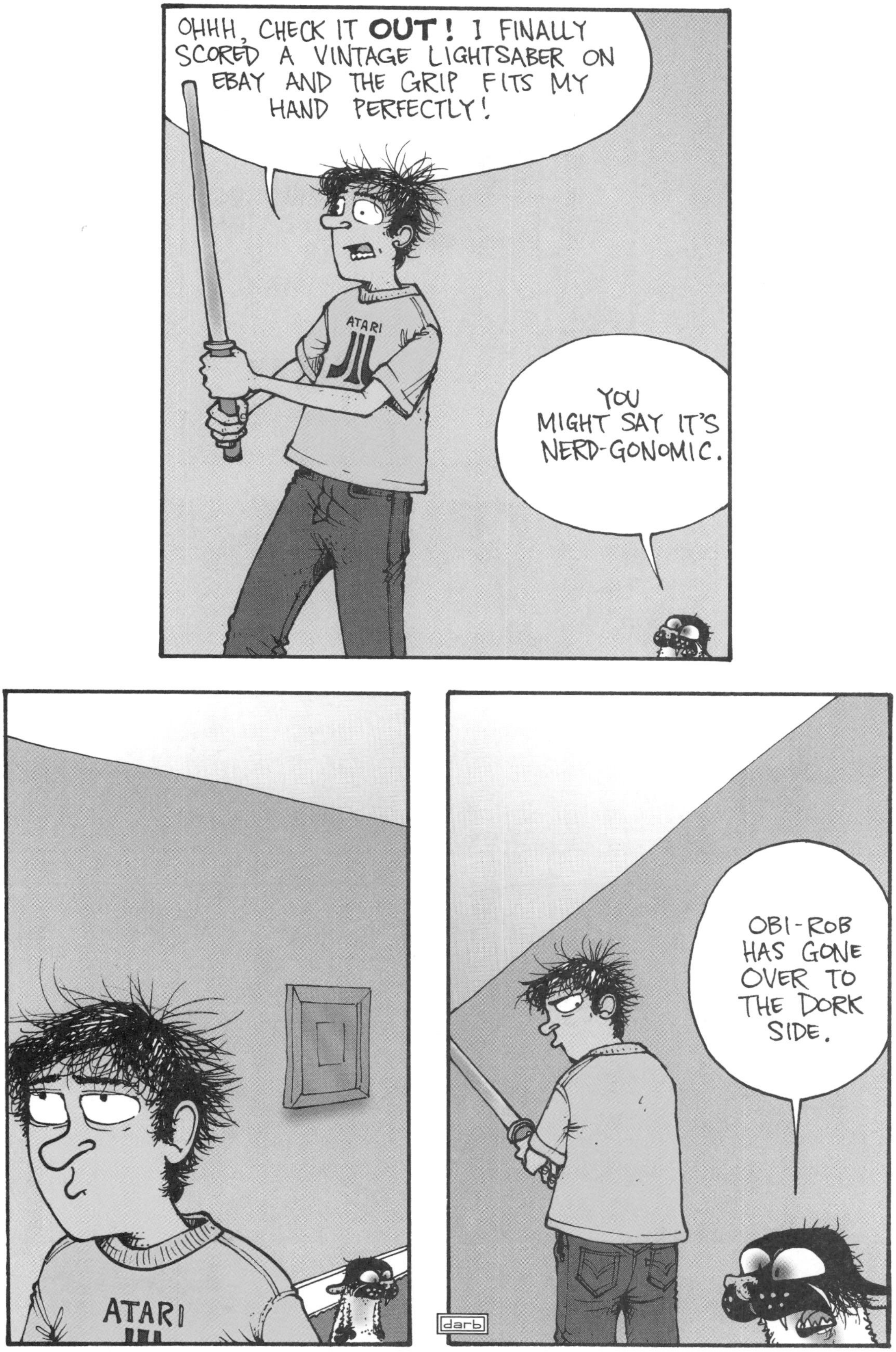
OHHH, CHECK IT OUT! I FINALLY SCORED A VINTAGE LIGHTSABER ON EBAY AND THE GRIP FITS MY HAND PERFECTLY!
ATARI
YOU MIGHT SAY IT'S NERD-GONOMIC.
ATARI
darb
OBI-ROB HAS GONE OVER TO THE DORK SIDE.

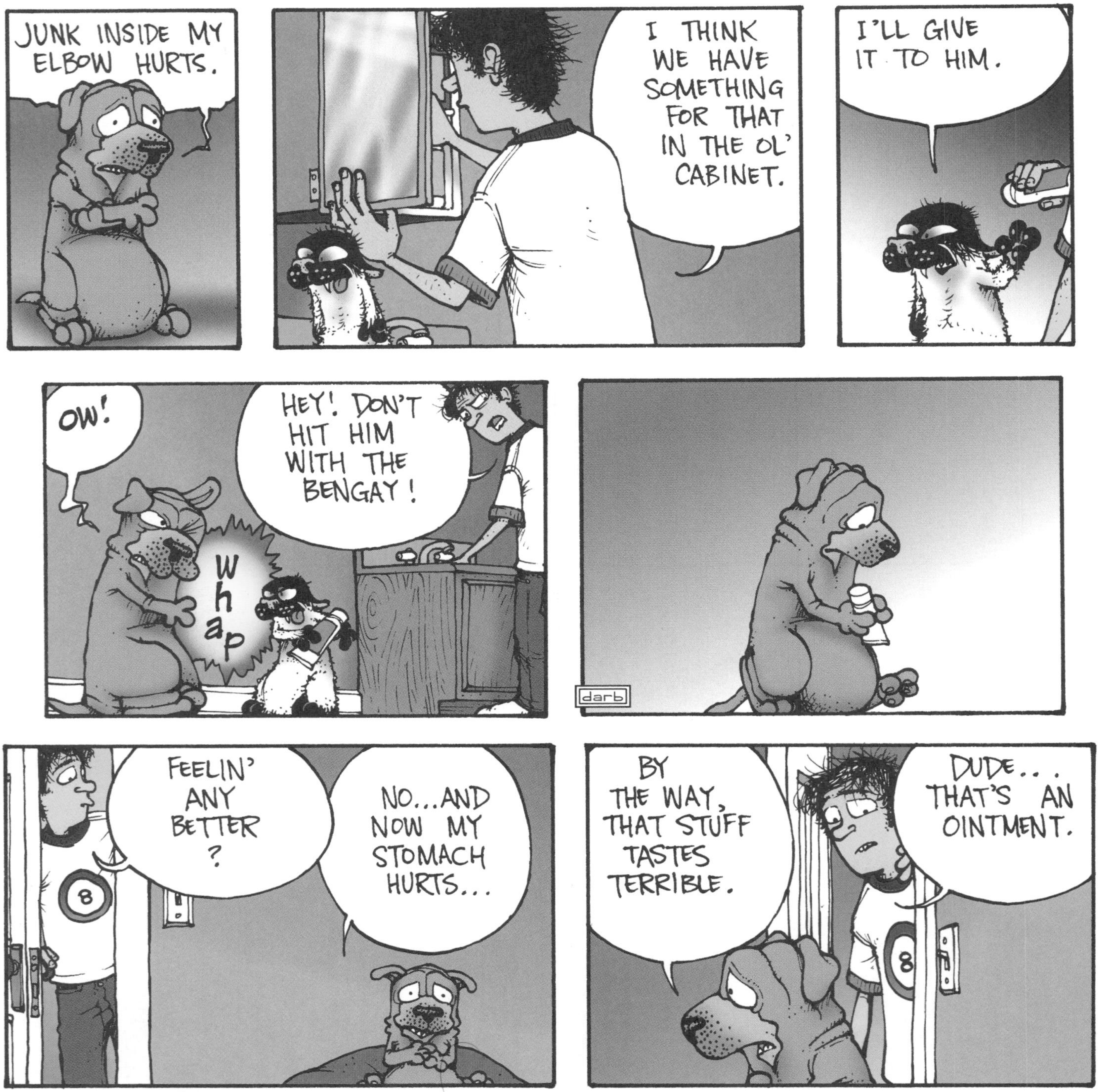
JUNK INSIDE MY ELBOW HURTS.
I THINK WE HAVE SOMETHING FOR THAT IN THE OL' CABINET.
I'LL GIVE IT TO HIM.
OW!
HEY! DON'T HIT HIM WITH THE BENGAY!
whap
darb
FEELIN' ANY BETTER ?
NO...AND NOW MY STOMACH HURTS...
BY THE WAY, THAT STUFF TASTES TERRIBLE.
DUDE... THAT'S AN OINTMENT.

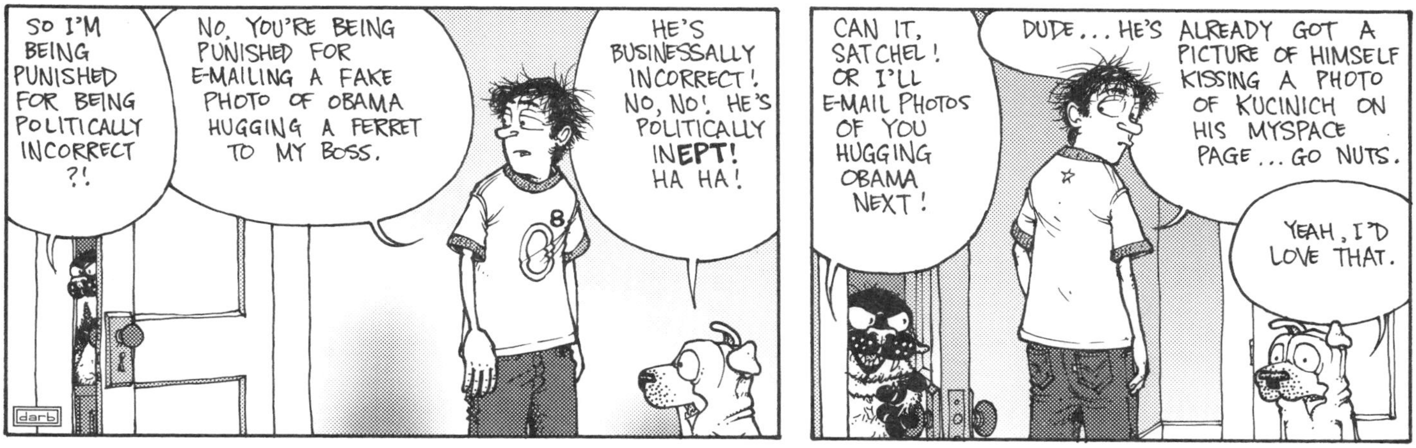
SO I'M BEING PUNISHED FOR BEING POLITICALLY INCORRECT ?!
NO, YOU'RE BEING PUNISHED FOR E-MAILING A FAKE PHOTO OF OBAMA HUGGING A FERRET TO MY BOSS.
HE'S BUSINESSALLY INCORRECT! NO, NO! HE'S POLITICALLY IN**EPT!** HA HA!
CAN IT, SATCHEL! OR I'LL E-MAIL PHOTOS OF YOU HUGGING OBAMA NEXT!
DUDE... HE'S ALREADY GOT A PICTURE OF HIMSELF KISSING A PHOTO OF KUCINICH ON HIS MYSPACE PAGE... GO NUTS.
YEAH, I'D LOVE THAT.
darb

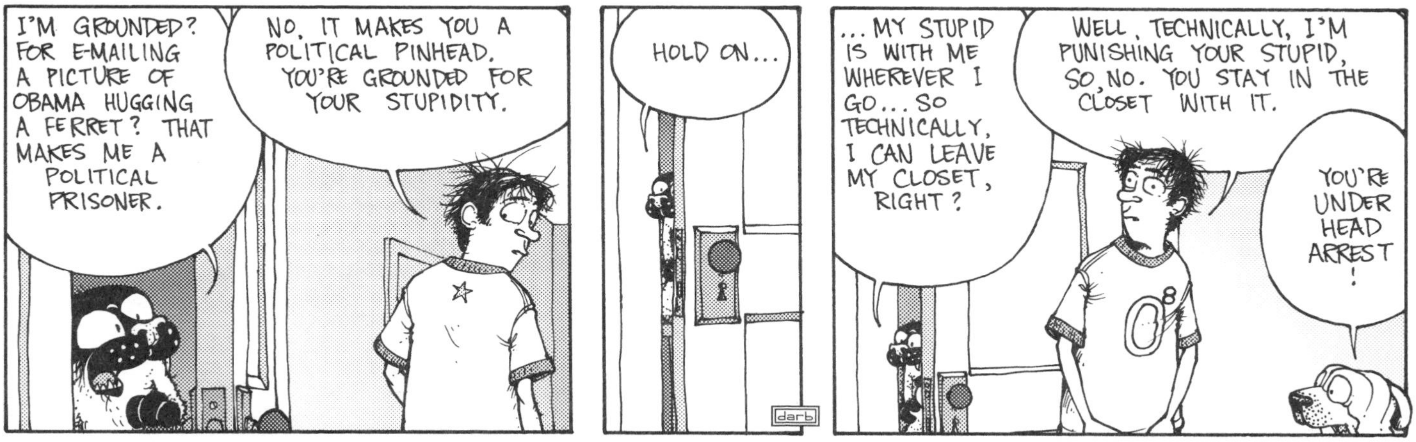
I'M GROUNDED? FOR E-MAILING A PICTURE OF OBAMA HUGGING A FERRET? THAT MAKES ME A POLITICAL PRISONER.
NO, IT MAKES YOU A POLITICAL PINHEAD. YOU'RE GROUNDED FOR YOUR STUPIDITY.
HOLD ON...
...MY STUPID IS WITH ME WHEREVER I GO... SO TECHNICALLY, I CAN LEAVE MY CLOSET, RIGHT?
WELL, TECHNICALLY, I'M PUNISHING YOUR STUPID, SO, NO. YOU STAY IN THE CLOSET WITH IT.
YOU'RE UNDER HEAD ARREST!
darb

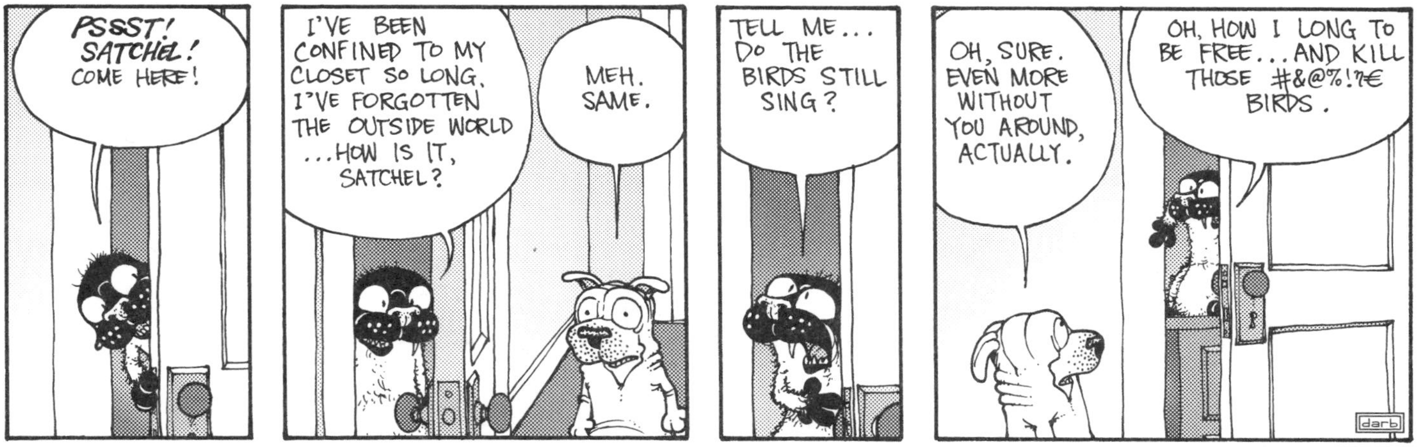
PSSST! SATCHEL! COME HERE!
I'VE BEEN CONFINED TO MY CLOSET SO LONG, I'VE FORGOTTEN THE OUTSIDE WORLD ...HOW IS IT, SATCHEL?
MEH. SAME.
TELL ME... DO THE BIRDS STILL SING?
OH, SURE. EVEN MORE WITHOUT YOU AROUND, ACTUALLY.
OH, HOW I LONG TO BE FREE... AND KILL THOSE #&@%!?€ BIRDS.
darb

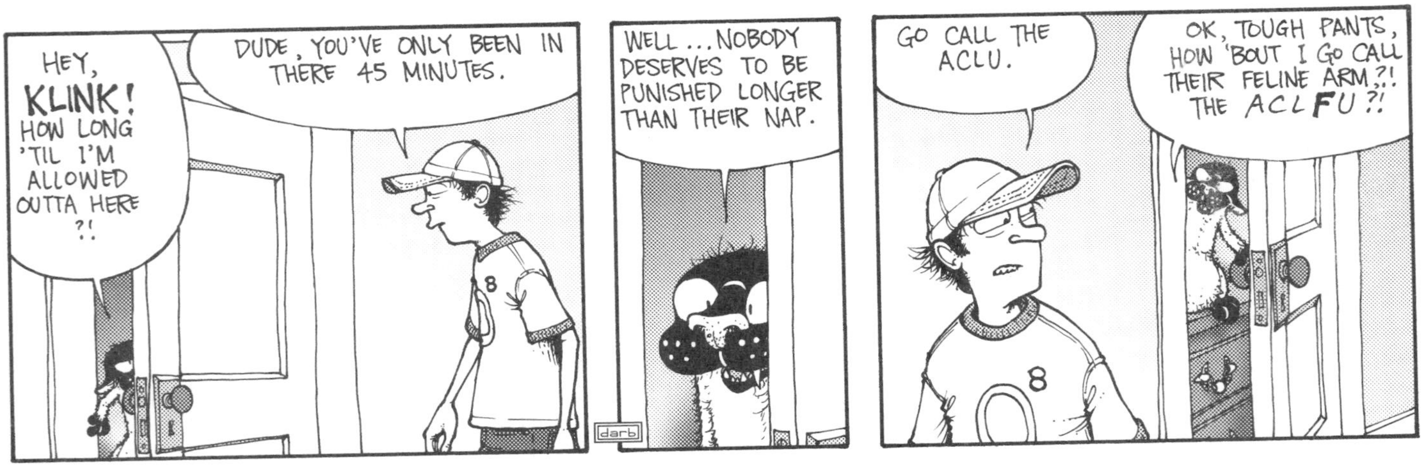
HEY, KLINK! HOW LONG 'TIL I'M ALLOWED OUTTA HERE ?!
DUDE, YOU'VE ONLY BEEN IN THERE 45 MINUTES.
WELL ... NOBODY DESERVES TO BE PUNISHED LONGER THAN THEIR NAP.
darb
GO CALL THE ACLU.
OK, TOUGH PANTS, HOW 'BOUT I GO CALL THEIR FELINE ARM ?! THE ACLFU ?!

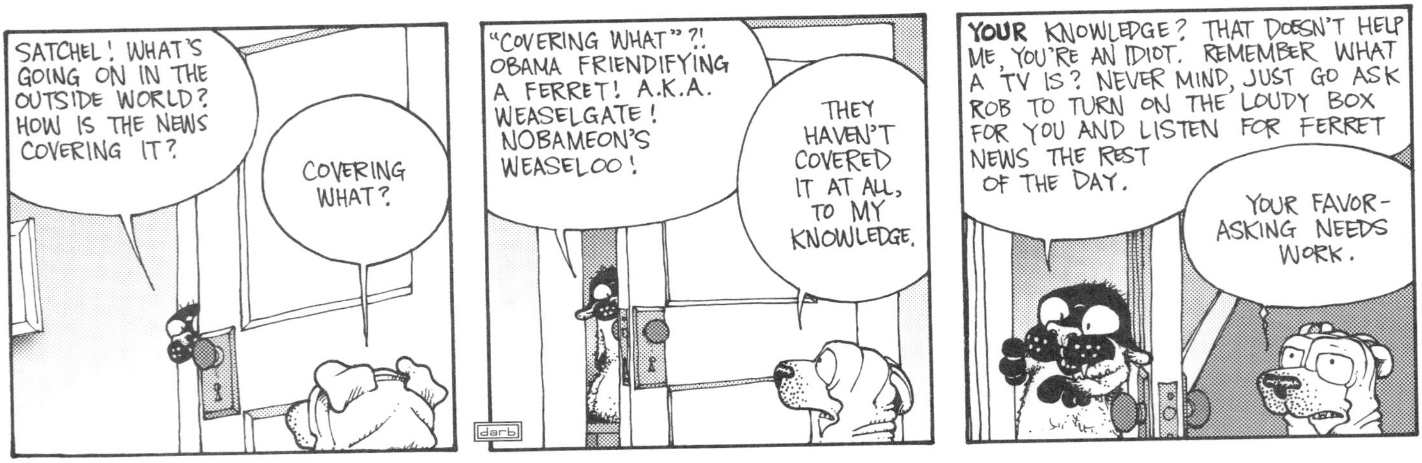
SATCHEL! WHAT'S GOING ON IN THE OUTSIDE WORLD? HOW IS THE NEWS COVERING IT?
COVERING WHAT?
darb
"COVERING WHAT"?! OBAMA FRIENDIFYING A FERRET! A.K.A. WEASELGATE! NOBAMEON'S WEASELOO!
THEY HAVEN'T COVERED IT AT ALL, TO MY KNOWLEDGE.
YOUR KNOWLEDGE? THAT DOESN'T HELP ME, YOU'RE AN IDIOT. REMEMBER WHAT A TV IS? NEVER MIND, JUST GO ASK ROB TO TURN ON THE LOUDY BOX FOR YOU AND LISTEN FOR FERRET NEWS THE REST OF THE DAY.
YOUR FAVOR-ASKING NEEDS WORK.

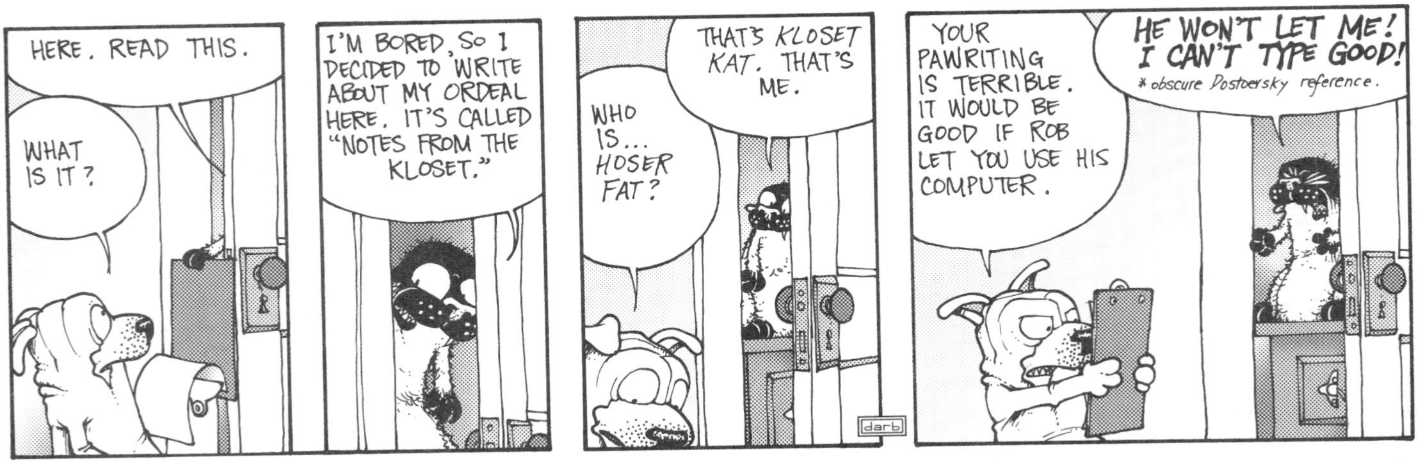
HERE. READ THIS.
WHAT IS IT?
I'M BORED, SO I DECIDED TO WRITE ABOUT MY ORDEAL HERE. IT'S CALLED "NOTES FROM THE KLOSET."
WHO IS... HOSER FAT?
THAT'S KLOSET KAT. THAT'S ME.
darb
YOUR PAWRITING IS TERRIBLE. IT WOULD BE GOOD IF ROB LET YOU USE HIS COMPUTER.
HE WON'T LET ME! I CAN'T TYPE GOOD!
* obscure Dostoevsky reference.

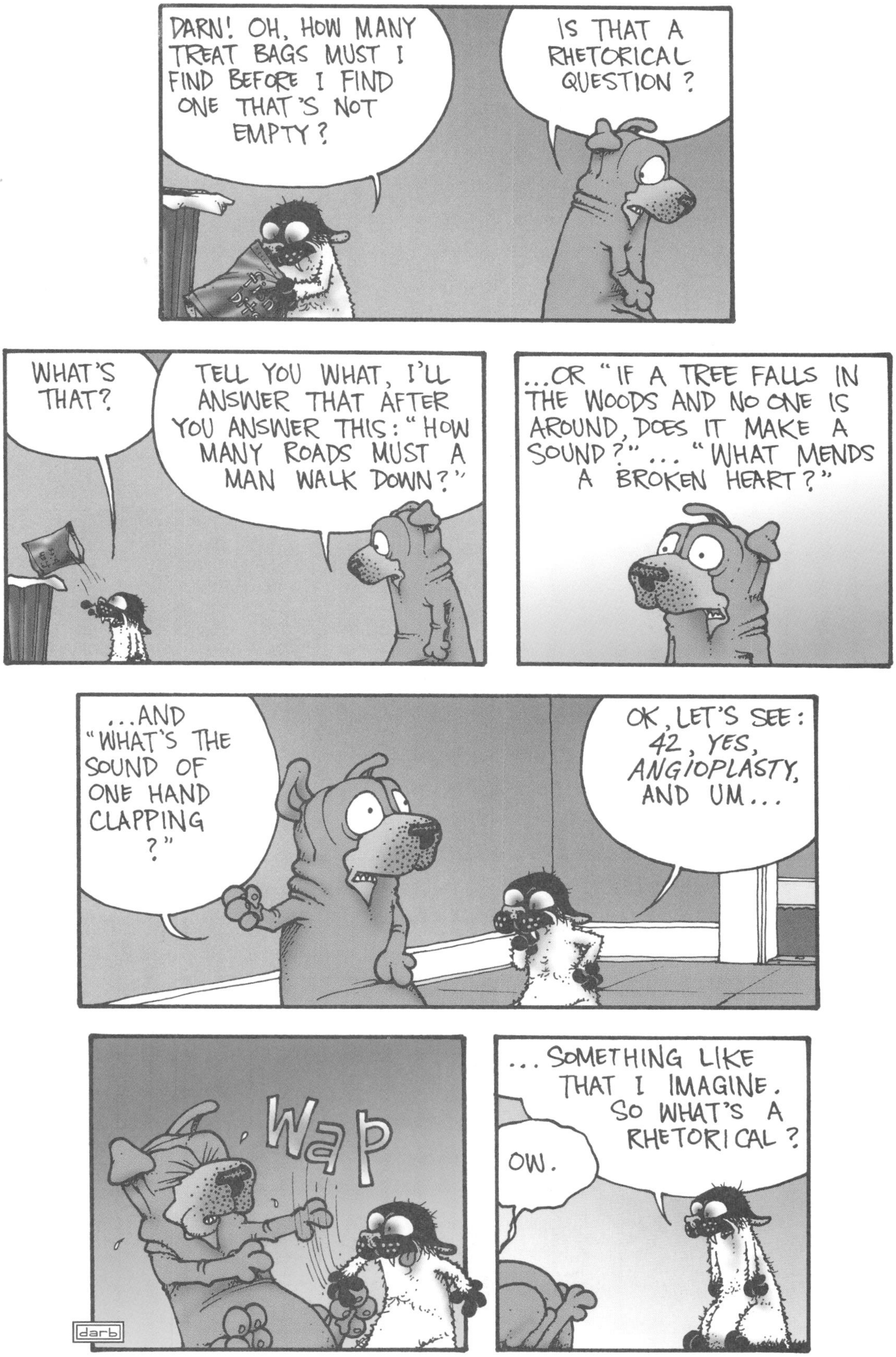
DARN! OH, HOW MANY TREAT BAGS MUST I FIND BEFORE I FIND ONE THAT'S NOT EMPTY?
IS THAT A RHETORICAL QUESTION?
WHAT'S THAT?
TELL YOU WHAT, I'LL ANSWER THAT AFTER YOU ANSWER THIS: "HOW MANY ROADS MUST A MAN WALK DOWN?"
...OR "IF A TREE FALLS IN THE WOODS AND NO ONE IS AROUND, DOES IT MAKE A SOUND?" ... "WHAT MENDS A BROKEN HEART?"
...AND "WHAT'S THE SOUND OF ONE HAND CLAPPING?"
OK, LET'S SEE: 42, YES, ANGIOPLASTY, AND UM...
Wap
darb
...SOMETHING LIKE THAT I IMAGINE. SO WHAT'S A RHETORICAL?
OW.

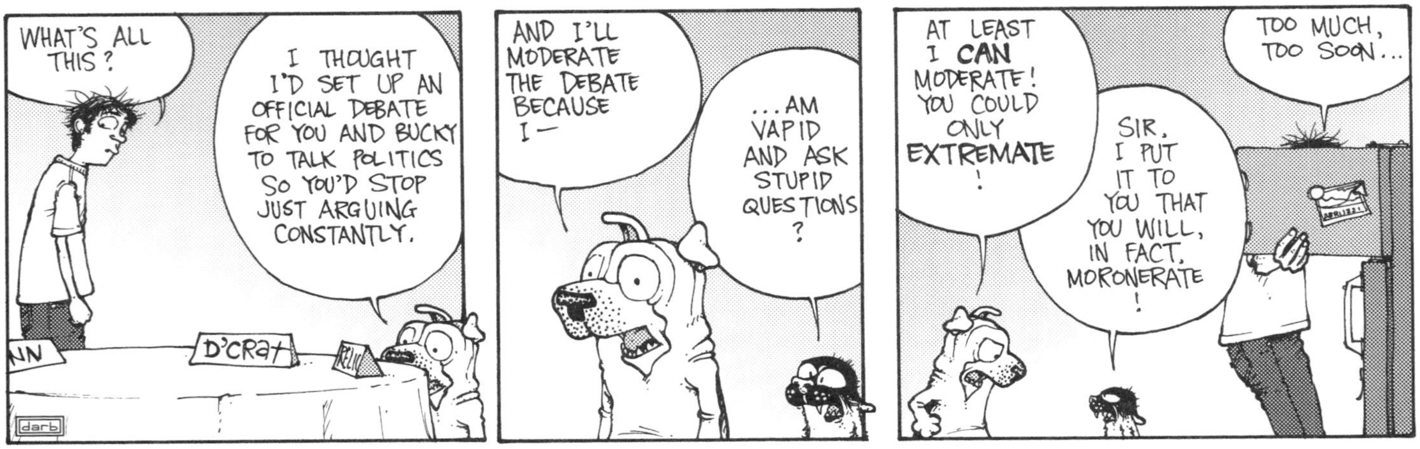
WHAT'S ALL THIS?
I THOUGHT I'D SET UP AN OFFICIAL DEBATE FOR YOU AND BUCKY TO TALK POLITICS SO YOU'D STOP JUST ARGUING CONSTANTLY.
NN
D'CRat
AND I'LL MODERATE THE DEBATE BECAUSE I—
...AM VAPID AND ASK STUPID QUESTIONS?
AT LEAST I **CAN** MODERATE! YOU COULD ONLY **EXTREMATE**!
SIR, I PUT IT TO YOU THAT YOU WILL, IN FACT, MORONERATE!
TOO MUCH, TOO SOON...

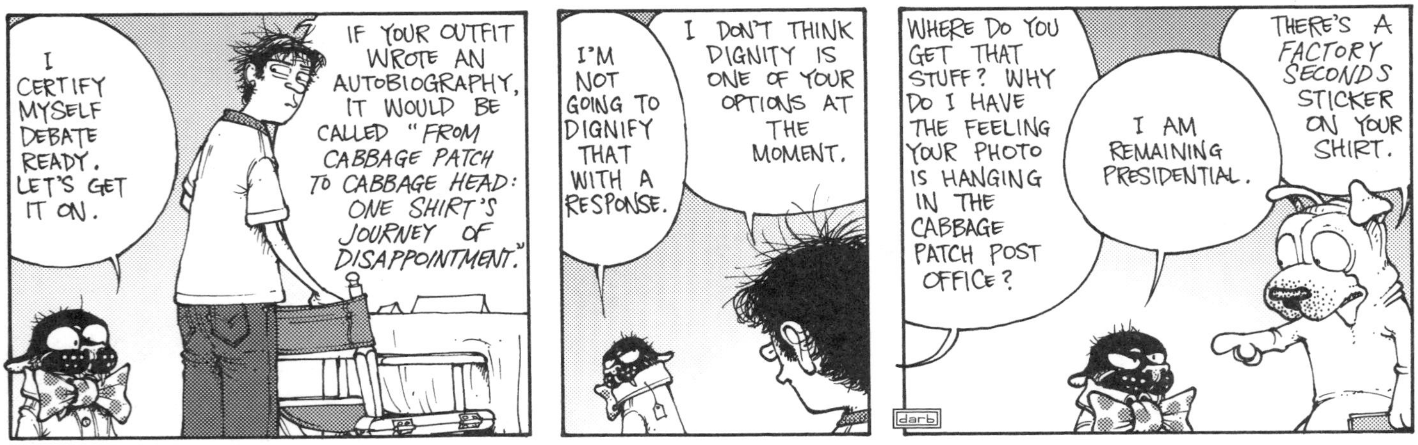
I CERTIFY MYSELF DEBATE READY. LET'S GET IT ON.
IF YOUR OUTFIT WROTE AN AUTOBIOGRAPHY, IT WOULD BE CALLED "*FROM CABBAGE PATCH TO CABBAGE HEAD: ONE SHIRT'S JOURNEY OF DISAPPOINTMENT*."
I'M NOT GOING TO DIGNIFY THAT WITH A RESPONSE.
I DON'T THINK DIGNITY IS ONE OF YOUR OPTIONS AT THE MOMENT.
WHERE DO YOU GET THAT STUFF? WHY DO I HAVE THE FEELING YOUR PHOTO IS HANGING IN THE CABBAGE PATCH POST OFFICE?
I AM REMAINING PRESIDENTIAL.
THERE'S A *FACTORY SECONDS* STICKER ON YOUR SHIRT.

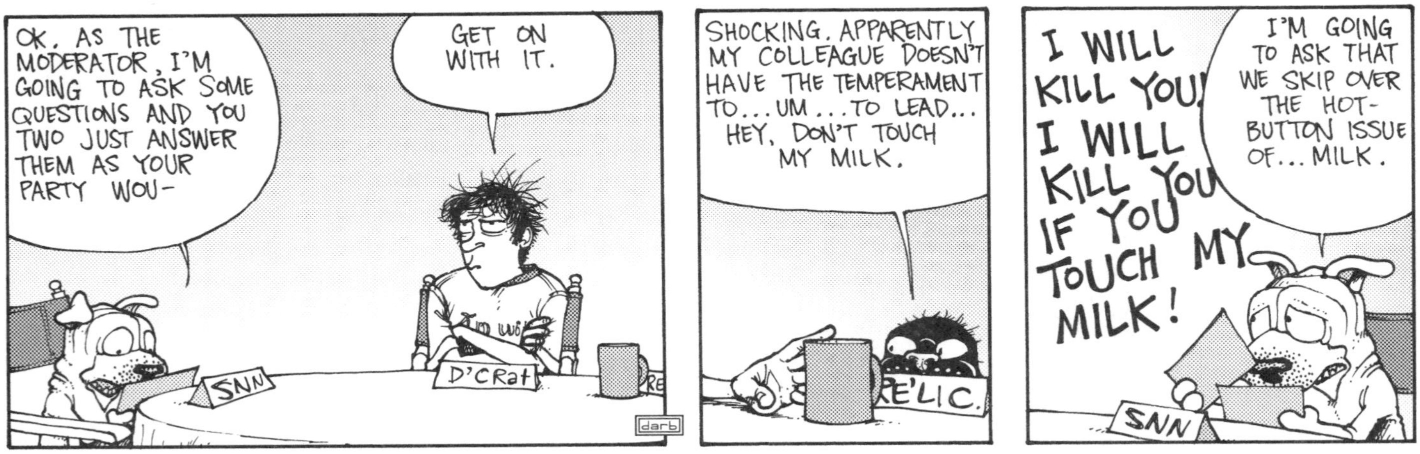
OK, AS THE MODERATOR, I'M GOING TO ASK SOME QUESTIONS AND YOU TWO JUST ANSWER THEM AS YOUR PARTY WOU-
GET ON WITH IT.
SNN
D'CRat
SHOCKING. APPARENTLY MY COLLEAGUE DOESN'T HAVE THE TEMPERAMENT TO...UM...TO LEAD... HEY, DON'T TOUCH MY MILK.
RE'LIC.
I WILL KILL YOU! I WILL KILL YOU IF YOU TOUCH MY MILK!
I'M GOING TO ASK THAT WE SKIP OVER THE HOT-BUTTON ISSUE OF... MILK.
SNN

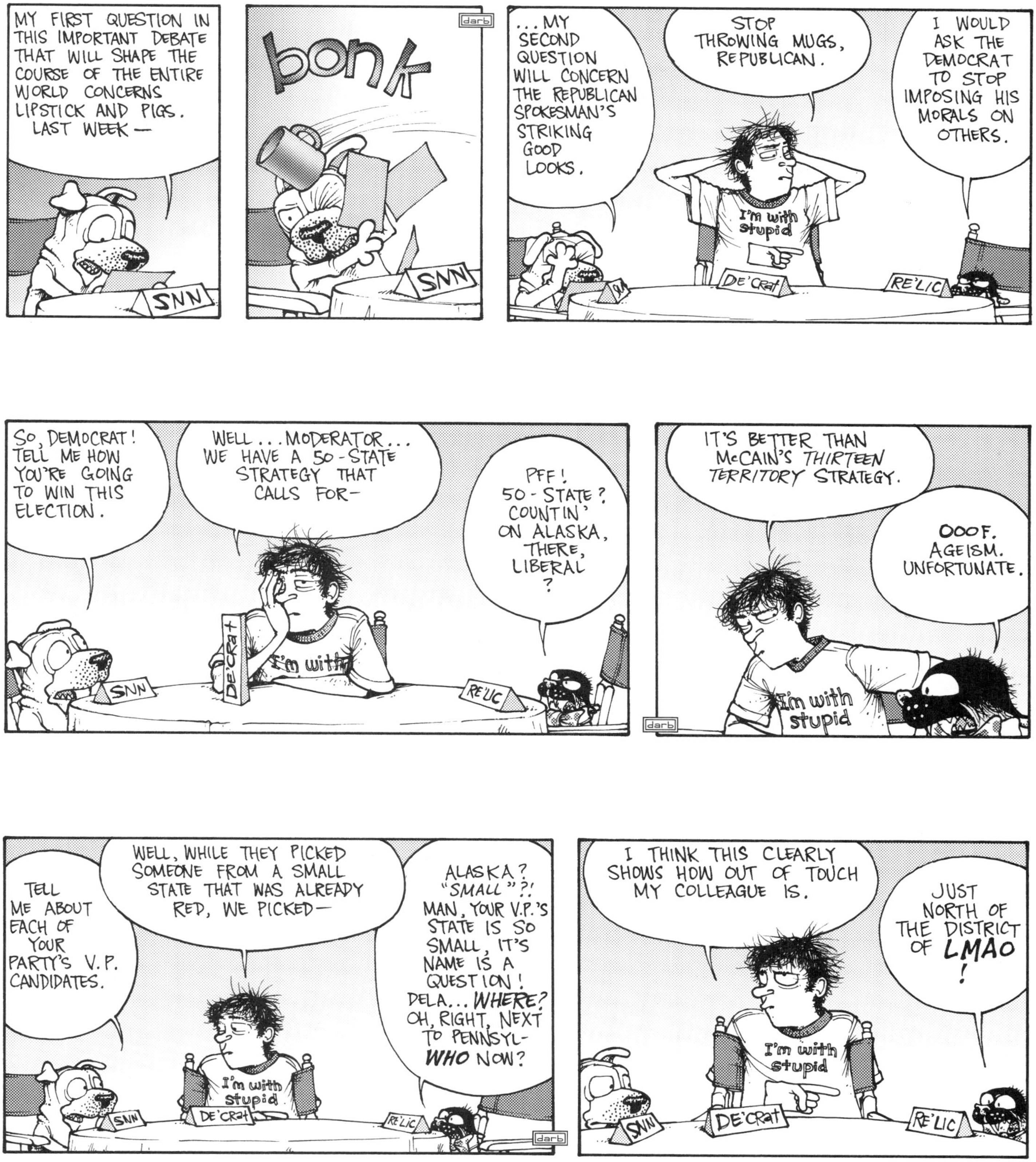
MY FIRST QUESTION IN THIS IMPORTANT DEBATE THAT WILL SHAPE THE COURSE OF THE ENTIRE WORLD CONCERNS LIPSTICK AND PIGS. LAST WEEK—
SNN
darb
bonk
SNN
...MY SECOND QUESTION WILL CONCERN THE REPUBLICAN SPOKESMAN'S STRIKING GOOD LOOKS.
STOP THROWING MUGS, REPUBLICAN.
I WOULD ASK THE DEMOCRAT TO STOP IMPOSING HIS MORALS ON OTHERS.
I'm with stupid
DE'CRAT
RE'LIC
SO, DEMOCRAT! TELL ME HOW YOU'RE GOING TO WIN THIS ELECTION.
WELL... MODERATOR... WE HAVE A 50-STATE STRATEGY THAT CALLS FOR—
PFF! 50-STATE? COUNTIN' ON ALASKA, THERE, LIBERAL?
SNN
DE'CRAT
I'm with
RE'LIC
IT'S BETTER THAN McCAIN'S *THIRTEEN TERRITORY* STRATEGY.
OOOF. AGEISM. UNFORTUNATE.
I'm with stupid
darb
TELL ME ABOUT EACH OF YOUR PARTY'S V.P. CANDIDATES.
WELL, WHILE THEY PICKED SOMEONE FROM A SMALL STATE THAT WAS ALREADY RED, WE PICKED—
ALASKA? "*SMALL*"?! MAN, YOUR V.P.'S STATE IS SO SMALL, IT'S NAME IS A QUESTION! DELA... **WHERE?** OH, RIGHT, NEXT TO PENNSYL-**WHO** NOW?
SNN
DE'CRAT
I'm with stupid
RE'LIC
darb
I THINK THIS CLEARLY SHOWS HOW OUT OF TOUCH MY COLLEAGUE IS.
JUST NORTH OF THE DISTRICT OF **LMAO**!
I'm with stupid
SNN
DE'CRAT
RE'LIC

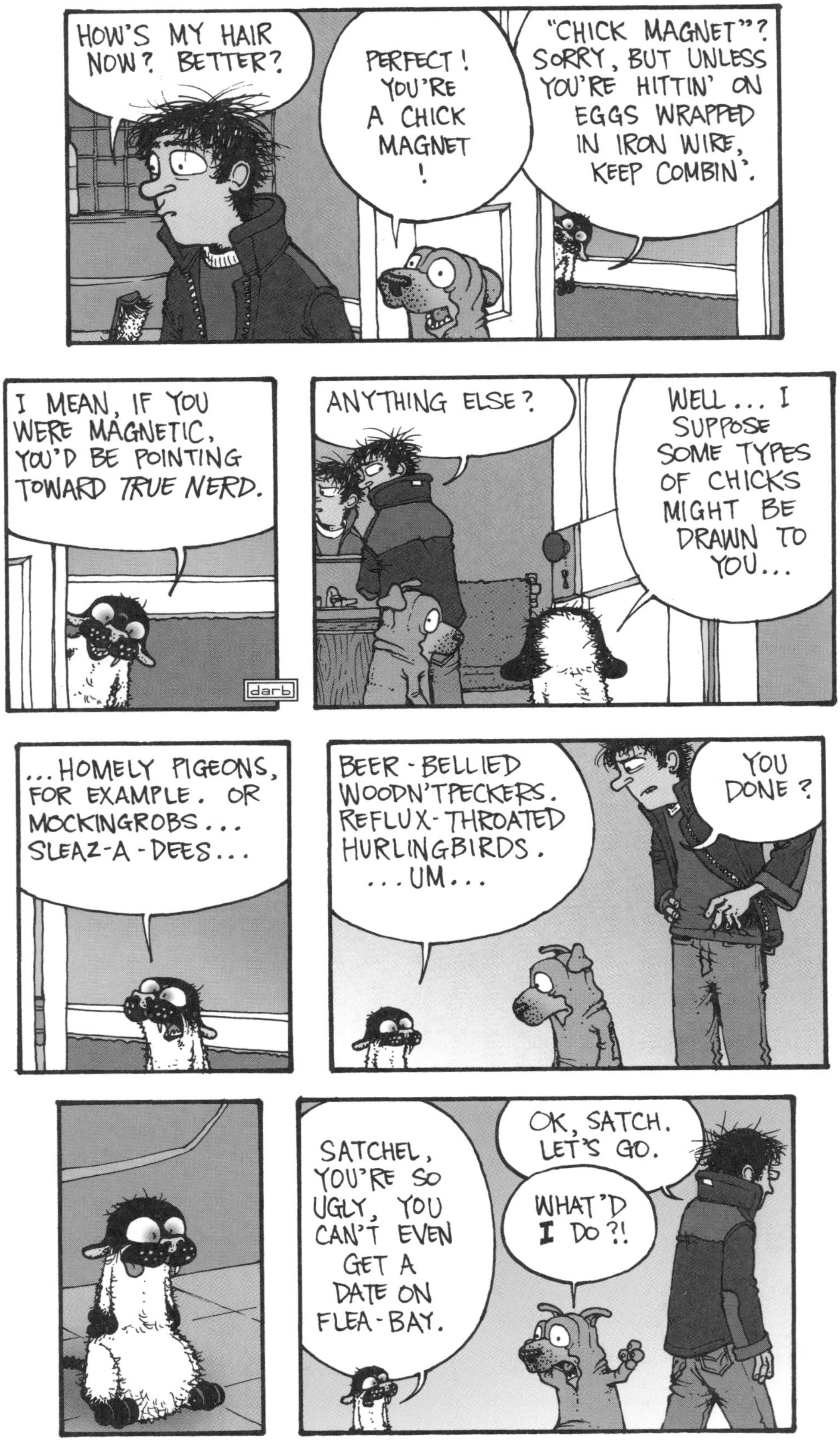
HOW'S MY HAIR NOW? BETTER?
PERFECT! YOU'RE A CHICK MAGNET!
"CHICK MAGNET"? SORRY, BUT UNLESS YOU'RE HITTIN' ON EGGS WRAPPED IN IRON WIRE, KEEP COMBIN'.
I MEAN, IF YOU WERE MAGNETIC, YOU'D BE POINTING TOWARD TRUE NERD.
darb
ANYTHING ELSE?
WELL... I SUPPOSE SOME TYPES OF CHICKS MIGHT BE DRAWN TO YOU...
...HOMELY PIGEONS, FOR EXAMPLE. OR MOCKINGROBS... SLEAZ-A-DEES...
BEER-BELLIED WOODN'TPECKERS. REFLUX-THROATED HURLINGBIRDS. ...UM...
YOU DONE?
SATCHEL, YOU'RE SO UGLY, YOU CAN'T EVEN GET A DATE ON FLEA-BAY.
OK, SATCH. LET'S GO.
WHAT'D I DO?!

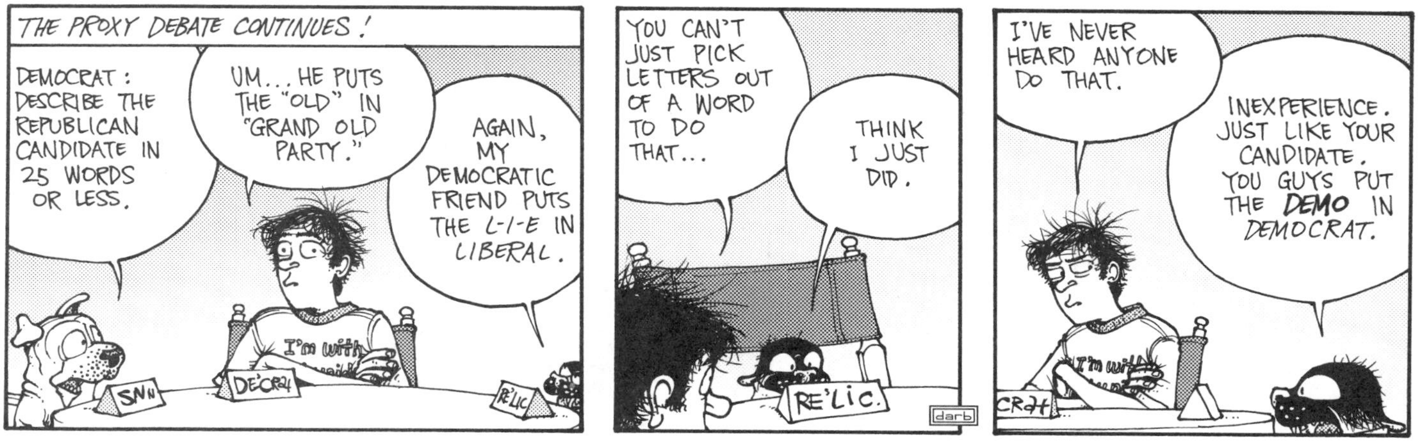
THE PROXY DEBATE CONTINUES!
DEMOCRAT: DESCRIBE THE REPUBLICAN CANDIDATE IN 25 WORDS OR LESS.
UM... HE PUTS THE "OLD" IN "GRAND OLD PARTY."
AGAIN, MY DEMOCRATIC FRIEND PUTS THE L-I-E IN LIBERAL.
YOU CAN'T JUST PICK LETTERS OUT OF A WORD TO DO THAT...
THINK I JUST DID.
RE'LIC.
I'VE NEVER HEARD ANYONE DO THAT.
INEXPERIENCE. JUST LIKE YOUR CANDIDATE. YOU GUYS PUT THE DEMO IN DEMOCRAT.

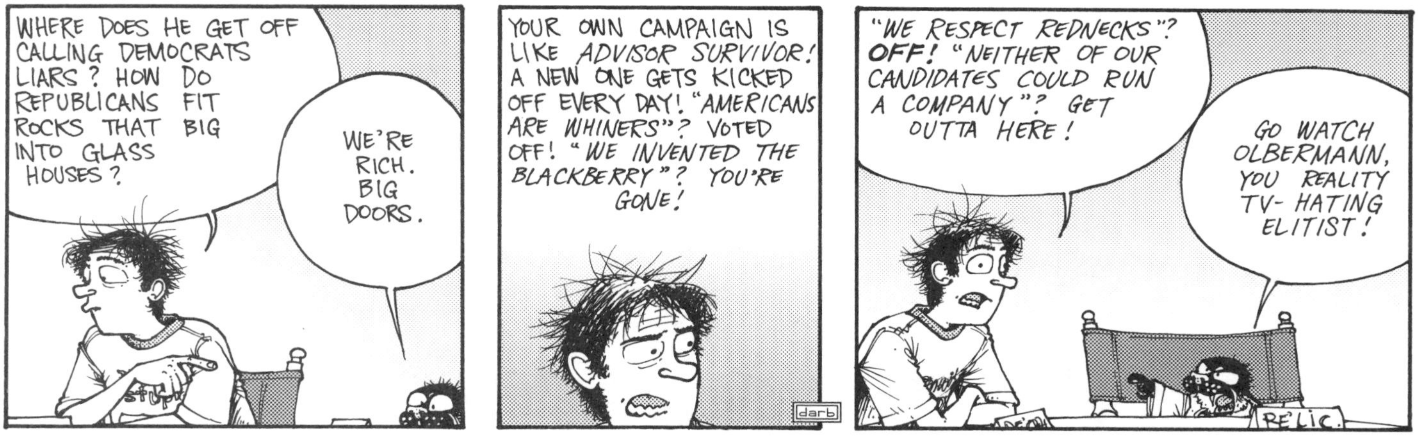
WHERE DOES HE GET OFF CALLING DEMOCRATS LIARS? HOW DO REPUBLICANS FIT ROCKS THAT BIG INTO GLASS HOUSES?
WE'RE RICH. BIG DOORS.
YOUR OWN CAMPAIGN IS LIKE ADVISOR SURVIVOR! A NEW ONE GETS KICKED OFF EVERY DAY! "AMERICANS ARE WHINERS"? VOTED OFF! "WE INVENTED THE BLACKBERRY"? YOU'RE GONE!
"WE RESPECT REDNECKS"? OFF! "NEITHER OF OUR CANDIDATES COULD RUN A COMPANY"? GET OUTTA HERE!
GO WATCH OLBERMANN, YOU REALITY TV-HATING ELITIST!
RE'LIC.

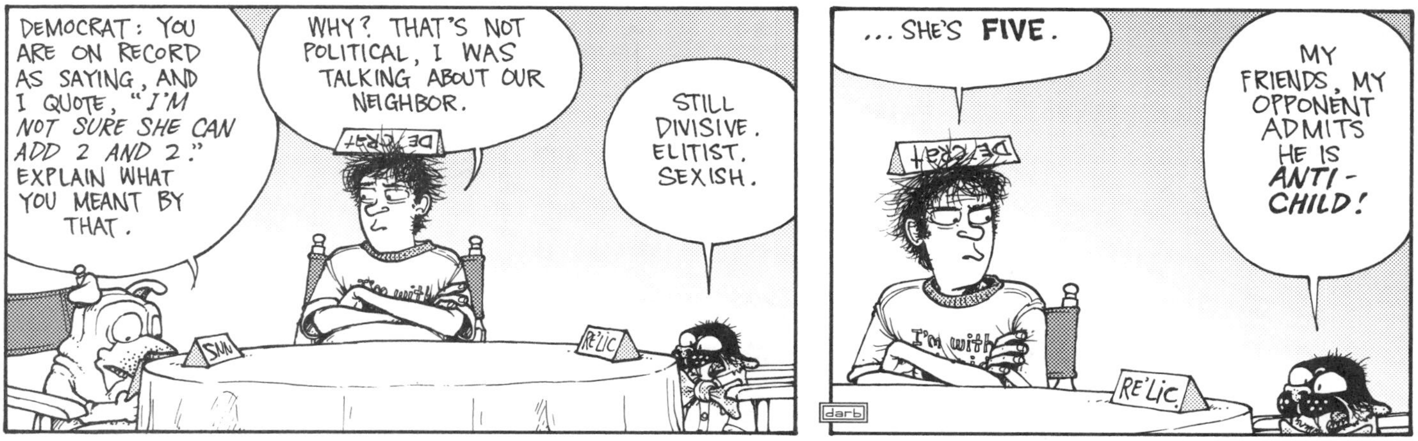
DEMOCRAT: YOU ARE ON RECORD AS SAYING, AND I QUOTE, "I'M NOT SURE SHE CAN ADD 2 AND 2." EXPLAIN WHAT YOU MEANT BY THAT.
WHY? THAT'S NOT POLITICAL, I WAS TALKING ABOUT OUR NEIGHBOR.
STILL DIVISIVE. ELITIST. SEXISH.
...SHE'S FIVE.
MY FRIENDS, MY OPPONENT ADMITS HE IS ANTI-CHILD!
RE'LIC.

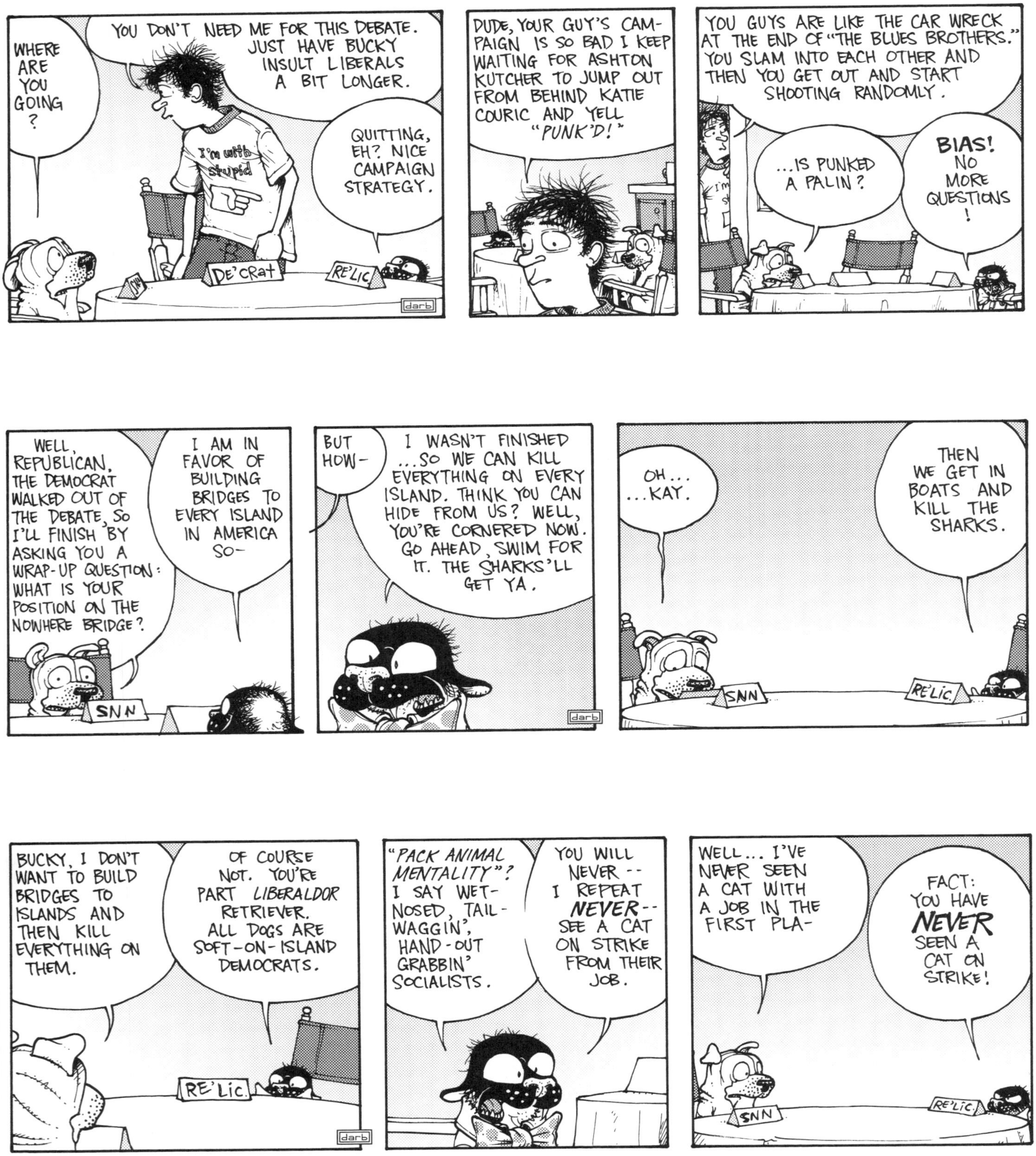
WHERE ARE YOU GOING?
YOU DON'T NEED ME FOR THIS DEBATE. JUST HAVE BUCKY INSULT LIBERALS A BIT LONGER.
I'm with stupid
QUITTING, EH? NICE CAMPAIGN STRATEGY.
DE'CRAT
RE'LIC
DUDE, YOUR GUY'S CAMPAIGN IS SO BAD I KEEP WAITING FOR ASHTON KUTCHER TO JUMP OUT FROM BEHIND KATIE COURIC AND YELL "PUNK'D!"
YOU GUYS ARE LIKE THE CAR WRECK AT THE END OF "THE BLUES BROTHERS." YOU SLAM INTO EACH OTHER AND THEN YOU GET OUT AND START SHOOTING RANDOMLY.
...IS PUNKED A PALIN?
BIAS! NO MORE QUESTIONS!
WELL, REPUBLICAN, THE DEMOCRAT WALKED OUT OF THE DEBATE, SO I'LL FINISH BY ASKING YOU A WRAP-UP QUESTION: WHAT IS YOUR POSITION ON THE NOWHERE BRIDGE?
I AM IN FAVOR OF BUILDING BRIDGES TO EVERY ISLAND IN AMERICA SO-
SNN
BUT HOW-
I WASN'T FINISHED ...SO WE CAN KILL EVERYTHING ON EVERY ISLAND. THINK YOU CAN HIDE FROM US? WELL, YOU'RE CORNERED NOW. GO AHEAD, SWIM FOR IT. THE SHARKS'LL GET YA.
OH... ...KAY.
THEN WE GET IN BOATS AND KILL THE SHARKS.
SNN
RE'LIC
BUCKY, I DON'T WANT TO BUILD BRIDGES TO ISLANDS AND THEN KILL EVERYTHING ON THEM.
OF COURSE NOT. YOU'RE PART LIBERALDOR RETRIEVER. ALL DOGS ARE SOFT-ON-ISLAND DEMOCRATS.
RE'LIC
"PACK ANIMAL MENTALITY"? I SAY WET-NOSED, TAIL-WAGGIN', HAND-OUT GRABBIN' SOCIALISTS.
YOU WILL NEVER -- I REPEAT NEVER -- SEE A CAT ON STRIKE FROM THEIR JOB.
WELL... I'VE NEVER SEEN A CAT WITH A JOB IN THE FIRST PLA-
FACT: YOU HAVE NEVER SEEN A CAT ON STRIKE!
SNN
RE'LIC

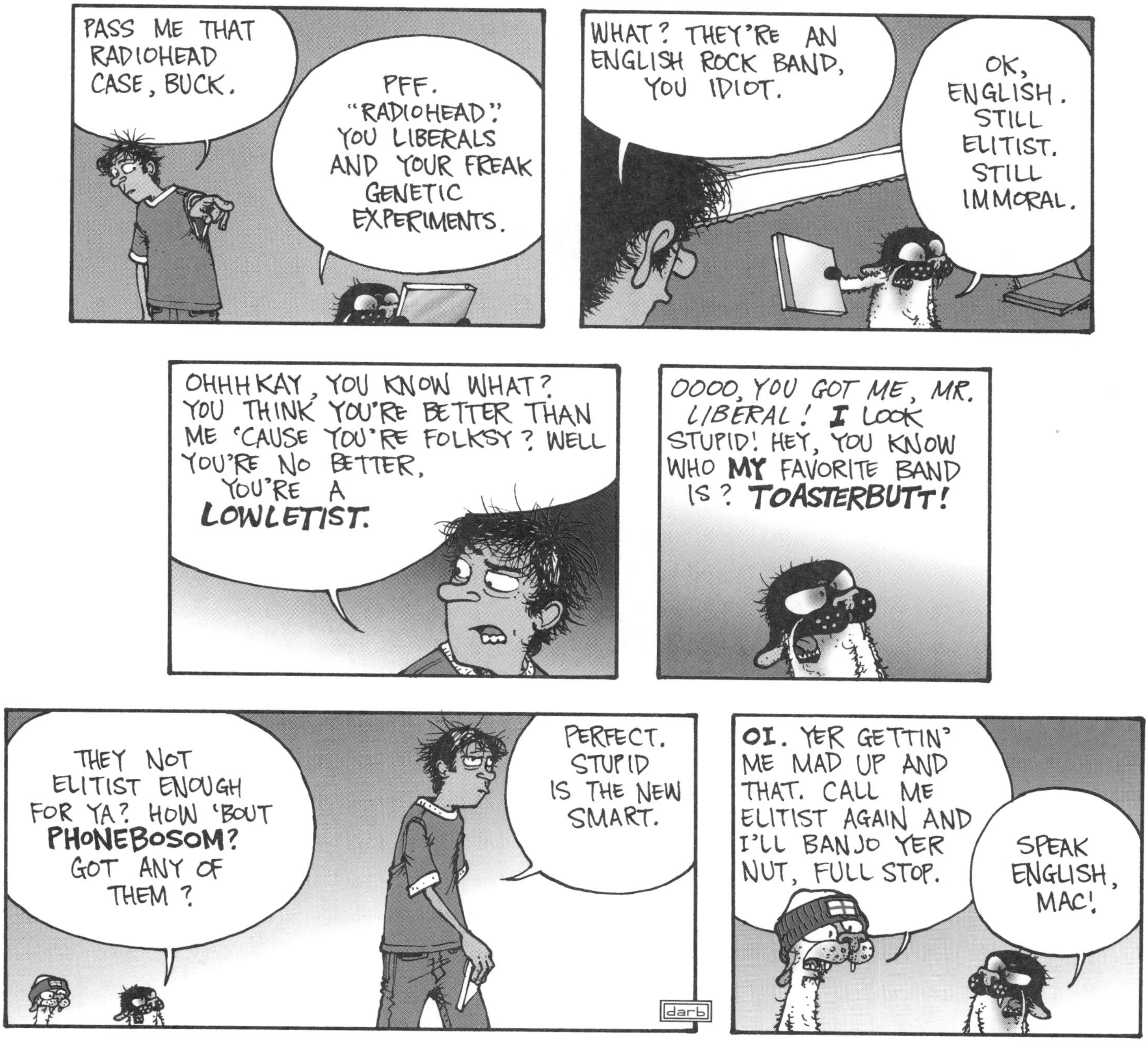
PASS ME THAT RADIOHEAD CASE, BUCK.
PFF. "RADIOHEAD." YOU LIBERALS AND YOUR FREAK GENETIC EXPERIMENTS.
WHAT? THEY'RE AN ENGLISH ROCK BAND, YOU IDIOT.
OK, ENGLISH. STILL ELITIST. STILL IMMORAL.
OHHHKAY, YOU KNOW WHAT? YOU THINK YOU'RE BETTER THAN ME 'CAUSE YOU'RE FOLKSY? WELL YOU'RE NO BETTER. YOU'RE A **LOWLETIST.**
OOOO, YOU GOT ME, MR. LIBERAL! **I** LOOK STUPID! HEY, YOU KNOW WHO **MY** FAVORITE BAND IS? **TOASTERBUTT!**
THEY NOT ELITIST ENOUGH FOR YA? HOW 'BOUT **PHONEBOSOM?** GOT ANY OF THEM?
PERFECT. STUPID IS THE NEW SMART.
darb
OI. YER GETTIN' ME MAD UP AND THAT. CALL ME ELITIST AGAIN AND I'LL BANJO YER NUT, FULL STOP.
SPEAK ENGLISH, MAC!

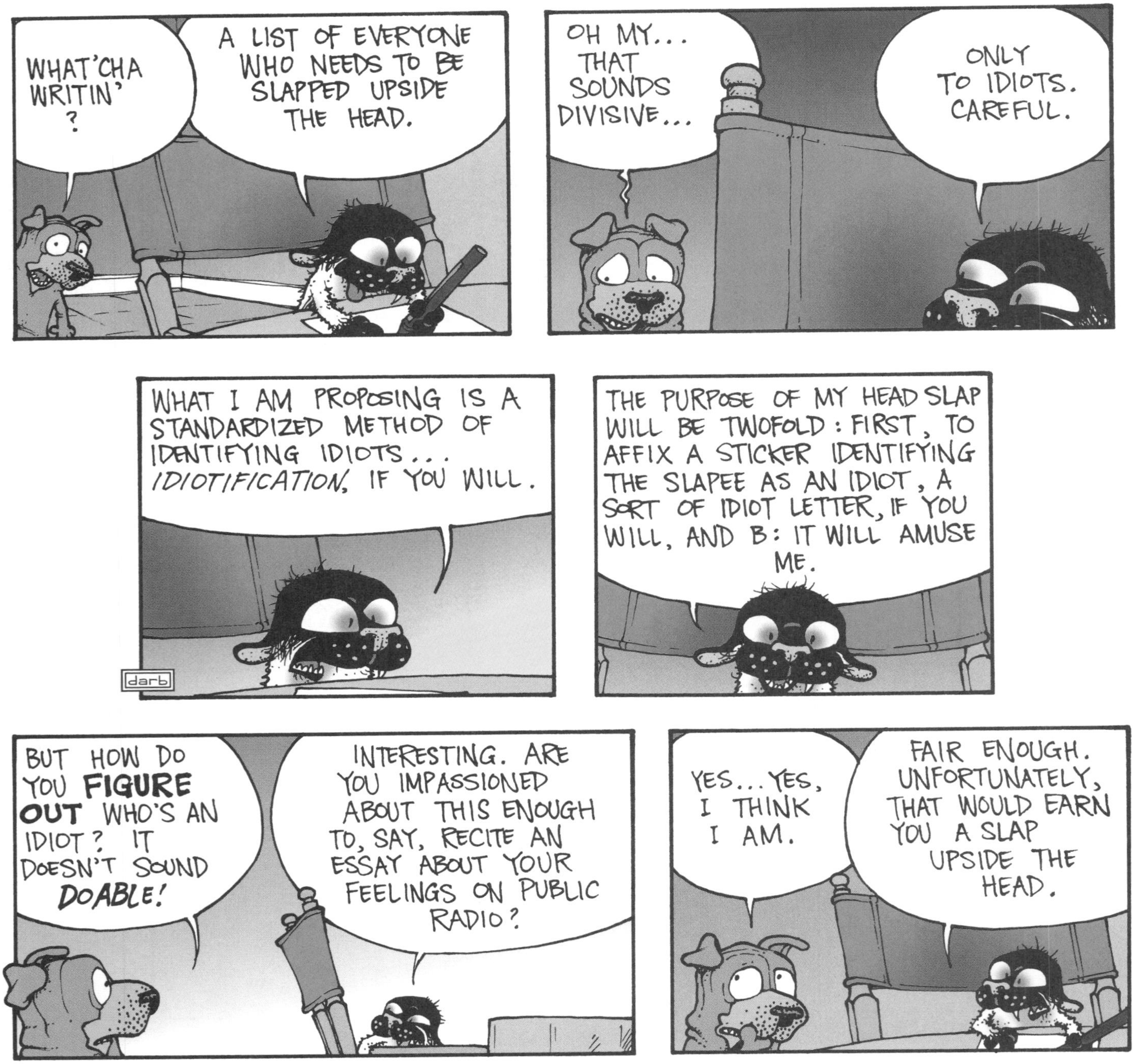
WHAT'CHA WRITIN' ?
A LIST OF EVERYONE WHO NEEDS TO BE SLAPPED UPSIDE THE HEAD.
OH MY... THAT SOUNDS DIVISIVE...
ONLY TO IDIOTS. CAREFUL.
WHAT I AM PROPOSING IS A STANDARDIZED METHOD OF IDENTIFYING IDIOTS... *IDIOTIFICATION*, IF YOU WILL.
darb
THE PURPOSE OF MY HEAD SLAP WILL BE TWOFOLD: FIRST, TO AFFIX A STICKER IDENTIFYING THE SLAPEE AS AN IDIOT, A SORT OF IDIOT LETTER, IF YOU WILL, AND B: IT WILL AMUSE ME.
BUT HOW DO YOU **FIGURE OUT** WHO'S AN IDIOT? IT DOESN'T SOUND ***DOABLE***!
INTERESTING. ARE YOU IMPASSIONED ABOUT THIS ENOUGH TO, SAY, RECITE AN ESSAY ABOUT YOUR FEELINGS ON PUBLIC RADIO?
YES... YES, I THINK I AM.
FAIR ENOUGH. UNFORTUNATELY, THAT WOULD EARN YOU A SLAP UPSIDE THE HEAD.

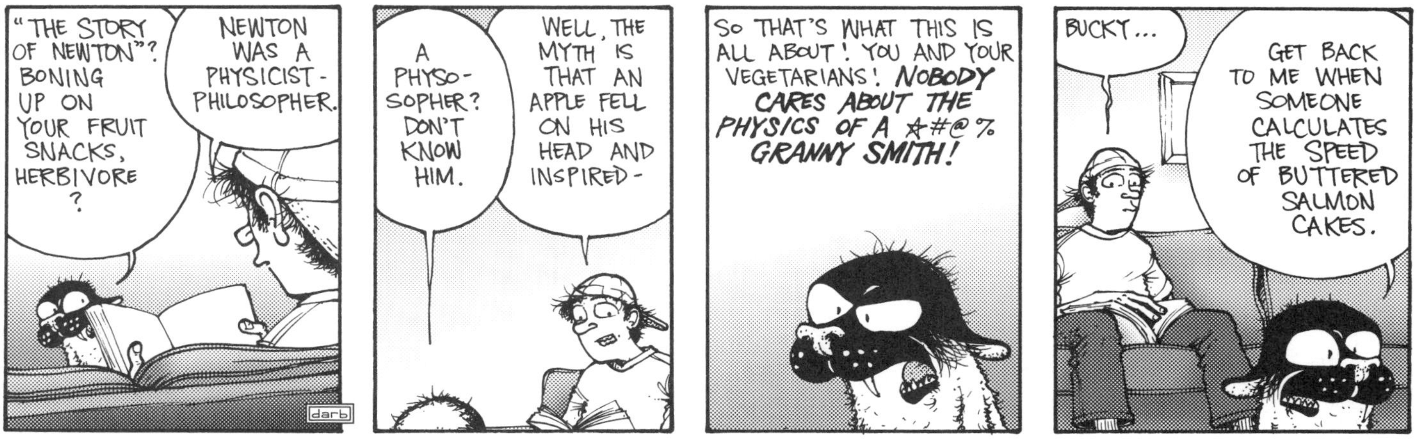
"THE STORY OF NEWTON"? BONING UP ON YOUR FRUIT SNACKS, HERBIVORE ?
NEWTON WAS A PHYSICIST-PHILOSOPHER.
darb
A PHYSO-SOPHER? DON'T KNOW HIM.
WELL, THE MYTH IS THAT AN APPLE FELL ON HIS HEAD AND INSPIRED-
SO THAT'S WHAT THIS IS ALL ABOUT! YOU AND YOUR VEGETARIANS! **NOBODY CARES ABOUT THE PHYSICS OF A ☆#@% GRANNY SMITH!**
BUCKY...
GET BACK TO ME WHEN SOMEONE CALCULATES THE SPEED OF BUTTERED SALMON CAKES.

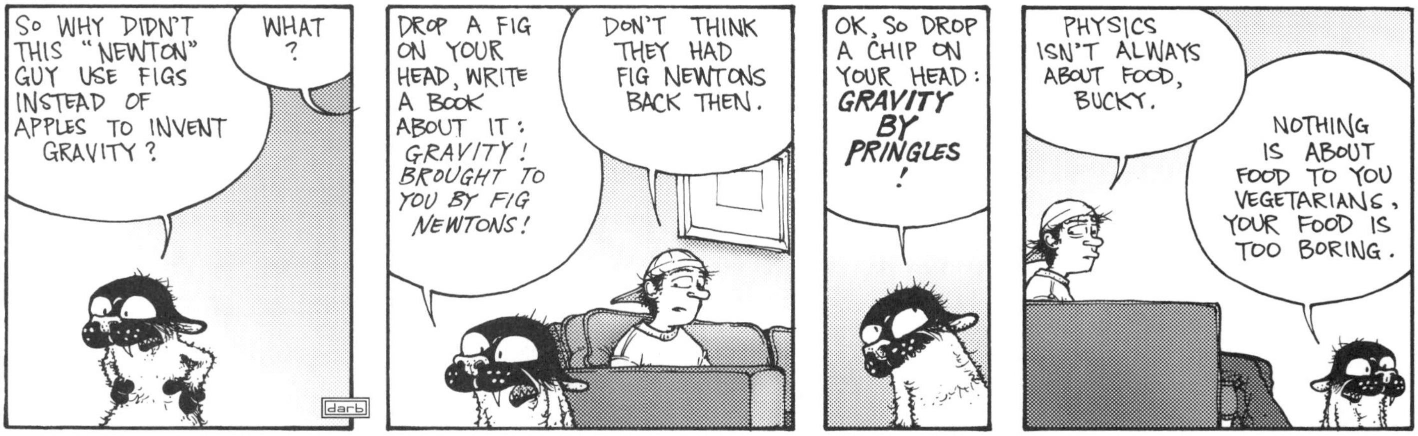
SO WHY DIDN'T THIS "NEWTON" GUY USE FIGS INSTEAD OF APPLES TO INVENT GRAVITY ?
WHAT ?
darb
DROP A FIG ON YOUR HEAD, WRITE A BOOK ABOUT IT: *GRAVITY! BROUGHT TO YOU BY FIG NEWTONS!*
DON'T THINK THEY HAD FIG NEWTONS BACK THEN.
OK, SO DROP A CHIP ON YOUR HEAD: **GRAVITY BY PRINGLES !**
PHYSICS ISN'T ALWAYS ABOUT FOOD, BUCKY.
NOTHING IS ABOUT FOOD TO YOU VEGETARIANS, YOUR FOOD IS TOO BORING.

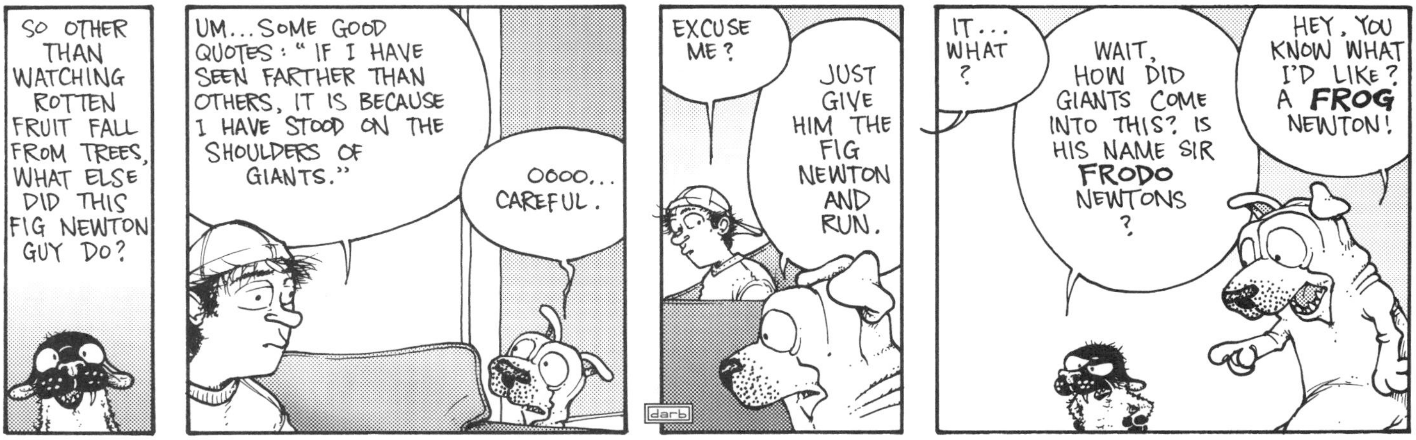
SO OTHER THAN WATCHING ROTTEN FRUIT FALL FROM TREES, WHAT ELSE DID THIS FIG NEWTON GUY DO?
UM...SOME GOOD QUOTES: "IF I HAVE SEEN FARTHER THAN OTHERS, IT IS BECAUSE I HAVE STOOD ON THE SHOULDERS OF GIANTS."
OOOO... CAREFUL.
darb
EXCUSE ME?
JUST GIVE HIM THE FIG NEWTON AND RUN.
IT... WHAT ?
WAIT, HOW DID GIANTS COME INTO THIS? IS HIS NAME SIR **FRODO** NEWTONS ?
HEY, YOU KNOW WHAT I'D LIKE? A **FROG** NEWTON!

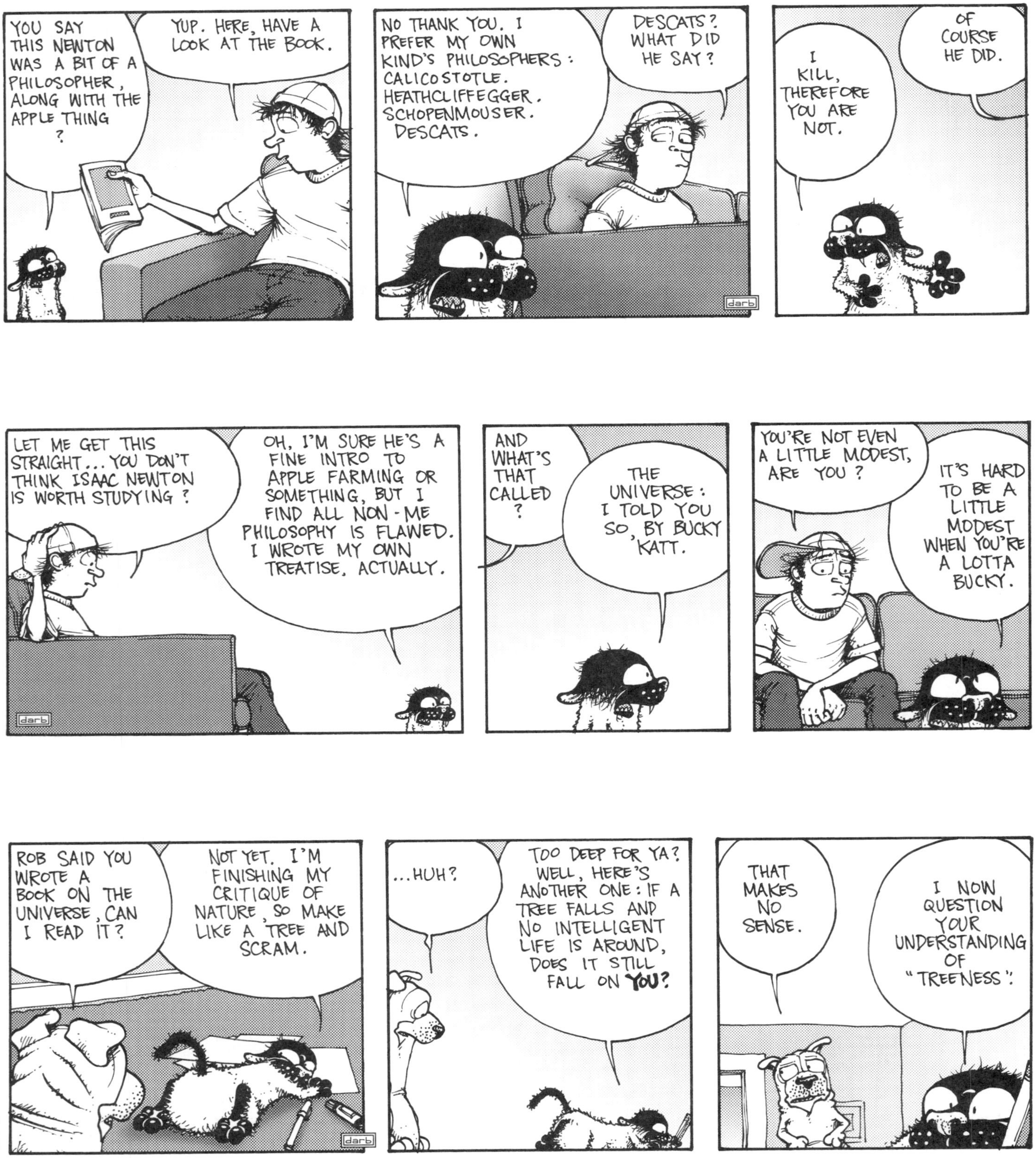
YOU SAY THIS NEWTON WAS A BIT OF A PHILOSOPHER, ALONG WITH THE APPLE THING?
YUP. HERE, HAVE A LOOK AT THE BOOK.
NO THANK YOU. I PREFER MY OWN KIND'S PHILOSOPHERS: CALICOSTOTLE. HEATHCLIFFEGGER. SCHOPENMOUSER. DESCATS.
DESCATS? WHAT DID HE SAY?
I KILL, THEREFORE YOU ARE NOT.
OF COURSE HE DID.
darb
LET ME GET THIS STRAIGHT... YOU DON'T THINK ISAAC NEWTON IS WORTH STUDYING?
OH, I'M SURE HE'S A FINE INTRO TO APPLE FARMING OR SOMETHING, BUT I FIND ALL NON-ME PHILOSOPHY IS FLAWED. I WROTE MY OWN TREATISE, ACTUALLY.
AND WHAT'S THAT CALLED?
THE UNIVERSE: I TOLD YOU SO, BY BUCKY KATT.
YOU'RE NOT EVEN A LITTLE MODEST, ARE YOU?
IT'S HARD TO BE A LITTLE MODEST WHEN YOU'RE A LOTTA BUCKY.
darb
ROB SAID YOU WROTE A BOOK ON THE UNIVERSE, CAN I READ IT?
NOT YET. I'M FINISHING MY CRITIQUE OF NATURE, SO MAKE LIKE A TREE AND SCRAM.
...HUH?
TOO DEEP FOR YA? WELL, HERE'S ANOTHER ONE: IF A TREE FALLS AND NO INTELLIGENT LIFE IS AROUND, DOES IT STILL FALL ON YOU?
THAT MAKES NO SENSE.
I NOW QUESTION YOUR UNDERSTANDING OF "TREENESS".
darb

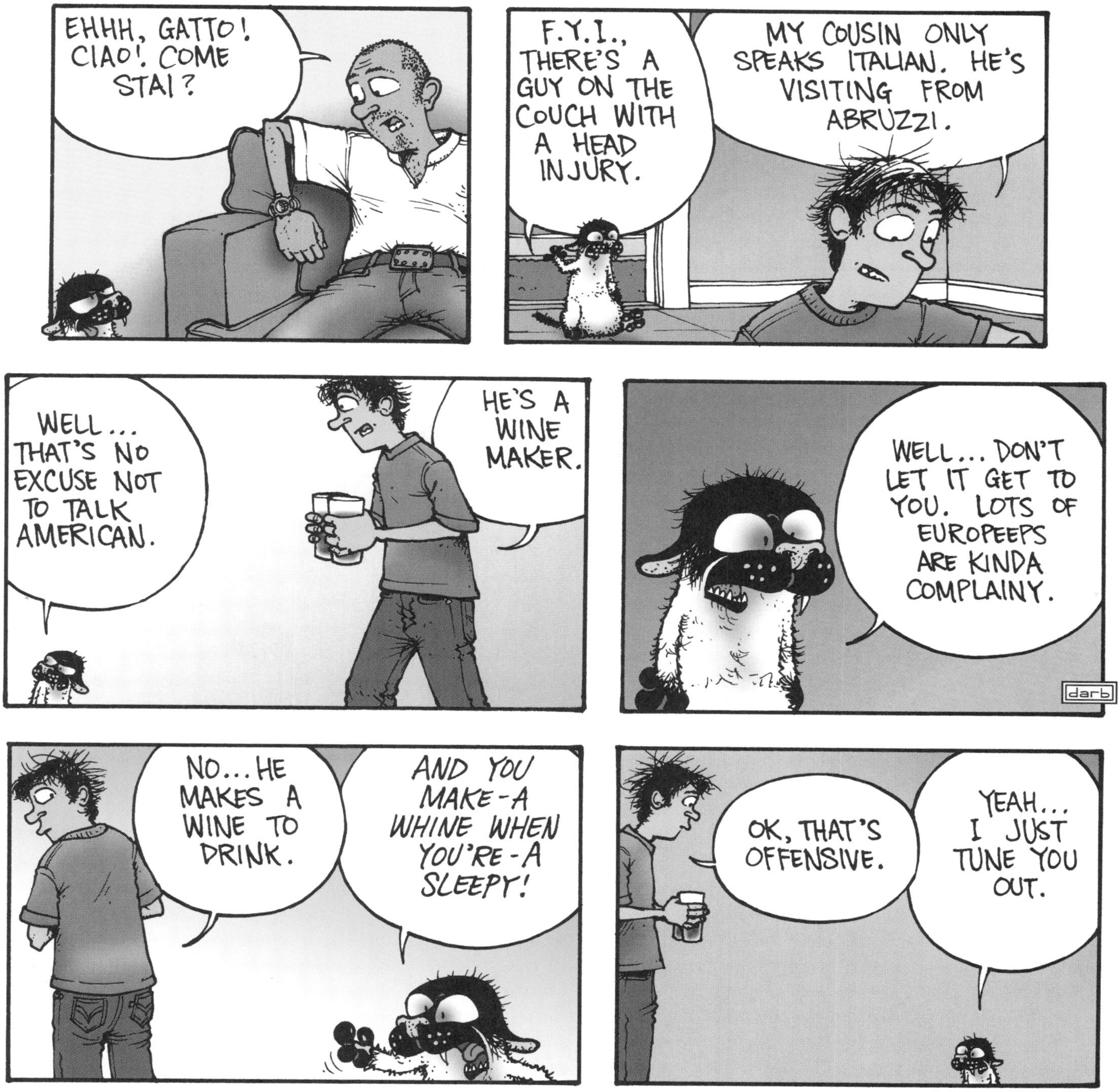
EHHH, GATTO! CIAO! COME STAI?
F.Y.I., THERE'S A GUY ON THE COUCH WITH A HEAD INJURY.
MY COUSIN ONLY SPEAKS ITALIAN. HE'S VISITING FROM ABRUZZI.
WELL... THAT'S NO EXCUSE NOT TO TALK AMERICAN.
HE'S A WINE MAKER.
WELL... DON'T LET IT GET TO YOU. LOTS OF EUROPEEPS ARE KINDA COMPLAINY.
darb
NO... HE MAKES A WINE TO DRINK.
AND YOU MAKE-A WHINE WHEN YOU'RE-A SLEEPY!
OK, THAT'S OFFENSIVE.
YEAH... I JUST TUNE YOU OUT.

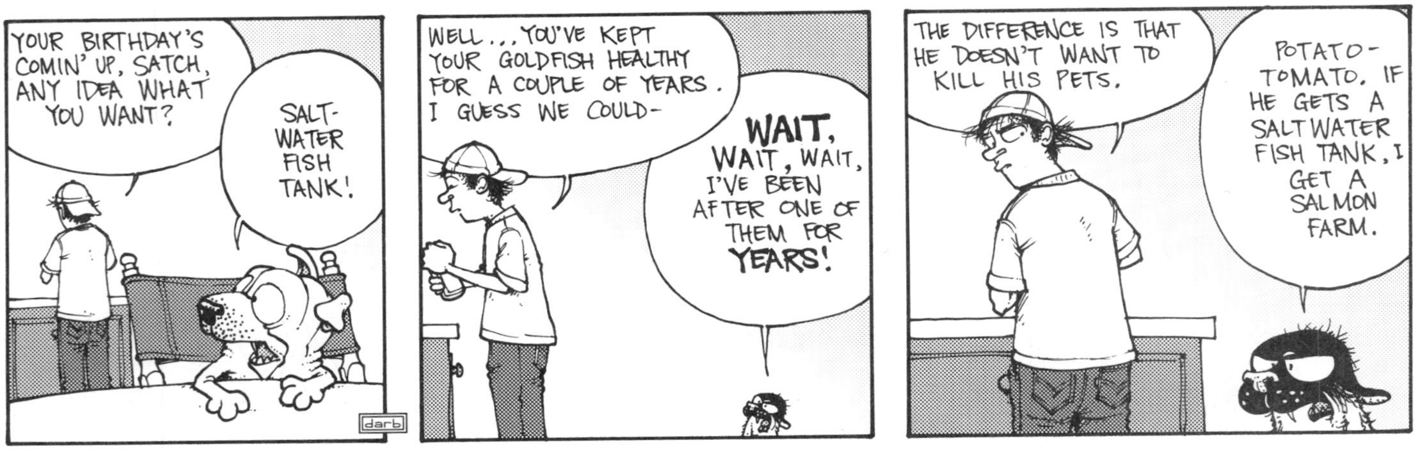
YOUR BIRTHDAY'S COMIN' UP, SATCH, ANY IDEA WHAT YOU WANT?
SALT-WATER FISH TANK!
WELL... YOU'VE KEPT YOUR GOLDFISH HEALTHY FOR A COUPLE OF YEARS. I GUESS WE COULD-
WAIT, WAIT, WAIT, I'VE BEEN AFTER ONE OF THEM FOR YEARS!
THE DIFFERENCE IS THAT HE DOESN'T WANT TO KILL HIS PETS.
POTATO-TOMATO. IF HE GETS A SALTWATER FISH TANK, I GET A SALMON FARM.
darb

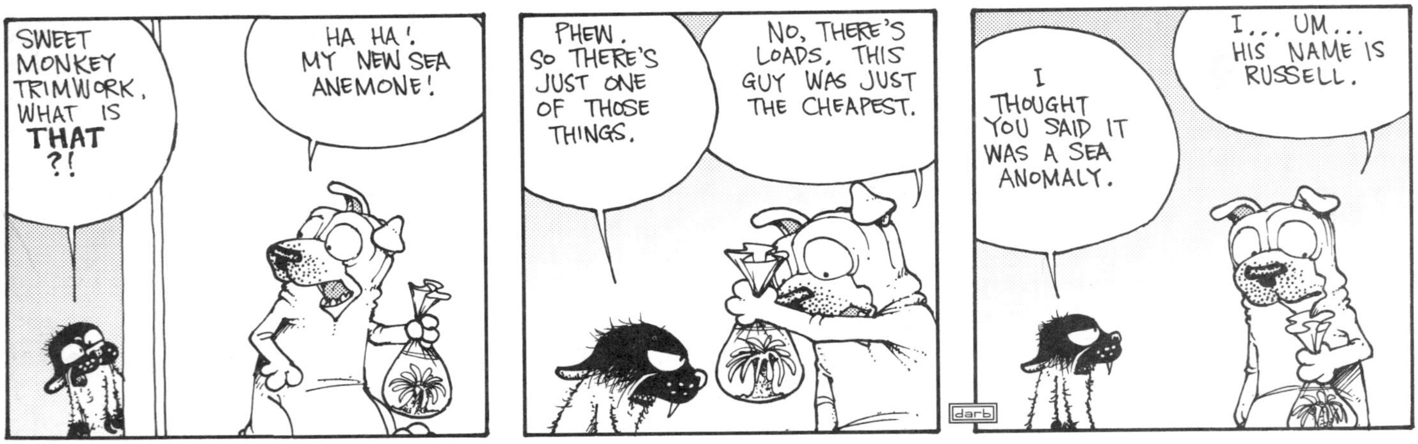
SWEET MONKEY TRIMWORK, WHAT IS THAT ?!
HA HA! MY NEW SEA ANEMONE!
PHEW. SO THERE'S JUST ONE OF THOSE THINGS.
NO, THERE'S LOADS. THIS GUY WAS JUST THE CHEAPEST.
I THOUGHT YOU SAID IT WAS A SEA ANOMALY.
I... UM... HIS NAME IS RUSSELL.
darb

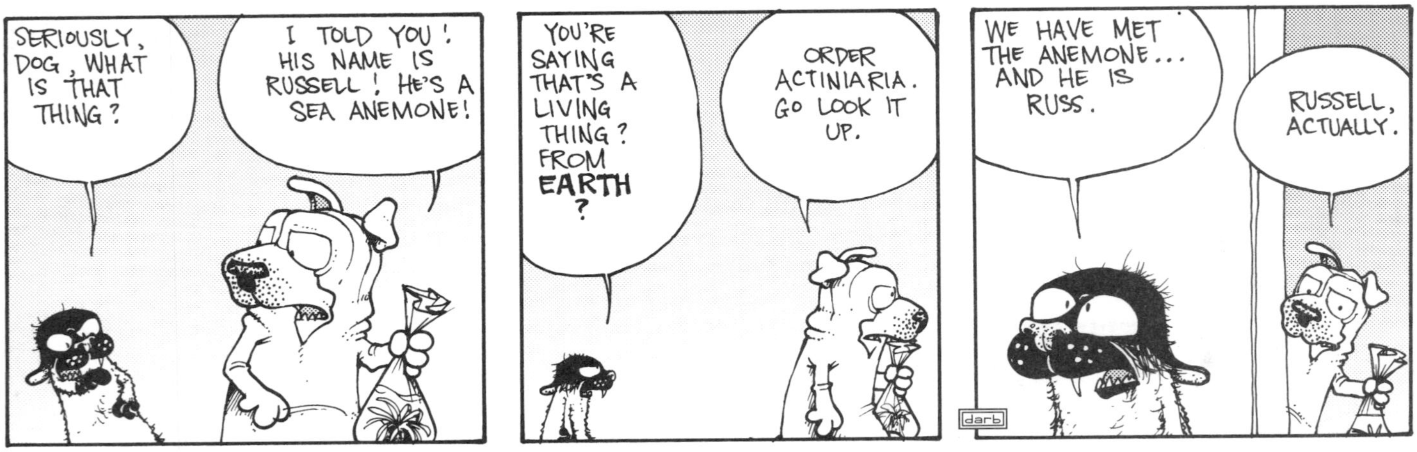
SERIOUSLY, DOG, WHAT IS THAT THING?
I TOLD YOU! HIS NAME IS RUSSELL! HE'S A SEA ANEMONE!
YOU'RE SAYING THAT'S A LIVING THING? FROM EARTH ?
ORDER ACTINIARIA. GO LOOK IT UP.
WE HAVE MET THE ANEMONE... AND HE IS RUSS.
RUSSELL, ACTUALLY.
darb

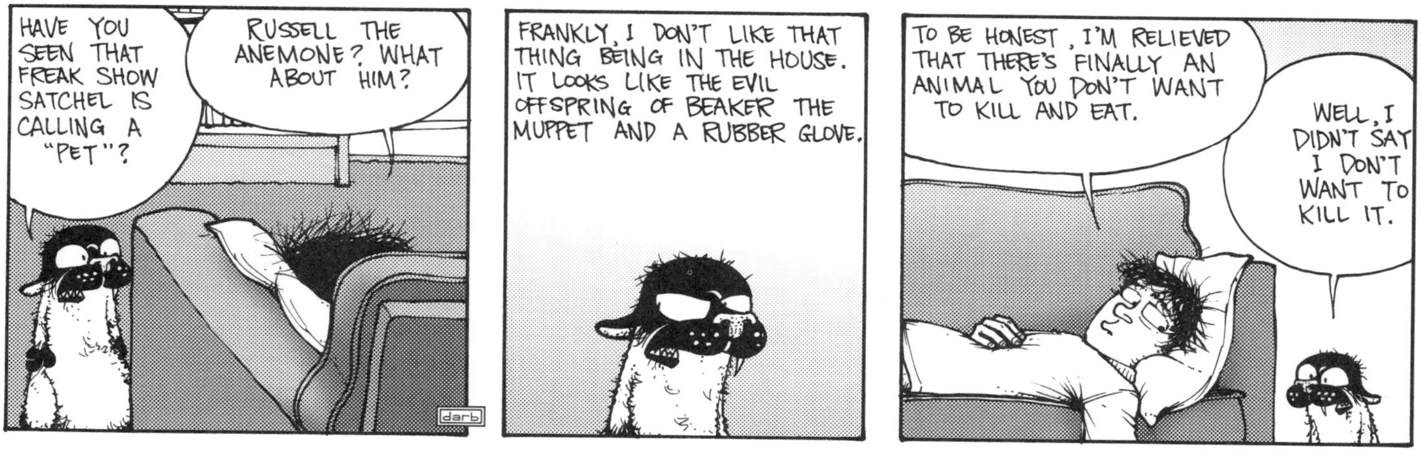
HAVE YOU SEEN THAT FREAK SHOW SATCHEL IS CALLING A "PET"?
RUSSELL THE ANEMONE? WHAT ABOUT HIM?
FRANKLY, I DON'T LIKE THAT THING BEING IN THE HOUSE. IT LOOKS LIKE THE EVIL OFFSPRING OF BEAKER THE MUPPET AND A RUBBER GLOVE.
TO BE HONEST, I'M RELIEVED THAT THERE'S FINALLY AN ANIMAL YOU DON'T WANT TO KILL AND EAT.
WELL, I DIDN'T SAY I DON'T WANT TO KILL IT.
darb

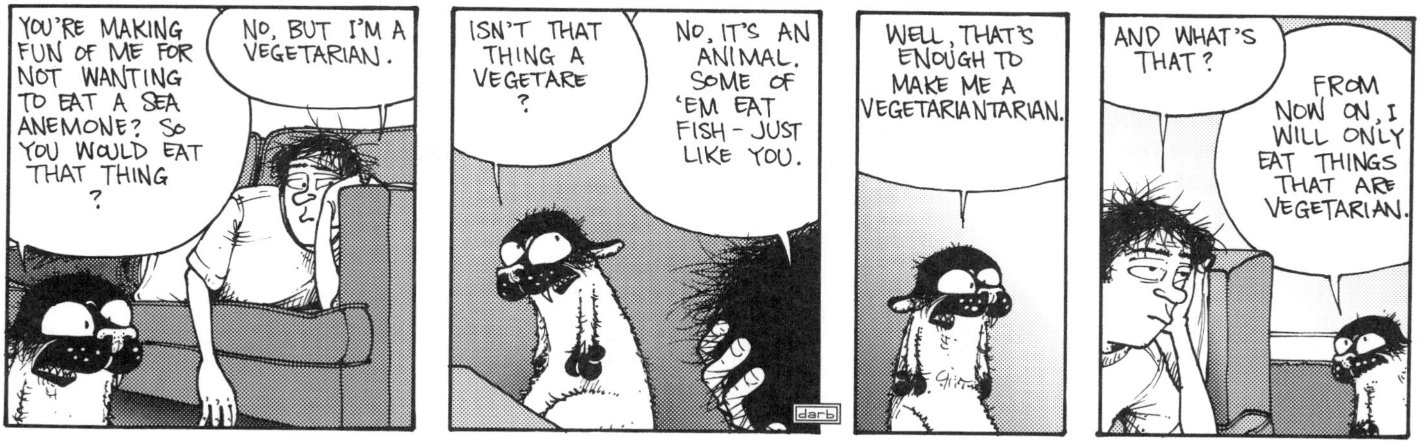
YOU'RE MAKING FUN OF ME FOR NOT WANTING TO EAT A SEA ANEMONE? SO YOU WOULD EAT THAT THING?
NO, BUT I'M A VEGETARIAN.
ISN'T THAT THING A VEGETARE?
NO, IT'S AN ANIMAL. SOME OF 'EM EAT FISH - JUST LIKE YOU.
darb
WELL, THAT'S ENOUGH TO MAKE ME A VEGETARIANTARIAN.
AND WHAT'S THAT?
FROM NOW ON, I WILL ONLY EAT THINGS THAT ARE VEGETARIAN.

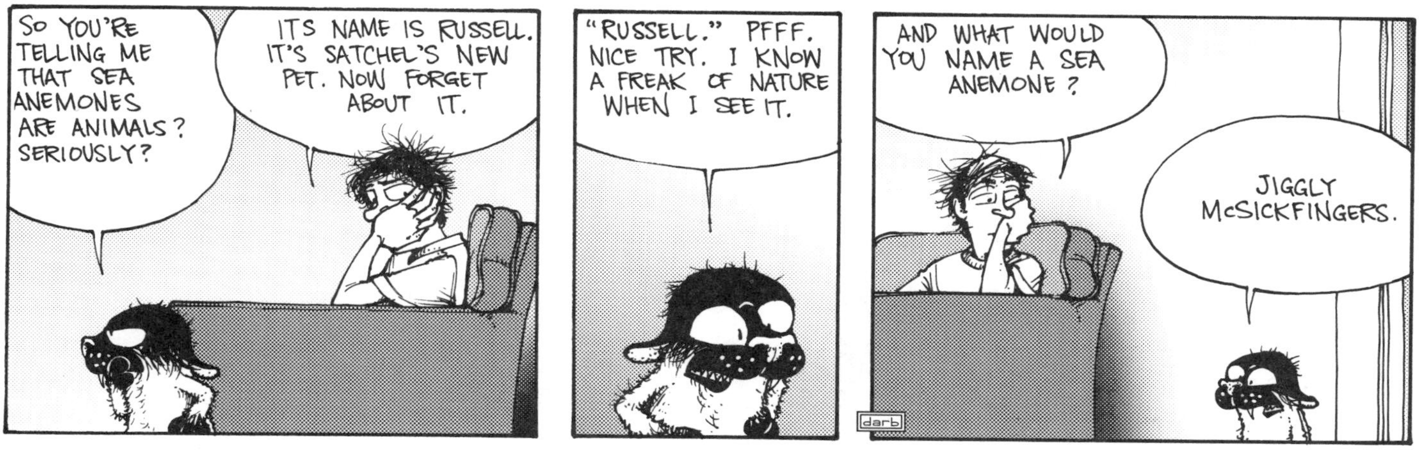
SO YOU'RE TELLING ME THAT SEA ANEMONES ARE ANIMALS? SERIOUSLY?
ITS NAME IS RUSSELL. IT'S SATCHEL'S NEW PET. NOW FORGET ABOUT IT.
"RUSSELL." PFFF. NICE TRY. I KNOW A FREAK OF NATURE WHEN I SEE IT.
darb
AND WHAT WOULD YOU NAME A SEA ANEMONE?
JIGGLY McSICKFINGERS.

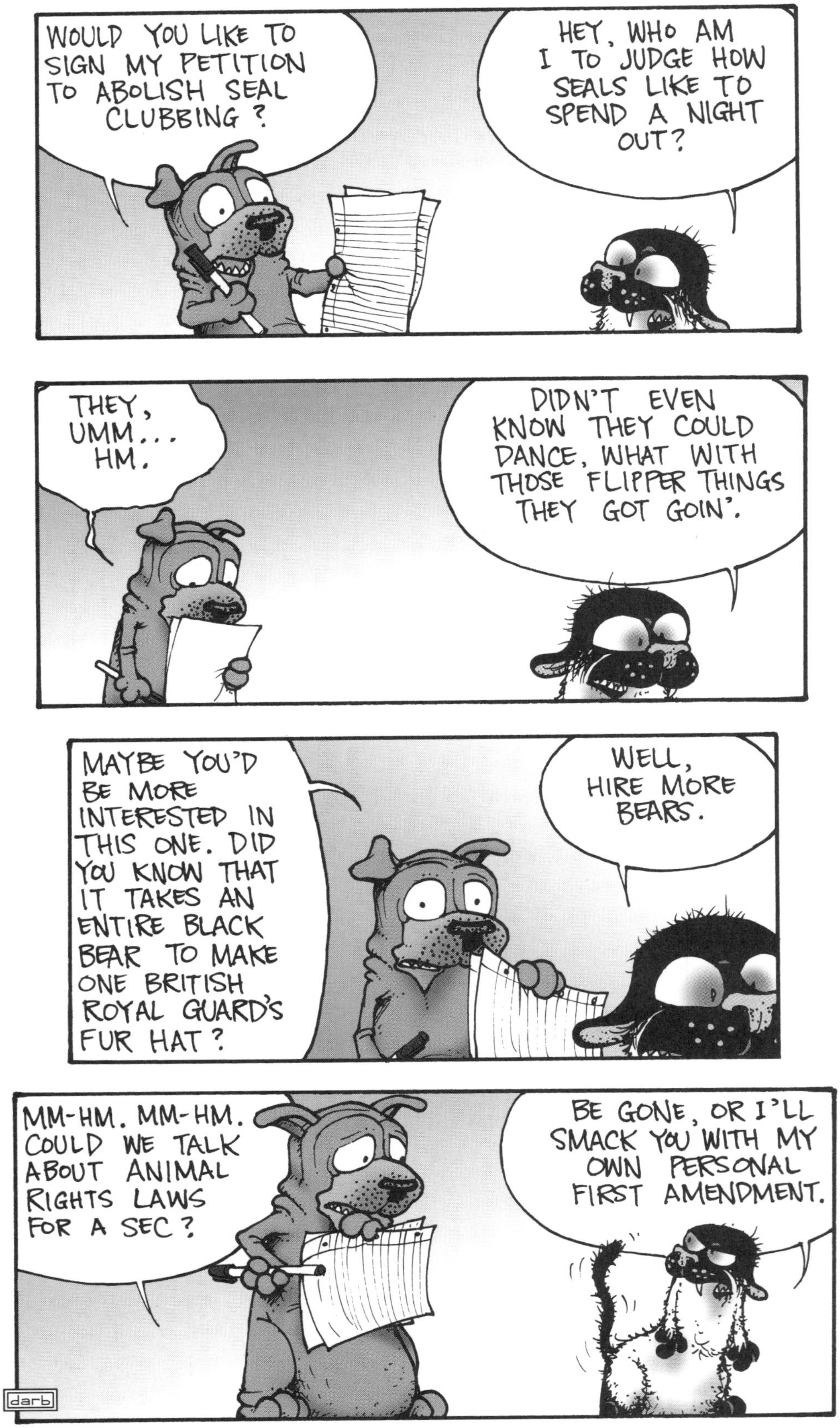
WOULD YOU LIKE TO SIGN MY PETITION TO ABOLISH SEAL CLUBBING?
HEY, WHO AM I TO JUDGE HOW SEALS LIKE TO SPEND A NIGHT OUT?
THEY, UMM... HM.
DIDN'T EVEN KNOW THEY COULD DANCE, WHAT WITH THOSE FLIPPER THINGS THEY GOT GOIN'.
MAYBE YOU'D BE MORE INTERESTED IN THIS ONE. DID YOU KNOW THAT IT TAKES AN ENTIRE BLACK BEAR TO MAKE ONE BRITISH ROYAL GUARD'S FUR HAT?
WELL, HIRE MORE BEARS.
MM-HM. MM-HM. COULD WE TALK ABOUT ANIMAL RIGHTS LAWS FOR A SEC?
BE GONE, OR I'LL SMACK YOU WITH MY OWN PERSONAL FIRST AMENDMENT.
darb

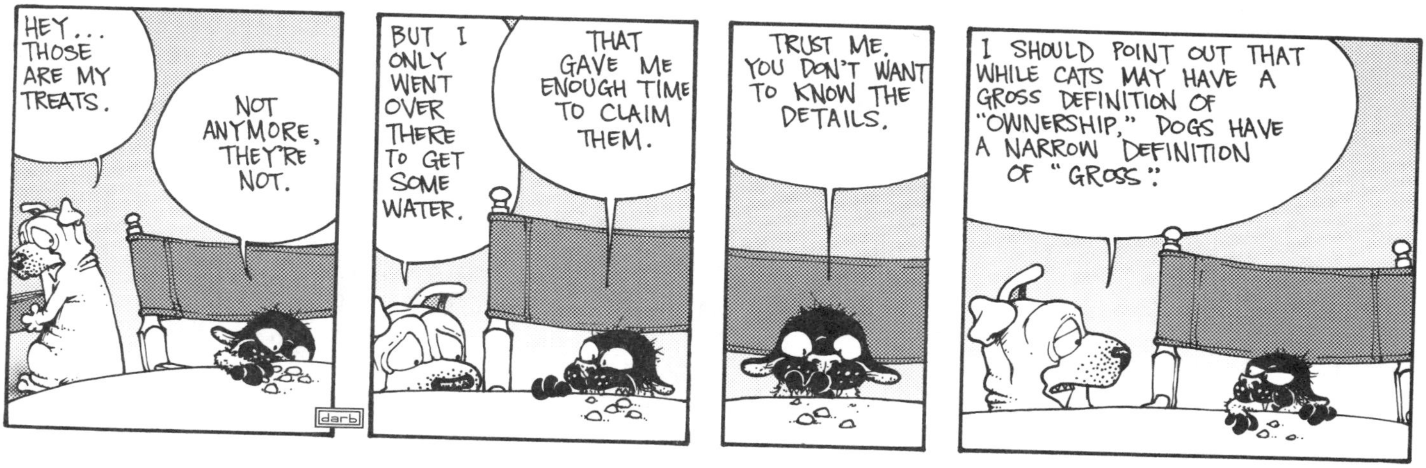
HEY... THOSE ARE MY TREATS.
NOT ANYMORE, THEY'RE NOT.
BUT I ONLY WENT OVER THERE TO GET SOME WATER.
THAT GAVE ME ENOUGH TIME TO CLAIM THEM.
TRUST ME. YOU DON'T WANT TO KNOW THE DETAILS.
I SHOULD POINT OUT THAT WHILE CATS MAY HAVE A GROSS DEFINITION OF "OWNERSHIP," DOGS HAVE A NARROW DEFINITION OF "GROSS."
darb

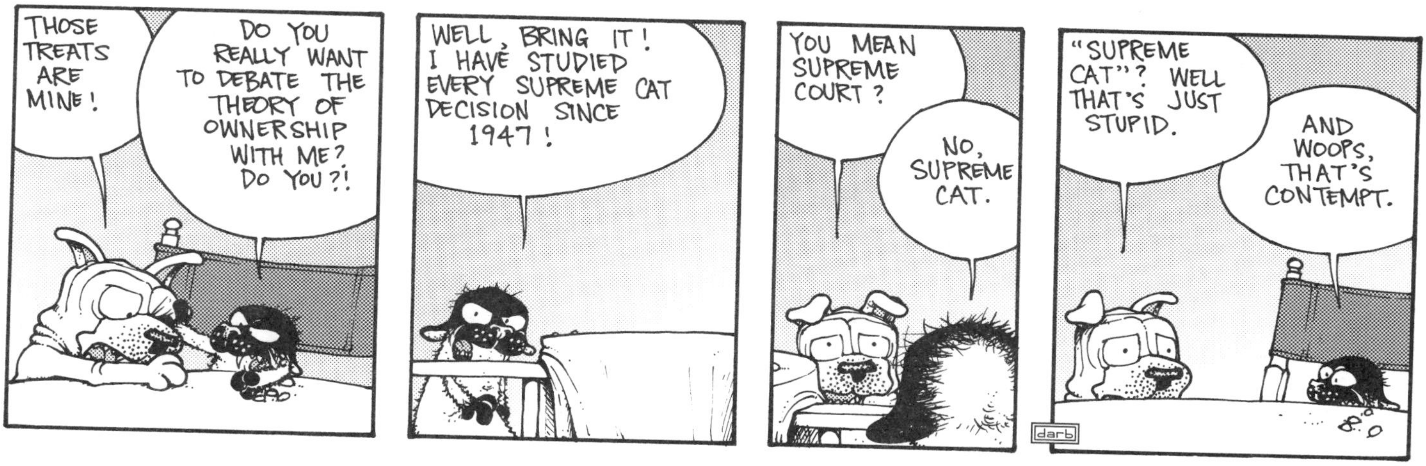
THOSE TREATS ARE MINE!
DO YOU REALLY WANT TO DEBATE THE THEORY OF OWNERSHIP WITH ME? DO YOU?!
WELL, BRING IT! I HAVE STUDIED EVERY SUPREME CAT DECISION SINCE 1947!
YOU MEAN SUPREME COURT?
NO, SUPREME CAT.
"SUPREME CAT"? WELL THAT'S JUST STUPID.
AND WOOPS, THAT'S CONTEMPT.
darb

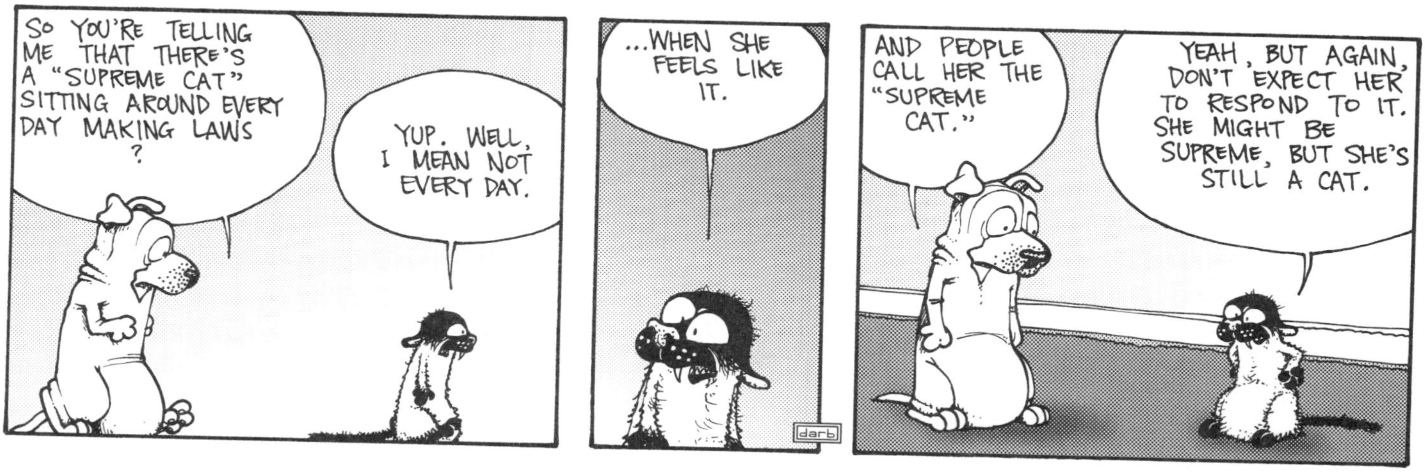
SO YOU'RE TELLING ME THAT THERE'S A "SUPREME CAT" SITTING AROUND EVERY DAY MAKING LAWS?
YUP. WELL, I MEAN NOT EVERY DAY.
...WHEN SHE FEELS LIKE IT.
darb
AND PEOPLE CALL HER THE "SUPREME CAT."
YEAH, BUT AGAIN, DON'T EXPECT HER TO RESPOND TO IT. SHE MIGHT BE SUPREME, BUT SHE'S STILL A CAT.

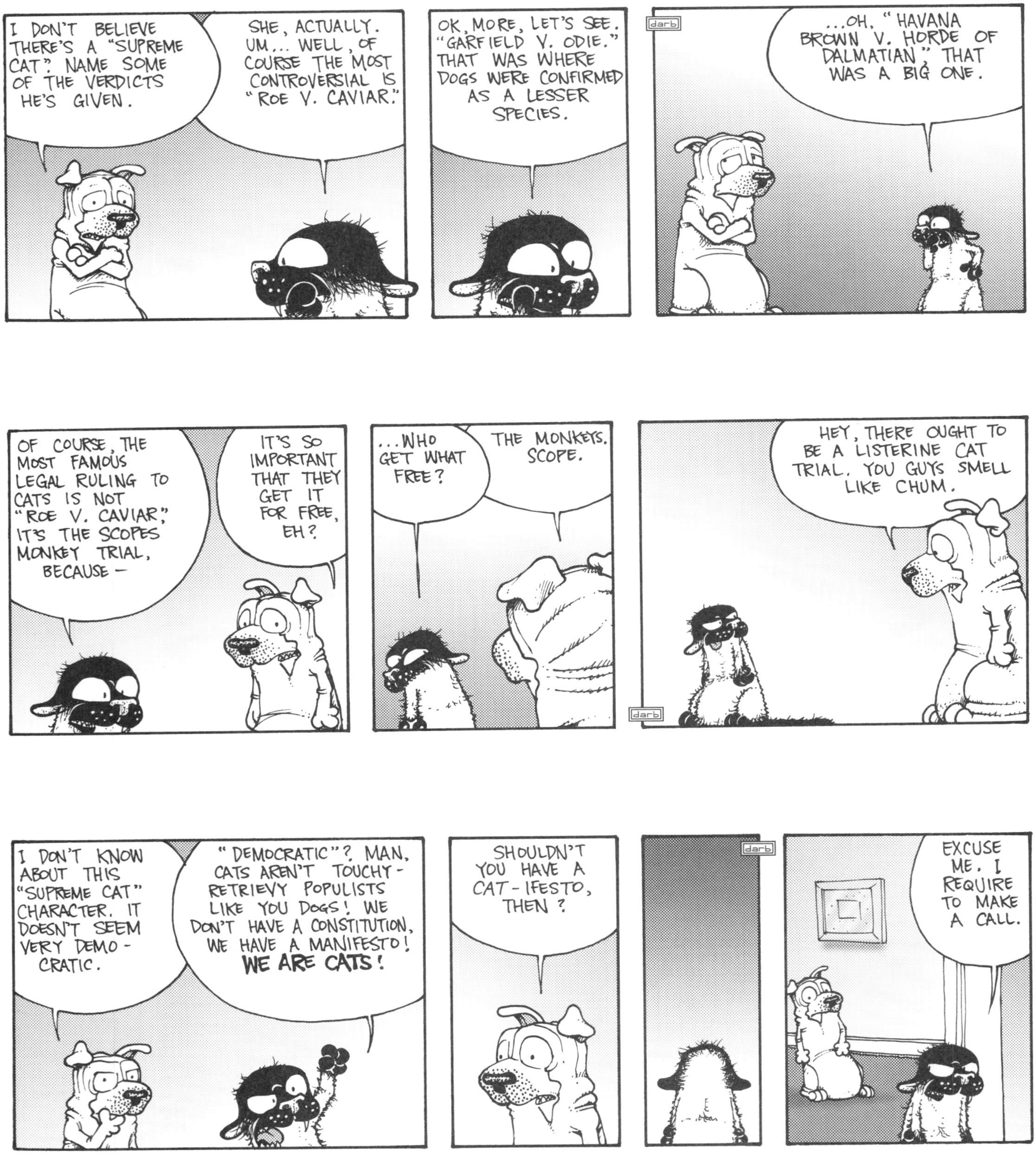
I DON'T BELIEVE THERE'S A "SUPREME CAT." NAME SOME OF THE VERDICTS HE'S GIVEN.
SHE, ACTUALLY. UM... WELL, OF COURSE THE MOST CONTROVERSIAL IS "ROE V. CAVIAR."
OK, MORE, LET'S SEE. "GARFIELD V. ODIE." THAT WAS WHERE DOGS WERE CONFIRMED AS A LESSER SPECIES.
...OH, "HAVANA BROWN V. HORDE OF DALMATIAN." THAT WAS A BIG ONE.
OF COURSE, THE MOST FAMOUS LEGAL RULING TO CATS IS NOT "ROE V. CAVIAR," IT'S THE SCOPES MONKEY TRIAL, BECAUSE –
IT'S SO IMPORTANT THAT THEY GET IT FOR FREE, EH?
...WHO GET WHAT FREE?
THE MONKEYS. SCOPE.
HEY, THERE OUGHT TO BE A LISTERINE CAT TRIAL. YOU GUYS SMELL LIKE CHUM.
I DON'T KNOW ABOUT THIS "SUPREME CAT" CHARACTER. IT DOESN'T SEEM VERY DEMO-CRATIC.
"DEMOCRATIC"? MAN, CATS AREN'T TOUCHY-RETRIEVY POPULISTS LIKE YOU DOGS! WE DON'T HAVE A CONSTITUTION, WE HAVE A MANIFESTO! WE ARE CATS!
SHOULDN'T YOU HAVE A CAT-IFESTO, THEN?
EXCUSE ME. I REQUIRE TO MAKE A CALL.

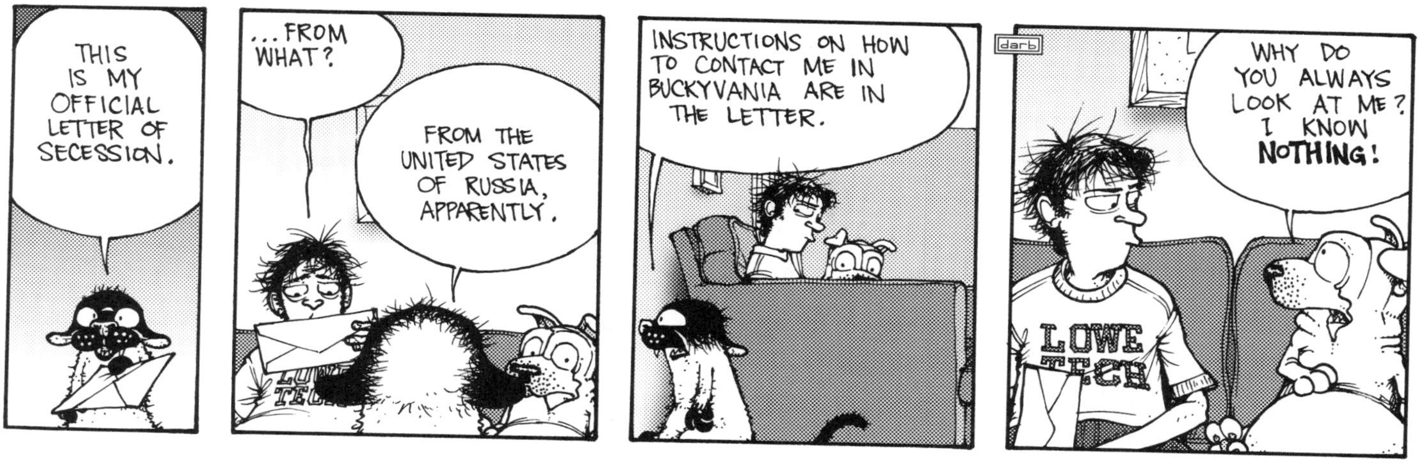
THIS IS MY OFFICIAL LETTER OF SECESSION.
...FROM WHAT?
FROM THE UNITED STATES OF RUSSIA, APPARENTLY.
INSTRUCTIONS ON HOW TO CONTACT ME IN BUCKYVANIA ARE IN THE LETTER.
darb
WHY DO YOU ALWAYS LOOK AT ME? I KNOW **NOTHING**!
LOWE TECH

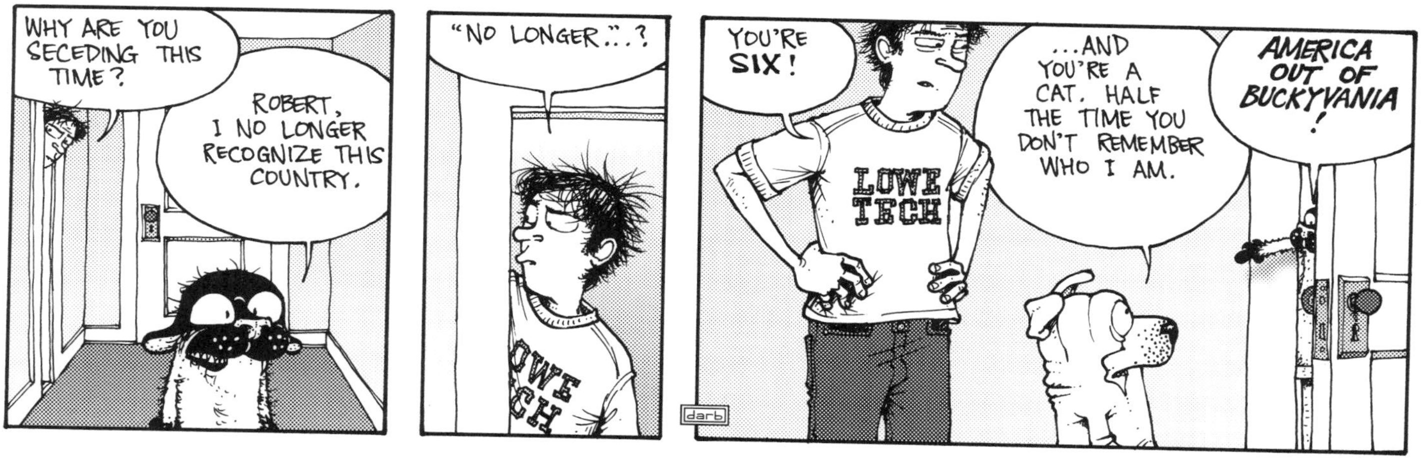
WHY ARE YOU SECEDING THIS TIME?
ROBERT, I NO LONGER RECOGNIZE THIS COUNTRY.
"NO LONGER..."?
darb
YOU'RE **SIX**!
...AND YOU'RE A CAT. HALF THE TIME YOU DON'T REMEMBER WHO I AM.
AMERICA OUT OF BUCKYVANIA!
LOWE TECH

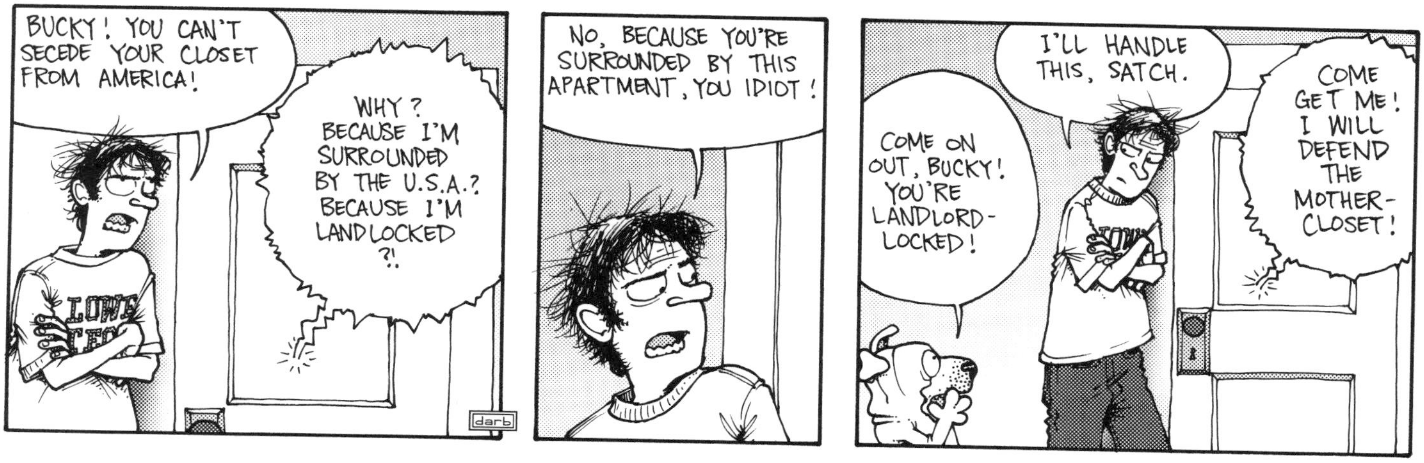
BUCKY! YOU CAN'T SECEDE YOUR CLOSET FROM AMERICA!
WHY? BECAUSE I'M SURROUNDED BY THE U.S.A.? BECAUSE I'M LANDLOCKED?!
darb
NO, BECAUSE YOU'RE SURROUNDED BY THIS APARTMENT, YOU IDIOT!
I'LL HANDLE THIS, SATCH.
COME ON OUT, BUCKY! YOU'RE LANDLORD-LOCKED!
COME GET ME! I WILL DEFEND THE MOTHER-CLOSET!

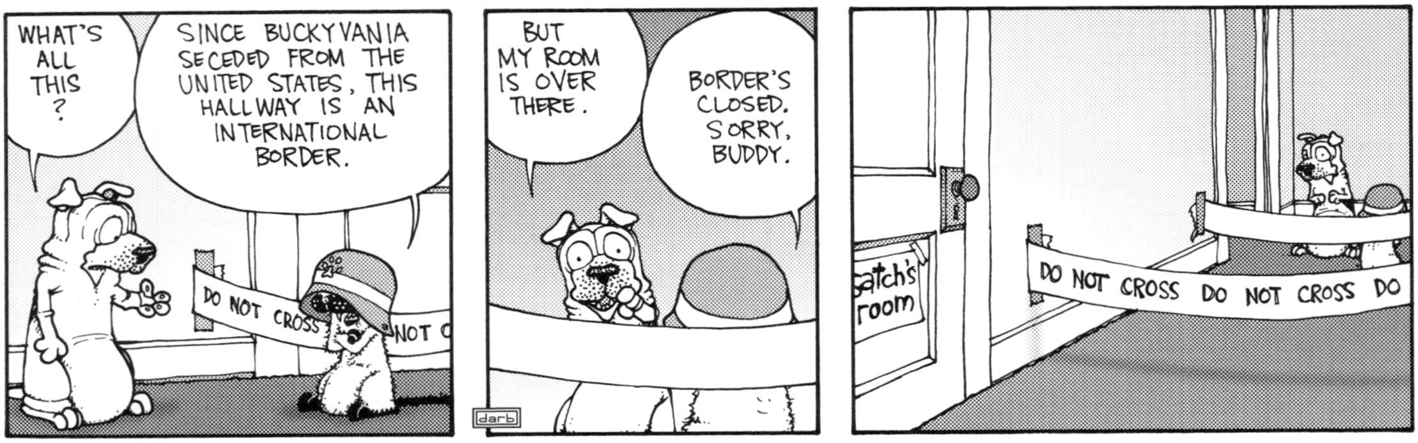
WHAT'S ALL THIS ?
SINCE BUCKYVANIA SECEDED FROM THE UNITED STATES, THIS HALLWAY IS AN INTERNATIONAL BORDER.
DO NOT CROSS
NOT C
BUT MY ROOM IS OVER THERE.
BORDER'S CLOSED. SORRY, BUDDY.
darb
Satch's room
DO NOT CROSS DO NOT CROSS DO

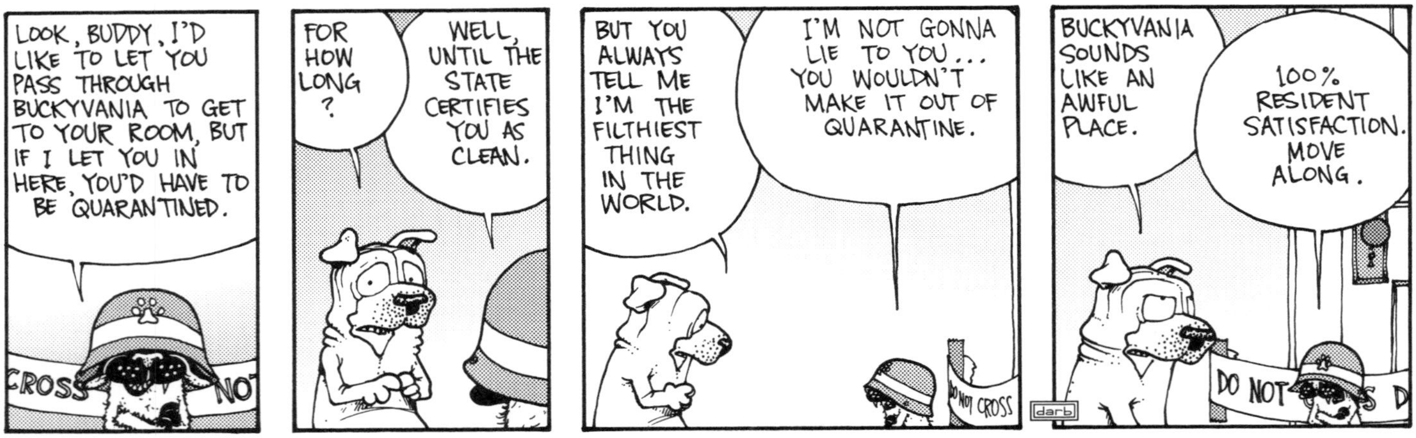
LOOK, BUDDY, I'D LIKE TO LET YOU PASS THROUGH BUCKYVANIA TO GET TO YOUR ROOM, BUT IF I LET YOU IN HERE, YOU'D HAVE TO BE QUARANTINED.
CROSS
NO
FOR HOW LONG ?
WELL, UNTIL THE STATE CERTIFIES YOU AS CLEAN.
BUT YOU ALWAYS TELL ME I'M THE FILTHIEST THING IN THE WORLD.
I'M NOT GONNA LIE TO YOU... YOU WOULDN'T MAKE IT OUT OF QUARANTINE.
DO NOT CROSS
darb
BUCKYVANIA SOUNDS LIKE AN AWFUL PLACE.
100% RESIDENT SATISFACTION. MOVE ALONG.
DO NOT

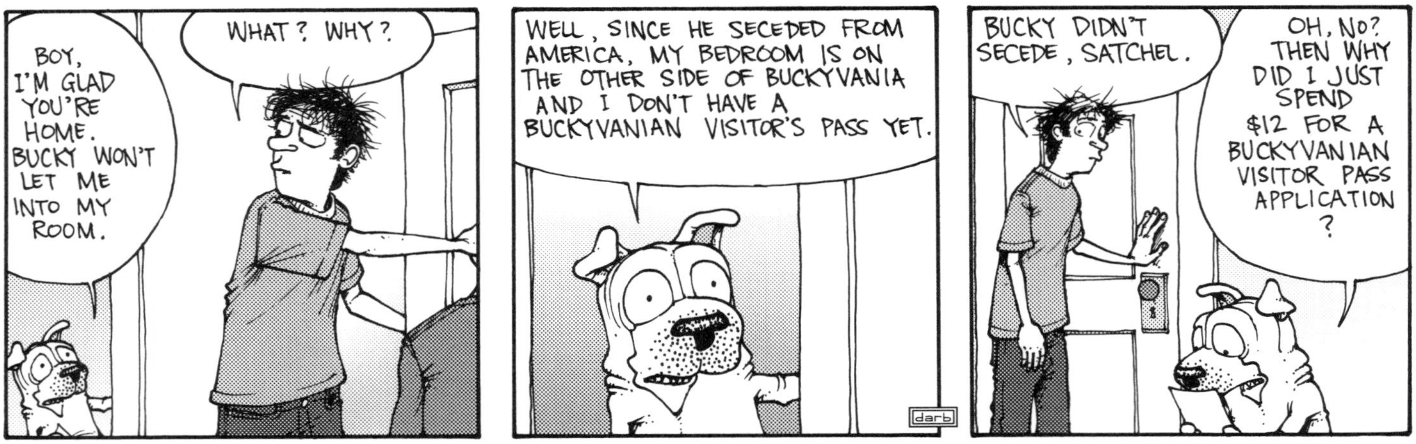
BOY, I'M GLAD YOU'RE HOME. BUCKY WON'T LET ME INTO MY ROOM.
WHAT? WHY?
WELL, SINCE HE SECEDED FROM AMERICA, MY BEDROOM IS ON THE OTHER SIDE OF BUCKYVANIA AND I DON'T HAVE A BUCKYVANIAN VISITOR'S PASS YET.
darb
BUCKY DIDN'T SECEDE, SATCHEL.
OH, NO? THEN WHY DID I JUST SPEND $12 FOR A BUCKYVANIAN VISITOR PASS APPLICATION ?

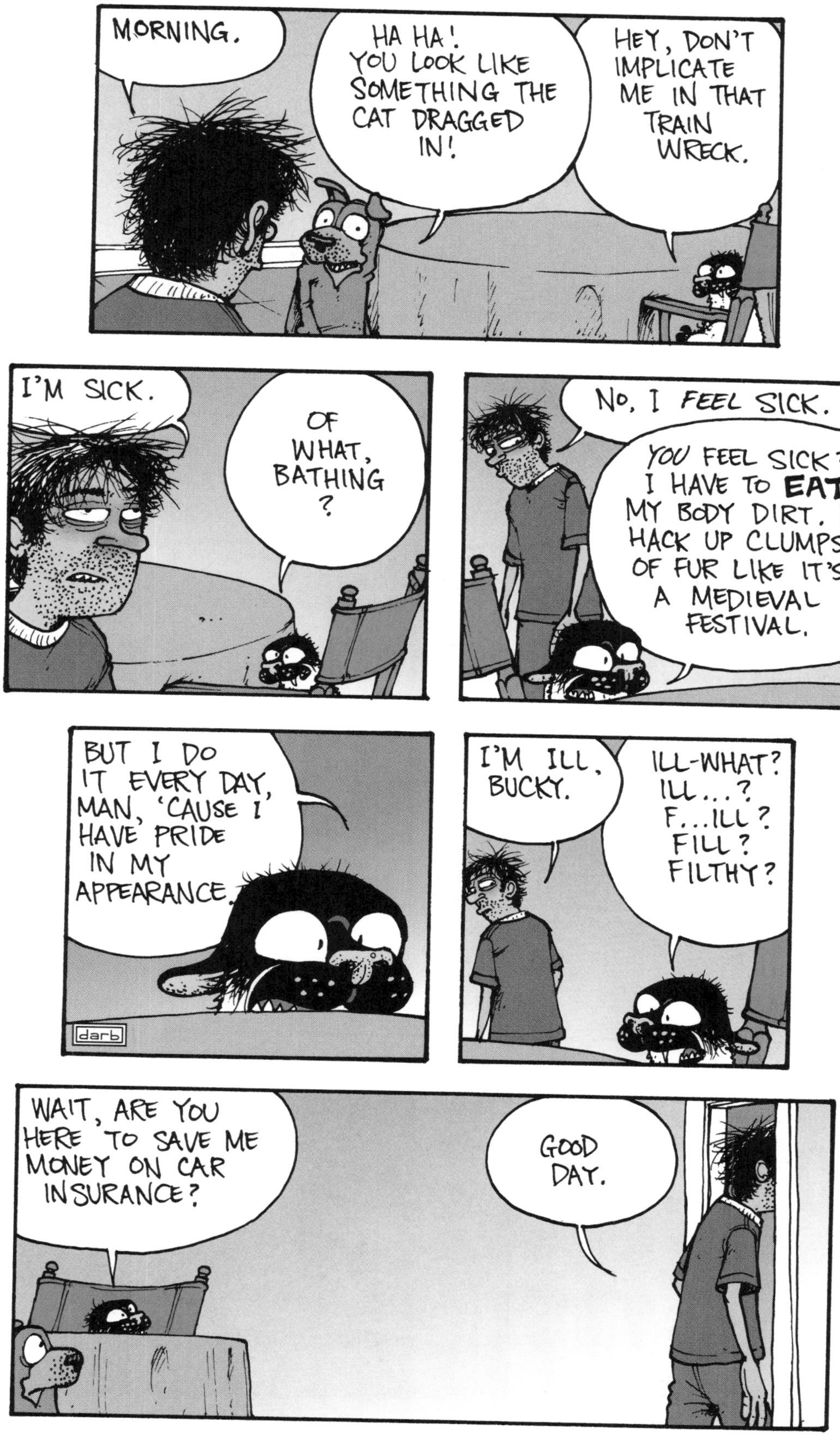
MORNING.
HA HA! YOU LOOK LIKE SOMETHING THE CAT DRAGGED IN!
HEY, DON'T IMPLICATE ME IN THAT TRAIN WRECK.
I'M SICK.
OF WHAT, BATHING?
...
NO, I *FEEL* SICK.
YOU FEEL SICK? I HAVE TO **EAT** MY BODY DIRT. I HACK UP CLUMPS OF FUR LIKE IT'S A MEDIEVAL FESTIVAL.
BUT I DO IT EVERY DAY, MAN, 'CAUSE I HAVE PRIDE IN MY APPEARANCE.
darb
I'M ILL, BUCKY.
ILL-WHAT? ILL...? F...ILL? FILL? FILTHY?
WAIT, ARE YOU HERE TO SAVE ME MONEY ON CAR INSURANCE?
GOOD DAY.

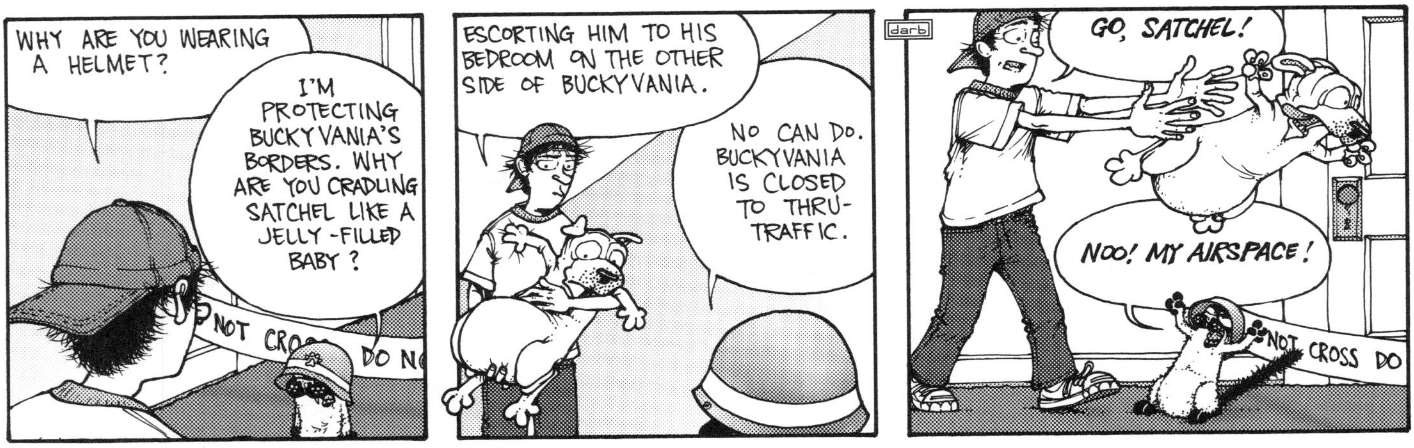
WHY ARE YOU WEARING A HELMET?
I'M PROTECTING BUCKYVANIA'S BORDERS. WHY ARE YOU CRADLING SATCHEL LIKE A JELLY-FILLED BABY?
ESCORTING HIM TO HIS BEDROOM ON THE OTHER SIDE OF BUCKYVANIA.
NO CAN DO. BUCKYVANIA IS CLOSED TO THRU-TRAFFIC.
GO, SATCHEL!
NOO! MY AIRSPACE!

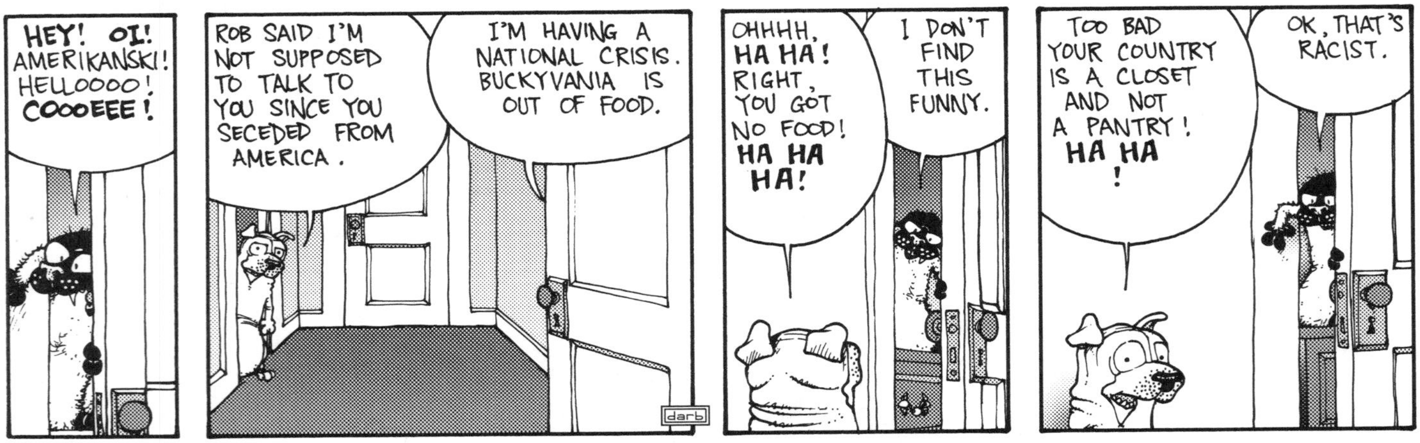
HEY! OI! AMERIKANSKI! HELLOOOO! COOOEEE!
ROB SAID I'M NOT SUPPOSED TO TALK TO YOU SINCE YOU SECEDED FROM AMERICA.
I'M HAVING A NATIONAL CRISIS. BUCKYVANIA IS OUT OF FOOD.
OHHHH, HA HA! RIGHT, YOU GOT NO FOOD! HA HA HA!
I DON'T FIND THIS FUNNY.
TOO BAD YOUR COUNTRY IS A CLOSET AND NOT A PANTRY! HA HA!
OK, THAT'S RACIST.

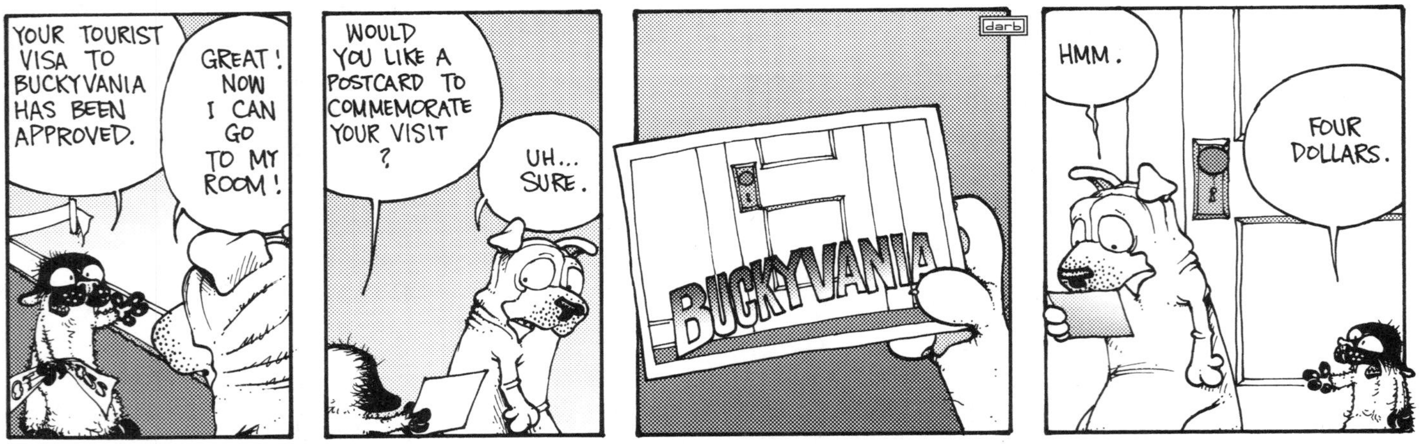
YOUR TOURIST VISA TO BUCKYVANIA HAS BEEN APPROVED.
GREAT! NOW I CAN GO TO MY ROOM!
WOULD YOU LIKE A POSTCARD TO COMMEMORATE YOUR VISIT?
UH... SURE.
BUCKYVANIA
HMM.
FOUR DOLLARS.

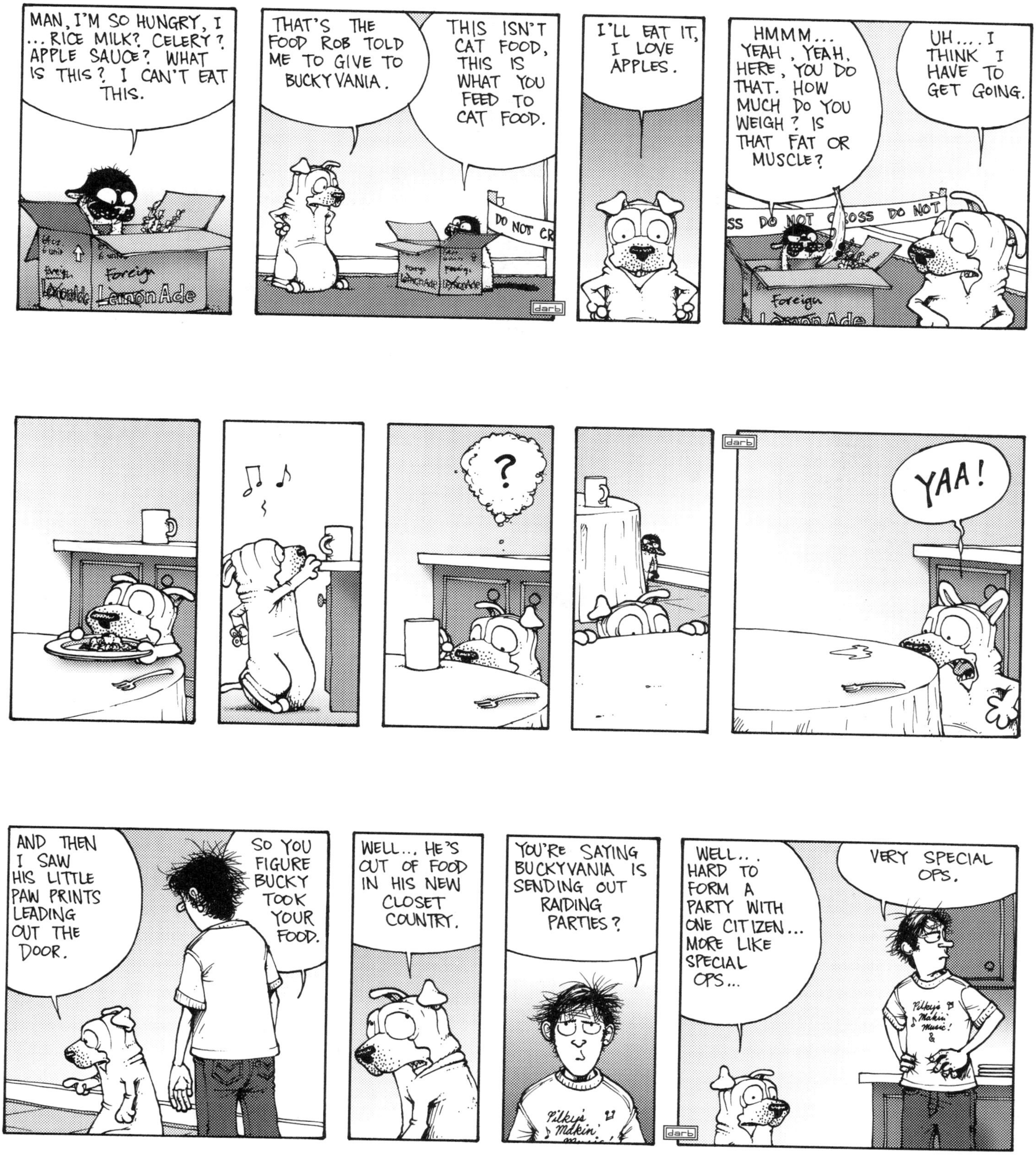
MAN, I'M SO HUNGRY, I ... RICE MILK? CELERY? APPLE SAUCE? WHAT IS THIS? I CAN'T EAT THIS.
Foreign LemonAde
THAT'S THE FOOD ROB TOLD ME TO GIVE TO BUCKYVANIA.
THIS ISN'T CAT FOOD, THIS IS WHAT YOU FEED TO CAT FOOD.
DO NOT CR
darb
I'LL EAT IT, I LOVE APPLES.
HMMM... YEAH, YEAH. HERE, YOU DO THAT. HOW MUCH DO YOU WEIGH? IS THAT FAT OR MUSCLE?
UH.... I THINK I HAVE TO GET GOING.
SS DO NOT CROSS DO NOT
Foreign
?
darb
YAA!
AND THEN I SAW HIS LITTLE PAW PRINTS LEADING OUT THE DOOR.
SO YOU FIGURE BUCKY TOOK YOUR FOOD.
WELL... HE'S OUT OF FOOD IN HIS NEW CLOSET COUNTRY.
YOU'RE SAYING BUCKYVANIA IS SENDING OUT RAIDING PARTIES?
darb
WELL... HARD TO FORM A PARTY WITH ONE CITIZEN... MORE LIKE SPECIAL OPS...
VERY SPECIAL OPS.
Pilkey's Makin' Music!

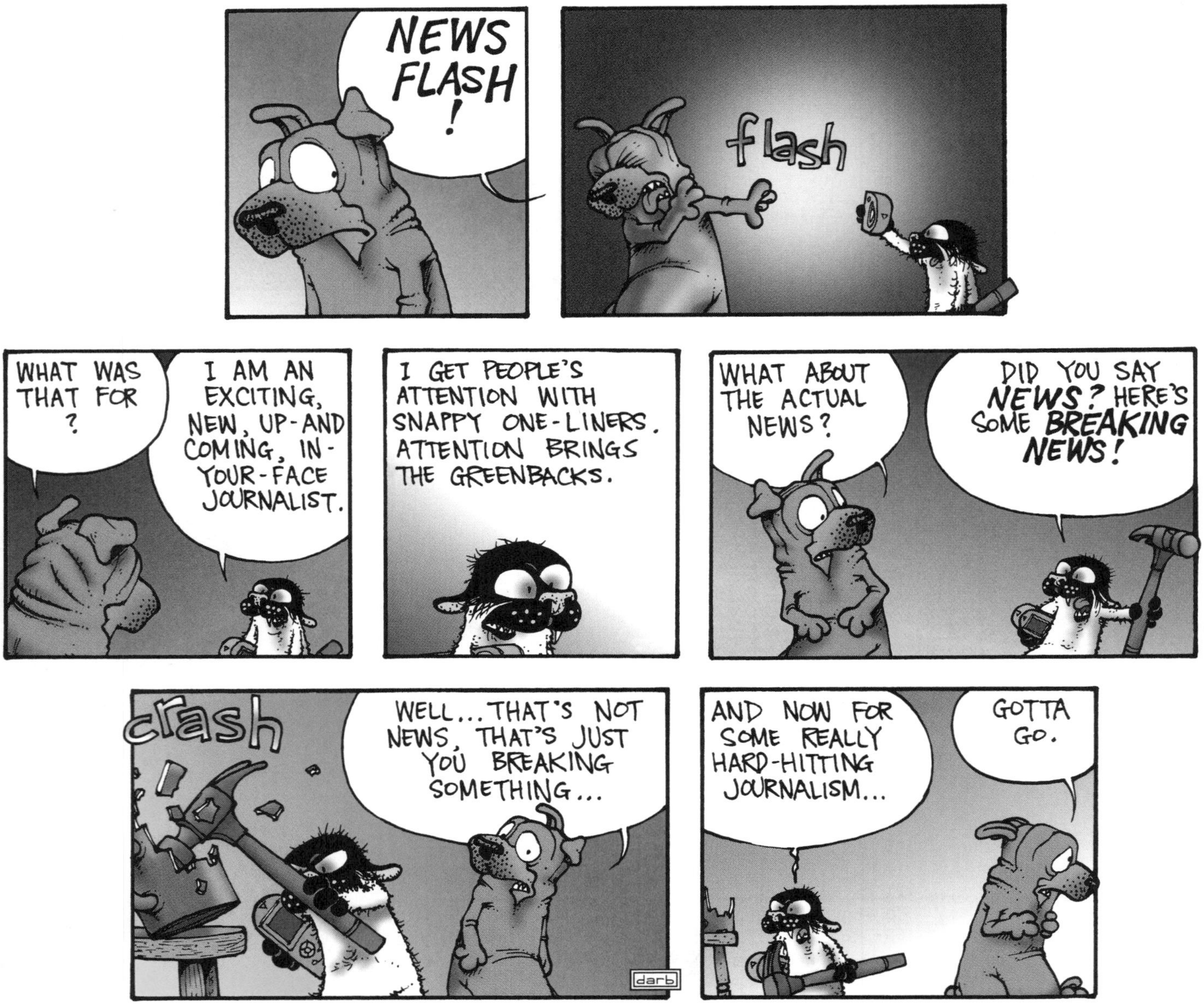
NEWS FLASH !
flash
WHAT WAS THAT FOR ?
I AM AN EXCITING, NEW, UP-AND COMING, IN-YOUR-FACE JOURNALIST.
I GET PEOPLE'S ATTENTION WITH SNAPPY ONE-LINERS. ATTENTION BRINGS THE GREENBACKS.
WHAT ABOUT THE ACTUAL NEWS ?
DID YOU SAY NEWS? HERE'S SOME BREAKING NEWS!
crash
WELL... THAT'S NOT NEWS, THAT'S JUST YOU BREAKING SOMETHING...
darb
AND NOW FOR SOME REALLY HARD-HITTING JOURNALISM...
GOTTA GO.

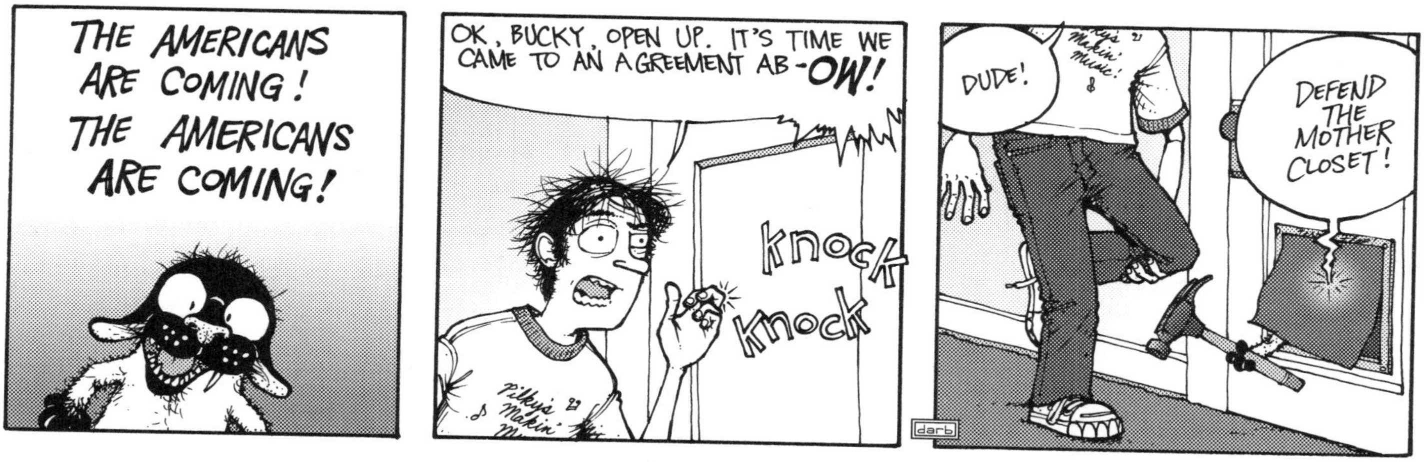
THE AMERICANS ARE COMING! THE AMERICANS ARE COMING!
OK, BUCKY, OPEN UP. IT'S TIME WE CAME TO AN AGREEMENT AB-OW!
knock knock
DUDE!
DEFEND THE MOTHER CLOSET!

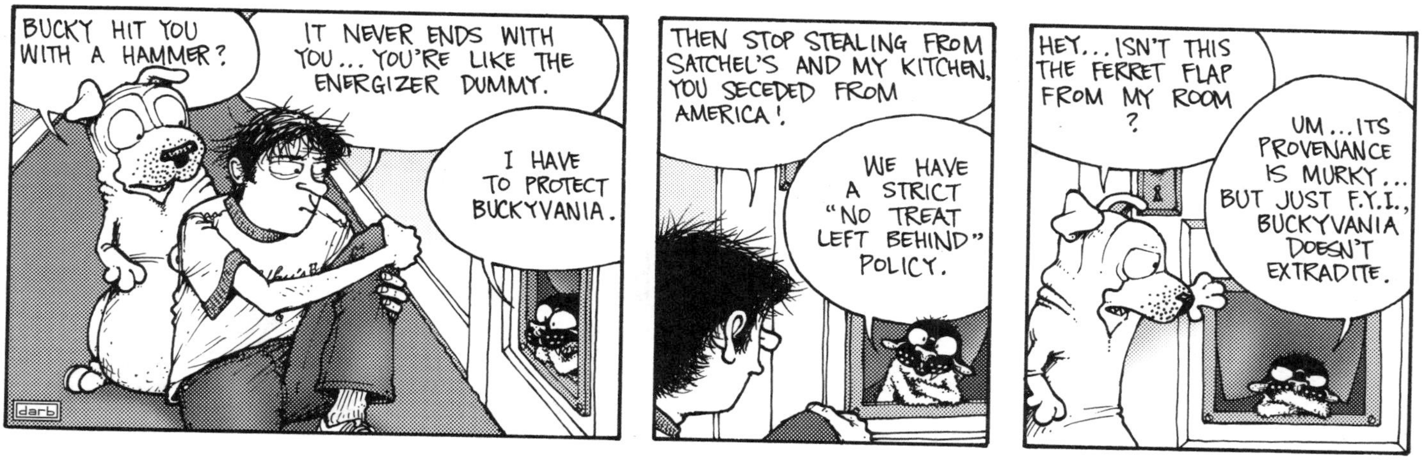
BUCKY HIT YOU WITH A HAMMER?
IT NEVER ENDS WITH YOU... YOU'RE LIKE THE ENERGIZER DUMMY.
I HAVE TO PROTECT BUCKYVANIA.
THEN STOP STEALING FROM SATCHEL'S AND MY KITCHEN. YOU SECEDED FROM AMERICA!
WE HAVE A STRICT "NO TREAT LEFT BEHIND" POLICY.
HEY... ISN'T THIS THE FERRET FLAP FROM MY ROOM?
UM... ITS PROVENANCE IS MURKY... BUT JUST F.Y.I., BUCKYVANIA DOESN'T EXTRADITE.

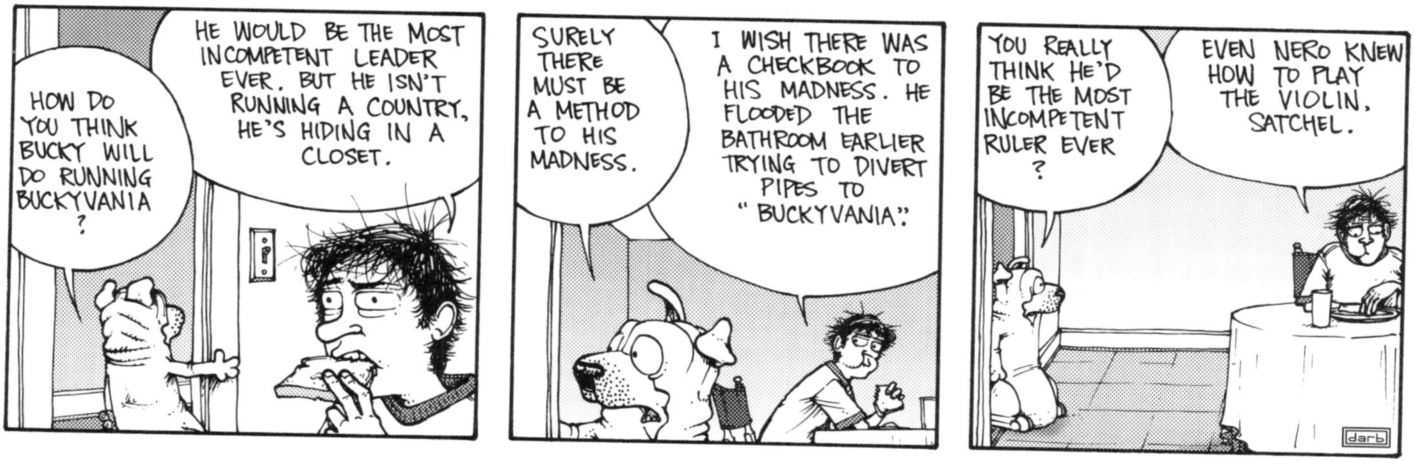
HOW DO YOU THINK BUCKY WILL DO RUNNING BUCKYVANIA?
HE WOULD BE THE MOST INCOMPETENT LEADER EVER. BUT HE ISN'T RUNNING A COUNTRY, HE'S HIDING IN A CLOSET.
SURELY THERE MUST BE A METHOD TO HIS MADNESS.
I WISH THERE WAS A CHECKBOOK TO HIS MADNESS. HE FLOODED THE BATHROOM EARLIER TRYING TO DIVERT PIPES TO "BUCKYVANIA."
YOU REALLY THINK HE'D BE THE MOST INCOMPETENT RULER EVER?
EVEN NERO KNEW HOW TO PLAY THE VIOLIN, SATCHEL.

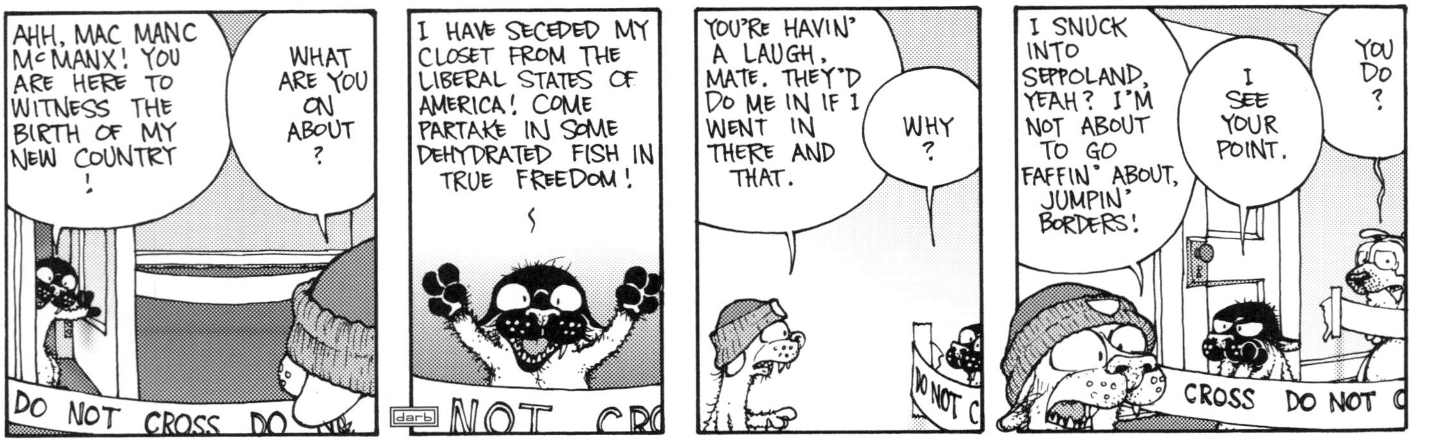
AHH, MAC MANC McMANX! YOU ARE HERE TO WITNESS THE BIRTH OF MY NEW COUNTRY!
WHAT ARE YOU ON ABOUT?
DO NOT CROSS
I HAVE SECEDED MY CLOSET FROM THE LIBERAL STATES OF AMERICA! COME PARTAKE IN SOME DEHYDRATED FISH IN TRUE FREEDOM!
darb
YOU'RE HAVIN' A LAUGH, MATE. THEY'D DO ME IN IF I WENT IN THERE AND THAT.
WHY?
I SNUCK INTO SEPPOLAND, YEAH? I'M NOT ABOUT TO GO FAFFIN' ABOUT, JUMPIN' BORDERS!
I SEE YOUR POINT.
YOU DO?
CROSS DO NOT

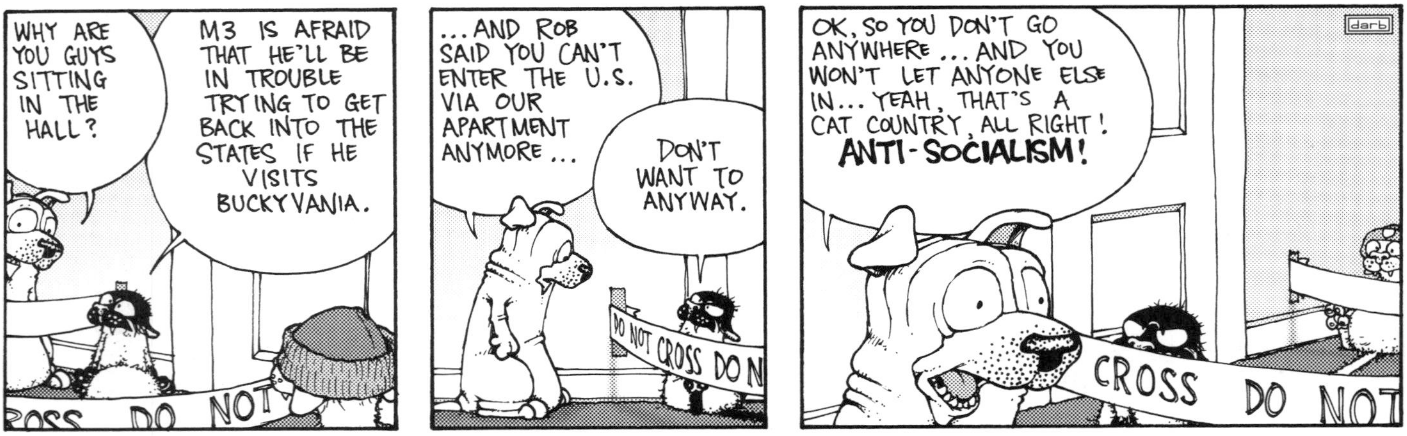
WHY ARE YOU GUYS SITTING IN THE HALL?
M3 IS AFRAID THAT HE'LL BE IN TROUBLE TRYING TO GET BACK INTO THE STATES IF HE VISITS BUCKYVANIA.
...AND ROB SAID YOU CAN'T ENTER THE U.S. VIA OUR APARTMENT ANYMORE...
DON'T WANT TO ANYWAY.
DO NOT CROSS
OK, SO YOU DON'T GO ANYWHERE... AND YOU WON'T LET ANYONE ELSE IN... YEAH, THAT'S A CAT COUNTRY, ALL RIGHT!
ANTI-SOCIALISM!
darb
CROSS DO

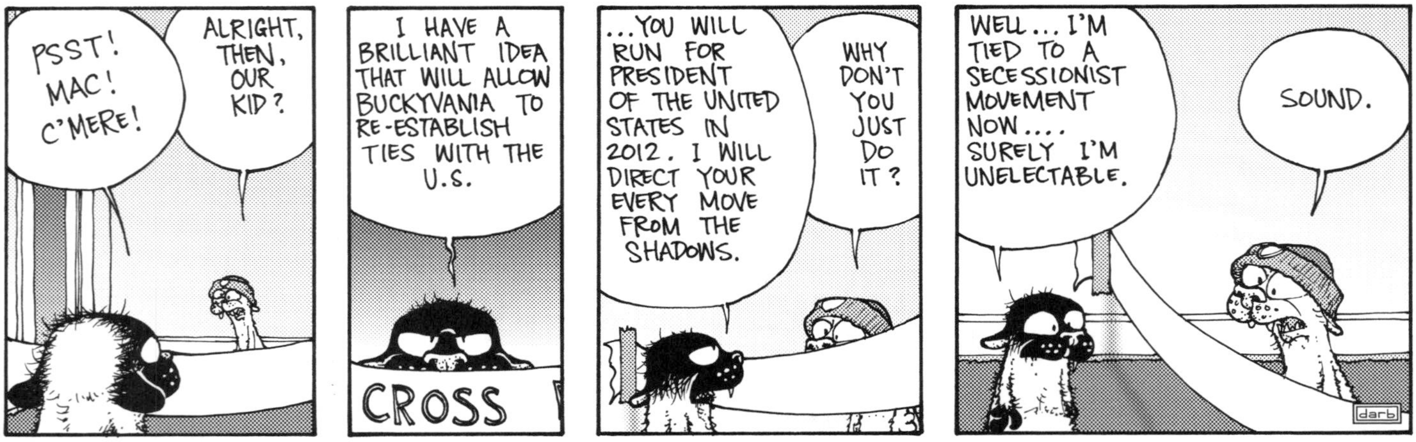
PSST! MAC! C'MERE!
ALRIGHT, THEN, OUR KID?
I HAVE A BRILLIANT IDEA THAT WILL ALLOW BUCKYVANIA TO RE-ESTABLISH TIES WITH THE U.S.
CROSS
...YOU WILL RUN FOR PRESIDENT OF THE UNITED STATES IN 2012. I WILL DIRECT YOUR EVERY MOVE FROM THE SHADOWS.
WHY DON'T YOU JUST DO IT?
WELL... I'M TIED TO A SECESSIONIST MOVEMENT NOW.... SURELY I'M UNELECTABLE.
SOUND.
darb

GREETINGS, SIR, CAN I INTEREST YOU IN THE LATEST IN PERSONAL ENTERTAINMENT TECHNOLOGY?

IT JUST LOOKS LIKE AN IPOD WITH EXTRA BATTERIES...

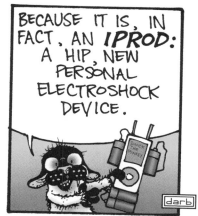

BECAUSE IT IS, IN FACT, AN *IPROD*: A HIP, NEW PERSONAL ELECTROSHOCK DEVICE.

darb

HOW IS THAT AN ENTERTAINMENT DEVICE?

HAVE YOU NEVER SEEN SOMEONE GET SHOCKED? IT'S QUITE ENTERTAINING.

SO ALL IT DOES IS SHOCK PEOPLE?

WELL... DON'T DOWNPLAY IT, IT IS CAPABLE OF SHOCKING ANY SPECIES.

THAT IS THE MOST RIDICULOUS THING I'VE EVER SEEN.

I AM AN IDEA MAN.

"IDEA", YEAH. YOU'RE CERTAINLY NOT ABLE TO EXECUTE.

NOT JUST YET, BUT I AM TAKING PRE-ORDERS FOR THAT VERSION.

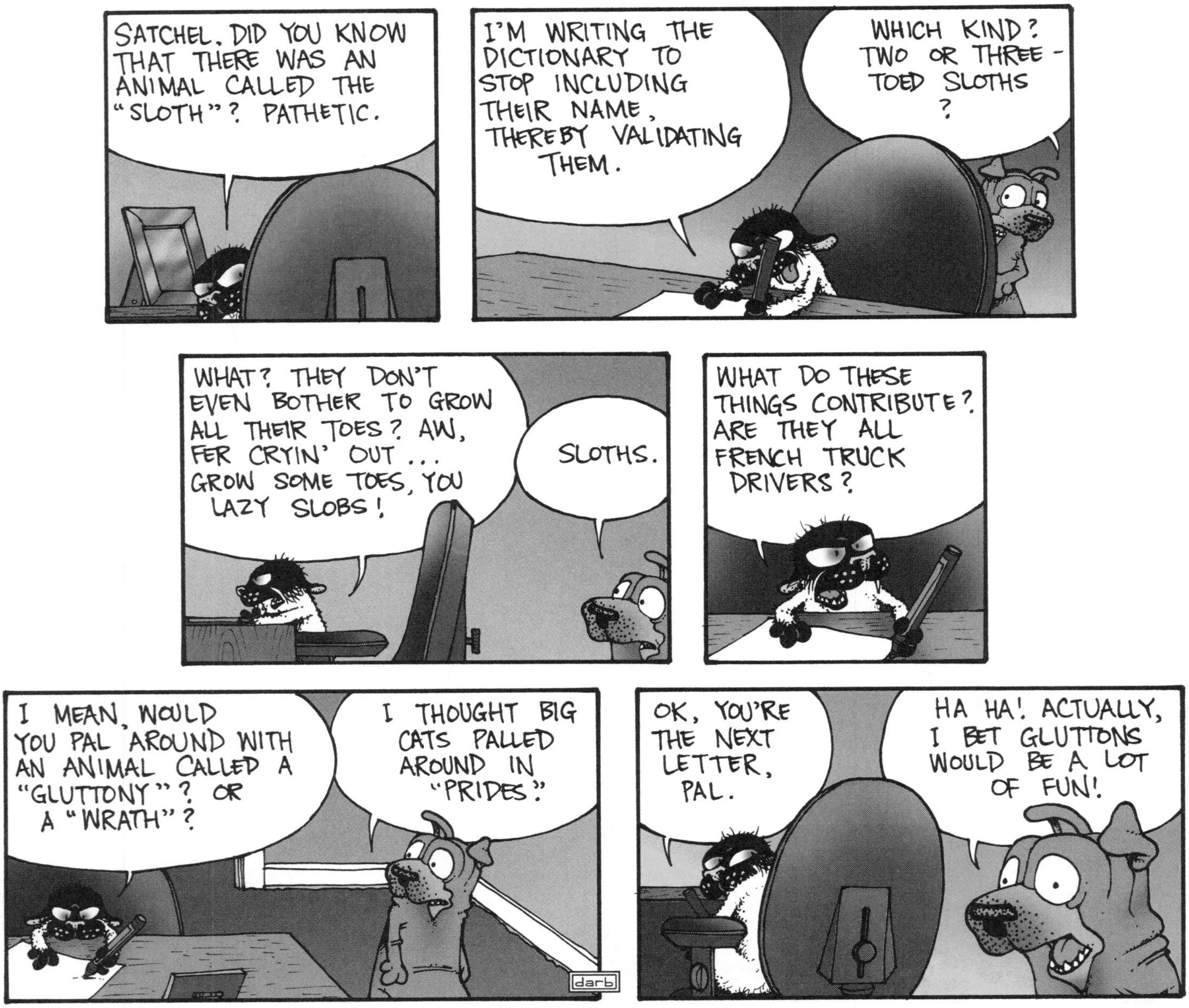
SATCHEL, DID YOU KNOW THAT THERE WAS AN ANIMAL CALLED THE "SLOTH"? PATHETIC.
I'M WRITING THE DICTIONARY TO STOP INCLUDING THEIR NAME, THEREBY VALIDATING THEM.
WHICH KIND? TWO OR THREE-TOED SLOTHS?
WHAT? THEY DON'T EVEN BOTHER TO GROW ALL THEIR TOES? AW, FER CRYIN' OUT ... GROW SOME TOES, YOU LAZY SLOBS!
SLOTHS.
WHAT DO THESE THINGS CONTRIBUTE? ARE THEY ALL FRENCH TRUCK DRIVERS?
I MEAN, WOULD YOU PAL AROUND WITH AN ANIMAL CALLED A "GLUTTONY"? OR A "WRATH"?
I THOUGHT BIG CATS PALLED AROUND IN "PRIDES."
darb
OK, YOU'RE THE NEXT LETTER, PAL.
HA HA! ACTUALLY, I BET GLUTTONS WOULD BE A LOT OF FUN!

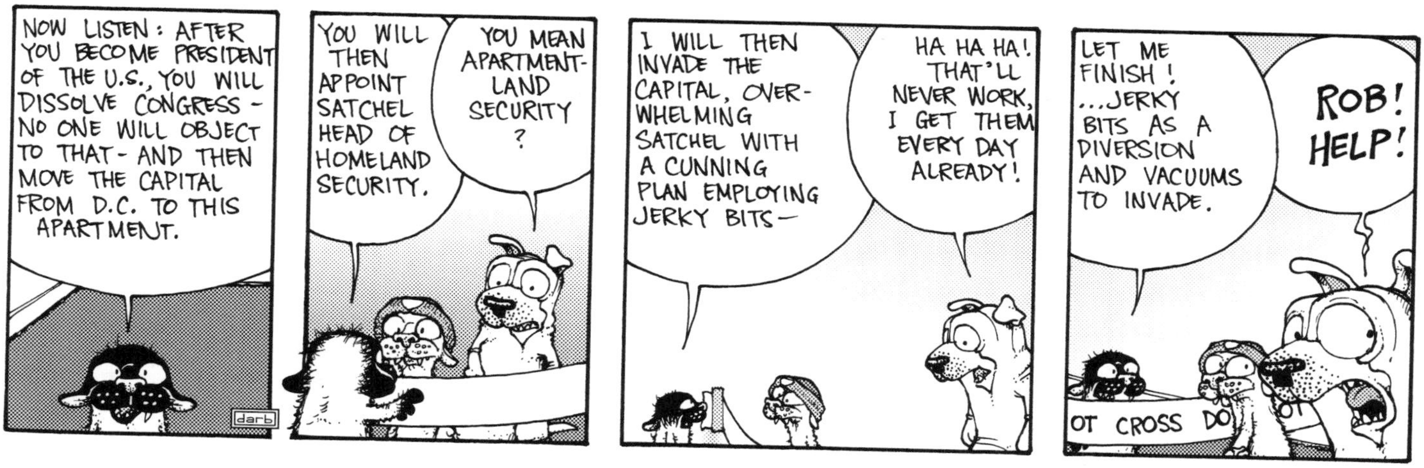
NOW LISTEN: AFTER YOU BECOME PRESIDENT OF THE U.S., YOU WILL DISSOLVE CONGRESS - NO ONE WILL OBJECT TO THAT - AND THEN MOVE THE CAPITAL FROM D.C. TO THIS APARTMENT.
darb
YOU WILL THEN APPOINT SATCHEL HEAD OF HOMELAND SECURITY.
YOU MEAN APARTMENT-LAND SECURITY ?
I WILL THEN INVADE THE CAPITAL, OVER-WHELMING SATCHEL WITH A CUNNING PLAN EMPLOYING JERKY BITS—
HA HA HA! THAT'LL NEVER WORK, I GET THEM EVERY DAY ALREADY!
LET ME FINISH! ...JERKY BITS AS A DIVERSION AND VACUUMS TO INVADE.
ROB! HELP!
OT CROSS DO

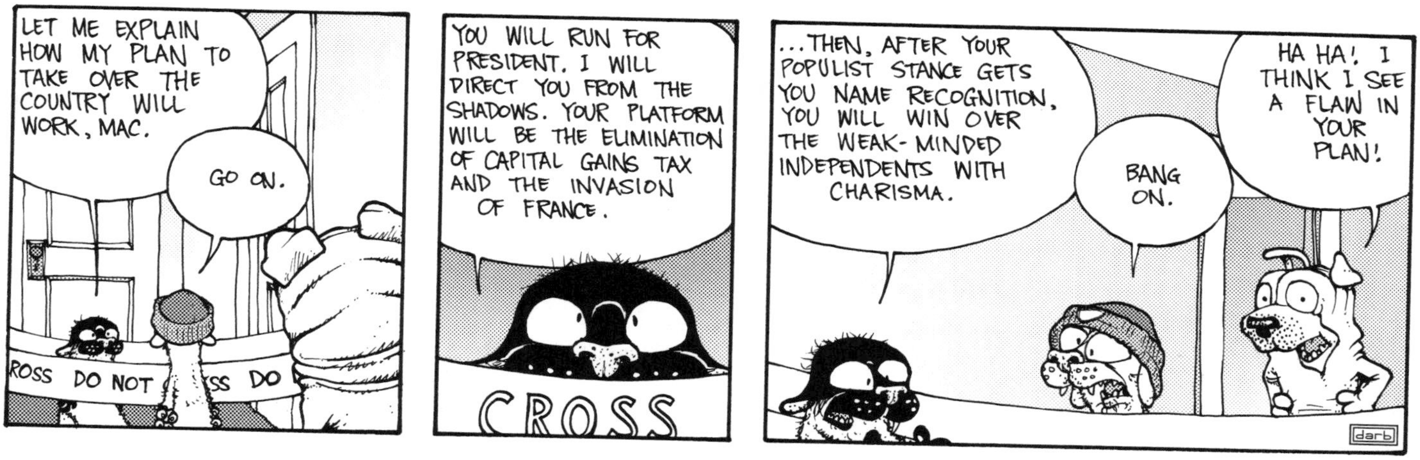
LET ME EXPLAIN HOW MY PLAN TO TAKE OVER THE COUNTRY WILL WORK, MAC.
GO ON.
ROSS DO NOT
YOU WILL RUN FOR PRESIDENT. I WILL DIRECT YOU FROM THE SHADOWS. YOUR PLATFORM WILL BE THE ELIMINATION OF CAPITAL GAINS TAX AND THE INVASION OF FRANCE.
CROSS
...THEN, AFTER YOUR POPULIST STANCE GETS YOU NAME RECOGNITION, YOU WILL WIN OVER THE WEAK-MINDED INDEPENDENTS WITH CHARISMA.
BANG ON.
HA HA! I THINK I SEE A FLAW IN YOUR PLAN!
darb

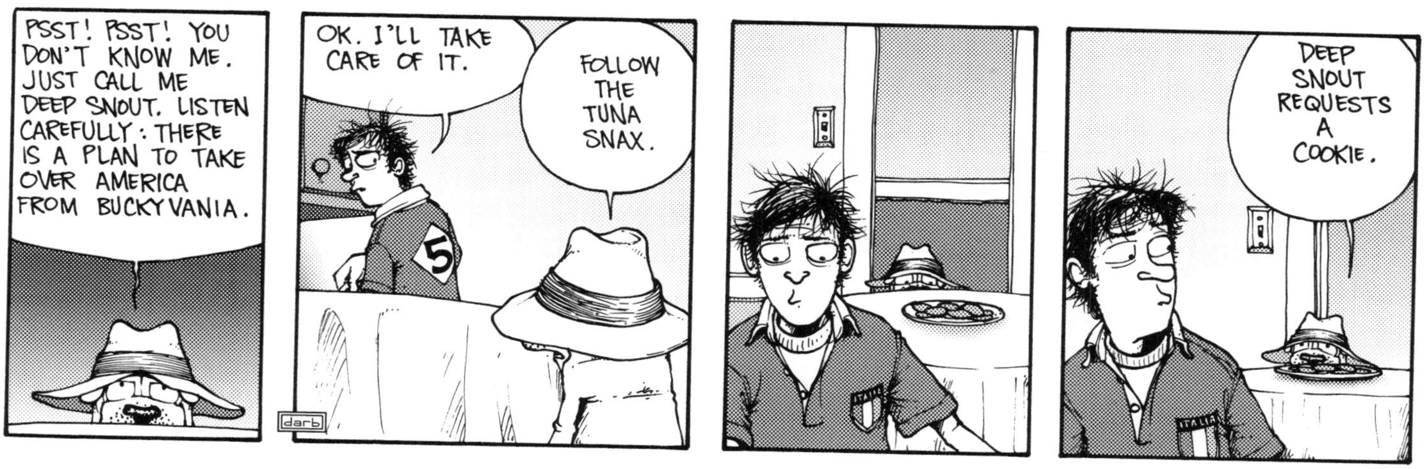
PSST! PSST! YOU DON'T KNOW ME. JUST CALL ME DEEP SNOUT. LISTEN CAREFULLY: THERE IS A PLAN TO TAKE OVER AMERICA FROM BUCKYVANIA.
darb
OK. I'LL TAKE CARE OF IT.
FOLLOW THE TUNA SNAX.
5
DEEP SNOUT REQUESTS A COOKIE.

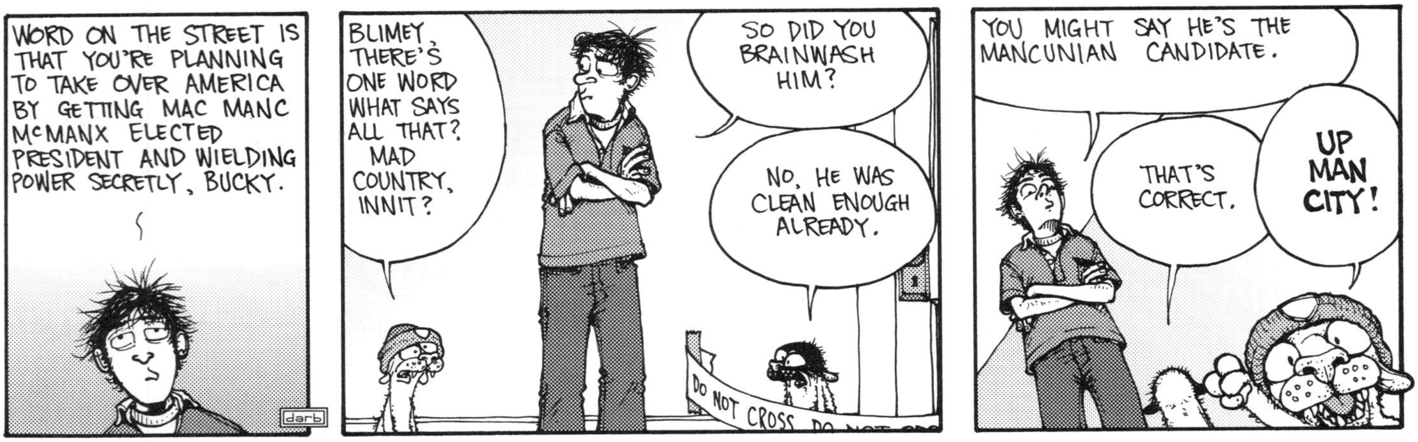
WORD ON THE STREET IS THAT YOU'RE PLANNING TO TAKE OVER AMERICA BY GETTING MAC MANC McMANX ELECTED PRESIDENT AND WIELDING POWER SECRETLY, BUCKY.
BLIMEY, THERE'S ONE WORD WHAT SAYS ALL THAT? MAD COUNTRY, INNIT?
SO DID YOU BRAINWASH HIM?
NO, HE WAS CLEAN ENOUGH ALREADY.
DO NOT CROSS
YOU MIGHT SAY HE'S THE MANCUNIAN CANDIDATE.
THAT'S CORRECT.
UP MAN CITY!
darb

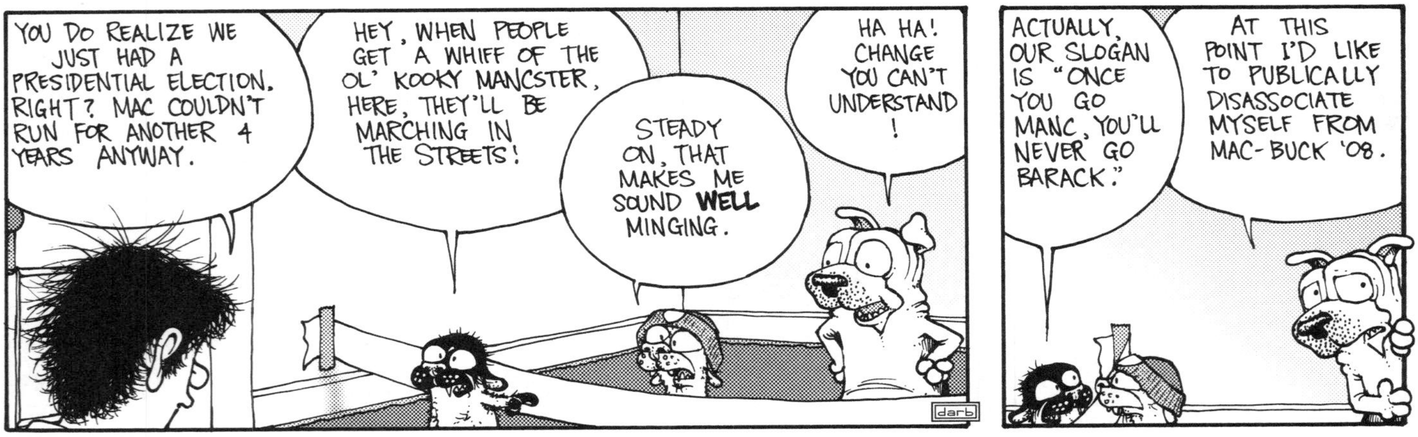
YOU DO REALIZE WE JUST HAD A PRESIDENTIAL ELECTION, RIGHT? MAC COULDN'T RUN FOR ANOTHER 4 YEARS ANYWAY.
HEY, WHEN PEOPLE GET A WHIFF OF THE OL' KOOKY MANCSTER, HERE, THEY'LL BE MARCHING IN THE STREETS!
STEADY ON, THAT MAKES ME SOUND **WELL** MINGING.
HA HA! CHANGE YOU CAN'T UNDERSTAND!
darb
ACTUALLY, OUR SLOGAN IS "ONCE YOU GO MANC, YOU'LL NEVER GO BARACK."
AT THIS POINT I'D LIKE TO PUBLICALLY DISASSOCIATE MYSELF FROM MAC-BUCK '08.

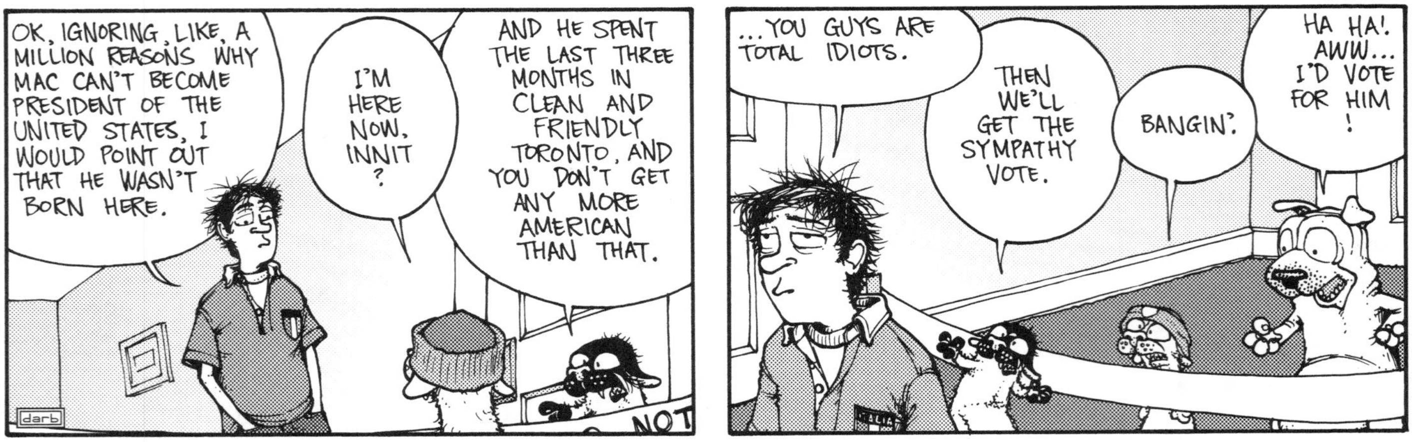
OK, IGNORING, LIKE, A MILLION REASONS WHY MAC CAN'T BECOME PRESIDENT OF THE UNITED STATES, I WOULD POINT OUT THAT HE WASN'T BORN HERE.
I'M HERE NOW, INNIT?
AND HE SPENT THE LAST THREE MONTHS IN CLEAN AND FRIENDLY TORONTO, AND YOU DON'T GET ANY MORE AMERICAN THAN THAT.
darb
NOT
...YOU GUYS ARE TOTAL IDIOTS.
THEN WE'LL GET THE SYMPATHY VOTE.
BANGIN'.
HA HA! AWW... I'D VOTE FOR HIM!

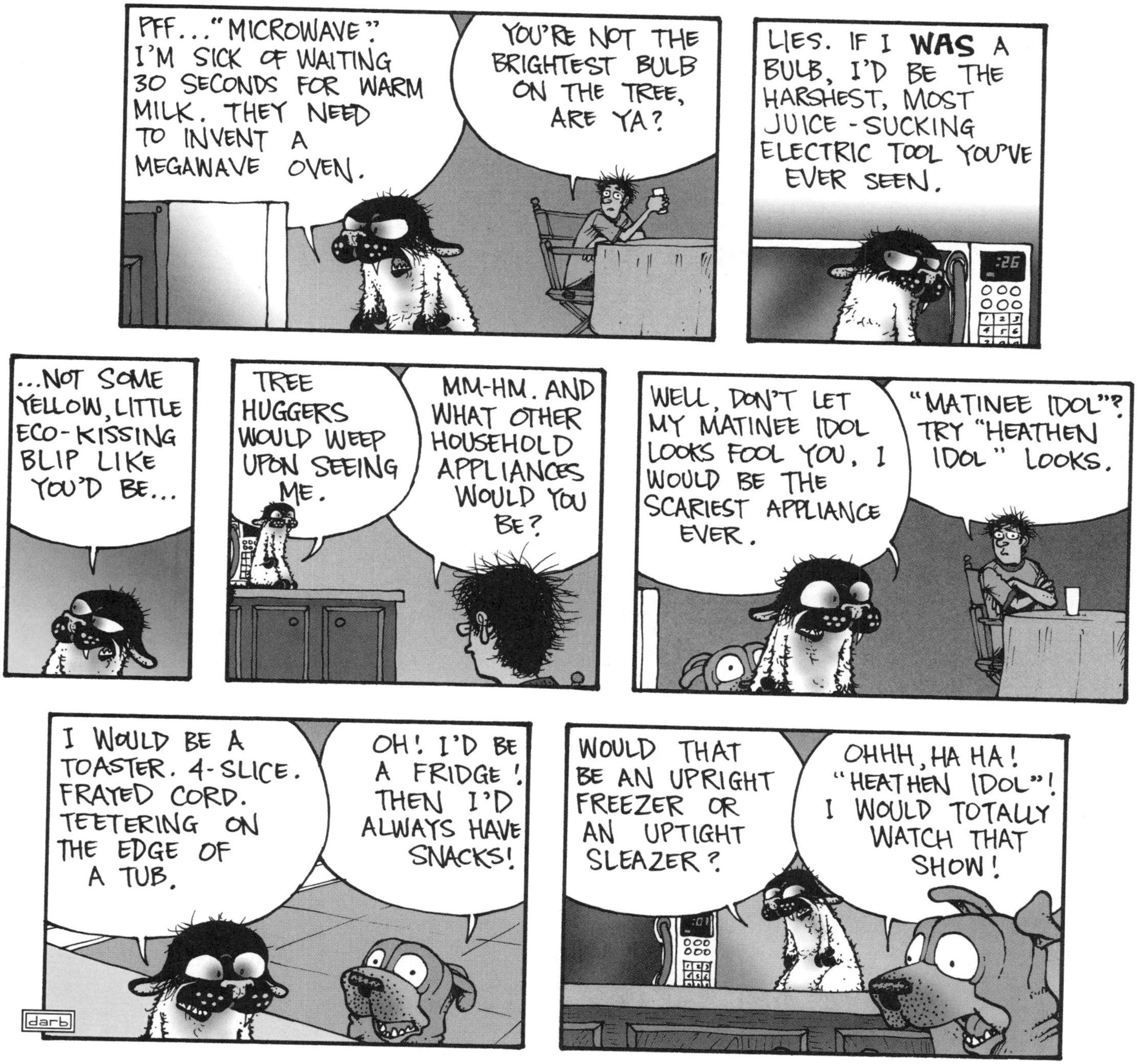
PFF..."MICROWAVE." I'M SICK OF WAITING 30 SECONDS FOR WARM MILK. THEY NEED TO INVENT A MEGAWAVE OVEN.
YOU'RE NOT THE BRIGHTEST BULB ON THE TREE, ARE YA?
LIES. IF I **WAS** A BULB, I'D BE THE HARSHEST, MOST JUICE-SUCKING ELECTRIC TOOL YOU'VE EVER SEEN.
...NOT SOME YELLOW, LITTLE ECO-KISSING BLIP LIKE YOU'D BE...
TREE HUGGERS WOULD WEEP UPON SEEING ME.
MM-HM. AND WHAT OTHER HOUSEHOLD APPLIANCES WOULD YOU BE?
WELL, DON'T LET MY MATINEE IDOL LOOKS FOOL YOU. I WOULD BE THE SCARIEST APPLIANCE EVER.
"MATINEE IDOL"? TRY "HEATHEN IDOL" LOOKS.
I WOULD BE A TOASTER. 4-SLICE. FRAYED CORD. TEETERING ON THE EDGE OF A TUB.
OH! I'D BE A FRIDGE! THEN I'D ALWAYS HAVE SNACKS!
WOULD THAT BE AN UPRIGHT FREEZER OR AN UPTIGHT SLEAZER?
OHHH, HA HA! "HEATHEN IDOL"! I WOULD TOTALLY WATCH THAT SHOW!
darb

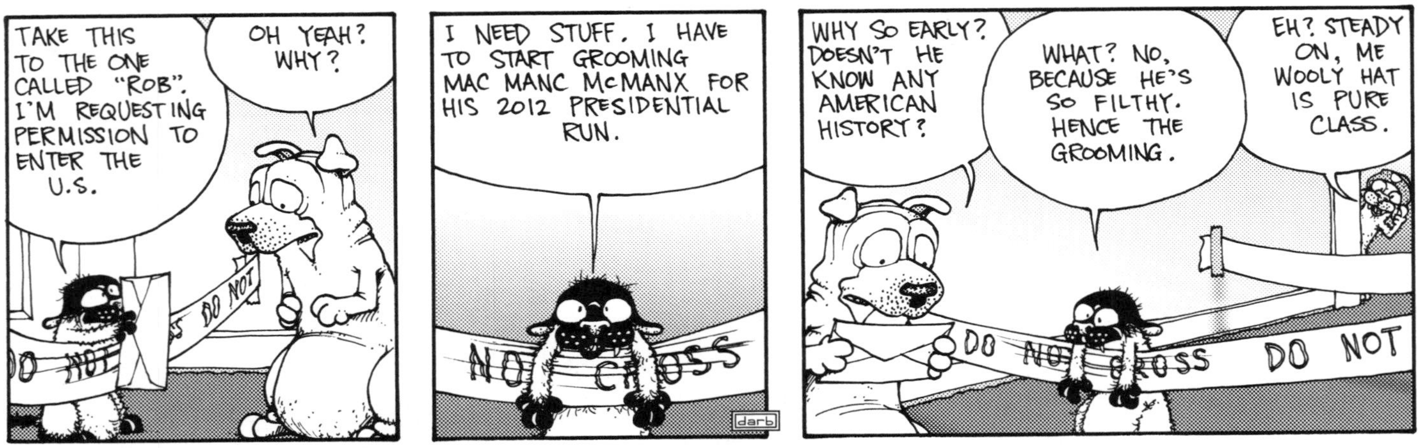
TAKE THIS TO THE ONE CALLED "ROB". I'M REQUESTING PERMISSION TO ENTER THE U.S.
OH YEAH? WHY?
I NEED STUFF. I HAVE TO START GROOMING MAC MANC McMANX FOR HIS 2012 PRESIDENTIAL RUN.
WHY SO EARLY? DOESN'T HE KNOW ANY AMERICAN HISTORY?
WHAT? NO, BECAUSE HE'S SO FILTHY. HENCE THE GROOMING.
EH? STEADY ON, ME WOOLY HAT IS PURE CLASS.
DO NOT CROSS
darb

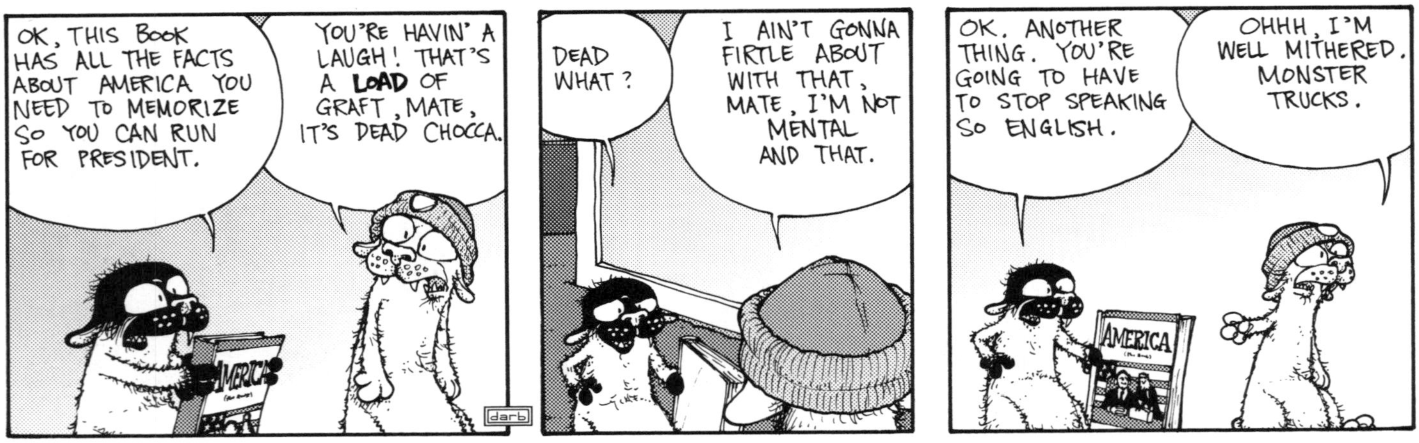
OK, THIS BOOK HAS ALL THE FACTS ABOUT AMERICA YOU NEED TO MEMORIZE SO YOU CAN RUN FOR PRESIDENT.
YOU'RE HAVIN' A LAUGH! THAT'S A LOAD OF GRAFT, MATE, IT'S DEAD CHOCCA.
DEAD WHAT?
I AIN'T GONNA FIRTLE ABOUT WITH THAT, MATE, I'M NOT MENTAL AND THAT.
OK. ANOTHER THING. YOU'RE GOING TO HAVE TO STOP SPEAKING SO ENGLISH.
OHHH, I'M WELL MITHERED. MONSTER TRUCKS.
AMERICA
darb

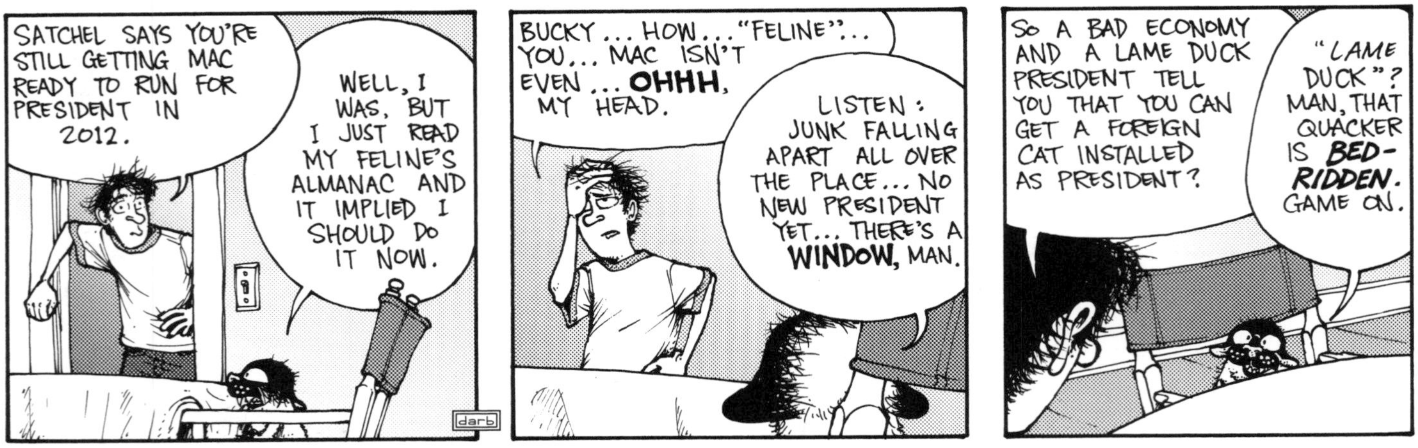
SATCHEL SAYS YOU'RE STILL GETTING MAC READY TO RUN FOR PRESIDENT IN 2012.
WELL, I WAS, BUT I JUST READ MY FELINE'S ALMANAC AND IT IMPLIED I SHOULD DO IT NOW.
BUCKY... HOW... "FELINE"... YOU... MAC ISN'T EVEN... OHHH, MY HEAD.
LISTEN: JUNK FALLING APART ALL OVER THE PLACE... NO NEW PRESIDENT YET... THERE'S A WINDOW, MAN.
SO A BAD ECONOMY AND A LAME DUCK PRESIDENT TELL YOU THAT YOU CAN GET A FOREIGN CAT INSTALLED AS PRESIDENT?
"LAME DUCK"? MAN, THAT QUACKER IS BED-RIDDEN. GAME ON.
darb

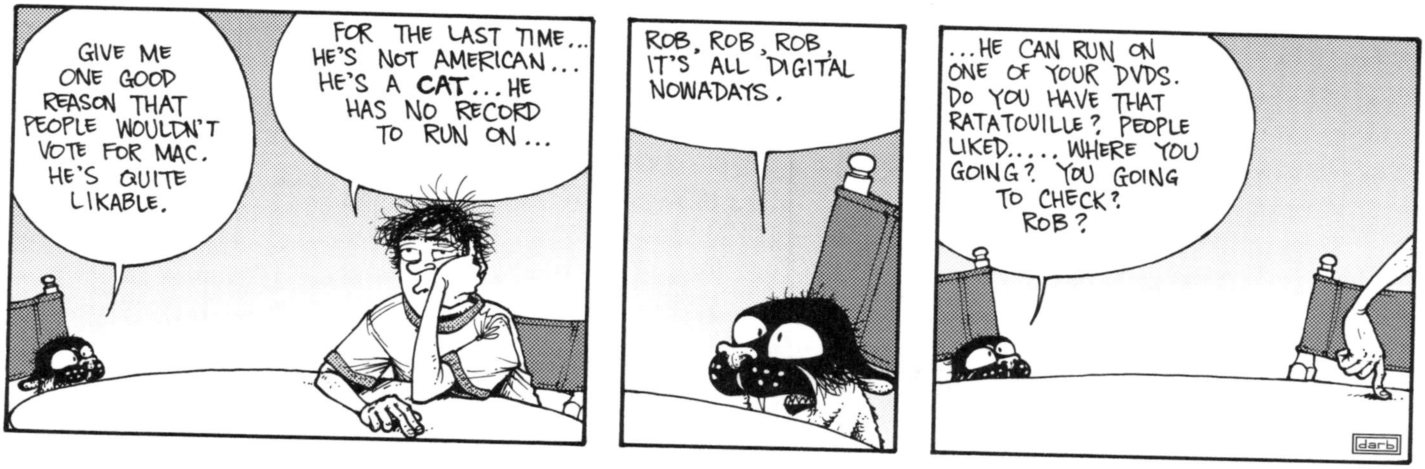
GIVE ME ONE GOOD REASON THAT PEOPLE WOULDN'T VOTE FOR MAC. HE'S QUITE LIKABLE.
FOR THE LAST TIME... HE'S NOT AMERICAN... HE'S A **CAT**... HE HAS NO RECORD TO RUN ON...
ROB, ROB, ROB, IT'S ALL DIGITAL NOWADAYS.
...HE CAN RUN ON ONE OF YOUR DVDS. DO YOU HAVE THAT RATATOUILLE? PEOPLE LIKED..... WHERE YOU GOING? YOU GOING TO CHECK? ROB?
darb

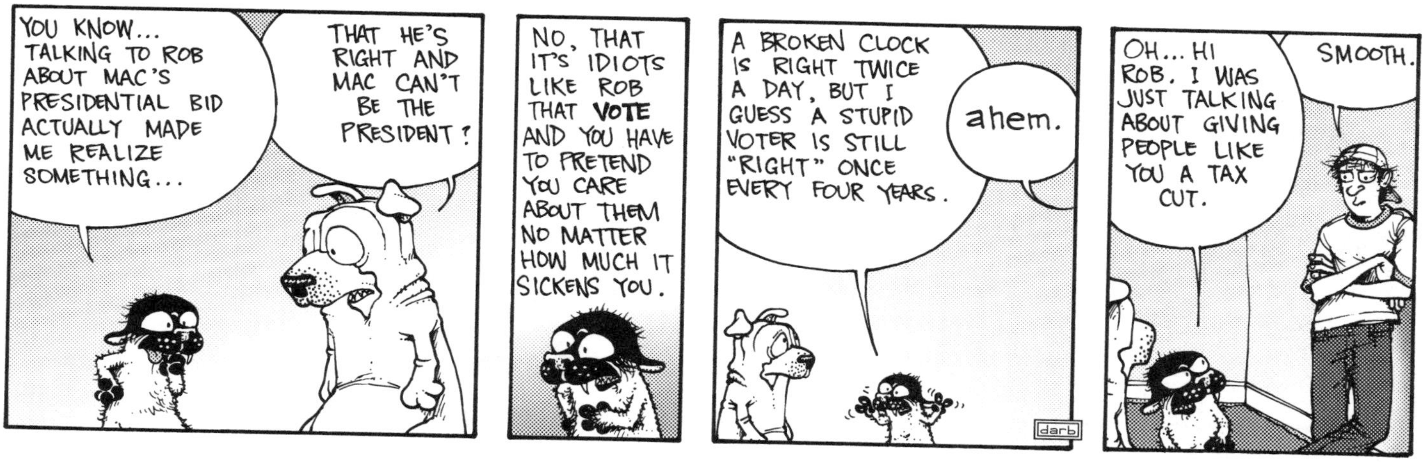
YOU KNOW... TALKING TO ROB ABOUT MAC'S PRESIDENTIAL BID ACTUALLY MADE ME REALIZE SOMETHING...
THAT HE'S RIGHT AND MAC CAN'T BE THE PRESIDENT?
NO, THAT IT'S IDIOTS LIKE ROB THAT **VOTE** AND YOU HAVE TO PRETEND YOU CARE ABOUT THEM NO MATTER HOW MUCH IT SICKENS YOU.
A BROKEN CLOCK IS RIGHT TWICE A DAY, BUT I GUESS A STUPID VOTER IS STILL "RIGHT" ONCE EVERY FOUR YEARS.
ahem.
darb
OH... HI ROB. I WAS JUST TALKING ABOUT GIVING PEOPLE LIKE YOU A TAX CUT.
SMOOTH.

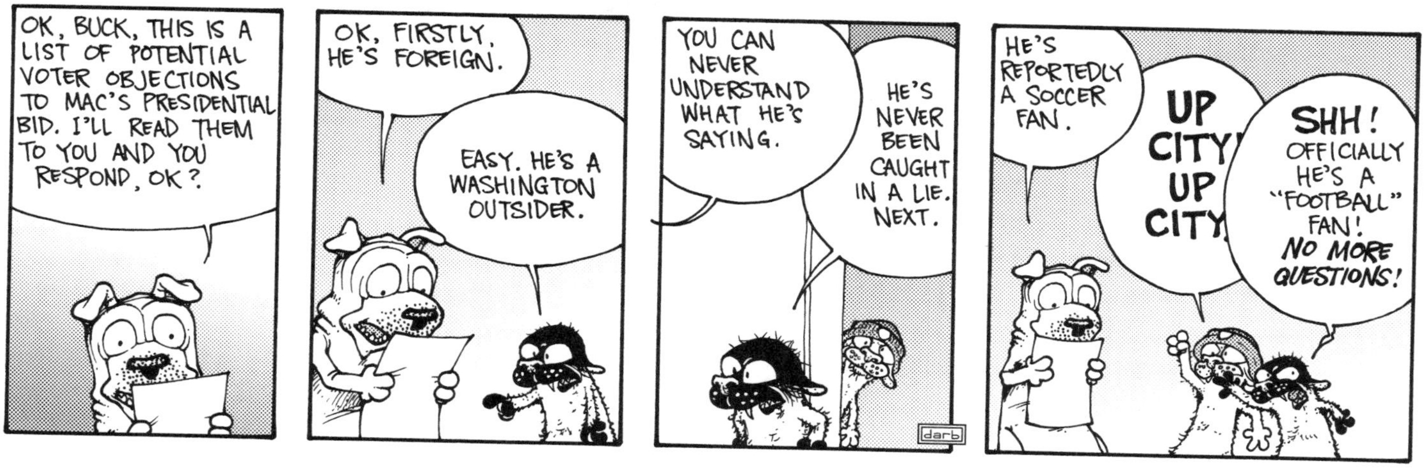
OK, BUCK, THIS IS A LIST OF POTENTIAL VOTER OBJECTIONS TO MAC'S PRESIDENTIAL BID. I'LL READ THEM TO YOU AND YOU RESPOND, OK?
OK, FIRSTLY, HE'S FOREIGN.
EASY. HE'S A WASHINGTON OUTSIDER.
YOU CAN NEVER UNDERSTAND WHAT HE'S SAYING.
HE'S NEVER BEEN CAUGHT IN A LIE. NEXT.
darb
HE'S REPORTEDLY A SOCCER FAN.
UP CITY! UP CITY!
SHH! OFFICIALLY HE'S A "FOOTBALL" FAN! NO MORE QUESTIONS!

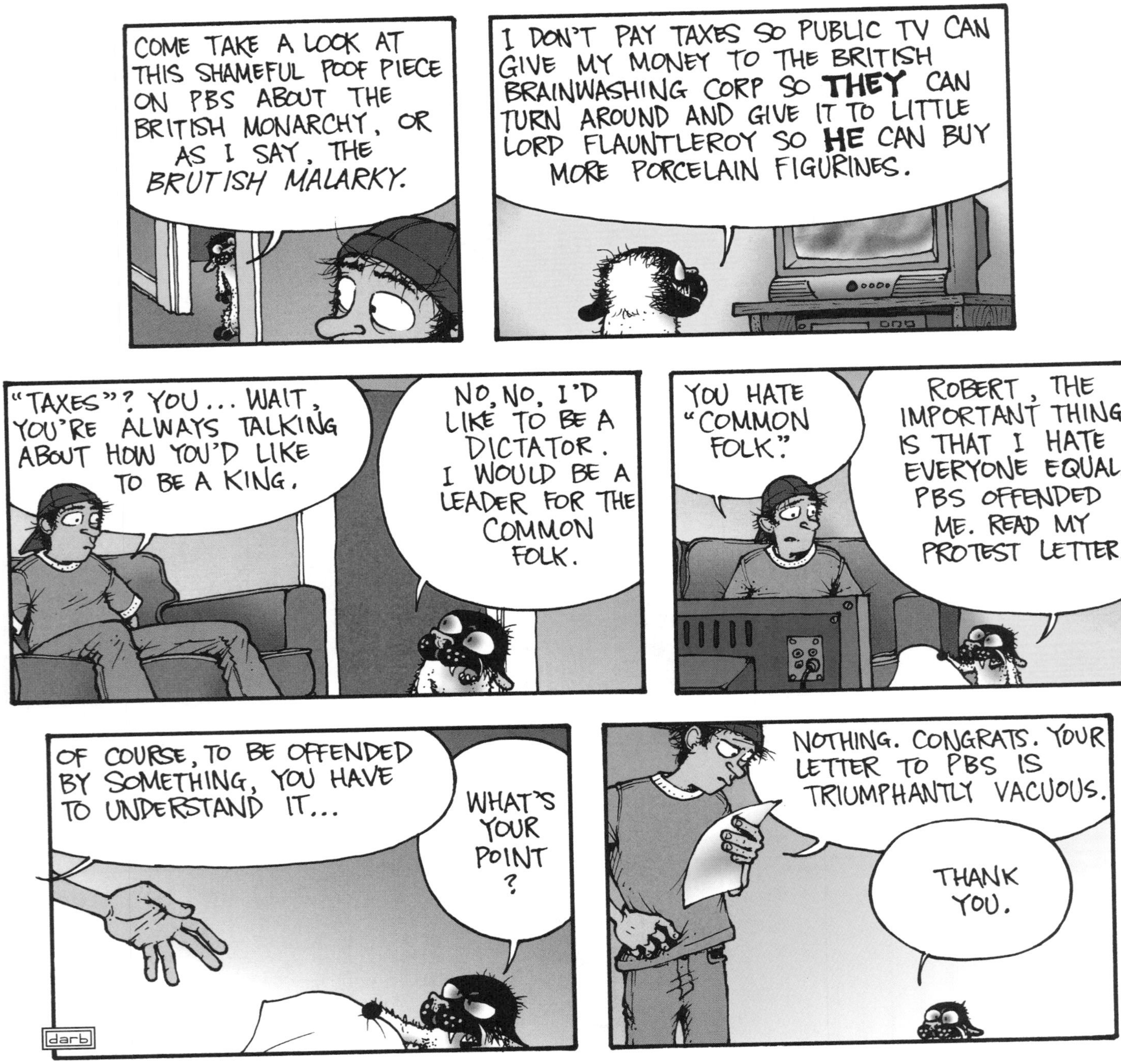
COME TAKE A LOOK AT THIS SHAMEFUL POOF PIECE ON PBS ABOUT THE BRITISH MONARCHY, OR AS I SAY, THE *BRUTISH MALARKY.*
I DON'T PAY TAXES SO PUBLIC TV CAN GIVE MY MONEY TO THE BRITISH BRAINWASHING CORP SO **THEY** CAN TURN AROUND AND GIVE IT TO LITTLE LORD FLAUNTLEROY SO **HE** CAN BUY MORE PORCELAIN FIGURINES.
"TAXES"? YOU... WAIT, YOU'RE ALWAYS TALKING ABOUT HOW YOU'D LIKE TO BE A KING.
NO, NO, I'D LIKE TO BE A DICTATOR. I WOULD BE A LEADER FOR THE COMMON FOLK.
YOU HATE "COMMON FOLK."
ROBERT, THE IMPORTANT THING IS THAT I HATE EVERYONE EQUAL. PBS OFFENDED ME. READ MY PROTEST LETTER.
OF COURSE, TO BE OFFENDED BY SOMETHING, YOU HAVE TO UNDERSTAND IT...
WHAT'S YOUR POINT ?
darb
NOTHING. CONGRATS. YOUR LETTER TO PBS IS TRIUMPHANTLY VACUOUS.
THANK YOU.

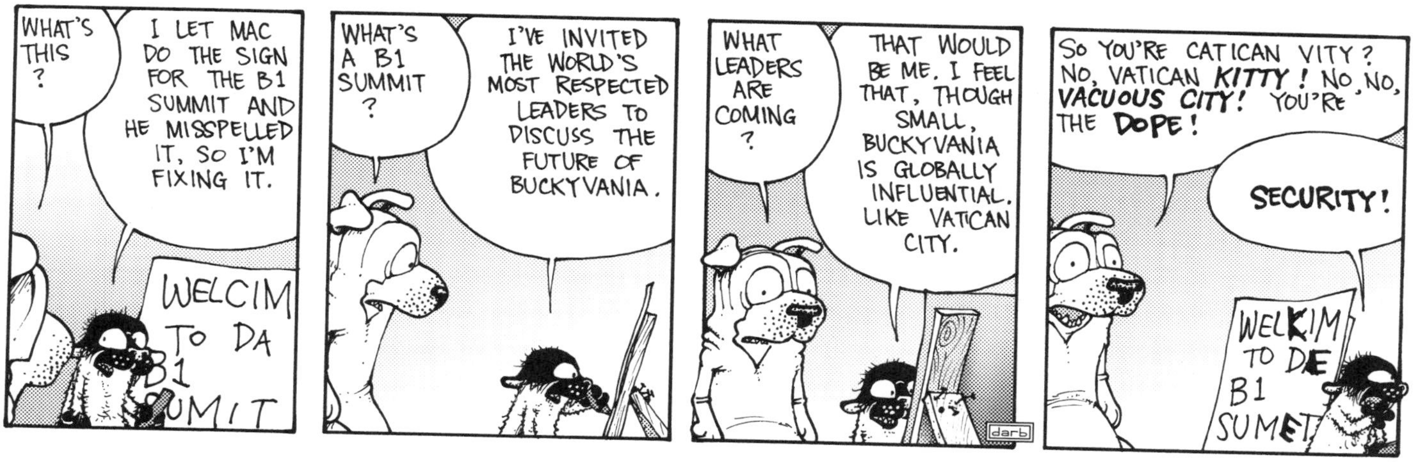
WHAT'S THIS ?
I LET MAC DO THE SIGN FOR THE B1 SUMMIT AND HE MISSPELLED IT, SO I'M FIXING IT.
WELCIM TO DA
WHAT'S A B1 SUMMIT ?
I'VE INVITED THE WORLD'S MOST RESPECTED LEADERS TO DISCUSS THE FUTURE OF BUCKYVANIA.
WHAT LEADERS ARE COMING ?
THAT WOULD BE ME. I FEEL THAT, THOUGH SMALL, BUCKYVANIA IS GLOBALLY INFLUENTIAL. LIKE VATICAN CITY.
darb
SO YOU'RE CATICAN VITY ? NO, VATICAN KITTY ! NO, NO, VACUOUS CITY! YOU'RE THE DOPE!
SECURITY!
WELKIM TO DE B1 SUMET

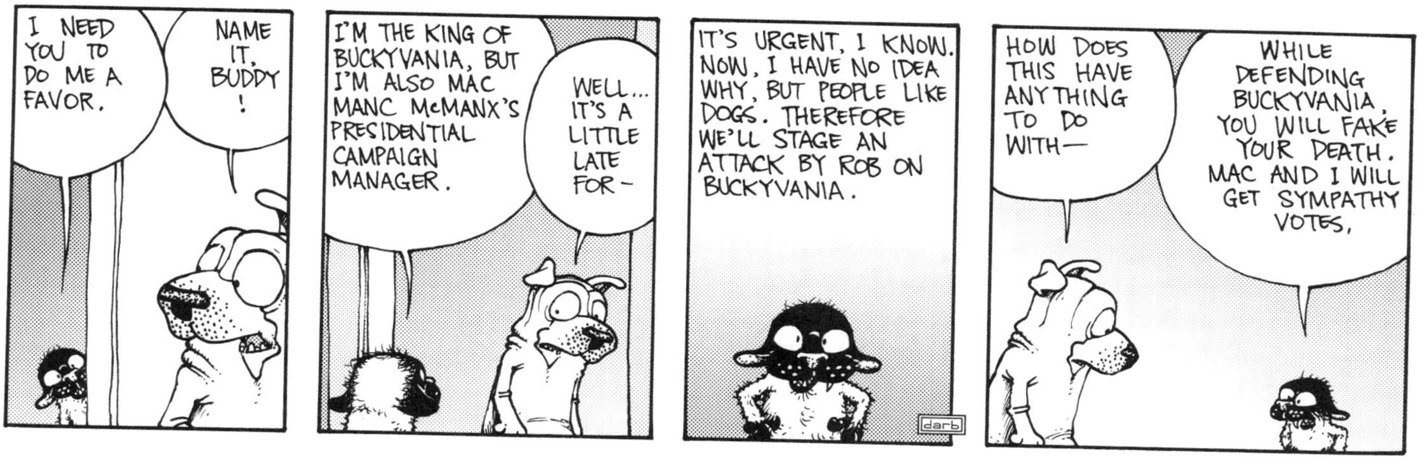
I NEED YOU TO DO ME A FAVOR.
NAME IT, BUDDY !
I'M THE KING OF BUCKYVANIA, BUT I'M ALSO MAC MANC McMANX'S PRESIDENTIAL CAMPAIGN MANAGER.
WELL... IT'S A LITTLE LATE FOR-
IT'S URGENT, I KNOW. NOW, I HAVE NO IDEA WHY, BUT PEOPLE LIKE DOGS. THEREFORE WE'LL STAGE AN ATTACK BY ROB ON BUCKYVANIA.
darb
HOW DOES THIS HAVE ANYTHING TO DO WITH—
WHILE DEFENDING BUCKYVANIA, YOU WILL FAKE YOUR DEATH. MAC AND I WILL GET SYMPATHY VOTES.

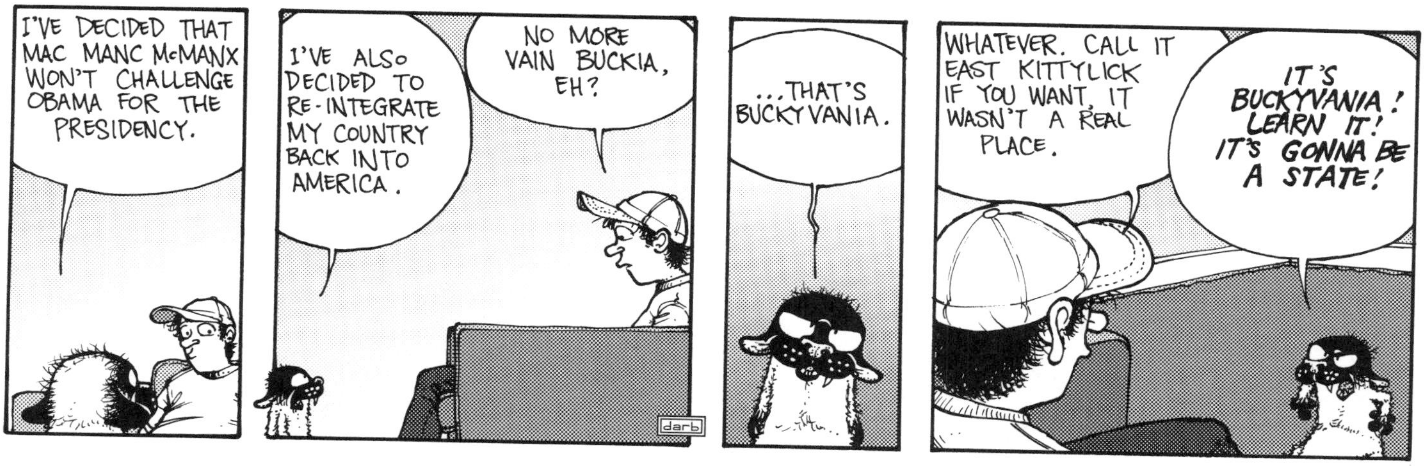
I'VE DECIDED THAT MAC MANC McMANX WON'T CHALLENGE OBAMA FOR THE PRESIDENCY.
I'VE ALSO DECIDED TO RE-INTEGRATE MY COUNTRY BACK INTO AMERICA.
NO MORE VAIN BUCKIA, EH?
darb
...THAT'S BUCKYVANIA.
WHATEVER. CALL IT EAST KITTYLICK IF YOU WANT, IT WASN'T A REAL PLACE.
IT'S BUCKYVANIA! LEARN IT! IT'S GONNA BE A STATE!

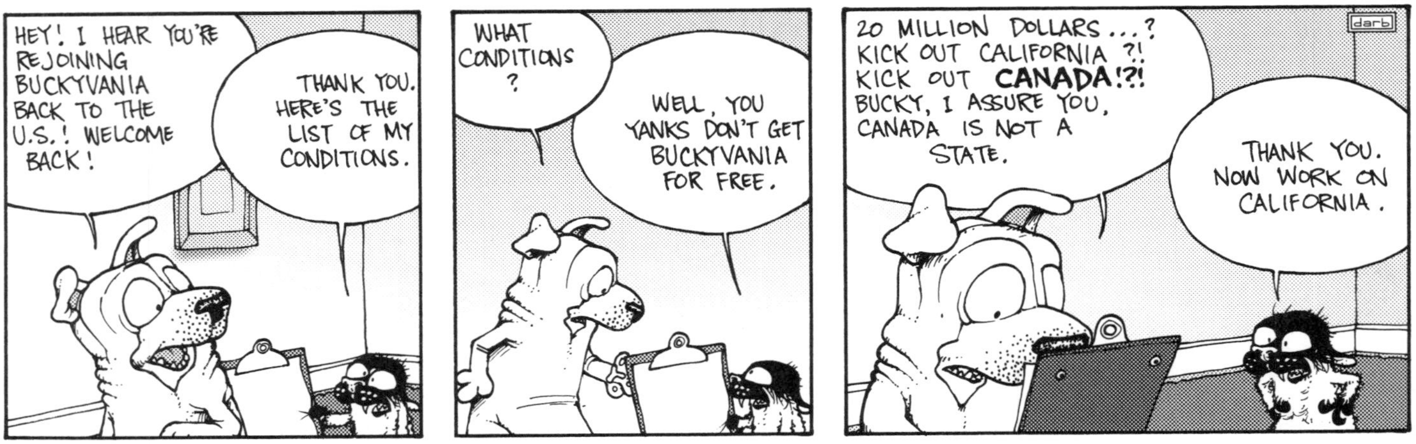
HEY! I HEAR YOU'RE REJOINING BUCKYVANIA BACK TO THE U.S.! WELCOME BACK!
THANK YOU. HERE'S THE LIST OF MY CONDITIONS.
WHAT CONDITIONS?
WELL, YOU YANKS DON'T GET BUCKYVANIA FOR FREE.
20 MILLION DOLLARS...? KICK OUT CALIFORNIA ?! KICK OUT CANADA!?! BUCKY, I ASSURE YOU, CANADA IS NOT A STATE.
THANK YOU. NOW WORK ON CALIFORNIA.
darb

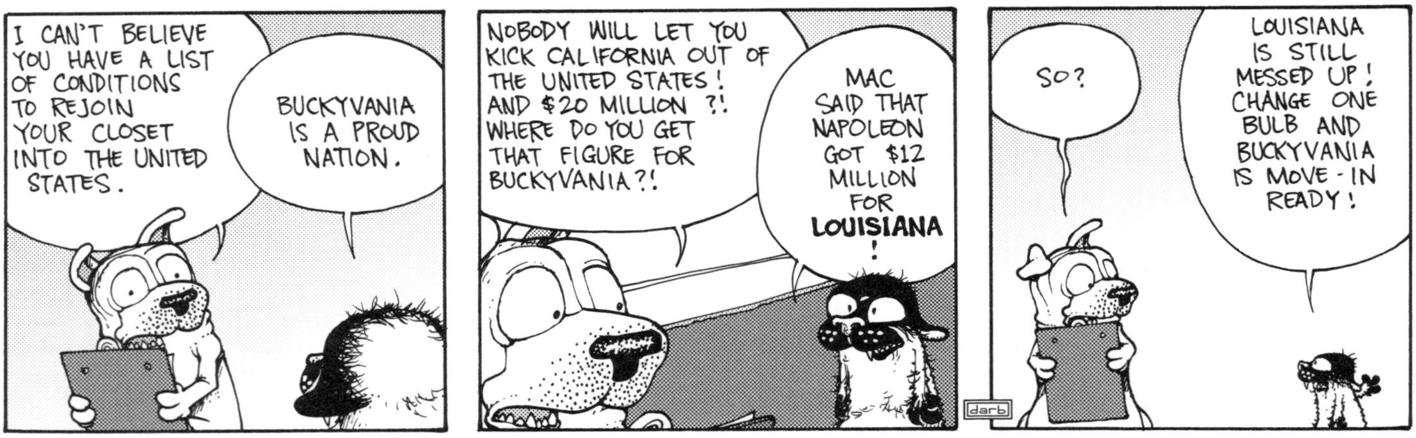
I CAN'T BELIEVE YOU HAVE A LIST OF CONDITIONS TO REJOIN YOUR CLOSET INTO THE UNITED STATES.
BUCKYVANIA IS A PROUD NATION.
NOBODY WILL LET YOU KICK CALIFORNIA OUT OF THE UNITED STATES! AND $20 MILLION ?! WHERE DO YOU GET THAT FIGURE FOR BUCKYVANIA?!
MAC SAID THAT NAPOLEON GOT $12 MILLION FOR LOUISIANA!
darb
SO?
LOUISIANA IS STILL MESSED UP! CHANGE ONE BULB AND BUCKYVANIA IS MOVE-IN READY!

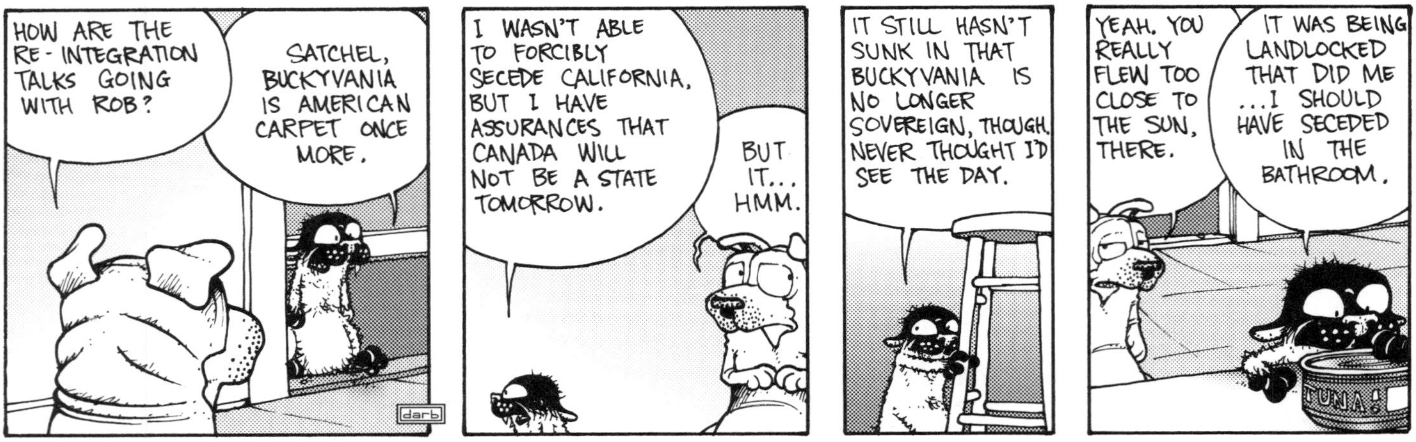
HOW ARE THE RE-INTEGRATION TALKS GOING WITH ROB?
SATCHEL, BUCKYVANIA IS AMERICAN CARPET ONCE MORE.
darb
I WASN'T ABLE TO FORCIBLY SECEDE CALIFORNIA, BUT I HAVE ASSURANCES THAT CANADA WILL NOT BE A STATE TOMORROW.
BUT IT... HMM.
IT STILL HASN'T SUNK IN THAT BUCKYVANIA IS NO LONGER SOVEREIGN, THOUGH. NEVER THOUGHT I'D SEE THE DAY.
YEAH. YOU REALLY FLEW TOO CLOSE TO THE SUN, THERE.
IT WAS BEING LANDLOCKED THAT DID ME ...I SHOULD HAVE SECEDED IN THE BATHROOM.
TUNA!

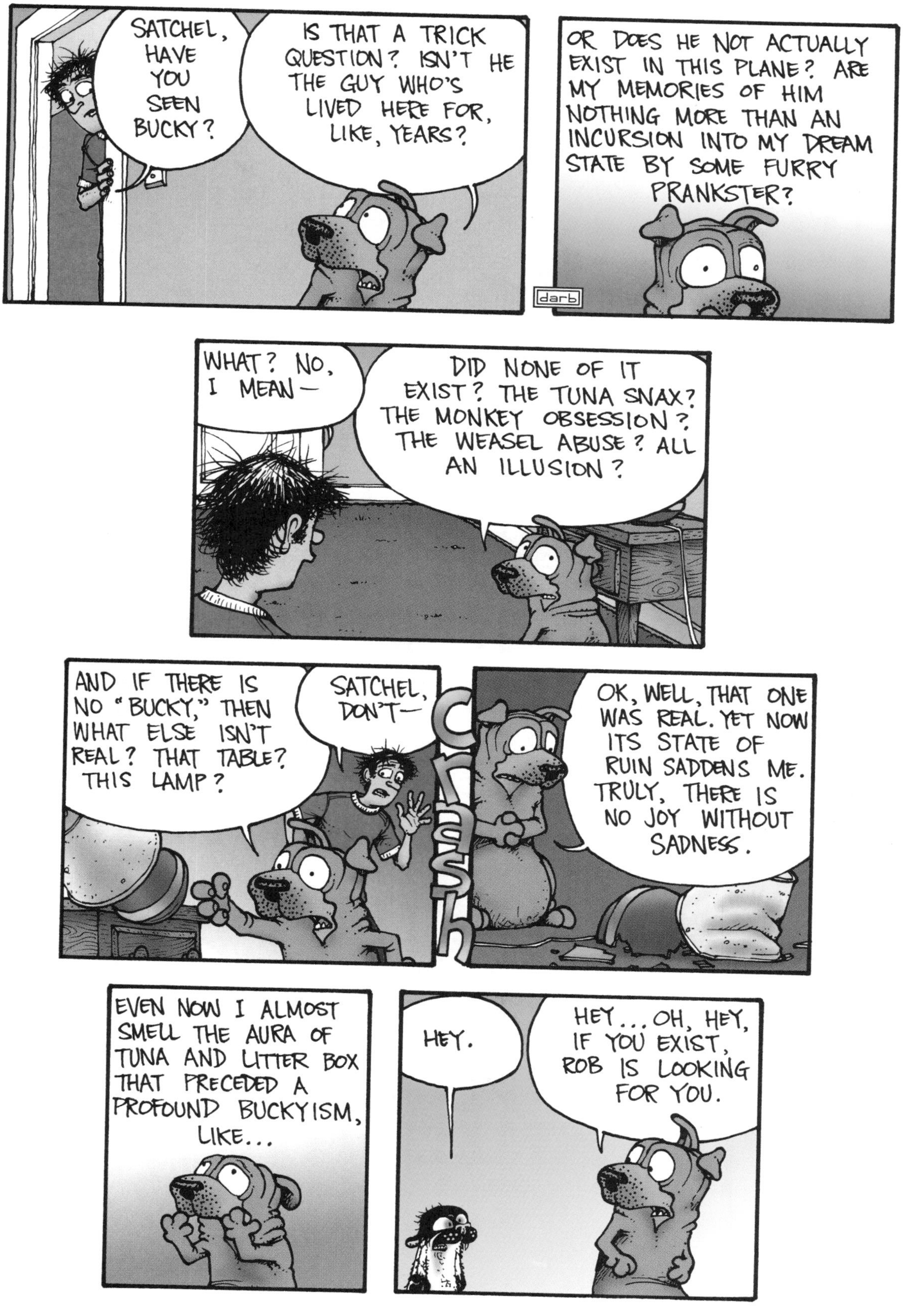
SATCHEL, HAVE YOU SEEN BUCKY?
IS THAT A TRICK QUESTION? ISN'T HE THE GUY WHO'S LIVED HERE FOR, LIKE, YEARS?
darb
OR DOES HE NOT ACTUALLY EXIST IN THIS PLANE? ARE MY MEMORIES OF HIM NOTHING MORE THAN AN INCURSION INTO MY DREAM STATE BY SOME FURRY PRANKSTER?
WHAT? NO, I MEAN—
DID NONE OF IT EXIST? THE TUNA SNAX? THE MONKEY OBSESSION? THE WEASEL ABUSE? ALL AN ILLUSION?
AND IF THERE IS NO "BUCKY," THEN WHAT ELSE ISN'T REAL? THAT TABLE? THIS LAMP?
SATCHEL, DON'T—
crash
OK, WELL, THAT ONE WAS REAL. YET NOW ITS STATE OF RUIN SADDENS ME. TRULY, THERE IS NO JOY WITHOUT SADNESS.
EVEN NOW I ALMOST SMELL THE AURA OF TUNA AND LITTER BOX THAT PRECEDED A PROFOUND BUCKYISM, LIKE...
HEY.
HEY... OH, HEY, IF YOU EXIST, ROB IS LOOKING FOR YOU.

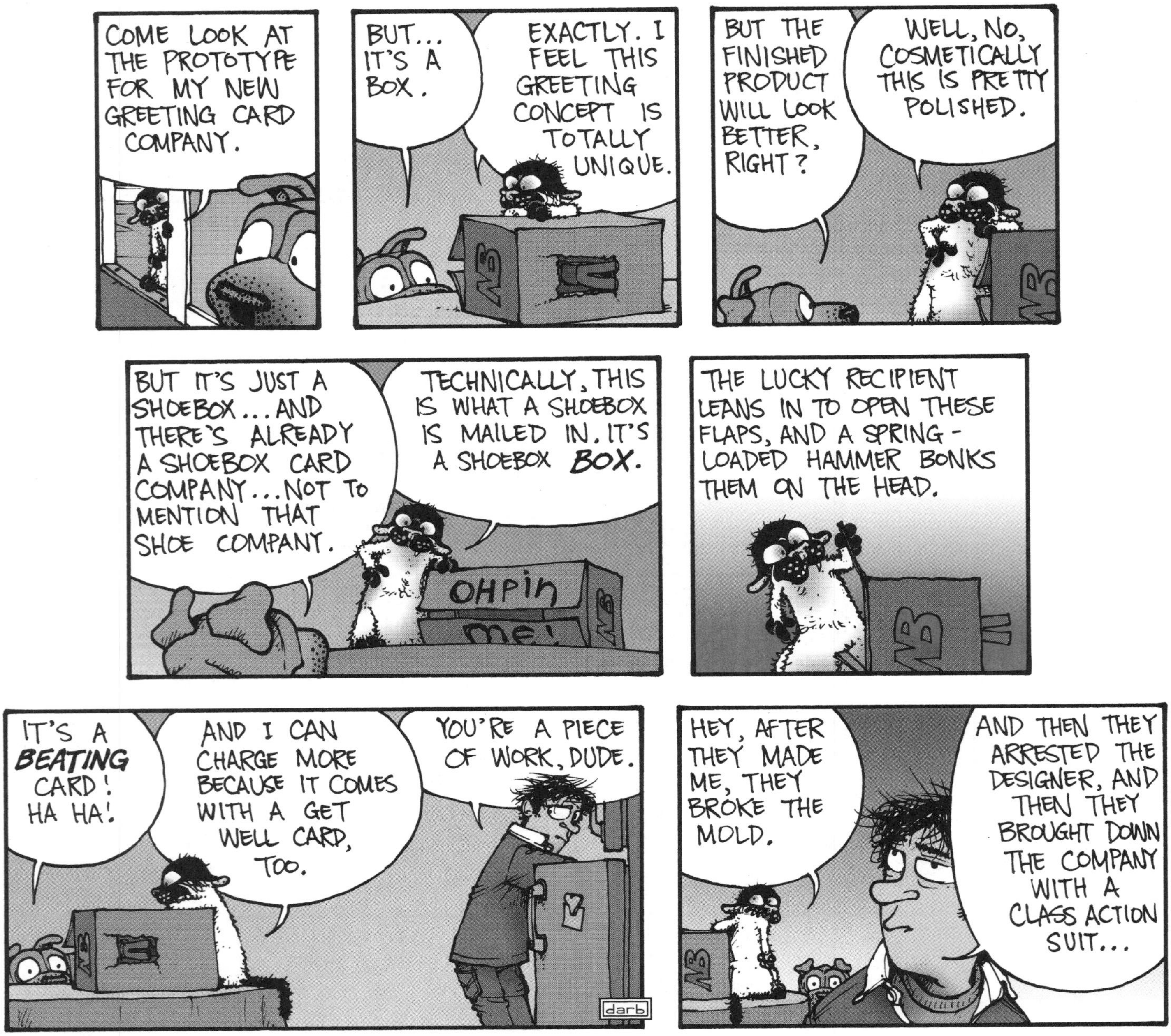
COME LOOK AT THE PROTOTYPE FOR MY NEW GREETING CARD COMPANY.
BUT... IT'S A BOX.
EXACTLY. I FEEL THIS GREETING CONCEPT IS TOTALLY UNIQUE.
BUT THE FINISHED PRODUCT WILL LOOK BETTER, RIGHT?
WELL, NO, COSMETICALLY THIS IS PRETTY POLISHED.
BUT IT'S JUST A SHOEBOX... AND THERE'S ALREADY A SHOEBOX CARD COMPANY... NOT TO MENTION THAT SHOE COMPANY.
TECHNICALLY, THIS IS WHAT A SHOEBOX IS MAILED IN. IT'S A SHOEBOX **BOX**.
OHPin
me!
THE LUCKY RECIPIENT LEANS IN TO OPEN THESE FLAPS, AND A SPRING-LOADED HAMMER BONKS THEM ON THE HEAD.
IT'S A **BEATING** CARD! HA HA!
AND I CAN CHARGE MORE BECAUSE IT COMES WITH A GET WELL CARD, TOO.
YOU'RE A PIECE OF WORK, DUDE.
darb
HEY, AFTER THEY MADE ME, THEY BROKE THE MOLD.
AND THEN THEY ARRESTED THE DESIGNER, AND THEN THEY BROUGHT DOWN THE COMPANY WITH A CLASS ACTION SUIT...

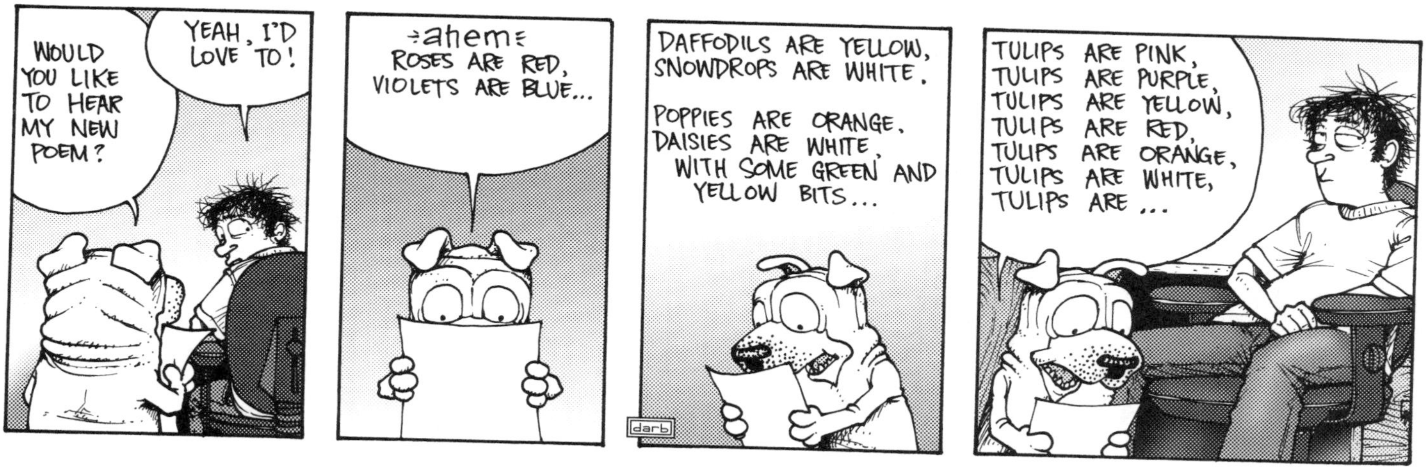
WOULD YOU LIKE TO HEAR MY NEW POEM?
YEAH, I'D LOVE TO!
ahem
ROSES ARE RED, VIOLETS ARE BLUE...
DAFFODILS ARE YELLOW, SNOWDROPS ARE WHITE.
POPPIES ARE ORANGE. DAISIES ARE WHITE, WITH SOME GREEN AND YELLOW BITS...
TULIPS ARE PINK, TULIPS ARE PURPLE, TULIPS ARE YELLOW, TULIPS ARE RED, TULIPS ARE ORANGE, TULIPS ARE WHITE, TULIPS ARE...
darb

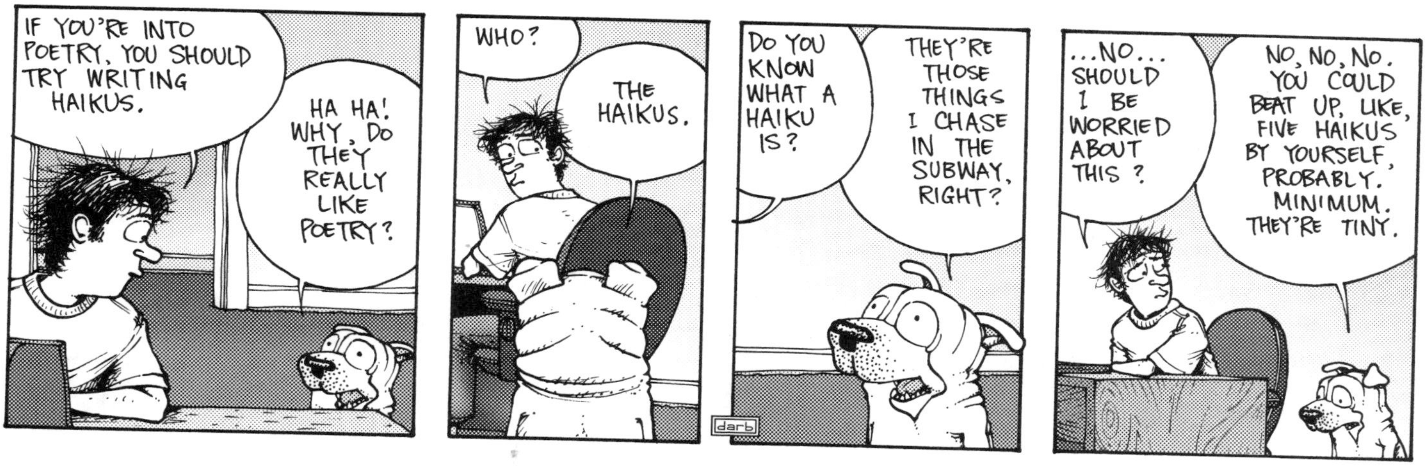
IF YOU'RE INTO POETRY, YOU SHOULD TRY WRITING HAIKUS.
HA HA! WHY, DO THEY REALLY LIKE POETRY?
WHO?
THE HAIKUS.
DO YOU KNOW WHAT A HAIKU IS?
THEY'RE THOSE THINGS I CHASE IN THE SUBWAY, RIGHT?
darb
...NO... SHOULD I BE WORRIED ABOUT THIS?
NO, NO, NO. YOU COULD BEAT UP, LIKE, FIVE HAIKUS BY YOURSELF, PROBABLY. MINIMUM. THEY'RE TINY.

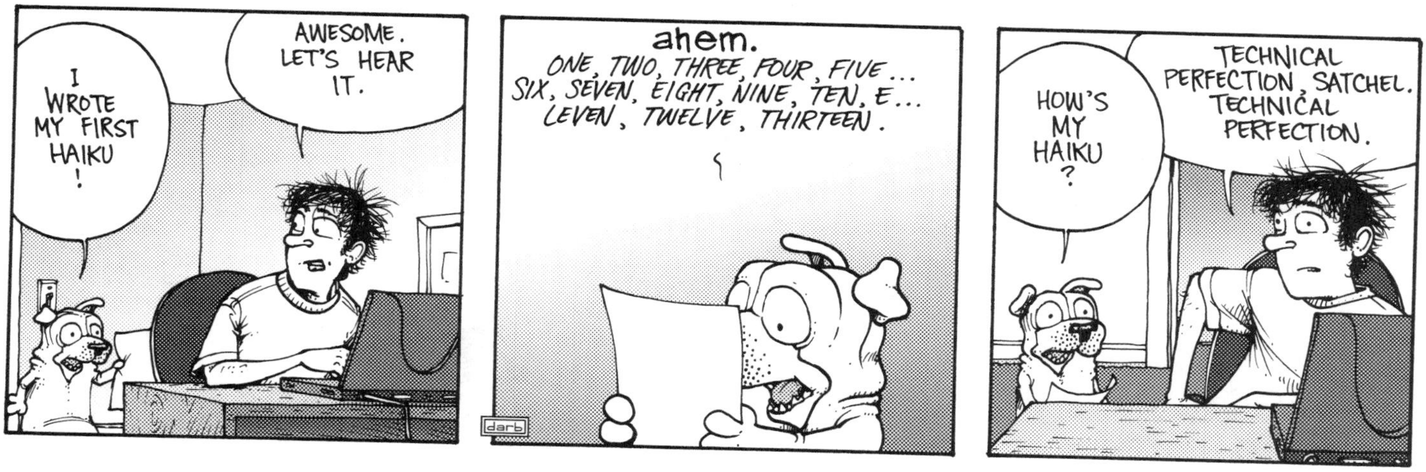
I WROTE MY FIRST HAIKU!
AWESOME. LET'S HEAR IT.
ahem.
ONE, TWO, THREE, FOUR, FIVE... SIX, SEVEN, EIGHT, NINE, TEN, E... LEVEN, TWELVE, THIRTEEN.
darb
HOW'S MY HAIKU?
TECHNICAL PERFECTION, SATCHEL. TECHNICAL PERFECTION.

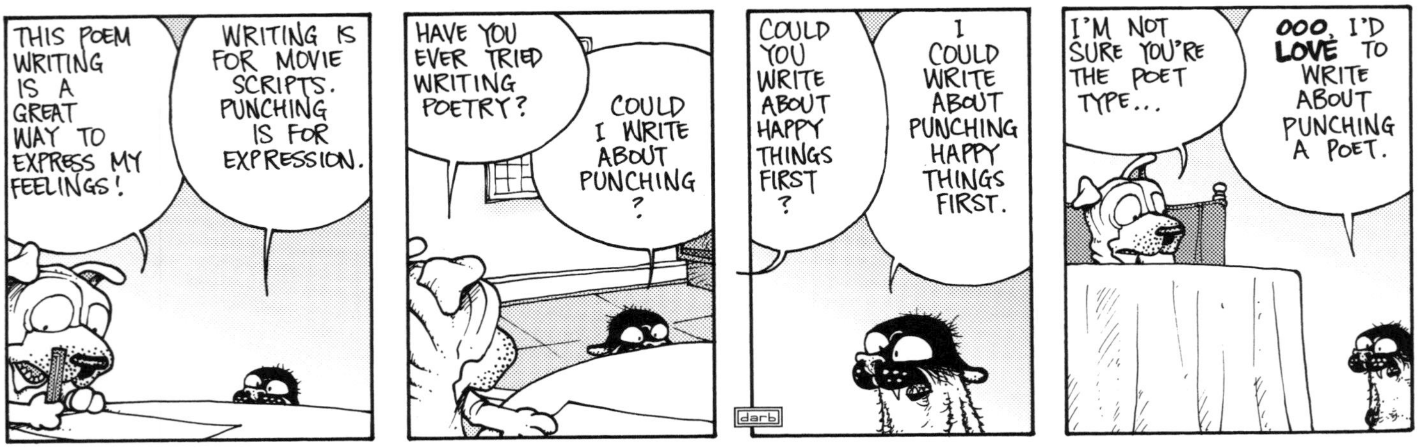
THIS POEM WRITING IS A GREAT WAY TO EXPRESS MY FEELINGS!
WRITING IS FOR MOVIE SCRIPTS. PUNCHING IS FOR EXPRESSION.
HAVE YOU EVER TRIED WRITING POETRY?
COULD I WRITE ABOUT PUNCHING?
COULD YOU WRITE ABOUT HAPPY THINGS FIRST?
I COULD WRITE ABOUT PUNCHING HAPPY THINGS FIRST.
I'M NOT SURE YOU'RE THE POET TYPE...
OOO, I'D LOVE TO WRITE ABOUT PUNCHING A POET.
darb

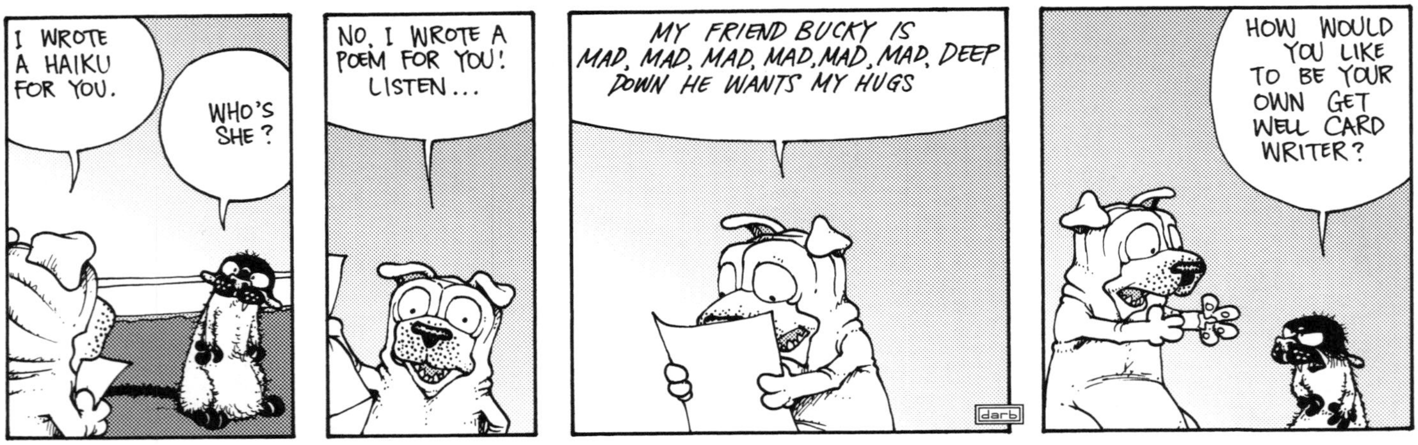
I WROTE A HAIKU FOR YOU.
WHO'S SHE?
NO, I WROTE A POEM FOR YOU! LISTEN...
MY FRIEND BUCKY IS MAD, MAD, MAD, MAD, MAD, MAD, DEEP DOWN HE WANTS MY HUGS
HOW WOULD YOU LIKE TO BE YOUR OWN GET WELL CARD WRITER?
darb

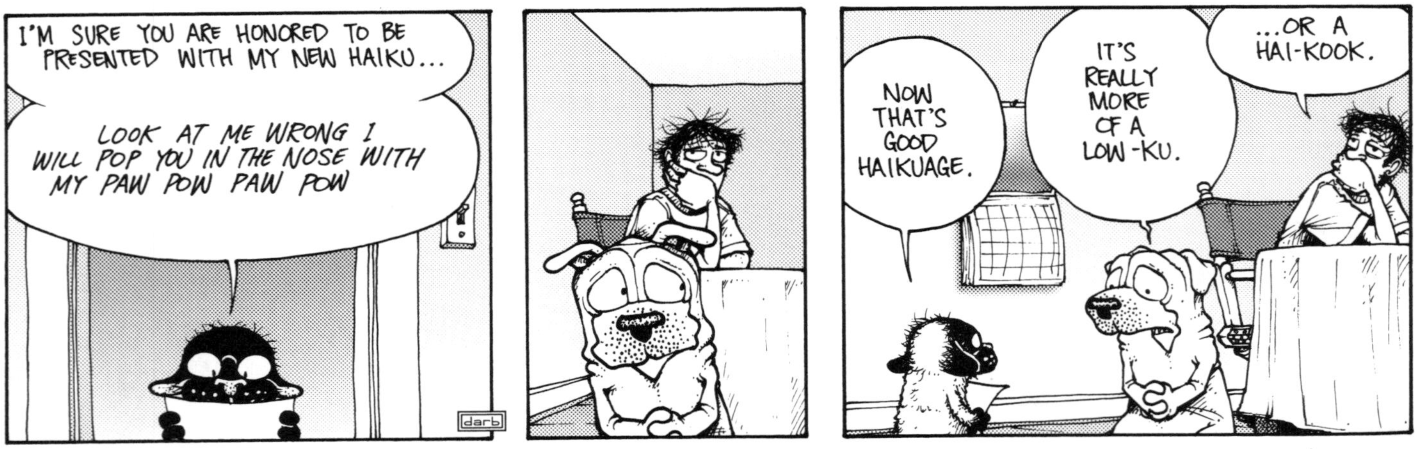
I'M SURE YOU ARE HONORED TO BE PRESENTED WITH MY NEW HAIKU...
LOOK AT ME WRONG I WILL POP YOU IN THE NOSE WITH MY PAW POW PAW POW
NOW THAT'S GOOD HAIKUAGE.
IT'S REALLY MORE OF A LOW-KU.
...OR A HAI-KOOK.
darb

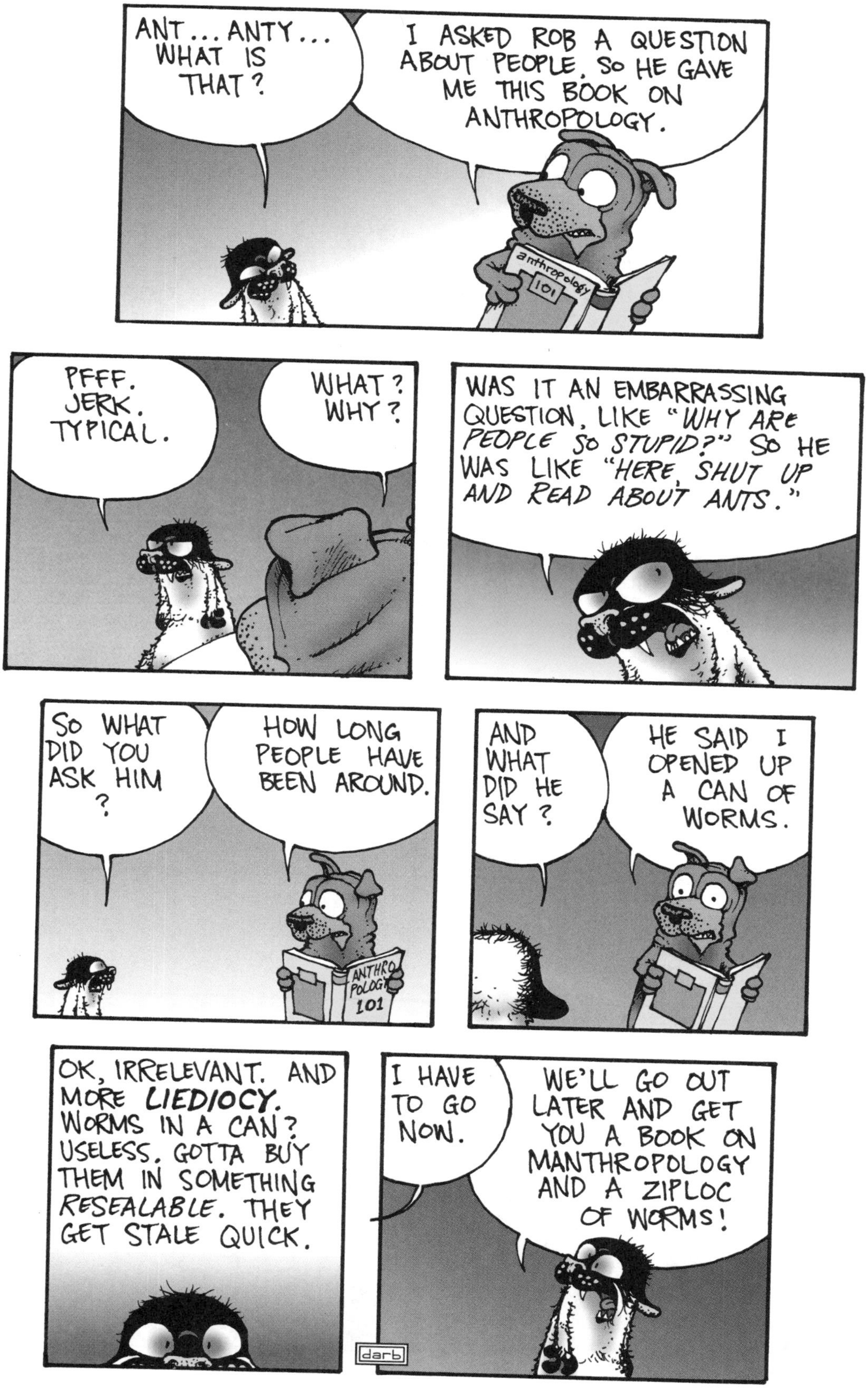
ANT... ANTY... WHAT IS THAT?
I ASKED ROB A QUESTION ABOUT PEOPLE, SO HE GAVE ME THIS BOOK ON ANTHROPOLOGY.
anthropology 101
PFFF. JERK. TYPICAL.
WHAT? WHY?
WAS IT AN EMBARRASSING QUESTION, LIKE "WHY ARE PEOPLE SO STUPID?" SO HE WAS LIKE "HERE, SHUT UP AND READ ABOUT ANTS."
SO WHAT DID YOU ASK HIM?
HOW LONG PEOPLE HAVE BEEN AROUND.
ANTHRO POLOGY 101
AND WHAT DID HE SAY?
HE SAID I OPENED UP A CAN OF WORMS.
OK, IRRELEVANT. AND MORE LIEDIOCY. WORMS IN A CAN? USELESS. GOTTA BUY THEM IN SOMETHING RESEALABLE. THEY GET STALE QUICK.
darb
I HAVE TO GO NOW.
WE'LL GO OUT LATER AND GET YOU A BOOK ON MANTHROPOLOGY AND A ZIPLOC OF WORMS!

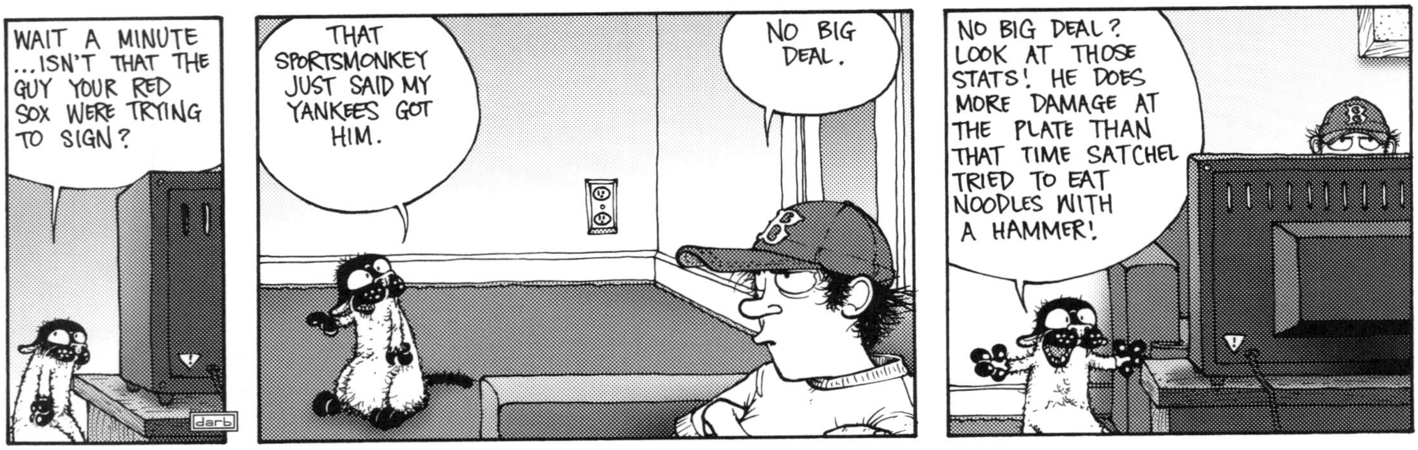
WAIT A MINUTE ...ISN'T THAT THE GUY YOUR RED SOX WERE TRYING TO SIGN?
darb
THAT SPORTSMONKEY JUST SAID MY YANKEES GOT HIM.
NO BIG DEAL.
NO BIG DEAL? LOOK AT THOSE STATS! HE DOES MORE DAMAGE AT THE PLATE THAN THAT TIME SATCHEL TRIED TO EAT NOODLES WITH A HAMMER!

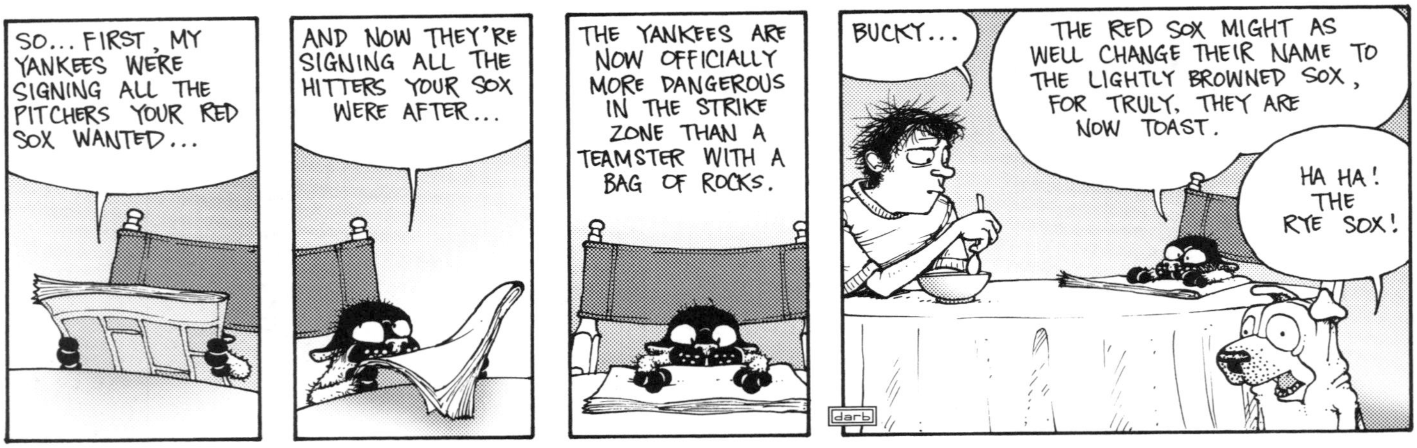
SO... FIRST, MY YANKEES WERE SIGNING ALL THE PITCHERS YOUR RED SOX WANTED...
AND NOW THEY'RE SIGNING ALL THE HITTERS YOUR SOX WERE AFTER...
THE YANKEES ARE NOW OFFICIALLY MORE DANGEROUS IN THE STRIKE ZONE THAN A TEAMSTER WITH A BAG OF ROCKS.
darb
BUCKY...
THE RED SOX MIGHT AS WELL CHANGE THEIR NAME TO THE LIGHTLY BROWNED SOX, FOR TRULY, THEY ARE NOW TOAST.
HA HA! THE RYE SOX!

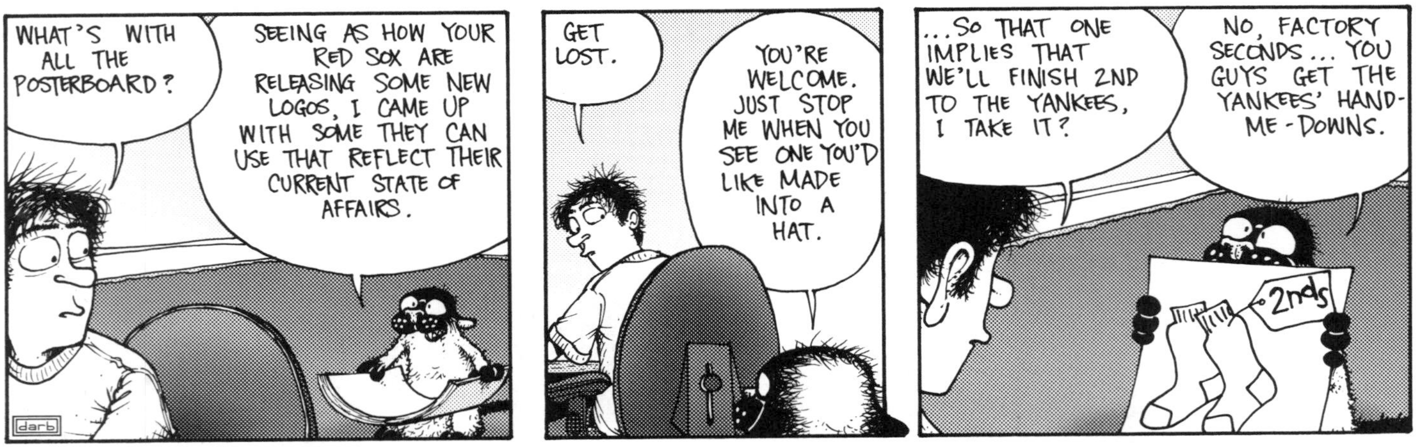
WHAT'S WITH ALL THE POSTERBOARD?
SEEING AS HOW YOUR RED SOX ARE RELEASING SOME NEW LOGOS, I CAME UP WITH SOME THEY CAN USE THAT REFLECT THEIR CURRENT STATE OF AFFAIRS.
darb
GET LOST.
YOU'RE WELCOME. JUST STOP ME WHEN YOU SEE ONE YOU'D LIKE MADE INTO A HAT.
...SO THAT ONE IMPLIES THAT WE'LL FINISH 2ND TO THE YANKEES, I TAKE IT?
NO, FACTORY SECONDS... YOU GUYS GET THE YANKEES' HAND-ME-DOWNS.
2nds

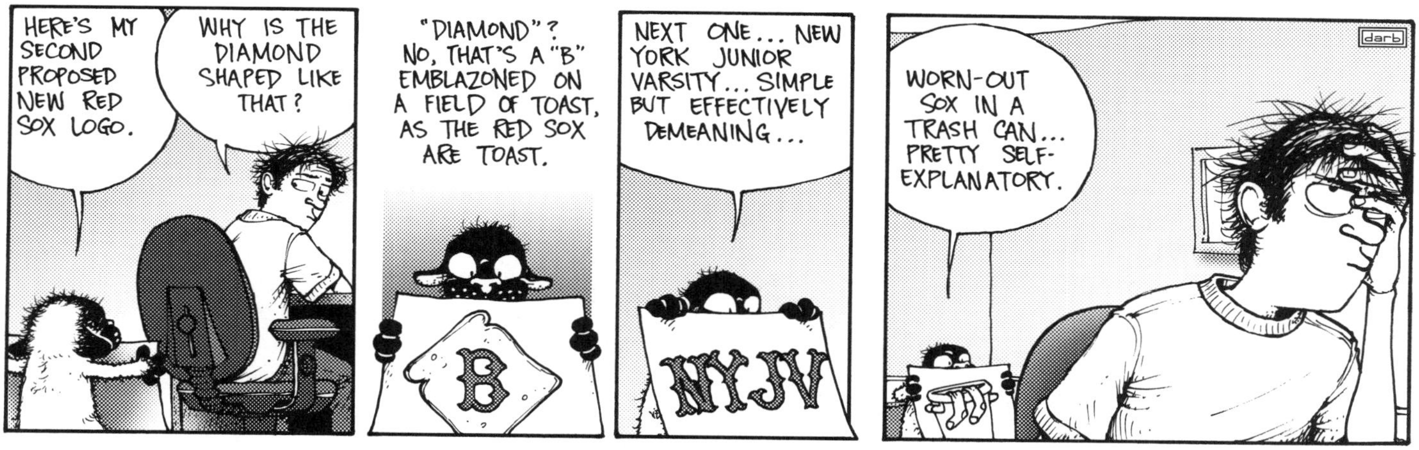
HERE'S MY SECOND PROPOSED NEW RED SOX LOGO.
WHY IS THE DIAMOND SHAPED LIKE THAT?
"DIAMOND"? NO, THAT'S A "B" EMBLAZONED ON A FIELD OF TOAST, AS THE RED SOX ARE TOAST.
B
NEXT ONE... NEW YORK JUNIOR VARSITY... SIMPLE BUT EFFECTIVELY DEMEANING...
NYJV
WORN-OUT SOX IN A TRASH CAN... PRETTY SELF-EXPLANATORY.
darb

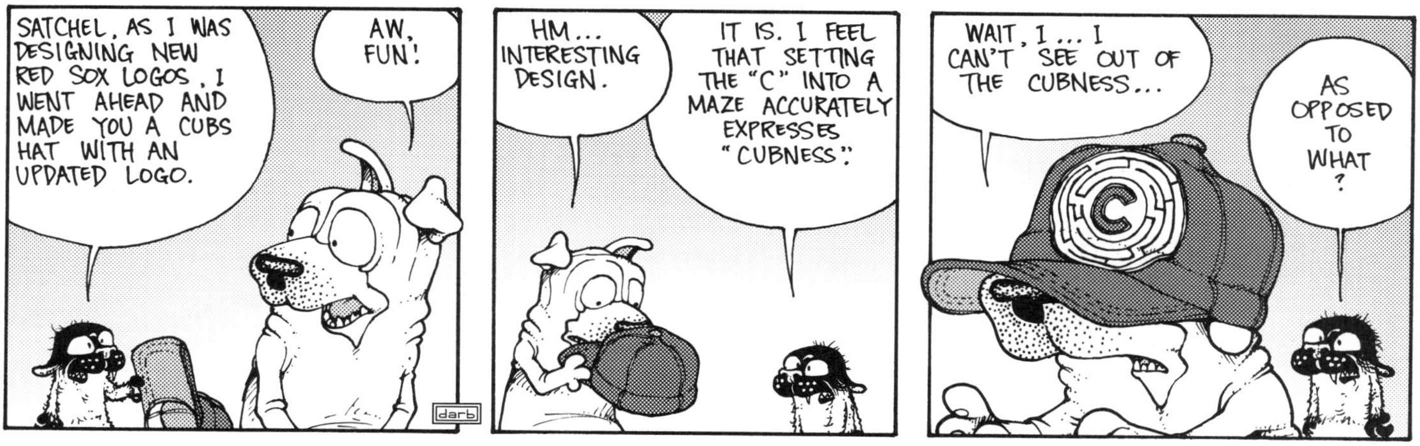
SATCHEL, AS I WAS DESIGNING NEW RED SOX LOGOS, I WENT AHEAD AND MADE YOU A CUBS HAT WITH AN UPDATED LOGO.
AW, FUN!
darb
HM... INTERESTING DESIGN.
IT IS. I FEEL THAT SETTING THE "C" INTO A MAZE ACCURATELY EXPRESSES "CUBNESS."
WAIT, I... I CAN'T SEE OUT OF THE CUBNESS...
AS OPPOSED TO WHAT?

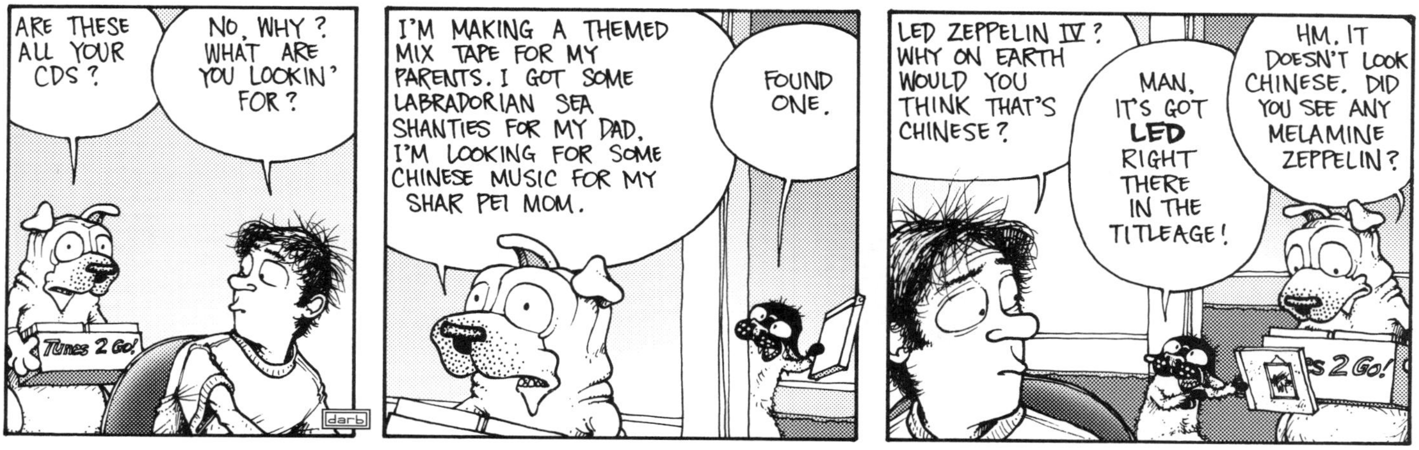
ARE THESE ALL YOUR CDS?
NO, WHY? WHAT ARE YOU LOOKIN' FOR?
Tunes 2 Go!
darb
I'M MAKING A THEMED MIX TAPE FOR MY PARENTS. I GOT SOME LABRADORIAN SEA SHANTIES FOR MY DAD. I'M LOOKING FOR SOME CHINESE MUSIC FOR MY SHAR PEI MOM.
FOUND ONE.
LED ZEPPELIN IV? WHY ON EARTH WOULD YOU THINK THAT'S CHINESE?
MAN, IT'S GOT **LED** RIGHT THERE IN THE TITLEAGE!
HM. IT DOESN'T LOOK CHINESE. DID YOU SEE ANY MELAMINE ZEPPELIN?

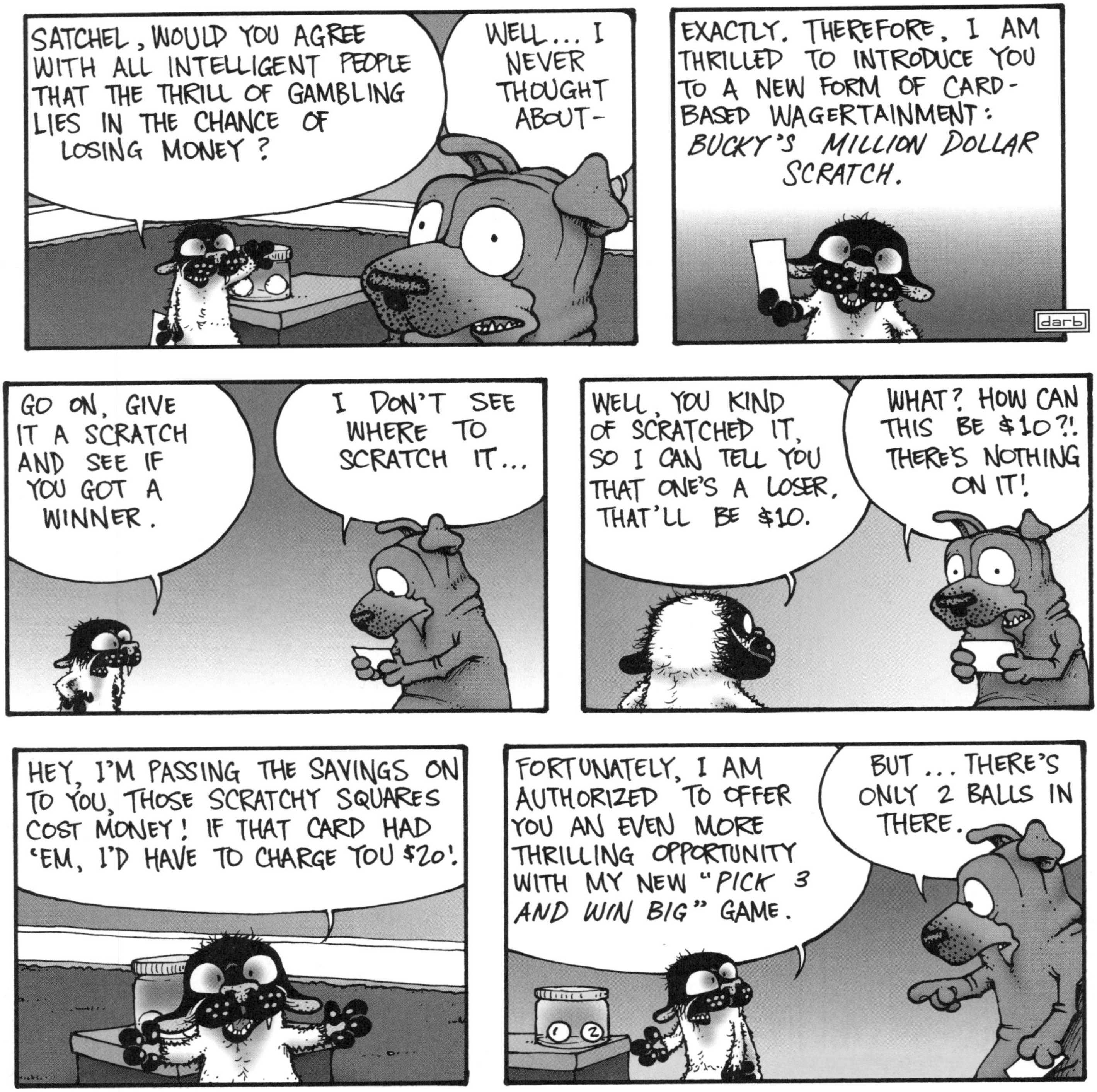
SATCHEL, WOULD YOU AGREE WITH ALL INTELLIGENT PEOPLE THAT THE THRILL OF GAMBLING LIES IN THE CHANCE OF LOSING MONEY?
WELL... I NEVER THOUGHT ABOUT-
EXACTLY. THEREFORE, I AM THRILLED TO INTRODUCE YOU TO A NEW FORM OF CARD-BASED WAGERTAINMENT: BUCKY'S MILLION DOLLAR SCRATCH.
darb
GO ON, GIVE IT A SCRATCH AND SEE IF YOU GOT A WINNER.
I DON'T SEE WHERE TO SCRATCH IT...
WELL, YOU KIND OF SCRATCHED IT, SO I CAN TELL YOU THAT ONE'S A LOSER. THAT'LL BE $10.
WHAT? HOW CAN THIS BE $10?! THERE'S NOTHING ON IT!
HEY, I'M PASSING THE SAVINGS ON TO YOU, THOSE SCRATCHY SQUARES COST MONEY! IF THAT CARD HAD 'EM, I'D HAVE TO CHARGE YOU $20!
FORTUNATELY, I AM AUTHORIZED TO OFFER YOU AN EVEN MORE THRILLING OPPORTUNITY WITH MY NEW "PICK 3 AND WIN BIG" GAME.
BUT... THERE'S ONLY 2 BALLS IN THERE.

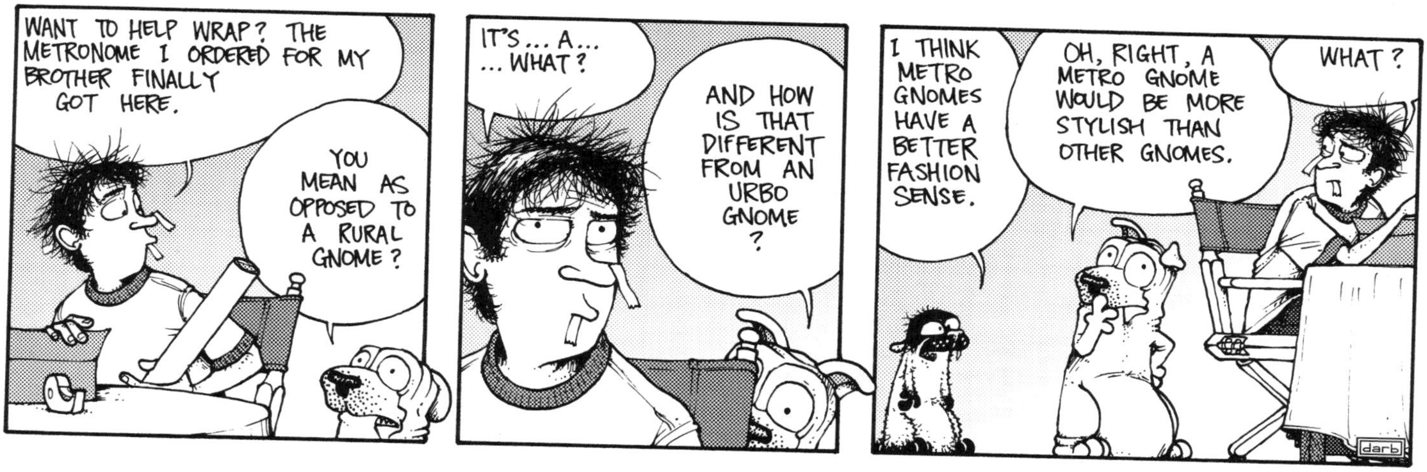
WANT TO HELP WRAP? THE METRONOME I ORDERED FOR MY BROTHER FINALLY GOT HERE.
YOU MEAN AS OPPOSED TO A RURAL GNOME?
IT'S... A... ...WHAT?
AND HOW IS THAT DIFFERENT FROM AN URBO GNOME?
I THINK METRO GNOMES HAVE A BETTER FASHION SENSE.
OH, RIGHT, A METRO GNOME WOULD BE MORE STYLISH THAN OTHER GNOMES.
WHAT?
darb

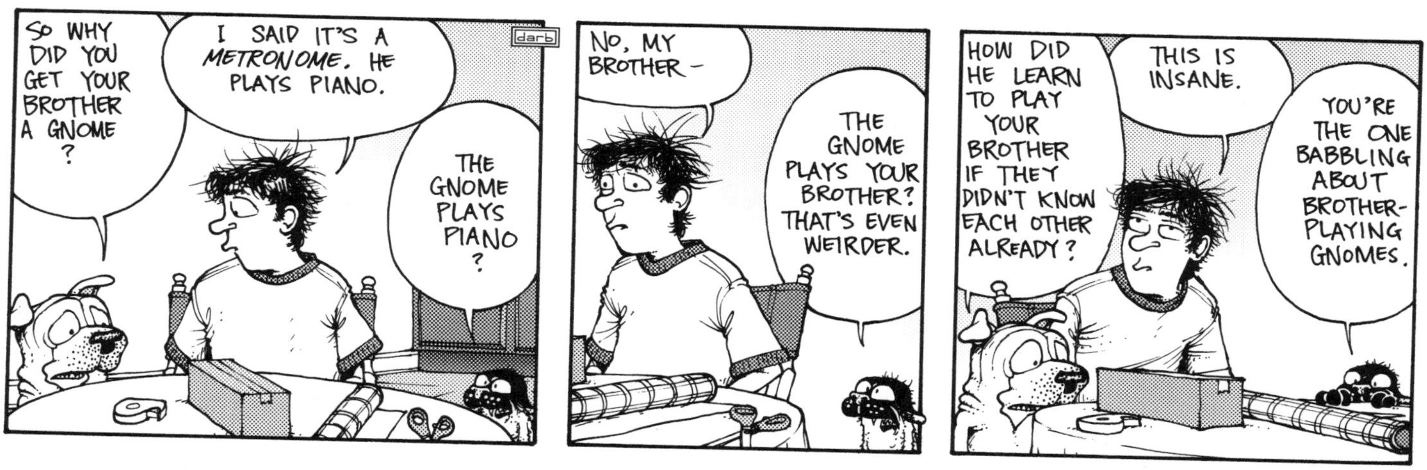
SO WHY DID YOU GET YOUR BROTHER A GNOME?
I SAID IT'S A *METRONOME*. HE PLAYS PIANO.
THE GNOME PLAYS PIANO?
darb
NO, MY BROTHER–
THE GNOME PLAYS YOUR BROTHER? THAT'S EVEN WEIRDER.
HOW DID HE LEARN TO PLAY YOUR BROTHER IF THEY DIDN'T KNOW EACH OTHER ALREADY?
THIS IS INSANE.
YOU'RE THE ONE BABBLING ABOUT BROTHER-PLAYING GNOMES.

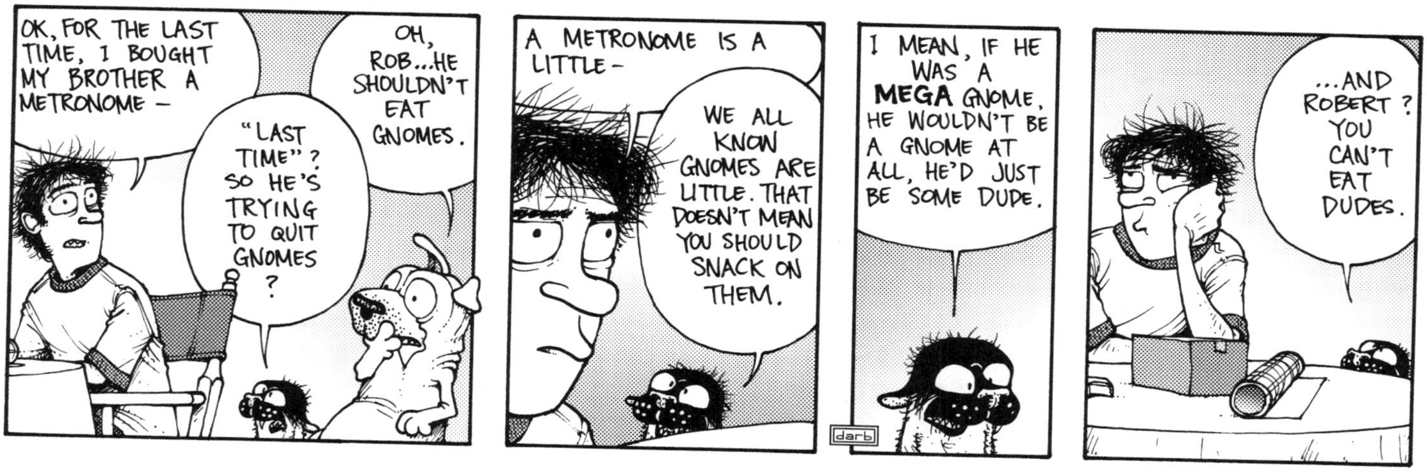
OK, FOR THE LAST TIME, I BOUGHT MY BROTHER A METRONOME–
OH, ROB...HE SHOULDN'T EAT GNOMES.
"LAST TIME"? SO HE'S TRYING TO QUIT GNOMES?
A METRONOME IS A LITTLE–
WE ALL KNOW GNOMES ARE LITTLE. THAT DOESN'T MEAN YOU SHOULD SNACK ON THEM.
I MEAN, IF HE WAS A **MEGA** GNOME, HE WOULDN'T BE A GNOME AT ALL, HE'D JUST BE SOME DUDE.
darb
...AND ROBERT? YOU CAN'T EAT DUDES.

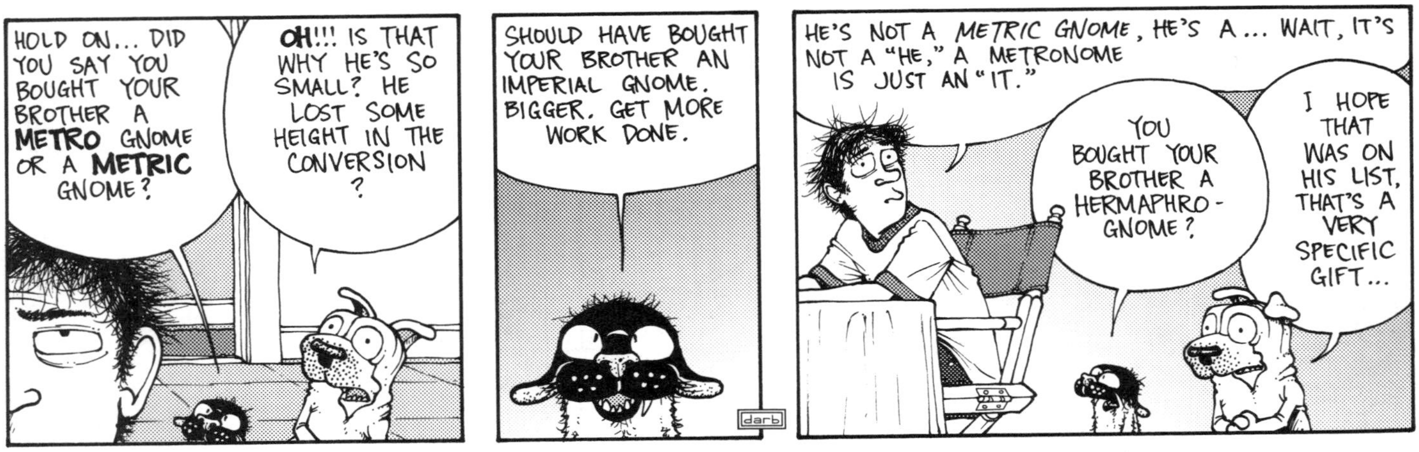
HOLD ON... DID YOU SAY YOU BOUGHT YOUR BROTHER A **METRO** GNOME OR A **METRIC** GNOME?
OH!!! IS THAT WHY HE'S SO SMALL? HE LOST SOME HEIGHT IN THE CONVERSION?
SHOULD HAVE BOUGHT YOUR BROTHER AN IMPERIAL GNOME. BIGGER. GET MORE WORK DONE.
darb
HE'S NOT A *METRIC GNOME*, HE'S A... WAIT, IT'S NOT A "HE," A METRONOME IS JUST AN "IT."
YOU BOUGHT YOUR BROTHER A HERMAPHRO-GNOME?
I HOPE THAT WAS ON HIS LIST, THAT'S A VERY SPECIFIC GIFT...

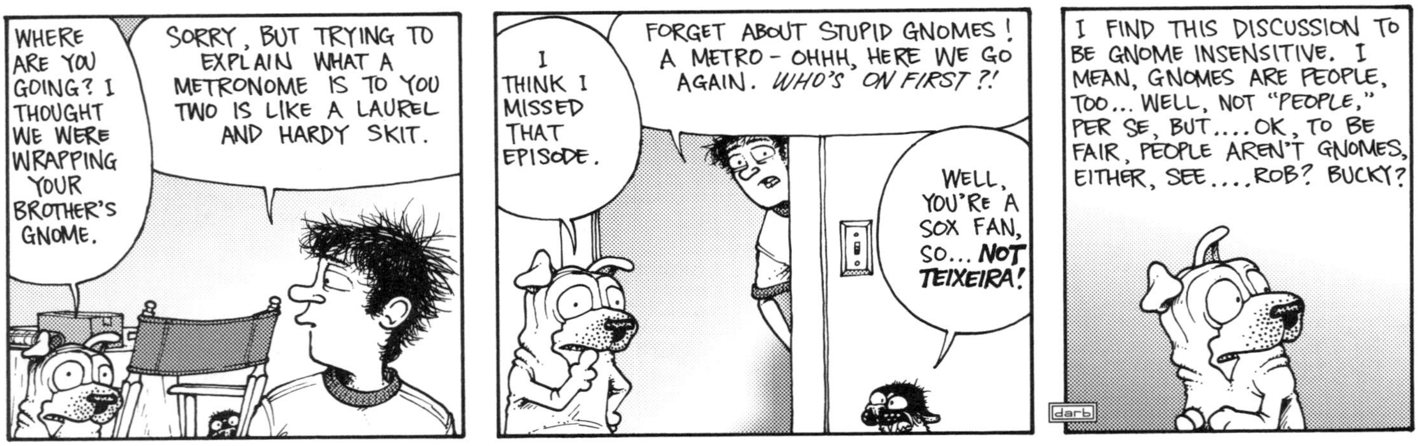
WHERE ARE YOU GOING? I THOUGHT WE WERE WRAPPING YOUR BROTHER'S GNOME.
SORRY, BUT TRYING TO EXPLAIN WHAT A METRONOME IS TO YOU TWO IS LIKE A LAUREL AND HARDY SKIT.
FORGET ABOUT STUPID GNOMES! A METRO- OHHH, HERE WE GO AGAIN. *WHO'S ON FIRST?!*
I THINK I MISSED THAT EPISODE.
WELL, YOU'RE A SOX FAN, SO... ***NOT TEIXEIRA!***
I FIND THIS DISCUSSION TO BE GNOME INSENSITIVE. I MEAN, GNOMES ARE PEOPLE, TOO... WELL, NOT "PEOPLE," PER SE, BUT....OK, TO BE FAIR, PEOPLE AREN'T GNOMES, EITHER, SEE....ROB? BUCKY?
darb

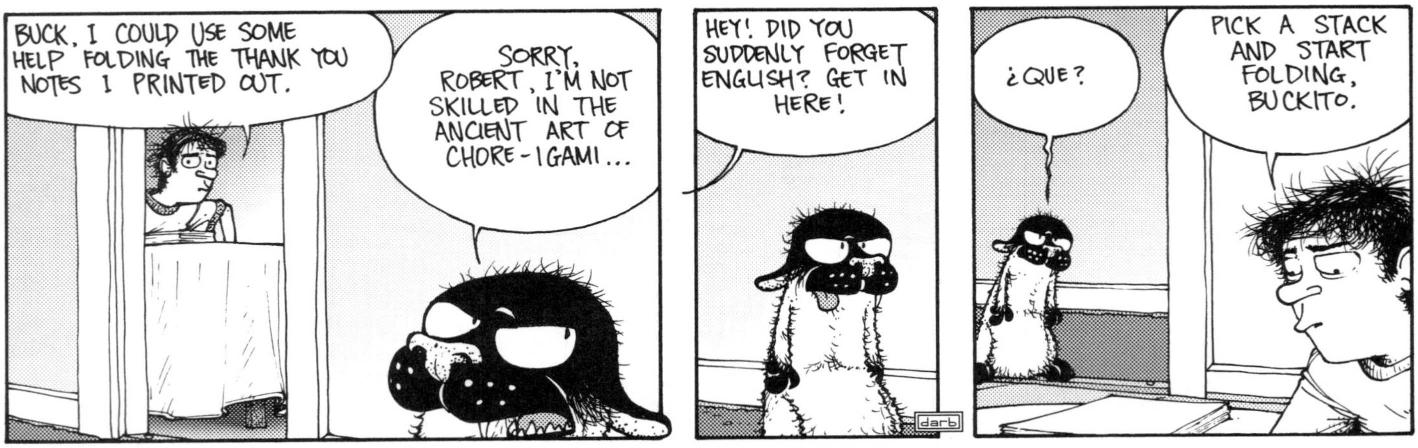
BUCK, I COULD USE SOME HELP FOLDING THE THANK YOU NOTES I PRINTED OUT.
SORRY, ROBERT, I'M NOT SKILLED IN THE ANCIENT ART OF CHORE-IGAMI...
HEY! DID YOU SUDDENLY FORGET ENGLISH? GET IN HERE!
darb
¿QUE?
PICK A STACK AND START FOLDING, BUCKITO.

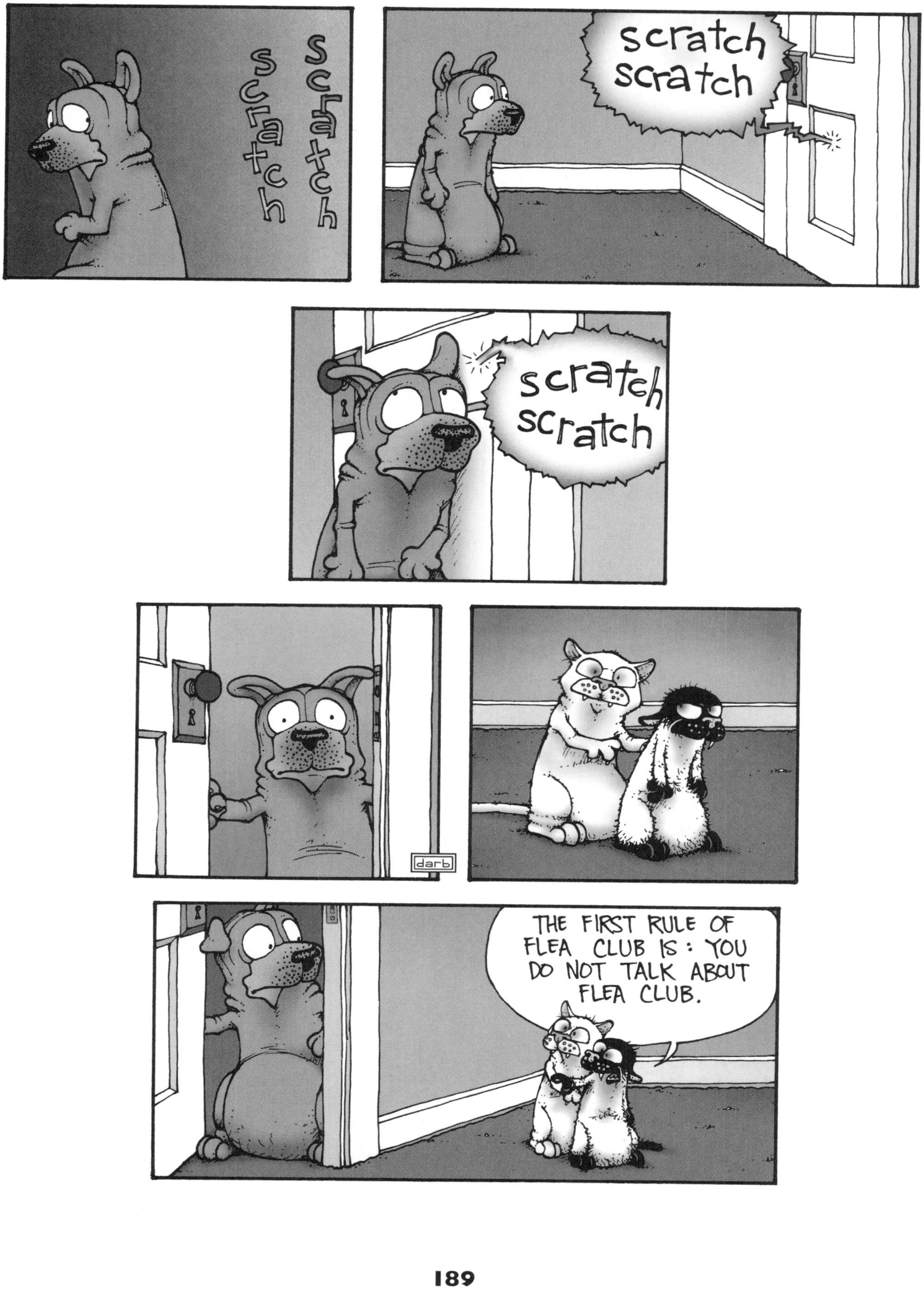
scratch scratch
scratch scratch
scratch scratch
scratch scratch
darb
THE FIRST RULE OF FLEA CLUB IS: YOU DO NOT TALK ABOUT FLEA CLUB.

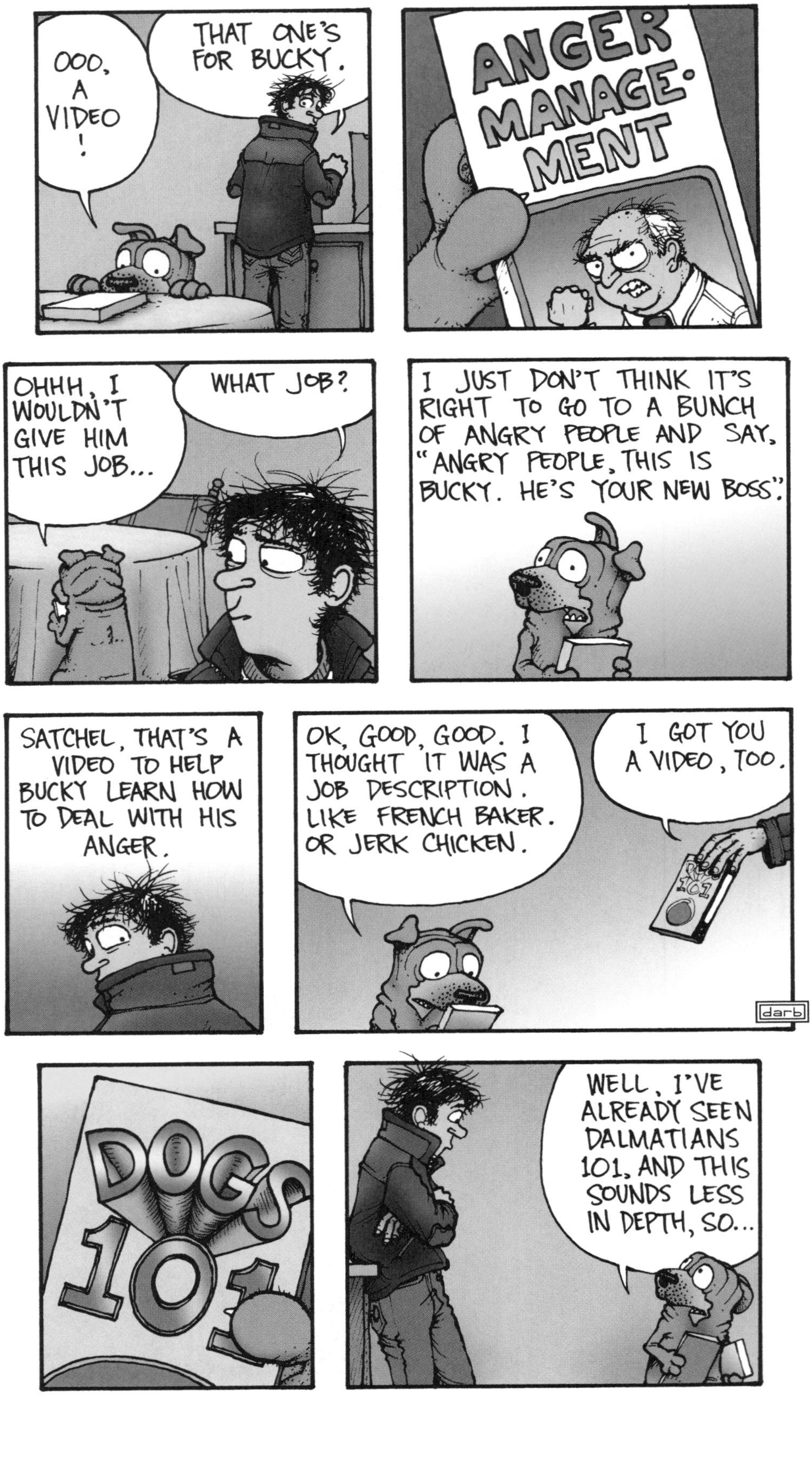
OOO, A VIDEO!
THAT ONE'S FOR BUCKY.
ANGER MANAGE-MENT
OHHH, I WOULDN'T GIVE HIM THIS JOB...
WHAT JOB?
I JUST DON'T THINK IT'S RIGHT TO GO TO A BUNCH OF ANGRY PEOPLE AND SAY, "ANGRY PEOPLE, THIS IS BUCKY. HE'S YOUR NEW BOSS."
SATCHEL, THAT'S A VIDEO TO HELP BUCKY LEARN HOW TO DEAL WITH HIS ANGER.
OK, GOOD, GOOD. I THOUGHT IT WAS A JOB DESCRIPTION. LIKE FRENCH BAKER. OR JERK CHICKEN.
I GOT YOU A VIDEO, TOO.
darb
DOGS 101
WELL, I'VE ALREADY SEEN DALMATIANS 101, AND THIS SOUNDS LESS IN DEPTH, SO...

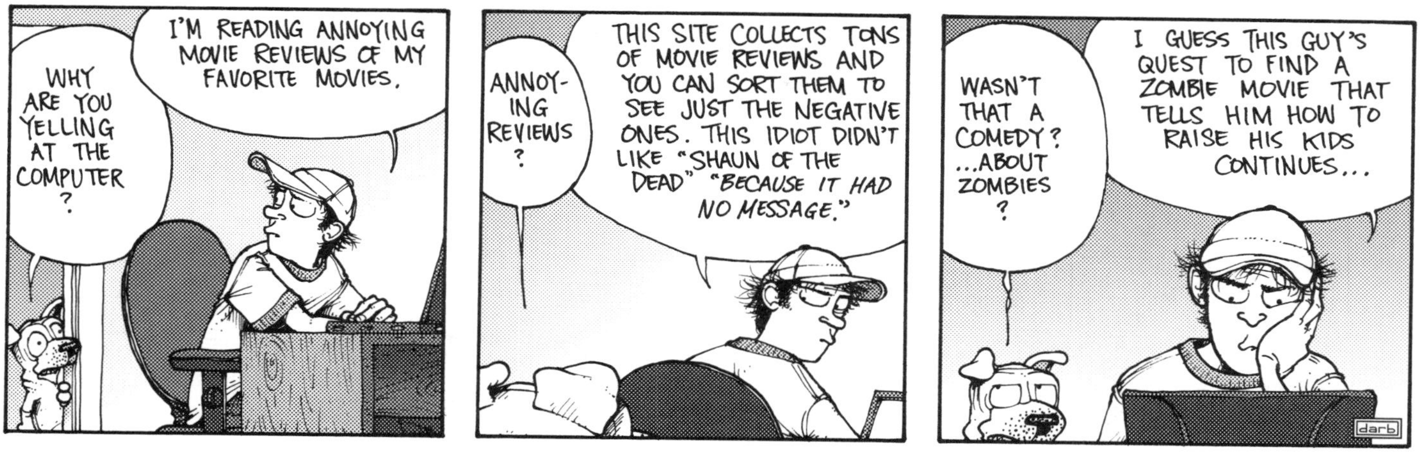
WHY ARE YOU YELLING AT THE COMPUTER?
I'M READING ANNOYING MOVIE REVIEWS OF MY FAVORITE MOVIES.
ANNOYING REVIEWS?
THIS SITE COLLECTS TONS OF MOVIE REVIEWS AND YOU CAN SORT THEM TO SEE JUST THE NEGATIVE ONES. THIS IDIOT DIDN'T LIKE "SHAUN OF THE DEAD" "BECAUSE IT HAD NO MESSAGE."
WASN'T THAT A COMEDY? ...ABOUT ZOMBIES?
I GUESS THIS GUY'S QUEST TO FIND A ZOMBIE MOVIE THAT TELLS HIM HOW TO RAISE HIS KIDS CONTINUES...
darb

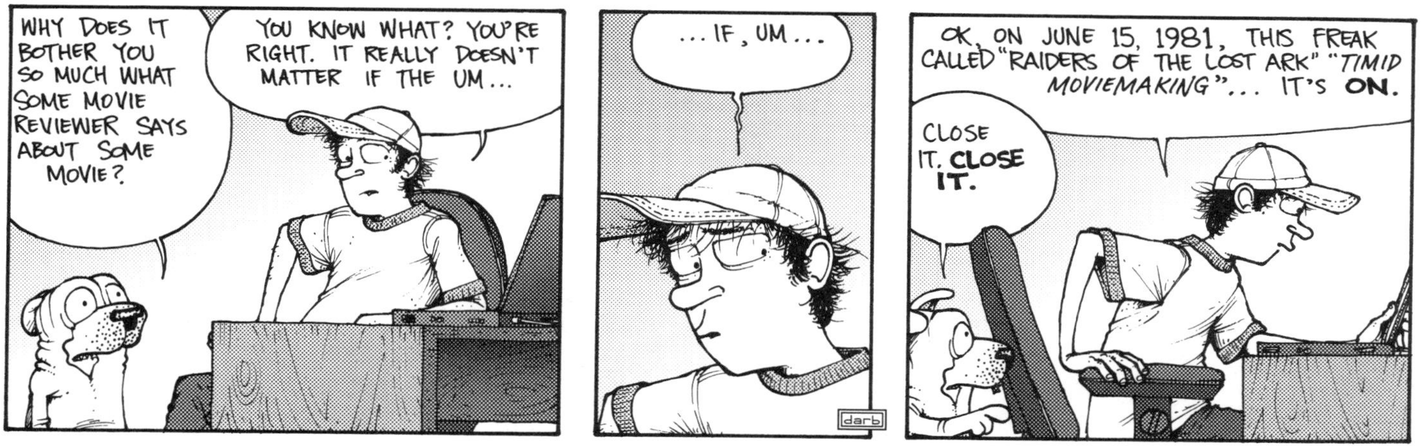
WHY DOES IT BOTHER YOU SO MUCH WHAT SOME MOVIE REVIEWER SAYS ABOUT SOME MOVIE?
YOU KNOW WHAT? YOU'RE RIGHT. IT REALLY DOESN'T MATTER IF THE UM...
...IF, UM...
darb
OK, ON JUNE 15, 1981, THIS FREAK CALLED "RAIDERS OF THE LOST ARK" "TIMID MOVIEMAKING"... IT'S ON.
CLOSE IT. CLOSE IT.

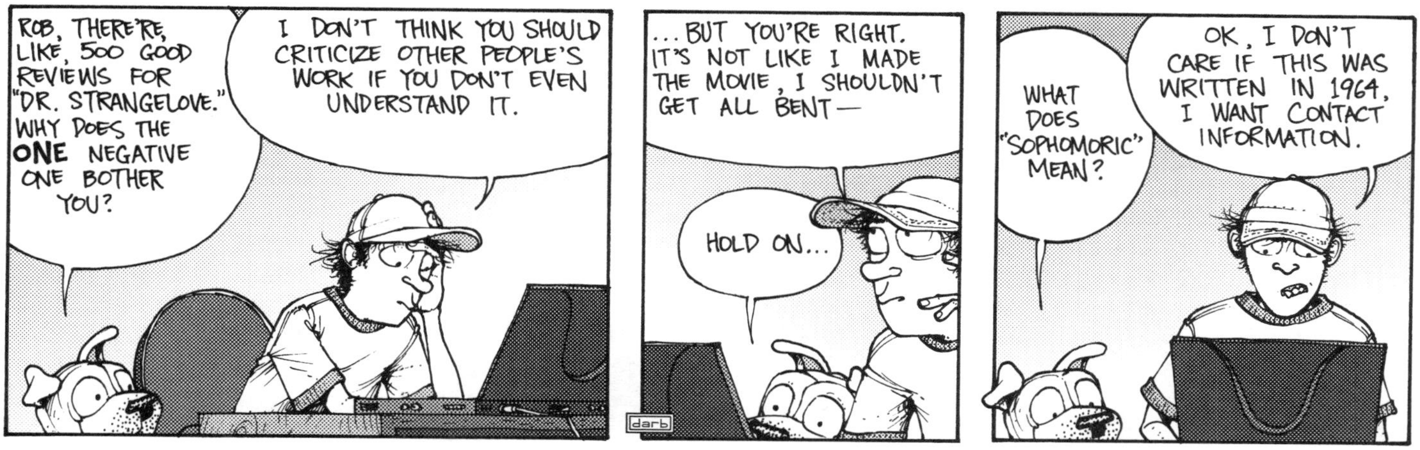
ROB, THERE'RE, LIKE, 500 GOOD REVIEWS FOR "DR. STRANGELOVE." WHY DOES THE ONE NEGATIVE ONE BOTHER YOU?
I DON'T THINK YOU SHOULD CRITICIZE OTHER PEOPLE'S WORK IF YOU DON'T EVEN UNDERSTAND IT.
darb
...BUT YOU'RE RIGHT. IT'S NOT LIKE I MADE THE MOVIE, I SHOULDN'T GET ALL BENT—
HOLD ON...
WHAT DOES "SOPHOMORIC" MEAN?
OK, I DON'T CARE IF THIS WAS WRITTEN IN 1964, I WANT CONTACT INFORMATION.

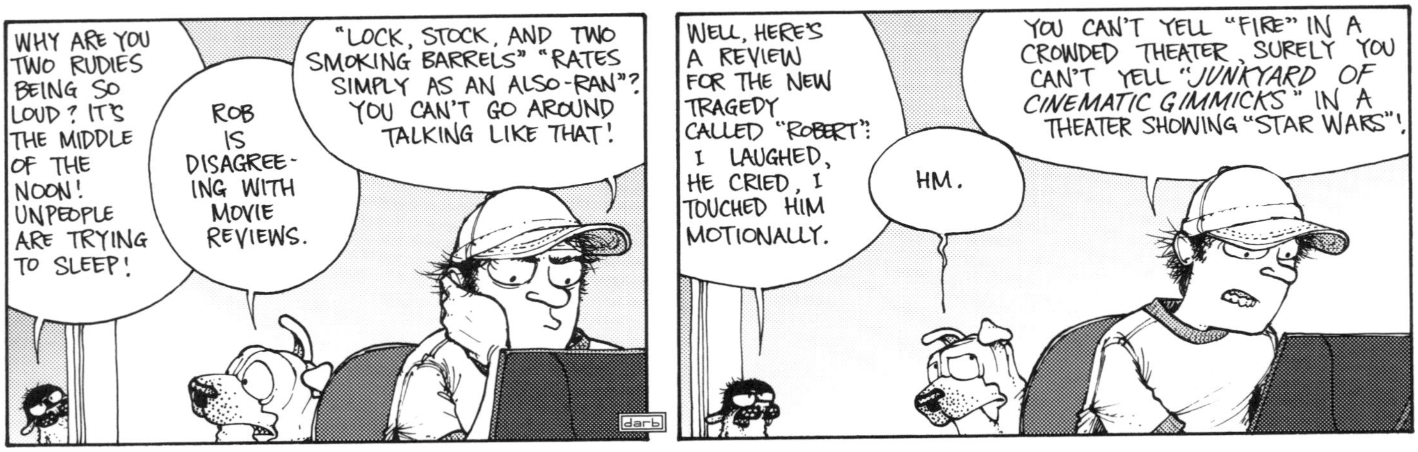
WHY ARE YOU TWO RUDIES BEING SO LOUD? IT'S THE MIDDLE OF THE NOON! UNPEOPLE ARE TRYING TO SLEEP!
ROB IS DISAGREE-ING WITH MOVIE REVIEWS.
"LOCK, STOCK, AND TWO SMOKING BARRELS" "RATES SIMPLY AS AN ALSO-RAN"? YOU CAN'T GO AROUND TALKING LIKE THAT!
darb
WELL, HERE'S A REVIEW FOR THE NEW TRAGEDY CALLED "ROBERT": I LAUGHED, HE CRIED, I TOUCHED HIM MOTIONALLY.
HM.
YOU CAN'T YELL "FIRE" IN A CROWDED THEATER, SURELY YOU CAN'T YELL "*JUNKYARD OF CINEMATIC GIMMICKS*" IN A THEATER SHOWING "STAR WARS"!

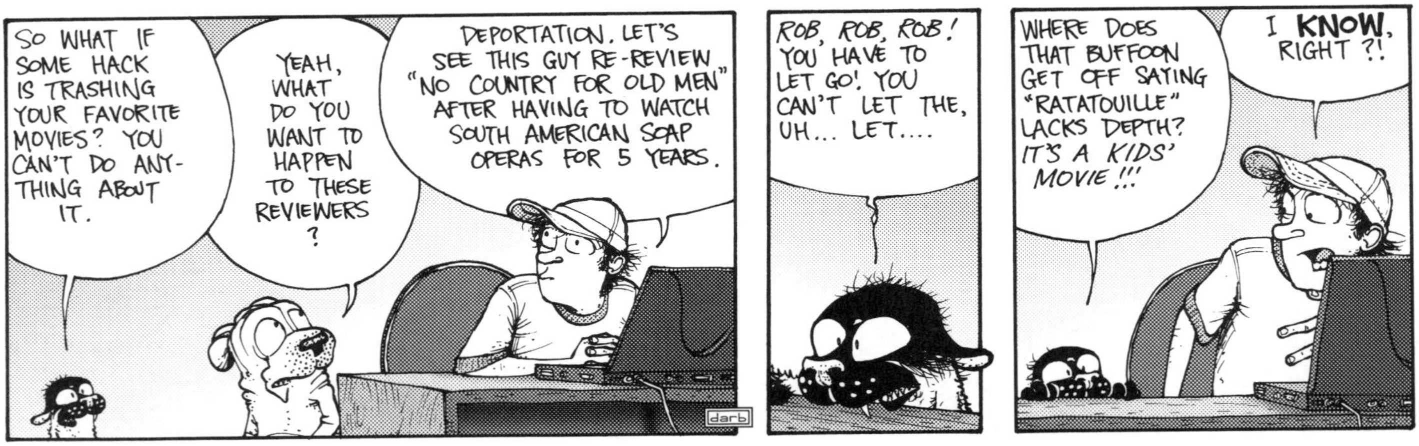
SO WHAT IF SOME HACK IS TRASHING YOUR FAVORITE MOVIES? YOU CAN'T DO ANY-THING ABOUT IT.
YEAH, WHAT DO YOU WANT TO HAPPEN TO THESE REVIEWERS?
DEPORTATION. LET'S SEE THIS GUY RE-REVIEW "NO COUNTRY FOR OLD MEN" AFTER HAVING TO WATCH SOUTH AMERICAN SOAP OPERAS FOR 5 YEARS.
darb
ROB, ROB, ROB! YOU HAVE TO LET GO! YOU CAN'T LET THE, UH... LET....
WHERE DOES THAT BUFFOON GET OFF SAYING "RATATOUILLE" LACKS DEPTH? *IT'S A KIDS' MOVIE!!!*
I **KNOW**, RIGHT?!

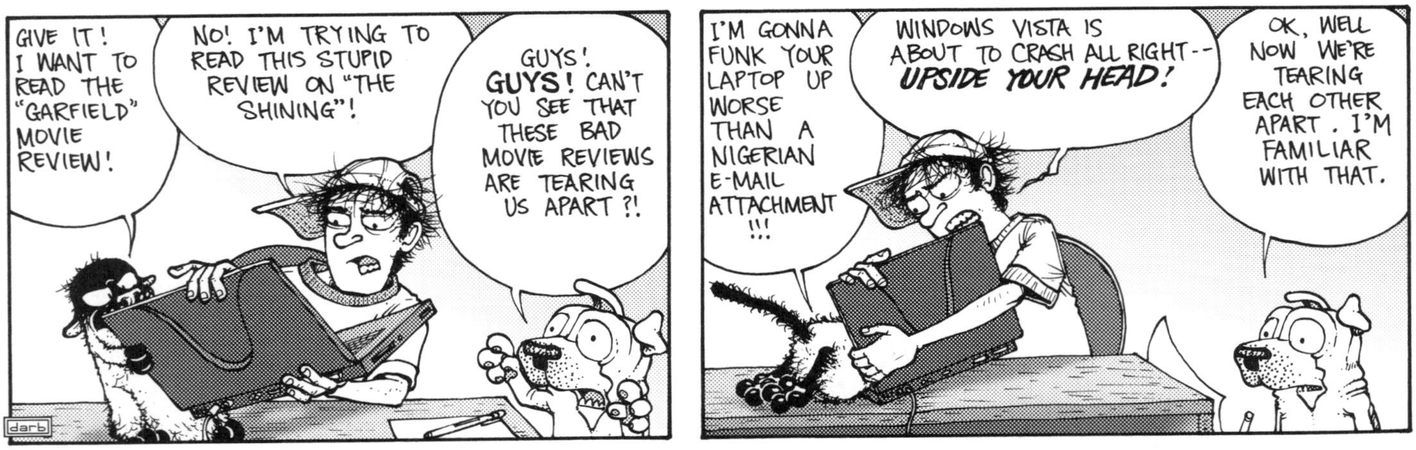
GIVE IT! I WANT TO READ THE "GARFIELD" MOVIE REVIEW!
NO! I'M TRYING TO READ THIS STUPID REVIEW ON "THE SHINING"!
GUYS! **GUYS!** CAN'T YOU SEE THAT THESE BAD MOVIE REVIEWS ARE TEARING US APART?!
darb
I'M GONNA FUNK YOUR LAPTOP UP WORSE THAN A NIGERIAN E-MAIL ATTACHMENT!!!
WINDOWS VISTA IS ABOUT TO CRASH ALL RIGHT-- ***UPSIDE YOUR HEAD!***
OK, WELL NOW WE'RE TEARING EACH OTHER APART. I'M FAMILIAR WITH THAT.

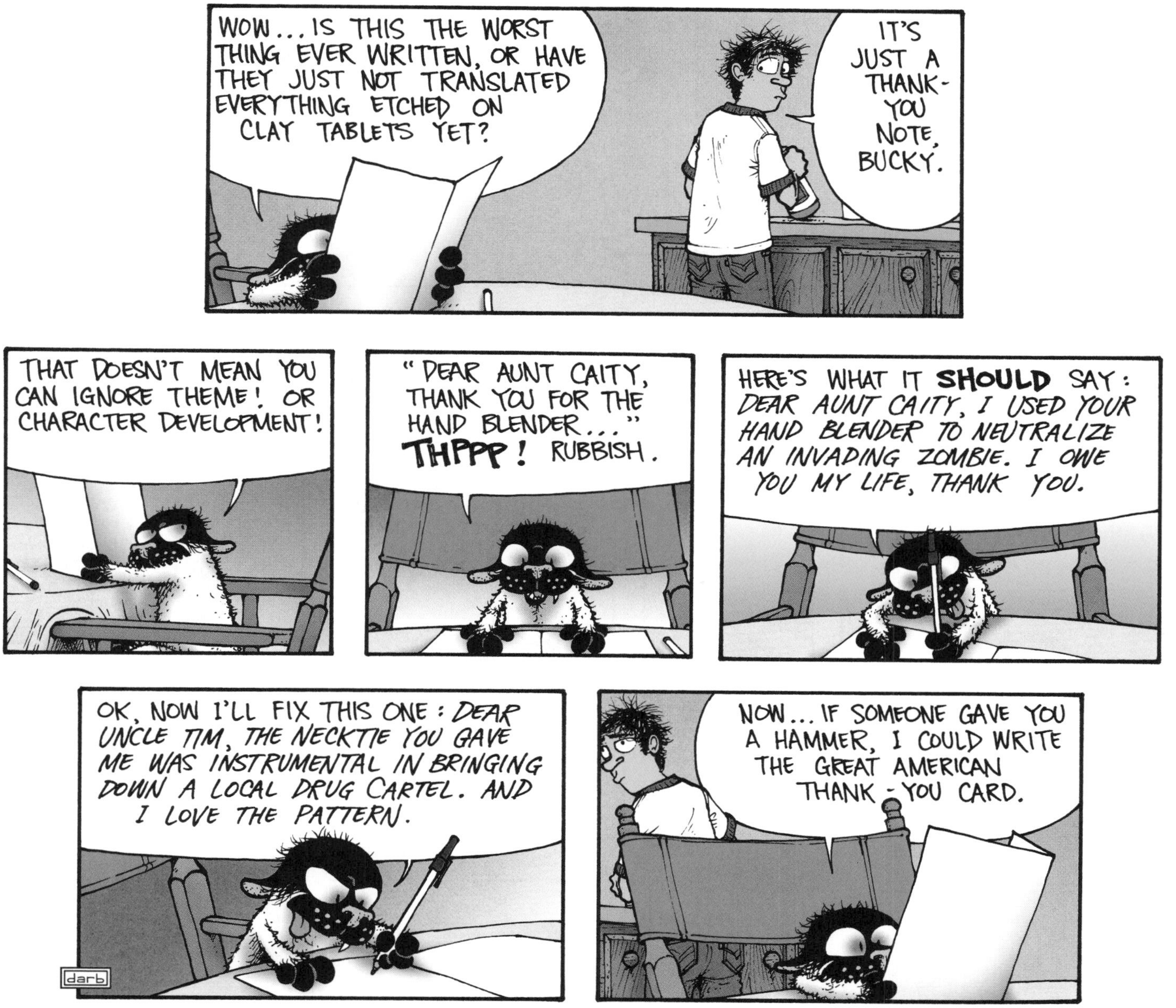
WOW... IS THIS THE WORST THING EVER WRITTEN, OR HAVE THEY JUST NOT TRANSLATED EVERYTHING ETCHED ON CLAY TABLETS YET?
IT'S JUST A THANK-YOU NOTE, BUCKY.
THAT DOESN'T MEAN YOU CAN IGNORE THEME! OR CHARACTER DEVELOPMENT!
"DEAR AUNT CAITY, THANK YOU FOR THE HAND BLENDER..." THPPP! RUBBISH.
HERE'S WHAT IT SHOULD SAY: DEAR AUNT CAITY, I USED YOUR HAND BLENDER TO NEUTRALIZE AN INVADING ZOMBIE. I OWE YOU MY LIFE, THANK YOU.
OK, NOW I'LL FIX THIS ONE: DEAR UNCLE TIM, THE NECKTIE YOU GAVE ME WAS INSTRUMENTAL IN BRINGING DOWN A LOCAL DRUG CARTEL. AND I LOVE THE PATTERN.
darb
NOW... IF SOMEONE GAVE YOU A HAMMER, I COULD WRITE THE GREAT AMERICAN THANK-YOU CARD.

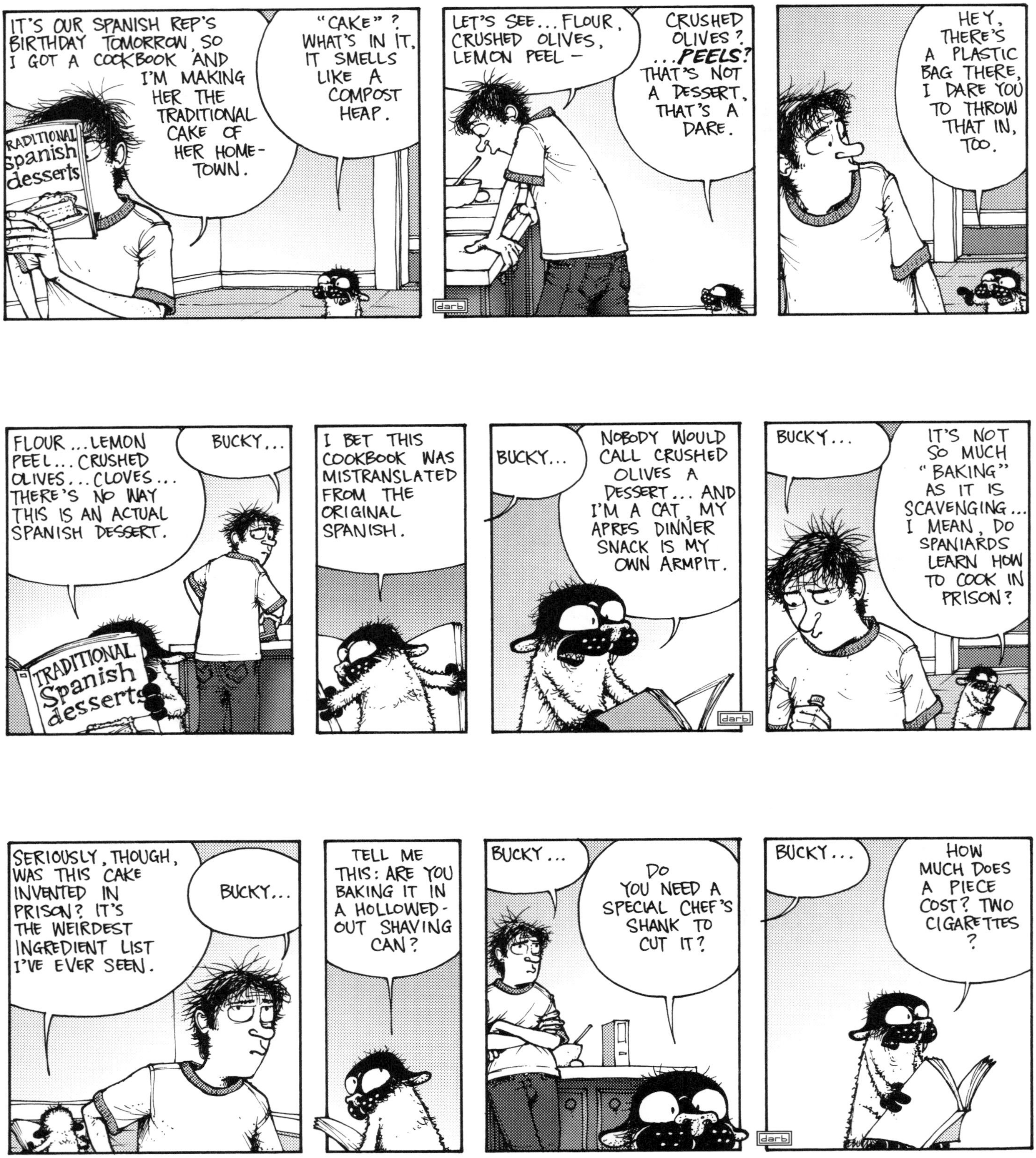
IT'S OUR SPANISH REP'S BIRTHDAY TOMORROW, SO I GOT A COOKBOOK AND I'M MAKING HER THE TRADITIONAL CAKE OF HER HOME-TOWN.
"CAKE"? WHAT'S IN IT, IT SMELLS LIKE A COMPOST HEAP.
TRADITIONAL spanish desserts
LET'S SEE... FLOUR, CRUSHED OLIVES, LEMON PEEL –
CRUSHED OLIVES? ...PEELS? THAT'S NOT A DESSERT, THAT'S A DARE.
darb
HEY, THERE'S A PLASTIC BAG THERE, I DARE YOU TO THROW THAT IN, TOO.
FLOUR... LEMON PEEL... CRUSHED OLIVES... CLOVES... THERE'S NO WAY THIS IS AN ACTUAL SPANISH DESSERT.
BUCKY...
TRADITIONAL Spanish desserts
I BET THIS COOKBOOK WAS MISTRANSLATED FROM THE ORIGINAL SPANISH.
BUCKY...
NOBODY WOULD CALL CRUSHED OLIVES A DESSERT... AND I'M A CAT, MY APRES DINNER SNACK IS MY OWN ARMPIT.
darb
BUCKY...
IT'S NOT SO MUCH "BAKING" AS IT IS SCAVENGING... I MEAN, DO SPANIARDS LEARN HOW TO COOK IN PRISON?
SERIOUSLY, THOUGH, WAS THIS CAKE INVENTED IN PRISON? IT'S THE WEIRDEST INGREDIENT LIST I'VE EVER SEEN.
BUCKY...
TELL ME THIS: ARE YOU BAKING IT IN A HOLLOWED-OUT SHAVING CAN?
BUCKY...
DO YOU NEED A SPECIAL CHEF'S SHANK TO CUT IT?
darb
BUCKY...
HOW MUCH DOES A PIECE COST? TWO CIGARETTES?

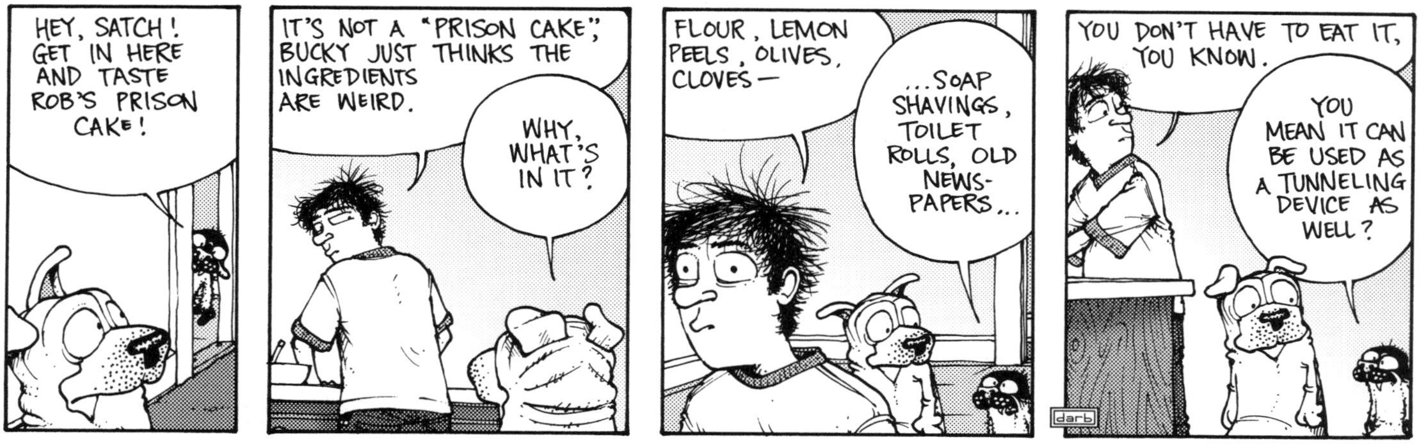
HEY, SATCH! GET IN HERE AND TASTE ROB'S PRISON CAKE!
IT'S NOT A "PRISON CAKE"; BUCKY JUST THINKS THE INGREDIENTS ARE WEIRD.
WHY, WHAT'S IN IT?
FLOUR, LEMON PEELS, OLIVES, CLOVES—
...SOAP SHAVINGS, TOILET ROLLS, OLD NEWS-PAPERS...
YOU DON'T HAVE TO EAT IT, YOU KNOW.
YOU MEAN IT CAN BE USED AS A TUNNELING DEVICE AS WELL?
darb

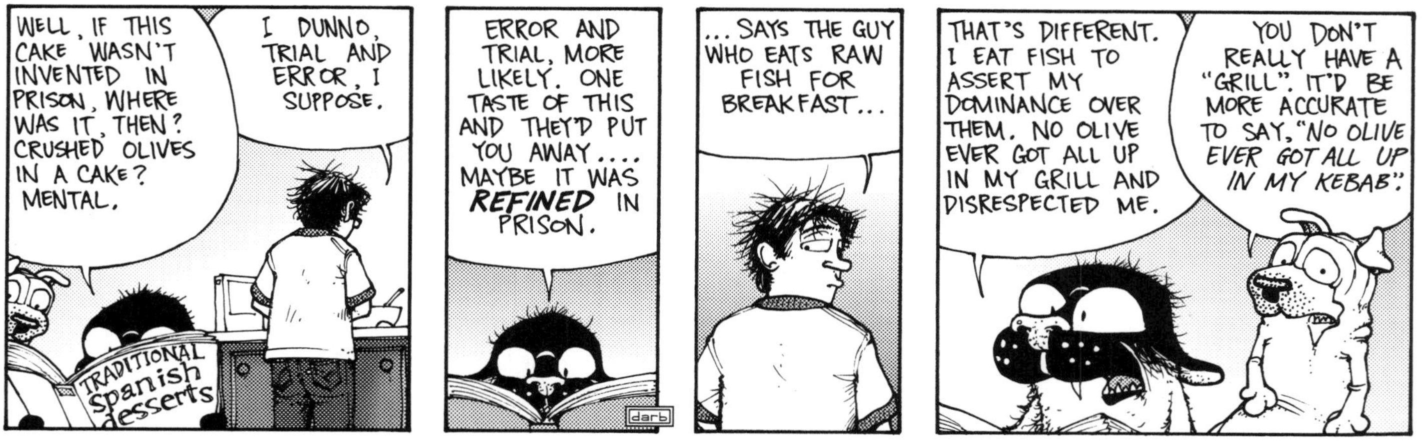
WELL, IF THIS CAKE WASN'T INVENTED IN PRISON, WHERE WAS IT, THEN? CRUSHED OLIVES IN A CAKE? MENTAL.
I DUNNO, TRIAL AND ERROR, I SUPPOSE.
TRADITIONAL spanish desserts
ERROR AND TRIAL, MORE LIKELY. ONE TASTE OF THIS AND THEY'D PUT YOU AWAY.... MAYBE IT WAS *REFINED* IN PRISON.
darb
...SAYS THE GUY WHO EATS RAW FISH FOR BREAKFAST...
THAT'S DIFFERENT. I EAT FISH TO ASSERT MY DOMINANCE OVER THEM. NO OLIVE EVER GOT ALL UP IN MY GRILL AND DISRESPECTED ME.
YOU DON'T REALLY HAVE A "GRILL". IT'D BE MORE ACCURATE TO SAY, "*NO OLIVE EVER GOT ALL UP IN MY KEBAB*".

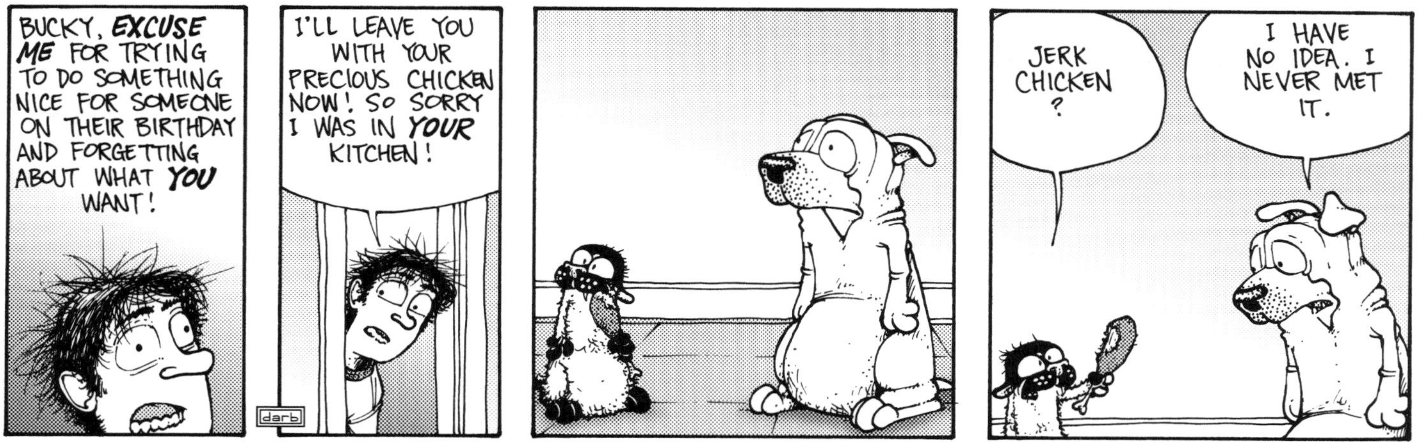
BUCKY, ***EXCUSE ME*** FOR TRYING TO DO SOMETHING NICE FOR SOMEONE ON THEIR BIRTHDAY AND FORGETTING ABOUT WHAT ***YOU*** WANT!
darb
I'LL LEAVE YOU WITH YOUR PRECIOUS CHICKEN NOW! SO SORRY I WAS IN ***YOUR*** KITCHEN!
JERK CHICKEN?
I HAVE NO IDEA. I NEVER MET IT.

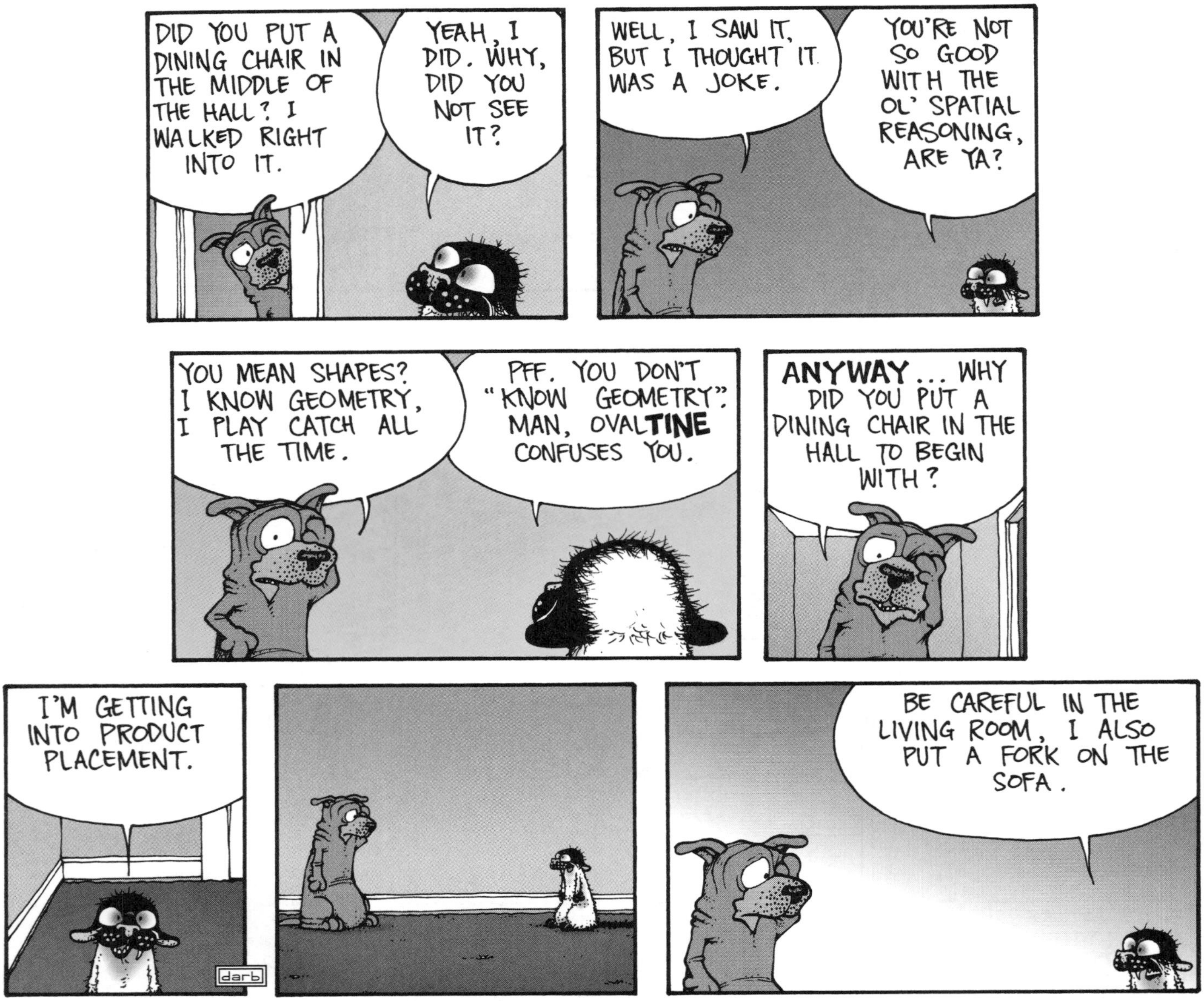
DID YOU PUT A DINING CHAIR IN THE MIDDLE OF THE HALL? I WALKED RIGHT INTO IT.
YEAH, I DID. WHY, DID YOU NOT SEE IT?
WELL, I SAW IT, BUT I THOUGHT IT WAS A JOKE.
YOU'RE NOT SO GOOD WITH THE OL' SPATIAL REASONING, ARE YA?
YOU MEAN SHAPES? I KNOW GEOMETRY, I PLAY CATCH ALL THE TIME.
PFF. YOU DON'T "KNOW GEOMETRY". MAN, OVALTINE CONFUSES YOU.
ANYWAY... WHY DID YOU PUT A DINING CHAIR IN THE HALL TO BEGIN WITH?
I'M GETTING INTO PRODUCT PLACEMENT.
darb
BE CAREFUL IN THE LIVING ROOM, I ALSO PUT A FORK ON THE SOFA.

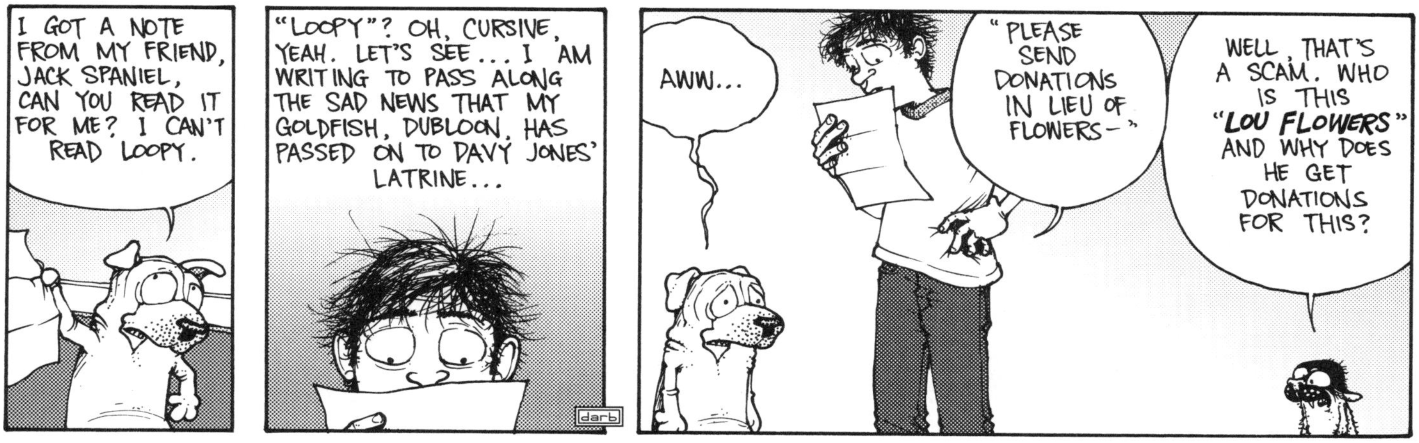
I GOT A NOTE FROM MY FRIEND, JACK SPANIEL, CAN YOU READ IT FOR ME? I CAN'T READ LOOPY.
"LOOPY"? OH, CURSIVE, YEAH. LET'S SEE... I AM WRITING TO PASS ALONG THE SAD NEWS THAT MY GOLDFISH, DUBLOON, HAS PASSED ON TO DAVY JONES' LATRINE...
darb
AWW...
"PLEASE SEND DONATIONS IN LIEU OF FLOWERS—"
WELL, THAT'S A SCAM. WHO IS THIS "LOU FLOWERS" AND WHY DOES HE GET DONATIONS FOR THIS?

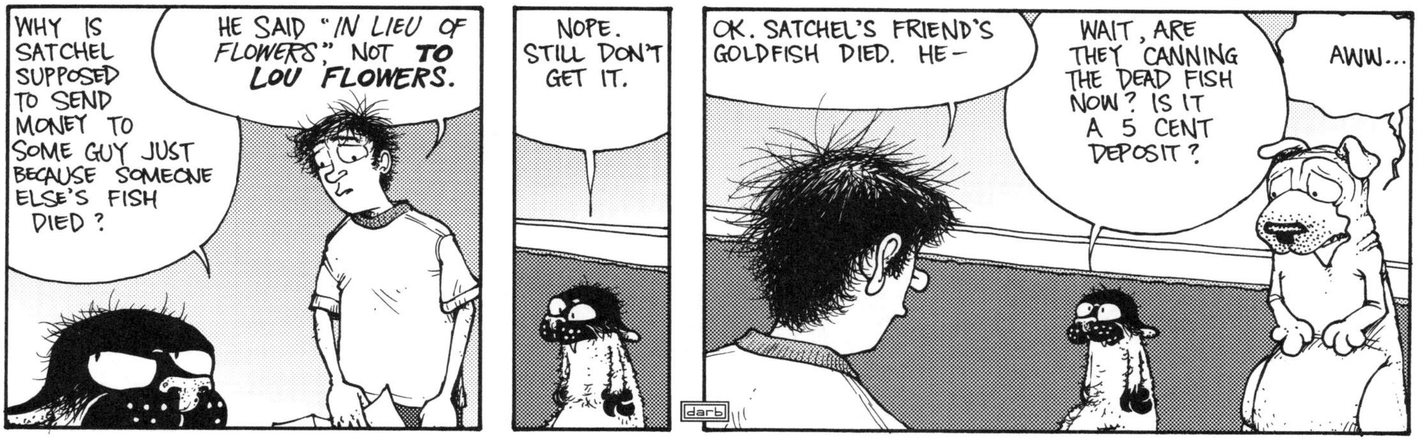
WHY IS SATCHEL SUPPOSED TO SEND MONEY TO SOME GUY JUST BECAUSE SOMEONE ELSE'S FISH DIED?
HE SAID "IN LIEU OF FLOWERS," NOT TO LOU FLOWERS.
NOPE. STILL DON'T GET IT.
darb
OK. SATCHEL'S FRIEND'S GOLDFISH DIED. HE—
WAIT, ARE THEY CANNING THE DEAD FISH NOW? IS IT A 5 CENT DEPOSIT?
AWW...

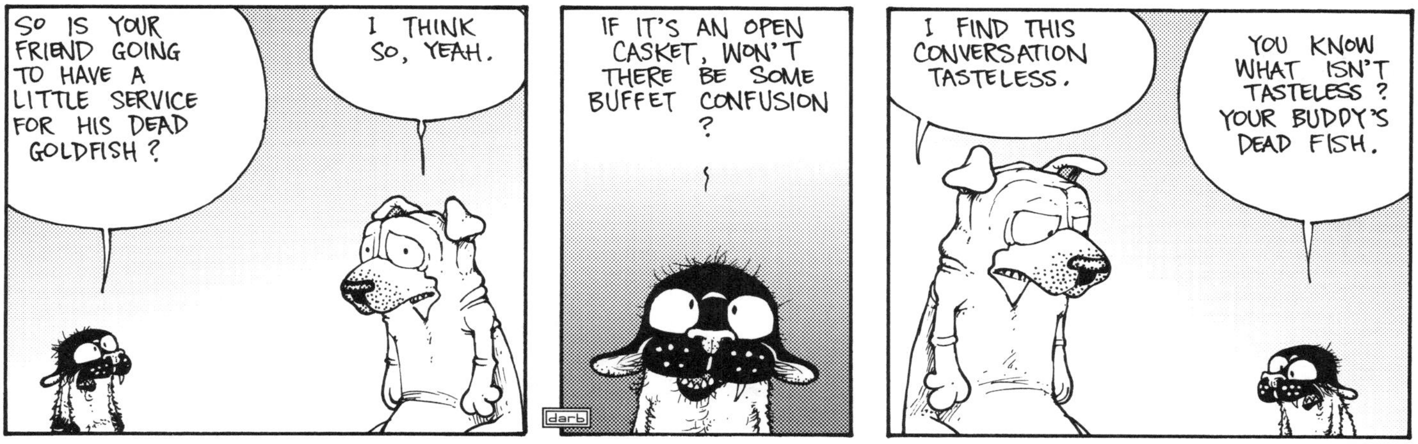
SO IS YOUR FRIEND GOING TO HAVE A LITTLE SERVICE FOR HIS DEAD GOLDFISH?
I THINK SO, YEAH.
darb
IF IT'S AN OPEN CASKET, WON'T THERE BE SOME BUFFET CONFUSION?
I FIND THIS CONVERSATION TASTELESS.
YOU KNOW WHAT ISN'T TASTELESS? YOUR BUDDY'S DEAD FISH.

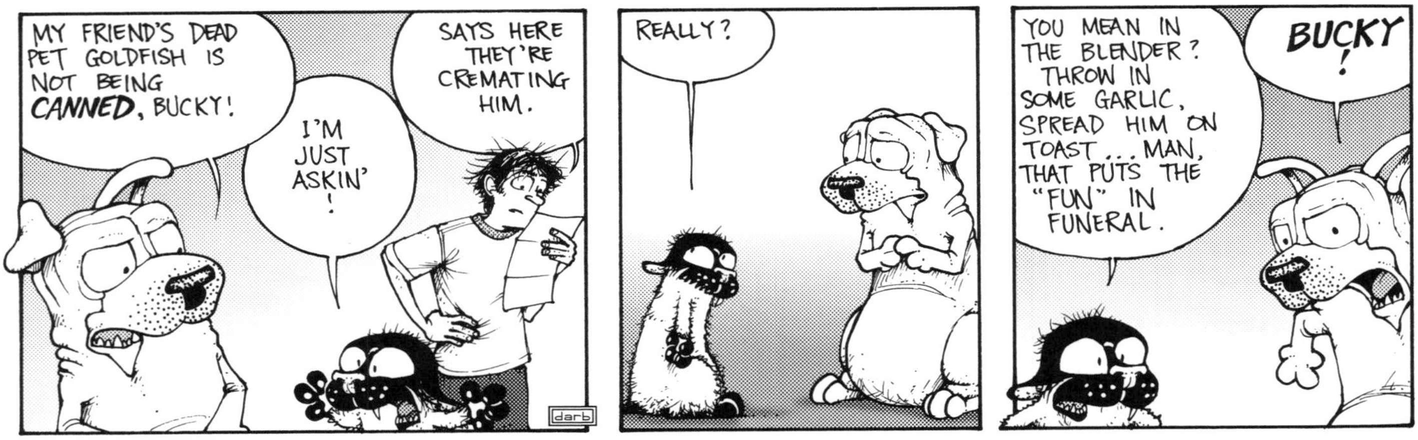
MY FRIEND'S DEAD PET GOLDFISH IS NOT BEING **CANNED**, BUCKY!
I'M JUST ASKIN'!
SAYS HERE THEY'RE CREMATING HIM.
REALLY?
YOU MEAN IN THE BLENDER? THROW IN SOME GARLIC, SPREAD HIM ON TOAST... MAN, THAT PUTS THE "FUN" IN FUNERAL.
BUCKY!
darb

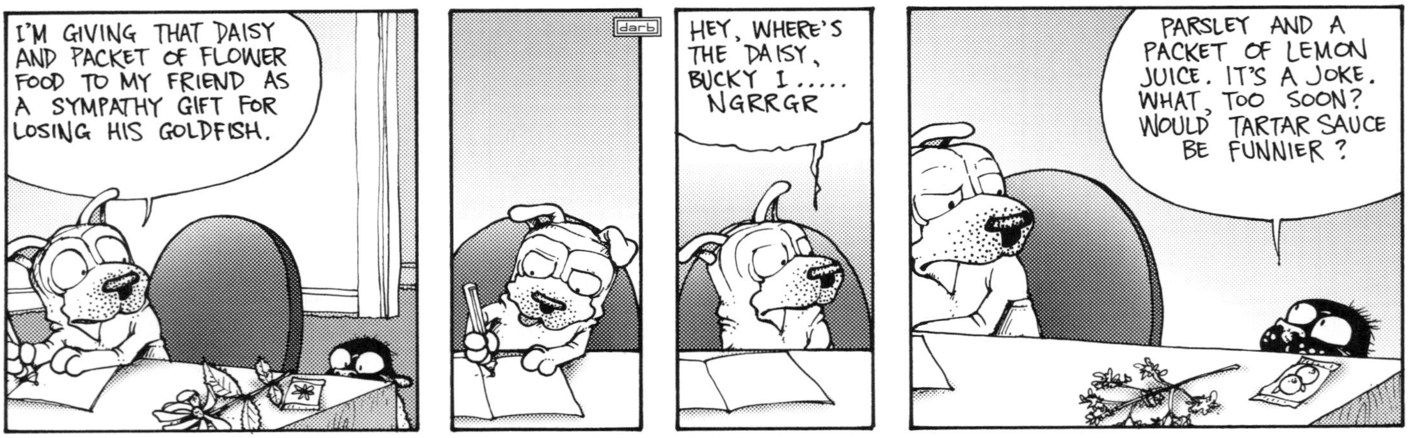
I'M GIVING THAT DAISY AND PACKET OF FLOWER FOOD TO MY FRIEND AS A SYMPATHY GIFT FOR LOSING HIS GOLDFISH.
darb
HEY, WHERE'S THE DAISY, BUCKY I..... NGRRGR
PARSLEY AND A PACKET OF LEMON JUICE. IT'S A JOKE. WHAT, TOO SOON? WOULD TARTAR SAUCE BE FUNNIER?

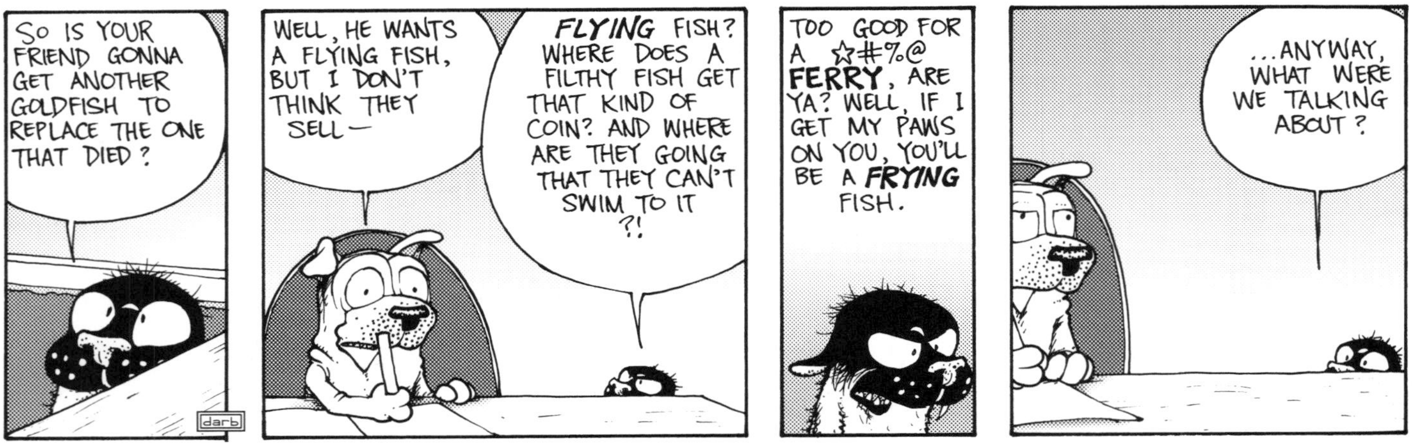
SO IS YOUR FRIEND GONNA GET ANOTHER GOLDFISH TO REPLACE THE ONE THAT DIED?
darb
WELL, HE WANTS A FLYING FISH, BUT I DON'T THINK THEY SELL—
FLYING FISH? WHERE DOES A FILTHY FISH GET THAT KIND OF COIN? AND WHERE ARE THEY GOING THAT THEY CAN'T SWIM TO IT?!
TOO GOOD FOR A ☆#%@ **FERRY**, ARE YA? WELL, IF I GET MY PAWS ON YOU, YOU'LL BE A ***FRYING*** FISH.
...ANYWAY, WHAT WERE WE TALKING ABOUT?

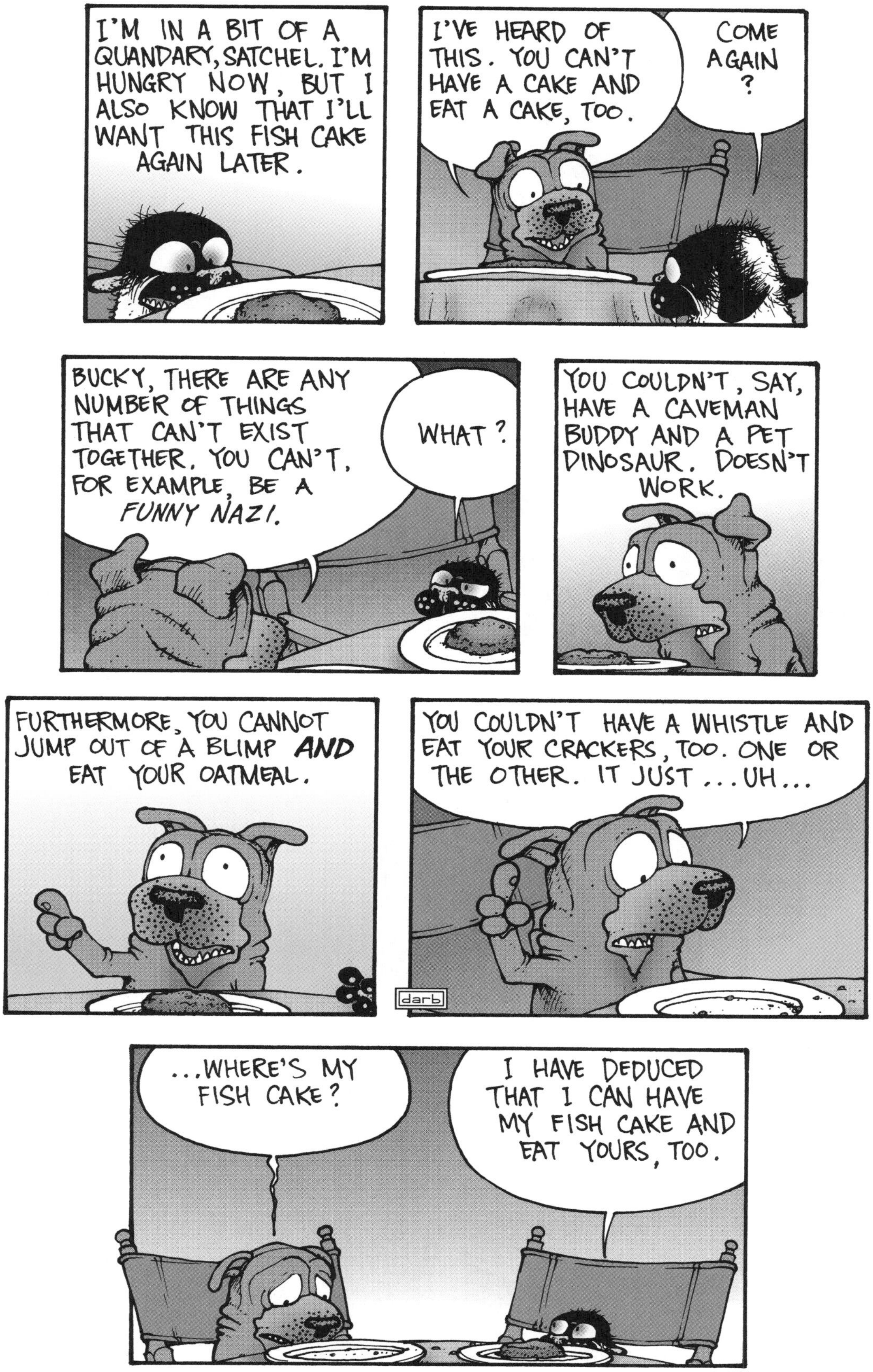
I'M IN A BIT OF A QUANDARY, SATCHEL. I'M HUNGRY NOW, BUT I ALSO KNOW THAT I'LL WANT THIS FISH CAKE AGAIN LATER.
I'VE HEARD OF THIS. YOU CAN'T HAVE A CAKE AND EAT A CAKE, TOO.
COME AGAIN ?
BUCKY, THERE ARE ANY NUMBER OF THINGS THAT CAN'T EXIST TOGETHER. YOU CAN'T, FOR EXAMPLE, BE A FUNNY NAZI.
WHAT ?
YOU COULDN'T, SAY, HAVE A CAVEMAN BUDDY AND A PET DINOSAUR. DOESN'T WORK.
FURTHERMORE, YOU CANNOT JUMP OUT OF A BLIMP AND EAT YOUR OATMEAL.
YOU COULDN'T HAVE A WHISTLE AND EAT YOUR CRACKERS, TOO. ONE OR THE OTHER. IT JUST ... UH ...
darb
...WHERE'S MY FISH CAKE?
I HAVE DEDUCED THAT I CAN HAVE MY FISH CAKE AND EAT YOURS, TOO.

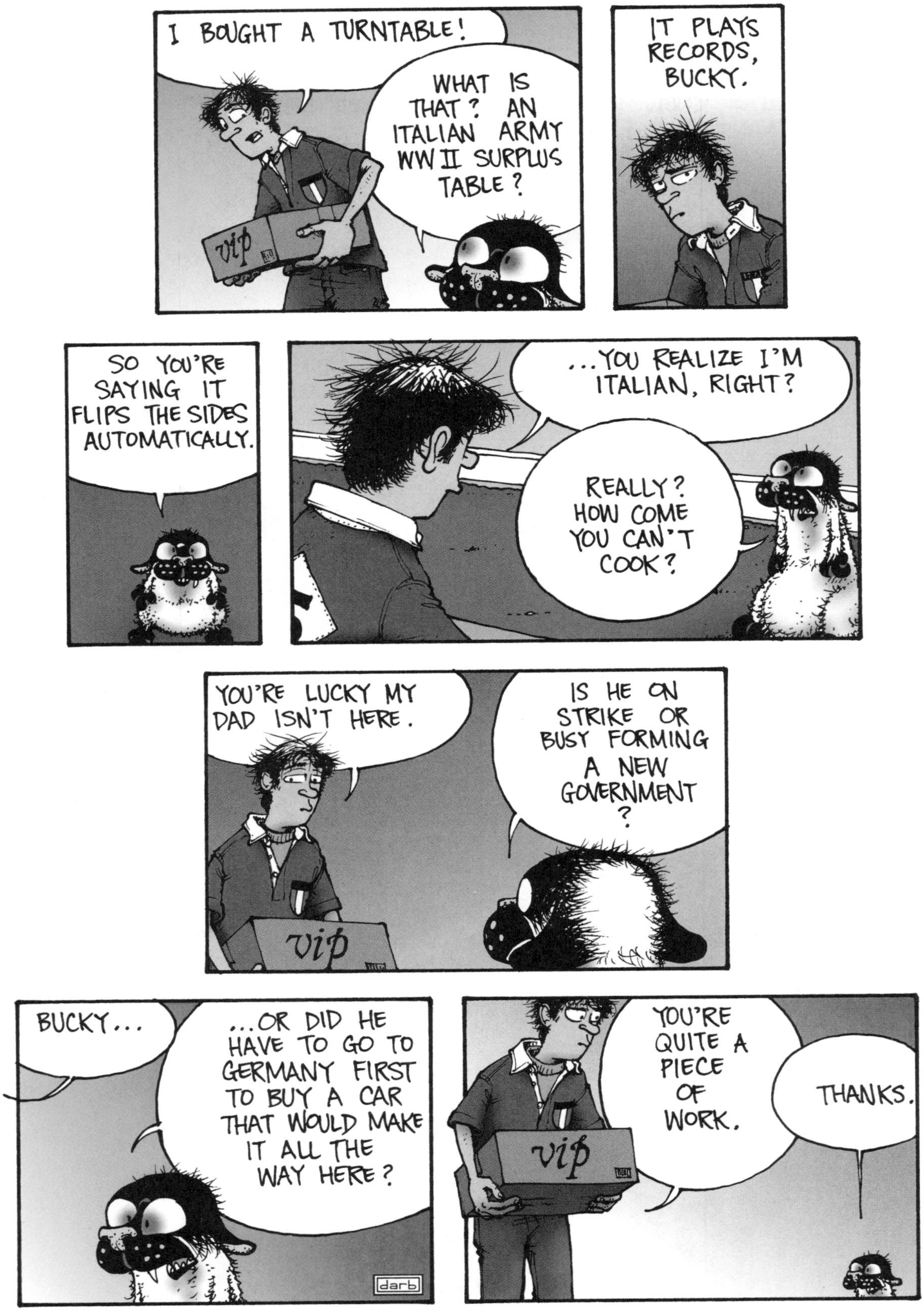
I BOUGHT A TURNTABLE!
WHAT IS THAT? AN ITALIAN ARMY WW II SURPLUS TABLE?
IT PLAYS RECORDS, BUCKY.
SO YOU'RE SAYING IT FLIPS THE SIDES AUTOMATICALLY.
...YOU REALIZE I'M ITALIAN, RIGHT?
REALLY? HOW COME YOU CAN'T COOK?
YOU'RE LUCKY MY DAD ISN'T HERE.
IS HE ON STRIKE OR BUSY FORMING A NEW GOVERNMENT?
BUCKY...
...OR DID HE HAVE TO GO TO GERMANY FIRST TO BUY A CAR THAT WOULD MAKE IT ALL THE WAY HERE?
darb
YOU'RE QUITE A PIECE OF WORK.
THANKS.

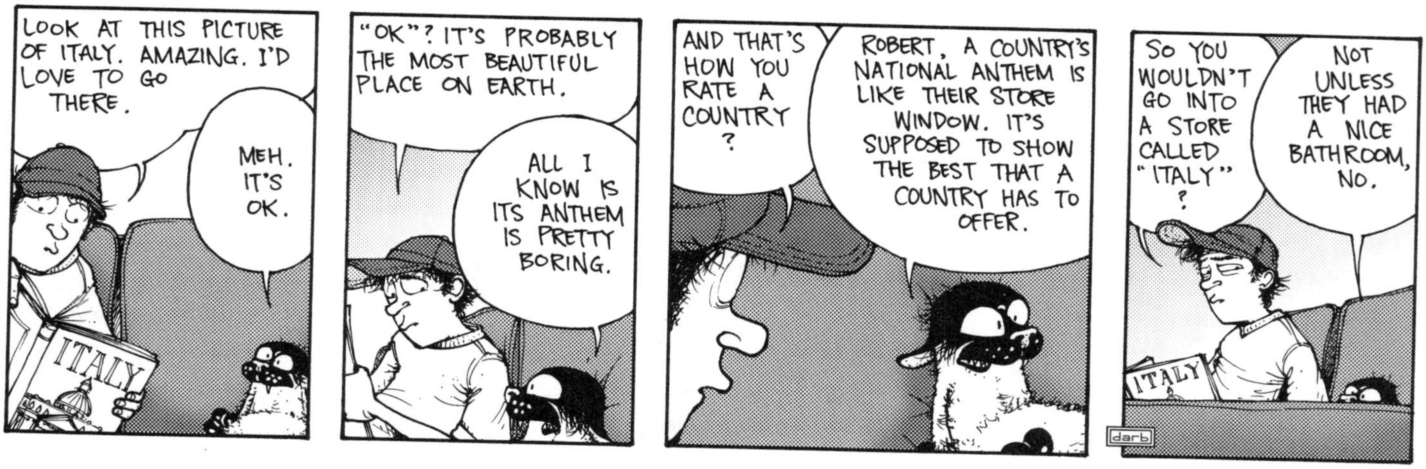
LOOK AT THIS PICTURE OF ITALY. AMAZING. I'D LOVE TO GO THERE.
MEH. IT'S OK.
ITALY
"OK"? IT'S PROBABLY THE MOST BEAUTIFUL PLACE ON EARTH.
ALL I KNOW IS ITS ANTHEM IS PRETTY BORING.
AND THAT'S HOW YOU RATE A COUNTRY?
ROBERT, A COUNTRY'S NATIONAL ANTHEM IS LIKE THEIR STORE WINDOW. IT'S SUPPOSED TO SHOW THE BEST THAT A COUNTRY HAS TO OFFER.
SO YOU WOULDN'T GO INTO A STORE CALLED "ITALY"?
NOT UNLESS THEY HAD A NICE BATHROOM, NO.
ITALY
darb

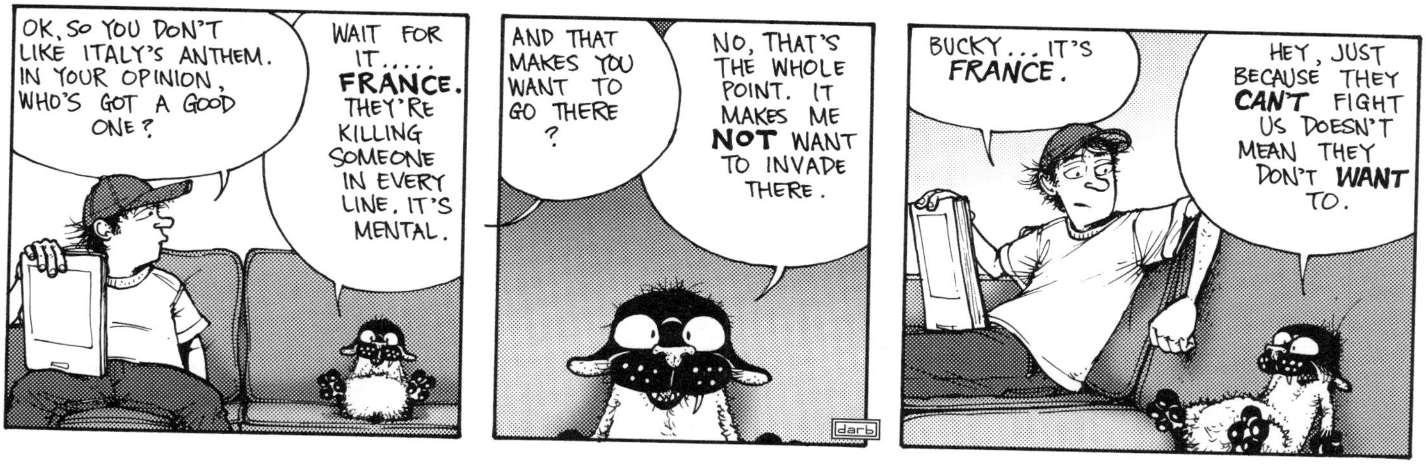
OK, SO YOU DON'T LIKE ITALY'S ANTHEM. IN YOUR OPINION, WHO'S GOT A GOOD ONE?
WAIT FOR IT..... FRANCE. THEY'RE KILLING SOMEONE IN EVERY LINE. IT'S MENTAL.
AND THAT MAKES YOU WANT TO GO THERE?
NO, THAT'S THE WHOLE POINT. IT MAKES ME NOT WANT TO INVADE THERE.
darb
BUCKY... IT'S FRANCE.
HEY, JUST BECAUSE THEY CAN'T FIGHT US DOESN'T MEAN THEY DON'T WANT TO.

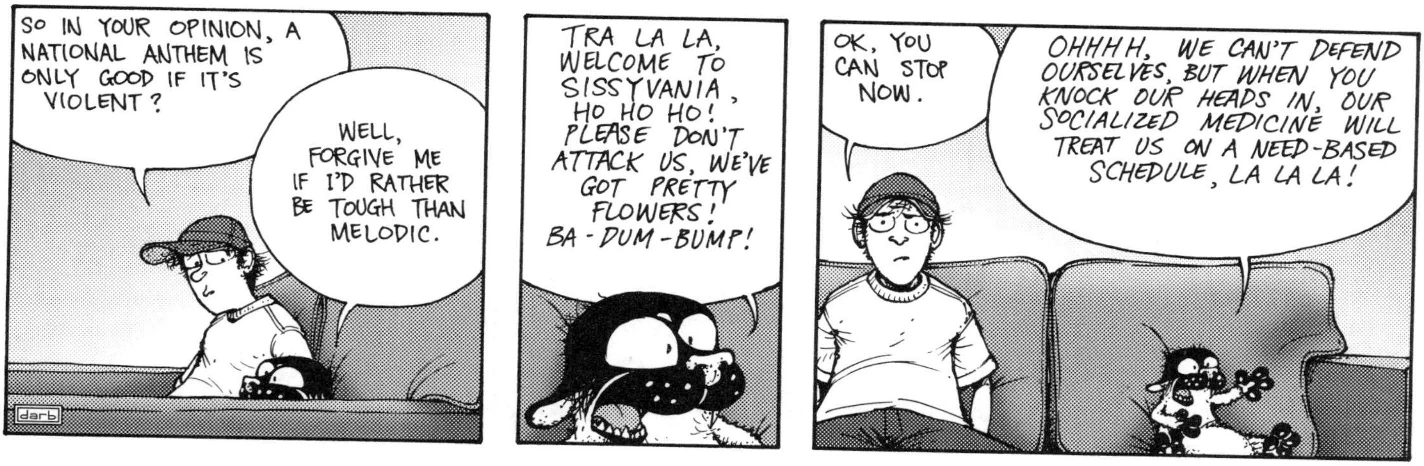
SO IN YOUR OPINION, A NATIONAL ANTHEM IS ONLY GOOD IF IT'S VIOLENT?
WELL, FORGIVE ME IF I'D RATHER BE TOUGH THAN MELODIC.
darb
TRA LA LA, WELCOME TO SISSYVANIA, HO HO HO! PLEASE DON'T ATTACK US, WE'VE GOT PRETTY FLOWERS! BA-DUM-BUMP!
OK, YOU CAN STOP NOW.
OHHHH, WE CAN'T DEFEND OURSELVES, BUT WHEN YOU KNOCK OUR HEADS IN, OUR SOCIALIZED MEDICINE WILL TREAT US ON A NEED-BASED SCHEDULE, LA LA LA!

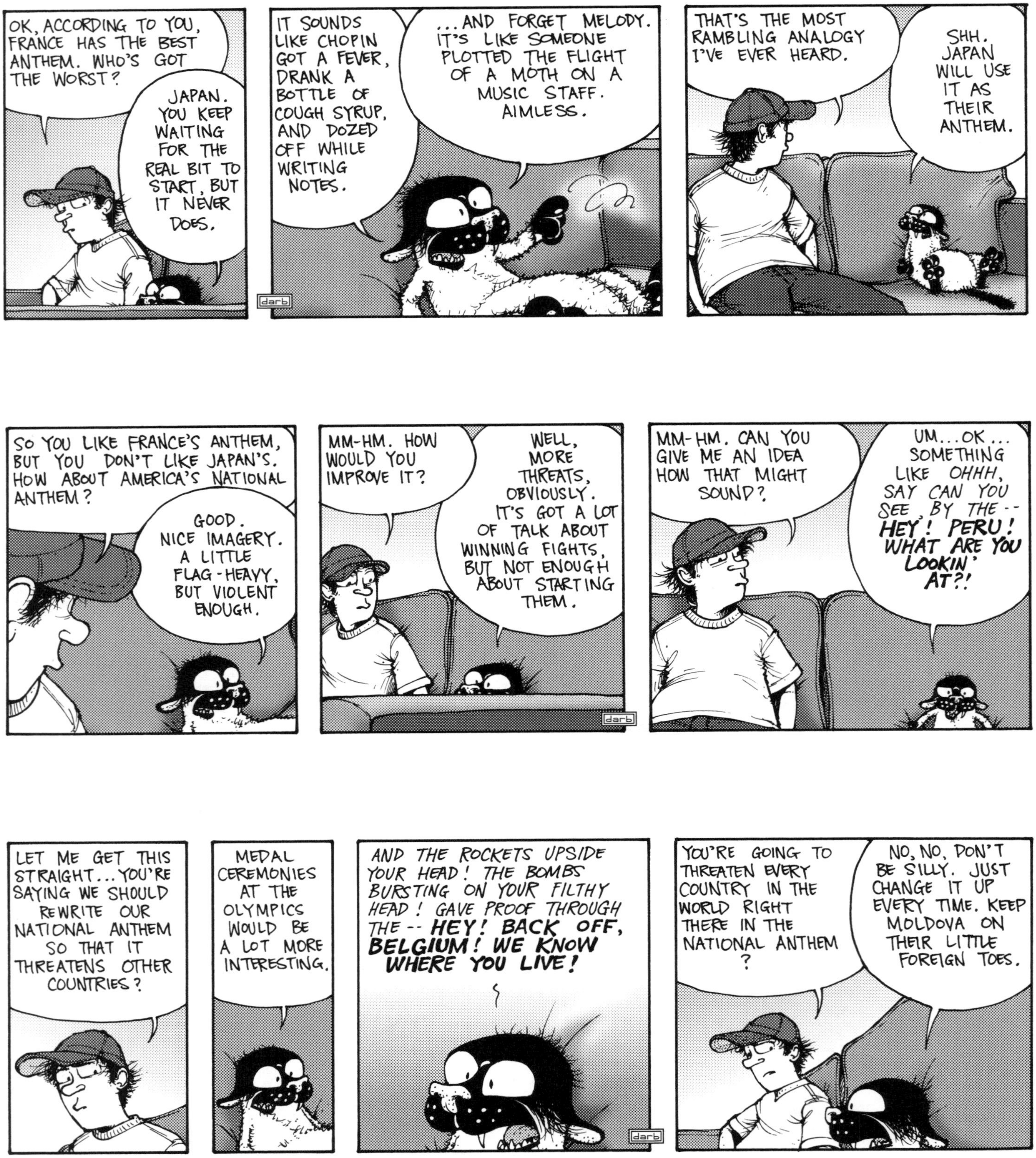
OK, ACCORDING TO YOU, FRANCE HAS THE BEST ANTHEM. WHO'S GOT THE WORST?
JAPAN. YOU KEEP WAITING FOR THE REAL BIT TO START, BUT IT NEVER DOES.
IT SOUNDS LIKE CHOPIN GOT A FEVER, DRANK A BOTTLE OF COUGH SYRUP, AND DOZED OFF WHILE WRITING NOTES.
...AND FORGET MELODY. IT'S LIKE SOMEONE PLOTTED THE FLIGHT OF A MOTH ON A MUSIC STAFF. AIMLESS.
darb
THAT'S THE MOST RAMBLING ANALOGY I'VE EVER HEARD.
SHH. JAPAN WILL USE IT AS THEIR ANTHEM.
SO YOU LIKE FRANCE'S ANTHEM, BUT YOU DON'T LIKE JAPAN'S. HOW ABOUT AMERICA'S NATIONAL ANTHEM?
GOOD. NICE IMAGERY. A LITTLE FLAG-HEAVY, BUT VIOLENT ENOUGH.
MM-HM. HOW WOULD YOU IMPROVE IT?
WELL, MORE THREATS, OBVIOUSLY. IT'S GOT A LOT OF TALK ABOUT WINNING FIGHTS, BUT NOT ENOUGH ABOUT STARTING THEM.
darb
MM-HM. CAN YOU GIVE ME AN IDEA HOW THAT MIGHT SOUND?
UM...OK... SOMETHING LIKE *OHHH, SAY CAN YOU SEE, BY THE--* **HEY! PERU! WHAT ARE YOU LOOKIN' AT?!**
LET ME GET THIS STRAIGHT... YOU'RE SAYING WE SHOULD REWRITE OUR NATIONAL ANTHEM SO THAT IT THREATENS OTHER COUNTRIES?
MEDAL CEREMONIES AT THE OLYMPICS WOULD BE A LOT MORE INTERESTING.
AND THE ROCKETS UPSIDE YOUR HEAD! THE BOMBS BURSTING ON YOUR FILTHY HEAD! GAVE PROOF THROUGH THE-- **HEY! BACK OFF, BELGIUM! WE KNOW WHERE YOU LIVE!**
darb
YOU'RE GOING TO THREATEN EVERY COUNTRY IN THE WORLD RIGHT THERE IN THE NATIONAL ANTHEM?
NO, NO, DON'T BE SILLY. JUST CHANGE IT UP EVERY TIME. KEEP MOLDOVA ON THEIR LITTLE FOREIGN TOES.

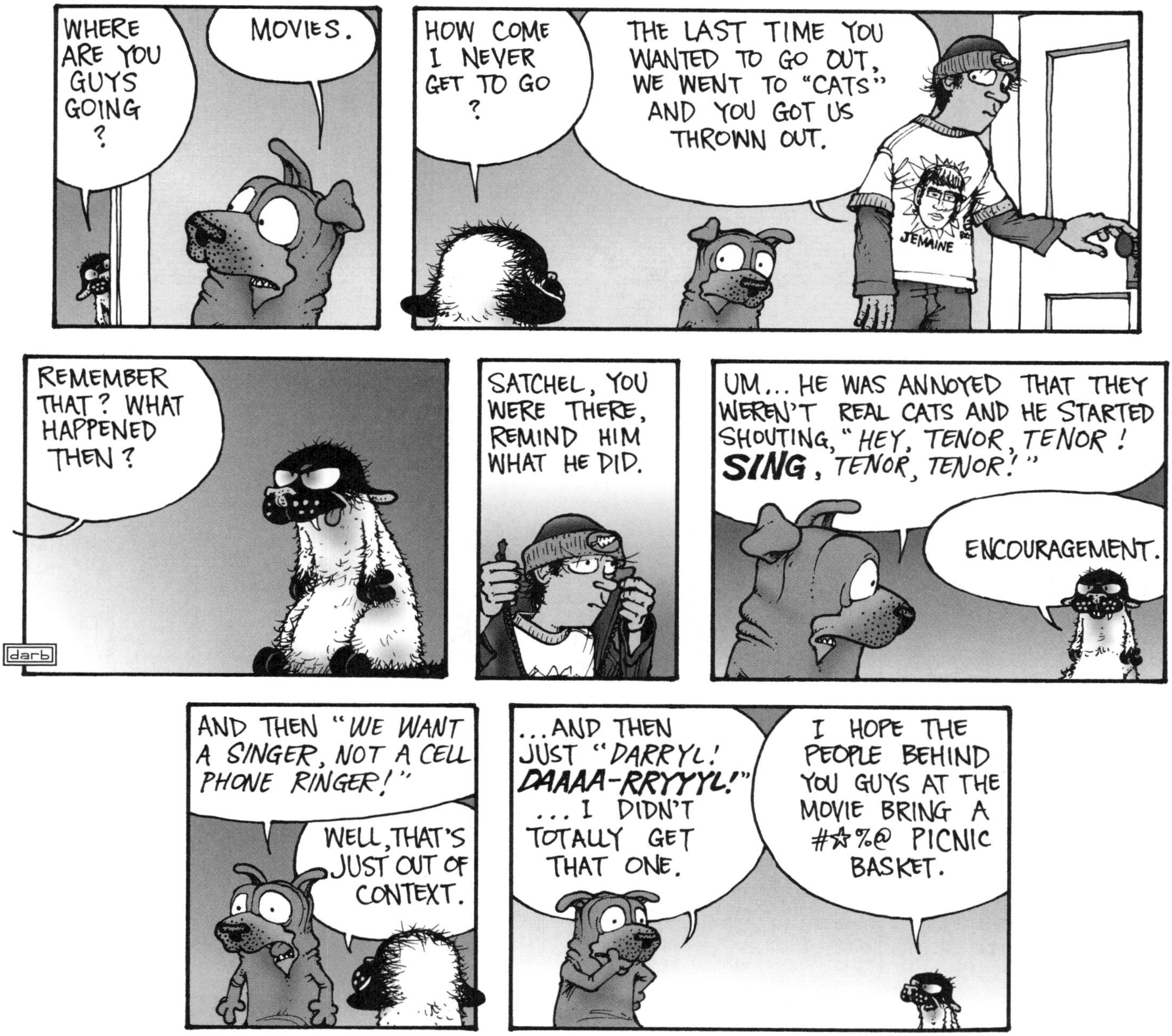
WHERE ARE YOU GUYS GOING ?
MOVIES.
HOW COME I NEVER GET TO GO ?
THE LAST TIME YOU WANTED TO GO OUT, WE WENT TO "CATS" AND YOU GOT US THROWN OUT.
JEMAINE
REMEMBER THAT? WHAT HAPPENED THEN?
darb
SATCHEL, YOU WERE THERE, REMIND HIM WHAT HE DID.
UM... HE WAS ANNOYED THAT THEY WEREN'T REAL CATS AND HE STARTED SHOUTING, "HEY, TENOR, TENOR! SING, TENOR, TENOR!"
ENCOURAGEMENT.
AND THEN "WE WANT A SINGER, NOT A CELL PHONE RINGER!"
WELL, THAT'S JUST OUT OF CONTEXT.
...AND THEN JUST "DARRYL! DAAAA-RRYYYL!" ...I DIDN'T TOTALLY GET THAT ONE.
I HOPE THE PEOPLE BEHIND YOU GUYS AT THE MOVIE BRING A #☆%@ PICNIC BASKET.

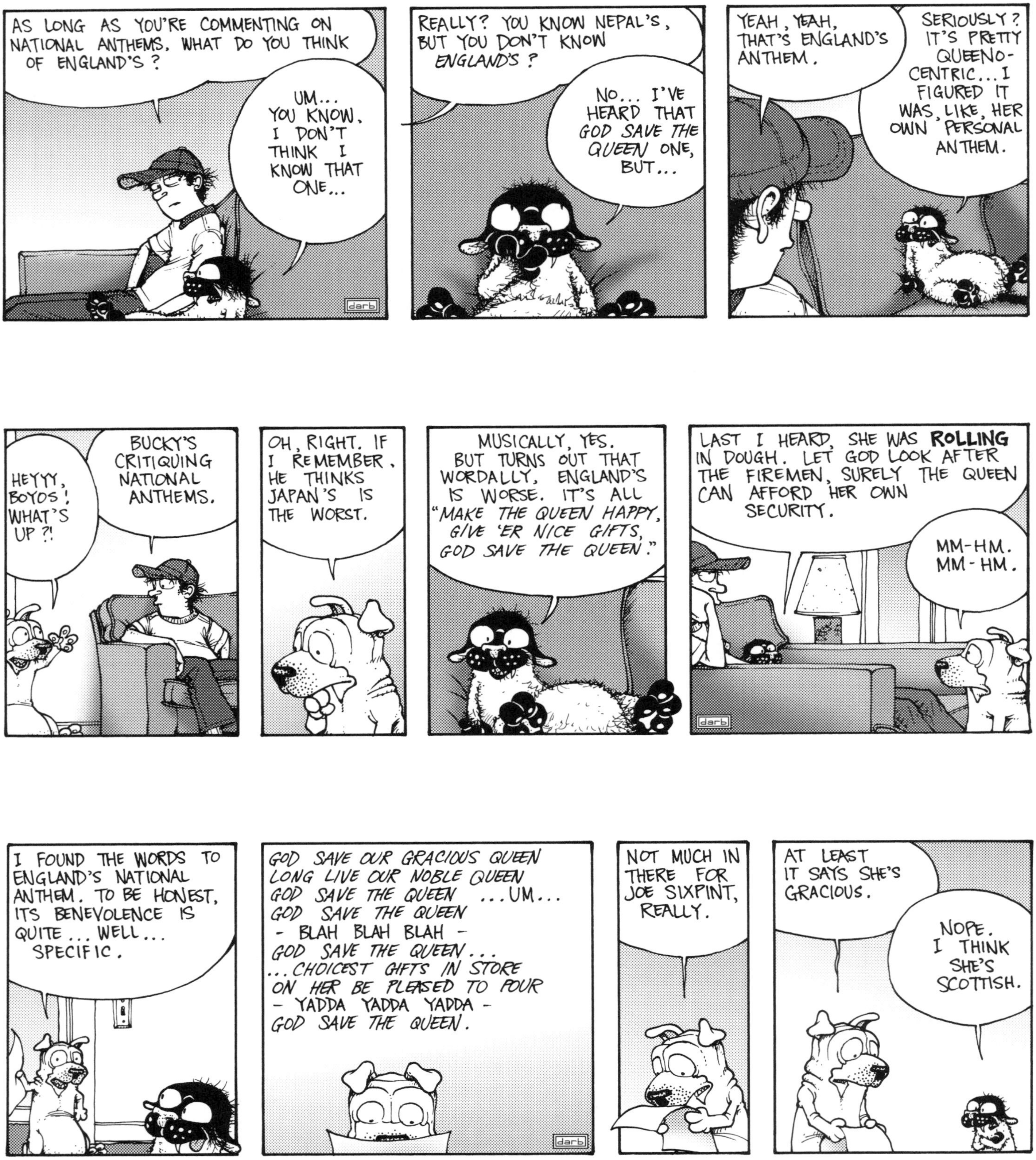
AS LONG AS YOU'RE COMMENTING ON NATIONAL ANTHEMS, WHAT DO YOU THINK OF ENGLAND'S?
UM... YOU KNOW, I DON'T THINK I KNOW THAT ONE...
darb
REALLY? YOU KNOW NEPAL'S, BUT YOU DON'T KNOW ENGLAND'S?
NO... I'VE HEARD THAT GOD SAVE THE QUEEN ONE, BUT...
YEAH, YEAH, THAT'S ENGLAND'S ANTHEM.
SERIOUSLY? IT'S PRETTY QUEENO-CENTRIC... I FIGURED IT WAS, LIKE, HER OWN PERSONAL ANTHEM.
HEYYY, BOYOS! WHAT'S UP?!
BUCKY'S CRITIQUING NATIONAL ANTHEMS.
OH, RIGHT. IF I REMEMBER, HE THINKS JAPAN'S IS THE WORST.
MUSICALLY, YES. BUT TURNS OUT THAT WORDALLY, ENGLAND'S IS WORSE. IT'S ALL "MAKE THE QUEEN HAPPY, GIVE 'ER NICE GIFTS, GOD SAVE THE QUEEN."
LAST I HEARD, SHE WAS **ROLLING** IN DOUGH. LET GOD LOOK AFTER THE FIREMEN, SURELY THE QUEEN CAN AFFORD HER OWN SECURITY.
MM-HM. MM-HM.
darb
I FOUND THE WORDS TO ENGLAND'S NATIONAL ANTHEM. TO BE HONEST, ITS BENEVOLENCE IS QUITE... WELL... SPECIFIC.
GOD SAVE OUR GRACIOUS QUEEN
LONG LIVE OUR NOBLE QUEEN
GOD SAVE THE QUEEN ...UM...
GOD SAVE THE QUEEN
- BLAH BLAH BLAH -
GOD SAVE THE QUEEN...
...CHOICEST GIFTS IN STORE
ON HER BE PLEASED TO POUR
- YADDA YADDA YADDA -
GOD SAVE THE QUEEN.
darb
NOT MUCH IN THERE FOR JOE SIXPINT, REALLY.
AT LEAST IT SAYS SHE'S GRACIOUS.
NOPE. I THINK SHE'S SCOTTISH.

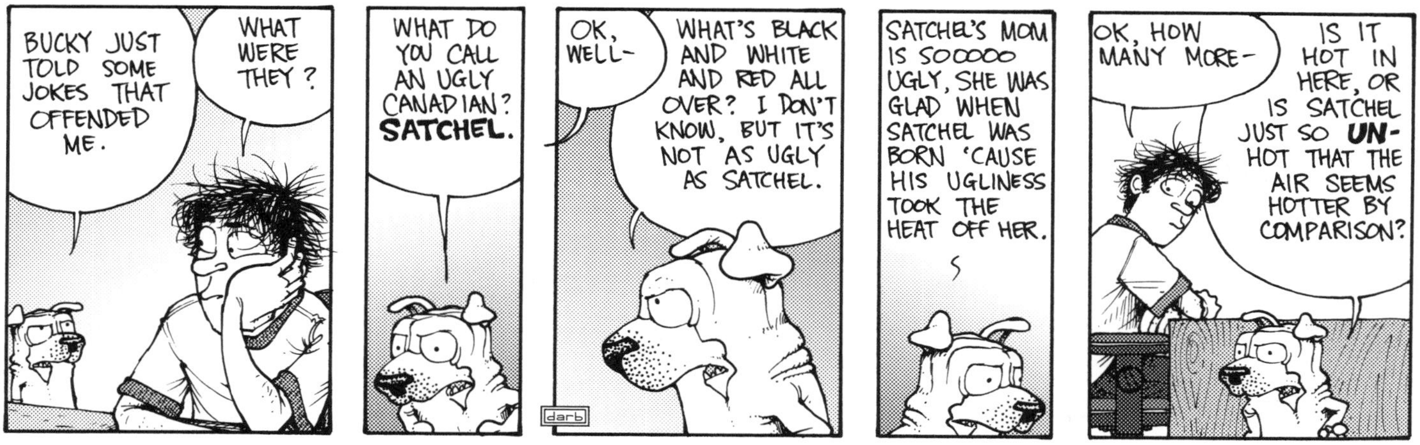
BUCKY JUST TOLD SOME JOKES THAT OFFENDED ME.
WHAT WERE THEY?
WHAT DO YOU CALL AN UGLY CANADIAN? **SATCHEL**.
OK, WELL-
WHAT'S BLACK AND WHITE AND RED ALL OVER? I DON'T KNOW, BUT IT'S NOT AS UGLY AS SATCHEL.
darb
SATCHEL'S MOM IS SOOOOO UGLY, SHE WAS GLAD WHEN SATCHEL WAS BORN 'CAUSE HIS UGLINESS TOOK THE HEAT OFF HER.
OK, HOW MANY MORE-
IS IT HOT IN HERE, OR IS SATCHEL JUST SO **UN**-HOT THAT THE AIR SEEMS HOTTER BY COMPARISON?

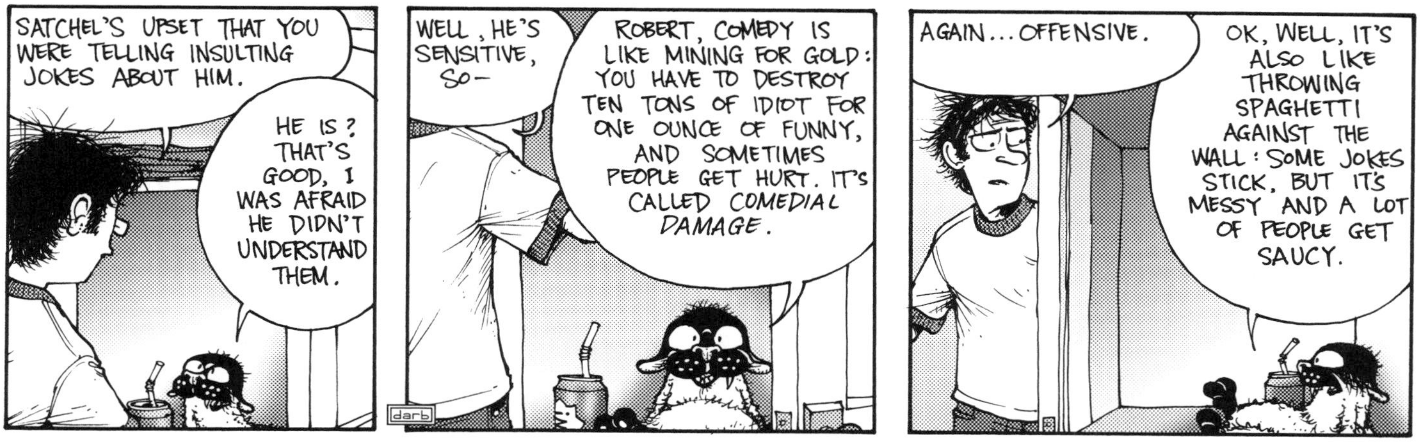
SATCHEL'S UPSET THAT YOU WERE TELLING INSULTING JOKES ABOUT HIM.
HE IS? THAT'S GOOD, I WAS AFRAID HE DIDN'T UNDERSTAND THEM.
WELL, HE'S SENSITIVE, SO-
ROBERT, COMEDY IS LIKE MINING FOR GOLD: YOU HAVE TO DESTROY TEN TONS OF IDIOT FOR ONE OUNCE OF FUNNY, AND SOMETIMES PEOPLE GET HURT. IT'S CALLED *COMEDIAL DAMAGE*.
darb
AGAIN... OFFENSIVE.
OK, WELL, IT'S ALSO LIKE THROWING SPAGHETTI AGAINST THE WALL: SOME JOKES STICK, BUT IT'S MESSY AND A LOT OF PEOPLE GET SAUCY.

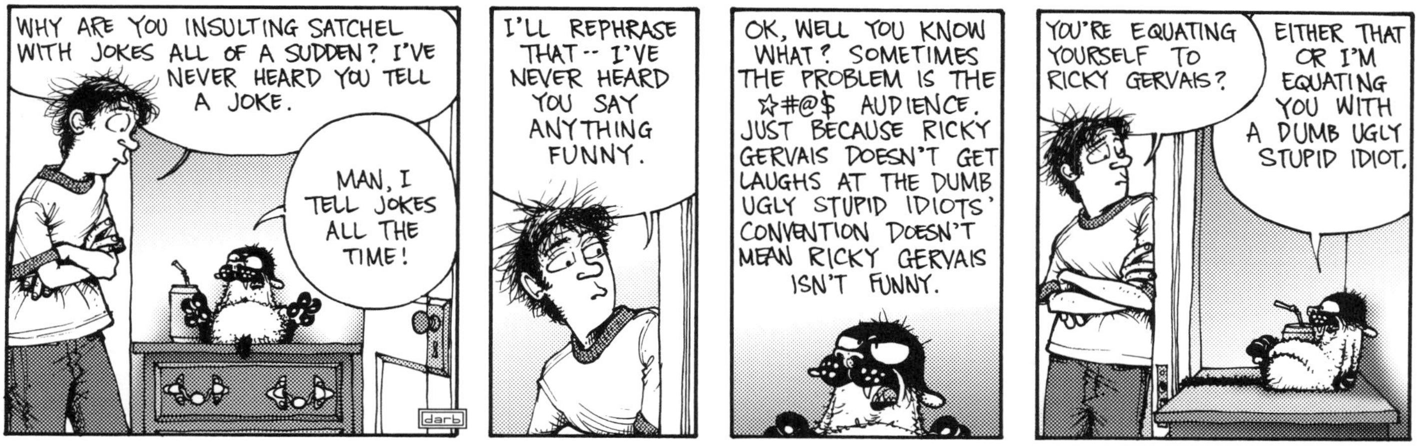
WHY ARE YOU INSULTING SATCHEL WITH JOKES ALL OF A SUDDEN? I'VE NEVER HEARD YOU TELL A JOKE.
MAN, I TELL JOKES ALL THE TIME!
darb
I'LL REPHRASE THAT-- I'VE NEVER HEARD YOU SAY ANYTHING FUNNY.
OK, WELL YOU KNOW WHAT? SOMETIMES THE PROBLEM IS THE ☆#@$ AUDIENCE. JUST BECAUSE RICKY GERVAIS DOESN'T GET LAUGHS AT THE DUMB UGLY STUPID IDIOTS' CONVENTION DOESN'T MEAN RICKY GERVAIS ISN'T FUNNY.
YOU'RE EQUATING YOURSELF TO RICKY GERVAIS?
EITHER THAT OR I'M EQUATING YOU WITH A DUMB UGLY STUPID IDIOT.

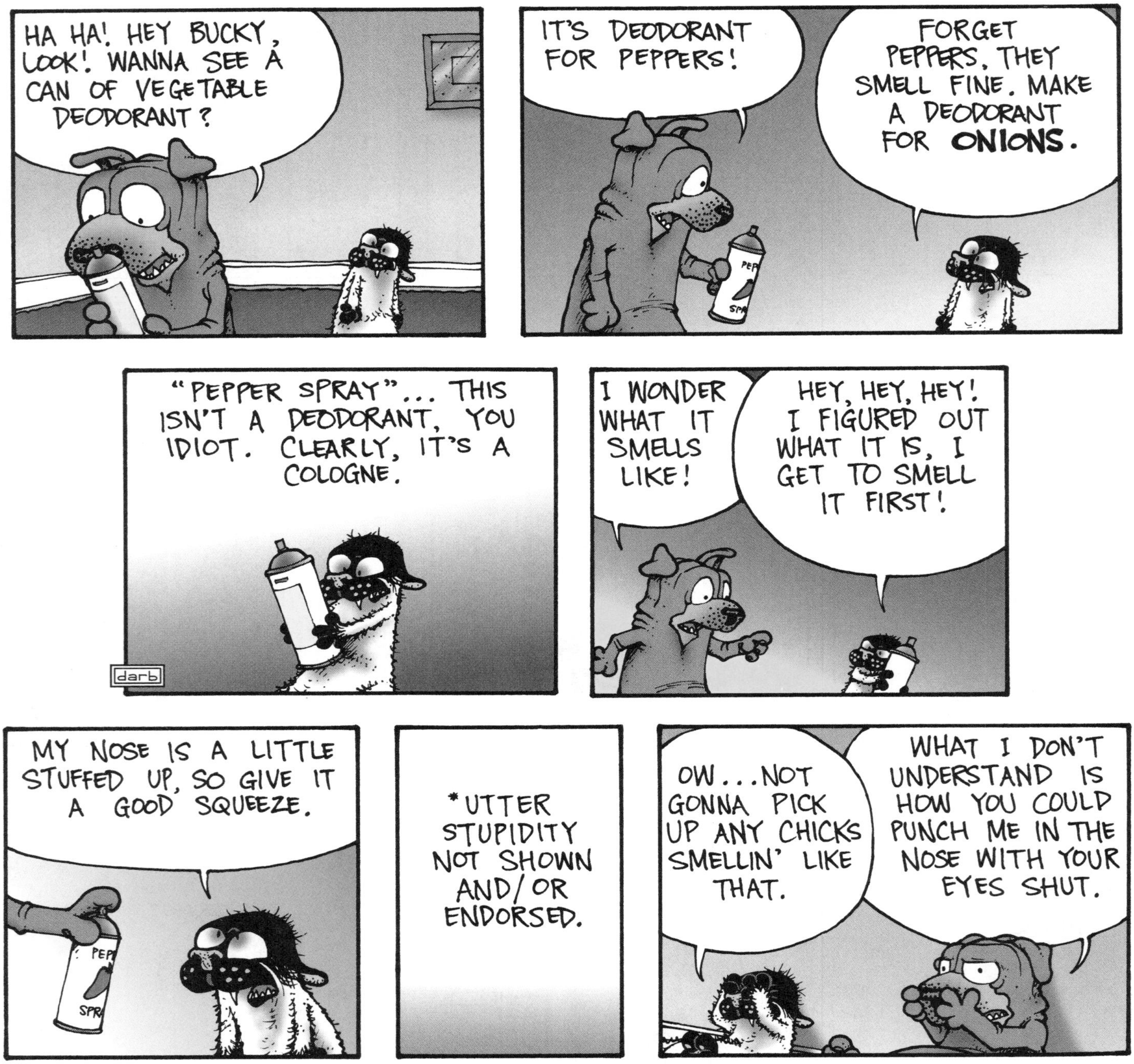
HA HA! HEY BUCKY, LOOK! WANNA SEE A CAN OF VEGETABLE DEODORANT?
IT'S DEODORANT FOR PEPPERS!
FORGET PEPPERS, THEY SMELL FINE. MAKE A DEODORANT FOR **ONIONS**.
"PEPPER SPRAY"... THIS ISN'T A DEODORANT, YOU IDIOT. CLEARLY, IT'S A COLOGNE.
darb
I WONDER WHAT IT SMELLS LIKE!
HEY, HEY, HEY! I FIGURED OUT WHAT IT IS, I GET TO SMELL IT FIRST!
MY NOSE IS A LITTLE STUFFED UP, SO GIVE IT A GOOD SQUEEZE.
*UTTER STUPIDITY NOT SHOWN AND/OR ENDORSED.
OW...NOT GONNA PICK UP ANY CHICKS SMELLIN' LIKE THAT.
WHAT I DON'T UNDERSTAND IS HOW YOU COULD PUNCH ME IN THE NOSE WITH YOUR EYES SHUT.

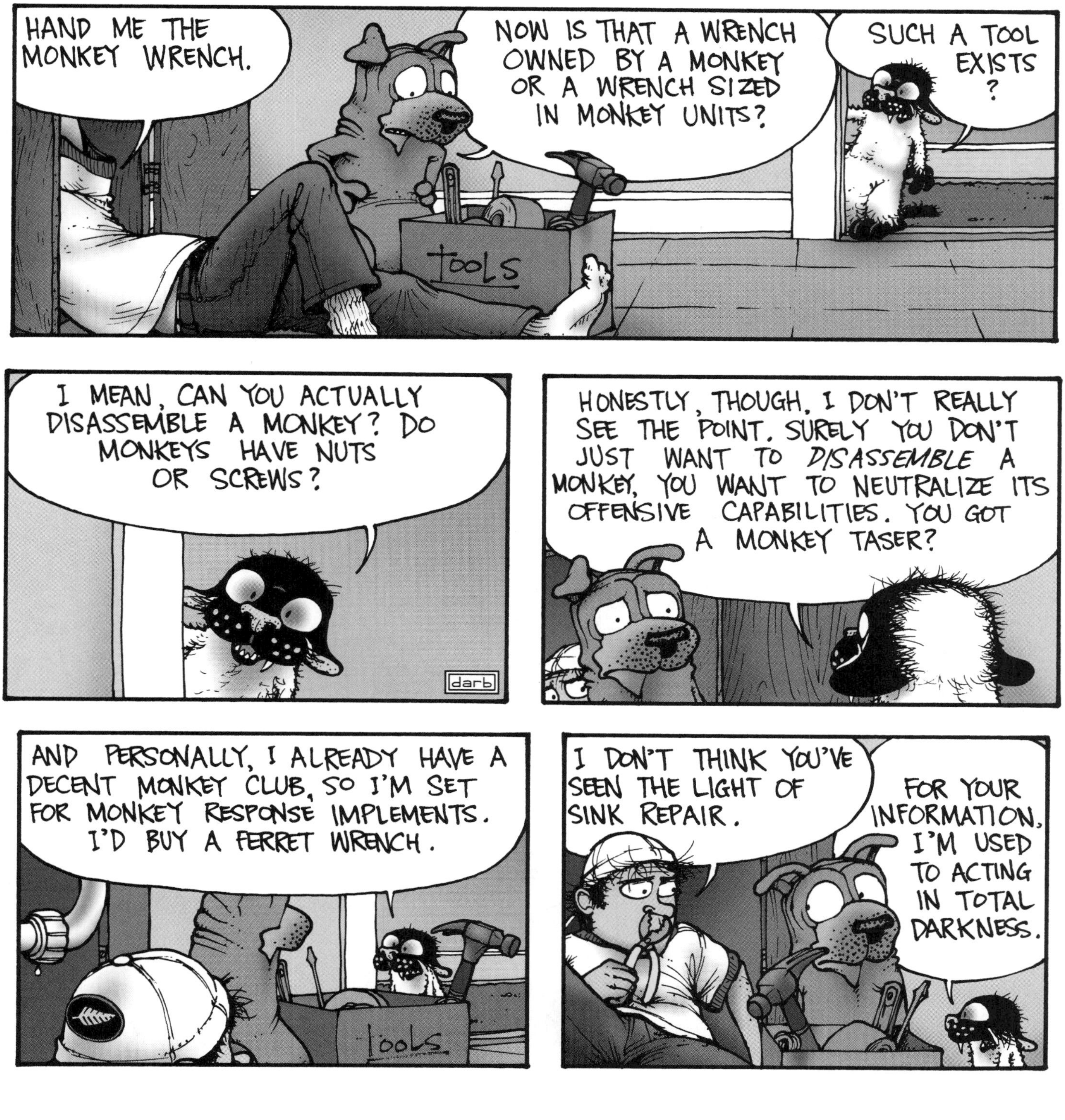
HAND ME THE MONKEY WRENCH.
NOW IS THAT A WRENCH OWNED BY A MONKEY OR A WRENCH SIZED IN MONKEY UNITS?
SUCH A TOOL EXISTS ?
TOOLS
I MEAN, CAN YOU ACTUALLY DISASSEMBLE A MONKEY? DO MONKEYS HAVE NUTS OR SCREWS?
darb
HONESTLY, THOUGH, I DON'T REALLY SEE THE POINT. SURELY YOU DON'T JUST WANT TO *DISASSEMBLE* A MONKEY, YOU WANT TO NEUTRALIZE ITS OFFENSIVE CAPABILITIES. YOU GOT A MONKEY TASER?
AND PERSONALLY, I ALREADY HAVE A DECENT MONKEY CLUB, SO I'M SET FOR MONKEY RESPONSE IMPLEMENTS. I'D BUY A FERRET WRENCH.
TOOLS
I DON'T THINK YOU'VE SEEN THE LIGHT OF SINK REPAIR.
FOR YOUR INFORMATION, I'M USED TO ACTING IN TOTAL DARKNESS.

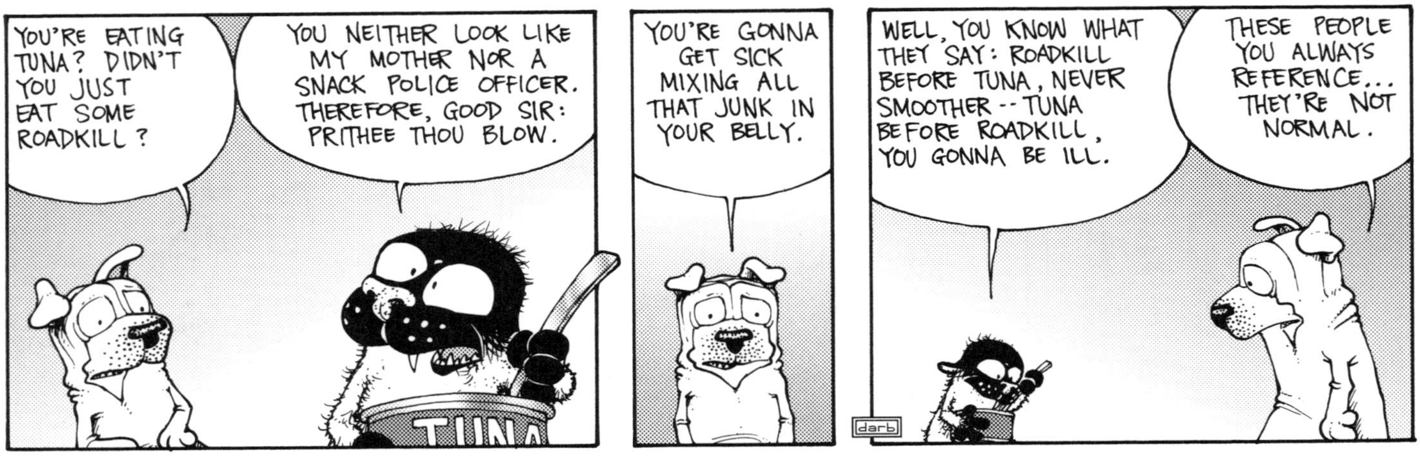
YOU'RE EATING TUNA? DIDN'T YOU JUST EAT SOME ROADKILL?
YOU NEITHER LOOK LIKE MY MOTHER NOR A SNACK POLICE OFFICER. THEREFORE, GOOD SIR: PRITHEE THOU BLOW.
TUNA
YOU'RE GONNA GET SICK MIXING ALL THAT JUNK IN YOUR BELLY.
WELL, YOU KNOW WHAT THEY SAY: ROADKILL BEFORE TUNA, NEVER SMOOTHER -- TUNA BEFORE ROADKILL, YOU GONNA BE ILL.
darb
THESE PEOPLE YOU ALWAYS REFERENCE... THEY'RE NOT NORMAL.

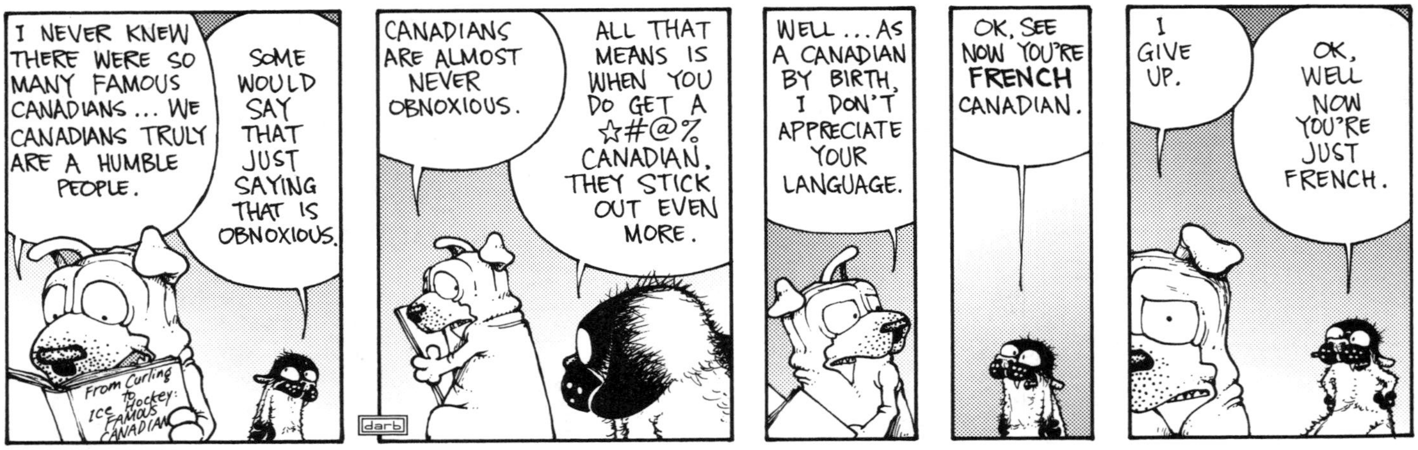
I NEVER KNEW THERE WERE SO MANY FAMOUS CANADIANS... WE CANADIANS TRULY ARE A HUMBLE PEOPLE.
SOME WOULD SAY THAT JUST SAYING THAT IS OBNOXIOUS.
From Curling to Ice Hockey: FAMOUS CANADIAN
darb
CANADIANS ARE ALMOST NEVER OBNOXIOUS.
ALL THAT MEANS IS WHEN YOU DO GET A ☆#@% CANADIAN, THEY STICK OUT EVEN MORE.
WELL... AS A CANADIAN BY BIRTH, I DON'T APPRECIATE YOUR LANGUAGE.
OK, SEE NOW YOU'RE **FRENCH** CANADIAN.
I GIVE UP.
OK, WELL NOW YOU'RE JUST FRENCH.

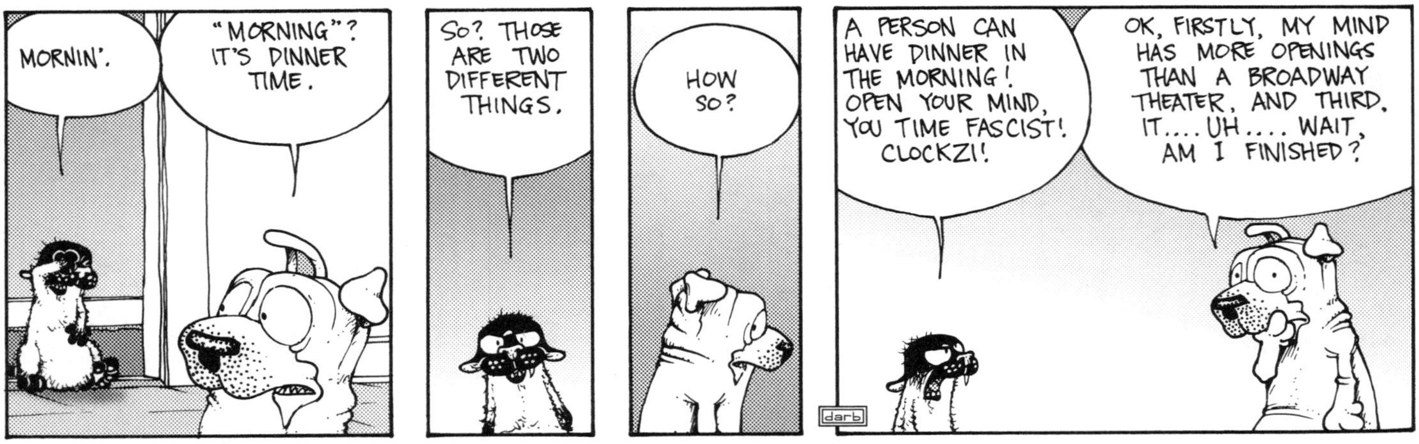
MORNIN'.
"MORNING"? IT'S DINNER TIME.
SO? THOSE ARE TWO DIFFERENT THINGS.
HOW SO?
darb
A PERSON CAN HAVE DINNER IN THE MORNING! OPEN YOUR MIND, YOU TIME FASCIST! CLOCKZI!
OK, FIRSTLY, MY MIND HAS MORE OPENINGS THAN A BROADWAY THEATER, AND THIRD, IT.... UH.... WAIT, AM I FINISHED?

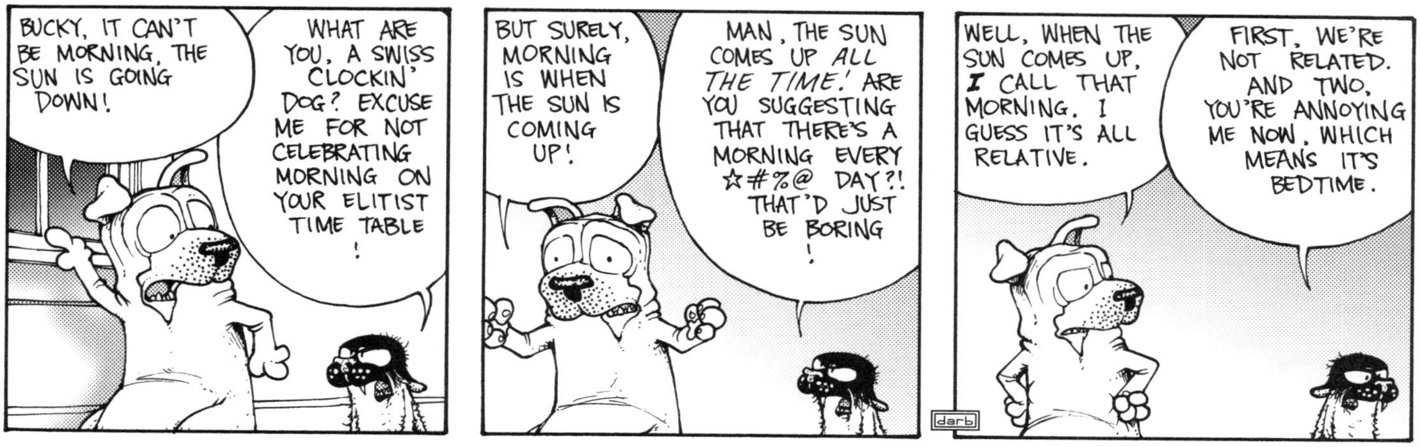
BUCKY, IT CAN'T BE MORNING, THE SUN IS GOING DOWN!
WHAT ARE YOU, A SWISS CLOCKIN' DOG? EXCUSE ME FOR NOT CELEBRATING MORNING ON YOUR ELITIST TIME TABLE!
BUT SURELY, MORNING IS WHEN THE SUN IS COMING UP!
MAN, THE SUN COMES UP *ALL THE TIME!* ARE YOU SUGGESTING THAT THERE'S A MORNING EVERY ☆#%@ DAY?! THAT'D JUST BE BORING!
WELL, WHEN THE SUN COMES UP, **I** CALL THAT MORNING. I GUESS IT'S ALL RELATIVE.
FIRST, WE'RE NOT RELATED. AND TWO, YOU'RE ANNOYING ME NOW, WHICH MEANS IT'S BEDTIME.
darb

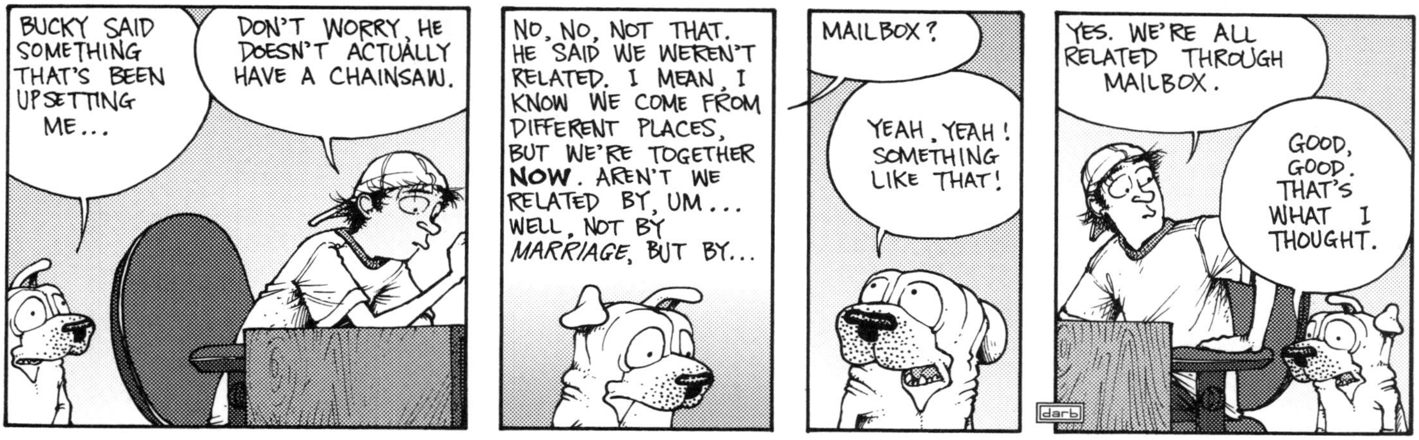
BUCKY SAID SOMETHING THAT'S BEEN UPSETTING ME...
DON'T WORRY, HE DOESN'T ACTUALLY HAVE A CHAINSAW.
NO, NO, NOT THAT. HE SAID WE WEREN'T RELATED. I MEAN, I KNOW WE COME FROM DIFFERENT PLACES, BUT WE'RE TOGETHER **NOW**. AREN'T WE RELATED BY, UM... WELL, NOT BY *MARRIAGE*, BUT BY...
MAILBOX?
YEAH, YEAH! SOMETHING LIKE THAT!
YES. WE'RE ALL RELATED THROUGH MAILBOX.
GOOD, GOOD. THAT'S WHAT I THOUGHT.
darb

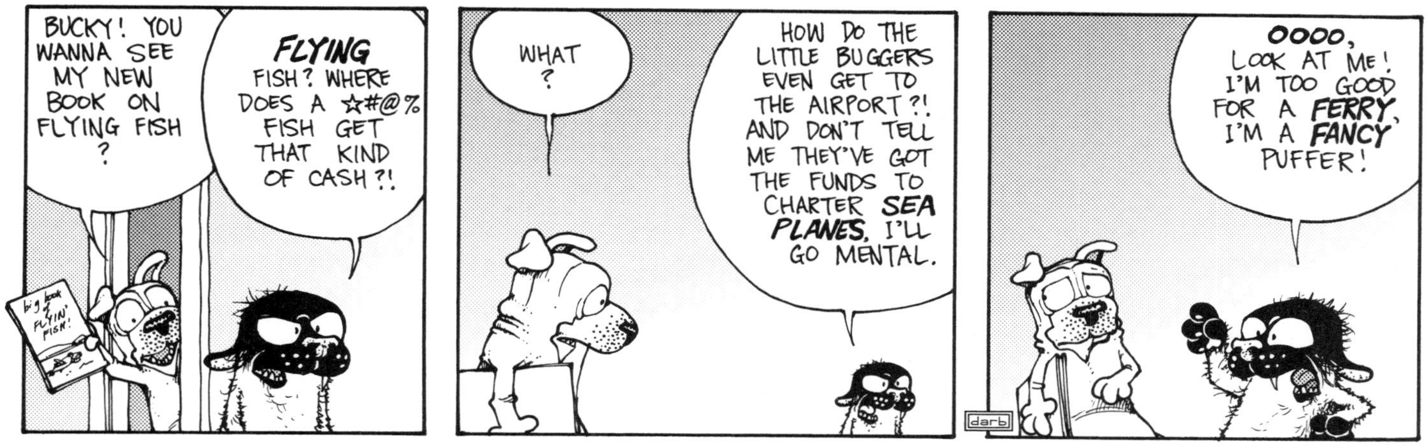
BUCKY! YOU WANNA SEE MY NEW BOOK ON FLYING FISH?
big book of FLYIN' FISH!
FLYING FISH? WHERE DOES A ☆#@% FISH GET THAT KIND OF CASH?!
WHAT?
HOW DO THE LITTLE BUGGERS EVEN GET TO THE AIRPORT?! AND DON'T TELL ME THEY'VE GOT THE FUNDS TO CHARTER **SEA PLANES**. I'LL GO MENTAL.
OOOO, LOOK AT ME! I'M TOO GOOD FOR A **FERRY**, I'M A **FANCY** PUFFER!
darb

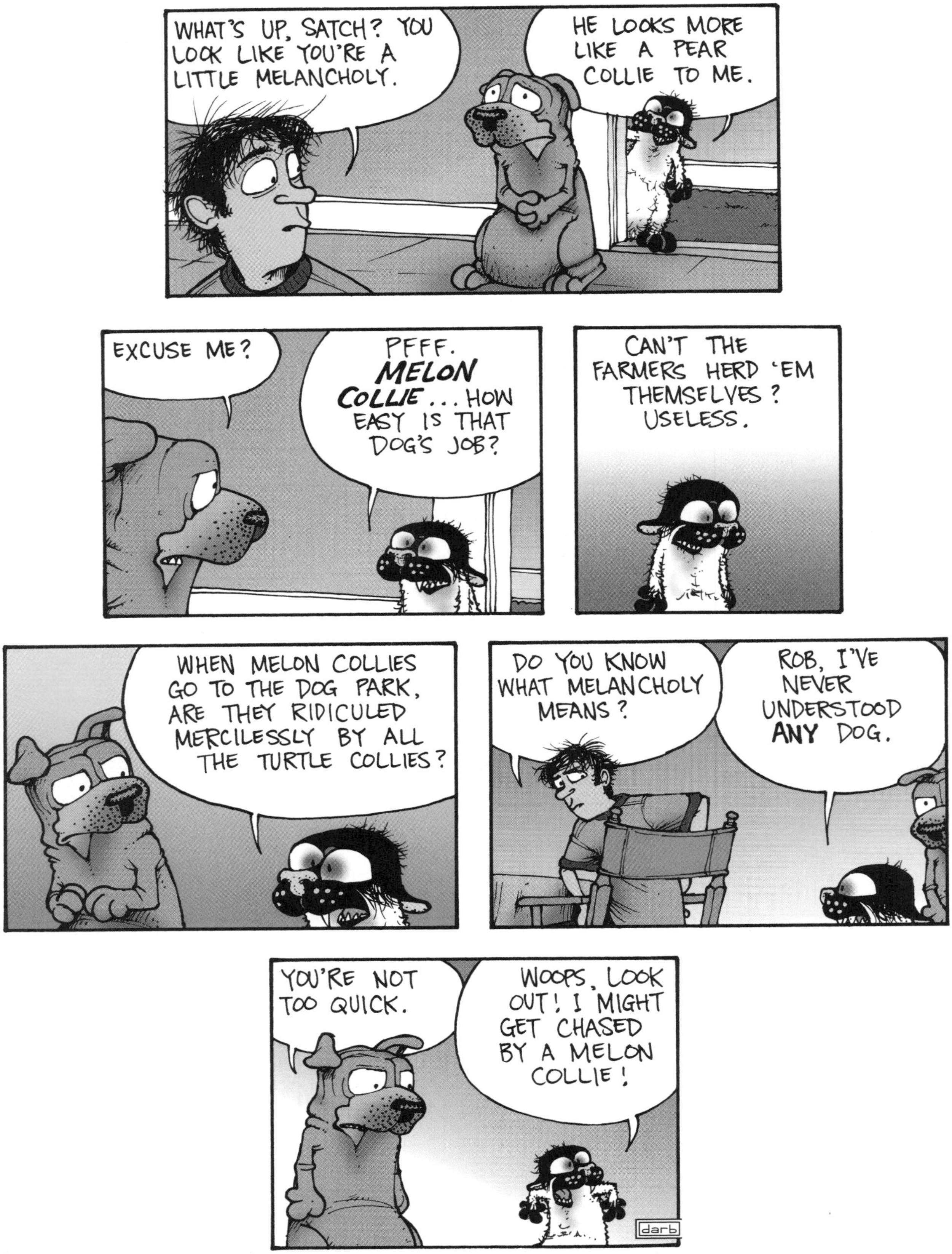
WHAT'S UP, SATCH? YOU LOOK LIKE YOU'RE A LITTLE MELANCHOLY.
HE LOOKS MORE LIKE A PEAR COLLIE TO ME.
EXCUSE ME?
PFFF. MELON COLLIE... HOW EASY IS THAT DOG'S JOB?
CAN'T THE FARMERS HERD 'EM THEMSELVES? USELESS.
WHEN MELON COLLIES GO TO THE DOG PARK, ARE THEY RIDICULED MERCILESSLY BY ALL THE TURTLE COLLIES?
DO YOU KNOW WHAT MELANCHOLY MEANS?
ROB, I'VE NEVER UNDERSTOOD ANY DOG.
YOU'RE NOT TOO QUICK.
WOOPS, LOOK OUT! I MIGHT GET CHASED BY A MELON COLLIE!
darb

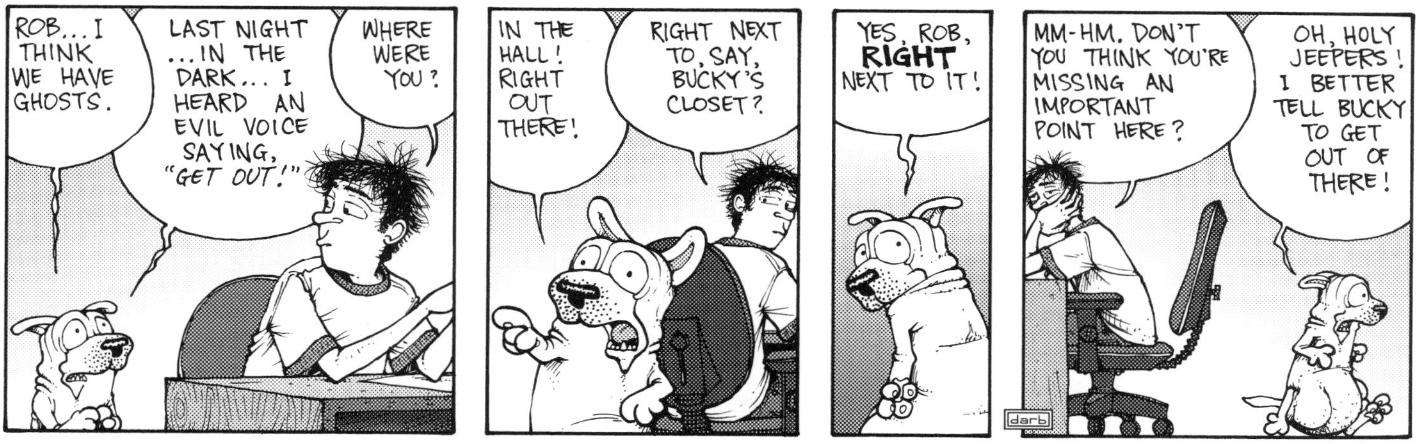
ROB... I THINK WE HAVE GHOSTS.
LAST NIGHT ...IN THE DARK... I HEARD AN EVIL VOICE SAYING, "GET OUT!"
WHERE WERE YOU?
IN THE HALL! RIGHT OUT THERE!
RIGHT NEXT TO, SAY, BUCKY'S CLOSET?
YES, ROB, **RIGHT** NEXT TO IT!
MM-HM. DON'T YOU THINK YOU'RE MISSING AN IMPORTANT POINT HERE?
OH, HOLY JEEPERS! I BETTER TELL BUCKY TO GET OUT OF THERE!

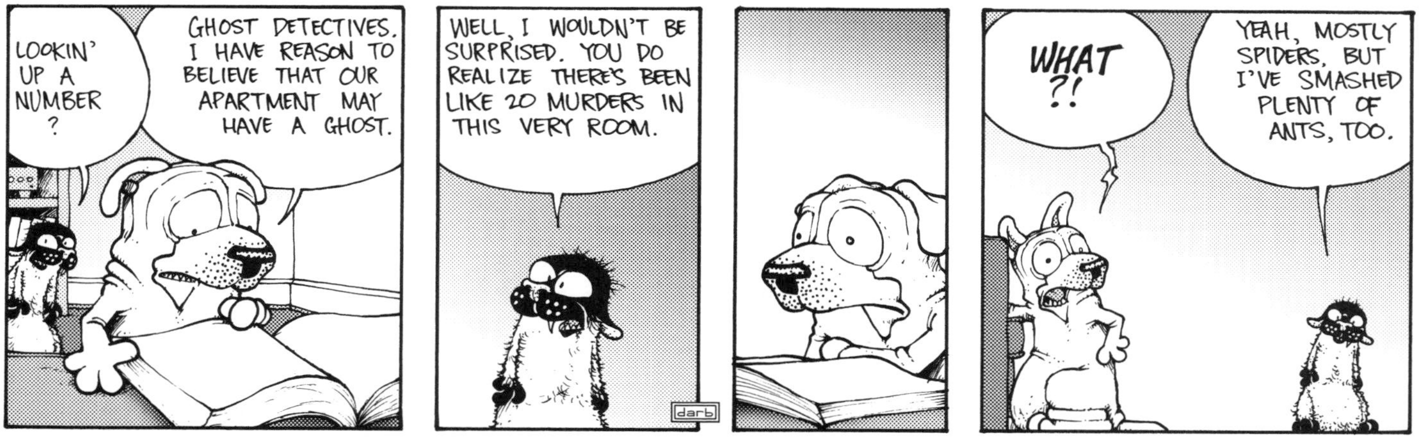
LOOKIN' UP A NUMBER?
GHOST DETECTIVES. I HAVE REASON TO BELIEVE THAT OUR APARTMENT MAY HAVE A GHOST.
WELL, I WOULDN'T BE SURPRISED. YOU DO REALIZE THERE'S BEEN LIKE 20 MURDERS IN THIS VERY ROOM.
WHAT ?!
YEAH, MOSTLY SPIDERS, BUT I'VE SMASHED PLENTY OF ANTS, TOO.

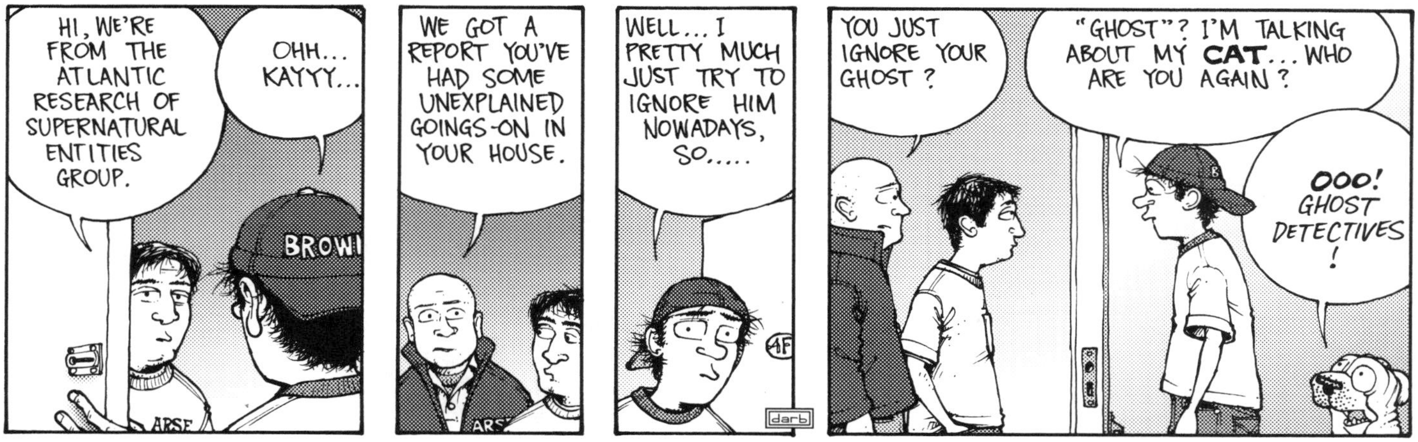
HI, WE'RE FROM THE ATLANTIC RESEARCH OF SUPERNATURAL ENTITIES GROUP.
OHH... KAYYY...
WE GOT A REPORT YOU'VE HAD SOME UNEXPLAINED GOINGS-ON IN YOUR HOUSE.
WELL... I PRETTY MUCH JUST TRY TO IGNORE HIM NOWADAYS, SO.....
YOU JUST IGNORE YOUR GHOST?
"GHOST"? I'M TALKING ABOUT MY **CAT**... WHO ARE YOU AGAIN?
OOO! GHOST DETECTIVES!

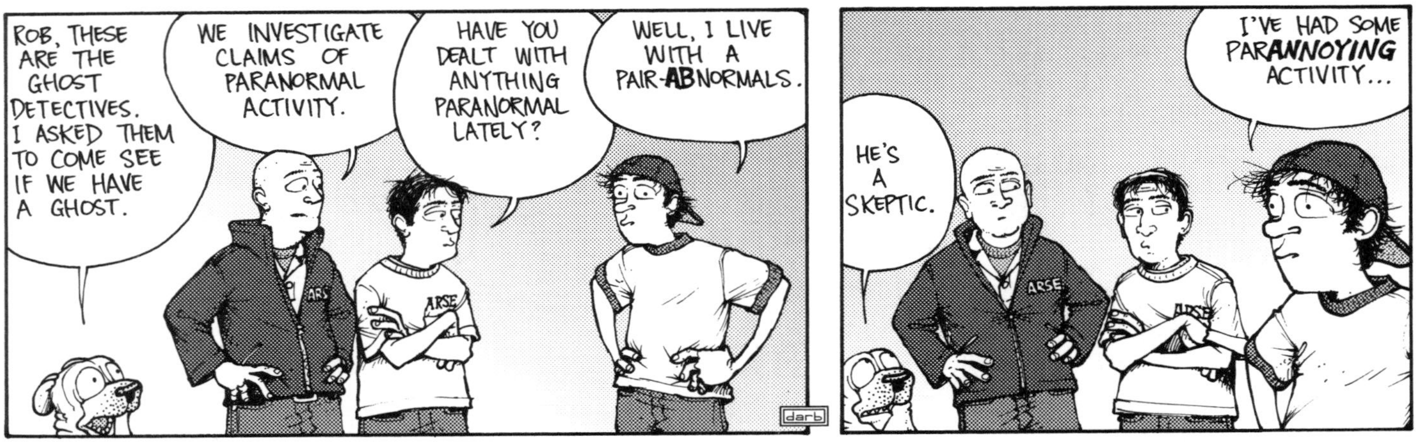
ROB, THESE ARE THE GHOST DETECTIVES. I ASKED THEM TO COME SEE IF WE HAVE A GHOST.
WE INVESTIGATE CLAIMS OF PARANORMAL ACTIVITY.
HAVE YOU DEALT WITH ANYTHING PARANORMAL LATELY?
WELL, I LIVE WITH A PAIR-AB NORMALS.
darb
HE'S A SKEPTIC.
I'VE HAD SOME PARANNOYING ACTIVITY...

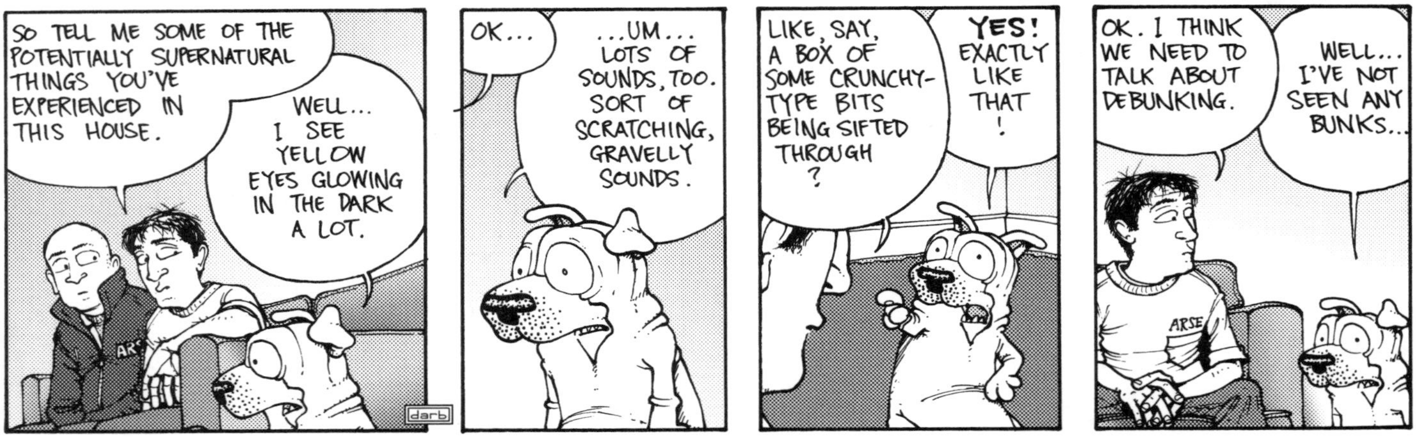
SO TELL ME SOME OF THE POTENTIALLY SUPERNATURAL THINGS YOU'VE EXPERIENCED IN THIS HOUSE.
WELL... I SEE YELLOW EYES GLOWING IN THE DARK A LOT.
darb
OK...
...UM... LOTS OF SOUNDS, TOO. SORT OF SCRATCHING, GRAVELLY SOUNDS.
LIKE, SAY, A BOX OF SOME CRUNCHY-TYPE BITS BEING SIFTED THROUGH?
YES! EXACTLY LIKE THAT!
OK. I THINK WE NEED TO TALK ABOUT DEBUNKING.
WELL... I'VE NOT SEEN ANY BUNKS...

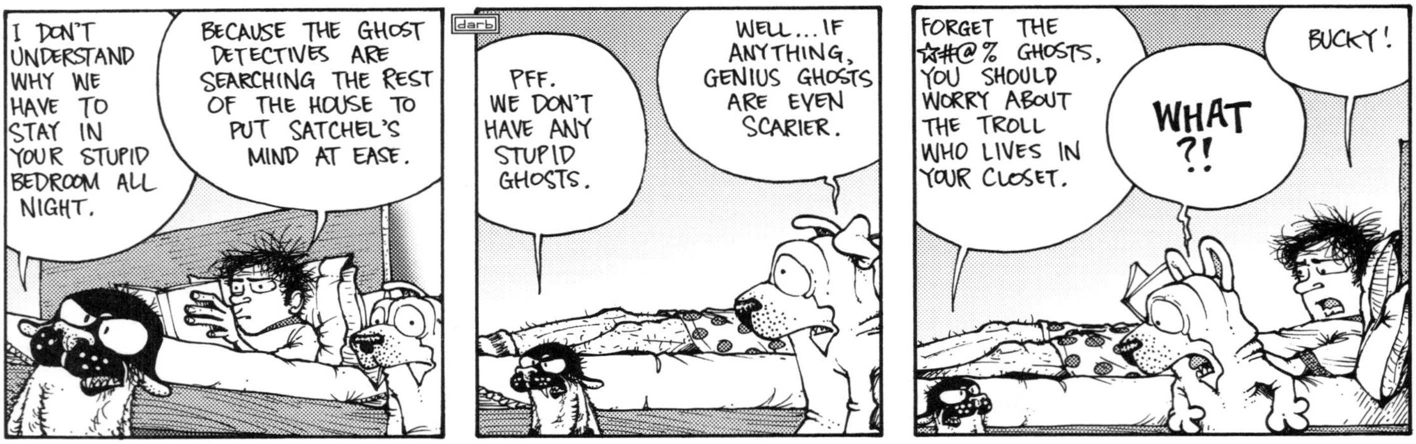
I DON'T UNDERSTAND WHY WE HAVE TO STAY IN YOUR STUPID BEDROOM ALL NIGHT.
BECAUSE THE GHOST DETECTIVES ARE SEARCHING THE REST OF THE HOUSE TO PUT SATCHEL'S MIND AT EASE.
darb
PFF. WE DON'T HAVE ANY STUPID GHOSTS.
WELL... IF ANYTHING, GENIUS GHOSTS ARE EVEN SCARIER.
FORGET THE ☆#@% GHOSTS, YOU SHOULD WORRY ABOUT THE TROLL WHO LIVES IN YOUR CLOSET.
WHAT?!
BUCKY!

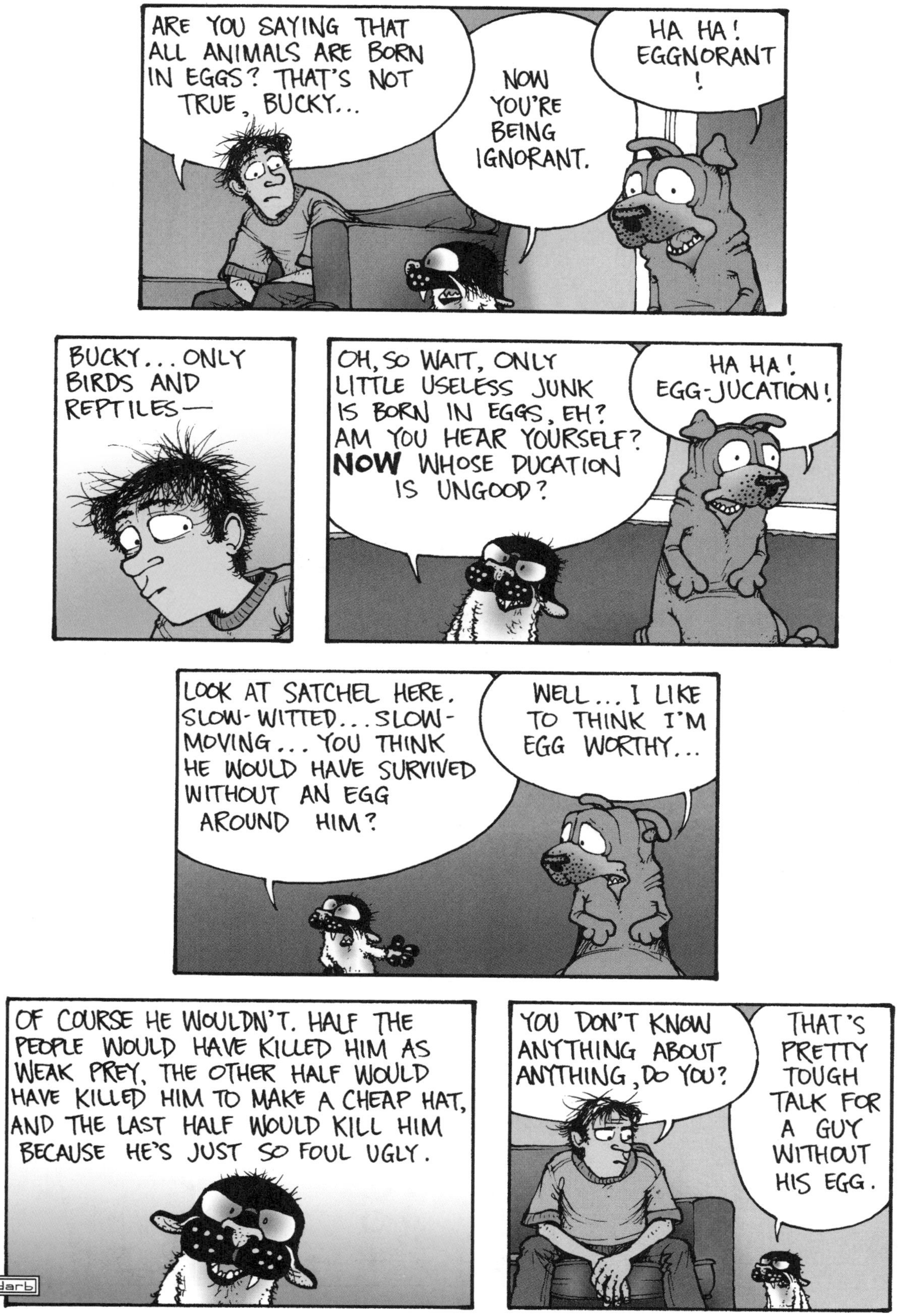
ARE YOU SAYING THAT ALL ANIMALS ARE BORN IN EGGS? THAT'S NOT TRUE, BUCKY...
NOW YOU'RE BEING IGNORANT.
HA HA! EGGNORANT!
BUCKY... ONLY BIRDS AND REPTILES—
OH, SO WAIT, ONLY LITTLE USELESS JUNK IS BORN IN EGGS, EH? AM YOU HEAR YOURSELF? NOW WHOSE DUCATION IS UNGOOD?
HA HA! EGG-JUCATION!
LOOK AT SATCHEL HERE. SLOW-WITTED... SLOW-MOVING... YOU THINK HE WOULD HAVE SURVIVED WITHOUT AN EGG AROUND HIM?
WELL... I LIKE TO THINK I'M EGG WORTHY...
OF COURSE HE WOULDN'T. HALF THE PEOPLE WOULD HAVE KILLED HIM AS WEAK PREY, THE OTHER HALF WOULD HAVE KILLED HIM TO MAKE A CHEAP HAT, AND THE LAST HALF WOULD KILL HIM BECAUSE HE'S JUST SO FOUL UGLY.
darb
YOU DON'T KNOW ANYTHING ABOUT ANYTHING, DO YOU?
THAT'S PRETTY TOUGH TALK FOR A GUY WITHOUT HIS EGG.

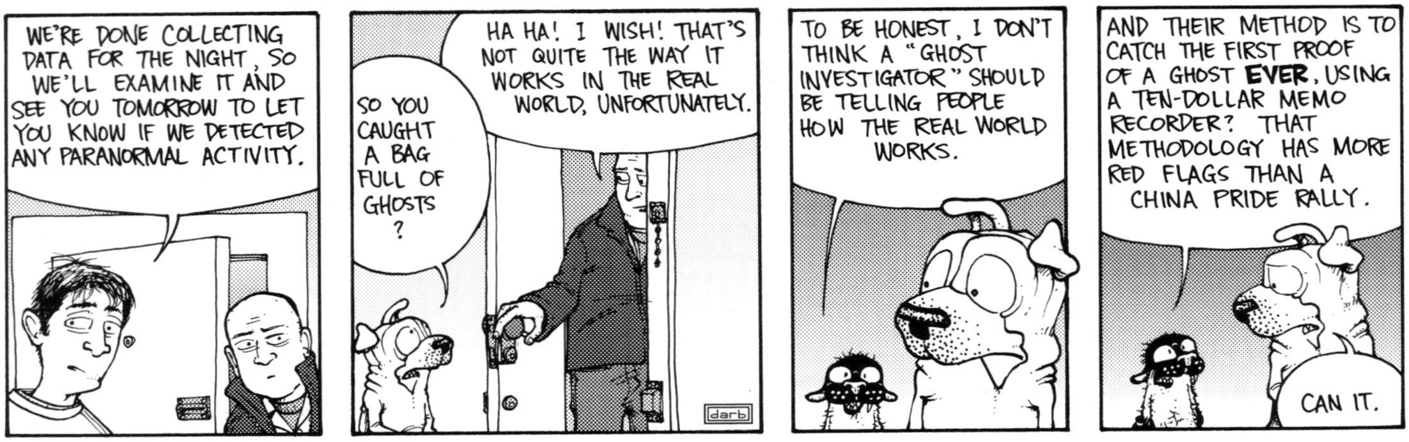
WE'RE DONE COLLECTING DATA FOR THE NIGHT, SO WE'LL EXAMINE IT AND SEE YOU TOMORROW TO LET YOU KNOW IF WE DETECTED ANY PARANORMAL ACTIVITY.
SO YOU CAUGHT A BAG FULL OF GHOSTS?
HA HA! I WISH! THAT'S NOT QUITE THE WAY IT WORKS IN THE REAL WORLD, UNFORTUNATELY.
darb
TO BE HONEST, I DON'T THINK A "GHOST INVESTIGATOR" SHOULD BE TELLING PEOPLE HOW THE REAL WORLD WORKS.
AND THEIR METHOD IS TO CATCH THE FIRST PROOF OF A GHOST EVER, USING A TEN-DOLLAR MEMO RECORDER? THAT METHODOLOGY HAS MORE RED FLAGS THAN A CHINA PRIDE RALLY.
CAN IT.

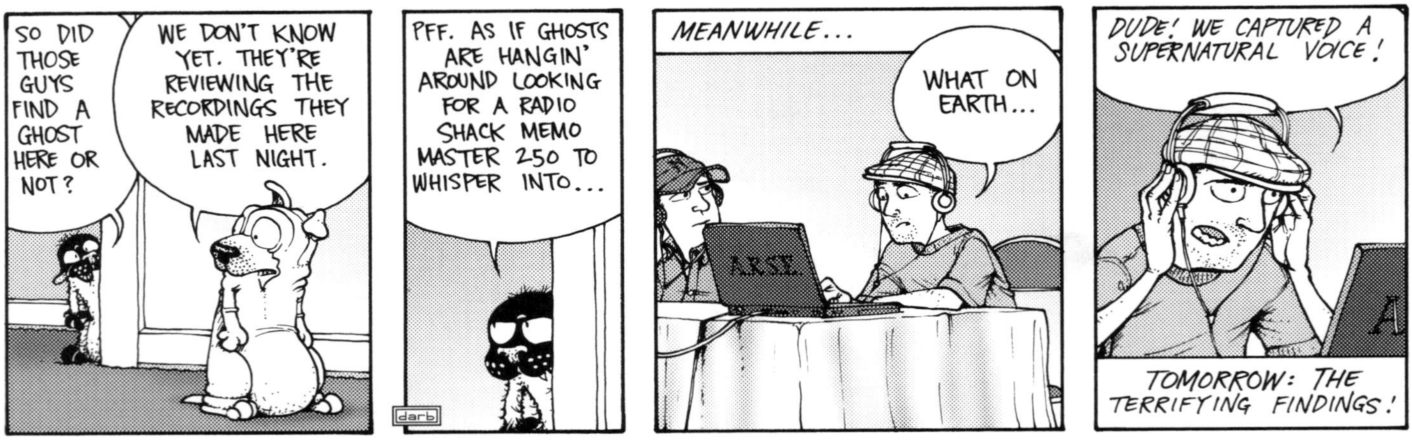
SO DID THOSE GUYS FIND A GHOST HERE OR NOT?
WE DON'T KNOW YET. THEY'RE REVIEWING THE RECORDINGS THEY MADE HERE LAST NIGHT.
PFF. AS IF GHOSTS ARE HANGIN' AROUND LOOKING FOR A RADIO SHACK MEMO MASTER 250 TO WHISPER INTO...
darb
MEANWHILE...
WHAT ON EARTH...
A.R.S.E.
DUDE! WE CAPTURED A SUPERNATURAL VOICE!
TOMORROW: THE TERRIFYING FINDINGS!

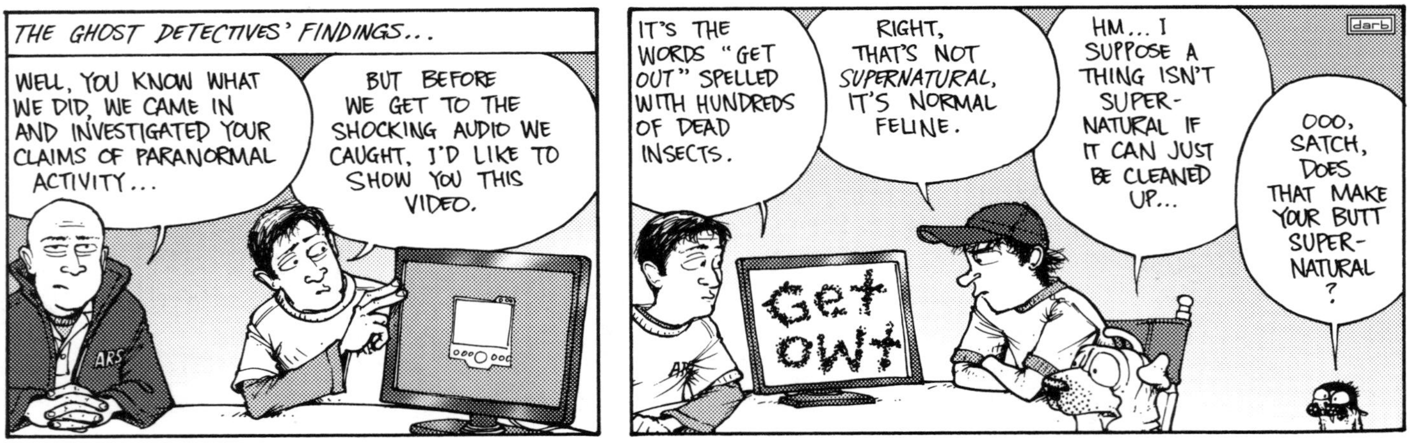
THE GHOST DETECTIVES' FINDINGS...
WELL, YOU KNOW WHAT WE DID, WE CAME IN AND INVESTIGATED YOUR CLAIMS OF PARANORMAL ACTIVITY...
BUT BEFORE WE GET TO THE SHOCKING AUDIO WE CAUGHT, I'D LIKE TO SHOW YOU THIS VIDEO.
IT'S THE WORDS "GET OUT" SPELLED WITH HUNDREDS OF DEAD INSECTS.
RIGHT, THAT'S NOT SUPERNATURAL, IT'S NORMAL FELINE.
HM... I SUPPOSE A THING ISN'T SUPER-NATURAL IF IT CAN JUST BE CLEANED UP...
OOO, SATCH, DOES THAT MAKE YOUR BUTT SUPER-NATURAL?
Get out
darb

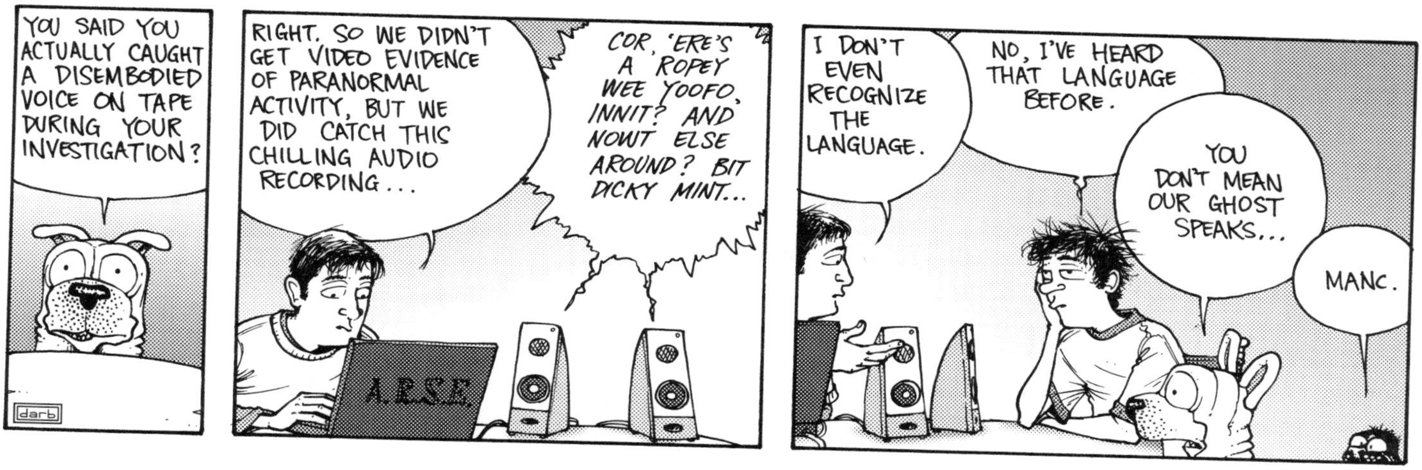

YOU SAID YOU ACTUALLY CAUGHT A DISEMBODIED VOICE ON TAPE DURING YOUR INVESTIGATION?
darb
RIGHT. SO WE DIDN'T GET VIDEO EVIDENCE OF PARANORMAL ACTIVITY, BUT WE DID CATCH THIS CHILLING AUDIO RECORDING...
COR, 'ERE'S A ROPEY WEE YOOFO, INNIT? AND NOWT ELSE AROUND? BIT DICKY MINT...
A.R.S.E.
I DON'T EVEN RECOGNIZE THE LANGUAGE.
NO, I'VE HEARD THAT LANGUAGE BEFORE.
YOU DON'T MEAN OUR GHOST SPEAKS...
MANC.

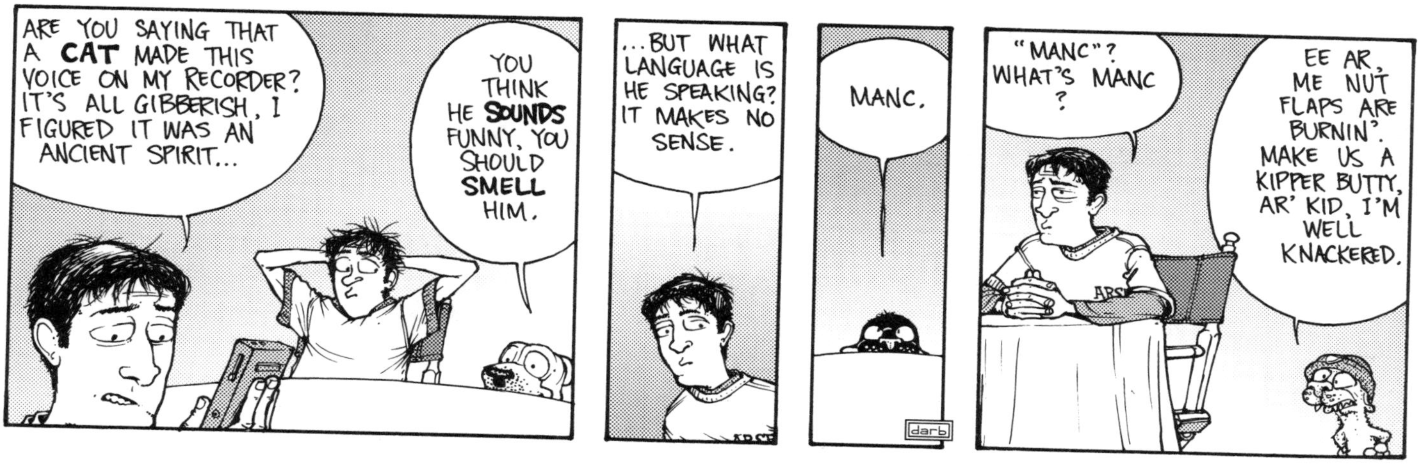

ARE YOU SAYING THAT A **CAT** MADE THIS VOICE ON MY RECORDER? IT'S ALL GIBBERISH, I FIGURED IT WAS AN ANCIENT SPIRIT...
YOU THINK HE **SOUNDS** FUNNY, YOU SHOULD **SMELL** HIM.
...BUT WHAT LANGUAGE IS HE SPEAKING? IT MAKES NO SENSE.
MANC.
darb
"MANC"? WHAT'S MANC?
EE AR, ME NUT FLAPS ARE BURNIN'. MAKE US A KIPPER BUTTY, AR' KID, I'M WELL KNACKERED.

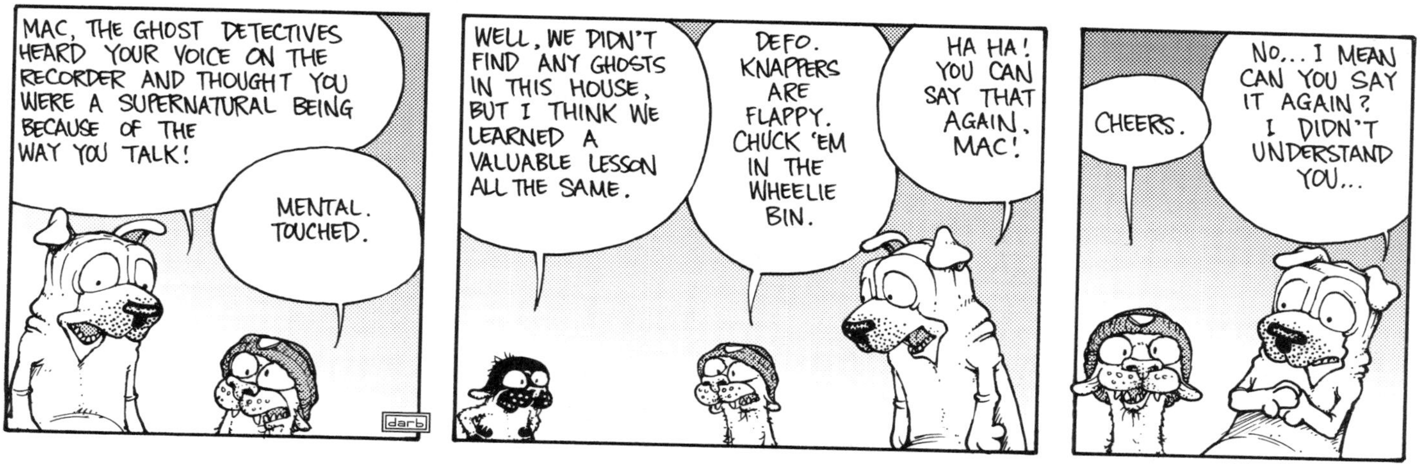

MAC, THE GHOST DETECTIVES HEARD YOUR VOICE ON THE RECORDER AND THOUGHT YOU WERE A SUPERNATURAL BEING BECAUSE OF THE WAY YOU TALK!
MENTAL. TOUCHED.
darb
WELL, WE DIDN'T FIND ANY GHOSTS IN THIS HOUSE, BUT I THINK WE LEARNED A VALUABLE LESSON ALL THE SAME.
DEFO. KNAPPERS ARE FLAPPY. CHUCK 'EM IN THE WHEELIE BIN.
HA HA! YOU CAN SAY THAT AGAIN, MAC!
CHEERS.
NO... I MEAN CAN YOU SAY IT AGAIN? I DIDN'T UNDERSTAND YOU...

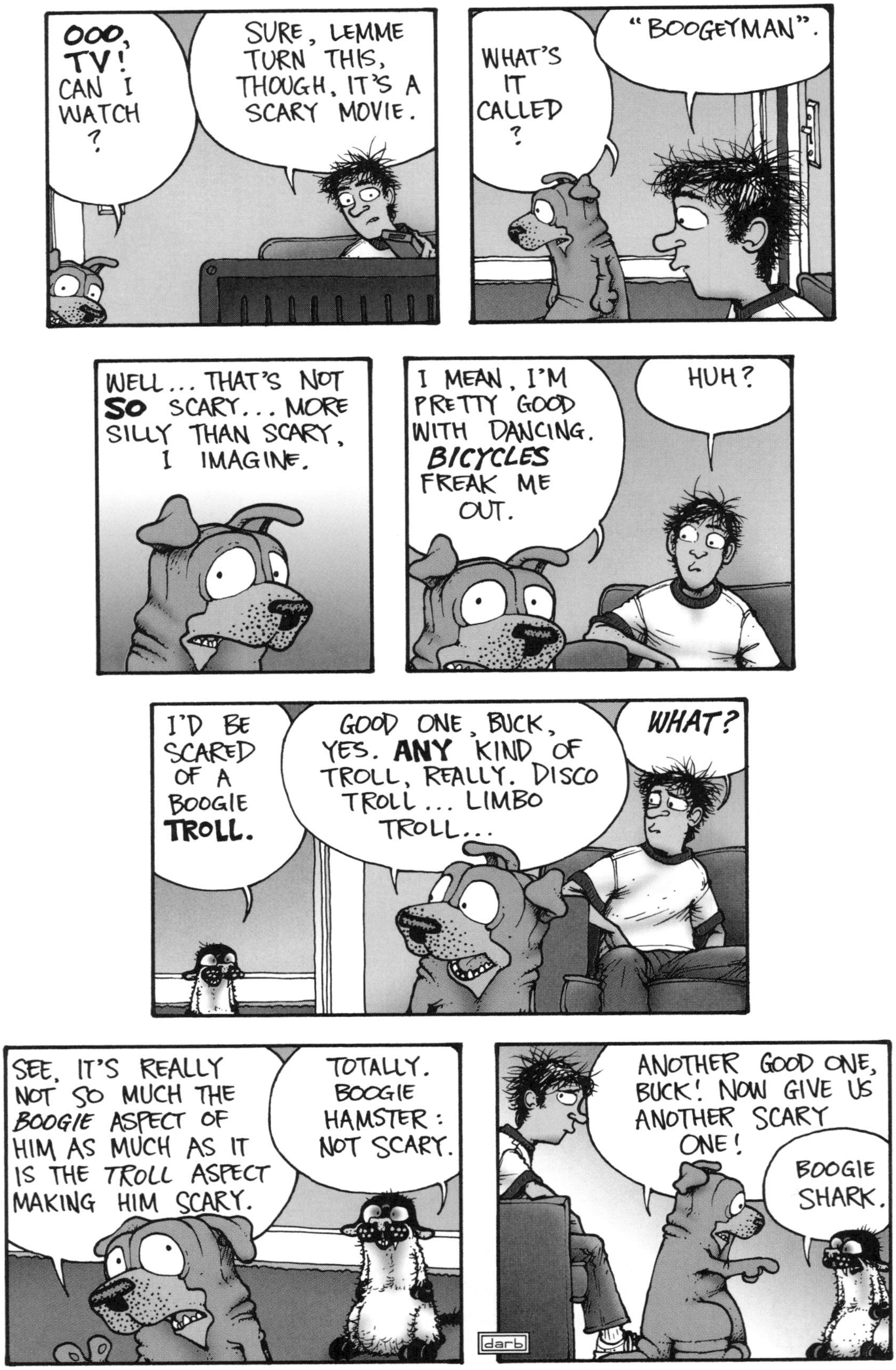
OOO, TV! CAN I WATCH ?
SURE, LEMME TURN THIS, THOUGH. IT'S A SCARY MOVIE.
WHAT'S IT CALLED ?
"BOOGEYMAN".
WELL... THAT'S NOT SO SCARY... MORE SILLY THAN SCARY, I IMAGINE.
I MEAN, I'M PRETTY GOOD WITH DANCING. BICYCLES FREAK ME OUT.
HUH?
I'D BE SCARED OF A BOOGIE TROLL.
GOOD ONE, BUCK, YES. ANY KIND OF TROLL, REALLY. DISCO TROLL... LIMBO TROLL...
WHAT?
SEE, IT'S REALLY NOT SO MUCH THE BOOGIE ASPECT OF HIM AS MUCH AS IT IS THE TROLL ASPECT MAKING HIM SCARY.
TOTALLY. BOOGIE HAMSTER: NOT SCARY.
ANOTHER GOOD ONE, BUCK! NOW GIVE US ANOTHER SCARY ONE!
BOOGIE SHARK.
darb

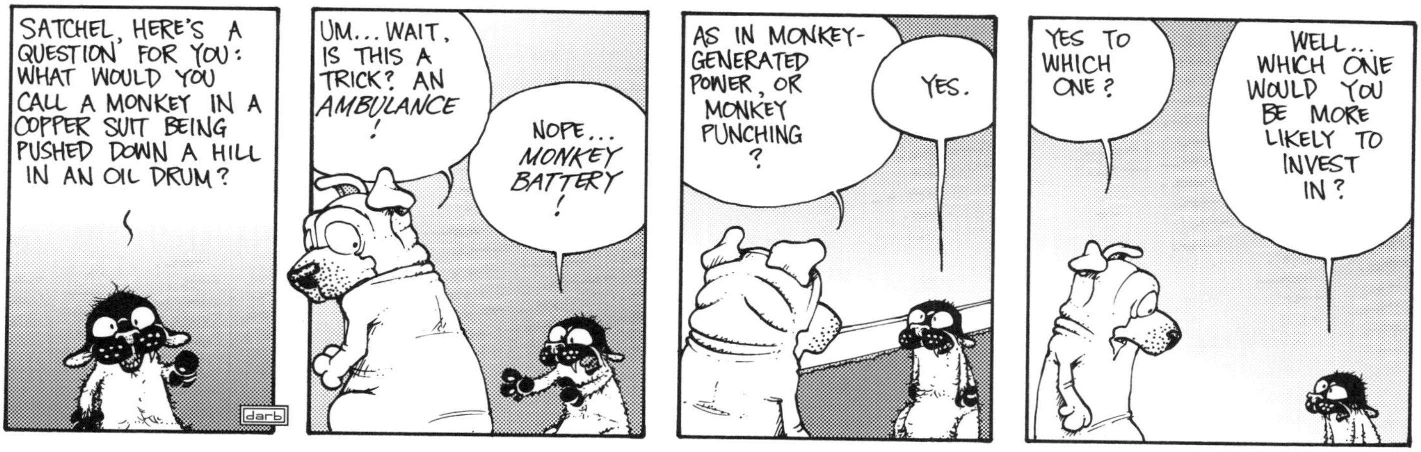
SATCHEL, HERE'S A QUESTION FOR YOU: WHAT WOULD YOU CALL A MONKEY IN A COPPER SUIT BEING PUSHED DOWN A HILL IN AN OIL DRUM?
UM... WAIT, IS THIS A TRICK? AN *AMBULANCE*!
NOPE... *MONKEY BATTERY*!
AS IN MONKEY-GENERATED POWER, OR MONKEY PUNCHING?
YES.
YES TO WHICH ONE?
WELL... WHICH ONE WOULD YOU BE MORE LIKELY TO INVEST IN?
darb

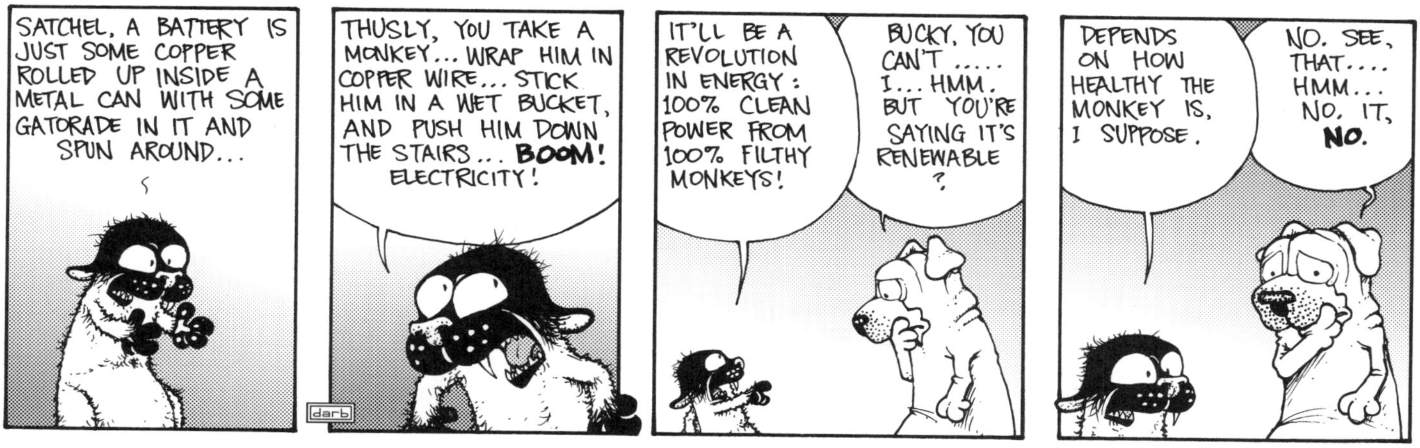
SATCHEL, A BATTERY IS JUST SOME COPPER ROLLED UP INSIDE A METAL CAN WITH SOME GATORADE IN IT AND SPUN AROUND...
THUSLY, YOU TAKE A MONKEY... WRAP HIM IN COPPER WIRE... STICK HIM IN A WET BUCKET, AND PUSH HIM DOWN THE STAIRS... **BOOM!** ELECTRICITY!
IT'LL BE A REVOLUTION IN ENERGY: 100% CLEAN POWER FROM 100% FILTHY MONKEYS!
BUCKY, YOU CAN'T..... I... HMM. BUT YOU'RE SAYING IT'S RENEWABLE?
DEPENDS ON HOW HEALTHY THE MONKEY IS, I SUPPOSE.
NO. SEE, THAT.... HMM... NO, IT, **NO**.
darb

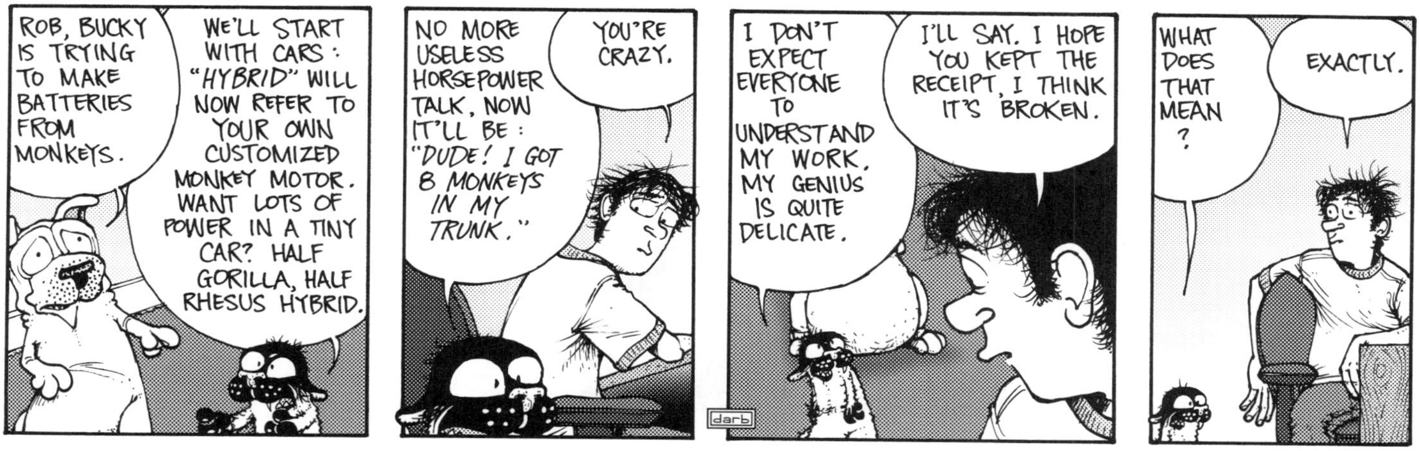
ROB, BUCKY IS TRYING TO MAKE BATTERIES FROM MONKEYS.
WE'LL START WITH CARS: "*HYBRID*" WILL NOW REFER TO YOUR OWN CUSTOMIZED MONKEY MOTOR. WANT LOTS OF POWER IN A TINY CAR? HALF GORILLA, HALF RHESUS HYBRID.
NO MORE USELESS HORSEPOWER TALK, NOW IT'LL BE: "*DUDE! I GOT 8 MONKEYS IN MY TRUNK.*"
YOU'RE CRAZY.
I DON'T EXPECT EVERYONE TO UNDERSTAND MY WORK, MY GENIUS IS QUITE DELICATE.
I'LL SAY. I HOPE YOU KEPT THE RECEIPT, I THINK IT'S BROKEN.
WHAT DOES THAT MEAN?
EXACTLY.
darb

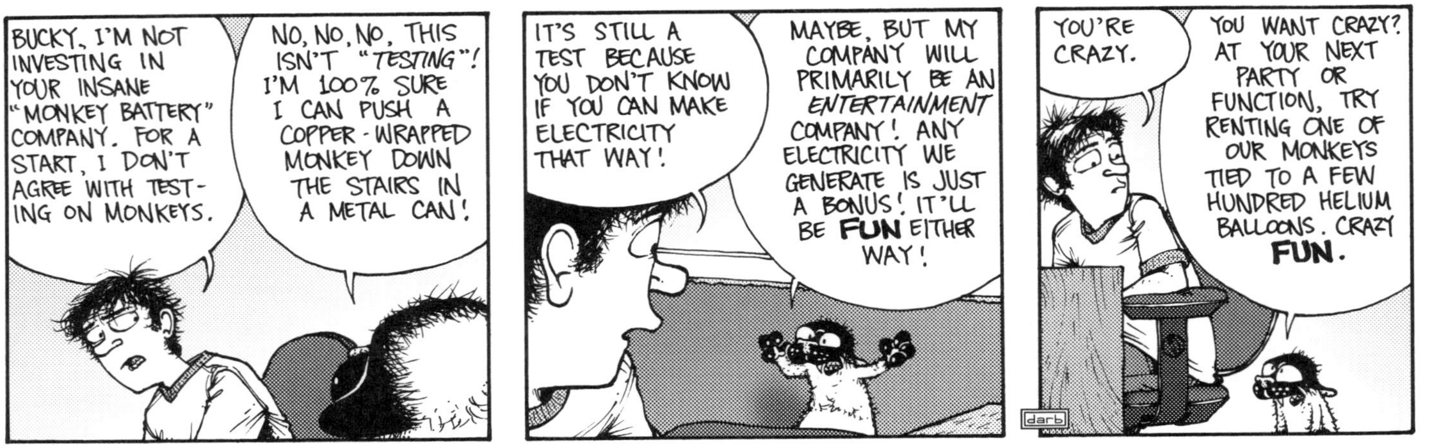
BUCKY, I'M NOT INVESTING IN YOUR INSANE "MONKEY BATTERY" COMPANY. FOR A START, I DON'T AGREE WITH TESTING ON MONKEYS.
NO, NO, NO, THIS ISN'T "TESTING"! I'M 100% SURE I CAN PUSH A COPPER-WRAPPED MONKEY DOWN THE STAIRS IN A METAL CAN!
IT'S STILL A TEST BECAUSE YOU DON'T KNOW IF YOU CAN MAKE ELECTRICITY THAT WAY!
MAYBE, BUT MY COMPANY WILL PRIMARILY BE AN ENTERTAINMENT COMPANY! ANY ELECTRICITY WE GENERATE IS JUST A BONUS! IT'LL BE FUN EITHER WAY!
YOU'RE CRAZY.
YOU WANT CRAZY? AT YOUR NEXT PARTY OR FUNCTION, TRY RENTING ONE OF OUR MONKEYS TIED TO A FEW HUNDRED HELIUM BALLOONS. CRAZY FUN.
darb

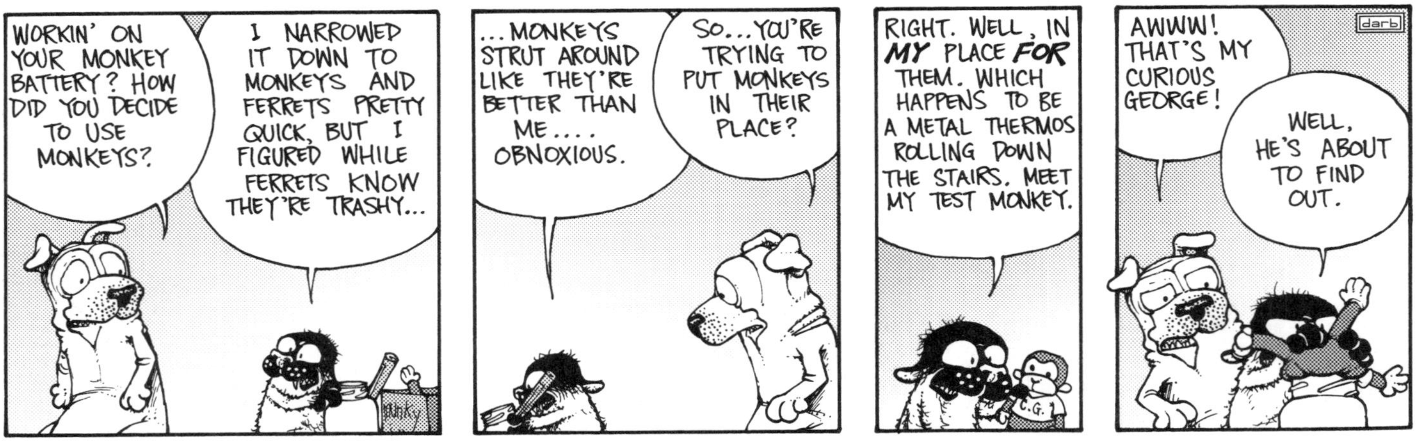
WORKIN' ON YOUR MONKEY BATTERY? HOW DID YOU DECIDE TO USE MONKEYS?
I NARROWED IT DOWN TO MONKEYS AND FERRETS PRETTY QUICK, BUT I FIGURED WHILE FERRETS KNOW THEY'RE TRASHY...
...MONKEYS STRUT AROUND LIKE THEY'RE BETTER THAN ME.... OBNOXIOUS.
SO...YOU'RE TRYING TO PUT MONKEYS IN THEIR PLACE?
RIGHT. WELL, IN MY PLACE FOR THEM. WHICH HAPPENS TO BE A METAL THERMOS ROLLING DOWN THE STAIRS. MEET MY TEST MONKEY.
AWWW! THAT'S MY CURIOUS GEORGE!
WELL, HE'S ABOUT TO FIND OUT.
darb

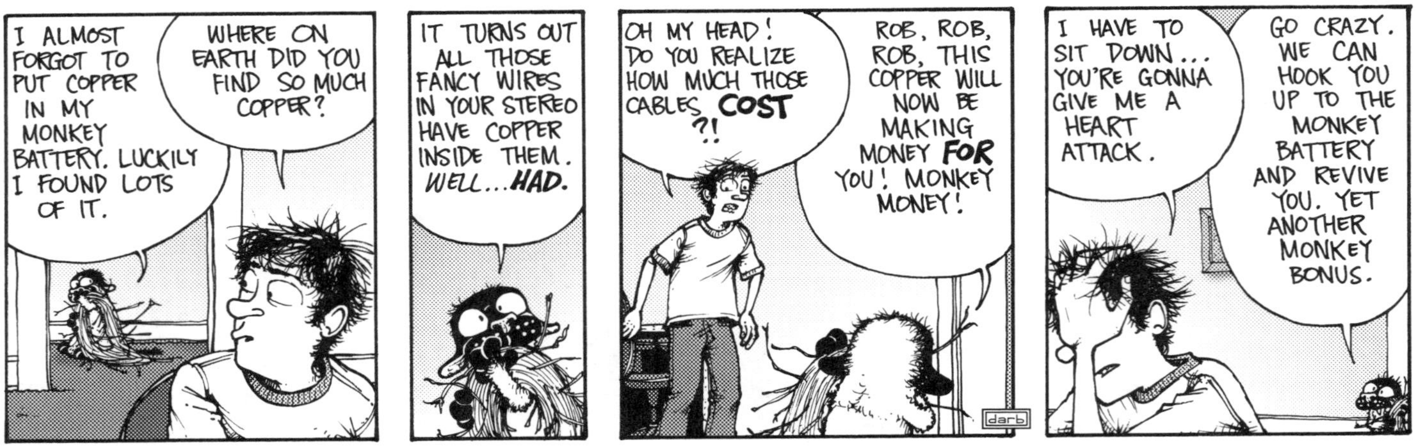
I ALMOST FORGOT TO PUT COPPER IN MY MONKEY BATTERY. LUCKILY I FOUND LOTS OF IT.
WHERE ON EARTH DID YOU FIND SO MUCH COPPER?
IT TURNS OUT ALL THOSE FANCY WIRES IN YOUR STEREO HAVE COPPER INSIDE THEM. WELL...HAD.
OH MY HEAD! DO YOU REALIZE HOW MUCH THOSE CABLES COST?!
ROB, ROB, ROB, THIS COPPER WILL NOW BE MAKING MONEY FOR YOU! MONKEY MONEY!
I HAVE TO SIT DOWN... YOU'RE GONNA GIVE ME A HEART ATTACK.
GO CRAZY. WE CAN HOOK YOU UP TO THE MONKEY BATTERY AND REVIVE YOU. YET ANOTHER MONKEY BONUS.
darb

WHERE YA GOIN' ALL DRESSED UP?

MY COLLEGE REUNION IS TONIGHT.

MM-HM. WHAT DO YOU DO AT THAT?

CHAT WITH OLD FRIENDS... HAVE A NICE DINNER... MAYBE EVEN DO A LITTLE DANCING.

YOU'RE GOING DANCING?

PROBLEM?

ONLY FOR **YOU**... MAN, YOU'RE SO OLD YOU'LL BE BODY POPPING WHILE YOU SLOW DANCE.

I'LL HAVE YOU KNOW I COULD BUST QUITE A MOVE IN MY DAY.

WELL, IN **THIS** DAY YOU'LL BE BUSTING QUITE A HIP.

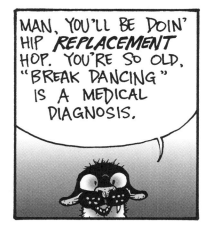

MAN, YOU'LL BE DOIN' HIP **REPLACEMENT** HOP. YOU'RE SO OLD, "BREAK DANCING" IS A MEDICAL DIAGNOSIS.

DON'T WAIT UP.

SLAM!

HOW BAD DO YOU THINK HE'S GONNA HURT HIMSELF?

PUT IT THIS WAY: I GET HIS ROOM.

darb

219

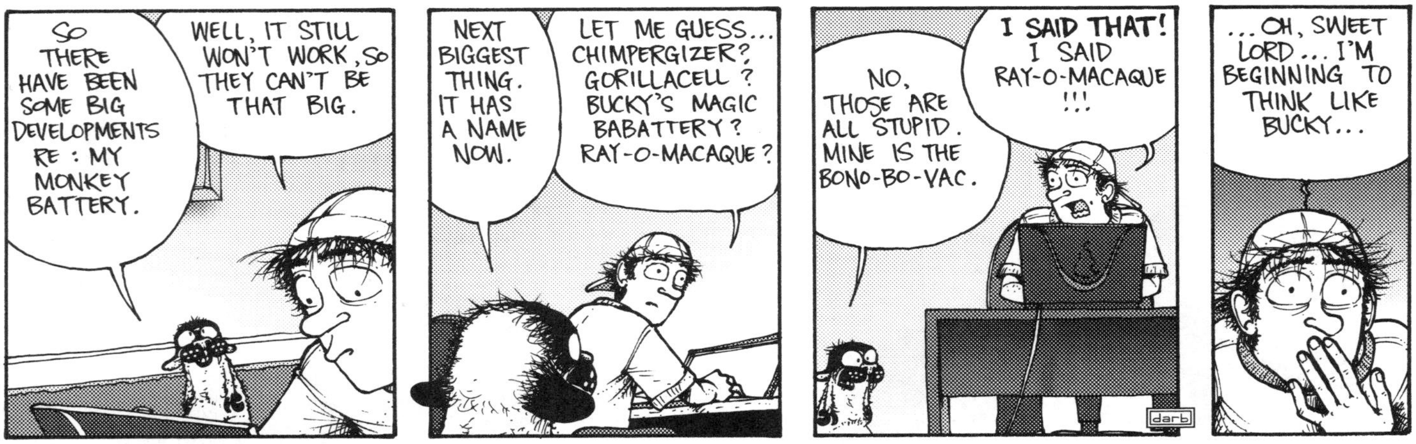
SO THERE HAVE BEEN SOME BIG DEVELOPMENTS RE: MY MONKEY BATTERY.
WELL, IT STILL WON'T WORK, SO THEY CAN'T BE THAT BIG.
NEXT BIGGEST THING. IT HAS A NAME NOW.
LET ME GUESS... CHIMPERGIZER? GORILLACELL? BUCKY'S MAGIC BABATTERY? RAY-O-MACAQUE?
NO, THOSE ARE ALL STUPID. MINE IS THE BONO-BO-VAC.
I SAID THAT! I SAID RAY-O-MACAQUE !!!
...OH, SWEET LORD... I'M BEGINNING TO THINK LIKE BUCKY...
darb

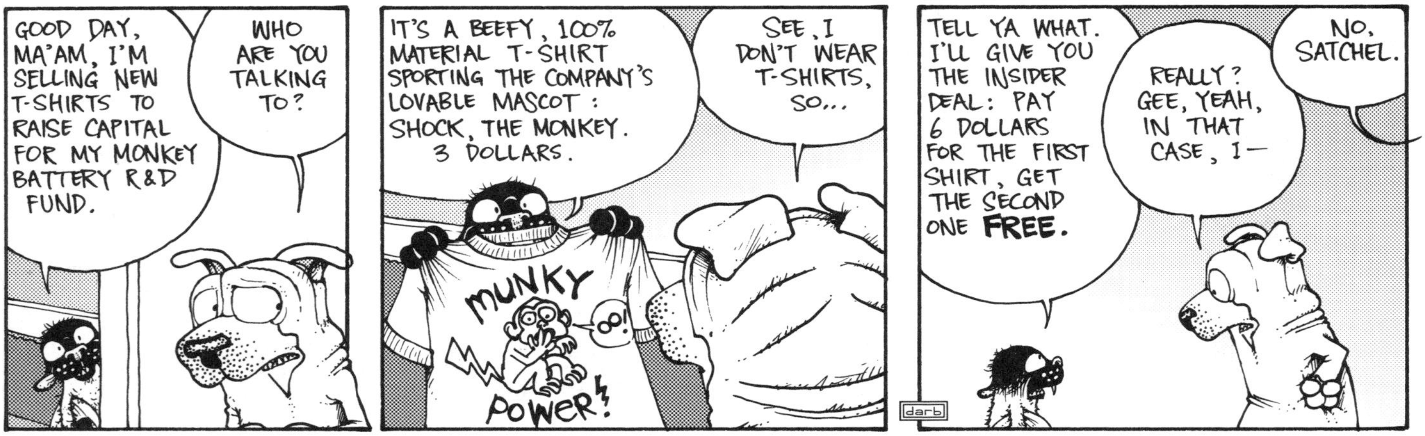
GOOD DAY, MA'AM, I'M SELLING NEW T-SHIRTS TO RAISE CAPITAL FOR MY MONKEY BATTERY R&D FUND.
WHO ARE YOU TALKING TO?
IT'S A BEEFY, 100% MATERIAL T-SHIRT SPORTING THE COMPANY'S LOVABLE MASCOT: SHOCK, THE MONKEY. 3 DOLLARS.
MUNKY POWER!
OO!
SEE, I DON'T WEAR T-SHIRTS, SO...
TELL YA WHAT. I'LL GIVE YOU THE INSIDER DEAL: PAY 6 DOLLARS FOR THE FIRST SHIRT, GET THE SECOND ONE FREE.
REALLY? GEE, YEAH, IN THAT CASE, I—
NO, SATCHEL.
darb

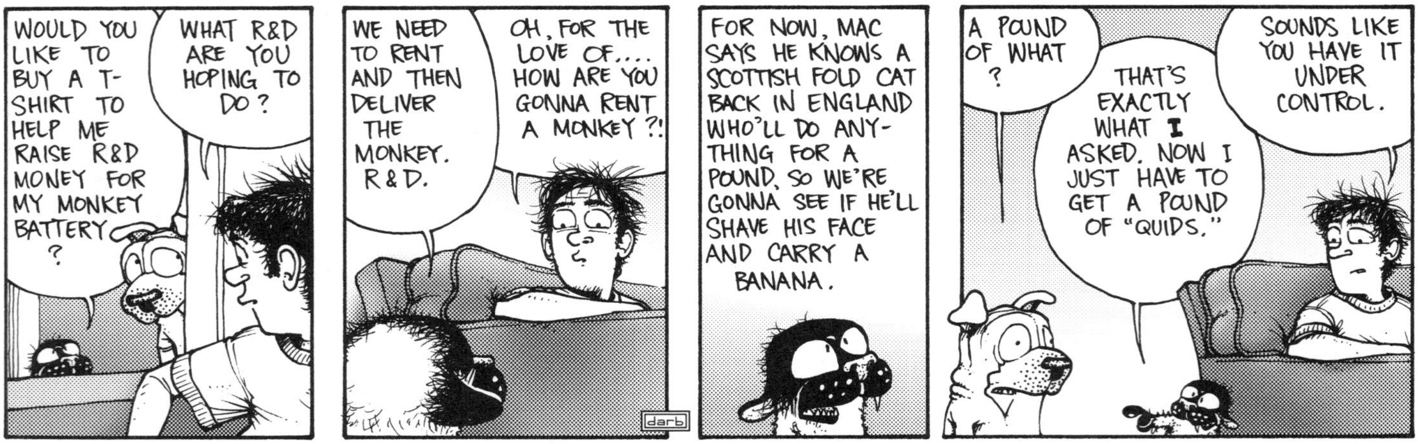
WOULD YOU LIKE TO BUY A T-SHIRT TO HELP ME RAISE R&D MONEY FOR MY MONKEY BATTERY ?
WHAT R&D ARE YOU HOPING TO DO?
WE NEED TO RENT AND THEN DELIVER THE MONKEY. R&D.
OH, FOR THE LOVE OF.... HOW ARE YOU GONNA RENT A MONKEY ?!
FOR NOW, MAC SAYS HE KNOWS A SCOTTISH FOLD CAT BACK IN ENGLAND WHO'LL DO ANYTHING FOR A POUND, SO WE'RE GONNA SEE IF HE'LL SHAVE HIS FACE AND CARRY A BANANA.
A POUND OF WHAT ?
THAT'S EXACTLY WHAT I ASKED. NOW I JUST HAVE TO GET A POUND OF "QUIDS."
SOUNDS LIKE YOU HAVE IT UNDER CONTROL.
darb

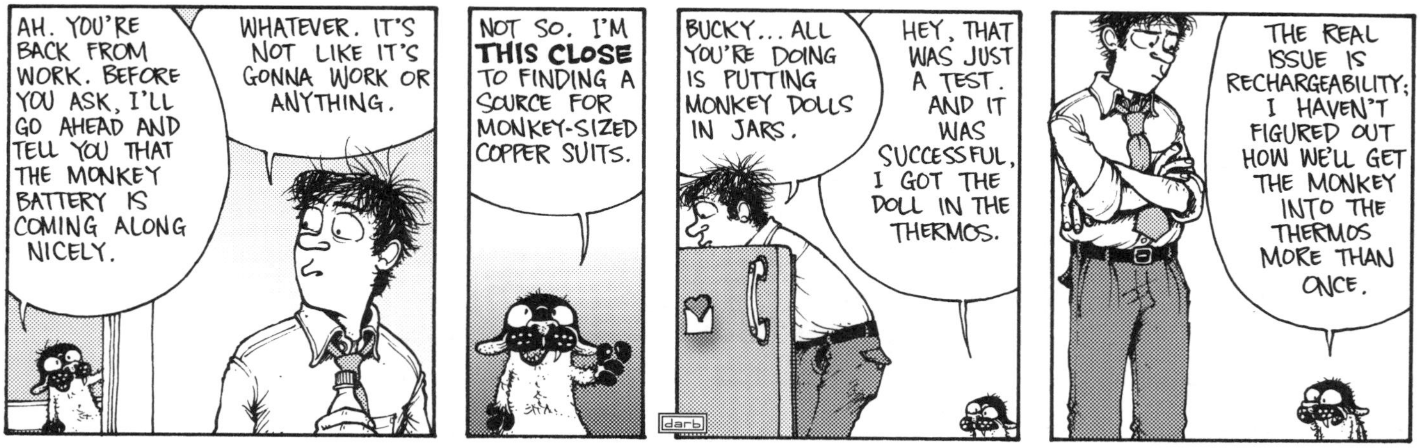
AH. YOU'RE BACK FROM WORK. BEFORE YOU ASK, I'LL GO AHEAD AND TELL YOU THAT THE MONKEY BATTERY IS COMING ALONG NICELY.
WHATEVER. IT'S NOT LIKE IT'S GONNA WORK OR ANYTHING.
NOT SO. I'M **THIS CLOSE** TO FINDING A SOURCE FOR MONKEY-SIZED COPPER SUITS.
darb
BUCKY... ALL YOU'RE DOING IS PUTTING MONKEY DOLLS IN JARS.
HEY, THAT WAS JUST A TEST. AND IT WAS SUCCESSFUL, I GOT THE DOLL IN THE THERMOS.
THE REAL ISSUE IS RECHARGEABILITY; I HAVEN'T FIGURED OUT HOW WE'LL GET THE MONKEY INTO THE THERMOS MORE THAN ONCE.

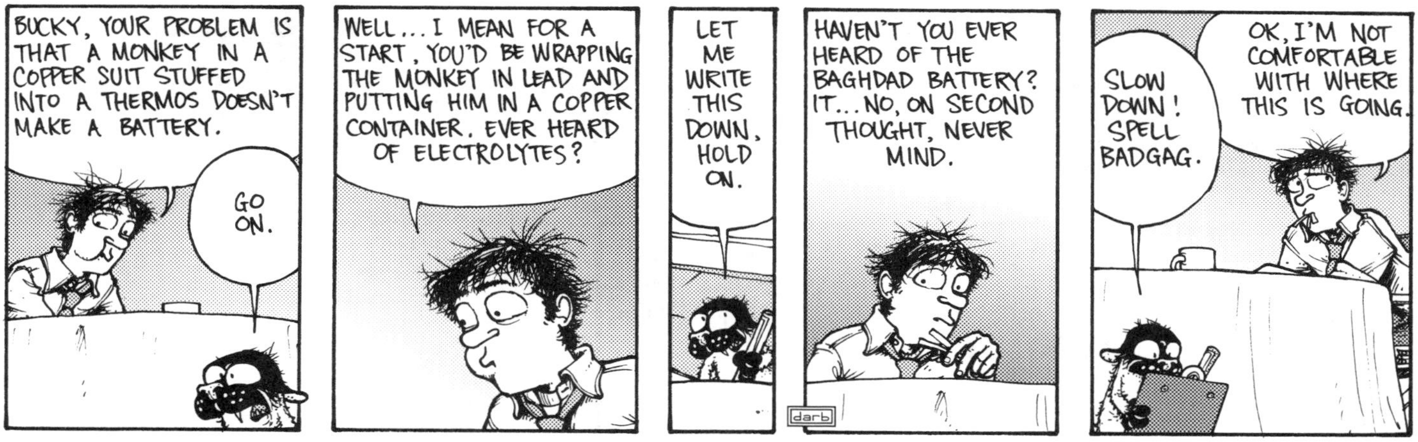
BUCKY, YOUR PROBLEM IS THAT A MONKEY IN A COPPER SUIT STUFFED INTO A THERMOS DOESN'T MAKE A BATTERY.
GO ON.
WELL... I MEAN FOR A START, YOU'D BE WRAPPING THE MONKEY IN LEAD AND PUTTING HIM IN A COPPER CONTAINER. EVER HEARD OF ELECTROLYTES?
LET ME WRITE THIS DOWN. HOLD ON.
darb
HAVEN'T YOU EVER HEARD OF THE BAGHDAD BATTERY? IT... NO, ON SECOND THOUGHT, NEVER MIND.
SLOW DOWN! SPELL BADGAG.
OK, I'M NOT COMFORTABLE WITH WHERE THIS IS GOING.

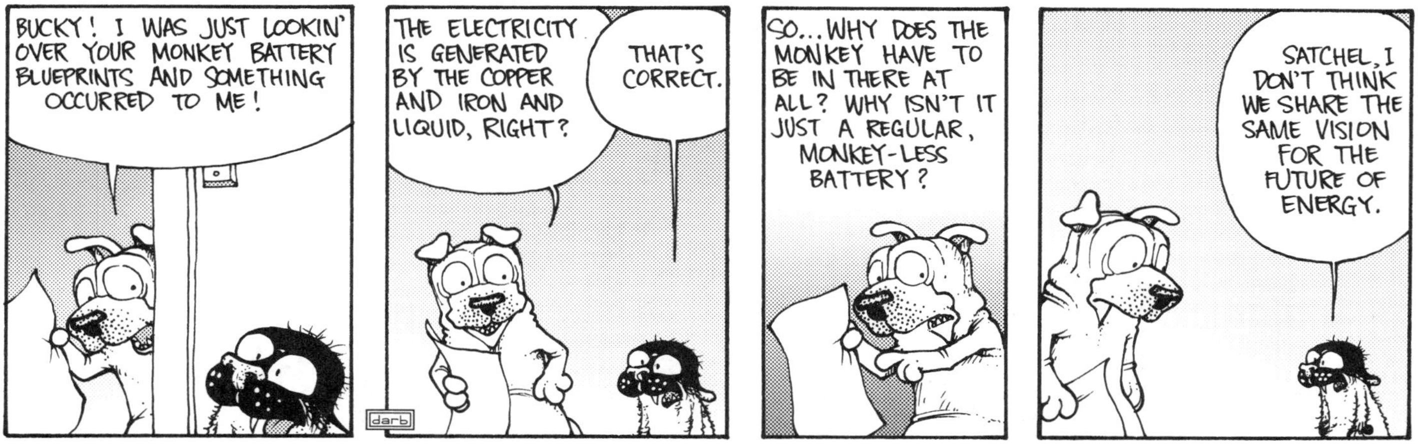
BUCKY! I WAS JUST LOOKIN' OVER YOUR MONKEY BATTERY BLUEPRINTS AND SOMETHING OCCURRED TO ME!
darb
THE ELECTRICITY IS GENERATED BY THE COPPER AND IRON AND LIQUID, RIGHT?
THAT'S CORRECT.
SO... WHY DOES THE MONKEY HAVE TO BE IN THERE AT ALL? WHY ISN'T IT JUST A REGULAR, MONKEY-LESS BATTERY?
SATCHEL, I DON'T THINK WE SHARE THE SAME VISION FOR THE FUTURE OF ENERGY.

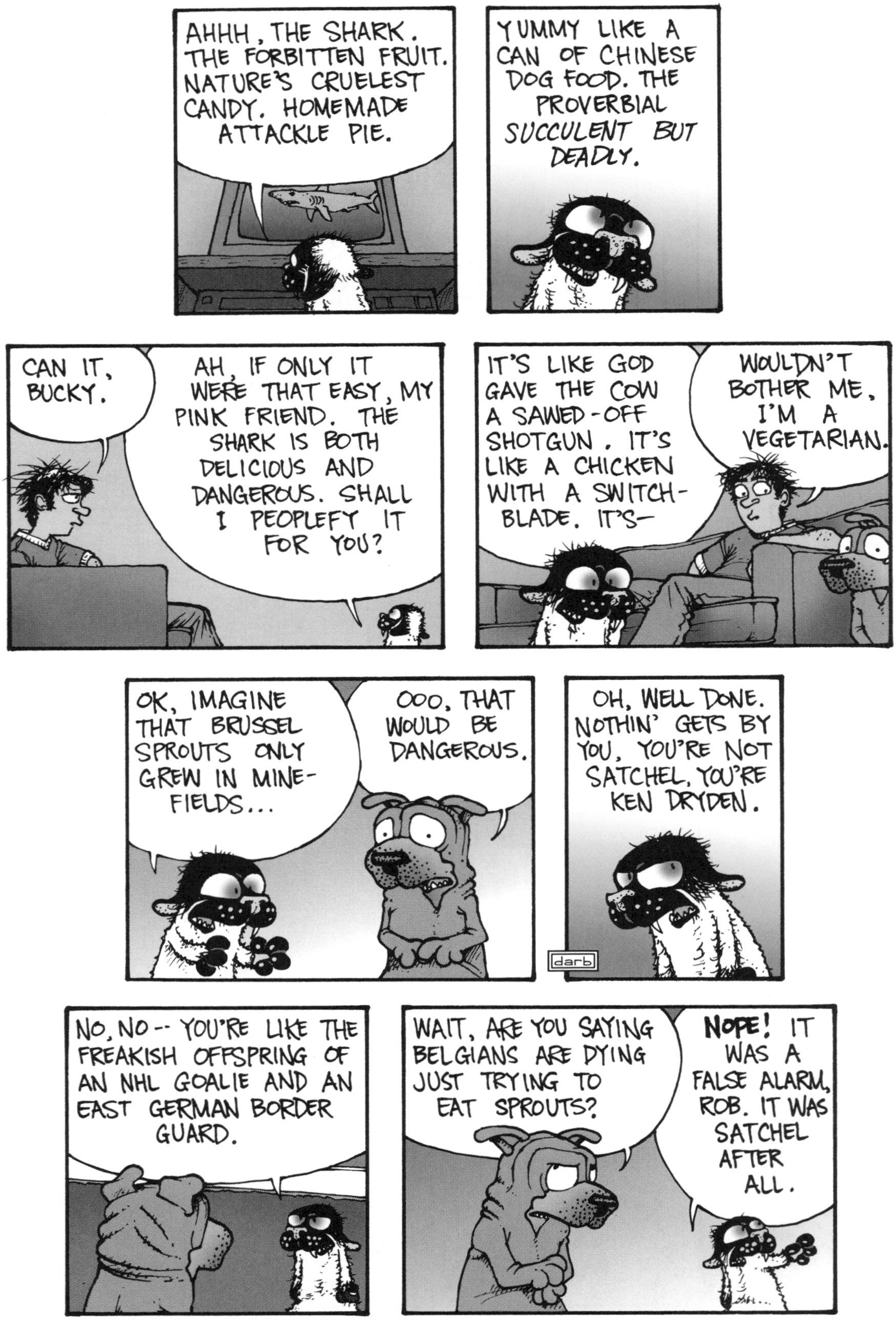
AHHH, THE SHARK. THE FORBITTEN FRUIT. NATURE'S CRUELEST CANDY. HOMEMADE ATTACKLE PIE.
YUMMY LIKE A CAN OF CHINESE DOG FOOD. THE PROVERBIAL SUCCULENT BUT DEADLY.
CAN IT, BUCKY.
AH, IF ONLY IT WERE THAT EASY, MY PINK FRIEND. THE SHARK IS BOTH DELICIOUS AND DANGEROUS. SHALL I PEOPLEFY IT FOR YOU?
IT'S LIKE GOD GAVE THE COW A SAWED-OFF SHOTGUN. IT'S LIKE A CHICKEN WITH A SWITCH-BLADE. IT'S—
WOULDN'T BOTHER ME. I'M A VEGETARIAN.
OK, IMAGINE THAT BRUSSEL SPROUTS ONLY GREW IN MINE-FIELDS...
OOO, THAT WOULD BE DANGEROUS.
OH, WELL DONE. NOTHIN' GETS BY YOU, YOU'RE NOT SATCHEL, YOU'RE KEN DRYDEN.
darb
NO, NO -- YOU'RE LIKE THE FREAKISH OFFSPRING OF AN NHL GOALIE AND AN EAST GERMAN BORDER GUARD.
WAIT, ARE YOU SAYING BELGIANS ARE DYING JUST TRYING TO EAT SPROUTS?
NOPE! IT WAS A FALSE ALARM, ROB. IT WAS SATCHEL AFTER ALL.

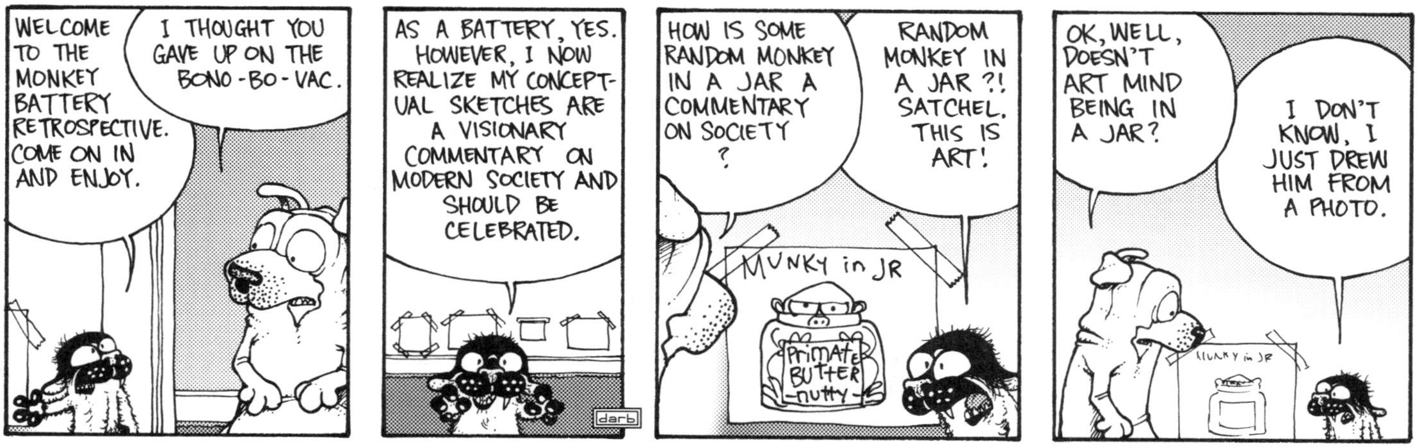
WELCOME TO THE MONKEY BATTERY RETROSPECTIVE. COME ON IN AND ENJOY.
I THOUGHT YOU GAVE UP ON THE BONO-BO-VAC.
AS A BATTERY, YES. HOWEVER, I NOW REALIZE MY CONCEPTUAL SKETCHES ARE A VISIONARY COMMENTARY ON MODERN SOCIETY AND SHOULD BE CELEBRATED.
darb
HOW IS SOME RANDOM MONKEY IN A JAR A COMMENTARY ON SOCIETY ?
RANDOM MONKEY IN A JAR ?! SATCHEL. THIS IS ART!
MUNKY in JR
Primate BUTter -nutty-
OK, WELL, DOESN'T ART MIND BEING IN A JAR?
I DON'T KNOW, I JUST DREW HIM FROM A PHOTO.

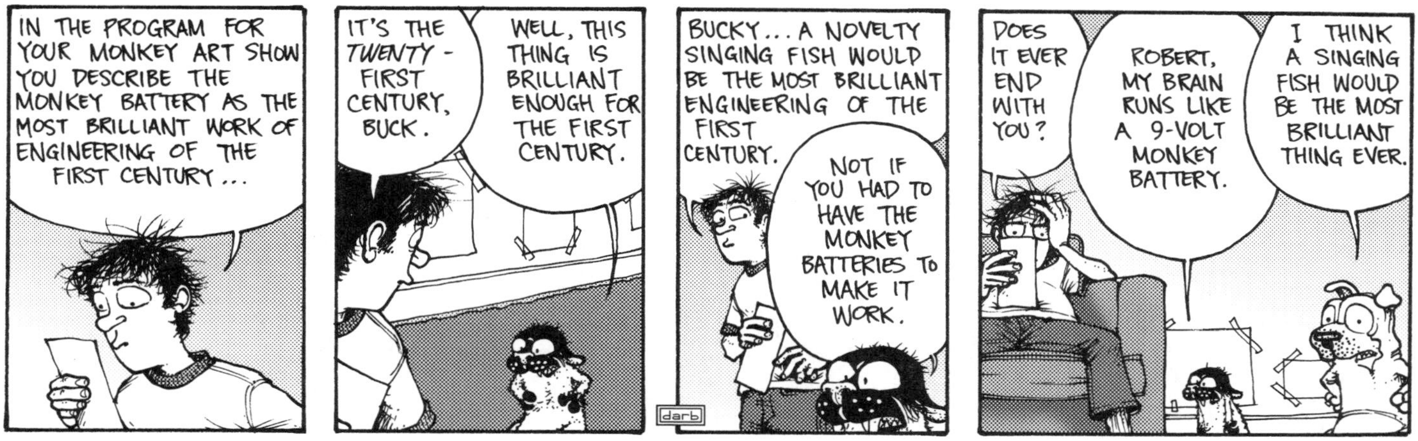
IN THE PROGRAM FOR YOUR MONKEY ART SHOW YOU DESCRIBE THE MONKEY BATTERY AS THE MOST BRILLIANT WORK OF ENGINEERING OF THE FIRST CENTURY...
IT'S THE *TWENTY*-FIRST CENTURY, BUCK.
WELL, THIS THING IS BRILLIANT ENOUGH FOR THE FIRST CENTURY.
darb
BUCKY... A NOVELTY SINGING FISH WOULD BE THE MOST BRILLIANT ENGINEERING OF THE FIRST CENTURY.
NOT IF YOU HAD TO HAVE THE MONKEY BATTERIES TO MAKE IT WORK.
DOES IT EVER END WITH YOU?
ROBERT, MY BRAIN RUNS LIKE A 9-VOLT MONKEY BATTERY.
I THINK A SINGING FISH WOULD BE THE MOST BRILLIANT THING EVER.

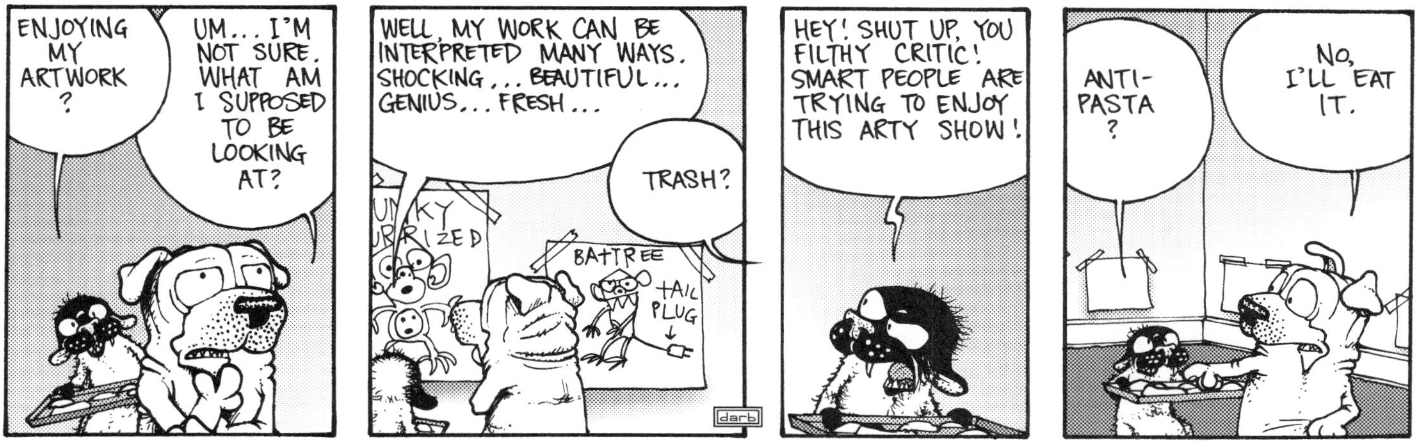
ENJOYING MY ARTWORK ?
UM... I'M NOT SURE. WHAT AM I SUPPOSED TO BE LOOKING AT?
WELL, MY WORK CAN BE INTERPRETED MANY WAYS. SHOCKING... BEAUTIFUL... GENIUS... FRESH...
TRASH?
BATTREE
TAIL PLUG
darb
HEY! SHUT UP, YOU FILTHY CRITIC! SMART PEOPLE ARE TRYING TO ENJOY THIS ARTY SHOW!
ANTI-PASTA ?
NO, I'LL EAT IT.

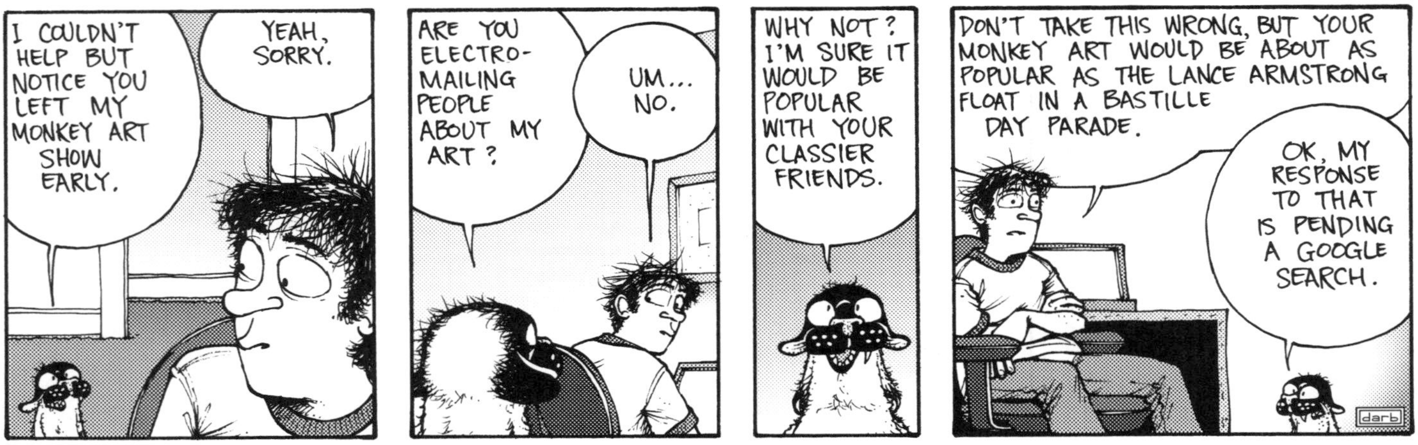
I COULDN'T HELP BUT NOTICE YOU LEFT MY MONKEY ART SHOW EARLY.
YEAH, SORRY.
ARE YOU ELECTRO-MAILING PEOPLE ABOUT MY ART?
UM... NO.
WHY NOT? I'M SURE IT WOULD BE POPULAR WITH YOUR CLASSIER FRIENDS.
DON'T TAKE THIS WRONG, BUT YOUR MONKEY ART WOULD BE ABOUT AS POPULAR AS THE LANCE ARMSTRONG FLOAT IN A BASTILLE DAY PARADE.
OK, MY RESPONSE TO THAT IS PENDING A GOOGLE SEARCH.
darb

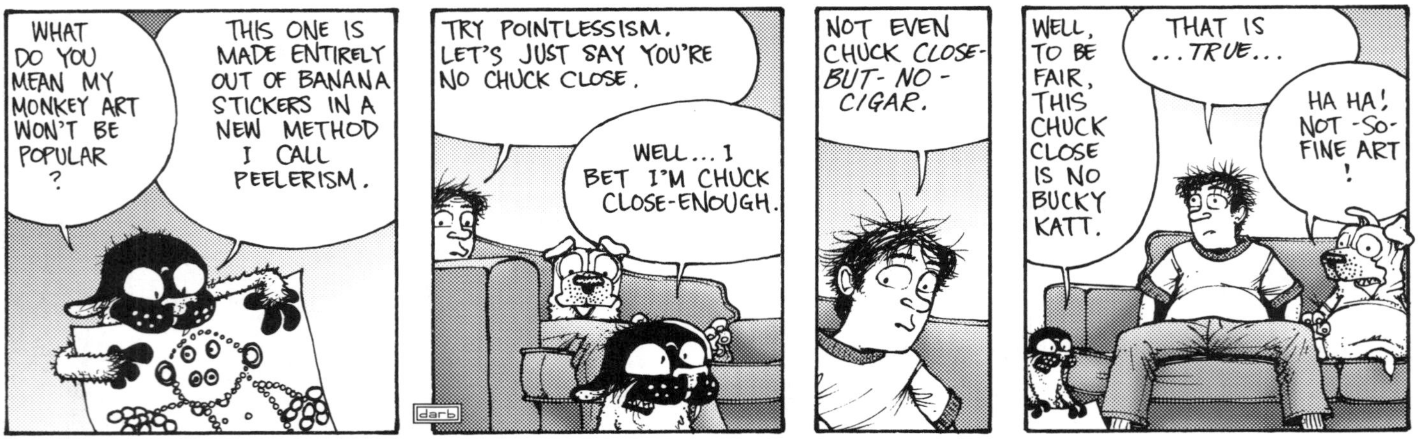
WHAT DO YOU MEAN MY MONKEY ART WON'T BE POPULAR?
THIS ONE IS MADE ENTIRELY OUT OF BANANA STICKERS IN A NEW METHOD I CALL PEELERISM.
darb
TRY POINTLESSISM. LET'S JUST SAY YOU'RE NO CHUCK CLOSE.
WELL... I BET I'M CHUCK CLOSE-ENOUGH.
NOT EVEN CHUCK *CLOSE-BUT-NO-CIGAR*.
WELL, TO BE FAIR, THIS CHUCK CLOSE IS NO BUCKY KATT.
THAT IS ...*TRUE*...
HA HA! NOT-SO-FINE ART!

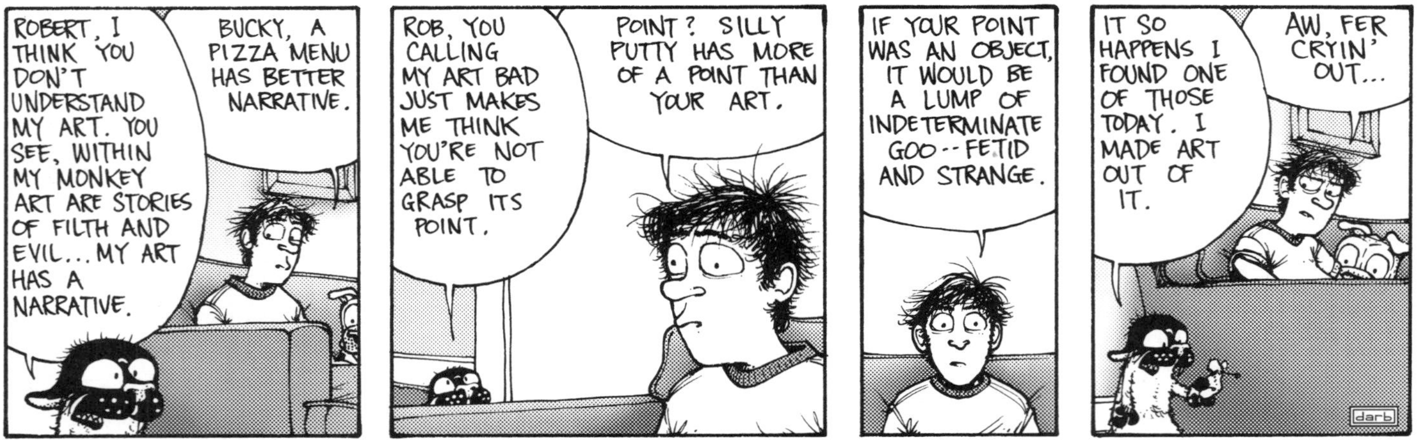
ROBERT, I THINK YOU DON'T UNDERSTAND MY ART. YOU SEE, WITHIN MY MONKEY ART ARE STORIES OF FILTH AND EVIL... MY ART HAS A NARRATIVE.
BUCKY, A PIZZA MENU HAS BETTER NARRATIVE.
ROB, YOU CALLING MY ART BAD JUST MAKES ME THINK YOU'RE NOT ABLE TO GRASP ITS POINT.
POINT? SILLY PUTTY HAS MORE OF A POINT THAN YOUR ART.
IF YOUR POINT WAS AN OBJECT, IT WOULD BE A LUMP OF INDETERMINATE GOO--FETID AND STRANGE.
IT SO HAPPENS I FOUND ONE OF THOSE TODAY. I MADE ART OUT OF IT.
AW, FER CRYIN' OUT...
darb

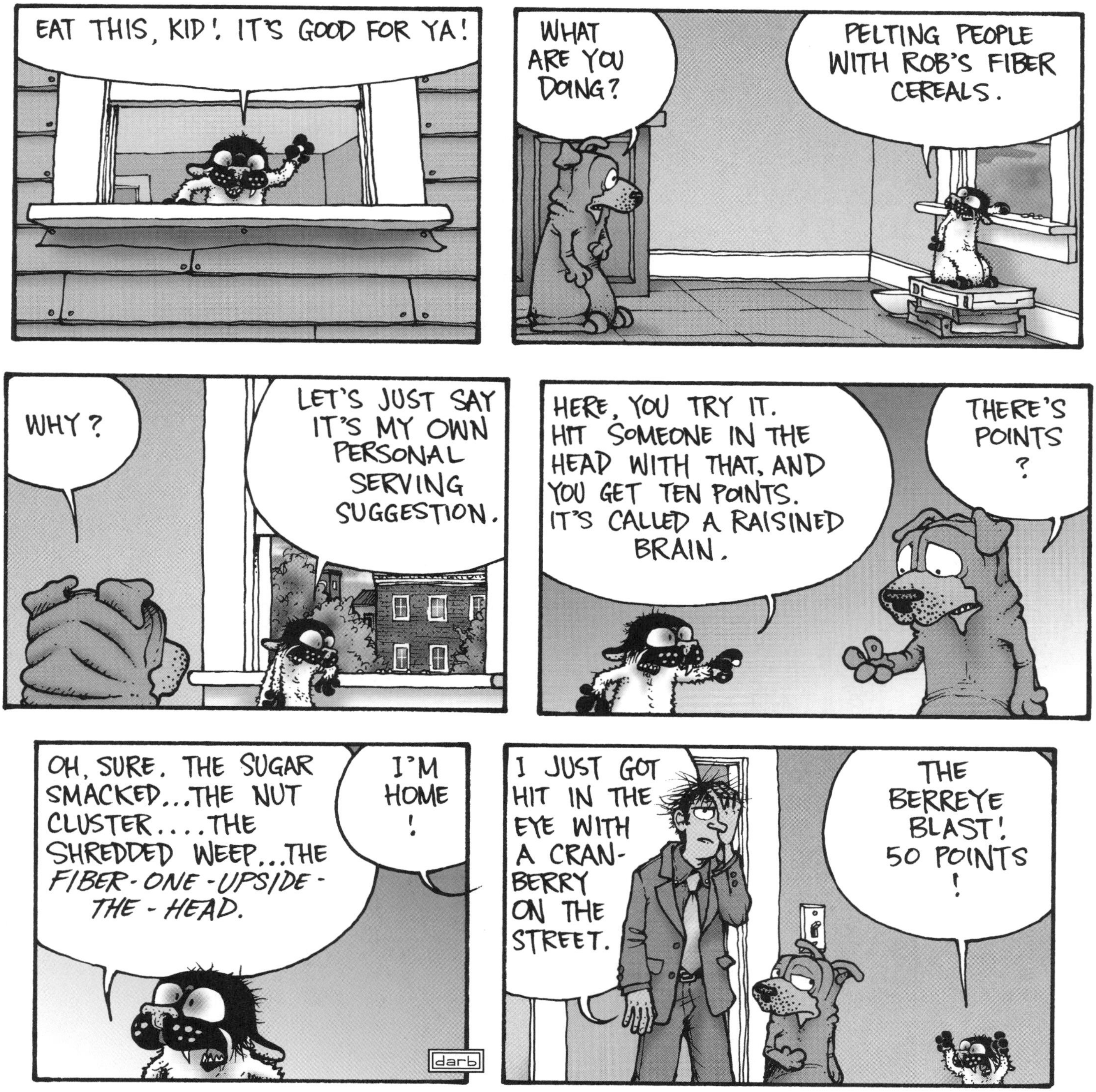

EAT THIS, KID! IT'S GOOD FOR YA!
WHAT ARE YOU DOING?
PELTING PEOPLE WITH ROB'S FIBER CEREALS.
WHY?
LET'S JUST SAY IT'S MY OWN PERSONAL SERVING SUGGESTION.
HERE, YOU TRY IT. HIT SOMEONE IN THE HEAD WITH THAT, AND YOU GET TEN POINTS. IT'S CALLED A RAISINED BRAIN.
THERE'S POINTS?
OH, SURE. THE SUGAR SMACKED...THE NUT CLUSTER....THE SHREDDED WEEP...THE *FIBER-ONE-UPSIDE-THE-HEAD.*
I'M HOME!
darb
I JUST GOT HIT IN THE EYE WITH A CRAN-BERRY ON THE STREET.
THE BERREYE BLAST! 50 POINTS!

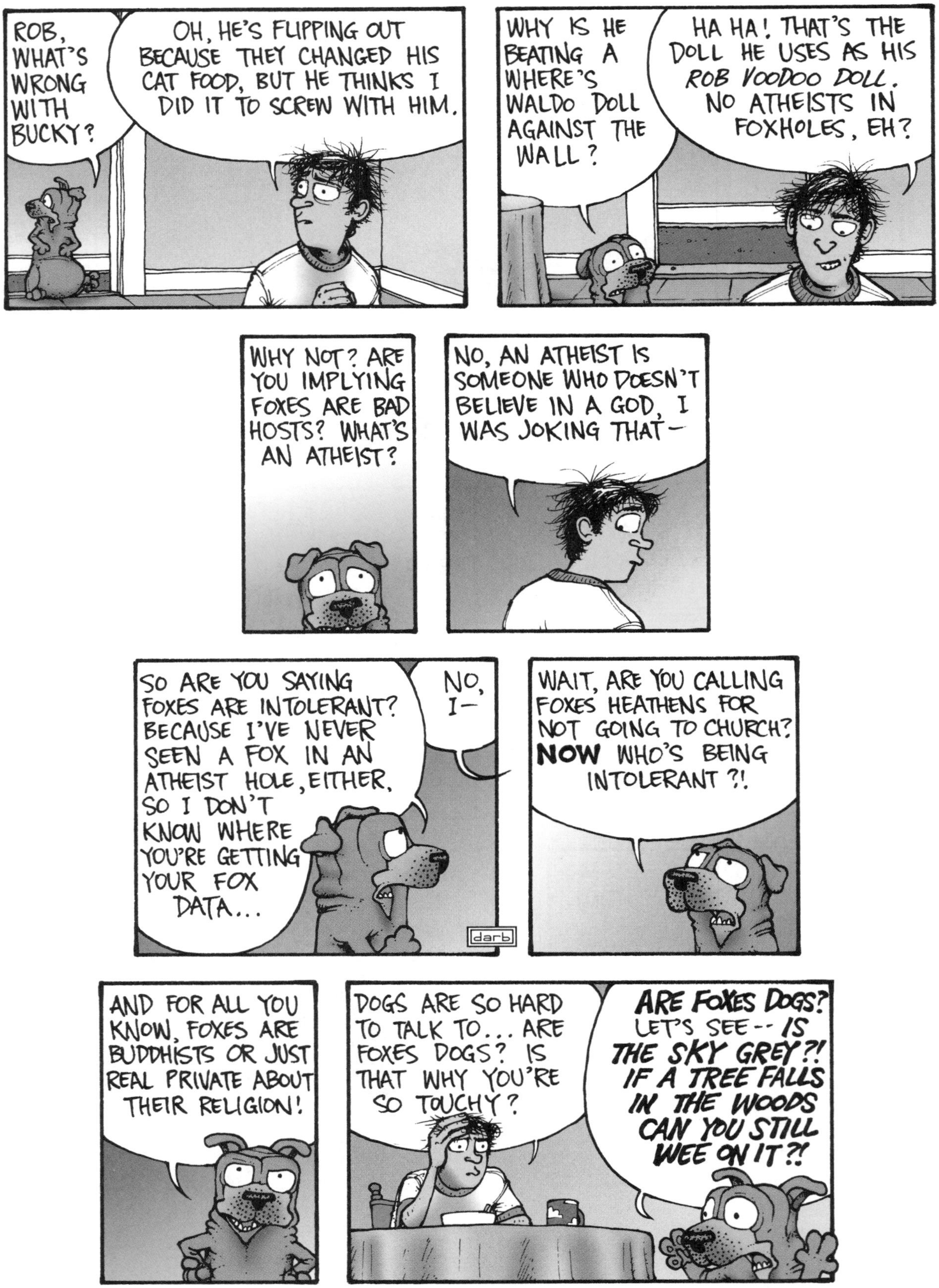
ROB, WHAT'S WRONG WITH BUCKY?
OH, HE'S FLIPPING OUT BECAUSE THEY CHANGED HIS CAT FOOD, BUT HE THINKS I DID IT TO SCREW WITH HIM.
WHY IS HE BEATING A WHERE'S WALDO DOLL AGAINST THE WALL?
HA HA! THAT'S THE DOLL HE USES AS HIS *ROB VOODOO DOLL*. NO ATHEISTS IN FOXHOLES, EH?
WHY NOT? ARE YOU IMPLYING FOXES ARE BAD HOSTS? WHAT'S AN ATHEIST?
NO, AN ATHEIST IS SOMEONE WHO DOESN'T BELIEVE IN A GOD, I WAS JOKING THAT—
SO ARE YOU SAYING FOXES ARE INTOLERANT? BECAUSE I'VE NEVER SEEN A FOX IN AN ATHEIST HOLE, EITHER, SO I DON'T KNOW WHERE YOU'RE GETTING YOUR FOX DATA...
NO, I—
darb
WAIT, ARE YOU CALLING FOXES HEATHENS FOR NOT GOING TO CHURCH? **NOW** WHO'S BEING INTOLERANT?!
AND FOR ALL YOU KNOW, FOXES ARE BUDDHISTS OR JUST REAL PRIVATE ABOUT THEIR RELIGION!
DOGS ARE SO HARD TO TALK TO... ARE FOXES DOGS? IS THAT WHY YOU'RE SO TOUCHY?
ARE FOXES DOGS? LET'S SEE-- ***IS THE SKY GREY?! IF A TREE FALLS IN THE WOODS CAN YOU STILL WEE ON IT?!***

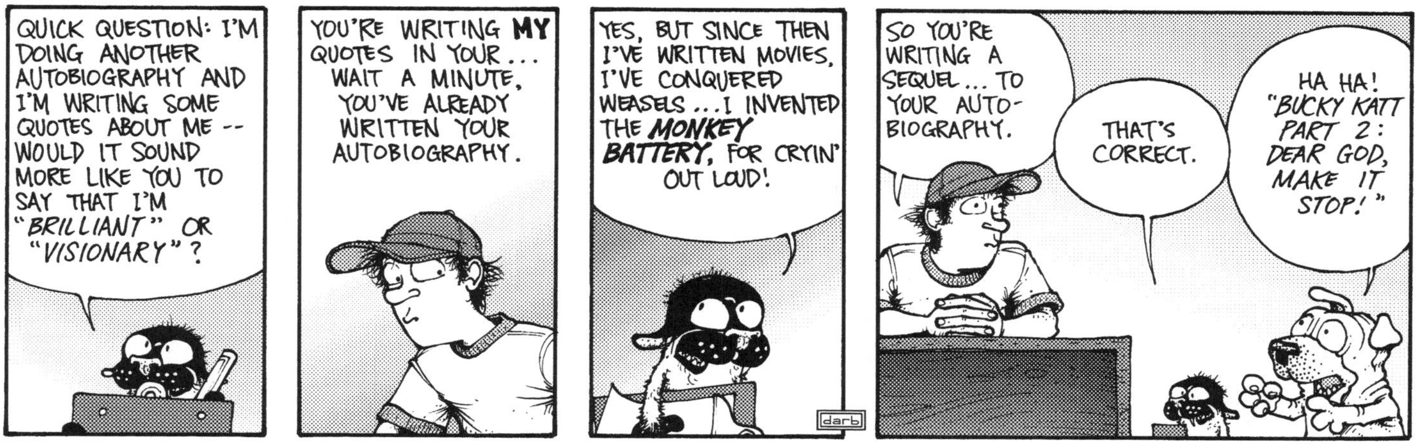
QUICK QUESTION: I'M DOING ANOTHER AUTOBIOGRAPHY AND I'M WRITING SOME QUOTES ABOUT ME -- WOULD IT SOUND MORE LIKE YOU TO SAY THAT I'M "BRILLIANT" OR "VISIONARY"?
YOU'RE WRITING MY QUOTES IN YOUR... WAIT A MINUTE, YOU'VE ALREADY WRITTEN YOUR AUTOBIOGRAPHY.
YES, BUT SINCE THEN I'VE WRITTEN MOVIES, I'VE CONQUERED WEASELS... I INVENTED THE MONKEY BATTERY, FOR CRYIN' OUT LOUD!
darb
SO YOU'RE WRITING A SEQUEL... TO YOUR AUTOBIOGRAPHY.
THAT'S CORRECT.
HA HA! "BUCKY KATT PART 2: DEAR GOD, MAKE IT STOP!"

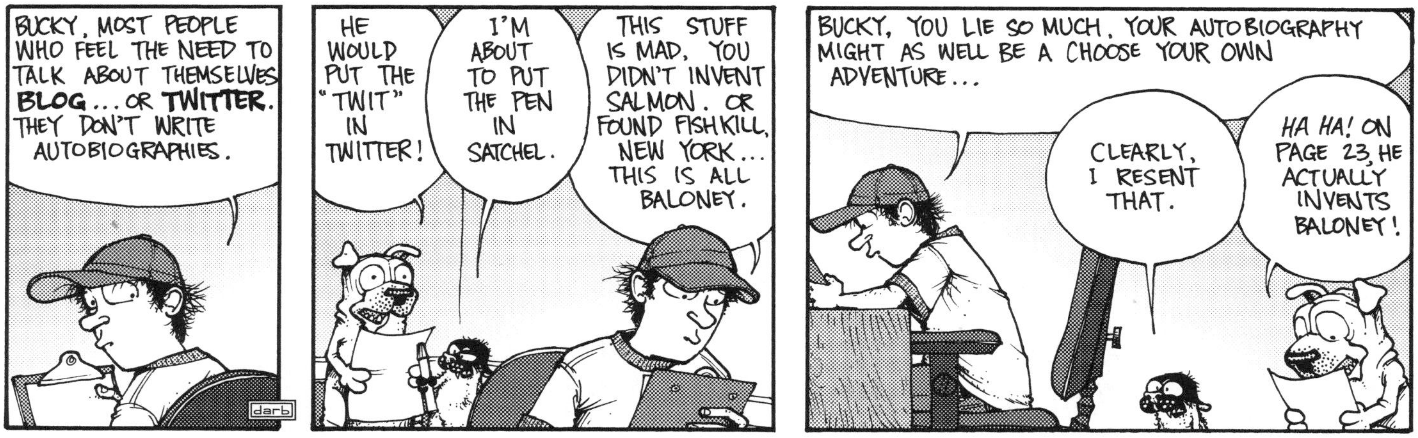
BUCKY, MOST PEOPLE WHO FEEL THE NEED TO TALK ABOUT THEMSELVES BLOG... OR TWITTER. THEY DON'T WRITE AUTOBIOGRAPHIES.
darb
HE WOULD PUT THE "TWIT" IN TWITTER!
I'M ABOUT TO PUT THE PEN IN SATCHEL.
THIS STUFF IS MAD. YOU DIDN'T INVENT SALMON. OR FOUND FISHKILL, NEW YORK... THIS IS ALL BALONEY.
BUCKY, YOU LIE SO MUCH, YOUR AUTOBIOGRAPHY MIGHT AS WELL BE A CHOOSE YOUR OWN ADVENTURE...
CLEARLY, I RESENT THAT.
HA HA! ON PAGE 23, HE ACTUALLY INVENTS BALONEY!

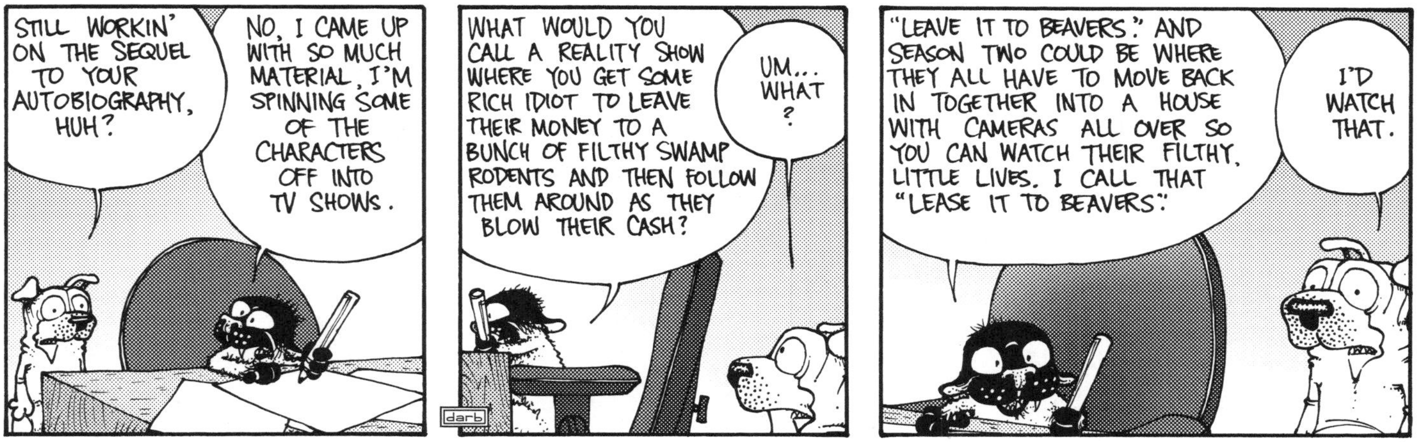
STILL WORKIN' ON THE SEQUEL TO YOUR AUTOBIOGRAPHY, HUH?
NO, I CAME UP WITH SO MUCH MATERIAL, I'M SPINNING SOME OF THE CHARACTERS OFF INTO TV SHOWS.
WHAT WOULD YOU CALL A REALITY SHOW WHERE YOU GET SOME RICH IDIOT TO LEAVE THEIR MONEY TO A BUNCH OF FILTHY SWAMP RODENTS AND THEN FOLLOW THEM AROUND AS THEY BLOW THEIR CASH?
UM... WHAT?
darb
"LEAVE IT TO BEAVERS." AND SEASON TWO COULD BE WHERE THEY ALL HAVE TO MOVE BACK IN TOGETHER INTO A HOUSE WITH CAMERAS ALL OVER SO YOU CAN WATCH THEIR FILTHY, LITTLE LIVES. I CALL THAT "LEASE IT TO BEAVERS."
I'D WATCH THAT.

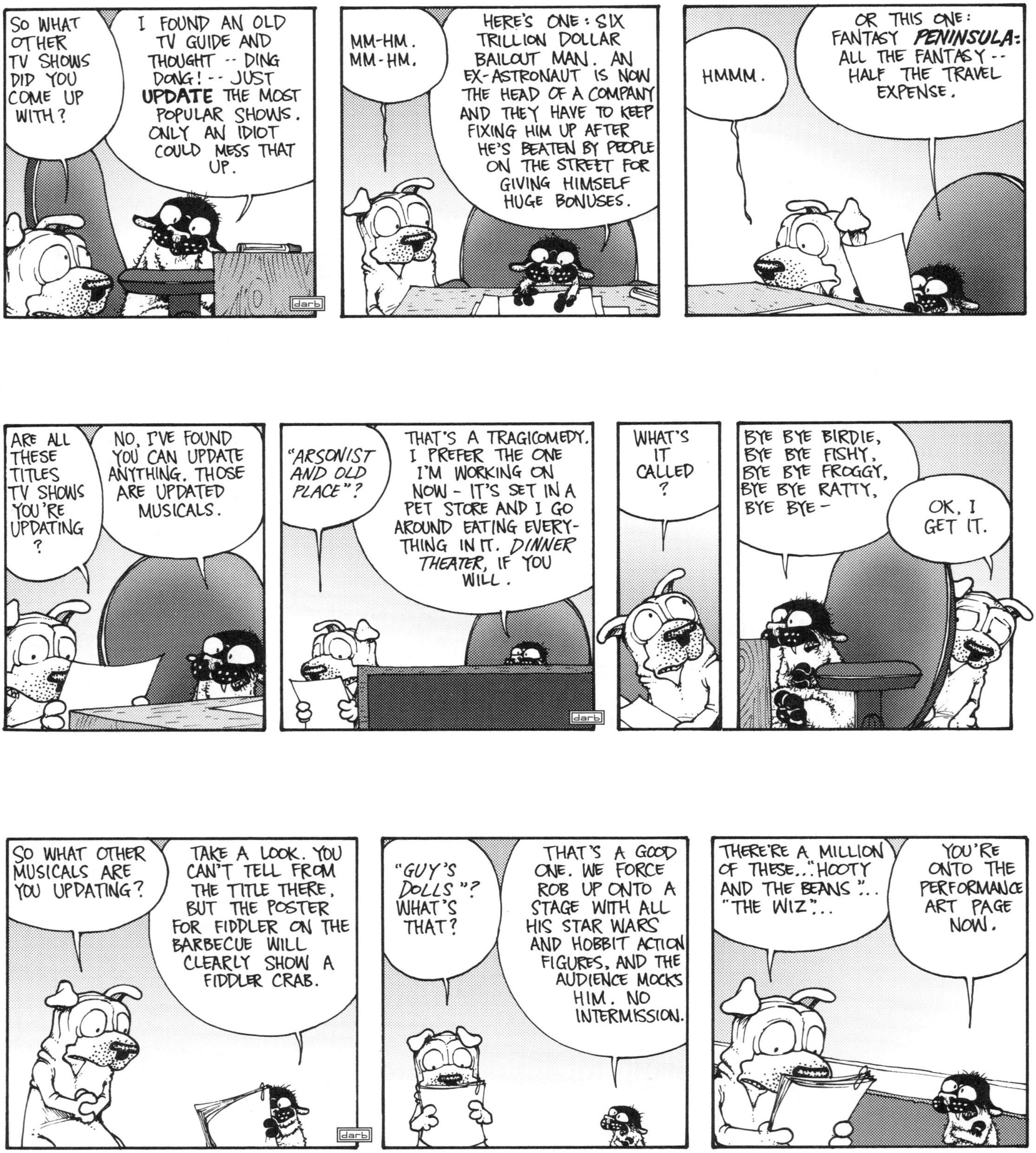
SO WHAT OTHER TV SHOWS DID YOU COME UP WITH?
I FOUND AN OLD TV GUIDE AND THOUGHT -- DING DONG! -- JUST **UPDATE** THE MOST POPULAR SHOWS. ONLY AN IDIOT COULD MESS THAT UP.
darb
MM-HM. MM-HM.
HERE'S ONE: SIX TRILLION DOLLAR BAILOUT MAN. AN EX-ASTRONAUT IS NOW THE HEAD OF A COMPANY AND THEY HAVE TO KEEP FIXING HIM UP AFTER HE'S BEATEN BY PEOPLE ON THE STREET FOR GIVING HIMSELF HUGE BONUSES.
HMMM.
OR THIS ONE: FANTASY ***PENINSULA***: ALL THE FANTASY -- HALF THE TRAVEL EXPENSE.
ARE ALL THESE TITLES TV SHOWS YOU'RE UPDATING?
NO, I'VE FOUND YOU CAN UPDATE ANYTHING. THOSE ARE UPDATED MUSICALS.
"*ARSONIST AND OLD PLACE*"?
THAT'S A TRAGICOMEDY. I PREFER THE ONE I'M WORKING ON NOW - IT'S SET IN A PET STORE AND I GO AROUND EATING EVERYTHING IN IT. *DINNER THEATER*, IF YOU WILL.
darb
WHAT'S IT CALLED?
BYE BYE BIRDIE, BYE BYE FISHY, BYE BYE FROGGY, BYE BYE RATTY, BYE BYE -
OK, I GET IT.
SO WHAT OTHER MUSICALS ARE YOU UPDATING?
TAKE A LOOK. YOU CAN'T TELL FROM THE TITLE THERE, BUT THE POSTER FOR FIDDLER ON THE BARBECUE WILL CLEARLY SHOW A FIDDLER CRAB.
darb
"*GUY'S DOLLS*"? WHAT'S THAT?
THAT'S A GOOD ONE. WE FORCE ROB UP ONTO A STAGE WITH ALL HIS STAR WARS AND HOBBIT ACTION FIGURES, AND THE AUDIENCE MOCKS HIM. NO INTERMISSION.
THERE'RE A MILLION OF THESE..."HOOTY AND THE BEANS"... "THE WIZ"...
YOU'RE ONTO THE PERFORMANCE ART PAGE NOW.

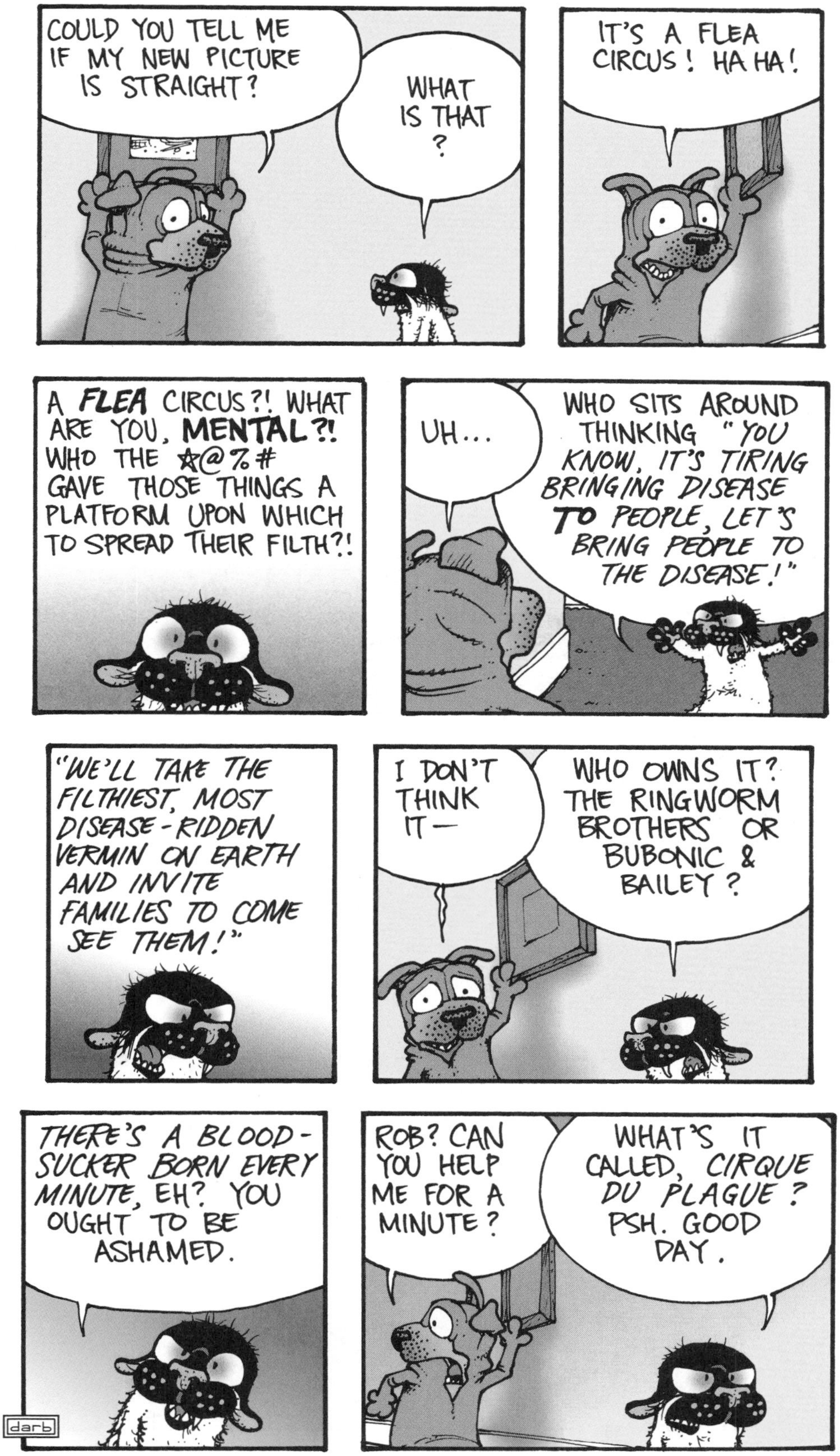
COULD YOU TELL ME IF MY NEW PICTURE IS STRAIGHT?
WHAT IS THAT ?
IT'S A FLEA CIRCUS! HA HA!
A FLEA CIRCUS?! WHAT ARE YOU, MENTAL?! WHO THE ☆@%# GAVE THOSE THINGS A PLATFORM UPON WHICH TO SPREAD THEIR FILTH?!
UH...
WHO SITS AROUND THINKING "YOU KNOW, IT'S TIRING BRINGING DISEASE TO PEOPLE, LET'S BRING PEOPLE TO THE DISEASE!"
"WE'LL TAKE THE FILTHIEST, MOST DISEASE-RIDDEN VERMIN ON EARTH AND INVITE FAMILIES TO COME SEE THEM!"
I DON'T THINK IT—
WHO OWNS IT? THE RINGWORM BROTHERS OR BUBONIC & BAILEY?
THERE'S A BLOOD-SUCKER BORN EVERY MINUTE, EH? YOU OUGHT TO BE ASHAMED.
darb
ROB? CAN YOU HELP ME FOR A MINUTE?
WHAT'S IT CALLED, CIRQUE DU PLAGUE? PSH. GOOD DAY.

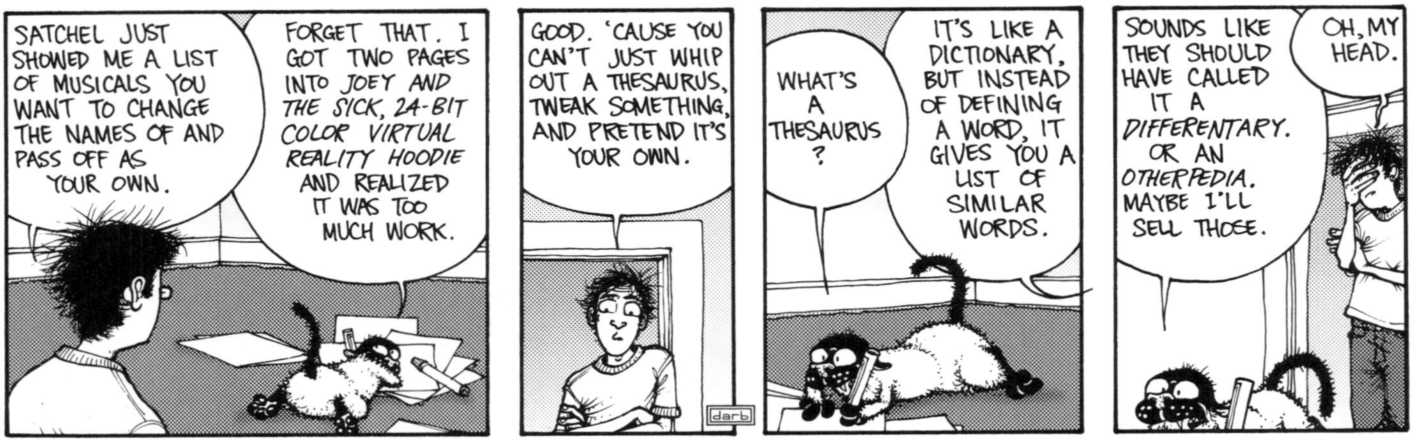
SATCHEL JUST SHOWED ME A LIST OF MUSICALS YOU WANT TO CHANGE THE NAMES OF AND PASS OFF AS YOUR OWN.
FORGET THAT. I GOT TWO PAGES INTO *JOEY AND THE SICK, 24-BIT COLOR VIRTUAL REALITY HOODIE* AND REALIZED IT WAS TOO MUCH WORK.
GOOD. 'CAUSE YOU CAN'T JUST WHIP OUT A THESAURUS, TWEAK SOMETHING, AND PRETEND IT'S YOUR OWN.
WHAT'S A THESAURUS?
IT'S LIKE A DICTIONARY, BUT INSTEAD OF DEFINING A WORD, IT GIVES YOU A LIST OF SIMILAR WORDS.
SOUNDS LIKE THEY SHOULD HAVE CALLED IT A *DIFFERENTARY*. OR AN *OTHERPEDIA*. MAYBE I'LL SELL THOSE.
OH, MY HEAD.
darb

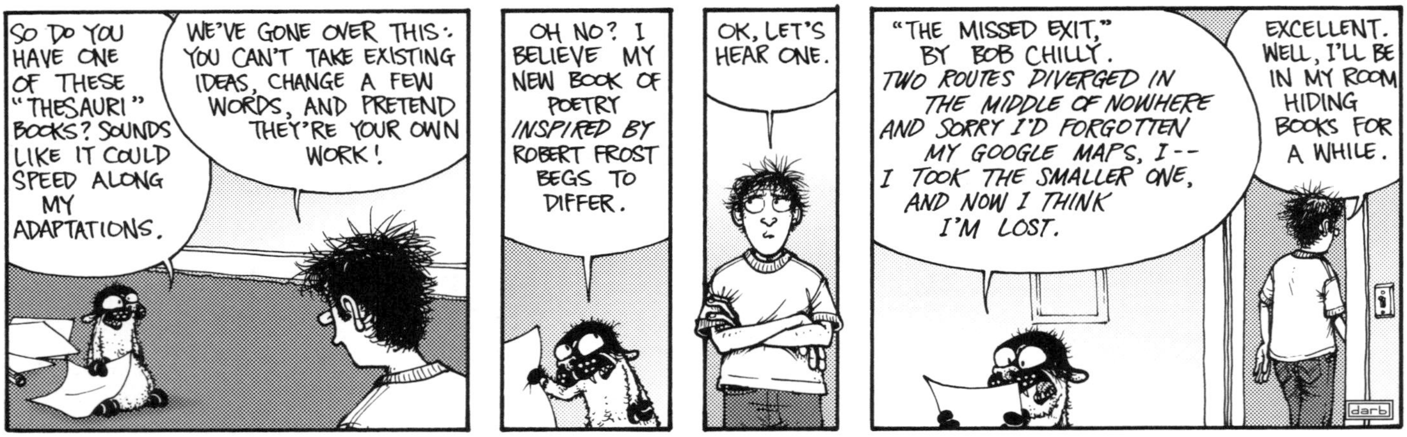
SO DO YOU HAVE ONE OF THESE "THESAURI" BOOKS? SOUNDS LIKE IT COULD SPEED ALONG MY ADAPTATIONS.
WE'VE GONE OVER THIS: YOU CAN'T TAKE EXISTING IDEAS, CHANGE A FEW WORDS, AND PRETEND THEY'RE YOUR OWN WORK!
OH NO? I BELIEVE MY NEW BOOK OF POETRY *INSPIRED BY* ROBERT FROST BEGS TO DIFFER.
OK, LET'S HEAR ONE.
"THE MISSED EXIT," BY BOB CHILLY. *TWO ROUTES DIVERGED IN THE MIDDLE OF NOWHERE AND SORRY I'D FORGOTTEN MY GOOGLE MAPS, I-- I TOOK THE SMALLER ONE, AND NOW I THINK I'M LOST.*
EXCELLENT. WELL, I'LL BE IN MY ROOM HIDING BOOKS FOR A WHILE.
darb

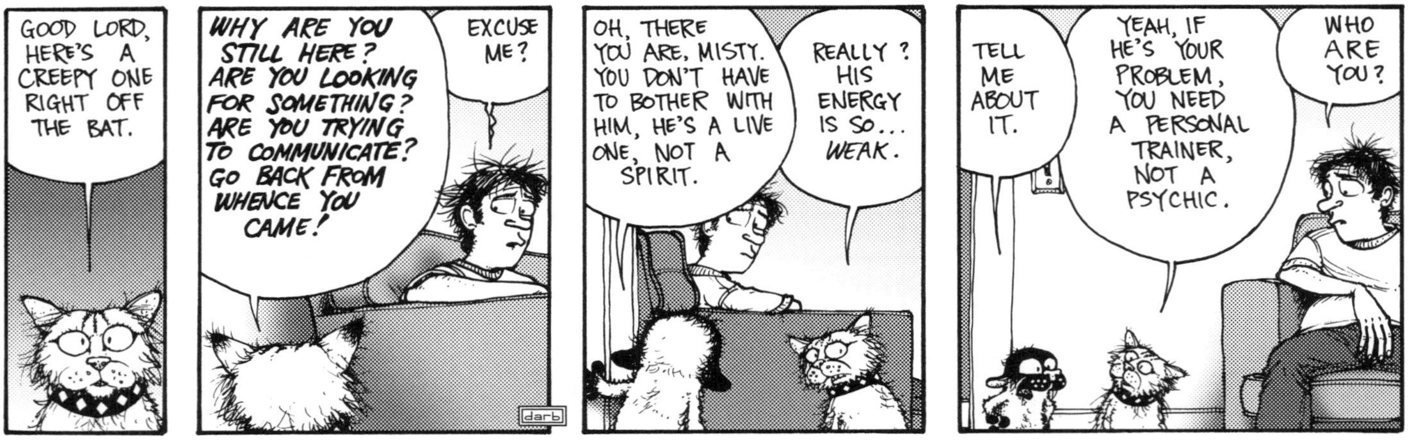
GOOD LORD, HERE'S A CREEPY ONE RIGHT OFF THE BAT.
WHY ARE YOU STILL HERE? ARE YOU LOOKING FOR SOMETHING? ARE YOU TRYING TO COMMUNICATE? GO BACK FROM WHENCE YOU CAME!
EXCUSE ME?
darb
OH, THERE YOU ARE, MISTY. YOU DON'T HAVE TO BOTHER WITH HIM, HE'S A LIVE ONE, NOT A SPIRIT.
REALLY? HIS ENERGY IS SO... *WEAK*.
TELL ME ABOUT IT.
YEAH, IF HE'S YOUR PROBLEM, YOU NEED A PERSONAL TRAINER, NOT A PSYCHIC.
WHO ARE YOU?

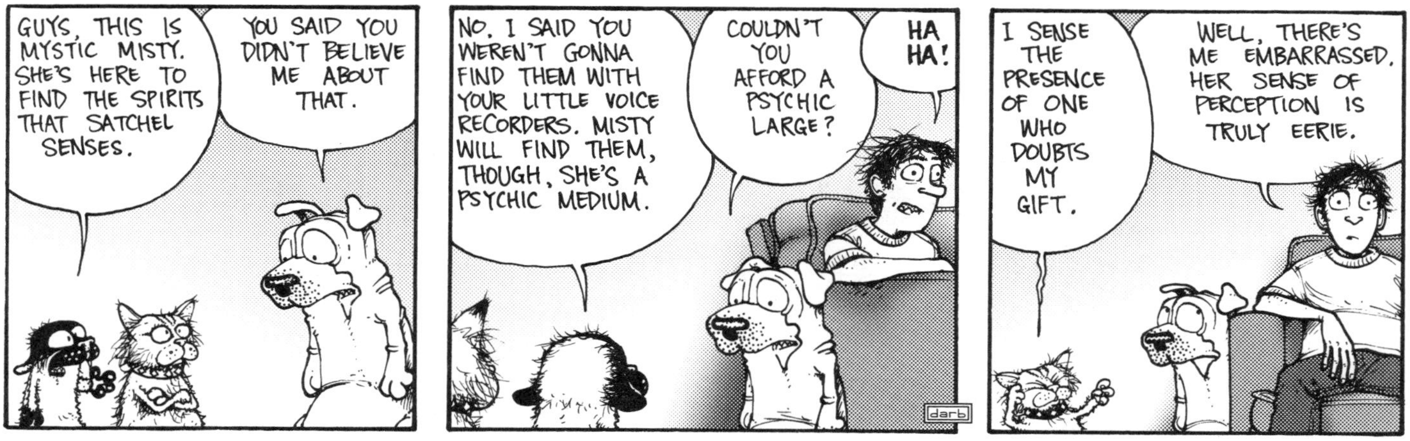
GUYS, THIS IS MYSTIC MISTY. SHE'S HERE TO FIND THE SPIRITS THAT SATCHEL SENSES.
YOU SAID YOU DIDN'T BELIEVE ME ABOUT THAT.
NO. I SAID YOU WEREN'T GONNA FIND THEM WITH YOUR LITTLE VOICE RECORDERS. MISTY WILL FIND THEM, THOUGH. SHE'S A PSYCHIC MEDIUM.
COULDN'T YOU AFFORD A PSYCHIC LARGE?
HA HA!
I SENSE THE PRESENCE OF ONE WHO DOUBTS MY GIFT.
WELL, THERE'S ME EMBARRASSED. HER SENSE OF PERCEPTION IS TRULY EERIE.
darb

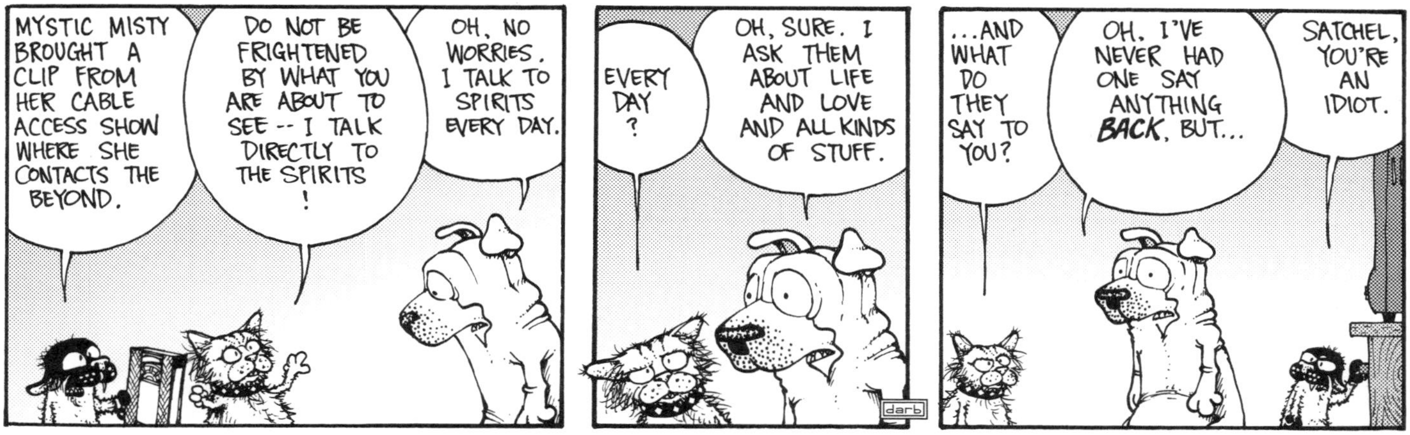
MYSTIC MISTY BROUGHT A CLIP FROM HER CABLE ACCESS SHOW WHERE SHE CONTACTS THE BEYOND.
DO NOT BE FRIGHTENED BY WHAT YOU ARE ABOUT TO SEE -- I TALK DIRECTLY TO THE SPIRITS!
OH, NO WORRIES. I TALK TO SPIRITS EVERY DAY.
EVERY DAY?
OH, SURE. I ASK THEM ABOUT LIFE AND LOVE AND ALL KINDS OF STUFF.
...AND WHAT DO THEY SAY TO YOU?
OH. I'VE NEVER HAD ONE SAY ANYTHING BACK, BUT...
SATCHEL, YOU'RE AN IDIOT.
darb

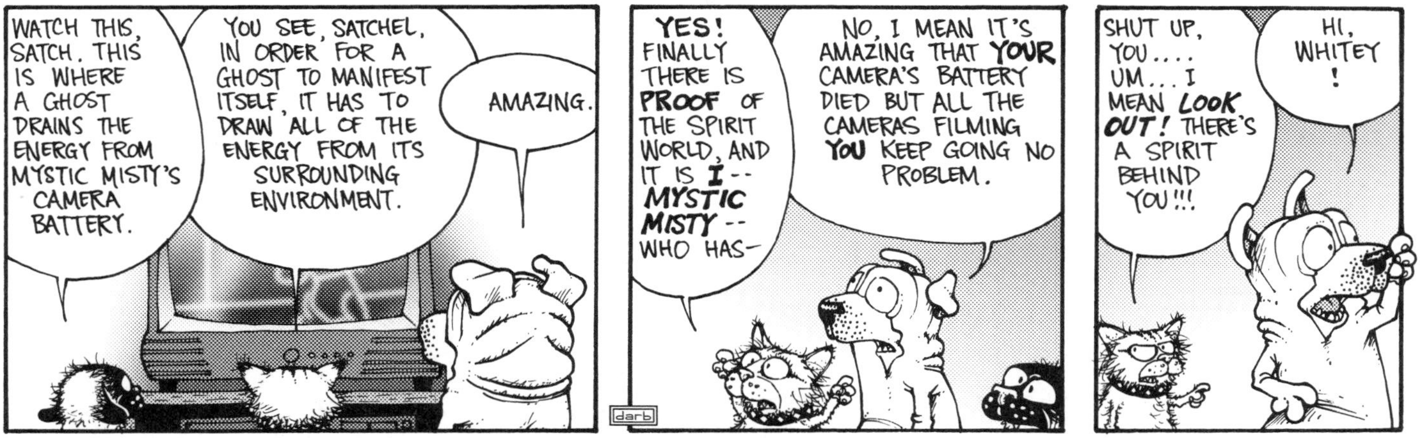
WATCH THIS, SATCH. THIS IS WHERE A GHOST DRAINS THE ENERGY FROM MYSTIC MISTY'S CAMERA BATTERY.
YOU SEE, SATCHEL, IN ORDER FOR A GHOST TO MANIFEST ITSELF, IT HAS TO DRAW ALL OF THE ENERGY FROM ITS SURROUNDING ENVIRONMENT.
AMAZING.
YES! FINALLY THERE IS PROOF OF THE SPIRIT WORLD, AND IT IS I -- MYSTIC MISTY -- WHO HAS—
NO, I MEAN IT'S AMAZING THAT YOUR CAMERA'S BATTERY DIED BUT ALL THE CAMERAS FILMING YOU KEEP GOING NO PROBLEM.
SHUT UP, YOU.... UM... I MEAN LOOK OUT! THERE'S A SPIRIT BEHIND YOU!!!
HI, WHITEY!
darb

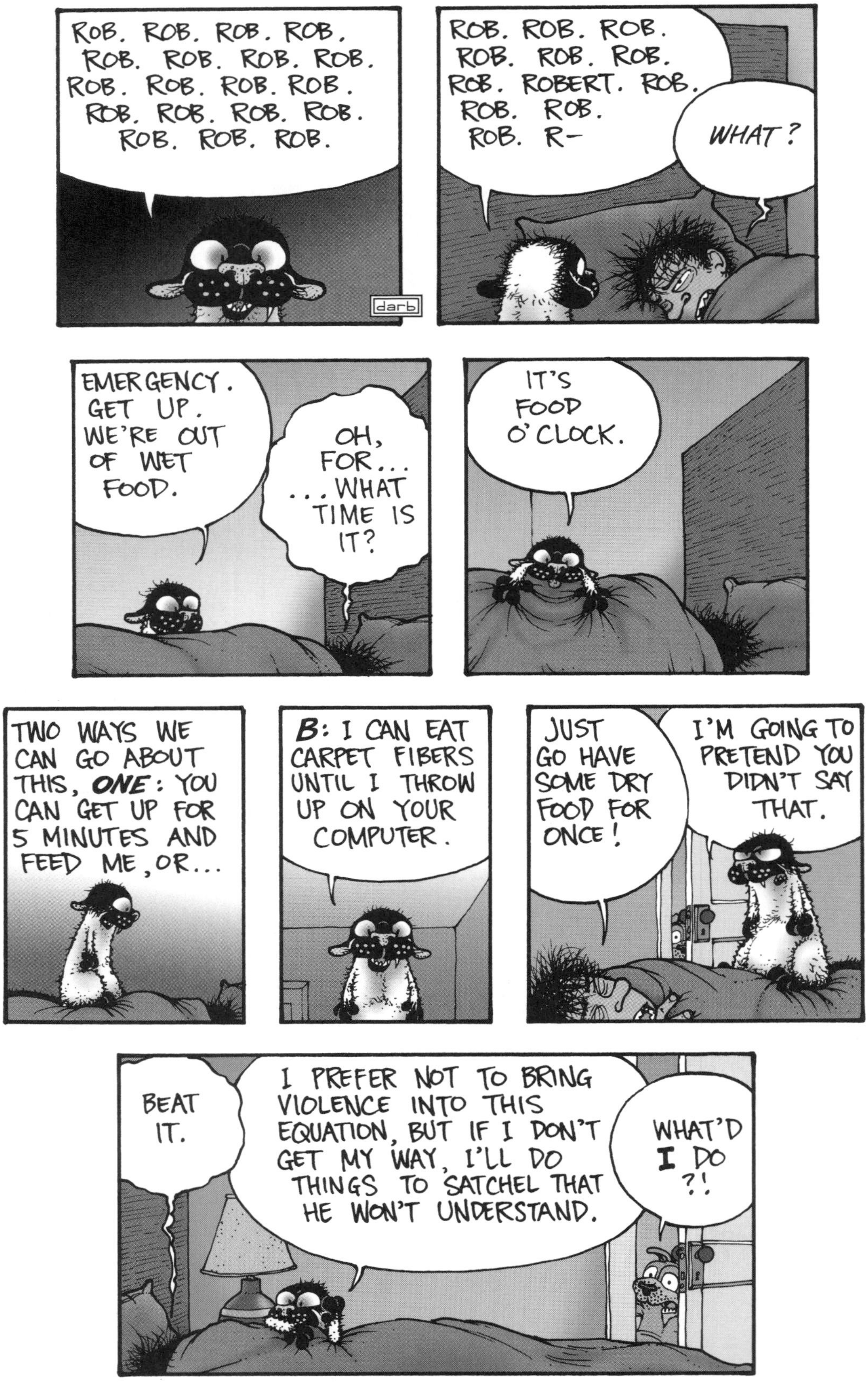
ROB. ROB. ROB. ROB. ROB. ROB. ROB. ROB. ROB. ROB. ROB. ROB. ROB. ROB. ROB. ROB. ROB. ROB. ROB.
darb
ROB. ROB. ROB. ROB. ROB. ROB. ROB. ROBERT. ROB. ROB. ROB. ROB. R-
WHAT?
EMERGENCY. GET UP. WE'RE OUT OF WET FOOD.
OH, FOR... ...WHAT TIME IS IT?
IT'S FOOD O'CLOCK.
TWO WAYS WE CAN GO ABOUT THIS, ONE: YOU CAN GET UP FOR 5 MINUTES AND FEED ME, OR...
B: I CAN EAT CARPET FIBERS UNTIL I THROW UP ON YOUR COMPUTER.
JUST GO HAVE SOME DRY FOOD FOR ONCE!
I'M GOING TO PRETEND YOU DIDN'T SAY THAT.
BEAT IT.
I PREFER NOT TO BRING VIOLENCE INTO THIS EQUATION, BUT IF I DON'T GET MY WAY, I'LL DO THINGS TO SATCHEL THAT HE WON'T UNDERSTAND.
WHAT'D I DO?!

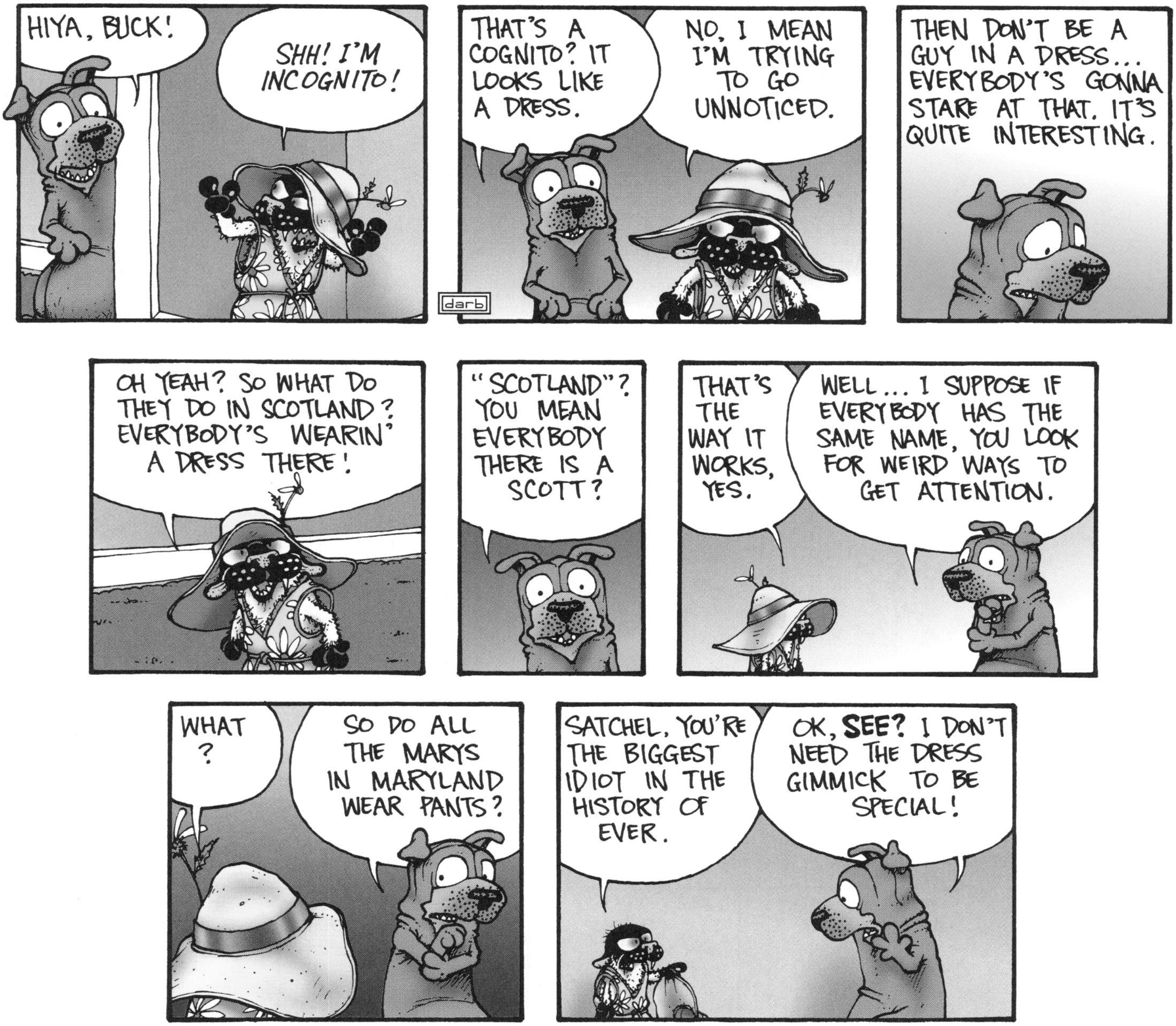
HIYA, BUCK!
SHH! I'M INCOGNITO!
THAT'S A COGNITO? IT LOOKS LIKE A DRESS.
NO, I MEAN I'M TRYING TO GO UNNOTICED.
darb
THEN DON'T BE A GUY IN A DRESS... EVERYBODY'S GONNA STARE AT THAT. IT'S QUITE INTERESTING.
OH YEAH? SO WHAT DO THEY DO IN SCOTLAND? EVERYBODY'S WEARIN' A DRESS THERE!
"SCOTLAND"? YOU MEAN EVERYBODY THERE IS A SCOTT?
THAT'S THE WAY IT WORKS, YES.
WELL... I SUPPOSE IF EVERYBODY HAS THE SAME NAME, YOU LOOK FOR WEIRD WAYS TO GET ATTENTION.
WHAT?
SO DO ALL THE MARYS IN MARYLAND WEAR PANTS?
SATCHEL, YOU'RE THE BIGGEST IDIOT IN THE HISTORY OF EVER.
OK, **SEE?** I DON'T NEED THE DRESS GIMMICK TO BE SPECIAL!

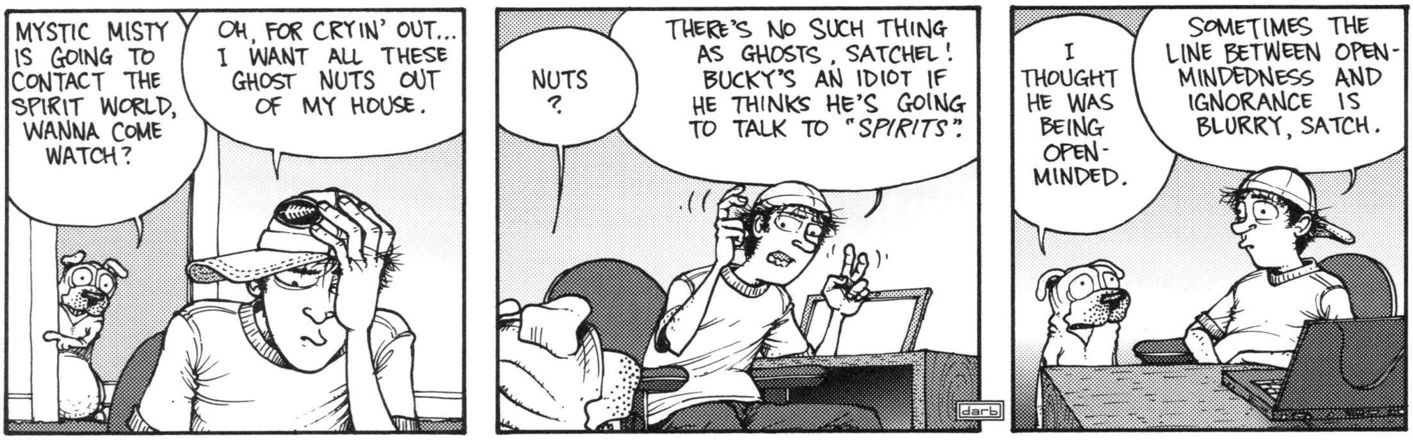
MYSTIC MISTY IS GOING TO CONTACT THE SPIRIT WORLD, WANNA COME WATCH?
OH, FOR CRYIN' OUT... I WANT ALL THESE GHOST NUTS OUT OF MY HOUSE.
NUTS?
THERE'S NO SUCH THING AS GHOSTS, SATCHEL! BUCKY'S AN IDIOT IF HE THINKS HE'S GOING TO TALK TO "SPIRITS".
I THOUGHT HE WAS BEING OPEN-MINDED.
SOMETIMES THE LINE BETWEEN OPEN-MINDEDNESS AND IGNORANCE IS BLURRY, SATCH.
darb

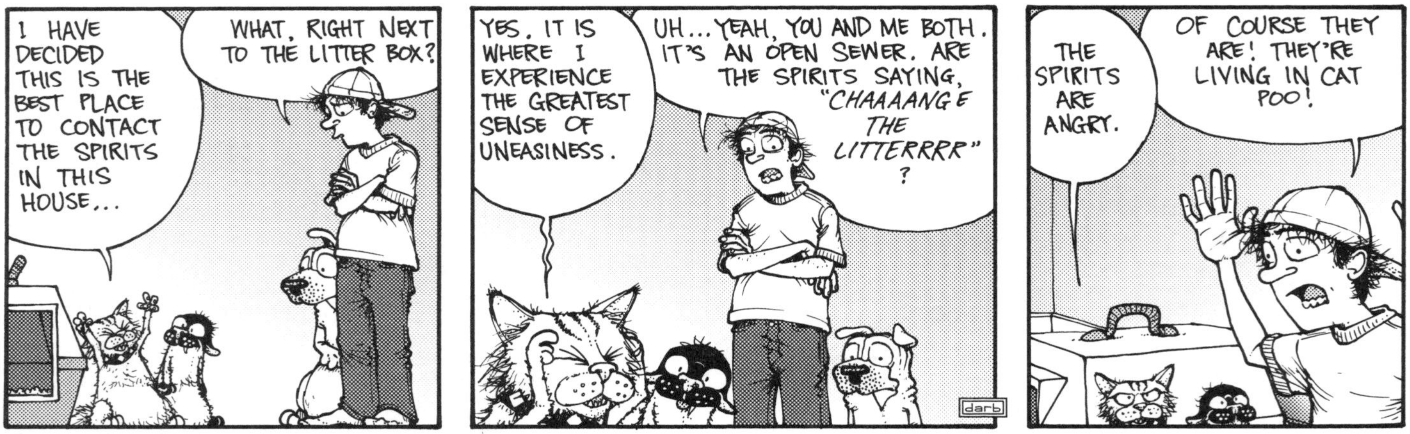
I HAVE DECIDED THIS IS THE BEST PLACE TO CONTACT THE SPIRITS IN THIS HOUSE...
WHAT, RIGHT NEXT TO THE LITTER BOX?
YES. IT IS WHERE I EXPERIENCE THE GREATEST SENSE OF UNEASINESS.
UH... YEAH, YOU AND ME BOTH. IT'S AN OPEN SEWER. ARE THE SPIRITS SAYING, "CHAAAANGE THE LITTERRRR"?
THE SPIRITS ARE ANGRY.
OF COURSE THEY ARE! THEY'RE LIVING IN CAT POO!
darb

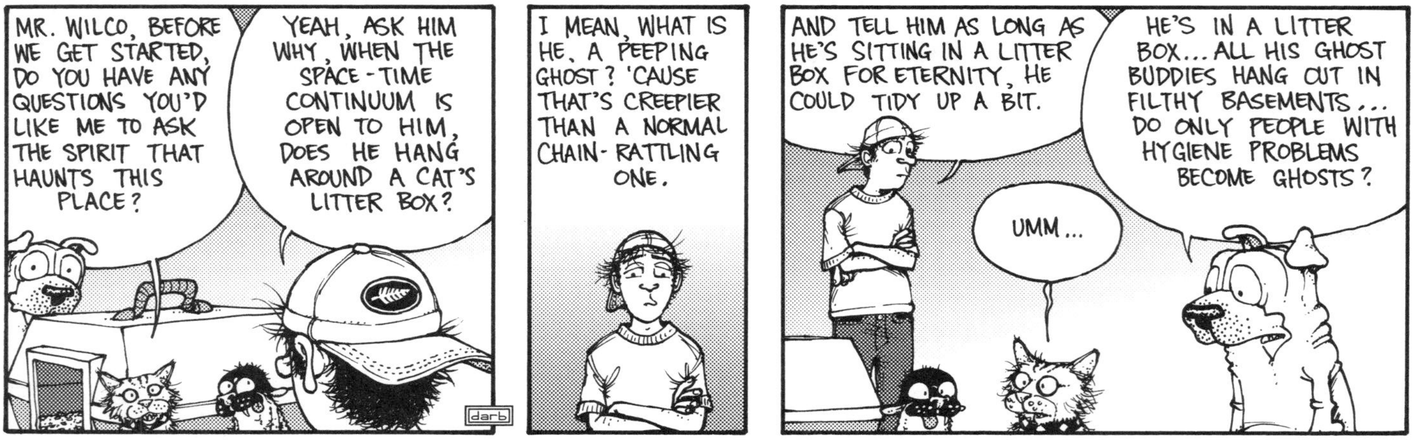
MR. WILCO, BEFORE WE GET STARTED, DO YOU HAVE ANY QUESTIONS YOU'D LIKE ME TO ASK THE SPIRIT THAT HAUNTS THIS PLACE?
YEAH, ASK HIM WHY, WHEN THE SPACE-TIME CONTINUUM IS OPEN TO HIM, DOES HE HANG AROUND A CAT'S LITTER BOX?
I MEAN, WHAT IS HE, A PEEPING GHOST? 'CAUSE THAT'S CREEPIER THAN A NORMAL CHAIN-RATTLING ONE.
AND TELL HIM AS LONG AS HE'S SITTING IN A LITTER BOX FOR ETERNITY, HE COULD TIDY UP A BIT.
HE'S IN A LITTER BOX... ALL HIS GHOST BUDDIES HANG OUT IN FILTHY BASEMENTS... DO ONLY PEOPLE WITH HYGIENE PROBLEMS BECOME GHOSTS?
UMM...
darb

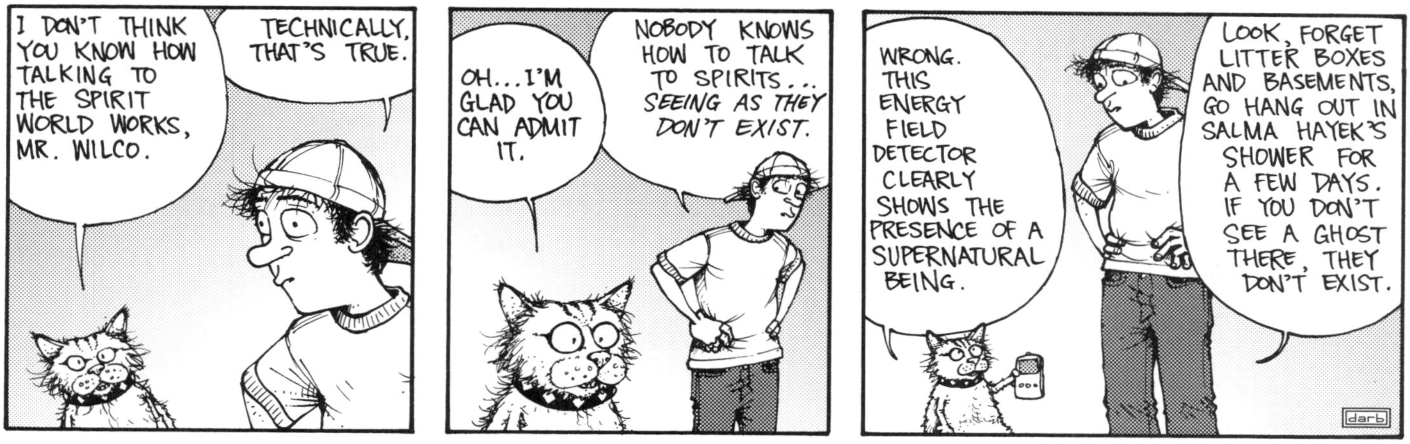
I DON'T THINK YOU KNOW HOW TALKING TO THE SPIRIT WORLD WORKS, MR. WILCO.
TECHNICALLY, THAT'S TRUE.
OH... I'M GLAD YOU CAN ADMIT IT.
NOBODY KNOWS HOW TO TALK TO SPIRITS... *SEEING AS THEY DON'T EXIST.*
WRONG. THIS ENERGY FIELD DETECTOR CLEARLY SHOWS THE PRESENCE OF A SUPERNATURAL BEING.
LOOK, FORGET LITTER BOXES AND BASEMENTS, GO HANG OUT IN SALMA HAYEK'S SHOWER FOR A FEW DAYS. IF YOU DON'T SEE A GHOST THERE, THEY DON'T EXIST.
darb

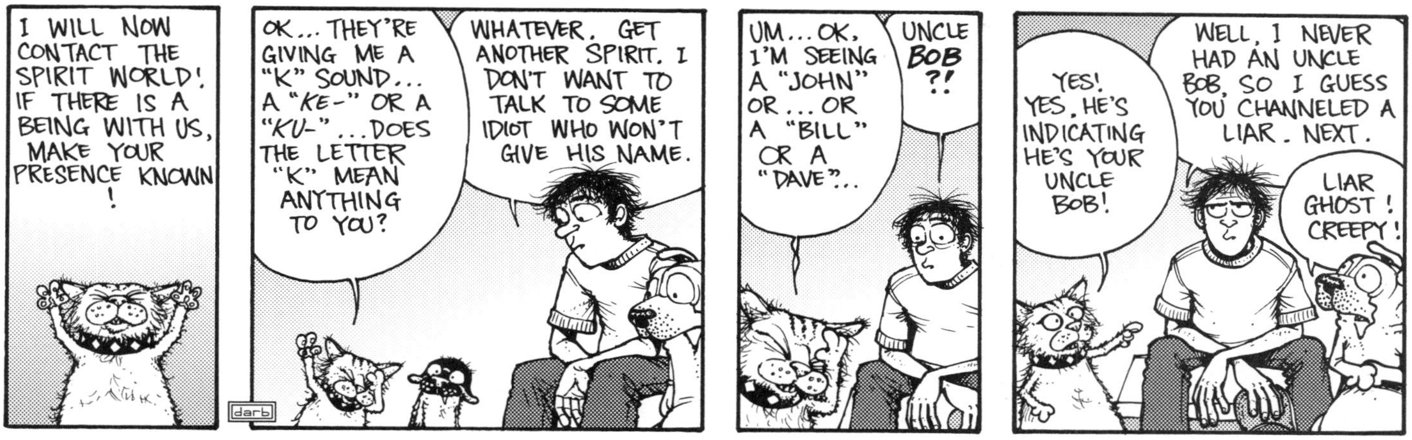
I WILL NOW CONTACT THE SPIRIT WORLD! IF THERE IS A BEING WITH US, MAKE YOUR PRESENCE KNOWN!
darb
OK... THEY'RE GIVING ME A "K" SOUND... A "*KE-*" OR A "*KU-*"... DOES THE LETTER "K" MEAN ANYTHING TO YOU?
WHATEVER. GET ANOTHER SPIRIT. I DON'T WANT TO TALK TO SOME IDIOT WHO WON'T GIVE HIS NAME.
UM... OK, I'M SEEING A "JOHN" OR... OR A "BILL" OR A "DAVE"?...
UNCLE **BOB** ?!
YES! YES, HE'S INDICATING HE'S YOUR UNCLE BOB!
WELL, I NEVER HAD AN UNCLE BOB, SO I GUESS YOU CHANNELED A LIAR. NEXT.
LIAR GHOST! CREEPY!

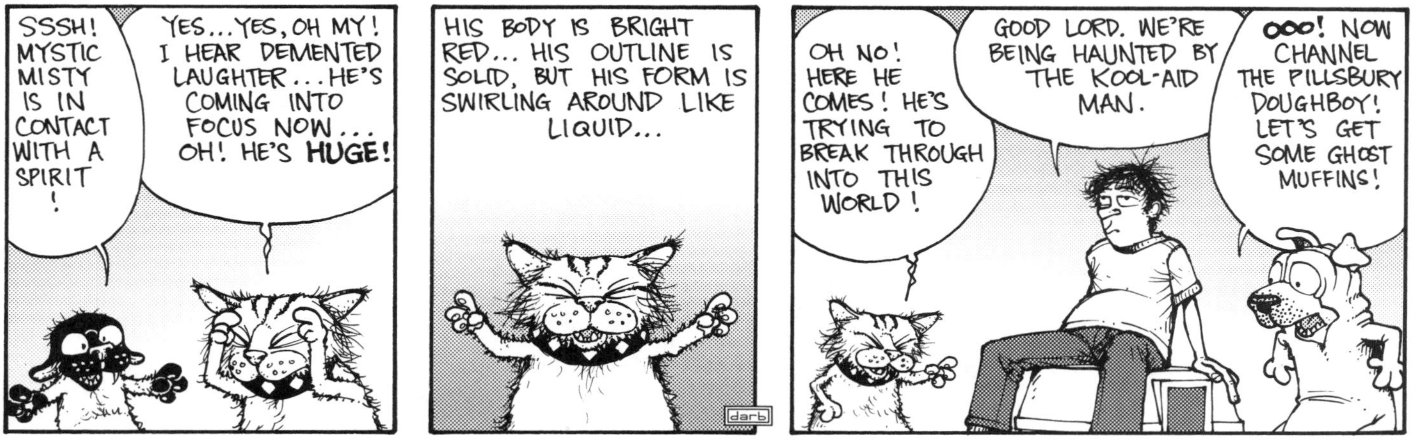
SSSH! MYSTIC MISTY IS IN CONTACT WITH A SPIRIT!
YES... YES, OH MY! I HEAR DEMENTED LAUGHTER... HE'S COMING INTO FOCUS NOW... OH! HE'S **HUGE**!
HIS BODY IS BRIGHT RED... HIS OUTLINE IS SOLID, BUT HIS FORM IS SWIRLING AROUND LIKE LIQUID...
darb
OH NO! HERE HE COMES! HE'S TRYING TO BREAK THROUGH INTO THIS WORLD!
GOOD LORD. WE'RE BEING HAUNTED BY THE KOOL-AID MAN.
OOO! NOW CHANNEL THE PILLSBURY DOUGHBOY! LET'S GET SOME GHOST MUFFINS!

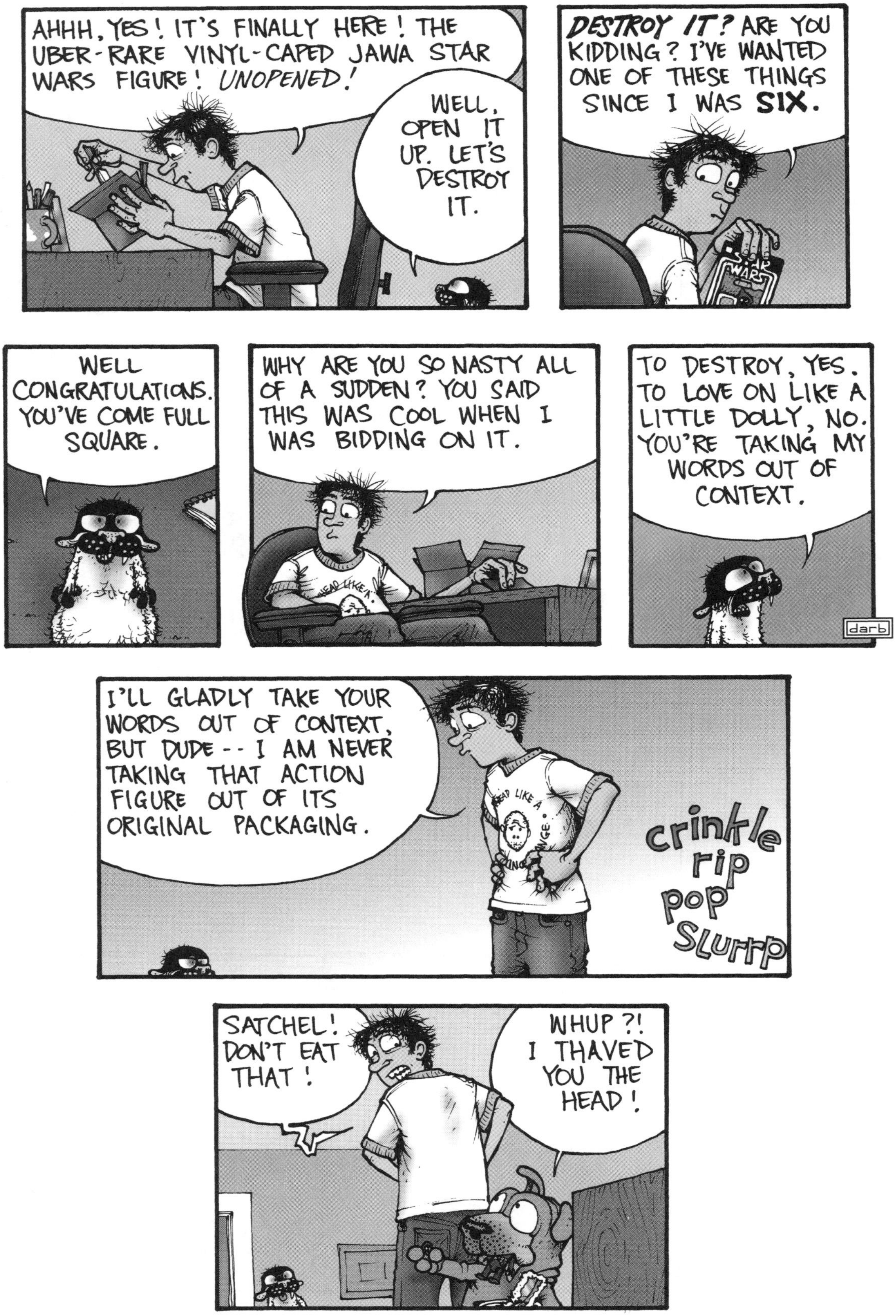
AHHH, YES! IT'S FINALLY HERE! THE UBER-RARE VINYL-CAPED JAWA STAR WARS FIGURE! UNOPENED!
WELL, OPEN IT UP. LET'S DESTROY IT.
DESTROY IT? ARE YOU KIDDING? I'VE WANTED ONE OF THESE THINGS SINCE I WAS SIX.
STAR WARS
WELL CONGRATULATIONS. YOU'VE COME FULL SQUARE.
WHY ARE YOU SO NASTY ALL OF A SUDDEN? YOU SAID THIS WAS COOL WHEN I WAS BIDDING ON IT.
TO DESTROY, YES. TO LOVE ON LIKE A LITTLE DOLLY, NO. YOU'RE TAKING MY WORDS OUT OF CONTEXT.
darb
I'LL GLADLY TAKE YOUR WORDS OUT OF CONTEXT, BUT DUDE -- I AM NEVER TAKING THAT ACTION FIGURE OUT OF ITS ORIGINAL PACKAGING.
crinkle
rip
pop
SLURRP
SATCHEL! DON'T EAT THAT!
WHUP?! I THAVED YOU THE HEAD!

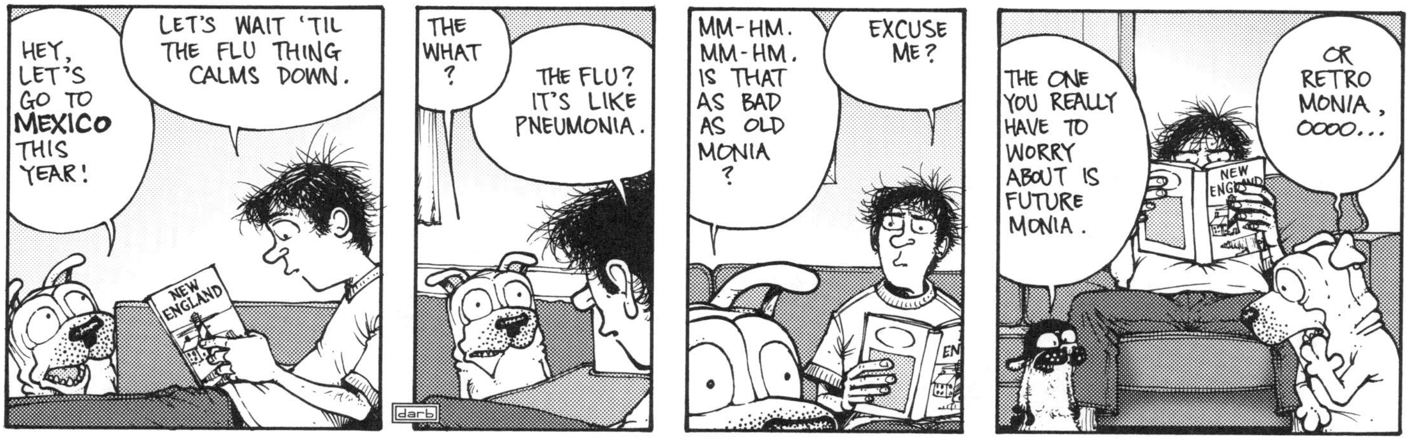
HEY, LET'S GO TO **MEXICO** THIS YEAR!
LET'S WAIT 'TIL THE FLU THING CALMS DOWN.
NEW ENGLAND
THE WHAT ?
THE FLU? IT'S LIKE PNEUMONIA.
darb
MM-HM. MM-HM. IS THAT AS BAD AS OLD MONIA ?
EXCUSE ME?
THE ONE YOU REALLY HAVE TO WORRY ABOUT IS FUTURE MONIA.
OR RETRO MONIA, OOOO...
NEW ENGLAND

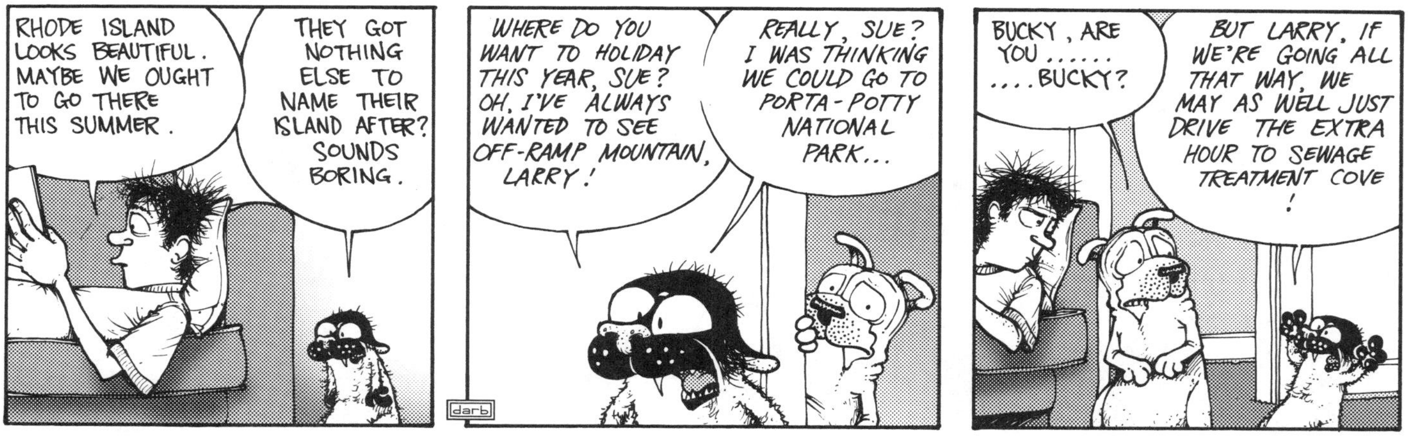
RHODE ISLAND LOOKS BEAUTIFUL. MAYBE WE OUGHT TO GO THERE THIS SUMMER.
THEY GOT NOTHING ELSE TO NAME THEIR ISLAND AFTER? SOUNDS BORING.
darb
WHERE DO YOU WANT TO HOLIDAY THIS YEAR, SUE? OH, I'VE ALWAYS WANTED TO SEE OFF-RAMP MOUNTAIN, LARRY!
REALLY, SUE? I WAS THINKING WE COULD GO TO PORTA-POTTY NATIONAL PARK...
BUCKY, ARE YOU...... ....BUCKY?
BUT LARRY, IF WE'RE GOING ALL THAT WAY, WE MAY AS WELL JUST DRIVE THE EXTRA HOUR TO SEWAGE TREATMENT COVE !

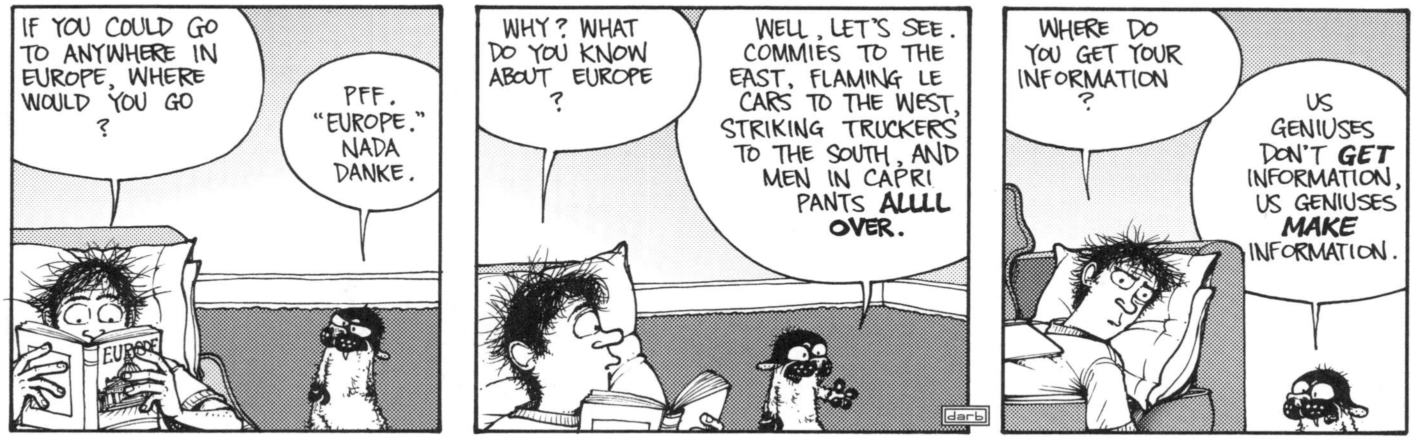
IF YOU COULD GO TO ANYWHERE IN EUROPE, WHERE WOULD YOU GO ?
PFF. "EUROPE." NADA DANKE.
EUROPE
WHY? WHAT DO YOU KNOW ABOUT EUROPE ?
WELL, LET'S SEE. COMMIES TO THE EAST, FLAMING LE CARS TO THE WEST, STRIKING TRUCKERS TO THE SOUTH, AND MEN IN CAPRI PANTS **ALLLL OVER.**
darb
WHERE DO YOU GET YOUR INFORMATION ?
US GENIUSES DON'T **GET** INFORMATION, US GENIUSES **MAKE** INFORMATION.

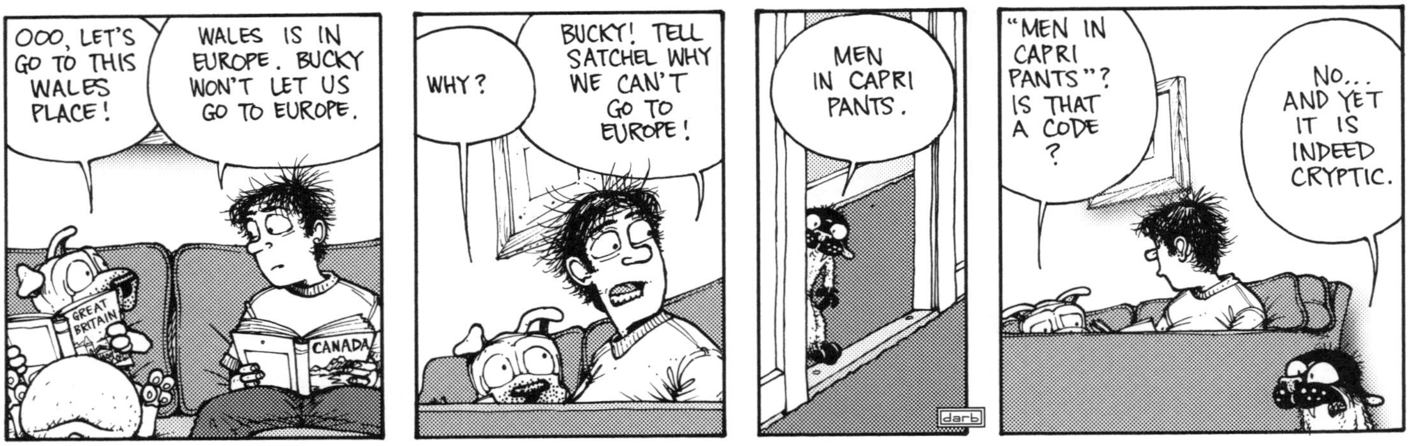
OOO, LET'S GO TO THIS WALES PLACE!
WALES IS IN EUROPE. BUCKY WON'T LET US GO TO EUROPE.
GREAT BRITAIN
CANADA
WHY?
BUCKY! TELL SATCHEL WHY WE CAN'T GO TO EUROPE!
MEN IN CAPRI PANTS.
darb
"MEN IN CAPRI PANTS"? IS THAT A CODE?
NO... AND YET IT IS INDEED CRYPTIC.

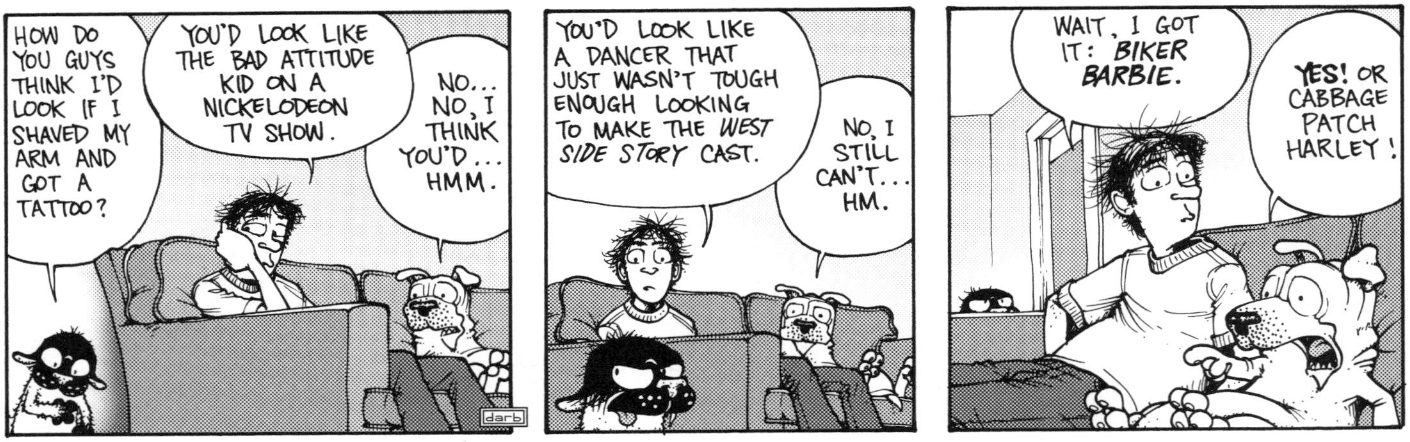
HOW DO YOU GUYS THINK I'D LOOK IF I SHAVED MY ARM AND GOT A TATTOO?
YOU'D LOOK LIKE THE BAD ATTITUDE KID ON A NICKELODEON TV SHOW.
NO... NO, I THINK YOU'D... HMM.
darb
YOU'D LOOK LIKE A DANCER THAT JUST WASN'T TOUGH ENOUGH LOOKING TO MAKE THE *WEST SIDE STORY* CAST.
NO, I STILL CAN'T... HM.
WAIT, I GOT IT: ***BIKER BARBIE.***
YES! OR CABBAGE PATCH HARLEY!

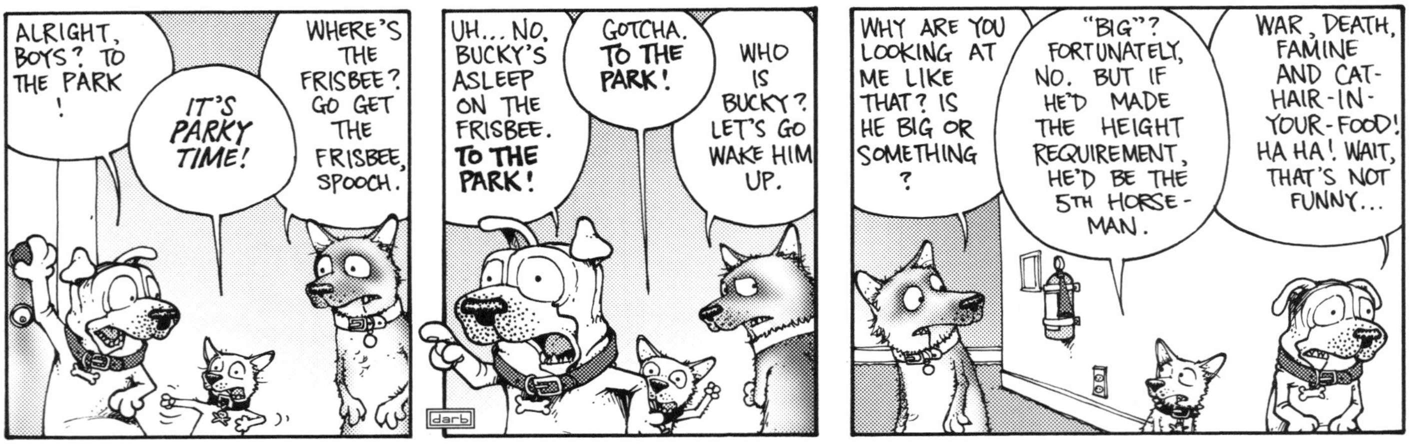
ALRIGHT, BOYS? TO THE PARK!
*IT'S **PARKY** TIME!*
WHERE'S THE FRISBEE? GO GET THE FRISBEE, SPOOCH.
darb
UH... NO. BUCKY'S ASLEEP ON THE FRISBEE. **TO THE PARK!**
GOTCHA. **TO THE PARK!**
WHO IS BUCKY? LET'S GO WAKE HIM UP.
WHY ARE YOU LOOKING AT ME LIKE THAT? IS HE BIG OR SOMETHING?
"BIG"? FORTUNATELY, NO. BUT IF HE'D MADE THE HEIGHT REQUIREMENT, HE'D BE THE 5TH HORSE-MAN.
WAR, DEATH, FAMINE AND CAT-HAIR-IN-YOUR-FOOD! HA HA! WAIT, THAT'S NOT FUNNY...

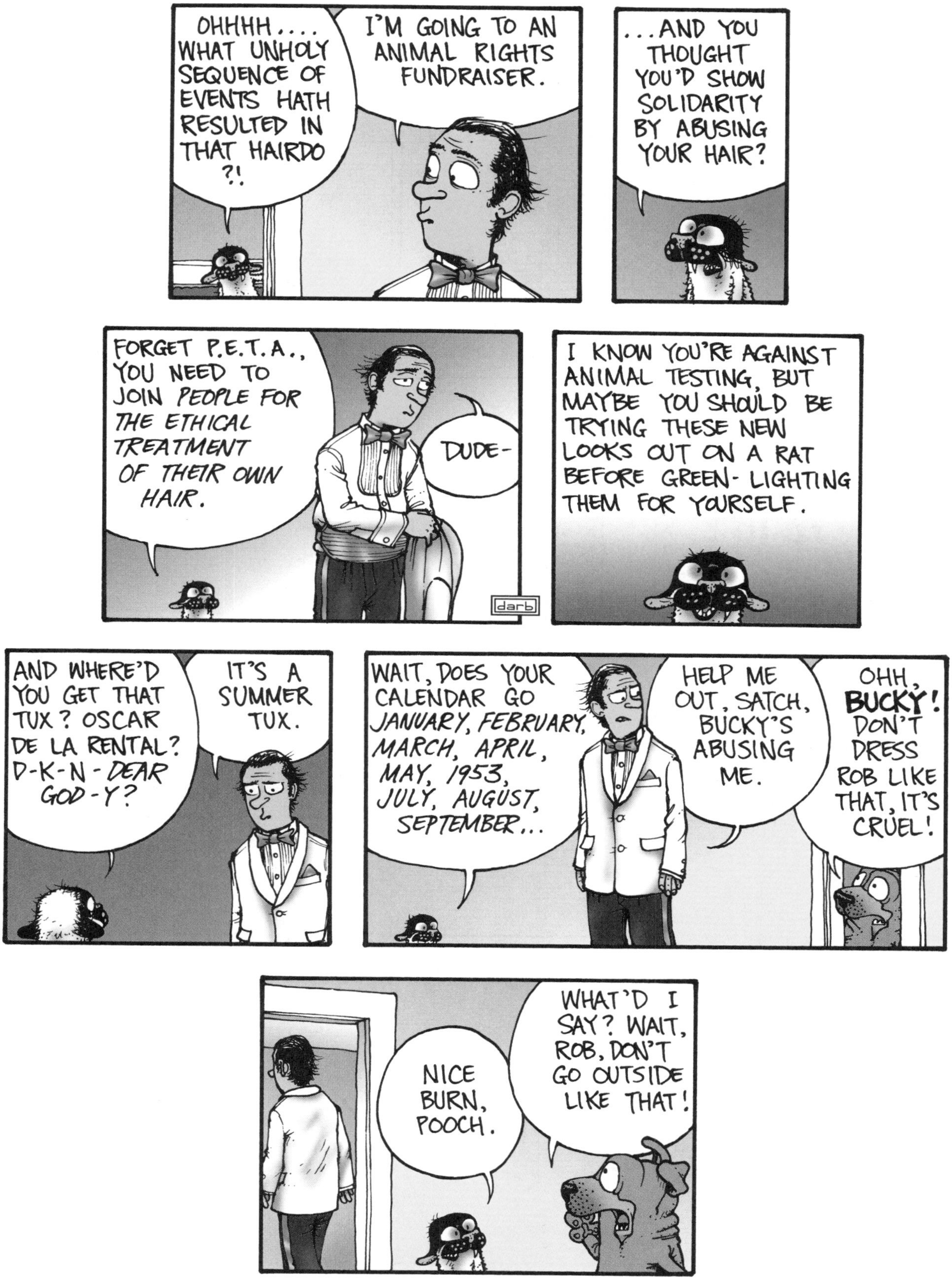
OHHHH.... WHAT UNHOLY SEQUENCE OF EVENTS HATH RESULTED IN THAT HAIRDO ?!
I'M GOING TO AN ANIMAL RIGHTS FUNDRAISER.
...AND YOU THOUGHT YOU'D SHOW SOLIDARITY BY ABUSING YOUR HAIR?
FORGET P.E.T.A., YOU NEED TO JOIN *PEOPLE FOR THE ETHICAL TREATMENT OF THEIR OWN HAIR.*
DUDE-
darb
I KNOW YOU'RE AGAINST ANIMAL TESTING, BUT MAYBE YOU SHOULD BE TRYING THESE NEW LOOKS OUT ON A RAT BEFORE GREEN-LIGHTING THEM FOR YOURSELF.
AND WHERE'D YOU GET THAT TUX? OSCAR DE LA RENTAL? D-K-N-*DEAR GOD*-Y?
IT'S A SUMMER TUX.
WAIT, DOES YOUR CALENDAR GO *JANUARY, FEBRUARY, MARCH, APRIL, MAY, 1953, JULY, AUGUST, SEPTEMBER...*
HELP ME OUT, SATCH, BUCKY'S ABUSING ME.
OHH, **BUCKY!** DON'T DRESS ROB LIKE THAT, IT'S CRUEL!
NICE BURN, POOCH.
WHAT'D I SAY? WAIT, ROB, DON'T GO OUTSIDE LIKE THAT!

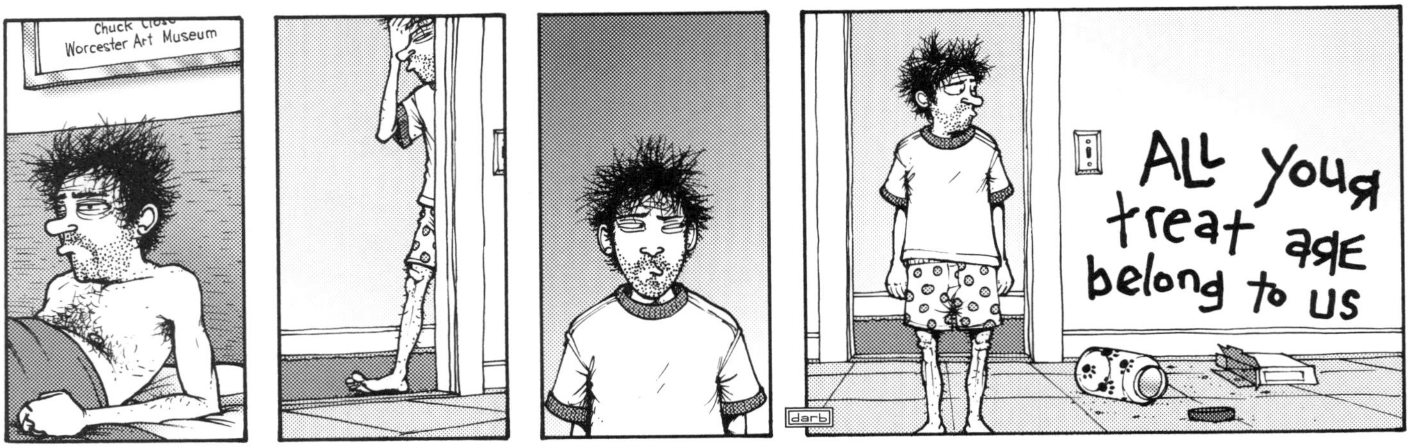
Worcester Art Museum
ALL your treat aRE belong to us
darb

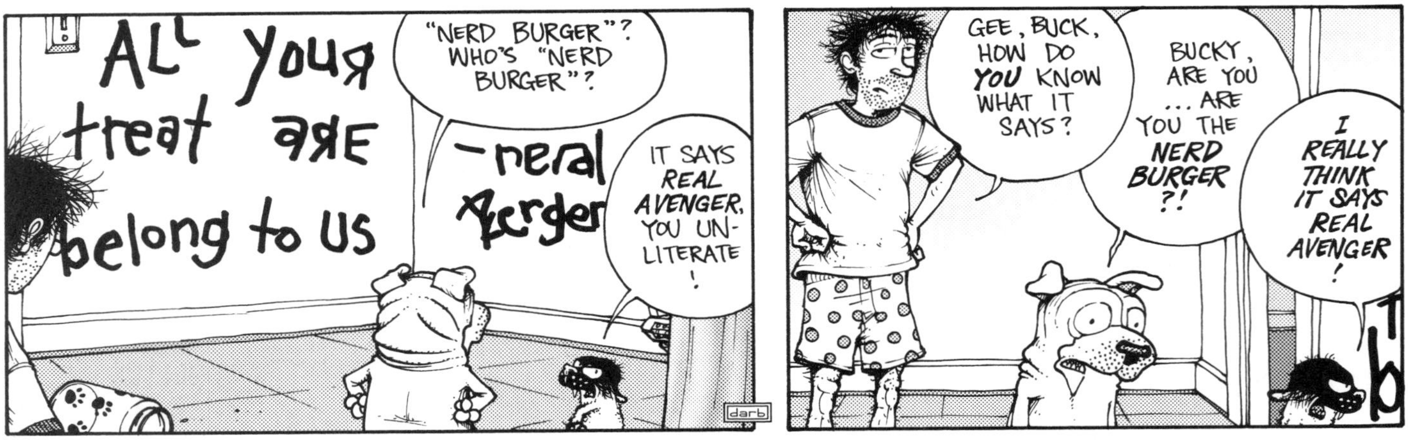
ALL your treat aRE belong to us
"NERD BURGER"? WHO'S "NERD BURGER"?
-neral
IT SAYS REAL AVENGER, YOU UN-LITERATE!
darb
GEE, BUCK, HOW DO YOU KNOW WHAT IT SAYS?
BUCKY, ARE YOU ... ARE YOU THE NERD BURGER?!
I REALLY THINK IT SAYS REAL AVENGER!

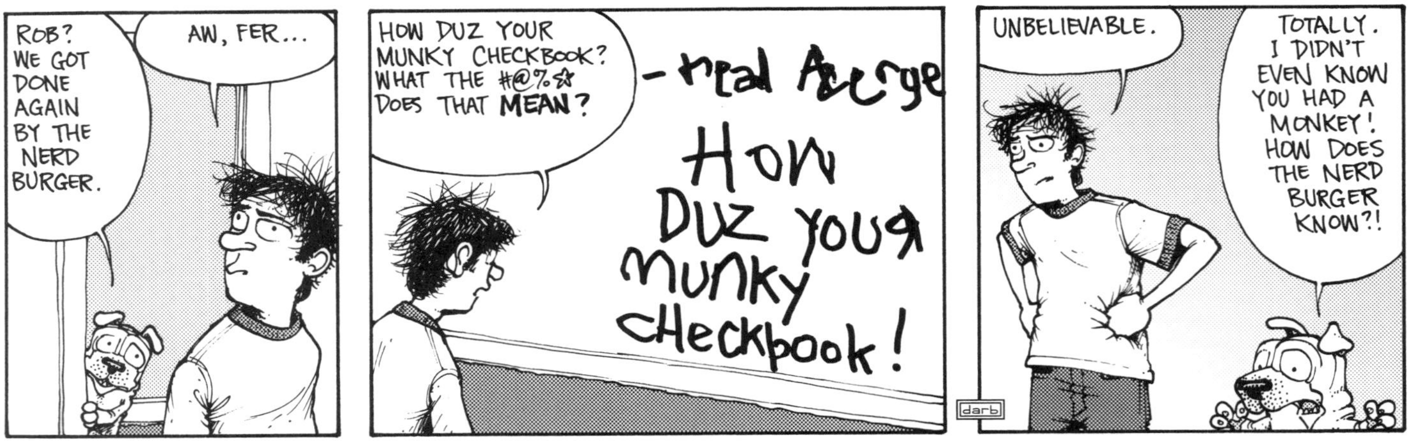
ROB? WE GOT DONE AGAIN BY THE NERD BURGER.
AW, FER...
HOW DUZ YOUR MUNKY CHECKBOOK? WHAT THE #@%☆ DOES THAT MEAN?
How DUZ your munky checkbook!
darb
UNBELIEVABLE.
TOTALLY. I DIDN'T EVEN KNOW YOU HAD A MONKEY! HOW DOES THE NERD BURGER KNOW?!

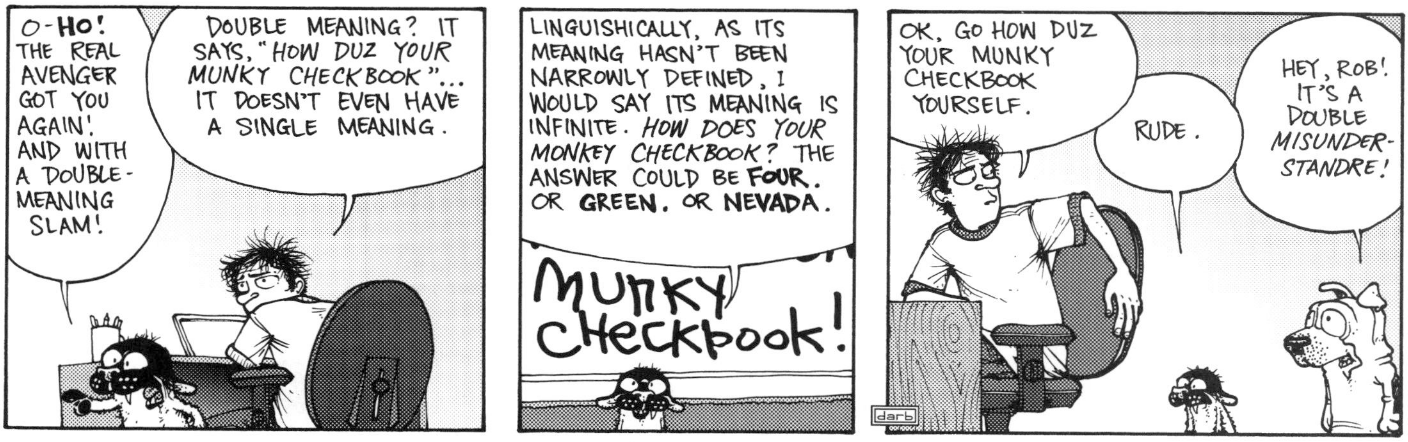
O-HO! THE REAL AVENGER GOT YOU AGAIN! AND WITH A DOUBLE-MEANING SLAM!
DOUBLE MEANING? IT SAYS, "HOW DUZ YOUR MUNKY CHECKBOOK"... IT DOESN'T EVEN HAVE A SINGLE MEANING.
LINGUISHICALLY, AS ITS MEANING HASN'T BEEN NARROWLY DEFINED, I WOULD SAY ITS MEANING IS INFINITE. HOW DOES YOUR MONKEY CHECKBOOK? THE ANSWER COULD BE FOUR. OR GREEN. OR NEVADA.
Munky Checkbook!
OK. GO HOW DUZ YOUR MUNKY CHECKBOOK YOURSELF.
RUDE.
HEY, ROB! IT'S A DOUBLE MISUNDER-STANDRE!
darb

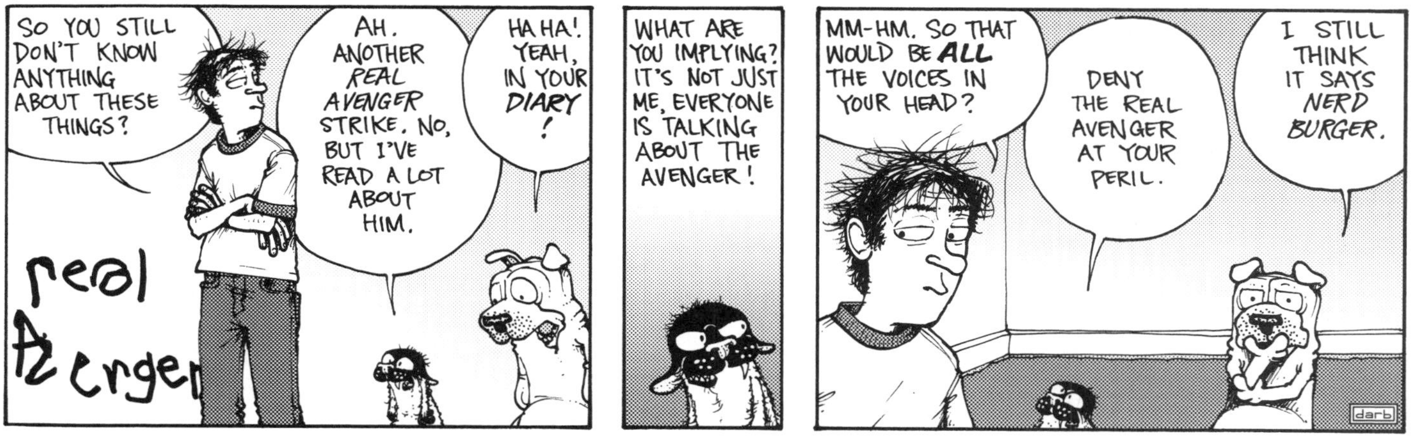
SO YOU STILL DON'T KNOW ANYTHING ABOUT THESE THINGS?
AH. ANOTHER REAL AVENGER STRIKE. NO, BUT I'VE READ A LOT ABOUT HIM.
HA HA! YEAH, IN YOUR DIARY!
real Avenger
WHAT ARE YOU IMPLYING? IT'S NOT JUST ME, EVERYONE IS TALKING ABOUT THE AVENGER!
MM-HM. SO THAT WOULD BE ALL THE VOICES IN YOUR HEAD?
DENY THE REAL AVENGER AT YOUR PERIL.
I STILL THINK IT SAYS NERD BURGER.
darb

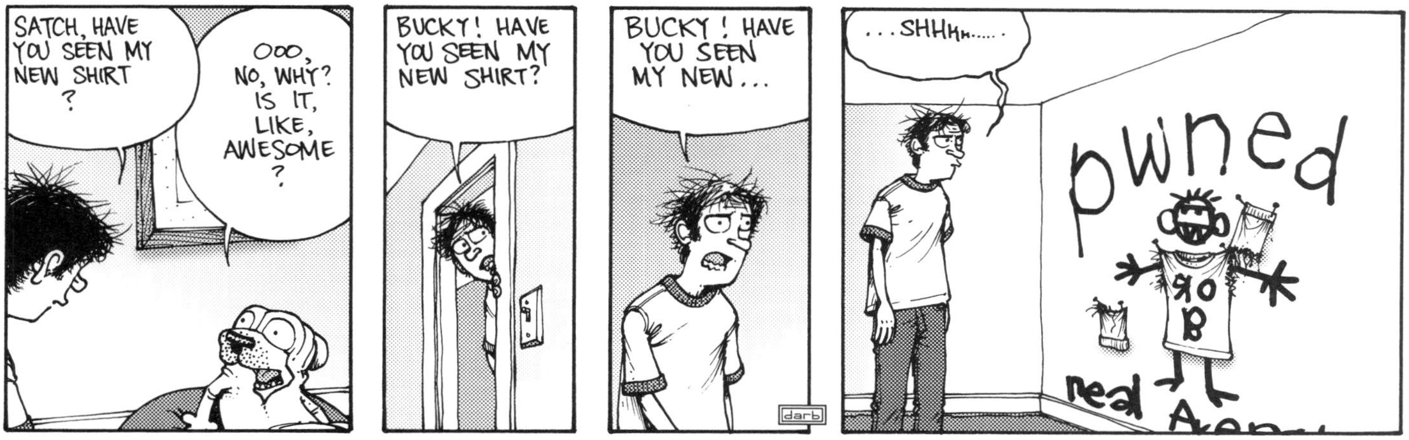
SATCH, HAVE YOU SEEN MY NEW SHIRT?
OOO, NO, WHY? IS IT, LIKE, AWESOME?
BUCKY! HAVE YOU SEEN MY NEW SHIRT?
darb
BUCKY! HAVE YOU SEEN MY NEW...
...SHHhh.....
pwned
ROB
real

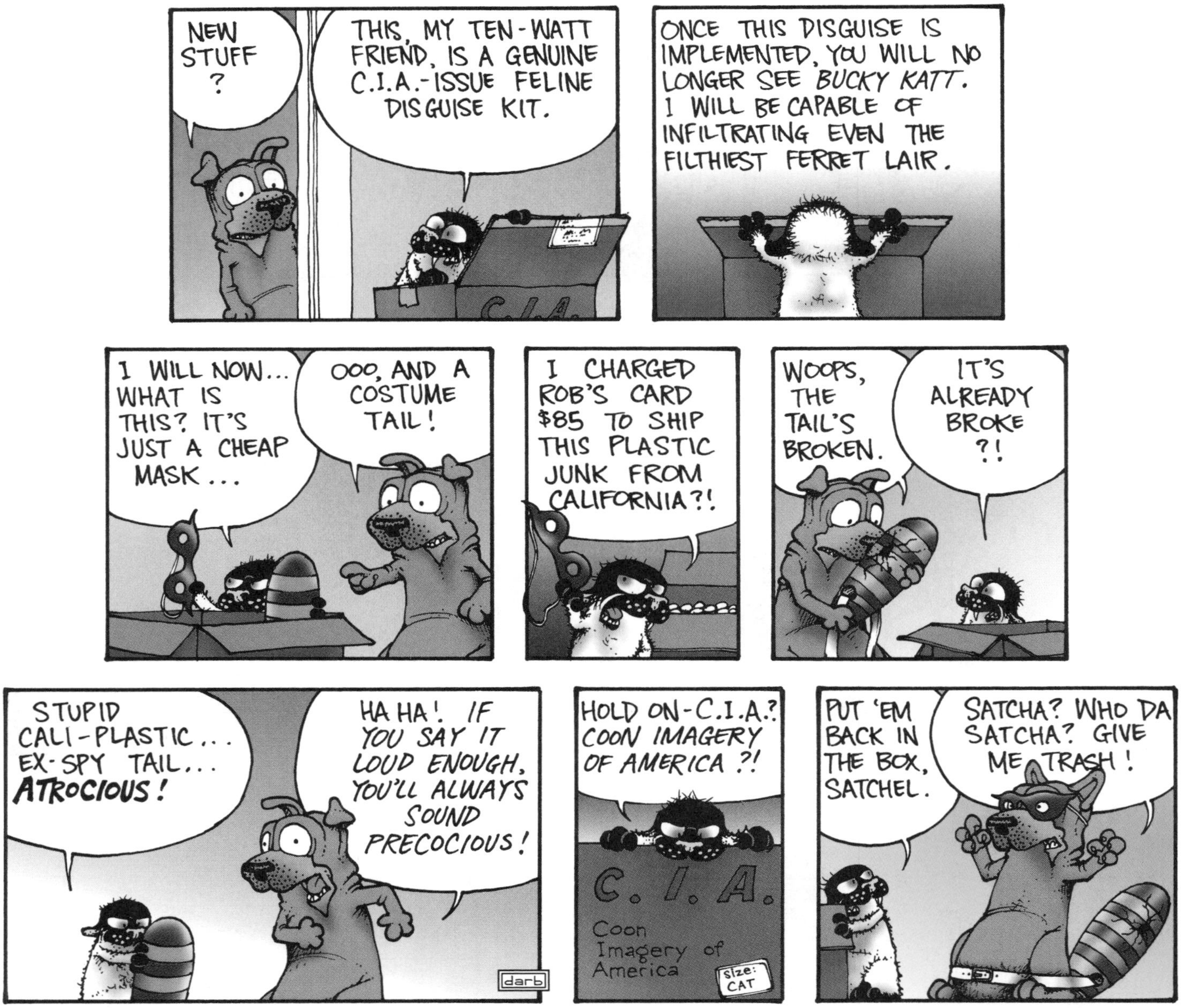
NEW STUFF ?
THIS, MY TEN-WATT FRIEND, IS A GENUINE C.I.A.-ISSUE FELINE DISGUISE KIT.
C.I.A.
ONCE THIS DISGUISE IS IMPLEMENTED, YOU WILL NO LONGER SEE *BUCKY KATT*. I WILL BE CAPABLE OF INFILTRATING EVEN THE FILTHIEST FERRET LAIR.
I WILL NOW... WHAT IS THIS? IT'S JUST A CHEAP MASK...
OOO, AND A COSTUME TAIL!
I CHARGED ROB'S CARD $85 TO SHIP THIS PLASTIC JUNK FROM CALIFORNIA?!
WOOPS, THE TAIL'S BROKEN.
IT'S ALREADY BROKE ?!
STUPID CALI-PLASTIC... EX-SPY TAIL... **ATROCIOUS!**
HA HA! *IF YOU SAY IT LOUD ENOUGH, YOU'LL ALWAYS SOUND PRECOCIOUS!*
darb
HOLD ON-C.I.A.? *COON IMAGERY OF AMERICA ?!*
C. I. A.
Coon Imagery of America
size: CAT
PUT 'EM BACK IN THE BOX, SATCHEL.
SATCHA? WHO DA SATCHA? GIVE ME TRASH!

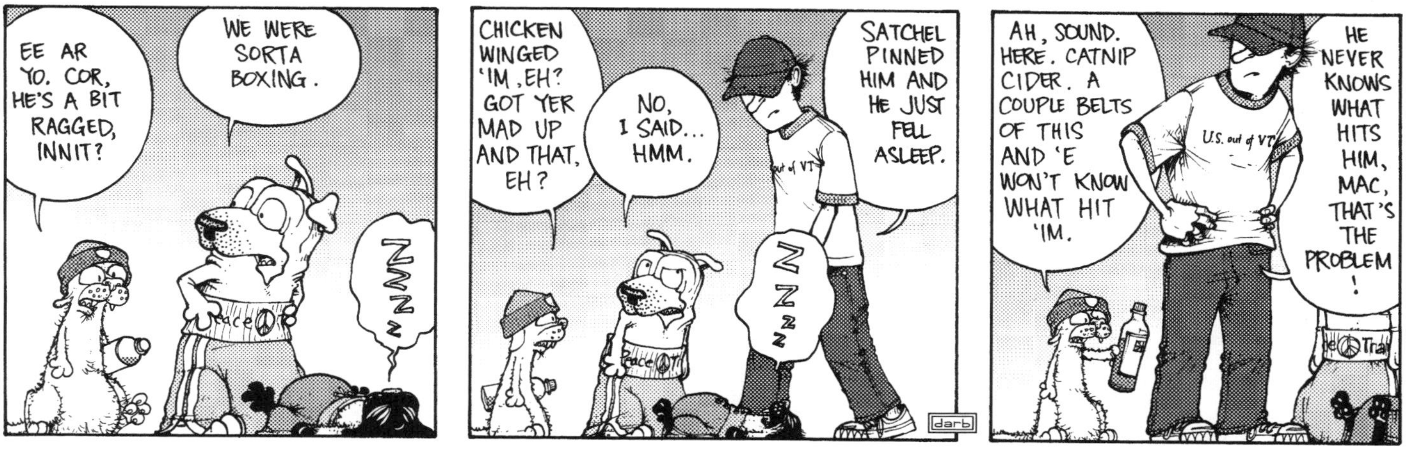
EE AR YO. COR, HE'S A BIT RAGGED, INNIT?
WE WERE SORTA BOXING.
ZZZZ
CHICKEN WINGED 'IM, EH? GOT YER MAD UP AND THAT, EH?
NO, I SAID... HMM.
SATCHEL PINNED HIM AND HE JUST FELL ASLEEP.
ZZZZ
AH, SOUND. HERE. CATNIP CIDER. A COUPLE BELTS OF THIS AND 'E WON'T KNOW WHAT HIT 'IM.
HE NEVER KNOWS WHAT HITS HIM, MAC, THAT'S THE PROBLEM!

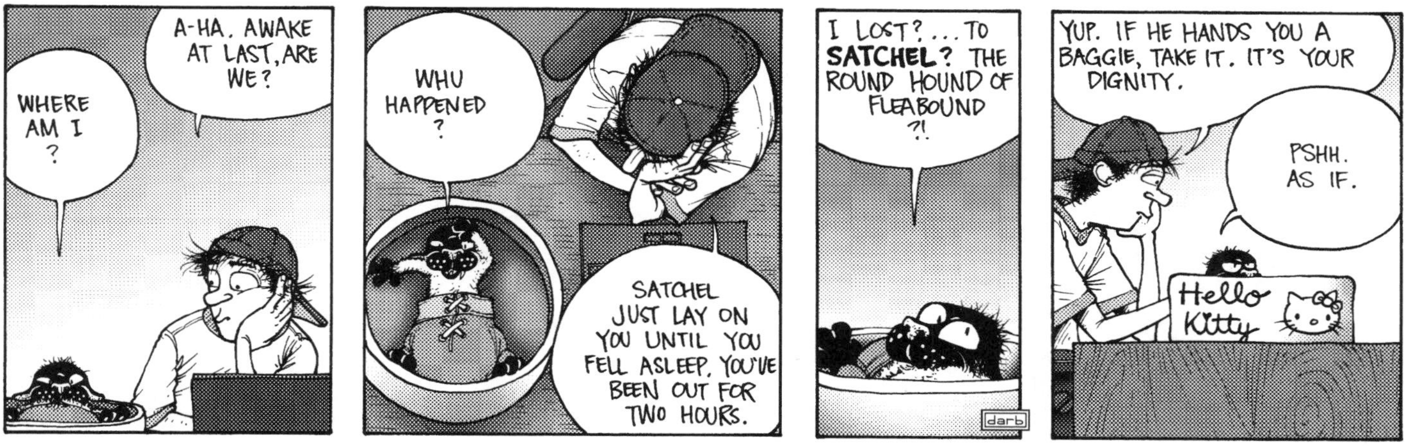
WHERE AM I?
A-HA. AWAKE AT LAST, ARE WE?
WHU HAPPENED?
SATCHEL JUST LAY ON YOU UNTIL YOU FELL ASLEEP. YOU'VE BEEN OUT FOR TWO HOURS.
I LOST?... TO **SATCHEL**? THE ROUND HOUND OF FLEABOUND?!
YUP. IF HE HANDS YOU A BAGGIE, TAKE IT. IT'S YOUR DIGNITY.
PSHH. AS IF.
Hello Kitty

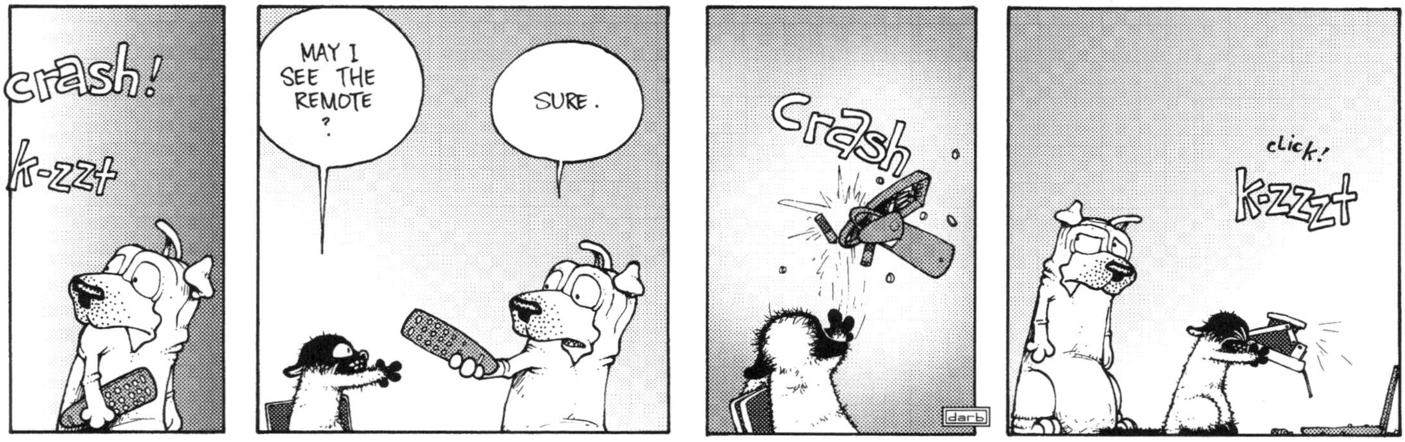
crash!
k-zzt
MAY I SEE THE REMOTE?
SURE.
crash
click!
k-zzzt

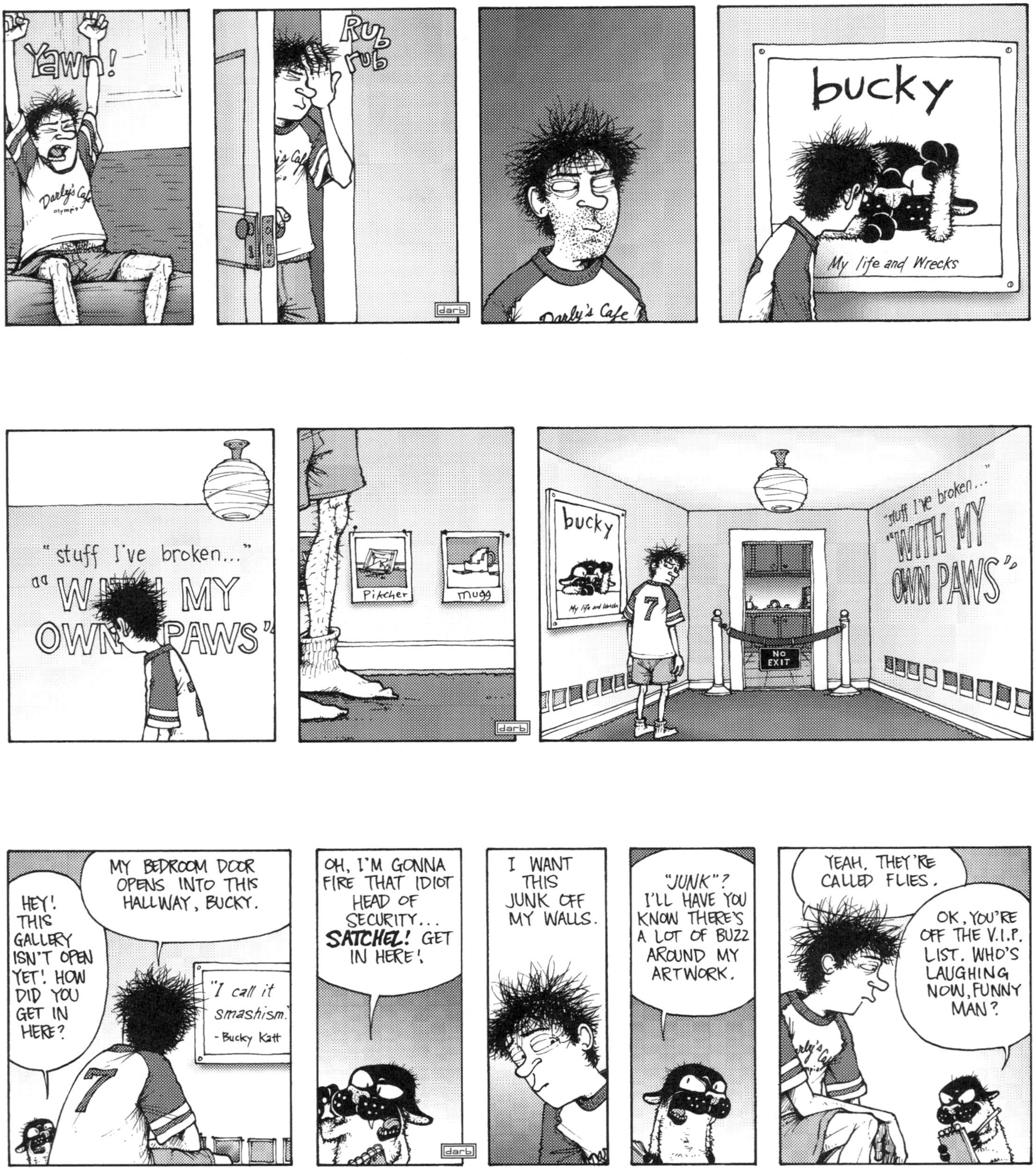

Yawn!
Rub rub
bucky
My life and Wrecks
"stuff I've broken..."
"WITH MY OWN PAWS"
Pitcher
Mugg
bucky
"stuff I've broken..."
"WITH MY OWN PAWS"
NO EXIT
HEY! THIS GALLERY ISN'T OPEN YET! HOW DID YOU GET IN HERE?
MY BEDROOM DOOR OPENS INTO THIS HALLWAY, BUCKY.
"I call it smashism." - Bucky Katt
OH, I'M GONNA FIRE THAT IDIOT HEAD OF SECURITY... SATCHEL! GET IN HERE!
I WANT THIS JUNK OFF MY WALLS.
"JUNK"? I'LL HAVE YOU KNOW THERE'S A LOT OF BUZZ AROUND MY ARTWORK.
YEAH, THEY'RE CALLED FLIES.
OK, YOU'RE OFF THE V.I.P. LIST. WHO'S LAUGHING NOW, FUNNY MAN?

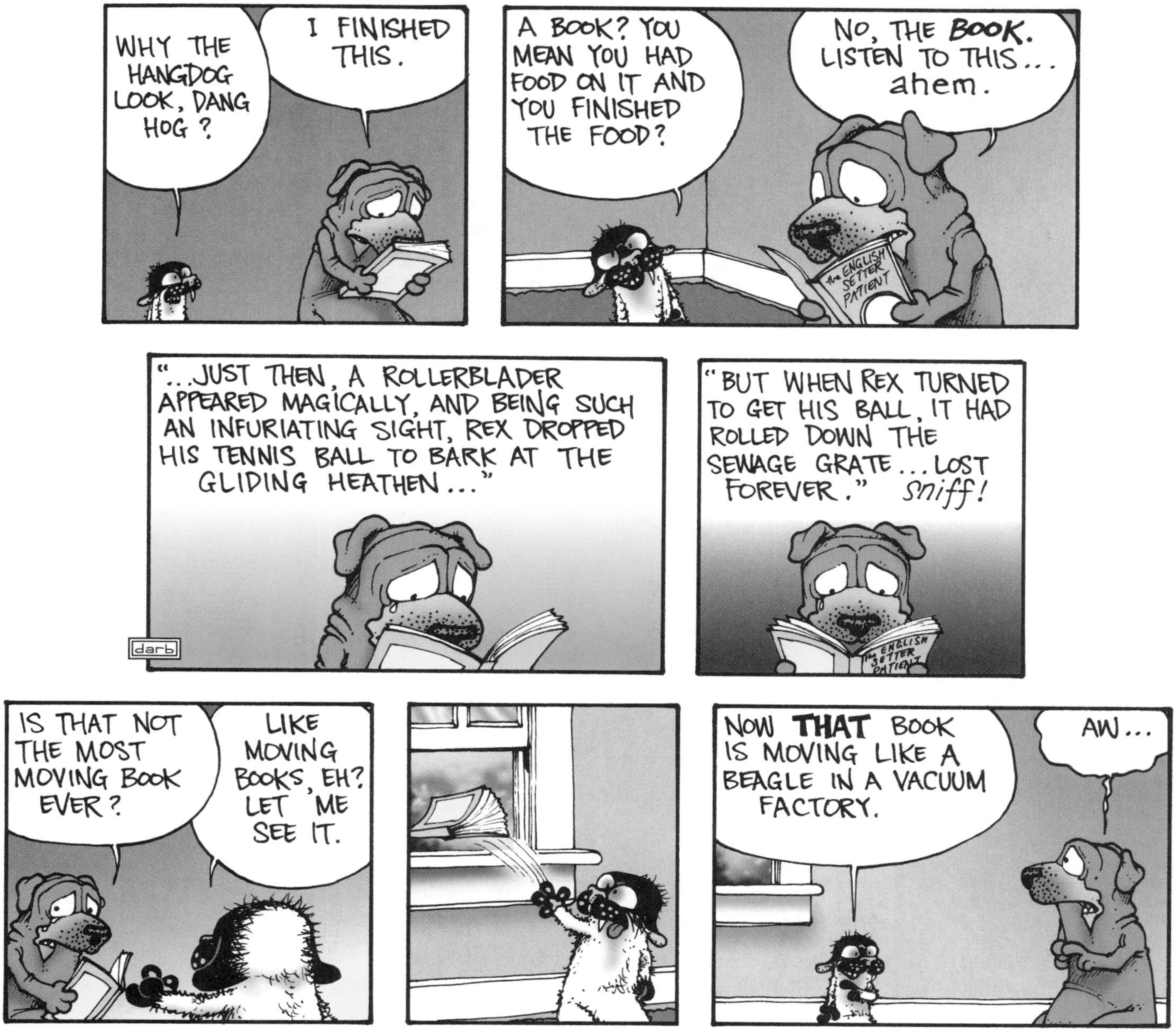
WHY THE HANGDOG LOOK, DANG HOG?
I FINISHED THIS.
A BOOK? YOU MEAN YOU HAD FOOD ON IT AND YOU FINISHED THE FOOD?
NO, THE BOOK. LISTEN TO THIS... ahem.
the ENGLISH SETTER PATIENT
"...JUST THEN, A ROLLERBLADER APPEARED MAGICALLY, AND BEING SUCH AN INFURIATING SIGHT, REX DROPPED HIS TENNIS BALL TO BARK AT THE GLIDING HEATHEN..."
darb
"BUT WHEN REX TURNED TO GET HIS BALL, IT HAD ROLLED DOWN THE SEWAGE GRATE... LOST FOREVER." sniff!
the ENGLISH SETTER PATIENT
IS THAT NOT THE MOST MOVING BOOK EVER?
LIKE MOVING BOOKS, EH? LET ME SEE IT.
NOW THAT BOOK IS MOVING LIKE A BEAGLE IN A VACUUM FACTORY.
AW...

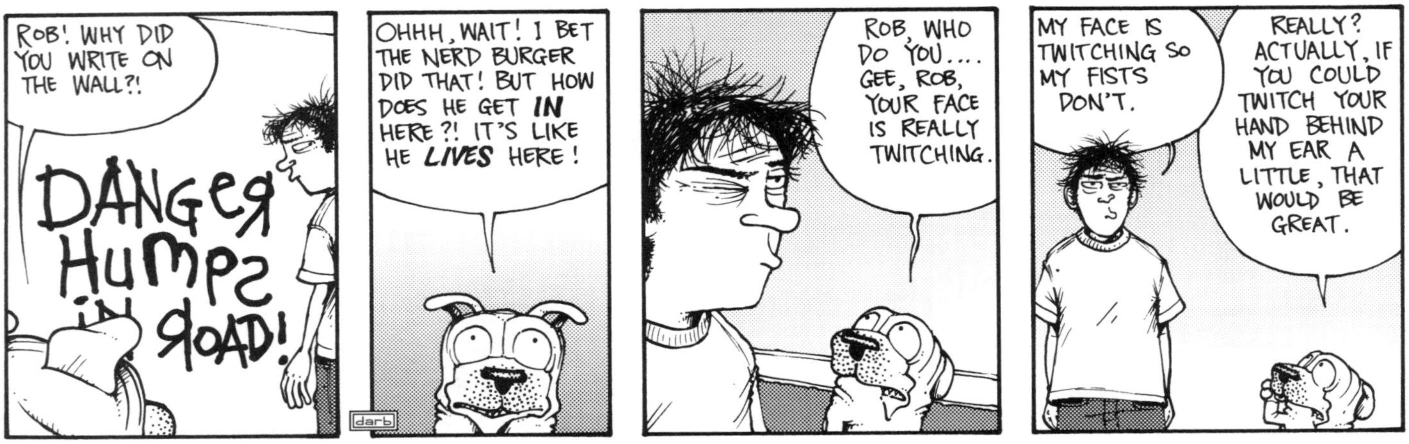
ROB! WHY DID YOU WRITE ON THE WALL?!
DANGER HUMPS
ROAD!
OHHH, WAIT! I BET THE NERD BURGER DID THAT! BUT HOW DOES HE GET **IN** HERE?! IT'S LIKE HE ***LIVES*** HERE!
darb
ROB, WHO DO YOU.... GEE, ROB, YOUR FACE IS REALLY TWITCHING.
MY FACE IS TWITCHING SO MY FISTS DON'T.
REALLY? ACTUALLY, IF YOU COULD TWITCH YOUR HAND BEHIND MY EAR A LITTLE, THAT WOULD BE GREAT.

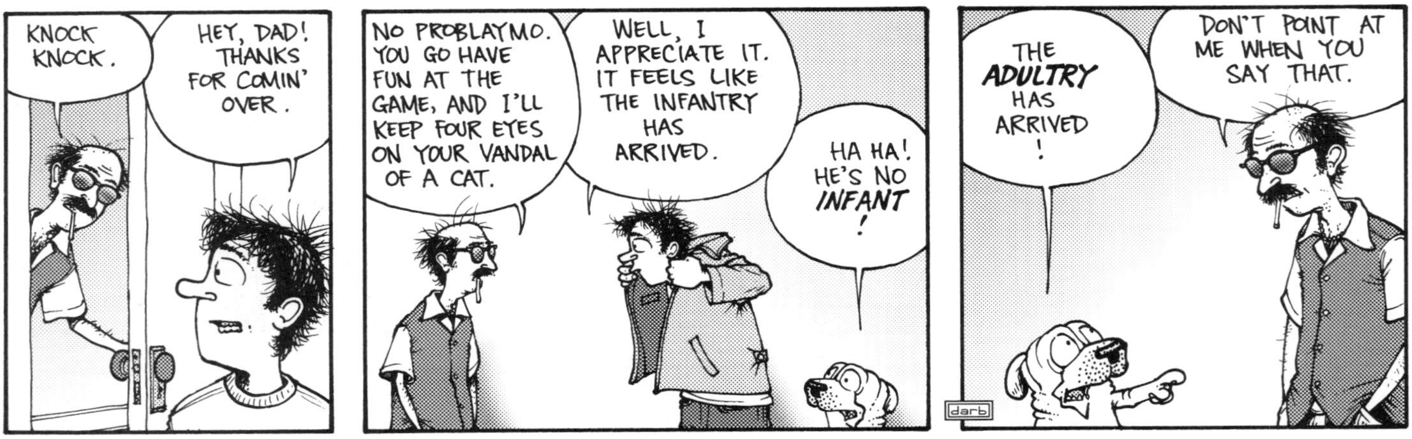
KNOCK KNOCK.
HEY, DAD! THANKS FOR COMIN' OVER.
NO PROBLAYMO. YOU GO HAVE FUN AT THE GAME, AND I'LL KEEP FOUR EYES ON YOUR VANDAL OF A CAT.
WELL, I APPRECIATE IT. IT FEELS LIKE THE INFANTRY HAS ARRIVED.
HA HA! HE'S NO ***INFANT***!
THE ***ADULTRY*** HAS ARRIVED!
DON'T POINT AT ME WHEN YOU SAY THAT.
darb

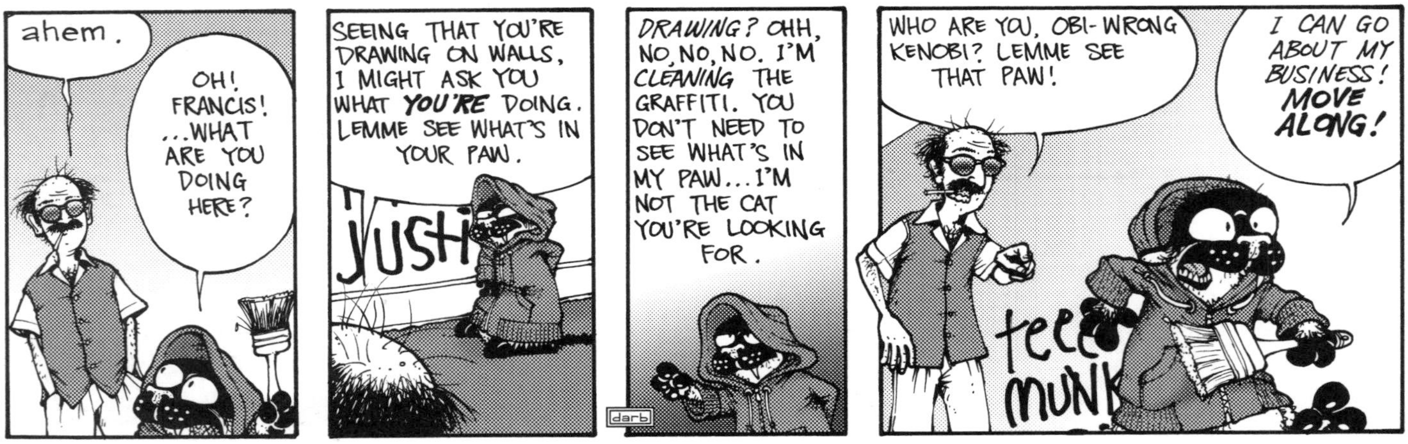
ahem.
OH! FRANCIS! ...WHAT ARE YOU DOING HERE?
SEEING THAT YOU'RE DRAWING ON WALLS, I MIGHT ASK YOU WHAT ***YOU'RE*** DOING. LEMME SEE WHAT'S IN YOUR PAW.
JUSTI
DRAWING? OHH, NO, NO, NO. I'M *CLEANING* THE GRAFFITI. YOU DON'T NEED TO SEE WHAT'S IN MY PAW... I'M NOT THE CAT YOU'RE LOOKING FOR.
darb
WHO ARE YOU, OBI-WRONG KENOBI? LEMME SEE THAT PAW!
I CAN GO ABOUT MY BUSINESS! ***MOVE ALONG!***
teee
MUNK

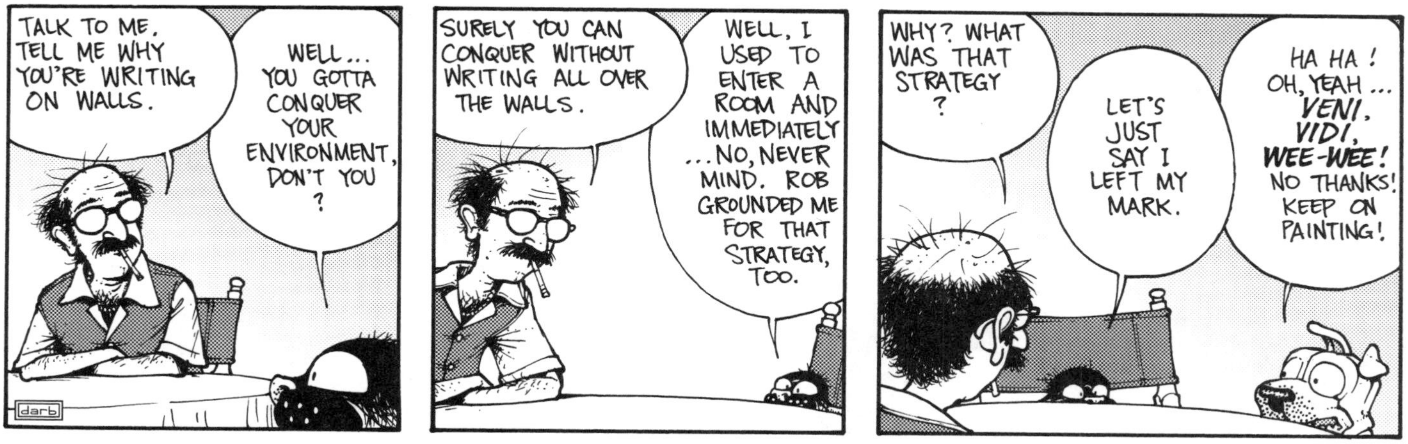
TALK TO ME. TELL ME WHY YOU'RE WRITING ON WALLS.
WELL... YOU GOTTA CONQUER YOUR ENVIRONMENT, DON'T YOU ?
darb
SURELY YOU CAN CONQUER WITHOUT WRITING ALL OVER THE WALLS.
WELL, I USED TO ENTER A ROOM AND IMMEDIATELY ...NO, NEVER MIND. ROB GROUNDED ME FOR THAT STRATEGY, TOO.
WHY? WHAT WAS THAT STRATEGY ?
LET'S JUST SAY I LEFT MY MARK.
HA HA ! OH, YEAH ... ***VENI, VIDI, WEE-WEE!*** NO THANKS! KEEP ON PAINTING!

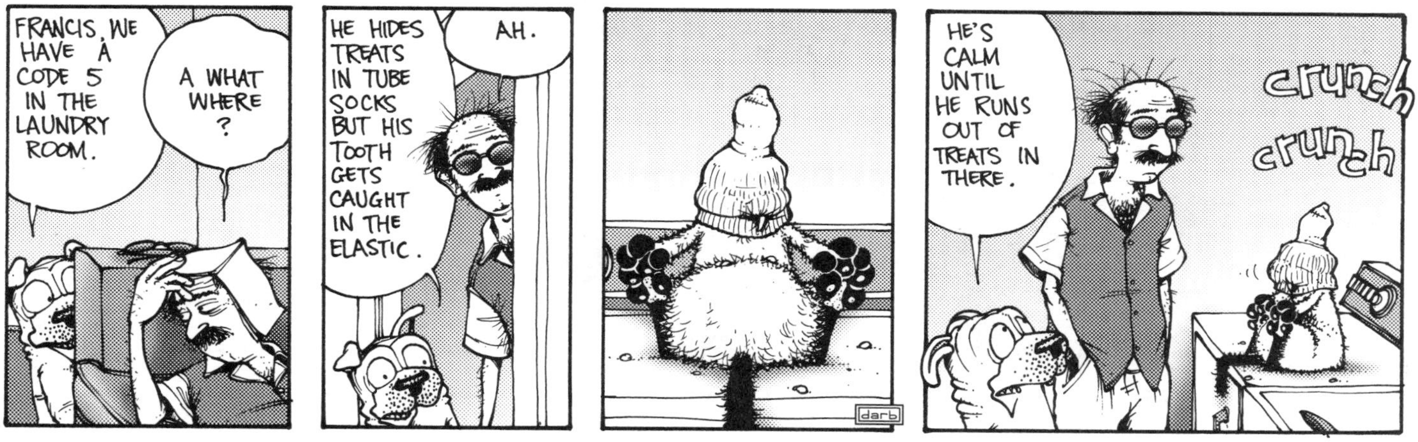
FRANCIS, WE HAVE A CODE 5 IN THE LAUNDRY ROOM.
A WHAT WHERE ?
HE HIDES TREATS IN TUBE SOCKS BUT HIS TOOTH GETS CAUGHT IN THE ELASTIC.
AH.
darb
HE'S CALM UNTIL HE RUNS OUT OF TREATS IN THERE.
crunch
crunch

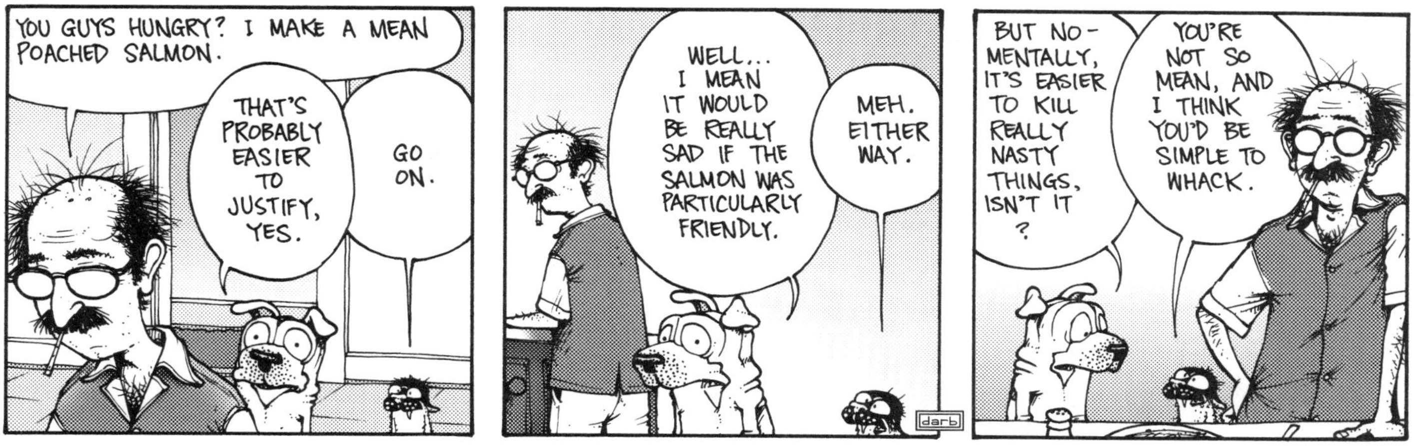
YOU GUYS HUNGRY? I MAKE A MEAN POACHED SALMON.
THAT'S PROBABLY EASIER TO JUSTIFY, YES.
GO ON.
WELL... I MEAN IT WOULD BE REALLY SAD IF THE SALMON WAS PARTICULARLY FRIENDLY.
MEH. EITHER WAY.
darb
BUT NO— MENTALLY, IT'S EASIER TO KILL REALLY NASTY THINGS, ISN'T IT ?
YOU'RE NOT SO MEAN, AND I THINK YOU'D BE SIMPLE TO WHACK.

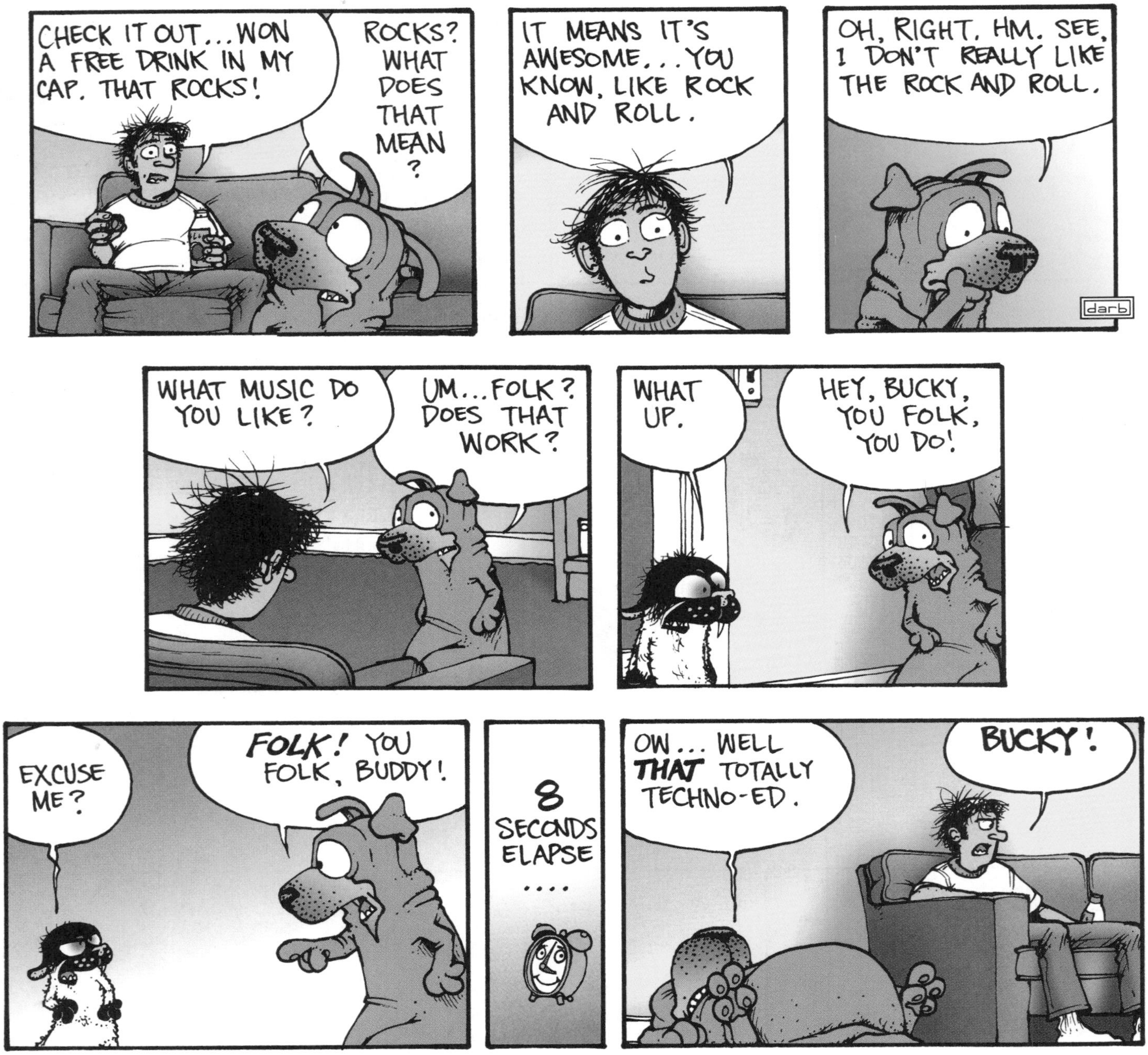
CHECK IT OUT... WON A FREE DRINK IN MY CAP. THAT ROCKS!
ROCKS? WHAT DOES THAT MEAN?
IT MEANS IT'S AWESOME... YOU KNOW, LIKE ROCK AND ROLL.
OH, RIGHT. HM. SEE, I DON'T REALLY LIKE THE ROCK AND ROLL.
darb
WHAT MUSIC DO YOU LIKE?
UM... FOLK? DOES THAT WORK?
WHAT UP.
HEY, BUCKY, YOU FOLK, YOU DO!
EXCUSE ME?
FOLK! YOU FOLK, BUDDY!
8 SECONDS ELAPSE ....
OW... WELL THAT TOTALLY TECHNO-ED.
BUCKY!